HOSEA, AMOS, MICAH

THE NIV APPLICATION COMMENTARY

From biblical text . . . to contemporary life

THE NIV APPLICATION COMMENTARY

From biblical text . . . to contemporary life

GARY V. SMITH

ZONDERVAN™

GRAND RAPIDS, MICHIGAN 49530 USA

The NIV Application Commentary: Hosea, Amos, Micah
Copyright © 2001 by Gary V. Smith

Requests for information should be addressed to:

Zondervan, *Grand Rapids, Michigan 49530*

Library of Congress Cataloging-in-Publication Data

Smith, Gary V., 1943
    Hosea, Amos, Micah / Gary V. Smith
        p. cm. — (The NIV application commentary)
    Includes bibliographical references and indexes.
    ISBN: 0–310–20614–6
    1. Bible. O.T. Hosea — Commentaries. 2. Bible. O.T. Amos — Commentaries.
    3. Bible. O.T. Micah — Commentaries. I. Title. II. Series.
    BS 1565.53.S55 2001
    224'.077 — dc21   00–047717
                                                      CIP

This edition printed on acid-free paper.

Printed in the United States of America

---

04 05 /❖ DC/ 10 9 8 7 6 5

Contents

The NIV Application Commentary Series

When complete, the NIV Application Commentary
will include the following volumes:

To see which titles are available,
visit our web site at www.zondervan.com

NIV Application Commentary
Series Introduction

THE NIV APPLICATION COMMENTARY SERIES is unique. Most commentaries help us make the journey from our world back to the world of the Bible. They enable us to cross the barriers of time, culture, language, and geography that separate us from the biblical world. Yet they only offer a one-way ticket to the past and assume that we can somehow make the return journey on our own. Once they have explained the *original meaning* of a book or passage, these commentaries give us little or no help in exploring its *contemporary significance*. The information they offer is valuable, but the job is only half done.

Recently, a few commentaries have included some contemporary application as *one* of their goals. Yet that application is often sketchy or moralistic, and some volumes sound more like printed sermons than commentaries.

The primary goal of the NIV Application Commentary Series is to help you with the difficult but vital task of bringing an ancient message into a modern context. The series not only focuses on application as a finished product but also helps you think through the *process* of moving from the original meaning of a passage to its contemporary significance. These are commentaries, not popular expositions. They are works of reference, not devotional literature.

The format of the series is designed to achieve the goals of the series. Each passage is treated in three sections: *Original Meaning, Bridging Contexts,* and *Contemporary Significance.*

THIS SECTION HELPS you understand the meaning of the biblical text in its original context. All of the elements of traditional exegesis—in concise form—are discussed here. These include the historical, literary, and cultural context of the passage. The authors discuss matters related to grammar and syntax and the meaning of biblical words.[1] They also seek to explore the main ideas of the passage and how the biblical author develops those ideas.

---

1. Please note that in general, when the authors discuss words in the original biblical languages, the series uses a general rather than a scholarly method of transliteration.

After reading this section, you will understand the problems, questions, and concerns of the *original audience* and how the biblical author addressed those issues. This understanding is foundational to any legitimate application of the text today.

 THIS SECTION BUILDS a bridge between the world of the Bible and the world of today, between the original context and the contemporary context, by focusing on both the timely and timeless aspects of the text.

God's Word is *timely*. The authors of Scripture spoke to specific situations, problems, and questions. The author of Joshua encouraged the faith of his original readers by narrating the destruction of Jericho, a seemingly impregnable city, at the hands of an angry warrior God (Josh. 6). Paul warned the Galatians about the consequences of circumcision and the dangers of trying to be justified by law (Gal. 5:2–5). The author of Hebrews tried to convince his readers that Christ is superior to Moses, the Aaronic priests, and the Old Testament sacrifices. John urged his readers to "test the spirits" of those who taught a form of incipient Gnosticism (1 John 4:1–6). In each of these cases, the timely nature of Scripture enables us to hear God's Word in situations that were *concrete* rather than abstract.

Yet the timely nature of Scripture also creates problems. Our situations, difficulties, and questions are not always directly related to those faced by the people in the Bible. Therefore, God's word to them does not always seem relevant to us. For example, when was the last time someone urged you to be circumcised, claiming that it was a necessary part of justification? How many people today care whether Christ is superior to the Aaronic priests? And how can a "test" designed to expose incipient Gnosticism be of any value in a modern culture?

Fortunately, Scripture is not only timely but *timeless*. Just as God spoke to the original audience, so he still speaks to us through the pages of Scripture. Because we share a common humanity with the people of the Bible, we discover a *universal dimension* in the problems they faced and the solutions God gave them. The timeless nature of Scripture enables it to speak with power in every time and in every culture.

Those who fail to recognize that Scripture is both timely and timeless run into a host of problems. For example, those who are intimidated by timely books such as Hebrews, Galatians, or Deuteronomy might avoid reading them because they seem meaningless today. At the other extreme, those who are convinced of the timeless nature of Scripture, but who fail to discern

Author's Preface

THE PROPHETIC BOOKS always cause me to wonder, "What would Hosea, Amos, or Micah say if they came to my church or saw what was happening in our culture?" Would their message to the political leaders, merchants, denominational leaders, and the average person on the street be much different? Of course, there would be differences between the worship in modern churches and the worship in the temples at Bethel and Jerusalem, but do not people have the same need to seek to know God? Hosea would still find prostitution rampant in our culture, Amos would still find the poor being oppressed, and Micah would still be talking about corruption in high places. Has anything changed?

Although modern culture has "progressed" with new medicines, fast transportation, worldwide communication, and fantastic inventions, the role of the modern messenger of God still boils down to the essential task of speaking God's words to a needy and sinful world. As one reads the prophetic sermons recorded in Scripture, one can begin to identify with the enormous prophetic task of transforming the thinking and behavior of a mixed-up group of religious people.

That also is our task. God has roared, so we must speak, and people must respond in fear (Amos 3:8). These prophetic sermons provide the inspiration and the foundation blocks for interacting with some of the basic problems of our generation. What does one say to persuade church people that they are not pleasing to God—look at Hosea 4:4–14; Amos 4:4–13; 5:21–27; or Micah 6:1–8. What things do please God? Micah would answer that we need justice, mercy, and a humble walk with God (Mic. 6:8), while Hosea would emphasize faithfulness, truth, steadfast covenant love, and an intimate relational knowledge of God (Hos. 4:1). Hosea realized his audience was in big trouble because the priests and prophets had forgotten God's divine revelation and led the people astray (4:6). Will not the same thing happen to people in our day if we fail to share with them the wisdom God has revealed through these prophets?

I want to thank Zondervan, especially Terry Muck and Jack Kuhatschak, the general editors; my Old Testament editor, Andrew Dearman, of Austin Presbyterian Seminary; and Verlyn Verbrugge, my Zondervan editor, for their assistance. Their insight, guidance, and critical attention to detail has greatly enhanced this work. I also want to thank the administration and trustees of Bethel Theological Seminary and Midwestern Baptist Theological Seminary for providing time for me to work on this project. I also want to thank my wife, Susan, for her long-suffering patience and support.

Gary V. Smith
Professor of Old Testament
Midwestern Baptist Theological Seminary
Kansas City, Missouri

Abbreviations

AASOR	Annual of the American Schools of Oriental Research
AB	Anchor Bible
ABD	*Anchor Bible Dictionary*
AnBib	Analecta Biblica
ANET	*Ancient Near Eastern Texts*, ed. J. B. Pritchard
BA	*Biblical Archeologist*
BCBC	Believers Church Bible Commentary
BDB	*Hebrew and English Lexicon of the Old Testament*, ed. F. Brown, S. R. Driver, C. A. Briggs
BECNT	Baker's Exegetical Commentary on the New Testament
Bib	*Biblica*
BibSac	*Bibliotheca Sacra*
BKAT	Biblischer Kommentar: Altes Testament
BR	*Bible Review*
BT	*Bible Translator*
BZAW	Beihefte zur Zeitschrift für die alttestamentliche Wissenschaft
CBQ	*Catholic Biblical Quarterly*
CC	Continental Commentaries
CT	*Christianity Today*
CTJ	*Calvin Theological Journal*
DSS	Dead Sea Scrolls
EBC	*Expositor's Bible Commentary*
Enc	*Encounter*
ExpT	*Expository Times*
GKC	*Gesenius: Hebrew Grammar*, ed. E. Kautzsch
HBT	Horizons in Biblical Theology
HTR	*Harvard Theological Review*
HUCA	*Hebrew Union College Annual*
IB	*Interpreter's Bible*
ICC	International Critical Commentary
IDB	*Interpreter's Dictionary of the Bible*, ed. G. A. Buttrick
IEJ	*Israel Exploration Journal*

Abbreviations

Int	*Interpretation*
Interp	Interpretation: A Bible Commentary for Teaching and Preaching
ISBE	*International Standard Bible Encyclopedia*, ed. G. W. Bromiley
ITC	International Theological Commentary
JAOS	*Journal of the American Oriental Society*
JBL	*Journal of Biblical Literature*
JETS	*Journal of the Evangelical Theological Society*
JJS	*Journal of Jewish Studies*
JNES	*Journal of Near Eastern Studies*
JNSL	*Journal of Northwest Semitic Languages*
JR	*Journal of Religion*
JSOT	*Journal for the Study of the Old Testament*
JSS	*Journal of Semitic Studies*
JTS	*Journal of Theological Studies*
KAT	Kommentar zum Alten Testament
LXX	Septuagint
MT	Masoretic Text
NAC	New American Commentary
NASB	New American Standard Bible
NCBC	New Century Bible Commentary
NEB	New English Bible
NIB	*New Interpreter's Bible*
NICOT	New International Commentary on the Old Testament
NIDNTT	*New International Dictionary of New Testament Theology*, ed. C. Brown
NIDOTTE	*New International Dictionary of Old Testament Theology and Exegesis*, ed. W. VanGemeren
NIV	New International Version
NIVAC	NIV Application Commentary
NovT	*Novum Testamentum*
Or	*Orientalia*
OTL	Old Testament Library
OtSt	*Oudtestamentische Studiën*
OTWSA	*Ou-Testamentiese Werkgemeenskap in Suid-Afrika*
PEQ	*Palestine Exploration Quarterly*
RevExp	*Review and Expositor*
RSV	Revised Standard Version

SEÅ	Svensk exegetisk årsbok
SJT	*Scottish Journal of Theology*
TDNT	*Theological Dictionary of the New Testament*, ed. G. Kittel
TDOT	*Theological Dictionary of the Old Testament*, ed. G. J. Botterweck and H. Ringgren
THAT	*Theologisches Handwörterbuch zum Alten Testament*, ed. E. Jenni, with C. Westermann
Tg	Targum
TOTC	Tyndale Old Testament Commentaries
TrinJ	*Trinity Journal*
TS	*Theological Studies*
TynBul	*Tyndale Bulletin*
VT	*Vetus Testamentum*
VTSup	Supplements to Vetus Testamentum
WBC	Word Biblical Commentary
WEC	Wycliffe Exegetical Commentary
WTJ	*Westminster Theological Journal*
ZAW	*Zeitschrift für die alttestamentliche Wissenschaft*

Introduction to Hosea

ONE OF THE MOST important factors that influences personal relationships between individuals is that warm, caring sense of acceptance and commitment that is sometimes called love. In ethics textbooks it is one of the central principles that motivates ethical behavior, in erotic romance novels and television talk shows it is a spicy sensual thrill that is trivialized, and in the counselor's office it is the fundamental foundation for good family life. Some might jokingly suggest that "love is what makes the world go round," but others see a serious lack of love exhibited between the sexes, between parents and children, between the races, and between the nations of the world.

One does not need to read many letters written to Ann Landers to realize that some people suffer because they love someone deeply, while others are selfishly motivated and show little love for others. Many of these letters tell of the bitterness and tragic consequences of someone failing to love and truly respect a friend or family member. Why is it so hard for people to deal with others in loving ways? Why do people fail to honor their marriage and family commitments? Why do individuals allow small differences of opinion or minor arguments to sour their relationships with someone they once loved?

Since the topic of love is so misunderstood, there is likely to be much confusion in the minds of unbelievers, and even some believers, when they read a biblical passage talking about love. What does the Bible mean when it says that a man is to love his wife as Christ loved the church (Eph. 5:25)? Equally confusing are all the different Greek terms that ministers keep referring to in sermons, plus the odd ways other cultures claim to legitimately express love. What does the love of God mean, and how can it be so powerful that nothing can separate us from it (Rom. 8:39)? Some even question the very idea of God's love because they have seen the horrors of war, the thousands who die in natural disasters, and the senseless violence of the strong against the weak. How can God allow such things to continue if he is a God of love?

First, one needs to define what one means by love and what the Bible means by love. One dictionary defines love as "1. strong affection or liking for someone or something; 2. a passionate affection for one of the opposite sex."[1]

---

1. D. B. Guralink, ed., *Webster's New World Dictionary of the American Language* (New York: Warner, 1987), 357.

In contrast, W. Eichrodt defines one kind of biblical love (*ḥesed*) as "the brotherly comradeship and loyalty which one party to a covenant must render to the other."[2] As applied to God's love relationship to the Israelites, "there was a strong, living conviction in Israel that Yahweh's kindness and readiness to succour was something which could be expected of him in view of his having established the covenant relationship."[3]

The other main Hebrew term for love (*'ahab*) "retains the passionate overtones of complete engagement of the will accompanied by strong emotion."[4] This kind of divine love is not based on covenant commitments but is a more "irrational power" that is unexplainable and paradoxical, since it is undeserved. It is a free giving of love to another person to care for, forgive, and protect that person—without strings or conditions attached. Human language can never adequately define or surround the concept of divine love; it can only point to acts or evidence of it with amazement and respond with either disbelief or warm acceptance, joy, and praise.

Since it is difficult to comprehend God's love and hard for people to know exactly what it means to love God, illustrations of divine love are powerful ways of demonstrating some of the characteristics of love. God's redemption of the nation Israel from Egyptian bondage is one of the greatest Old Testament examples of God's love, and Christ's death on the cross is the prime New Testament illustration. Yet for many people, the most vital and only real definition of love is impersonated in the attitudes and actions of some person they know today, not some event that took place thousands of years ago. These living experiences communicate the concept of love with a reality that goes beyond textbook definitions, rational formulas, secondhand experience, or lists of things to do or not to do. Love is something that must be experienced because it includes feelings that cannot be expressed in a cold dictionary definition.

The life of the prophet Hosea is special because people can identify with him and sense the joy and frustration of this living illustration of God's love. His tender and devastating experiences with his wife, Gomer, explicate the ins and outs of love in a more real way than a thousand definitions. He, like God, irrationally loved someone who was not very lovely (lit., "a woman of prostitution," 1:2), stayed committed to that love relationship in spite of great unfaithfulness by his covenant partner, and out of deep love forgave and took back a lover who betrayed him (3:1–3).

---

2. W. Eichrodt, *Theology of the Old Testament*, trans. J A. Beker, 2 vols. (OTL; Philadelphia: Westminster, 1961, 1967), 1:232.

3. Ibid., 1:233.

4. Ibid., 1:250.

Hosea felt something of God's sense of agony when people reject God's love. He experienced how a lack of an intimate relationship, unfaithfulness, and deceit can undermine a love relationship. He also came to understand something of God's great grace and forgiveness when he forgave his wife for her prostitution and brought her back to his home. He was able to preach the sermons God gave him with much greater passion because he identified with God's situation. Both had loved and gotten burned by their lover. He knew the difference between play-acting and real love. He knew that love is not just a warm, fuzzy feeling but involves a deep commitment and a willingness to forgive.

The message of Hosea should open the eyes of readers today not only to the awesome nature of God's love for us, but also to the terrible harm human sinfulness causes to anyone's personal relationship with God. Hosea helps us understand that unfaithfulness to a commitment to love God is like prostitution, not just a minor, insignificant slip that has no consequences. Some people think it is their personal right to express their faith in their own ways; thus, they neither keep their commitments to maintain a relationship with God nor follow his standards of justice and holiness. These are free choices, but they must be labeled acts of rebellion against the love and will of God. God looks at such acts as hypocritical deceit and theological lies—the kind of behavior that characterizes the life of an unfaithful spouse or prostitute. Coldness or an impersonal relationship with God is a sign that there is no love relationship with him.

Hosea challenges readers to examine the nature of their love relationship to God. Is it a passionate personal relationship with a living being? Is love characterized by faithfulness and by devotion to God alone? Is it authentic and not just a performance or charade of following some acceptable religious behavior? If one falls short of loving God with all one's heart and soul, how does this affect a person's relationship to God? Do people today believe their unfaithfulness in their love affair with God is as serious as a charge of prostitution? If Hosea were to come and evaluate the contemporary church, would he find things much different from Israel in his day?

The challenge of Hosea to his listeners is parallel to the challenge a preacher or teacher can deliver to God's people today. Do people in the church have a problem with developing an intimate knowledge of God? Do they have trouble maintaining faithfulness to their covenant commitment to love God and following his will for their lives? Are people truthful about their love for God, or is there a level of deceit in worship? Do people show greater love for the material things of this world or for God? Hosea challenges us to examine the nature of our love.

The Setting of Hosea's Ministry

The Political Situation

HOSEA'S MINISTRY IN ISRAEL came shortly after the preaching of Amos in Israel (765–760 B.C.) and partially overlapped with Micah's and Isaiah's ministries in Judah. Although the superscription of the book of Hosea lists only one Israelite king, Jeroboam II, the parallel list of Judean kings (Uzziah, Jotham, Ahaz, and Hezekiah) demonstrates that Hosea preached during the reign of several kings after Jeroboam II died. This information allows us to posit a ministry extending from about 755 during the final years of Jeroboam II until around 722 B.C., just before the fall of Samaria and the exile of the people of Israel (2 Kings 17:1–6).

For most of Hosea's ministry, life in Israel was politically insecure because of several weak kings who lived under the thumb of strong Assyrian rulers. Hosea's ministry falls into three periods: (1) the last few years of the prosperous reign of Jeroboam II, when Assyria was weak; (2) times of anarchy in Israel because of Assyrian strength under Tiglath–Pileser III, including Israel's defeat in the Syro-Ephraimite war in the reign of Pekah; (3) the final years during the reign of Hoshea, when Samaria was captured and the Israelites exiled. A chart of these periods reveals the following relationships:

	Judah	*Israel*	*Assyria*
Early period	Uzziah strong	Jeroboam II strong	Ashur-dan weak
Middle period	Jotham /Ahaz weak	Pekah weak	Tiglath-Pileser III strong
Late period	Ahaz weak	Hoshea weak	Tiglath-Pileser III / Shalmaneser strong

Early prosperous times. Hosea 1:4 looks at a future time when Jeroboam II and his sons, the heirs of Jehu, would die. This suggests that Hosea married Gomer and some of their children were born when times were good and the nation was enjoying its prosperity of wool, silver and gold, and abundant harvests (2:8–12). Jeroboam II had expanded the borders of the nation (2 Kings 14:25; Amos 6:12–14), Israel had a strong army, and a wealthy class of rich landlords were controlling the economy of Israel (Amos 3:15–4:1; 6:1–8).[5] Everything was going great for the upper class, but God's revelation through Amos and Hosea warned that the end of the nation of Israel was at hand (2:13–16; 3:11–12; 5:27; 8:1–3). These conditions are reflected in Hosea 1–3.

---

5. J. Bright, *A History of Israel*, 3d ed. (Philadelphia: Westminster, 1981), 269–74.

Middle period of war and anarchy. After the death of Jeroboam II, a time of government chaos and military anarchy followed. Kings Zechariah and Shallum were assassinated after brief reigns (2 Kings 15:8–14). The Assyrian king Tiglath-Pileser III imposed heavy tribute on Israel (15:19–29) during the reign of Menahem and Pekah,[6] and Israel was defeated by the Assyrians in the Syro-Ephraimite war (734–732 B.C.; see 2 Kings 16; Isa. 7:1–16). At that time Rezin, king of Syria, joined Pekah, king of Israel, in attacking Ahaz, king of Judah. They wanted to replace Ahaz (Isa. 7:6) or to force him to join their coalition against Tiglath-Pileser III and his Assyrian army.

After Rezin and Pekah's forces killed 120,000 of Ahaz's troops and took 200,000 people captive (2 Chron. 28:6–8), Ahaz asked Tiglath-Pileser III to rescue him from his adversaries. The Assyrian king defeated Syria and Israel and then required a heavy tax from Ahaz (28:20–21). Hosea warned the people about these battles (Hos. 5:8–11), condemned the assassinations of Israel's kings (7:3, 7), and predicted the approaching defeat and exile of the nation (5:14).

These were difficult political times to be involved in any kind of prophetic ministry. The nation was literally falling apart before Hosea's eyes, and the ruling class did not have the political leaders to provide a stable government. Most people who heard Hosea preach probably did not think his religious analysis of their political problems was a credible evaluation of the nation's situation; thus, most did not turn from their evil ways. This time period corresponded to the reigns of Jotham and the early years of Ahaz in Judah—also the days when Isaiah and Micah were preaching in Judah. Hosea 4–11 probably come from this period.

Last days before destruction. The third period was not as difficult because Hoshea, the final ruler in Israel, was able to play a political game of Russian roulette by making secret political alliances with both Egypt and Assyria (Hos. 12:1). When the Assyrians discovered this conspiracy, kings Shalmaneser and Sargon II destroyed Samaria and exiled the people (722/721 B.C.; 2 Kings 17:1–6). Although Hosea probably lived through this disastrous military defeat of Israel, it appears that his prophetic ministry in the northern nation ended prior to this event.

There is no information about the final years of Hosea's life after the fall of Israel, but many assume he took refuge in Judah when the Assyrians defeated Israel and exiled its people. Ahaz was ruling in Judah at this time. Hezekiah, the crowned prince, was probably functioning as coregent since he was still fairly young. Micah and Isaiah were continuing to preach in Judah.

---

6. W. Kaiser, *A History of Israel from the Bronze Age Through the Jewish Wars* (Nashville: Broadman and Holman, 1998), 357–64.

The Social and Economic Context

ECONOMIC CONDITIONS WERE excellent during the reign of Jeroboam II, especially for the upper class (Hos. 2:5, 8, 12; Amos 3:15; 6:1–8). Although the poor were oppressed and cheated by the powerful through corrupt judges, high rents, and deceitful merchants (Amos 5:10–12; 8:4–6), the land produced good crops, and most had enough to eat. After the death of Jeroboam II this comfortable world fell apart. The political unrest and military defeats of the nation undermined any attempt to establish a strong economy, and heavy taxation by the Assyrians compounded the harshness of making a living (Hos. 8:7, 10). Enemy troops stole grain and ate people's animals, fellow Israelites robbed and killed one another (6:8–9; 7:1), and crops failed because of God's curse on the land (9:2; 13:15).

Life was difficult, and thousands of husbands and sons were killed both in the Syro-Ephraimite war and in the wars with Assyria (2 Chron. 28:6). Although one might think that such economic and social disorder would cause people to see the error of their ways and turn to God, most were so blinded by their sins that they were unable to turn and seek the Lord (Hos. 4:6; 5:4).

The Worship of God

ONE OF THE main reasons why Israel was in such bad shape was the perversity of their theological understanding of God and their wide acceptance of Canaanite culture with its religion of Baalism. The worship of Yahweh, Israel's God, was so syncretized with Baalism over the years that some people thought Yahweh and Baal were just two different names for one divine being (Hos. 2:16). The two golden calves in the Israelite temples at Dan and Bethel (1 Kings 11–12; Hos. 8:5–6; 10:5) only added to the confusion, for Baal was also pictured as a bull. Consequently, many people thought Baal (or Yahweh) was a god who should be honored, so they participated in the sacrificial system and prostitution during festival events at pagan temples (Hos. 2:13; 4:11–14; 11:2; 13:2).[7] They believed that through their worship of Baal (or Yahweh), he would provide fertility to their crops and animals.

These Canaanite gods existed in Palestine at least as far back as the time of the judges (Judg. 2:11–14). After the golden calves were built, the acceptance of Baalism increased. In the time of Ahab and Jezebel Baalism became the dominant state religion in Israel (1 Kings 16:29–33), and this confusion of the worship of Yahweh and Baal continued throughout Hosea's ministry

---

7. J. Day ("Baal," *ABD*, 1:548) supports the view that sacred prostitution was part of the Baal cult, though nothing is said of this in the Ugaritic epic myths about Baal. K. van der Toorn ("Prostitution," *ABD*, 5:510–13) presents some of the arguments that dispute the biblical connection between Baalism and prostitution.

(2 Kings 17:7–18). No wonder God was angry that the people were prostituting themselves by worshiping another god and not remaining faithful to the covenant responsibility to love the God of Israel with all their heart and soul (Deut. 6:5; 10:12). Many Israelites accepted the Canaanite social and religious worldview rather than maintaining themselves as a separate people dedicated to God and his way of life as outlined in the Torah.

The Ministry of the Prophet Hosea

His Background

THE BOOK OF Hosea says nothing about the prophet's early life, where he was born, what his occupation was before he was called to be a prophet,[8] or his age when he became a prophet. Most assume he was a young adult, based on his not being married and the length of his prophetic career after his call (about thirty years). His repeated mentioning of cities in Israel (Samaria in 7:1; 8:5–6; 10:5, 7; 13:16) and the strange peculiarities of his Hebrew dialect suggest that he was a native of Israel, who gave all his sermons in and around the capital city of Samaria, or possibly at the main temple at Bethel.[9]

Detailed information is given about his wife, Gomer, but commentators interpret the phrase "woman of adultery/prostitution" (1:2, lit. trans.) in different ways. It seems odd, if not immoral, that God would require someone to marry an ungodly spouse. Consequently, many attempt to minimize this moral problem by not interpreting the story literally. At least six theories have arisen to explain this problem.

(1) J. L. Mays makes Gomer out to be "one of the sacred prostitutes of the fertility cult"[10] of Baal.

(2) Others, like E. J. Young, thought that there never was a marriage between Hosea and Gomer. Instead, the whole story was a symbolic vision revealed to the prophet to help him teach a lesson (like a parable).[11]

---

8. G. A. F. Knight, *Hosea* (London: SCM, 1960), 13, thought he was a baker, based on 7:4–7; H. W. Wolff, *Hosea* (Hermeneia; Philadelphia: Fortress, 1974), 79–80, thought he was a Levite. Neither option is convincing. The fact is, we just do not know.

9. Hosea usually does not tell where he was when he was delivering his sermons, or who he was speaking to, so it is not wise to put a lot of weight on this point. The theme of his messages can be identified without knowing exactly where he was in the nation of Israel.

10. J. L. Mays, *Hosea* (OTL; Philadelphia: Westminster, 1969), 3, 26, also suggests she could have been a common harlot.

11. E. J. Young, *An Introduction to the Old Testament* (London: Tyndale, 1960), 253, maintains that if this was a real marriage, it would have destroyed Hosea's credibility.

(3) A few think the sin of Gomer was "spiritual prostitution" rather than physical immorality; that is, she was one who worshiped other gods.[12]

(4) L. Wood takes a proleptic view of the phrase "woman of prostitution," concluding that Gomer was pure at the time of her marriage. This phrase about Gomer reflects Hosea's later retrospective view of God's command in light of her behavior after the marriage.[13]

(5) D. Stuart concludes that the promiscuous woman in Hosea 3 was not Gomer, but another woman he married.[14]

(6) We believe it is best to accept a literal historical interpretation and conclude that Gomer was sexually involved with other men before and after her marriage with Hosea. There is little to support the idea that she was a temple prostitute, that this was all just a dream, or that Hosea married two different women.[15]

It is impossible to trace the prophet's life history in any kind of clarity. The story simply looks forward to and then records the marriage and the birth of three children. There is no statement indicating that Hosea was the father of all the children, so some assume that the second and third children were not fathered by Hosea. After an unknown length of time, Hosea bought his degraded wife from the slave market and returned her to his home (3:1–3). The purpose of Hosea 1–3 is to draw out the comparisons between the sinful actions of Gomer and the people of Israel. These events highlight the love of Hosea and God for undeserving partners. The chapters do not provide a detailed biography of the prophet's troubled family life but draw out comparative theological lessons from his experience with Gomer and God's with Israel.

Although this failed marriage may seem like a major stumbling block for the prophet's ministry, Hosea's family problems did not disqualify him from prophetic service for God. In fact, they gave him a new understanding (from God's point of view) into the grossness of Israel's sins (it was comparable to Gomer's prostitution) and the depths of God's love (it was comparable to Hosea's love for the undeserving Gomer). This strengthened the conviction of his preaching, for he knew firsthand what he was talking about. He knew how God hurt when he was rejected, and from his own experience he knew how deeply God loved his people. Usually people learn a great deal about God through the trials of life.

---

12. See D. Stuart, *Hosea–Jonah* (WBC; Waco, Tex.: Word, 1987), 10–12.

13. L. Wood, *The Prophets of Israel* (Grand Rapids: Baker, 1979), 279.

14. Stuart, *Hosea–Jonah*, 11.

15. H. H. Rowley, "The Marriage of Hosea," *Men of God* (New York: Nelson, 1963), 66–97, surveys a variety of approaches commentaries take.

His Preaching

THE GENERAL TIME period for Hosea's ministry in Israel was from about 755 to 722 B.C. Since each sermon is not dated individually, it is difficult to connect each message with specific historical events. The references to the approaching threat of wars in 5:8 and 8:1 may give some help, but it is impossible to know how long before or after these wars each sermon was preached. One can assume that Hosea repeated some of his messages at different places throughout Israel or hypothesize that these were only given once. Since this data is missing, it is necessary to relate passages to general periods of Israelite history rather than exact dates.

The sermons of Hosea are constructed around a three-part structure of accusations, judgment, and hope (see esp. chs. 1–3; 12–14). These three emphases fit into the general structure of a covenant lawsuit against Israel (4:1–3; 12:2), but Hosea's way of presenting the covenant lawsuit is unique when compared to similar sermons in other prophets (cf. Mic. 6).[16] Hosea also includes judgment speeches (Hos. 13:1–3), the summons to repent (14:1–3), and the salvation oracle (14:4–7) to communicate his message. These were well-known types of speech at that time and widely accepted ways of communicating in culturally sensitive ways.

In the midst of these persuasive messages Hosea legitimated the accusations and punishment statements by repeatedly referring to Israel's earlier theological traditions.[17] He reminded the people about God's dealing with Sodom, Gomorrah, Admah, and Zeboiim in 11:8 (using Gen. 18–19; Deut. 29:23), the deceptive ways of Jacob in 12:3–4 (using Gen. 25–35), and the exodus from Egypt in 8:13; 9:3; 11:1, 5; 12:9; 13:4 (using Ex. 14–15). He mentions several of the Ten Commandments in 4:2 (using Ex. 20:1–17), alludes to the story of Achan's sin at Jericho in 2:15 (using Josh. 7), and possibly the preaching of Amos in 8:14 and 11:10 (using Amos 1:2, 4).[18]

Many in Hosea's audience knew about these authoritative traditions; therefore, he could appeal to what God had done in the past to legitimate

---

16. F. I. Andersen and D. N. Freedman, *Hosea* (AB; Garden City, N.Y.: Doubleday, 1980), 71–73, 315–16, downplay the use of known literary structures identified by form critics because Hosea's use of these is so unusual. W. Brueggemann, however, *Tradition for Crisis* (Richmond: John Knox, 1968), 55–90, illustrates the use of the covenant lawsuit in Hosea's messages.

17. See G. V. Smith, *An Introduction to the Hebrew Prophets: The Prophets as Preachers* (Nashville: Broadman and Holman, 1994), 5–25, for a study of the role of prophetic persuasion in the process of theological and social transformation.

18. See the extensive discussion of traditions used by Hosea in Brueggemann, *Tradition for Crisis*, 26–54.

his predictions of God's action in the future.[19] Hosea was demonstrating that his words from God were consistent with God's past revelation, so they should be accepted as a valid basis for rethinking the theological beliefs of his audience. Hosea reminded the people they had agreed to a covenant of loyalty to God and their breaking of this covenant agreement had serious consequences. The nature of the covenant relationship was not totally unknown, for the consequences of blessing (salvation) and cursing (judgment) had been explained long ago in the Torah (see Lev. 26; Deut. 27–28).[20]

Three of the most distinctive aspects of Hosea's preaching are: (1) his creative use of bold imagery to describe the covenant relationship that Israel was destroying by its unfaithfulness; (2) his use of emotions to portray God and describe Israel's problems; and (3) his distinctive vocabulary and grammatical constructions.

(1) How do people react to someone who dares to characterize sin as prostitution? Who would think to compare God to pus in a wound (5:12), a lion or leopard (13:7), or a pine tree (14:8)? Who would imagine Israel to be like an oven (7:4–7), a stubborn heifer (4:16), dew (6:4), a vessel (8:8), wild grapes (9:10), a stick (10:7), silly birds (11:11), and chaff or smoke (13:3)? Hosea used every imaginable comparison to make his point. It almost seems as if he relishes the idea of shocking his audience into thinking outside the box of their normal theology. He wants to jar them loose from their careless way of thinking about themselves and God. He also uses assonance, puns, and wordplays that make sense to the Hebrew listener.[21]

(2) The very nature of Hosea's devastating experience with Gomer was emotional. The agony and misery of both Hosea and Gomer can probably be best understood by those who have had an experience with an unfaithful partner, or by those who have gone through a divorce. No doubt there was fear, anger, disappointment, shame, and frustration. Signs of these powerful emotional feelings are also found when Hosea describes Israel's failure to remain faithful to its covenant relationship with God.

Particularly powerful are those passages that picture God's yearning not to give up on his beloved people. In 6:4 he wonders what he should do with his disloyal people. One might normally expect God to conclude his covenant lawsuit by destroying these sinful people. But to our astonishment, he does not give up on those he loves (11:8). Instead, he seeks to be com-

---

19. See G. V. Smith, *Introduction to the Hebrew Prophets*, 32–45, for a discussion of how the prophets legitimated their messages through the use of past authoritative tradition.

20. Stuart, *Hosea–Jonah*, xxxi–xlii, gives a long list of categories of curses, many of which are related to judgments in Hosea's sermons.

21. A. A. Macintosh, *A Critical and Exegetical Commentary on Hosea* (ICC; Edinburgh: T. & T. Clark, 1997), lxiv, gives many examples of these.

passionate again and again so that they will eventually return to him and follow him (11:10–11). Yes, he is angry at Israel's unfaithfulness and deceitfulness, but in his great love he wants to forgive the people, heal them, and bless them again (14:1–7). This powerful pathos is evident in almost every section of the book. If one misses this distinctive spirit in the words of Hosea, one will eviscerate the heart from the body of each message.

(3) The third aspect of these messages is their unusual vocabulary and grammatical constructions. The Hebrew text is problematic, and the footnotes in this commentary will briefly highlight for the reader some of the more important problems. English readers become aware of these problems when they discover very different translations of verses in their modern translations of the Bible.

There are many Hebrew words found only in Hosea (*hapax legomena* are found, e.g., in 2:12, 15; 5:2, 13; 8:6, 13), and some verses are so difficult that they are frequently emended.[22] We will avoid emendations as much as possible and stick to the difficult Hebrew dialect of Hosea. In many places there is little convincing support for the educated guesses people have proposed. At times one must just honestly admit that the meaning of a text is unclear. Usually this does not destroy the thrust of the message of a passage, but it may confuse the exact point being made in one-half of a verse.

Perhaps these problems stem from poor scribal copying, but the explanation that these issues arose because of the distinctive dialect of Hebrew that Hosea spoke seems more likely. These technicalities of language are not insignificant issues to be ignored as only of concern to scholars. Every communicator of the message of Hosea must legitimate his or her exposition of God's Word on the basis of an understanding of what Hosea originally said and meant when he spoke or wrote his messages. Therefore, an accurate and understandable text is a practical necessity, not an optional academic luxury.

His Theology

HOSEA'S THEOLOGICAL UNDERPINNINGS are drawn from his understanding of God's covenant relationship with his people (8:1). Although he spends much rhetorical effort communicating his message in a creative way so as to be understandable to an audience that has syncretized the worship of Baal and Yahweh, his message is centered around two basic themes. (1) The Israelites have sinned against their covenant partner and therefore will suffer God's judgment. (2) God loves his covenant people dearly and will forgive their sins and bring in a new age of blessing.

---

22. See some of the emendations of 4:4 in E. Tov, *Textual Criticism of the Hebrew Bible* (Minneapolis: Fortress, 1992), 359.

These conclusions seem to conflict with one another so much that some commentators suggest that a later editor, not Hosea, added the positive ideas of hope.[23] Since it was common for the prophets to legitimate repentance, both by reviewing the disadvantages of suffering under the wrath of God's judgment and by recounting the tremendous advantages of enjoying God's blessing, our approach is close to the conclusions of F. I. Andersen and D. N. Freedman, that "the book is essentially the work of a single person"[24]; thus both aspects were central to his theology.

Israel's sinful prostitution. The comparison between the unfaithfulness of marriage partners and Israel's failure to maintain its covenant relationship with God frames Hosea's theology of sin. Using this analogy, Hosea maintains that sin is like the act of prostitution on the human level. Three main points are developed. (1) Sin, like prostitution, is an act of not truly knowing or acknowledging one's covenant partner on a personal level. The Israelites rejected their covenant partner as their exclusive partner. How can there be an intimate relationship between God and his covenant people if they do not know him in an intimate way (4:1)?

When the priests rejected and ignored God's revelation of himself in the Torah (4:6–7), the people were naturally led astray to become involved with worship that was filled with practices of Baalism (4:11–15). They knew Baal, but not the difference between Baal and the true God of Israel. To make matters worse, the people seemed to be ignorant of the fact that their syncretistic worship would lead to their ruin (4:14). This fundamental perversity led to the situation where it was almost impossible for the people to return to God in repentance (5:4). What was the solution to this problem? There must be a radical transformation of their theology. People should desire an intimate personal relationship with God alone (6:3) and reject Baalism. Hosea's sermons try to persuade his listeners to change their thinking and behavior.

(2) Sin, like prostitution, is an act of unfaithfulness to the covenant commitments that the people of Israel made long ago. They did not maintain a steadfast covenant love for God. They were easily led astray to focus more on outward acts of giving sacrifices (6:6). They did not put their complete trust in God for their political future but were unfaithful, making alliances with

---

23. W. R. Harper, *A Critical and Exegetical Commentary on Amos and Hosea* (ICC; Edinburgh: T. & T. Clark, 1905), clix–clxiii, discusses the various different types of later additions to Hosea. G. Yee, *Composition and Tradition in the Book of Hosea* (Atlanta: Scholars, 1987), 1–25, describes various theories concerning the composition of Hosea and hypothesizes two later redactors who added positive information to Hosea's words.

24. Andersen and Freedman, *Hosea*, 59, recognize the impossibility of proving there were later redactors.

other nations (7:8, 11). They broke the covenant (8:1), were unfaithful by worshiping the golden calf (8:5–6, 10), and trusted in armies and fortresses rather than God (8:14; 10:13–14). Those who are faithful to the covenant do not murder, ignore God's choice when they appoint a new king, or reject God's laws. Unfaithfulness involves pleasing another mistress rather than remaining faithful to the covenant partner.

(3) The third sin is deceit. A deceitful covenant partner says one thing but does another. Hosea saw that the Israelites were following the deceitful practices of their forefather Jacob (11:12–12:1). This lack of truthfulness was evident in the deceptive weights in the marketplace (12:7–8) and the worship of illusionary, man-made gods (13:1–3). The people did not commit themselves to God alone; their commitment lasted about as long as the dew in the morning.

These three characteristics of Israel's sins were evident in their political dealings with other nations, their economic dealings with one another, and their spiritual relationships with God. There was no sincerity or consistency in what they said or did. They somehow thought that they could love God and participate in Baal worship at the same time. They did not see any inconsistency between the values of their secular Baalistic culture and the demands of their covenant relationship with God. Rather than separating themselves from the world to become the holy people of God, they accepted a veneer of God-talk that covered a heart of unfaithful prostitution. Since the nation did not realize God looked at their sins so seriously, Hosea communicated both the true nature of sin in God's eyes and the horrible consequences of the prostitution of their loyalties. God would judge the people severely and destroy the nation.

The depth of God's love. We do Hosea a vast injustice if we suppose his theology was stuck in a negative hopelessness that saw no cure for the nation's prostitution. It is truly amazing to see the strength of God's love for his people in Hosea's sermons. God will not totally give up on his people but will allure them back to himself (2:14), restore his covenant relationship (2:19, 23), give them their messianic king (3:5), and cause the land to be fruitful again (2:21). Those who are not his people will become the sons of the living God (1:10–11).

Although the people do not deserve God's grace, how can he give up on his chosen people (11:8)? If they will but turn to him, he will forgive their sins, heal them, and love them once again (14:1–7). Since God's compassion outweighs the sins of the people, there is hope for them in the distant future. At that time they will intimately know him and will remain faithful to their covenant commitments.

The Challenge for the Church

IN MOST CHURCHES few messages are given on Hosea. Parts of the book can be hard to understand because of its odd and foreign symbolism, its difficult poetry, and its discussion of the embarrassing problem of prostitution in the family of a prophet—and in the family of God. Since Baalism is not a modern threat to the church and not many people in our neighborhoods fall down and worship idols, the setting and spiritual problems of Israel seem foreign to the struggles most believers face today.

Consequently, most preachers feel the difficulty of developing applications for the church from this series of prophetic sermons. After all, who would encourage the associate pastor in the church to marry a prostitute? How could the drunken worship at the Baal temples (4:11–14) be compared to anything that happens during a worship service today? Other than an occasional reference to God's love in Hosea 3 or 11, most of his messages are ignored because they appear to be irrelevant to the central issues people face in our modern technological culture.

Nevertheless, if one does not focus so much on the specifics of the ancient fertility beliefs or the sexual methods of worship in Baalism, one can begin to suggest areas where the theological message of Hosea relates to theological issues the church has struggled with in every era of its existence. If one views Baalism as a cultural expression of a Canaanite religious worldview, the true comparison for modern application is not limited to situations where pagans are worshiping idols in India or involved in some perverted sexual cult in some faraway country. The Canaanite culture needs to be compared to the British culture, the Hutu culture, the American culture, or the Brazilian culture.

Each of these countries has a popular "religious" philosophy of life that explains how the world works. Each culture includes ethical standards for appropriate conduct, economic ways of gaining prosperity (fertility in ancient Near Eastern terminology), and an explanation of how people are related to the divine powers. The questions that the church in every culture must ask are similar to the questions Hosea raises. Are the people who claim to be believers actually the people of God, or have they so accepted the popular religious culture of their day that they, like Israel, are "not my people"? Has the syncretism of the church with modern religious culture so infiltrated the fiber of the fellowship that people can no longer see a distinction between the two? Has the church lost its identity by compromising its beliefs and accepting the moral standards of the society that the church was supposed to transform?

Although believers are "in the world" and function in a culture that is shared with others, in another sense they are not "one" with all parts of that reality. The danger for Israel, and for the church today, is a double threat. One option is for people to withdraw totally into a conventlike existence or try to be separate (like the Amish) to maintain their purity. But this solution may so isolate believers from society that they will never reach the world with God's love or have a positive influence on the development of that culture. One cannot reach the world by retreating into a monastery so as to lose all contact with the world. Although purity may be maintained, is not the church to have a purifying effect as it goes into all the world to present the good news?

By contrast, those who fully participate in the culture face the danger of compromising some of their beliefs to the secular standards of the day. If education, business, entertainment, and ethics are framed by the cultural standards of ungodly people, most likely they will not be consistent with Christian standards. It is difficult for anyone to resist the temptation to compromise one's beliefs under such strong social pressure day after day.

Anyone over forty years of age knows that many people in churches have changed their ideas about what is right and wrong during that time period. When I was growing up, my parents did not even want me to go to a bowling hall that sold beer, but few make that a big issue when they raise teenagers today. The issue to be emphasized here is not who was right on this issue, but that believers are influenced for better or for worse by the cultural definition of "appropriate behavior" where they live.

In light of these factors it is important to recognize that Hosea does not just object to the theological system that honors Baal, nor does he just deal with the debased sexual ritual practiced at the Baal or Yahwistic temples (4:11–14). Behind these external signs of unfaithfulness to God lies the deeper problem of people's acceptance of a nonbiblical theological system from their culture. Hosea does not condemn or reject every aspect of that culture but does recognize that if people accept certain aspects, these can pervert their understanding of God and his relationship to humankind. This perversion led Israel to be unfaithful to its covenant relationship and caused it to be untruthful and deceptive to God. These are issues that can be investigated in each era of church history and in each denomination. Although the specific issues may be different, each generation faces the tension of knowing how to remain faithful to God in a world that loves to twist the truth—both in minor ways as well as direct affronts to the character and will of God.

Some people may deny that the culture of our day influences the religious ideas of people in the church, but there are too many subtle examples to ignore. It is not unusual to hear people say that the church needs to be run more like a business. Sometimes this is innocently expressed by those who say the church needs to have a mission statement and goals, as we do at work. Some constitutions overtly speak of the pastor as the CEO and have a business manager.

Yet these issues are minor in comparison to the attitudinal changes of some church attendees. Surely the consumer mentality of many Christians did not arise from reading about the operation of the early church in Acts. Opposition to guitars and drums or the raising of hands in worship was not an insight derived from reading about worship in Israel from the Psalms. The move to multimedia presentations in seeker-sensitive churches is not something derived from the worship Paul describes in his letters.

I am not suggesting that the church should condemn or resist all cultural innovations or that certain modern cultural methods are wrong in themselves; the church should adopt and adapt those things that make the presentation of the gospel more relevant to our culture. The difficulty is in determining which things to accept and which to reject. In this process one must continually ask whether a certain cultural phenomenon is consistent with scriptural principles, or whether there has been an attempt to lie and distort the truth in order to justify certain actions or attitudes.

Unfortunately, it is usually difficult to separate what is cultural from what is not, for many people do not even recognize the impact their culture has on their theological understanding. Yet all one has to do is to visit a Hispanic, a black, and a white church to observe the cultural differences. A messianic congregation in Israel will do things differently from a group of Korean believers in Minnesota. Although all these believers read the same Bible, they worship differently, think in unique theological ways, and develop separate methods of church polity. Such differences do not indicate that all truth is relative, nor do they prove that God's truth can be manipulated to say whatever we want it to say. It does mean that one can express the truth in different cultural ways so that it can make sense to people from different parts of the world.

Thus, God could reveal his truth to people like Abraham and David, who lived in a Semitic culture, as well as to Paul and Barnabas, who grew up in a Greco-Roman world. The problem of unfaithfulness to God arises not because of differences between cultures, but because of the misperceptions of God and his will for people within each culture.

In modern culture the forces of rationalism and science have eliminated the need to see God as the sovereign power in control of the weather, the sovereign force in charge of human health and the removal of disease, or the almighty king in control of world politics. L. Gilkey has complained that the idea of divine providence is a "rootless, disembodied ghost, flitting from footnote to footnote, but rarely finding secure lodgment in sustained theo-

logical discourse."[25] Although believers in the church may confess their belief
in the sovereignty of God over their souls after death, all too often they act
as if God actually has no role in determining what will happen today or
tomorrow. They have accepted the culture's view that the weather is controlled by wind, humidity, high and low pressure systems, and temperature,
rather than by God.

Yet one wonders, who controls the wind that directs the weather systems?
Who causes the jet stream to bend and dip? Who directs the currents in the
Pacific to produce the devastating global "El Niño" effect around the world?
Just how sovereign is God? Is he a wimp or the only one who actually has any
control over what happens on this earth? Have believers bought into the
humanistic explanations of the earth and restricted God's activity to heaven?

Hosea's message addresses issues where people have allowed their culture
to twist their theology into a deceptive illusion of the truth. The church
likewise needs to be vigilant to observe where the silent threat of cultural
accommodation may creep into the thought patterns of theological discourse and destroy its central connection to the truth. Is the message of
Scripture being adjusted to make it more popular? Does the formulation of
the truth change when it is packaged in new forms that the audience enjoys
hearing?

Recent studies of evangelicalism suggest that some evangelical Christians
have changed some of their theological and ethical beliefs.[26] H. Cox even
advocated "wasting little time thinking about 'ultimate' or 'religious questions.'"[27] As L. Sweet maintains, in the 1960s "being secular was not a way of
acknowledging defeat but a way of being authentically Christian in a new age.
Churches willingly relinquished their creeds, rituals, pieties, and beliefs to
accommodate new social attitudes."[28] When the church caves in to the authority of culture, people begin to believe the ideological notion that what is culturally normative must be theologically acceptable. They adopt the illusion
that the theological teaching of Scripture is outmoded and irrelevant in this
modern culture of relativism and pluralism; thus, devastating compromises
seem inevitable and the preferred approach to addressing problem issues.[29]

---

25. L. Gilkey, "The Concept of Providence in Contemporary Theology," *JR* 43 (1963): 171.

26. J. D. Hunter, *American Evangelicalism: Conservative Religion and the Quandary of Modernity* (New Brunswick: Rutgers Univ. Press, 1983); R. Quebedeux, *The Worldly Evangelicals* (San Francisco: Harper and Row, 1978).

27. H. Cox, *The Secular City* (New York: Macmillan, 1965).

28. L. I. Sweet, "The 1960s: The Crisis of Liberal Christianity and the Public Emer-
gence of Evangelicalism," *Evangelicalism and Modern America*, ed. G. Marsden (Grand Rapids: Eerdmans, 1984), 33.

29. Ibid., 34.

This issue of accommodation to cultural standards rather than to God's Word can also exhibit itself in settings where people allow "godly leaders" to create an almost cultic following they claim is biblical. These situations can then develop into a deceptive, mind-controlling culture enforced by a selfish and powerful charismatic leader who twists the truth as badly as some secular philosophers. The danger of being deceived into following some unfaithful system of thinking that is alien to God is present every time a person watches television, reads the newspaper, or hears a sermon.

Hosea's message requires us to ask: Is the message I am getting from this news story, sports information, comedy, or religious song one that I can accept, or is it contrary to what the Bible says about God? Would accepting it lead to unfaithfulness to God's will and my covenant relationship with him? Does this concept encourage a deceptive lifestyle, or does it clearly demonstrate the necessity of truthfulness with God and others? If we were to look at our relationship to God as a marriage (as Hosea does), how would God evaluate our love, our commitment to him, and our truthfulness? What should the proclaimers of God's words today be saying about what he expects of his future bride, the church? Is prostitution now acceptable, or does God still hate those who syncretize their faith with the pagan culture of the day?

Outline of Hosea

I. **Unfaithfulness in the Family of God** (1:1–3:5)
   A. Hosea's and God's Broken Family (1:1–2:1)
   B. Confronting Unfaithful Wives (2:2–23)
   C. Restoration of Broken Families (3:1–5)

II. **God's Lawsuit for No Knowledge of God** (4:1–6:6)
   A. The Priests Do Not Know God (4:1–19)
   B. Judgment of War (5:1–14)
   C. Possibilities of Restoration for the Seeker (5:15–6:6)

III. **God's Lawsuit for Lack of Steadfast Devotion to God** (6:7–11:11)
   A. Israel's Unfaithfulness to the Covenant (6:7–7:16)
   B. Destruction, Captivity, and an End to Israel (8:1–9:17)
   C. Sin is the Reason for Israel's Fall (10:1–15)
   D. God's Love Provides Hope for Restoration (11:1–11)

IV. **God's Lawsuit for Deceitfulness** (11:12–14:9)
   A. Charges of Deceit (11:12–13:3)
   B. Punishment of Destruction (13:4–16)
   C. Restoration for the Repentant (14:1–9)

Annotated Bibliography
on Hosea

Andersen, F. I, and D. N. Freedman. *Hosea.* AB 24. Garden City, N.Y.: Doubleday, 1980. An excellent but long and detailed study that uses Hebrew. They maintain that Hosea wrote this book and try to limit emendations of the text.

Brueggemann, W. *Tradition for Crisis: A Study in Hosea.* Richmond: John Knox, 1968. Shows how Hosea uses earlier traditions to support his points in this covenant lawsuit against Israel. This is not a verse-by-verse commentary.

Davies, G. I. *Hosea.* NCBC. Grand Rapids: Eerdmans, 1992. Explains Hosea's message, marriage, and historical context, seeing later redactors influencing the book.

Emmerson, G. I. *Hosea: An Israelite Prophet in Judean Perspective.* Sheffield: JSOT, 1984. A study of the Judean redaction of Hosea, which sees only moderate editing.

Garrett, D. *Hosea, Joel.* NAC. Nashville: Broadman and Holman, 1997. Has numerous footnotes that clarify the Hebrew text (and problems with the NIV) to support his exposition of Hosea's message. He does not think Hosea was using the covenant lawsuit form and rarely allows any emendations of the Hebrew text.

Guenther, A. *Hosea, Amos.* BCBC. Scottsdale: Herald, 1998. Provides a more pastoral reading that does not get involved with most of the technical data.

Harper, W. R. *A Critical and Exegetical Commentary on Amos and Hosea.* ICC. Edinburgh: T. & T. Clark, 1905. An older detailed and technical commentary that accepts later additions to Hosea.

Hubbard, D. A. *Hosea.* TOTC. Downers Grove: InterVarsity, 1989. Offers a brief exposition of Hosea.

Kidner, D. *Love to the Loveless: The Message of Hosea.* Downers Grove: InterVarsity, 1981. Another brief pastoral study of Hosea.

Limburg, J. *Hosea–Micah.* Interpretation. Atlanta: John Knox, 1988. While not a verse-by-verse treatment, it does include pastoral comments after each section. He accepts critical theories about the writing of the book.

Macintosh, A. A. *A Critical and Exegetical Commentary on Hosea.* ICC. Edinburgh: T. & T. Clark, 1997. Summarizes rabbinic thinking about the understanding of Hosea.

Mays, J. L. *Hosea*. OTL. Philadelphia: Westminster, 1969. Though a solid exposition of the text, Mays finds later authors adding material to the book of Hosea.

McComiskey, T. E. "Hosea." Pages 1–237 in *The Minor Prophets*, vol. 1. Grand Rapids: Baker, 1992. Contains a section on Hebrew and another on exposition. A solid study.

Stuart, D. *Hosea–Jonah*. WBC. Waco, Tex.: Word, 1987. Gives strong support to the use of the covenant lawsuit and covenant curses in Hosea. Does emend the text often to solve linguistic problems.

Ward, J. *Hosea: A Theological Commentary*. New York: Harper and Row, 1966. More of a theological summary of key themes in Hosea's preaching.

Wolff, H. W. *Hosea*. Hermeneia. Philadelphia: Fortress, 1974. A detailed critical study that accepts later redactional additions to Hosea.

Yee, G. *Composition and Tradition in the Book of Hosea*. Atlanta: Scholars, 1987. This is a critical study of the composition of the book by Hosea and several later redactors through four stages of writing.

_____. "The Book of Hosea." 197–297 in *New Interpreter's Bible*, vol. 7. Nashville: Abingdon, 1996. Provides both an exegetical commentary and pastoral reflections for use in communicating the text today.

Hosea 1:1–2:1

❧

THE WORD OF the LORD came to Hosea son of Berri during the reign of Uzziah, Jotham, Ahaz and Hezekiah, kings of Judah, and during the reign of Jeroboam son of Jehoash king of Israel.

²When the LORD began to speak through Hosea, the LORD said to him, "Go, take to yourself an adulterous wife and children of unfaithfulness, because the land is guilty of the vilest adultery in departing from the LORD." ³So he married Gomer daughter of Diblaim, and she conceived and bore him a son.

⁴Then the LORD said to Hosea, "Call him Jezreel, because I will soon punish the house of Jehu for the massacre at Jezreel, and I will put an end to the kingdom of Israel. ⁵In that day I will break Israel's bow in the Valley of Jezreel."

⁶Gomer conceived again and gave birth to a daughter. Then the Lord said to Hosea, "Call her Lo-Ruhamah, for I will no longer show love to the house of Israel, that I should at all forgive them. ⁷Yet I will show love to the house of Judah; and I will save them—not by bow, sword or battle, or by horses and horsemen, but by the LORD their God."

⁸After she had weaned Lo-Ruhamah, Gomer had another son. ⁹Then the LORD said, "Call him Lo-Ammi, for you are not my people, and I am not your God.

¹⁰"Yet the Israelites will be like the sand of the seashore, which cannot be measured or counted. In the place where it was said to them, 'You are not my people,' they will be called 'sons of the living God.' ¹¹The people of Judah and the people of Israel will be reunited, and they will appoint one leader and will come up out of the land, for great will be the day of Jezreel.

²:¹"Say to your brothers, 'My people,' and to your sisters, 'My loved one.'"

HOSEA 1:1–3:5 CONTAINS a direct analogy between the marriage of Hosea and Gomer and the covenant relationship between God and Israel. The story progresses through three stages: (1) the sinful adultery of Gomer and Israel destroys their covenant relationships (ch. 1); (2) confrontations and redemptive chastenings are begun (ch. 2); and (3) the restoration of the covenant relationship is accomplished through love (ch. 3). This representation of God's future dealing with Israel carries a dramatic and shocking message of callous betrayal by one party, an unwillingness to continue with the status quo by the other party, and the surprising undeserved mercy of God's love.

By setting Israel's sinful behavior in the framework of the vile behavior of a prostitute, Hosea reminds his audience both of the seriousness of sin (it destroys a mutual trusting relationship) and the amazing greatness of God's love. Unfaithfulness to God in Israel and the church cannot be ignored. Either people are believers and are faithful to their covenant commitments to God, or they are not a part of the family of God. Those who are unfaithful to God are really more like prostitutes. They are not and cannot be members of God's family unless two things happen. God must love them in spite of their sins (which he does), and they must respond to God's love with a new commitment of love for him. Hosea reveals that God has and will continue to give undeserved love to those who do not have a covenant relationship with God. The question is: How will people respond to his gracious gift of love?

Regarding 1:1–2:1, after the superscription (1:1), the structure of this narrative segment is ordered around Hosea's marriage and the subsequent birth of three children (1:2–9). Each sub-paragraph contains an initial imperative exhortation from God to Hosea (1:2b, 4a, 6b, 9a), followed by a divine explanation of how each name or action symbolically represents what is happening among the people in Israel (introduced by "because" [*ki*] in 1:2c, 4b–5, 6c, 9b). In something of a surprise ending, the negative implications of the children's names are dramatically reversed in the final paragraph (1:10–2:1; in the Heb. text these verses are 2:1–3) because a future time of covenant renewal and blessing is pictured.

The material in this story is not purely biographical, for the focus of attention is primarily on how God used the prophet's family as a symbolic representation of his dealings with the nation. The biographical details are in fact meager and give no indication of how this dysfunctional family coped with its symbolic role or the tragedy of an unfaithful spouse and mother. No words or emotional reactions (other than Hosea's obedience) from any member of the family are included.

The reference to the future fall of the dynasty of Jeroboam II (1:4–5) suggests that this material was spoken before the death of Jeroboam II.[1] The purposes for publishing these verses are: (1) to explain the peculiar symbolic names of Hosea's children; (2) to warn Hosea's audience about God's intentions to bring judgment on the nation of Israel; and (3) to encourage the righteous about God's intention to fulfill the Abrahamic covenant.[2] The prophet hopes he can persuade some unfaithful people in his audience to transform their thinking and behavior to avoid God's judgment on Israel.

God's and Hosea's Symbolic Marriage (1:1–3)

THE BRIEF HISTORICAL superscription places these events in the prosperous days of King Jeroboam II of Israel (1:1).[3] The first words the Lord God spoke "through Hosea" (1:2a) came at this time. Additional evidence of the prophetic role of Hosea is provided by the repeated emphasis on what "the LORD said" (1:2b, 4, 6, 9) to Hosea to help him and his readers understand the symbolic meaning of his marriage and children. These words revealed God's plan for Hosea's life. This idea of marrying an impure woman was probably not the family life that Hosea's proud parents planned for their son, but it was what God called him to do. Hosea did not just dream up this stuff about marrying a prostitute out of the rebelliousness of his youth; it was God's idea.

God instructed Hosea to marry an "adulterous wife" (1:2), an act that has caused great consternation among interpreters, but surprisingly no negative reaction from Hosea himself. The moral problem involved with this exhortation makes some think this whole story was just a vision or parable, while others conclude that Gomer was actually spiritually unfaithful rather than involved with sexual promiscuity.[4] Kaufmann thinks that Gomer merely put on the clothes of a harlot to symbolize the apostasy of Israel, much like the theatrical sign-acts of Isaiah (going naked in Isa. 20:1–4) and Ezekiel (cutting his hair and lying on his side in Ezek. 4–5).[5]

---

1. Wolff, *Hosea*, 12, and Stuart, *Hosea–Jonah*, 25, argue for an early date for this material.

2. The positive words of hope in 1:10–2:1 are sometimes identified as the words of a later redactor, but it is customary for Hosea to abruptly place paradoxical words of hope next to prophecies of judgment. The thematic connections between the original names of the children and the new names in the future require a close connection for the audience to see the great reversal that God will accomplish. See Yee, *Composition and Tradition in the Book of Hosea*, 68–72, who assigns these verses to a second deuteronomistic redactor after the exile. Stuart, *Hosea–Jonah*, 36, gives seven connections between 1:2–9 and 1:10–2:1 that indicate these two sections go together. G. I. Emmerson, *Hosea: An Israelite Prophet in Judean Perspective* (Sheffield: JSOT, 1984), 15–16, maintains these verses are a part of Hosea's preaching.

3. See the Introduction for the political, social, and religious background of this period.

4. See the earlier discussion and critique of these options in the Introduction.

5. Y. Kaufmann, *The Religion of Israel*, trans. M. Greenberg (Chicago: Univ. of Chicago Press, 1960), 370–71.

The plain meaning of these words cannot be easily escaped, however, for Gomer was to symbolize the fact that the land of Israel was full of people who had departed from the Lord and committed adultery by their involvement in the fertility religion of Baalism. Some scholars attempt to lessen the scandal by proposing that Gomer only had tendencies toward immoral behavior. Others suggest that God did not specifically ask Hosea to marry a harlot; instead, this verse is a retrospective realization by Hosea that God providentially led him to marry a woman who turned out to be unfaithful to her marriage vows.[6]

Although it sounds unusual and self-defeating for a prophet of God to marry a prostitute, the Bible only limits the wives a priest can choose. According to Leviticus 21:14 the priest must marry a virgin, not a harlot or a widow. No similar limitations are imposed on prophets or the average Hebrew citizen. Therefore, we conclude that Gomer[7] was sexually involved with other men before and after her marriage to Hosea and must have received some payment for her sexual favors (Hos. 2:5). Hosea's reception of these instructions from God helped him interpret his life and ministry as the divine plan of God. It changed how he looked at the sinful people in Israel and how he empathized with God's reaction to his sinful wife, Israel.

In accepting God's plan for his life, Hosea submitted his wishes to God's will. He set himself up to feel and know a little bit about the bitterness of God's pain, as well as the depth of his love for undeserving people. He understood how Gomer's adultery represented the behavior of the people in the nation of Israel, God's covenant partner. They were guilty of "the vilest adultery" (1:2). By their unfaithful worship of Baal and participation in the sexual activities in that fertility cult, they defiled themselves and rejected their own God. In God's eyes the nation's syncretism of the worship of Baal and Yahweh was not a minor problem of little significance; it was an affront to the exclusive covenant commitment God desires of those whom he loves.

God's and Hosea's Symbolic Children (1:4−9)

IF GOMER REPRESENTS the nation and its evil culture, the "children of unfaithfulness" (lit., "children of prostitution") represent the individual Israelites who later witness against their mother (2:2, 4). As the mother, Gomer symbolizes Israel's syncretistic religion that its leaders promote, while the children are those pressured to follow this cultural ideology. One should not conclude that

---

6. Harper, *Amos and Hosea*, 207, takes the first approach, while G. Archer, *A Survey of Old Testament Introduction* (Chicago: Moody, 1974), 323, calls the second the proleptic view.

7. We do not know if Gomer's father was Diblaim or if Diblaim was the village where she was raised.

the phrase about the children describes child prostitution; rather, it refers to the fact that at least some of Gomer's children (and the Israelites) were outside the covenant relationship. T. McComiskey thinks Hosea adopted the illegitimate children Gomer had before her marriage to Hosea,[8] but most interpreters prefer to explain "children of prostitution" by pointing to the fact that the text never connects Hosea to the conception of the second and third child (1:6, 8). Thus, perhaps the last two children were born because of Gomer's unfaithfulness to her marriage vows.

The first child was Hosea's (1:3, "she . . . bore him a son"), and God named him Jezreel. This child was to remind Hosea's audience of what had happened in the Valley of Jezreel, where king Jehu poured out the blood of innocent lives in order to solidify his political power (2 Kings 9–10, esp. 9:25–26; 10:11). The NIV and other translations connect this child's name with the idea that God "will soon punish" the house or dynasty of Jehu for this massacre and consequently bring an end to the kingdom of Israel (Hos. 1:4).

This interpretation does not make sense, however, for God approved what Jehu did in the Valley of Jezreel (2 Kings 10:30). Therefore, it seems better to follow D. Garrett and translate the text, "I will bring the bloodshed of Jezreel upon the house of Jehu."[9] This implies that a violent situation at the beginning of Jehu's reign will parallel a violent situation that will end the dynasty of Jehu. Indeed, after the death of Jeroboam II, his son Zechariah was assassinated after a short six-month reign (2 Kings 15:8). He was the last descendant of Jehu to rule in Israel. It was only about thirty years later that the "bow" (Hos. 1:5) or army of Israel was defeated and the nation was taken into exile by the Assyrians.

The second child (1:6–7) was a girl named "Lo-Ruhamah," a name that symbolically announces that God will have "no compassion, no love."[10] This child's name reveals that God will end his tender feelings of deep affection (like a mother's deep affection for the fruit of her womb) that are foundational to his covenant relationship with his people. The loving feeling between kinfolk will be missing; God will not pity or care what happens to them. This name represents a dramatic reversal of Israel's self-understanding (they thought they were the children of God) and will be a severe blow to their confidence in God's unfailing commitment to love his people. They will no longer be rescued when they are in trouble, for God's compassionate mercy will no longer be extended to them.

---

8. T. McComiskey, *The Minor Prophets*, 3 vols. (Grand Rapids: Baker, 1992, 1995, 1998), 1:12, but Andersen and Freedman, *Hosea*, 162, 167, argue convincingly against this proposal.
9. D. A. Garrett, *Hosea, Joel* (NAC; Nashville: Broadman & Holman, 1997), 56.
10. M. Butterworth, "רחם," *NIDOTTE*, 3:1093–95.

Verse 6 ends with the clause "that I should at all forgive them,"[11] which fits logically with an absence of divine mercy. But the verb *nś'* can also mean to lift up, take away, thus referring to God's plan to "take" the nation into exile. This idea makes a better translation since it provides a better contrast with God's commitment to save Judah in 1:7.[12] God will not abandon his love for all his people forever; he will only abandon those unfaithful to their covenant relationship with God at this time. In contrast to Israel, Judah will continue to receive God's deep affectionate love and protection from danger (1:7).[13] This love will be demonstrated by a great deed of divine deliverance—a deliverance that will not be accomplished through any military power. This prophecy may point ahead to God's miraculous deliverance of Hezekiah from the Assyrian king Sennacherib in 701 B.C., when 185,000 Assyrian troops were struck dead in a single night (Isa. 36−37).

These opposite ways (cursing and blessing) of dealing with different people naturally cause the listener in Israel to wish for the divine love that Judah will receive. If the prophet can create that desire, the listeners may then attempt to discover why God will deal with the two nations so differently and become jealous for God's grace. If people do not change, Israel's immediate future is hopeless, for "the vilest adultery" (1:2) pervades the land.

God gives the third child the name "Lo-Ammi . . . not my people" (1:8−9). Now it is official; the covenant connection is broken and God will no longer say, "I will . . . be your God, and you will be my people" (Lev. 26:12; cf. Ex. 6:7; Deut. 27:9). Israel's unfaithful adultery will lead to the dissolution of the covenant relationship. They will no longer be the children of God; their identity will change because they have committed themselves to another lover.

God's and Hosea's New Children (1:10−2:1)

THIS SECTION ENDS with a great paradoxical surprise and a reversal of the meaning of the children's names. The change is jarring and breathtakingly quick. At one moment God rejects his people, and in the next he accepts them back as his covenant partners. Some interpreters have great trouble accepting this abrupt change of attitude toward the nation when there is no

---

11. RSV, NEB, and NASB have a similar translation as NIV.

12. Stuart, *Hosea, Jonah*, 31, follows W. Kuhnigk, who suggested that *nś'* (to lift up, forgive) was confused with *nś'* (to reject). T. McComiskey, *Minor Prophets*, 1:25, and R. C. Ortlund, *Whoredom: God's Unfaithful Wife in Biblical Theology* (Grand Rapids: Eerdmans, 1996), 53, argue for "to take away."

13. Andersen and Freedman, *Hosea*, 5, 194, inappropriately continue the negatives of 1:6 into 1:7 and thus reverse the promises to Judah into curses by translating "nor for the state of Judah will I show pity or save them."

intercession by the prophet (cf. Amos 7:1–3) and no repentance by the people.[14]

In the editing of these messages for publication, it appears that Hosea chose this literary structure (putting opposite ideas side by side without any transitional phrases) in order to highlight the contrasts. He probably wants the reader to ask: How can total despair lead to total acceptance and hope for the future? Everyone knows you cannot get directly from one to the other. Only the miraculous power and love of God can bring grace to a vile and rejected people. The human mind cannot fully comprehend God's ways or justify his grace, for God's thoughts and ways are often beyond mortal explanation (Isa. 55:8–9). The interpreter must bow in humble amazement at that love rather than deny that God can ever reverse his actions so dramatically.

This positive promise begins with the reminder that in the future God will fulfill his promise to Abraham and Jacob and multiply the people in Israel like the sand of the sea (quoting portions of Gen. 22:17; 32:12). This present destruction will not prevent God from fulfilling his original plans. The time of God's wrath and destruction will one day end and God's blessing will revive the people. Then "in the place," that is, in the land of Israel, it will become apparent that these people are the "sons of the living God" (1:10). The "Lo-Ammi" ("not my people" in 1:9) of Hosea's day will be replaced by the true people of the living God.

J. L. Mays sees implicit in the title "living God" the recognition that it is God's miraculous life-giving power that makes new life possible for this new generation.[15] This title gives the people an identity as "sons," as well as an acknowledgment of their relationship to God. It implicitly signals the renewal of the covenant relationship between God and Israel.

The second promise relates to the unification of Judah and Israel (1:11). This rejuvenated people will be made up of two peoples who will join themselves together as one united nation, thus ending the suspicion and hatred that extended back to the original division of the nations by Jeroboam I (1 Kings 12) and even earlier (2 Sam. 2:3–11; 5:1–5). In one united effort they will appoint an unidentified leader (*ro᾿š*, leader, is used, not *melek*, king),

---

14. Wolff, *Hosea*, 25, relocates these verses beside 2:23–25, where these names reappear, while Yee, *Composition and Tradition in the Book of Hosea*, 55, 68–76, sees these verses as a redactional addition by a second exilic editor. These verses are repeatedly tied to the names of Hosea's children in 1:2–9; thus there is an inner unifying cohesion within its structure (see Stuart, *Hosea–Jonah*, 36, for some of these connections).

15. Mays, *Hosea*, 32. A second point of this title may be a purposeful contrast between "the living God" and Baal, the Canaanite fertility god who was so popular among those in Hosea's audience.

an idea that Hosea will clarify later in 3:5. Old conflicts and rivalries will be a thing of the past, and nationalism for the northern or southern tribes will disappear.

The third aspect of restoration describes the people's new relationship to their land (1:11). Andersen and Freedman see it as both a reference to a return from exile (a new historical exodus from exile) and a resurrection from the land of the dead (see 5:8–6:6).[16] If the last two lines of 1:11 are seen as a pair, then it makes more sense to follow T. McComiskey, who believes that Hosea is talking about the vegetation (similar to 2:22–23) that God will "sow" (using Jezreel in the next line) in the land. It will grow and multiply abundantly in the land, for great will be this positive day of Jezreel ("sowing") when God blesses his people and their land.[17]

As a result of God's powerful intervention, he will say (2:1) "Ammi—my people" instead of "not my people," and "Ruhamah—my loved one" instead of "not loved" (cf. 1:6, 9). This reflects God's complete acceptance of his people, his recognition of their new relationship, and a total reversal of the earlier status of the nation. These names reveal a tender connection between the parties because of God's compassion.

What effect would these words have on Hosea's audience? These promises should cause them to remember that the covenant relationship promises two possible destinies for Israel (curses and blessings), to realize that their harlotry will result in their judgment, and to understand that God's plans to bless his faithful people will happen after a period of judgment. His sermon may have encouraged some to recommit themselves in faith to God's future plans.

Bridging Contexts

THE USE OF **the marriage metaphor.** The main purpose of this story about Hosea's family is to represent symbolically in a real family both the positive and negative ways God relates to his people. Hosea 1:2–9 focuses on how God responds when his people forsake the commitments that are required of a covenant relationship, while 1:10–2:1 demonstrates God's compassion for his covenant people. Although sonship is an excellent biblical way of describing one's relationship to God (1:10), the

---

16. Andersen and Freedman, *Hosea*, 208–9, and Stuart, *Hosea–Jonah*, 39, follow this approach, but neither concept is usually expressed this way because "the land" usually refers to Israel, not the land of captivity or the place of the dead.

17. McComiskey, *Minor Prophets*, 1:30. This view seems to have fewer problems. Macintosh, *Hosea*, 31–32, surveys seven approaches to this problem and prefers to relate this line to the growing of vegetation.

marriage covenant relationship is one of the most powerful human analogies to compare with God's covenant relationship with his people.

Hosea boldly compares sin to adultery in order to demonstrate how terribly destructive it is to a person's relationship with God. Sin is not a minor incidental mistake that can be winked at, as if it really does not matter. Sin is a devastating affront to the exclusive love commitment one makes to God. Sin is a forsaking of loyalty to one person. Hosea does not give much detail in chapter 1 about the nature of Israel's specific sins (this will become clearer later), so it is inappropriate to draw specific theological principles about these issues. Instead the focus should be on this general point: The Israelites are sinners who flagrantly commit vile acts of prostitution.

Although sin is sin, this repulsive act of iniquity shows the level to which people can sink into the grip of sin. Thus a wife's sin of speeding on the highway will likely be seen by the husband as less threatening to their marriage than prostitution because the latter sin involves a direct rejection of an exclusive love relationship with her husband. Likewise, the sin of rejecting God and putting something in his place is a devastating act of unfaithfulness. This is especially true when one is pretending on the outside to be loyal (Gomer was still Hosea's wife) but is actually involved with disloyal activities.

Sin and the fulfillment of God's promises. The results of sin are pictured in the symbolic names of the children. The death and bloodshed symbolized by Jezreel (1:4) indicate that sin results in death and devastation (see Rom. 6:23). God cannot bless those who forsake a loving relationship with him. The theological implications of God's curse may even extend to the forsaking of his own beloved people (the meaning of Lo-Ammi, "not my people," in 1:9). Sin can cause God to postpone his blessing for another day (1:10–2:1), when people will love him with all their heart and soul (Deut. 6:5).

God is not obligated to bless any person who does not love him. When people reject their covenant commitment to God through sin, they destroy their special relationship with him and are in essence declaring that he is not their God and that they are not related to him (1:9). As a natural consequence, God will not treat the sinner in the same tender and compassionate way he treats someone who has a committed love relationship with him. When there is no compassion or love from God (1:6), life can become miserable.

Nevertheless, we must remember that sin and separation from God will not eradicate God's love completely or destroy his wonderful plans for this world. His promises of old will all come true in due time (1:10–2:1). The present failures will not keep God from calling out a great multitude of people for himself—as numerous as the sand on the seashore. This text does not adumbrate exactly how God will accomplish his plan, but there will be a revival and restoration of the people to him.

This group will be the "sons of the living God," and it will include people from both Judah and Israel. These people will be united together and committed to one leader, probably an oblique reference to the Messiah from the line of David (3:5). Then God will call them "my people" (2:1), and he will bless their land as he promised long ago (Lev. 26). There is no indication that these people will deserve any of these things; God's compassionate love and grace will be the means of accomplishing his plan.

Compassion and love. Studying this passage might encourage one to develop a theology of the compassionate love of God. This word (*rḥm*, compassion), which is connected to the root for "womb, inner part," draws its strength from the intense emotional involvement of one person with another (like a mother's love for her child). This deep positive emotion of attachment and care has nothing to do with an obligation toward another person, but focuses on the graciousness of a strong connection that comes from the heart.

Indeed, God's compassionate love is unlimited, unearned, and undeserved; thus, it is a paradoxical mystery and partially beyond human comprehension.[18] God's compassion may end and justice may prevail when people forsake him (Hos. 1:2–9), but this does not quench his will to be compassionate to those who do not deserve his grace (1:10–2:1). This love involves an eternal unselfish giving of his benefits to others (John 15:13), an affectionate demonstration of his loyalty and great kindness. This generosity demonstrates the "incomparable riches of his grace" (Eph. 2:7) toward others. Often this concept is in a context where the Lord sees the dire needs of someone and pities them by having compassion on them.[19]

The contrasting themes in Hosea 1 are paralleled in the blessings and the curses in Leviticus 26 and Deuteronomy 27–28. Israel's consistent sinfulness throughout its history is also marvelously contrasted in Nehemiah's prayer (Neh. 9) with the great compassion of God. God became known in the golden calf incident, to Jonah the reluctant missionary to Nineveh, and to the evangelist Joel as one who is forgiving, long-suffering, gracious, compassionate, and abundant in lovingkindness (Ex. 34:6–7; Neh. 9:17; Joel 2:13; Jonah 4:2). This compassionate reestablishment of the covenant with God's people sounds much like what Jeremiah calls the new covenant (Jer. 31:31–34).

In the New Testament the apostles Paul (Rom. 9:25–26) and Peter (1 Peter 2:10) unite the nearly identical terminology in Hosea 1:10 and 2:23 (using

---

18. See M. Butterworth, "רחם," *NIDOTTE*, 3:1093–95; "Mercy, Compassion," *NIDNTT*, 2:593–601.

19. See M. Erickson, *Christian Theology* (Grand Rapids: Baker, 1983), 1:292–96; W. Eichrodt, *Theology of the Old Testament*, 1:250–58.

the LXX translation) to demonstrate to their readers how God graciously and mercifully loved them and transformed those who were not the people of God into his people. All these passages from the Old and New Testaments demonstrate that there is hope for sinful humanity because of the compassionate love of God.

 OBEDIENCE TO GOD. The application of the message of Hosea can be approached from the biographical perspective to gain principles from the way God worked with Hosea himself. Hosea's experience demonstrates the importance of obeying God's will even when it may seem unusual or contrary to conventional wisdom. God instructed Hosea to marry a woman who seemingly would not enhance his prophetic career or his respect in the community. This woman with a checkered moral past would undoubtedly undermine some of the moral principles the prophet stood for and preached against. She would likely bring endless distress, sorrow, and embarrassment to him when she became unfaithful to him and their children.

Although the text tells us nothing about Hosea's possible negative reaction to this divine exhortation (there are no excuses similar to Moses in Ex. 3–5), it would seem natural for him to have had at least some questions or doubts about the sanity of this bizarre plan. After all, would any of us think it wise to advise a young person planning on going into ministry to marry a spouse involved in prostitution? Yet God's mysterious plans are not submitted to human opinion polls, based on what a mother and father idealize for their children, or brought to the deacon board for a vote. Human fears focus too much on what might not work, while God's bold plans accomplish much because they require people to risk much in faith.

Hosea did know this marriage would symbolically mirror God's relationship with Israel, so he realized God had a higher purpose for it. God's calling involved his whole family, his marriage, and even the naming of his children. Hosea knew that people would look at his family and learn something about the ways of God. To some extent, people today still learn something about God's transforming power through observing what God does in people's lives. Hosea's obedience to the unusual circumstances God planned for him presents a challenge for all who foresee great difficulty ahead if they are faithful to God's calling.

One who wishes to serve God cannot limit the unsearchable mysteries of God's wise plans to what makes sense to the common person. People must not let human fear overpower their trust in God's love for them. God can speak to others through the simple way we carry out our family relationships. In fact, family life is one of the key ways people can identify with others, so it is a natural way for others to see the compassionate love of God demonstrated in concrete ways.

By obediently following God's plan, Hosea came to understand and empathize in a much fuller way with God's deep hatred for sin and his unending love for those who deserve no compassion. Hosea felt the pain of God by having an unfaithful wife, and he came to experience a broken covenant relationship in more than an intellectual way. He knew how adultery destroys a relationship; he experienced the sorrow of raising a child that was not his. He also must have marveled at God's ability to love those who reject him. Although one would not suggest that this is the only way to appreciate the destructive power of sin in the lives of God's people, it is fundamentally important for people (and especially pastors) to identify with God's view of sin in our world (he hates it).

Of course, it is no less important to internalize the depth of God's love for people who presently are not children of God. We do not decide which persons God should show compassion to, and we do not pick the people who will become the "sons of the living God." God loved the whole world and each individual (John 3:16) while we were still sinners (Rom. 5:8). Thus, everyone should expect that God wants us to love the sinful people whom he loves—even when they act in unloving ways.

Maintaining loyal covenant commitment. Applications can also be drawn from the basic theological relationship between God and his people. Just as he was with the rebellious people of Israel and Gomer, God is not pleased with believers today who do not maintain a loyal covenant commitment to him. He still looks at sin as prostitution—a serious and disgusting breach of a love relationship. Although society has loosened the stigma of many sins and relativized morality to the level of individual personal preferences, God still sees sinful acts as serious as adultery.

The deceit and betrayal of trust caused by sin destroys our personal relationship with God (Isa. 59:1–2). Because of the seriousness of sin in his eyes, it ends his relationship with people (as it led to the end of Israel, cf. Hos. 1:4). While people may pretend or wish their sins will not cause God to remove his compassionate loving relationship with them, Hosea teaches that God's personal covenantal relationship with his lover (his people) does not allow sinful prostitution to go unnoticed.

The implications of sin are serious, not trivial. Some may feel that their good deeds, church membership, or baptism assures them of a positive relationship to God. They presume that their sins and lack of exclusive devotion to God will not interrupt his love for them. Hosea's theology raises questions with anyone who has a cavalier regard for sin. Sin is a destructive power and a deadly force that interrupts a person's relationship with God. In the eyes of God, sin is like prostitution.

The theology of Hosea 1 is not limited to the negative implications of sin in a person's life, however. Because of God's grace, people can be assured that his eternal plans and promises will be accomplished. In spite of the present destructive power of sin in this world, God's love and compassion will bring people who are not his people into a loving relationship with himself. The political, social, and religious problems that divide God's people into different cultural, denominational, or ethnic groups will be done away with; a messianic leader will lead the people, and the promises to God's people will all be fulfilled in a time of great blessing.

The salvation of Gentiles. Paul (Rom. 9:25–26) and Peter (1 Peter 2:10) both saw the application of the positive promises in Hosea 1:10 and 2:1 in the salvation of the Gentiles. By analogy they were a people who were not God's people, who then became God's people. This application sees a significance that goes beyond the limited meaning that Hosea spoke to his Hebrew audience. Although the New Testament points to a different referent, there is a parallelism between what Hosea says and the conversion of the Gentiles.[20]

Nevertheless, the complete fulfillment of these promises must include a future restoration of Hebrew people, an idea Paul mentions in Romans 11:11–32. The essence of the promise Hosea gives in Hosea 1:10–2:1 contains a general truth that can be applied to the salvation of the Gentiles because the same thing happens in both cases—people experience God's loving compassion, respond to it, and become his people. This task of bringing people into God's family is at the heart of his plan for the world, and it is the privilege of every believer to play a part in telling the world about his deep affection for them. People everywhere can become "my loved one" and "my people."

---

20. See the discussion of Paul's use of Hosea in T. Schreiner, *Romans*, (BECNT; Grand Rapids: Baker, 1998), 527–30.

Hosea 2:2–23

²"Rebuke your mother, rebuke her,
    for she is not my wife,
    and I am not her husband.
 Let her remove the adulterous look from her face
    and the unfaithfulness from between her breasts.
³Otherwise I will strip her naked
    and make her as bare as the day she was born;
 I will make her like a desert,
    turn her into a parched land,
    and slay her with thirst.
⁴I will not show my love to her children,
    because they are the children of adultery.
⁵Their mother has been unfaithful
    and has conceived them in disgrace.
 She said, 'I will go after my lovers,
    who give me my food and my water,
    my wool and my linen, my oil and my drink.'
⁶Therefore I will block her path with thornbushes;
    I will wall her in so that she cannot find her way.
⁷She will chase her lovers but will not catch them;
    she will look for them but will not find them.
 Then she will say,
    'I will go back to my husband as at the first,
    for then I was better off than now.'
⁸She will acknowledge that I was the one
    who gave her the grain, the new wine and oil,
 who lavished on her the silver and gold—
    which they used for Baal.
⁹Therefore I will take away my grain when it ripens,
    and my new wine when it is ready.
 I will take back my wool and my linen,
    intended to cover her nakedness.
¹⁰So now I will expose her lewdness
    before the eyes of her lovers;
    no one will take her out of my hands.
¹¹I will stop all her celebrations:
    her yearly festivals, her New Moons,
    her Sabbath days—all her appointed feasts.

¹² I will ruin her vines and her fig trees,
    which she said were pay from her lovers;
  I will make them a thicket,
    and wild animals will devour them.
¹³ I will punish her for the days
    she burned incense to the Baals;
  she decked herself with rings and jewelry,
    and went after her lovers,
    but me she forgot,"

                    declares the LORD.

¹⁴ "Therefore I am now going to allure her;
    I will lead her into the desert
    and speak tenderly to her.
¹⁵ There I will give her back her vineyards,
    and will make the Valley of Achor a door of hope.
  There she will sing as in the days of her youth,
    as in the days she came up out of Egypt.

¹⁶ "In that day," declares the LORD,
    "you will call me 'my husband';
    you will no longer call me 'my master.'
¹⁷ I will remove the names of the Baals from your lips;
    no longer will their names be invoked.
¹⁸ In that day I will make a covenant for them
    with the beasts of the field and the birds of the air
    and the creatures that move along the ground.
  Bow and sword and battle
    I will abolish from the land,
    so that all may lie down in safety.
¹⁹ I will betroth you to me forever;
    I will betroth you in righteousness and justice,
    in love and compassion.
²⁰ I will betroth you in faithfulness,
    and you will acknowledge the LORD.
²¹ "In that day I will respond,"
    declares the LORD—
  "I will respond to the skies,
    and they will respond to the earth;
²² and the earth will respond to the grain,
    the new wine and oil,
    and they will respond to Jezreel.

²³ I will plant her for myself in the land;
    I will show my love to the one I called 'Not my
        loved one.'
    I will say to those called 'Not my people,' 'You are
        my people';
    and they will say, 'You are my God.'"

 THIS LONG POETIC MESSAGE is structured into an initial series of accusations against an unfaithful wife and responses by God (2:2−15), and a series of promises concerning the restoration of the relationship between God and his people (2:16−23). The first section does not describe a linear progression of events but contains several accusations plus three "therefore" clauses (2:6, 9, 14). These latter clauses explain how God has attempted to change and heal his broken covenant relationship with his wife, Israel.

Chapter 2 centers on reflections concerning the problems described in chapter 1, though they focus more on the relationship between God and Israel rather than on Hosea and Gomer. The references to the prosperous production of grain, wine, oil, and wool indicate that this message comes during the last few years of Jeroboam II.[1] Unfortunately, many in the nation interpreted these good times not as the result of God's grace but as the blessing of Baal, the Canaanite god of fertility.

Several commentaries argue that Hosea and God are taking their wives to divorce court because accusations are brought against them (2:2), but this text lacks many of the usual indicators of a legal courtroom case (cf. 4:1−3, which is clearer).[2] The threat of formally ending this relationship is real, as the language of litigation suggests, so perhaps this should be seen as a last-ditch attempt to save the covenant relationship before it is legally terminated. If there are no changes in the wife's behavior, the marriage will be over, but God has not yet given up on his unfaithful wife. In the end he will win her back and reestablish his blessed covenantal relationship with his people (2:16−23).

---

1. Wolff, *Hosea*, 33, suggests "during the last years of Jeroboam II, i.e., around 750."

2. Andersen and Freedman, *Hosea*, 218−19; Macintosh, *Hosea*, 45; and Garrett, *Hosea, Joel*, 75, argue against a legal court procedure, while Mays, *Hosea*, 35; Stuart, *Hosea−Jonah*, 45; and Wolff, *Hosea*, 33, argue for it. Although we see legal talk reminding us of what happens in court, it seems that this is not a formal divorce proceeding in a court. These are the preliminary arguments that present the evidence for a case, but the purpose is primarily redemptive—to save the marriage rather than end it.

The Rejection of Adulterous Ways (2:2–5)

THE LORD INSTRUCTS the children to "rebuke" (lit., accuse, contend with) their mother, but it is really God who is doing all the talking. The accusation "she is not my wife, and I am not her husband" (2:2) is a statement of fact based on the wife's immoral behavior, but is probably not an official declaration of a divorce. This statement openly admits the obvious: Gomer is not behaving like Hosea's wife, so Hosea cannot act like her husband.

The basis for God's claim is the "adulterous look" and "unfaithfulness" between his wife's breasts. Some contend these expressions refer to outward signs of a prostitute (makeup, tattoos, or jewelry from the Baal cult) used as provocative attractions for sexual encounters.[3] But since the main thrust is to describe the people of Israel, not the prostitute Gomer, it is enough to see these as undeniable signs of their unfaithfulness. The reference to breasts suggests the sexual nature of the nation's unfaithfulness. The words of God are not just a legal accusation, but a call to transform the people's hearts and ways. God is trying to persuade Israel, his people, to remove the pagan culture of Canaan and its sexual fertility cult temples that dot the landscape.

This call for change is accompanied by a threat that God will bring shame on the nation and dry up the land so that there is no fertility (2:3). Like a dishonored husband who uncovers the nakedness of his wife,[4] God will humiliate his people and turn their fertile farmlands into bare deserts, which produce nothing. This is another way of predicting the coming humiliation of Israel through the exile of the nation. God warns of a divine curse on the land and the removal of life-giving rain. Since Baal was the god of rain and fertility, this would be a clear sign of his powerlessness and the extreme consequences of unfaithful prostitution with other gods.

The sins of the nation are present in the "children of adultery" (2:4) as well as in the "mother" (2:5). This is consistent with the imagery of 1:2, for Israel's (and Gomer's) prostitution has an effect on everyone. The connection between mother and children demonstrates that both share in the guilt, for most Israelites did not resist the introduction of Baalism into the culture by the spiritual and political leaders of Israel (Elijah and the 7,000 did resist, cf.

---

3. Mays, *Hosea*, 38, and D. A. Hubbard, *Hosea*, (TOTC; Downers Grove: InterVarsity, 1989), 73, argue for this interpretation, although there is little to confirm what prostitutes or the Baal cult functionaries looked like. Wolff, *Hosea*, 34, thinks these might refer to tattoos or cuts on the body from a cultic ceremony.

4. C. H. Gordon, "Hos 2:4–5 in the Light of New Semitic Inscriptions," *ZAW* 54 (1936): 277–80, found this practice of shaming a wife in a Nuzi tablet, so it may have existed in Israel (though there is no proof that this early Mesopotamian custom was ever used in Israel). The reference to this practice in Jer. 13:22–27 and Ezek. 16:37–39 at least suggests that the practice was well known, if it was not commonly practiced.

1 Kings 18–19). God will respond by withholding his love (2:4 picks up the symbolization of Lo-Ruhamah in 1:6) because these are not his people/children, but the followers of Baal (2:5). In fact, this unfaithfulness was a purposely planned pursuit of other lovers. Like a bold strutting prostitute hunting down customers, the people of Israel quickly invited and pursued the Baal fertility religion that promised to bring more fertility for their crops of grain, grapes, and oil (2:5).

God's Redemptive Plans for His Unfaithful People (2:6–15)

VERSE 6 BEGINS a series of three "therefore" clauses (see also vv. 9, 14) that describe what God plans to do to win back his unfaithful people. There is some indication that the nation will respond positively to God's discipline (vv. 7b, 15b). It is important to realize that God is actually acting in grace rather than in anger. He will symbolically hedge his wife, like a farm animal, within a confined area with stone walls and fences made of thornbushes. This is for her own good and for the good of their relationship (cf. 3:3). It will protect her from straying off and returning to love other gods.

Hosea does not interpret this metaphor for us, but D. Stuart believes that God restrained Israel when it was politically subjugated to Assyria, that is, when Tiglath-Pileser III began to take control of the nation (2 Kings 15:19, 29; 16:7).[5] The rise of Assyria did indeed limit Israel's freedom, but how did this keep the people from worshiping Baal? H. W. Wolff, F. Andersen, and D. Freedman conclude that God intends to somehow block the pathways that lead to Baal's temples around the land.[6] But in light of the next verses, it seems better to suggest that God is actually trying to block the theological connection between worshiping Baal and the rewards of blessing from Baal.

How? God will frustrate Israel's pursuit of Baal by discrediting the idol's power (2:7). It will appear as if Baal is not listening or has no power. This in turn will cause the Hebrew people to give up on him and decide to return to their first love—the God of Israel. God does this so that the people will realize that the God of Israel, not Baal, produces the fertility of the grain, wine, and oil (2:8).

The second "therefore" (2:9) reemphasizes how God will transform the people's thinking by reversing what he usually does. He will demonstrate his true sovereignty and ownership of nature (see Deut. 28:16, 38–40) and not allow the land to be fertile. When God takes away the gifts of his blessing (grain, wine, and wool), Baal will be shown to be impotent, a worthless god who

---

5. Stuart, *Hosea–Jonah*, 49.
6. Wolff, *Hosea*, 36; Andersen and Freedman, *Hosea*, 237–38.

cannot be trusted. This will bring shame on Israel and "expose her lewdness." Her foolish prostitution of herself to Baal will be seen for what it really is.

God will strip her naked by stripping the land of any agricultural produce. This could be accomplished by sending a drought or by having a military power take the agricultural produce from the land. In either case, God, not Baal, will sovereignly be in control of Israel's destiny.[7] His commitment to the restoration of his covenant relationship with his people is evident in the statement that "no one will take her out of my hands" (2:10).

Removing the fertility of Baal will eliminate any reason or theological basis for praising Baal at Israel's sexually perverse festivals or weekly religious celebrations at his temples (2:11). Instead of having fertile gardens and vineyards, God will show that it does not pay to worship Baal (2:12), for these fruitful lands will become thickets inhabited by wild animals. This will be God's way of punishing the nation for its worship of Baal. He will turn his back on Israel, just as Israel has jilted God by forgetting him (2:13).

The third "therefore" (2:14) describes a dramatic new step in God's tactics to win back his wife, Israel. Using sexual terminology, God will "allure" (romantically entice) Israel back to himself, a jarring and unexpected divine method of persuasion. He will speak the tender love language that the people understand, for he deeply cares for this wife who rejected him. The picture Hosea presents involves an encounter between the couple out in the desert, where they will be alone; it will be a place where they can start over.

This picture brings back memories of the wonderful commitment the Israelites made when they came up out of Egypt and depended on God during their journey through the desert (Deut. 8; Jer. 2:2).[8] It is unnecessary to know where this new desert will be. The concept is a metaphor for restoration after defeat. This new experience of complete dependence on God is what is important.

The resulting reversal of God's attitude toward his wife, Israel, and Israel's rejoicing (2:15) indicate that this meeting in the desert will bring about a renewal of the covenantal relationship of love between God and Israel (2:7 already hinted at this). God will pour out his covenant blessings of food and transform the negative memory of Achan's sin in the Valley of Achor (meaning "valley of trouble"; see Josh. 7) into a "door of hope." The Israelites will not be judged as they were after Achan's sin, but will be filled with hope, joy, and songs of praise to God. It will be like a new exodus experience; the

---

7. This contrast becomes clearer when one realizes that the name Baal means "lord, owner, master." God will show that he is their Master and the Lord of nature and history.

8. Garrett, *Hosea, Joel*, 88–91, has an excellent discussion of the various positive and negative ways the desert theme is used in the Old Testament.

power and might of God will be celebrated in a song similar to the one Moses sang in Exodus 15.[9] What a day of rejoicing that will be!

The New Covenantal Relationship (2:16–23)

THE SECOND HALF of this oracle is structured around three "in that day" promises, which refer to events at some unknown time in the future (2:16, 18, 21).[10] One is immediately struck with the total transformation of the relationship between God and his covenant people. They will relate to one another and the world around them in a new way. Harmony, love, and the renewal of God's covenant relationship will characterize this era.

This period will begin with the reaffirmation of Israel's covenant commitment to God (like repeating wedding vows[11]), in which she will cease to confuse God with Baal. God will be "my husband," not "my master" (*ba'al*, also possible to translate, "my Baal/my lord"); thus, they will no longer confuse the significant difference between God and Baal (2:16). In fact, Baal's name will not even be mentioned anymore (2:17). When the people worship and praise God, their devotion will be directed only to Israel's true covenant God. This change is not ascribed to the will of the Israelites; rather, God is the One who will remove the name of Baal from their lips. His love and miraculous transformational power will bring about this change in the hearts and minds of his covenant people.

The second thing God will do "in that day" will be to reestablish a covenant relationship with his people and with nature (2:18–20).[12] In contrast to the past, when God's judgment allowed animals to destroy things (2:12), this will be a time of peaceful relationships with the animals. Also in contrast to the past, when the sword and bow brought death to many on the earth, God's new covenant will remove the fear of death and war (cf. Isa. 2:4; Mic. 4:3) because peace and security will exist among all peoples.

This change implies a transformation of the behavior, character, and wishes of all creatures and a return to the conditions before the curse came

---

9. See Rev. 15:3–4 for a similar joyous singing of the Song of Moses.

10. I do not agree with Yee, *Composition and Tradition in the Book of Hosea*, 54–55, 86–90, who attributes most of this salvation oracle to a later redactor. G. I. Emmerson, *Hosea: An Israelite Prophet in Judean Perspective* (Sheffield: JSOT, 1984), 27–35, makes a detailed study of this section and concludes that there is nothing here that proves that this material did not come from Hosea.

11. Andersen and Freedman, *Hosea*, 278, maintain that "the eschaton is the wedding day," but it is hard to see this as the original wedding; it is more like a recommitment to the original covenant partner.

12. C. J. H. Wright, *An Eye for an Eye: The Place of Old Testament Ethics Today* (Downers Grove, Ill.: InterVarsity, 1983), 19, connects these three aspects in Israelite theology.

on the earth in Genesis 3.[13] Such a dramatic change is nothing but the miraculous work of a sovereign, loving God. It will involve God's reestablishment of his wedded relationship with his people (2:19–20 contrasts with 2:2). He will create an unconditional, everlasting, and unending connection between himself and his covenant people. This relationship will last because it will be based on, and will be an expression of, the qualities of righteousness, justice, love, compassion, and faithfulness.

These qualities are related to the final act of "paying the bride price" (ʾrś in 2:19) in an earthly wedding (not just the initial "betrothal," as NIV) at the end of the betrothal period and the beginning of the marriage. H. W. Wolff freely paraphrases the idea as, "I will eliminate your father's last objections to our marriage by paying the amount he demands."[14] Thus, God himself gives his gifts of righteousness, justice, love, compassion, and faithfulness to cement this relationship into an unbreakable union that will last forever.

In other words, the new relationship will not be achieved through any acts of human goodness, nor will it be conditioned by qualities people must achieve. This covenant relationship is initiated and made possible by God; it is a gift of his mysterious grace and a union based on godly qualities. The divine gift of "righteousness" makes the people righteous in God's eyes, the gift of "justice" ensures that their relationship will be characterized by equitable fairness, the gift of steadfast "love" will be revealed in the unfailing devotion of the parties for one another, the gift of "compassion" will surround the relationship with a deep caring affection, and the gift of "faithfulness" will ensure the consistency and reliability of this relationship.

The natural results will be that Israel will know (NIV "acknowledge") God (playing off the marital use of "know" in this context[15]) in a totally new and intimate way. She will freely acknowledge God as her covenant partner and respond appropriately (2:20). This will be a stark contrast from the nation's present ignoring of God and running after Baal (2:5).

The final "in that day" promises (2:21–23) describe the effects of this new relationship on life in this world. Once God's people know and love him (2:15, 20), he can respond to their love by restoring the natural bounty and beauty of the created universe. Thus, God in his magnificent power, not Baal, will reinvigorate the heavens above so that the sky will function as it was originally designed and give rain to the ground (2:21). God will also empower the earth to be fertile (Baal will not do this) by responding to the

---

13. See Isa. 11:6–8 and Ezek. 34:25–30, where similar secure conditions are described.

14. Wolff, *Hosea*, 52, shows from comparisons with human weddings in Israel that this verse is not pointing to the engagement, but to the consummation events; thus he translates 2:19, "I will make you my own" (46).

15. *yadaᶜ* (to know) can refer to cohabitation of a married couple (see, e.g., Gen. 4:1).

rain in the way it was designed. As a result, grain, grapes, and olive oil will be produced in abundance.

God will even be the One who will plant the seeds (Jezreel meaning "God sows"[16]), so there will be no doubt about the abundant results in the future (2:22). But the sowing of God will not be limited to just planting crops; he will also "plant" his people in their promised land (2:23). Like a good farmer, the Lord will lovingly care for his land and those who were once "unloved." These will now be proudly identified as "my people" rather than "not my people." Through his miraculous love his people will gladly say, "You are my God." These confessions of commitment almost sound like the "I take you as my wife/husband" of the marriage covenant ceremony. They demonstrate that God's beautiful plan for this world will be accomplished through his grace in spite of the present rebelliousness and unfaithfulness of his people.

Bridging Contexts

FEMINIST AND DECONSTRUCTIONIST approaches to Hosea 2. Few would suggest that Hosea 2 is easy to interpret, and many find it difficult to propose principles that can naturally be applied to the Christian in the twenty-first century. The problematic nature of this story has led those who follow feminist and deconstructionist hermeneutical approaches to suggest unusual interpretations of Hosea 2. Rather than generalize on how either of these methods interprets Hosea's poem in chapter 2, it is best to illustrate some of their strengths and weaknesses from several concrete examples.

G. Yee and other feminists are disturbed by the fact that this story metaphorically represents the sinful people in Israel as a woman because sometimes "the metaphorical character of the biblical image is forgotten and a husband's physical abuse of his wife becomes as justified as is God's retribution against Israel."[17] Although Yee finds the religious metaphors beautiful and profound, she has problems with these images because they support a common male strategy of wife control, justify physical abuse by a father and husband, and portray a seduction of the wife after the abuse.[18] T. Setel objects

---

16. This is consistent with the use of Jezreel in 1:11 and presents a sharp contrast to the negative meaning of Jezreel in 1:4.

17. G. Yee, "Hosea," *The Women's Bible Commentary*, ed. C. A. Newsom and S. H. Ringe (London: SPCK, 1992), 195; T. D. Setel, "Prophets and Pornography: Female Sexual Imagery in Hosea," *Feminist Interpretations of the Bible*, ed. L. M. Russell (Philadelphia: Westminster, 1985), 86, sees Hosea as the "first to use objectivized female sexuality as evil."

18. Yee, "Hosea," 199–200.

to the slanted portrayal of women as passive and dependent on males, without any portrayal of their positive roles of providing food and clothing for the family or their positive reproductive and nurturing contributions to the family.[19]

These studies have tried to be relevant by raising legitimate issues based on serious problems in modern marriages, but their concerns seem to be more related to fears about what some might read into the text of Hosea 2 rather than to what the text actually says. Hosea 2 is about God and Israel (which includes both male and female people); it is not primarily about Hosea and Gomer's marriage. This whole feminist approach is weakened by the fact that God does not abuse his wife, Israel, but shows his people that unfaithfulness to the covenant relationship has serious consequences. His goal is to remove the rewards of unfaithfulness and to restore the relationship he had with them at the beginning. Although I have never heard of anyone trying to justify wife abuse on the basis of Hosea's or God's behavior in this story, everyone would agree with Yee against any such misuse of this text.

A more serious threat to understanding the main point of God's revelation through Hosea is the deconstructionist twisting of what this text says. F. van Dijk-Hemmes distorts this text by turning it into Gomer's love song (parallel to the Song of Solomon), which Hosea has perverted to silence her, to stop her worship of the mother goddess, and to maintain his patriarchal control of her.[20] Not only does this hypothesis of a love song seem impossible, its deconstruction as Hosea's perversion of her sweet love song seems mostly imaginary and read into the text.[21]

Y. Sherwood's book-length study openly attacks the marginalization of women from a deconstructionist's and feminist's point of view. Her analysis notes that: (1) Gomer is not allowed to name her children; (2) God is irrational because he switches from punishing to tenderly loving his wife; (3) the author of the poem has a distorted sexual perversity because he enjoys the lascivious act of stripping the woman in 2:2–3; and (4) the woman's freedom is denied because her freedom threatens the patriarchal authority of the male.[22]

---

19. Setel, "Prophets and Pornography: Female Sexual Imagery in Hosea," 92–93.

20. F. van Dijk-Hemmes, "The Imagination of Power and the Power of Imagination: An Intertextual Analysis of Two Biblical Love Songs: The Song of Songs and Hosea 2," *JSOT* 44 (1989): 75–88.

21. See R. C. Ortlund, *Whoredom: God's Unfaithful Wife in Biblical Theology*, 177–85, for an extended critique of van Dijk-Hemmes's article.

22. Y. Sherwood, *The Prostitute and the Prophet: Hosea's Marriage in Literary-Theological Perspective* (Sheffield: Sheffield Academic Press, 1996), 33–40.

These lessons are drawn from the subversive voice of protest that undermines what the text says. That voice allows Sherwood to read into the text what she sees behind these factors, thus freeing her from what the text actually says. In this strange approach, Gomer's prostitution is actually turned into a good thing because it gives Gomer economic freedom from her husband. This, in turn, is good because her freedom undermines the patriarchal dominance of the husband. Sherwood believes the purpose of the whole story is to deconstruct the evils of the patriarchal system and to show that women actually were loving and independent people. In the process of her analysis she talks much more about sex than the text does, hyperbolizes any hints of abuse, and tends not to focus on the real point of this passage, namely, God's desire for a loving relationship with Israel.

Without getting into the weakness of the hermeneutics of deconstruction, it is evident that Sherwood frequently twists and turns the text's message into a subversive voice that comes from her own imagination and her own personal convictions about male and female relationships.[23] These modern readings of Hosea should not be taken lightly as unimportant, for they present to their adherents legitimate bridging principles that are then used to critique modern relationships between men and women. In addition, these ideological readings have a major influence on how these people view God and his relationship with his people. In contrast to these conclusions we will propose a different way of looking at Hosea 2.

Theological themes in Hosea 2. Although the graphic sexual images of the pagan Baal religion can initially intimidate the reader and complicate attempts to find abiding principles in this text, the shocking vulgarity of the text is purposely designed to open the interpreter's eyes to the surprising way God views the unfaithfulness of his people. Sin is not pretty or something one can just overlook; it is a devastating betrayal of trust that goes to the heart of any relationship.

If an accountant sins by stealing money, can the boss trust him to handle the company's money? If a babysitter is caught on video tape physically abusing the children, can a mother trust this person with her children? If a boss catches an employee lying about sales contacts, can that employee be trusted with an important new account? No, sin undermines the basis of any relationship between two people. Sin destroys a person's relationship with God, and it will bring about national decline because of his judgment.

A second theological theme in Hosea 2 is the loving and just discipline of God. Because God cares about his relationship with people and wants that covenant relationship to continue, he confronts action that threatens to ruin

---

23. See Garrett, *Hosea, Joel*, 124—33, for an extended critique of this approach to Hosea.

that relationship. He must first make people aware that those who follow the commonly accepted beliefs and behaviors of this world are sinners in his eyes. This transforming perspective on unfaithfulness to God may come about through the convicting power of the Holy Spirit (John 16:8), through the exhortation of another believer (a modern Hosea), or through removing what people depend on (see Hos. 2:9). Sometimes people get caught, and their shameful sin is exposed (as Gomer was shamed and exposed, 2:3, 10).

In the midst of this discipline God may try to hedge in a person's way to keep him or her from further sin (see 2:6). Certainly he will not accept the frail attempts to worship him by sinful people (see 2:11, 13). All of these efforts will attempt to show that the unfaithful person's present theological worldview and behavior are wrong.[24] By disrupting the people's present connection between their deceptive faith and their blessings, God will show that there is an error in their thinking. By demonstrating that their present behavior brings judgment rather than God's blessing, he instructs the attentive listener about his ways.

But God does not end his work with people with the theme of discipline, for hope in his eternal plans are not destroyed by the temporary failures of his people. Hosea contrasts the negative hopelessness of unfaithfulness and punishment with the allurement of a wonderful relationship with God, others, and all creation (2:14–23). God can tenderly speak to the deep desires and needs of people (see 2:14).

But the future is not dependent on the unknown possibility that people might or might not respond. No, God will so marvelously transform the thinking of people[25] that they will no longer confuse him with any other source of dependence or trust (see comments on 2:16). God can and will change people so much that they no longer think of those past deceptive ways (2:17). He can and will bring hope and rejoicing where failure and trouble formerly existed (2:15).

This transformation of people today and in the future will create a new vital and personal covenant relationship with God and a new peaceful relationship with the world (see 2:18, 20–21). This can happen because God's righteousness, justice, love, compassion, and faithfulness make it possible— not human abilities or characteristics (2:19–20). The only human activities that Hosea sees as significant are our identification with God alone (2:16), our praise of God for his mercy (2:15), and our acknowledgment of God as

---

24. P. Berger and T. Luckmann, *The Social Construction of Reality: A Treatise on the Sociology of Knowledge* (Garden City, N.Y.: Doubleday, 1966), discuss the process of developing a worldview through social contact with others.

25. Stuart, *Hosea–Jonah*, 58, sees that God imposes this new covenantal relationship.

our covenant partner (2:20b, 23b). How will such a dramatic change take place? It all boils down to one thing: The unfaithful and unworthy prostitutes (i.e., you and me) will one day be "sons of the living God" (cf. 1:10) because of God's deep, compassionate love (2:23).

THE DANGERS OF SYNCRETISM. The interpretation and application of Hosea 2 is complicated by the constant reference to the Baal fertility cult that was so popular in Canaan during Hosea's ministry. Since few if any perverse sexual religious cults honor pagan gods in most communities, Hosea's message creates a foreign analogy that is not helpful for communicating with people in the twenty-first century. In order to overcome this problem, one can consider two alternative approaches that may help people understand the central theological issues Hosea addresses.

(1) One can focus on Israel's basic misunderstanding of God's power and sufficiency to provide everything people need. The tendency is for people of all ages to misunderstand where life, prosperity, meaning, and hope for the future come from.[26] Can people really believe that God alone is sufficient to provide for all their needs? If people cannot trust God to meet their physical, emotional, and spiritual needs, then they will naturally look to other things—just as the Israelites looked to Baalism.

In an individualistic materialistic culture such as Western society today, we are constantly being tempted to depend on human abilities rather than on God. Moreover, it is easy to get sucked into the business worldview that places no reliance on God and substitutes for it an undue dependence on a job, the stock market, personal savings, or Social Security. Like Hosea, we must challenge our audiences to evaluate what their trust is based on. Do people actually see God as the final source of all economic blessing (Deut. 8:17–18)? Or is prosperity just the result of fortunately being at the right place at the right time, of smart farming procedures with the latest chemicals and fertilizers, of great investment advice, or of having the right genes to produce a high IQ? A central theme of Hosea 2 is that God is the only source who can meet people's needs. Any attempt to replace his proper role is seen as a prostitution of loyalties.

In Hosea, God's method of teaching people to recognize his all-sufficiency is to discipline them and remove their blessings; thus, today one might discuss different ways in which God "hints" that he is unhappy with the status quo of

---

26. Ortlund, *Whoredom: God's Unfaithful Wife in Biblical Theology*, 49, points to this idea as the basic theological problem Israel faced.

the sinner. Exhortations and commands in the Bible reveal in an unmistakable way what he approves of and hates. Equally important are the examples of biblical characters in the past who are a positive or negative example to all who live after them (1 Cor. 10:11). Failed marriages because of unfaithfulness, jail sentences for doing drugs, teenagers who have illegitimate children due to immorality, and the dead body of a college student who binge-drank himself to death are all indications that choices have consequences for anyone who might be tempted to experiment on the dangerous side of life.

Hosea teaches that God's discipline will persistently frustrate a person's evil desires and will remove the positive rewards people seek. Discipline is instructive and has the redemptive purpose of changing the way people think and act. God's discipline also involves the invitation (or "allurement") to try God's way. His way involves the discipline of total devotion to God and complete dependence on his gifts; it is not gained by any human effort or worth. Hosea makes it obvious that it is the sufficiency of God's righteousness, justice, love, compassion, and faithfulness (2:19–20) that transforms a sinful person into one of his covenantal children.

In the analogy, Gomer does not clean up her act so perfectly that she deserves to come back to her husband, and neither do we. It is only by God's grace that we are saved; it is a gift from him that no one deserves or earns (Eph. 2:8–9). In the end, complete dependence on the sufficiency of God is what trust and faith are all about. Any focus on self or dependence on anything else detracts from the marvelous sufficiency of Almighty God.

(2) Another way of approaching the tension that existed between Baalism and the worship of Israel's God in Hosea 2 is to deal with the problem of the syncretism of cultural ideas (modern Baalism) into the biblical worldview. Hosea's audience knew some things about God and worshiped at the Israelite temple at Bethel, so they had a form and the look of godliness about them. Their problem was that they gradually allowed theological ideas and practices from the Canaanite religion of their day to mix with their vague memories of biblical teachings.[27] This mixing soon resulted in many people seeing no difference between Baal and Yahweh (see 2:16). Israel's faith was adapted into Canaanite culture rather than transforming Canaanite culture.

Two opposite theologies and two contrasting moral ways of life were combined by ignoring both the holy requirements to be separated to God and the requirement to be separate from sin (see Lev. 18:24–30; 20:1–8, 22–27; Deut. 7:1–6). This syncretism of their culture led the Israelites to a religious way of thinking inconsistent with the ways of God.

---

27. Garrett, *Hosea, Joel*, 76, 79, also sees the mother of the story (Gomer) as symbolic of the Canaanite culture of Hosea's day.

A parallel struggle still exists today between the moral values of modern cultures and biblical teachings. Since almost everyone is raised and taught how to be worldly-wise, and since we are constantly impacted by immoral values of the mass media, it is hard to resist all of this enculturation. Not so subtle values such as the freedom to do your own thing, tolerance and pluralism, violence, materialism, lack of absolutes, and individual rights are affirmed over and over again by highly respected people. It is not surprising that some people who go to Christian churches have syncretized these ideas with the biblical message by reinterpreting the Bible to fit or support a worldview that is inconsistent with the Bible. Certainly Jesus did not try to fit in with the thinking of the people of his day. He chose to be different from the hypocritical, alms-giving Pharisees (Matt. 6:1–4); he even gave a more stringent command than the Old Testament law against committing adultery (5:27–28).

When serving on a summer missions program in Xatapa, Mexico, some years ago, I was surprised one day to see a native "holy man" carrying a pagan idol into the local Catholic church for a religious festival. Although I could not understand the local dialect to interpret what was happening, it was clear that the Catholic priest in that village had compromised portions of the biblical faith to the religious culture of the Indians to win their support. A similar syncretistic amalgamation of Israelite and Canaanite religion happened in Israel at the time of Hosea, and it still is happening in churches today. Although the church needs to speak to the issue of each era, it must resist any slanting of the message just to make it more palatable to the hearers.

The lines between Christianity and the cultures of the world vary from country to country. Many Western countries have had the broad influence of Catholic or Protestant Christianity for hundreds of years. Both modern and postmodern thought patterns have made major inroads into this Judeo-Christian approach to the Christian way of life. Consequently, people have begun to address the "culture wars" in which conflicting values are struggling to define life in the United States and other Western countries.[28]

This is a fight for the identity of Christianity. Will we accept homosexual marriages as normative? Will parents and local authorities control education? Will the values of some ideological group dictate what is normative? Will the media report the news impartially, or should it be allowed to create the news and sway public opinion by the way it presents only half the truth? What are the ethics of political compromise? Can any politician be trusted?

Writers like David Wells have responded by strongly opposing the postmodern trends that have infiltrated our daily lives and undercut orthodox

---

28. J. D. Hunter, *Culture Wars: The Struggle to Define America* (New York: Basic Books, 1991).

Christianity.[29] Certainly much of what he says about the disastrous state of the church is true because too many people have syncretized their beliefs with modern cultural trends and thus lost the distinctive heart of their faith. But we are in the world, and we must reach it with the transforming message of the gospel. Thus, we cannot just run off and hide in a cave by ourselves.

Many years ago H. Richard Niebuhr suggested that we have various choices: to take a stand against culture, to put Christ above culture, to leave Christ and culture in some sort of paradoxical relationship, to make Christ the transformer of culture, or to mix Christ with culture.[30] The choice between these options is not always clear, and there may not be only one model of operation for all believers in every culture. The central question that those who engage the culture must ask is: How can I maintain the purity of my faith in the midst of this foreign world?

All believers agree that denial of the existence of God in a materialistic culture must be resisted and opposed, but sometimes the more threatening problems are those that are less obvious. They innocently shade the truth by millimeters rather than miles and gradually wear down a person's logical objections because they seem so minor. Sometimes, like the Israelites and the Pharisees, people continue to worship, pray, and tithe, but they do not please God. Therefore, people need to be alert because the devil desires to devour them; they must examine their own lives for unhealthy compromises, confess their failures and turn from them, correct and forgive their fellow believers in a spirit of love, and strive for the unity and purity of the faith (Eph. 4:1–6).

People may not always know the extent to which they themselves have syncretized and compromised their beliefs with the philosophies of this world because each of us has an immense ability to be self-deceived (Jer. 17:9). Thus, it is important for us to immerse ourselves in the Word of God so that our minds can be transformed by the work of the Holy Spirit. As Hosea indicates, a belief system that simply accepts this world's thinking and combines it with a few Bible verses looks and acts like an unholy prostitution of true faith.

God's saving grace. A final application of Hosea 2 relates to God's great acts of grace when he restores his covenant relationship with his people and with nature (2:16–23). These great eschatological promises of a transformation of nature and people who do not know God give hope to the believer today. We have the great promise that God will one day restore this sinful

---

29. D. F. Wells, *No Place for Truth: Or Whatever Happened to Evangelical Theology* (Grand Rapids: Eerdmans, 1993).
30. H. R. Niebuhr, *Christ and Culture* (New York: Harper and Row, 1951).

world. In his sovereign power, he will act in righteousness, justice, love, compassion, and faithfulness to accomplish his plan.

There is nothing we can do to transform this world into a paradise; it is completely dependent on God. This will happen because we have the sure promise of God that he will take us as his bride. Such promises assure us that he will have victory over sin in the end. Although the world may be full of sinful people who cause great pain and suffering, God's original plan for creation will bring this evil world to an end.

Hosea 3:1–5

THE Lord SAID to me, "Go, show your love to your wife again, though she is loved by another and is an adulteress. Love her as the LORD loves the Israelites, though they turn to other gods and love the sacred raisin cakes."

²So I bought her for fifteen shekels of silver and about a homer and a lethek of barley. ³Then I told her, "You are to live with me many days; you must not be a prostitute or be intimate with any man, and I will live with you."

⁴For the Israelites will live many days without king or prince, without sacrifice or sacred stones, without ephod or idol. ⁵Afterward the Israelites will return and seek the LORD their God and David their king. They will come trembling to the LORD and to his blessings in the last days.

THIS SHORT NARRATIVE describes God's plans for restoring the relationship between Hosea and his wife (3:1–3) and between himself and his people (3:4–5). In contrast to chapter 1, which is a third-person account about Hosea's family, this story is told in the first-person singular. The unnamed "woman" in 3:1–3 is most likely Gomer,[1] and the restoration mentioned here happens after chapter 1. These events are a symbolic lesson to Hosea's audience that God's marvelous love will surely bring about a restoration of his covenant relationship with his people.[2]

The restoration process begins as an act commissioned and motivated by God (3:1), not as a human desire initiated by Hosea himself. The exhortation directs Hosea to love a woman of prostitution (or "an adulteress"), who is loved by another man. This is a call to reestablish his marriage relationship with Gomer even though she has already rejected him. The Hebrew

---

1. I disagree with Stuart, *Hosea-Jonah*, 64, who does not think the woman in 3:1–3 is Gomer. Such a proposal destroys the analogy between God and his people. God is not saying he will leave Israel and take a new wife. The fact that this woman is an adulterous woman (3:1) identifies her with Gomer.

2. Yee, *Composition and Tradition in the Book of Hosea*, 57–63, doubts that Hosea is the author of 3:1–5 (others only question 3:5), but Andersen and Freedman, *Hosea*, 292–93, reject this view.

word for "love" (*'hb*) has a broad spectrum of possible meanings: to have sexual relations, to fall in love, to express a deep emotional care and commitment, to make an alliance; here it must describe Hosea's acts and words that will win back his wife's affections.

Hosea's love is to be patterned after God's love, for God sets the model in his love for his adulterous people, who turned away from him to love other gods.[3] This divine comparison identifies the kind of love Hosea needs to exhibit. It is not selfish, remorseful, or a begrudged requirement, but an excited giving of one's self to people who do not deserve to be loved. This type of love is not lust or a brief emotional infatuation; it boldly expresses a yearning for a personal relationship that once existed in the past. This divine love for undeserving people is somewhat incomprehensible since both lovers (Gomer and Israel) willingly have betrayed their husbands and given their love to someone else.

Hosea's emotional response to this exhortation is missing because the story is not a chronicle about his own possible misgivings, doubts, or anger. The focus is on the positive act of loving and the restoration that love brings. When the people of Israel hear of the incredible love God has for them, his grace will make restoration possible.

Hosea's love is demonstrated by his action of buying his wife, an act that can be compared to paying the bride price. But why would Hosea need to make payments for someone who is already his wife? Possibly she is indebted in some way to someone else and is not free to go home with Hosea. Some compare the price of fifteen shekels of silver plus a homer and lethek of barley to the price of a slave[4] (thirty shekels of silver for a slave in Ex. 21:32, fifty shekels of silver for a bride price in Deut. 22:29), but we have no idea what a female slave cost in the time of Hosea. It is better to suppose that Hosea is simply paying off Gomer's debts. As a result of this gracious act of freeing the woman from her bondage, Gomer is now free to live with him for the foreseeable future (3:3).[5]

Some believe the series of restrictions on Gomer in 3:3 are acts of love designed to reform her.[6] This is partially due to the translation some give of the

---

3. The "raisin cakes" were some kind of sweet food made from dried grapes. They were something of a delicacy and apparently were eaten at religious ceremonies at the pagan temples (Jer. 7:18; 44:19).

4. Some suggest she sold herself into slavery or that she sold herself to a local temple as a prostitute. See Wolff, *Hosea*, 61.

5. "You shall dwell with me" is better than the NIV's "You are to live with me," although Andersen and Freedman, *Hosea*, 301, make a good case for "you must wait for me" because of the prepositional phrase "for me."

6. Stuart, *Hosea—Jonah*, 66; Mays, *Hosea*, 58, calls this love that imprisons a "strange tactic."

last line as "even I will not go in to you," rather than the positive assurance that "I will live with you" (NIV). The NIV is closer to the cryptic Hebrew text since there is no negative particle in this last line.[7] Therefore, it seems that Hosea is giving a balanced plan for the restoration of the marriage relationship rather than a harsh, punitive judgment that ends with the unsatisfying conclusion that they will never be intimate again. No, there is a positive restoration of relationships between God and Israel (3:4–5), and it is expected in Hosea's life too.

The three steps to restoration are: (1) Having won Gomer's release from a former creditor's control, Hosea gives her a positive message of his commitment to care for her for many days; (2) Hosea sets down the conditions of this new relationship—she must not have anything to do with her sinful past relationships with other men; and (3) Hosea will again be her husband.

This restoration of relationships between Hosea and Gomer is parallel to the restoration between God and Israel (3:4–5). No mention is made of punishment, only of Israel's living for "many days" without all those things that led them astray and away from God. Israel's political life (led by a wicked "king [and] prince") caused the people to stumble, so those leaders will be removed. Various religious practices ("sacrifice … sacred stones … ephod [and] idols") caused a break in the people's relationship with God, so they too will be removed. Just as Hosea cut Gomer off from the men who led her into adultery, so God will remove the factors that have caused Israel to destroy her relationship with him.

Then, "in the last days," the covenant relationship between God and Israel will be restored. Israel will seek to serve God and be willing to follow their messianic king from the line of David (3:5; cf. the similar but more general promise in 1:11). Both Hosea and God will love their wives and give them the blessings of their renewed covenant relationship (cf. the blessings in 2:21–23).[8]

---

7. The last line has no verb, so some insert "not live" from the preceding phrase, thus implying that others will not live with her and Hosea will not live with her either (see Wolff, *Hosea*, 56). This contradicts the first statement that "she will dwell with me"; therefore, it seems best to see the last line as a contrast to his statement that "she will not be a prostitute or belong to other men." The literal "and I will be to you" probably means "I will be yours." See Garrett, *Hosea, Joel*, 102.

8. Some object to the reference to David because it is part of Judah's eschatology, not Israel's; they claim it was added by a later Judean editor (Wolff, *Hosea*, 63). But Amos had no trouble talking to Israelites about the restoration of the Davidic kingdom (Amos 9:11–15). We do not believe the Davidic tradition is solely the property of Judah, for David made a covenant with the northern tribes (2 Sam. 5:1–3). In fact, the men of Israel felt that David belonged more to them than Judah in 2 Sam. 19:43. Ahijah even promised Jeroboam I the covenant God promised to David if he would serve God (1 Kings 11:30–38). At times the "house of David" may be a specific reference to the government in Jerusalem, but not all general references to David are from people in Judah.

THE PATHWAY OF LOVE. This short narrative describes the restoration of Gomer and Israel in the briefest terms. We must take care so that a minimal amount of information is implied between the lines. We do not have a complete compendium of chronological information that explains everything that happens. This story does not resolve the moral problems one might have with God's command that Hosea return to this unworthy spouse. In fact, the unloveliness of the one loved only emphasizes the depth of the love expressed by God and Hosea.

Since few people today will ever receive a specific exhortation from God to restore a spouse involved in prostitution, one must focus on the broader theological aspects of God's love for Israel and the practical implications of Hosea's love for Gomer in order to begin applying this passage today. God's love is not fully explained in the limited context of Hosea 3, but one does learn that it is not quenched by human failures or disloyalties (3:2).

God loved his people when they were few in number (Deut. 7:7–8), and he graciously gave them the land of Israel in spite of their stubbornness (9:4–6). His acts of love were regulated by his choices (7:7), his promises (7:8; 9:5), and his faithfulness to his covenant (7:9). God did not base his love on Israel's goodness or acceptance of a few religious ceremonies. Rather, it was a spontaneous force that has no justification or rationale;[9] it is an inexplicable mystery whereby God relates his grace, compassion, and commitment to people. First John 4:16 simply summarizes this point by saying that "God is love."

God's love is seen in the way he acts toward people. In this case he does not deal with Israel based on justice, but on the basis of undeserved love. His love is not blind, however; he knows when his people do not love him, and he makes every attempt to restore the love relationship between himself and his people. One method in the process of restoration is for people to humble themselves, confess their sins, and seek God's face for forgiveness (2 Chron. 7:14). God can also draw his people back to himself through chastening (Amos 4:6–13) or severe punishment (Ezek. 5–7). In Hosea, God encourages restoration by removing those stumbling blocks (evil kings and priests) that have caused his people not to love him with all their heart.

The final way in which God's love will be demonstrated is through the granting of the nation's great messianic hopes and dreams (3:5). The king from the line of David will reign in the last days (2 Sam. 7), and God will pour out his covenant blessings with abundance. This picture adds to the wonderful eschatological picture already presented in 1:10–11 and 2:16–23.

---

9. Eichrodt, *Theology of the Old Testament* (Philadelphia: Westminster, 1961), 1:250.

It is also helpful to reflect on the message that Hosea's love for Gomer sends to the prophet's audience. Although we do not know who that audience was or how they reacted, if one assumes that Hosea did what God commanded, a person can outline at least the basic changes people observed. They saw a man pay good money so that he could take back an undeserving wife who had betrayed him. They saw new love break out between two people; a broken marriage was restored. They saw a living human picture of God's love through the prophet's act of loving his unworthy wife.

This example of love probably did more to communicate God's love for his people than a hundred prophetic sermons. God's unbelievable commitment to his people also had a dramatic effect on Hosea's own understanding of God's love, on his view of his responsibility to love his wife, and on his agony over having a covenant partner who sinfully rejected his gift of love.

 SHOWING LOVE. In a world of war, violence, divorce, and all kinds of heartache, people do question the love of God. Although this passage does not directly address the issue of why there are so many problems in this world (sinful acts cause these problems in Hos. 1–3), it gives reassurance that God does graciously love his people even when they do not deserve it. Hosea is speaking of a situation where previous lovers (Gomer and Israel) have rejected their partner, so the most natural application is to deal with the question: If people fall into sin and turn their back on God, will he still love them? If people who have a relationship with God (like the Israelites) reject God's love and prostitute themselves by loving someone or something else more than God, will God totally reject them?

Hosea's answer is that no one has ever deserved or earned God's love; it is always a free gift to those who are unworthy. Hosea 3:3–4 shows that God's abundant blessings are interrupted by unfaithful actions, but his overpowering love is not quenched by temporary rejection. Since that love involves his emotional commitment of faithfulness to his people, he is steadfastly loyal to those whom he loves. It is overpoweringly persuasive and nearly irresistible; thus, it can soften and transform the hearts of rebellious people hardened by years of rejection. God's love provides the best for his people, and it energizes him faithfully to carry out all his promises (3:5).

No one should ever question the availability of God's love. The question, rather, is this: Will people respond to God's love? Scripture assures us that God loves everyone in the whole world and does not want any to perish (2 Peter 3:9). Paul also reassures the church at Rome that nothing can separate them from God's love (Rom. 8:38–39).

Although God's love is evident, one does not always see it illustrated in the lives of his people that cross our paths every day. Those who are hurt often look for revenge or try to figure out how they can sue someone. Instead of loving the unlovely, it is far more common to hear people condemn them with harsh arguments, trash talk, and severe criticisms not aimed at restoration. Certainly no one wants to support sinful behavior by evil people, but if one wants to win them back and transform their behavior, someone must care about them.

Even "good people" need to be concerned that love is a central part of their motivation. Although some try to impress people with their philanthropic gifts to charity and others demonstrate their "faith" by supporting a good social cause or a missionary in Africa, the most important thing that people can give is love to those around them (1 Cor. 13). In the end, loving or not loving people is a conscious choice we make. We can also choose to hate people, or we can ignore them and treat them as unimportant. When we love someone, we naturally get to know them, care for them, and invest our lives in them. In many ways the opposite of love is self-centeredness and pride. Love is what binds people together (Col. 2:2; 3:14).[10]

A more specific application can focus on the love a man should have for his wife (Eph. 5:25−33; Col. 3:18−19). Although New Testament passages compare a husband's love to Christ's love for the church, another good model is Hosea's love for Gomer. This means that a husband is not to act like the selfish and disrespectful Archie Bunker, the popular television husband who lorded it over his wife, Edith. Paul makes submission a central ingredient of marriage,[11] but his emphasis on love is the key that motivates each partner's desire to please and care for the other.

Although Hosea 3 says nothing about forgiveness, the prophet's love for his spouse surely includes forgiving her, helping her start a new life with him, and accepting her back as his lover. There are people in the average church who are now experiencing or have already experienced some of the agony Hosea went through. Their ability to forgive and love again after being betrayed is a modern illustration of the deep commitment and love that is needed in every marriage. Before one plans to teach or preach on Hosea, it might not be a bad idea to talk to one of these people in order to get a first-hand feel for the emotional turmoil Hosea went through.

---

10. P. T. O'Brien, *Colossians, Philemon* (WBC; Waco: Word, 1982), 204, emphasizes how important love is to the corporate life of the church if it is to function as a fellowship of believers.

11. D. E. Garland, *Colossians, Philemon* (NIVAC; Grand Rapids: Zondervan, 1998), 262−66, spends a great deal of space discussing submission but only a short final paragraph on love.

Finally, this passage emphasizes how the power of love and covenant commitment can overcome the horrors of sin in any relationship. Betrayal and rejection that is so personal is devastating, and it usually produces anger; but love can produce a much more powerful expression of grace and forgiveness. God has himself demonstrated this kind of love to us, and every believer is called to demonstrate it to others.

Hosea 4:1–19

¹ Hear the word of the LORD, you Israelites,
    because the LORD has a charge to bring
    against you who live in the land:
"There is no faithfulness, no love,
    no acknowledgment of God in the land.
² There is only cursing, lying and murder,
    stealing and adultery;
they break all bounds,
    and bloodshed follows bloodshed.
³ Because of this the land mourns,
    and all who live in it waste away:
the beasts of the field and the birds of the air
    and the fish of the sea are dying.

⁴ "But let no man bring a charge,
    let no man accuse another,
for your people are like those
    who bring charges against a priest.
⁵ You stumble day and night,
    and the prophets stumble with you.
So I will destroy your mother—
⁶   my people are destroyed from lack of knowledge.

"Because you have rejected knowledge,
    I also reject you as my priests;
Because you have ignored the law of your God.
    I also will ignore your children.
⁷ The more the priests increased,
    the more they sinned against me;
    they exchanged their Glory for something disgraceful.
⁸ They feed on the sins of my people
    and relish their wickedness.
⁹ And it will be: Like people, like priests.
    I will punish both of them for their ways
    and repay them for their deeds.

¹⁰ "They will eat but not have enough;
    they will engage in prostitution but not increase.

because they have deserted the LORD
    to give themselves ¹¹to prostitution,
to old wine and new,
    which take away the understanding ¹²of my people.
They consult a wooden idol
    and are answered by a stick of wood.
A spirit of prostitution leads them astray;
    they are unfaithful to their God.
¹³They sacrifice on the mountaintops
    and burn offerings on the hills,
under oak, poplar and terebinth,
    where the shade is pleasant.
Therefore your daughters turn to prostitution
    and your daughters-in-law to adultery.

¹⁴"I will not punish your daughters
    when they turn to prostitution,
nor your daughters-in-law
    when they commit adultery,
because the men themselves consort with harlots
    and sacrifice with shrine prostitutes—
    a people without understanding will come to ruin!

¹⁵"Though you commit adultery, O Israel,
    let not Judah become guilty.

"Do not go to Gilgal;
    do not go up to Beth Aven.
    And do not swear, 'As surely as the LORD lives!'
¹⁶The Israelites are stubborn,
    like a stubborn heifer.
How then can the Lord pasture them
    like lambs in a meadow?
¹⁷Ephraim is joined to idols;
    leave him alone!
¹⁸Even when their drinks are gone,
    they continue their prostitution;
    their rulers dearly love shameful ways.
¹⁹A whirlwind will sweep them away,
    and their sacrifices will bring them shame.

THE NEXT SECTION of Hosea (4:1–6:6) records the prophet's sermons to various audiences in Israel. The date for these prophecies is not well defined, but the rumors and warnings of war in 5:8 suggest that these messages should be dated close to the Syro-Ephraimite war, which lasted from 734 to 732 B.C.[1] In this war the nation of Syria and Ephraim (Israel) attacked Judah to try to force it to join a coalition of nations opposing the Assyrian empire (2 Kings 16). When Ahaz, the king of Judah, refused to join this coalition, most of Judah was defeated (2 Chron. 28). Foolishly refusing to trust God for deliverance, Ahaz called on the Assyrian king Tiglath-Pileser III to rescue him (Isa. 7:1–18). When Tiglath-Pileser III came, the Assyrians defeated King Rezin and the forces of Syria as well as King Pekah and the armies of Israel (see 2 Kings 16; 2 Chron. 28). These events may explain Hosea's reference to violence and bloodshed (Hos. 4:2), the warning that Ephraim will be laid waste and crushed (5:9, 11), and the trumpet warnings of war (5:8).

Hosea's main point is that God will discipline the nation of Israel because the priests (and the people) do not truly know God (4:6). A spirit of prostitution controls their hearts, which makes it difficult for them to acknowledge God as the Sovereign One who controls their future (5:4). If they will only return to God and have an intimate relationship with him, there will be a real hope of renewal (6:1–3). This message is communicated through words of accusation (4:1–19), threats of punishment (5:1–14), and promises of hope (6:1–6).

Hosea does not record his audience's response to his persuasive messages (unless 6:1–3 is understood as a response by some of his listeners). Since the nation suffers God's judgment a short time later, one should assume that only a few people repent and turn back to God.

Hosea begins the sermon in chapter 4 by mimicking words that would naturally be found in Israel's law courts or at a legal procedure at the city gate. God appears to be presenting parts of a "charge" (*rib*) or covenant lawsuit against his unfaithful people, similar to Micah 6.[2] As F. Andersen and D. N. Freedman have observed, only fragments of this lawsuit are obvious in the present text,[3]

---

1. Macintosh, *Hosea*, 194; Wolff, *Hosea*, 111; Stuart, *Hosea–Jonah*, 100; and Mays, *Hosea*, 86, all relate these events to this devastating war when Assyria took control of Syria, Israel, and Judah.

2. C. Westermann, *Basic Forms of Prophetic Speech*, trans. H. C. White (Philadelphia: Westminster, 1967), 199–201, finds similar legal procedures in Isa. 1 and 3. See also H. B. Houffmon, "The Covenant Lawsuit in the Prophets," *JBL* 78 (1959): 285–95.

3. Andersen and Freedman, *Hosea*, 335–36, shy away from a legal understanding of the text because it does not fit an ideal form of a lawsuit, while Garrett, *Hosea, Joel*, 107–8, dismisses this comparison with the lawsuit.

but one should not expect that a religious sermon would follow all the minor points of a literal court case. Rather, Hosea draws on legal terms, themes, and procedures to draw out the desired comparisons he wants to highlight. The prophet invites the audience to imagine what God might say if he were to take them to an imaginary court to prove their guilt. What charges would he bring? What verdict would he give at the end? Would there be any grace or leniency if they were pronounced guilty?

This strategy of mimicking a court case serves as a powerful mechanism to make Israel realize that her iniquity is serious in God's eyes—so serious that if the evidence were adjudicated in court, it would bring an end to the covenant relationship between God and Israel (cf. how Gomer's sin brought a temporary end to her marriage relationship with Hosea).

This section is divided into four subparagraphs: (1) the formal announcement of a lawsuit (4:1–3); (2) accusations against the priests (4:4–10); (3) accusations of pagan worship (4:11–14); and (4) a conclusion that Israel is hopeless (4:15–19). Each subparagraph is built around a series of accusations that presents the evidence and warns of punishment.[4]

God Has a Covenant Lawsuit Against His People (4:1–3)

HOSEA BEGINS BY calling the Israelites to attention (4:1a), announcing that God has a covenant lawsuit against his people (4:1b), and revealing the reasons for this dispute (4:1c). His complaint is that the people exhibit no true faithfulness to him, no steadfast covenant love toward him or others, and no acknowledgment of him as their divine overlord. These three elements have disrupted God's relationship with his covenant people.

The quality of "faithfulness" (*ʾemet*) or truth describes a firmness in the people's commitment (their yes cannot be a half-hearted or unresolved decision), a reliability in their responsibilities (they do not waver back and forth, but have integrity), and an honesty about what they say (there is no deception, but the people have made a lasting choice).[5] People who have this quality will be true and faithful to what they know and will give themselves to it completely. If the Israelites are untrustworthy, uncommitted, deceptive, and undecided about their devotion to God, how can God maintain a relationship with them?

The quality of "steadfast covenant love" (*ḥesed*) demonstrates a loving and compassionate attitude devoted to maintaining an existing relationship.

---

4. Stuart, *Hosea-Jonah*, 73–74, outlines the parts of each segment in detail.

5. H. Wildberger, "אמן *ʾmn*, firm, secure," *Theological Lexicon of the Old Testament*, ed. E. Jenni and C. Westermann, 2 vols. (Peabody, Mass.: Hendrickson, 1997): 1:34–57; R. W. Moberley, "אמן," *NIDOTTE*, 1:427–33.

Such people keep their obligations to their partners based on their care for them. They are loyal to the relationship, for *ḥesed* "is the 'essence' of the covenantal relationship."[6] They express their emotional heart connection to the one they love both by their actions and their words. Their love is deep and consistent. If the Israelites do not maintain a love relationship with God, how can their covenant relationship continue in any kind of meaningful way?

The concept of "knowing God" has both an objective aspect (truthful information about who he is) and a subjective aspect (a personal relationship with God that acknowledges him as the sovereign power over one's life and excludes any acknowledgment of Baal as deity).[7] This characteristic is especially important because some of the people were worshiping multiple gods and confusing God with Baal (2:16). They have not made the effort to really know God. Part of the reason for this ignorance and confusion was the general acceptance of Canaanite religious beliefs in Israelite culture, plus a lack of clear priestly teaching about God from the Torah (4:6).

Proof of this sad state of affairs is based on what the people are actually doing (4:2). They are breaking their covenant with God by doing what was prohibited in the Ten Commandments (Ex. 20:2–17), which summarize the covenant requirements. The people curse (take God's name in vain), lie, murder, steal, commit adultery, and break all the boundaries laid out to regulate their covenant relationship with God. Some may be surprised that Hosea brings up these types of issues rather than the worship of false gods, but to Hosea the prophet, religious faith and social action are mirrors of one another. One can argue all day about whether a person really believes or loves God; it is easier to decide the issue without argument by simply pointing to the way God's people are living. Faith and love are revealed by behavior.

This breakdown of covenant relationship results in the cursing of Israel's land, just as the covenant predicted (4:3; see Lev. 26; Deut. 28). The sign of this curse is the disappearance of vegetation, animals, birds, and even the fish. Hosea does not say whether this will happen through a drought, a military invasion, or a combination of these factors. What is important is that morality has an effect on the economic and political status of the nation. God has inserted into the fabric of covenantal theology a reciprocal relationship between loving or obeying God and blessing the land, and between unfaithfulness and cursing the land. Hosea warns that all who live on the land will feel the consequences of their sins.

---

6. D. A. Bear and R. P. Gordon, "חסד," *NIDOTTE*, 2:211–18.
7. Garrett, *Hosea, Joel*, 110, emphasizes both aspects.

Accusations Against the Priests (4:4–10)

GOD NOW HAS Hosea bring specific charges. Problems with understanding the Hebrew text and the difficulty of identifying the speaker(s) in 4:4 have produced a multitude of different translations. We need not list all the hypothetical emendations of the difficult Hebrew text, but the translation of 4:4b as "for with you is my contention, O priest" (RSV) makes the most sense of a difficult phrase.[8]

In 4:4a some interpreters suggest that a person in Hosea's audience objects to his bold attempt to present this case against Israel in 4:1–3. Like Amaziah's earlier attempt to quiet Amos (Amos 7:10–17, see comments), interpreters maintain that in 4:4a someone is telling Hosea not to bring a lawsuit or accuse anyone. The strong response in Hosea 4:4b is then Hosea's rejection of this admonition; he is determined to bring this case against Israel.[9] This view of 4:4a is not the best interpretation, since this verse gives no indication of any other speaker besides Hosea. It is better (following NIV, NASB) to see all of this verse as Hosea's report of what God has said. The prophet is encouraging the people to listen to what God has to say and not dispute his charges. The evidence will show that the priests, the spiritual leaders of the community, are guilty.

The prophets (4:5) and even the mothers and children of the priests will suffer under God's punishment (they will "stumble"; cf. Amos 7:17). This comes about because the priests have destroyed the people by failing to instruct the people concerning God's divine revelation in the Torah. How can they ever know God's character or ways if the priest never explains the "Bible" of that day? How can they distinguish God from Baal if the people are not taught the differences from the holy scrolls? How can the people have an intimate relationship with their covenant God and acknowledge him as their Lord if the priest never describes from Deuteronomy the close covenant relationship God desires?

It is impossible for God to continue his relationship with his chosen people if the priests keep increasing the people's sinfulness rather than leading them to God. If the truth were told, the priests actually enjoy sinning and relish their evil lifestyle (4:8). They encourage the people to exchange "their

---

8. It is difficult to understand what the NIV translation "for your people are like those who bring charges against a priest" means. The people were blindly following their evil priests, they were not bringing charges against them. By changing one vowel to make "your people" into "with you" and understanding the comparative "like" in the NIV as a dittography of the pronominal suffix "you" on the preceding word one gets the understandable "but with you is my contention, O priest."

9. Andersen and Freedman, *Hosea*, 345, think the objector in 4:4a is a priest.

Glory" (referring to God himself, who is the Glory of Israel) for some idolatrous false god like Baal (4:7).[10] What a despicable group of spiritual leaders the priests are. They are guilty of breaking the covenant with God.

God's response is to reciprocate by rejecting the priests (4:6). He will ignore their children, just as the priests have ignored his words. There is a certain level of justice in God's action. You get what you deserve. God will repay each one for his or her deeds in an appropriate manner (4:9). He cannot bless the families of those priests who have purposely deserted him. The priests are doubly accountable because they have prevented the people from hearing about the personal relationship God wants to have with his people (4:10). The priests have even gotten involved with the drinking and prostitution going on at these temples.[11] God will not reward these priests with any blessings, but instead will send a curse. Yes, both the priests and the people will be punished severely by God (4:9).

Accusations of Worthless Worship (4:11–14)

THE SECOND CHARGE explains how ignoring God's revelation is affecting the worship celebrations of the people. What is going on at the temples is astonishing: prostitution, drunkenness, idol worship, divination, and all the perversions that go with them.[12] These activities do not help the people reflect on life's values, draw out rational conclusions about right and wrong, or please God. Instead, they "take away the understanding of my people." These activities dull the mind so much that it is impossible for them truly to know Israel's God.

These practices describe the passionate sexuality of the Baal cult (some think such sexual activity will magically encourage Baal to give them fertility) and have nothing to do with maintaining a covenant relationship with

---

10. The Hebrew of 4:7b actually says, "I will change their glory into disgrace," which Macintosh, *Hosea* 141; Garrett, *Hosea, Joel,* 119; and McComiskey, *The Minor Prophets,* 1:62–63 (and RSV) keep, but most others (including NIV and NASB) follow the "emendation of the scribes" and other versions in order to read, "they exchanged their Glory for something disgraceful."

11. The NIV reads part of 4:11 with 4:10, hiding the change to a new topic in vv. 11–14. Stuart, *Hosea–Jonah,* 71, and others follow this same approach, but Garrett, *Hosea, Joel,* 121, wisely rejects this reconfiguration and properly translates the end of 4:10 as "for they have abandoned keeping faith with Yahweh." Although 4:10 only has "keeping," in Deuteronomy this verb is always associated with the positive act of maintaining one's relationship with God.

12. J. Day, "Baal," *ABD,* 1:548, supports the view that sacred prostitution was part of the Baal cult, though nothing is said of this in the Ugaritic epic myths about Baal. In a later article on "Prostitution" (*ABD,* 5:510–13), K. van der Toorn presents arguments that dispute the biblical connection between Baalism and prostitution.

Israel's true God. These practices lead people astray into unfaithful acts against God (4:12). Without proper teaching from Israel's priests, the population of Israel is filled with the "spirit of prostitution" and is blindly led away into a sensuous and selfish worldview that promotes debauchery rather than godliness.

Such worship does not take place at the temple of God, but at syncretistic Baalistic high places scattered throughout the countryside (4:13; elsewhere these are mentioned in 1 Kings 14:23; 2 Kings 17:10; Jer. 2:20). Here the people give their sacrifices to God/Baal (they apparently think these are two different names for the same god), enjoy the shade of the trees around these temples, and get involved with the sexual rites practiced at these outdoor places of worship. No doubt many who do this think they are reverencing God, being totally ignorant of what he actually requires in the Torah.

This paragraph ends with God's decision not to cast the primary blame on the young women (daughters and daughters-in-law) who are involved or who submit themselves to this sexual cultic activity at the Baal temples (4:14). Instead, God will punish the men (probably older) who set up, promote, and probably demand this perverse sexual activity. These sexual relations with cult prostitutes are designed to stimulate the fertility gods so that they will send fertility and blessing to the participants, but Hosea concludes that they only leave the people "without understanding" and in "ruin."[13] Of course, this is not just a sexual perversity, for it is all done in the name of and for the honor of the Canaanite gods.

Israel Is Hopeless (4:15–19)

THIS SECTION ENDS in great frustration and hopelessness. In a sense, God must give up on Israel and try to protect the innocent. He warns the Israelites not to influence the people of Judah with this unfaithful behavior of prostitution. Doing so will bring even greater guilt on them.

To ensure this does not happen, God gives three prohibitions to warn the people of Judah not to get involved with the adulterous worship at the Israelite temples (4:15). Hosea, like Amos (Amos 5:4–6), warns against worship at Gilgal (near Jericho, see Josh. 5:2–12; Hos. 9:15; 12:12) and against joining the worshipers at Beth Aven (probably Bethel).[14] They should also avoid swearing an oath like "as the LORD lives" at these places. Although the oath or vow (cf. similar cases in Deut. 6:13; Jer. 23:7; Amos 8:14) is to God,

---

13. See W. F. Albright, *Archaeology and the Religion of Israel* (Baltimore: Johns Hopkins Univ. Press, 1956), 75–76, for a fuller description of the pagan ritual of Baalism. Wolff, *Hosea*, 86–87, refers to Herodotus's account of a similar cult of prostitution in Babylon some years later.

14. See Amos 5:5 for a similar warning to the Israelites.

since the people think God and Baal are the same divine being, these oaths are actually being sworn in the name of a paganized Yahweh.

Because of these confusions, it is almost impossible for the stubborn people of Israel to change (4:16). They behave like a determined, self-willed, and obstinate heifer, not like a gentle lamb that can easily be led to enjoy the grass of a pleasant pasture. They are out of control and hopelessly determined to do whatever they want to do. The essential reasons for this hopeless situation are: (1) The people are spellbound by the idols that join with other forms of Baalism (4:17); (2) they deeply love the wine and the sexual prostitution at their temples (4:18); and (3) they are bound up by the adulterous spirit of their day (4:19).

When people are this hardened, about all one can do is to leave them alone (4:17b) and let them wallow in their shameful ways (4:18b).[15] They will wake up soon and realize the shamefulness of what they are doing. They have given themselves over to such a depraved way of thinking that there is not much Hosea or God can do.

THE MAJOR PROBLEM in bringing the ideas in Hosea 4 to people in the church today is the fact that people are not involved with anything similar to the Baal religion of Hosea's day. Thus, we must look beyond the idols and specific sexual aspects of the cultural representation of religion in Canaan to the broader and deeper problems destroying God's relationship to his people. As we have previously suggested, it is better to compare Baalism to the popular religious culture of our day rather than any specific set of beliefs or worship experiences. In that way every generation can ask: Have we so synthesized the popular religious ideas of our day into our faith that it has lost its true character?

Jesus himself called the religious people of his day "a wicked and adulterous generation" (Matt. 12:39; 16:4; Mark 8:38) because the people had prostituted their faith in God for something foreign to real faith. James warns his hearers about the dangers of syncretizing their faith with the culture of the day when he writes, "You adulterous people, don't you know that friendship with the world is hatred toward God?" (James 4:4). Paul also warned the

---

15. The NIV translates the last line in 4:18 as "their rulers dearly love shameful ways," but the word for rulers is actually the word "shields." Mays, *Hosea,* 76, translate it "shameless," and Stuart, *Hosea–Jonah,* 72, prefers "insolence." Most ancient readers would probably not take the reference to shields as a symbol of their rulers. Since God is called a shield (Gen. 15:1; Ps. 3:3; 7:10; 18:30), Garrett, *Hosea, Joel,* 139, proposes that this is a symbol of or appellation of one of their gods.

Corinthian believers about accepting the beliefs and standards of their culture. If they were members of the body of Christ, this would be the same as prostitution (1 Cor. 6:15–17).[16] Certainly the church today is threatened by this danger as much as the people in the Old and New Testaments. The real problem may be that we are as blind to our prostitution of the faith as the Israelites of Hosea's day and the Pharisees of Jesus' day.

The essentials of a relationship with God. The initial announcement of God's case against Israel (4:1–3) provides three criteria to evaluate the nature of the people's relationship to God. (1) We must look at the present characteristics of our beliefs and behaviors. If there is no faithfulness or truth to our relationship with God, if there is no steadfast covenant love for God and other people, and if there is no acknowledgment of God as Lord, then no positive reciprocal relationship with God can exist (4:1). We can claim many things when we talk, attempt to do many things for God to earn his favor, and be sincere (see Matt. 7:21–23), but without these fundamental principles working in our lives, there is no way to please God.

(2) If our lives are characterized by actions that run contrary to God's will (murder, stealing, lying, violence, and adultery are forbidden in the covenant documents in Ex. 20), one can legitimately conclude that we do not have a right relationship with God (Hos. 4:2). Such actions are a spiritual barometer of our true inner commitment to love and serve God.

(3) If the land where we live is continually suffering under the curse of no fertility, then perhaps we are not enjoying the blessings of a positive relationship with God.

As a point of caution, the critic who uses these criteria must be careful about misusing them for evaluating our true relationship with God, for no one wants to make the mistakes of Job's comforters. Nevertheless, Jesus, Paul, and James did use some of these ideas to critique and warn people about the dangers of internalizing too much of the deceptive thinking and sinful framework of the dominant culture of the day.

The centrality of the Word of God for spiritual leaders. When a people fail to follow God, it is always instructive to ask why. What did they do to displease God? Why did they miss the mark of doing what God requires? How can we learn from this incident so that we do not make the same mistakes (1 Cor. 10:11)?

In 4:4–10 Hosea explains one of the main reasons why the people in Israel were rejected by God. It was fundamentally a problem of not knowing

---

16. See Ortlund, *Whoredom: God's Unfaithful Wife in Biblical Theology*, 137–52, for a discussion of the New Testament usage of the marriage symbolism between Christ and the church. If the church is the bride, then it is natural to think of unfaithfulness to the bridegroom as prostitution.

God as their covenant Lord. If one were to ask why this had happened, the answer is clear. Israel's problem arose because the priests (and to some extent the prophets) were not teaching God's words of wisdom from the Torah (the five books of Moses). Although this might not be the reason for God's rejection of every group of people throughout history (some know God's words but do not follow them), several basic principles are established that serve as a warning to all spiritual leaders.

Of all the roles a pastor or any other spiritual leader has, the undergirding role is to help people know God (4:6). Israel's experience demonstrates that any acknowledgment of God as Lord is nearly impossible if spiritual leaders ignore God's revelation in the Bible. A leader will then tend to substitute some other "good" human cause that is culturally attractive but not nearly as important as the glorification of God (4:7). Jesus knew that the giving of charity and praying to God were "good" things, but he condemned the Pharisees who did not exhibit the more important characteristic of righteousness (Matt. 6:1–7). Eventually these "small" things lead to a perversion that destroys the true faith and involves people in things that God rejects (Hos. 4:10).

The powerfully persuasive warning throughout 4:4–10 is that God will destroy those teachers and preachers who reject him and lead his people astray. God's disapproval of false prophets who give dreams and false messages in his name is reported in Jeremiah 5:12–13; 14:14–15; 23:9–40. Jesus condemns the hypocritical Jewish teachers of his day in Matthew 23, and James warns about the serious responsibility of teachers (James 3:1). As Proverbs 29:18 says, where there is no revelation from God, the people perish.

The perversion of worship. The results of bad teaching nearly always show up in the way people worship God (4:11–14). If God is not presented as Redeemer, no one will come to him for forgiveness. If God is not seen as the Sovereign King of the universe, people will not honor and revere him as divine Lord, but will treat him as a casual buddy. If no one knows what God hates and is ignorant of what pleases him, it is not surprising if people do things that are contrary to his revealed will.

When people do not know God, they tend to do whatever seems culturally or socially acceptable. In Hosea's day that meant following the socially acceptable practices at the Baal temples. How could people go so wrong as to accept excessive drinking, idol worship, prostitution, and sacrifices to gods other than Israel's God? The simple explanation is that everyone around them was doing it; it was the cultural norm. If this principle is carried over to worship in churches today, the question we should be asking is: To what extent have our cultural norms determined what we do at church? What music, activities, messages, and methods do we use that do not glorify God but are done anyway since they seem so right?

Of course, not all modern cultural innovations are wrong, only those that lead people astray and involve acts of unfaithfulness to God (4:12). Twice Hosea condemns anything that "takes away the understanding" (4:11, 14). One should be suspicious of consulting anything or anyone other than God for divine wisdom (4:12) and of anything involving sexual impurity (4:13–14). Most people can spot an abusive cultic leader who demands absolute control over his followers so that he can indoctrinate them in his version of the truth,[17] but it is far more difficult to perceive the small ways in which many "respectable" groups accept the cultural values of our day and ignore what God's Word says. These perversions eventually have an impact on the nature of people's conception of God and their worship of him week by week.

Dealing with stubborn rebellion. The final paragraph (4:15–19) warns what can happen to any person or group who rejects God. Once a sinful perception of reality is viewed as normative and acceptable, it is difficult to bring about change. Stubborn persistence based on what people believe to be the truth can so blind our eyes that it is almost impossible to see the light. If my parents did it this way, if this is denominational policy, if this is what makes me comfortable, if this is something I think is okay, then it is hard to conceive of this action as a bad thing that God hates. When these perspectives become the keys to judging the normativity of anything, one has already lost the battle. It becomes a waste of time to lead people in a different way, for there is no ultimate authority (4:16).

The frightening fact is that some people can become so drawn into false religious beliefs that God seems to give up on them (cf. 4:17 with Rom. 1:18–32). In such cases about all one can do is to warn other individuals about not being involved with these sorts of people (4:15) and to encourage friends to stay away from the places of deception. Eventually a time may come where thoroughly deceived people must be left to their perverse ways until the shame of their ways finally catches up to them (4:18–19).

 **A DRAMATIC METHOD of presentation.** Part of the process of transforming people's lives is getting them to pay attention to what is being said. If the same old thing is said Sunday after Sunday, people drift off and daydream through the sermon. Sometimes a teacher/preacher must dare to do the unusual in order to wake people up and get them to understand the seriousness of God's unhappiness with them.

---

17. Even here, however, the process of indoctrination in a cult is often subtle; see Mary Alice Chrnalogar, *Twisted Scriptures* (Grand Rapids: Zondervan, 2000).

Hosea does this in 4:1–14 with the covenant lawsuit. He takes the chance to describe God's hatred of the people's sin in a new and potentially offensive way. But he cares little about those who may think he is a fool for doing this (9:7), since he is more concerned with communicating God's thoughts in a manner that the people will clearly understand. This raises the question: Should a person present a similar lawsuit against the church today?

Although not every church will be comfortable with hearing God's covenant lawsuit against them, the purest way to apply Hosea's method of teaching in this passage is to dramatize a comparable modern court case.[18] The most dramatic kind of presentation would be a complete courtroom reenactment with props and a small cast. One could replace the pulpit with a judge's bench and have a jury sitting in the choir loft. A prosecuting attorney would point out the failures of your church (attendance declines, fewer baptisms, difficulty of finding Sunday school teachers, cancellation of Wednesday prayer meetings, fewer people converted, etc.) and show how this has led to a decline in morality within the culture (more violence, adultery, stealing [cf. 4:2]).

The prosecutor would raise questions about the motives underlying this degeneration of morality. Perhaps people do not demonstrate a life of faithfulness to God that is reliable and firm in its commitment (cf. 4:1), or perhaps they have a deceptive commitment that goes hot and cold. Some may have a deeper commitment to their business or to sports events of their kids on Sunday. Are the people characterized by steadfast devotion to God (4:1) and their fellow human beings? What signs of steadfast love for God can be illustrated from the community? Is there a personal knowledge of God evident in people's lives, or do people have a one-sided and incomplete conception of the glory and majesty of Almighty God?

One could go on to raise questions about what or who is to blame for these problems, but in the end the spiritual leaders of the church must bear some responsibility. Following the example of Hosea 5–6, one could end the court proceedings with some sort of verdict (5:1–14), plus offer divine compassion on those who repent and truly seek God (5:15–6:3). Although this type of lesson or sermon may not be any more appreciated in the average church today than it was when Hosea first gave it, it would be a powerful mechanism of persuading people that God is deadly serious about his relationship with his people.

A dramatic assessment of responsibility. The blame for Israel's spiritual decline is put at the feet of her spiritual leaders, specifically her priests,

---

18. Getting permission from (or at least informing) the church council might be a wise step before attempting this kind of sermon.

although the prophets are also mentioned (4:4–10). It is always dangerous to generalize or oversimplify the complexities of life, but the failure of spiritual leadership is one of the top reasons why people in the church fail to acknowledge God, to have a steadfast devotion for God, and to be faithful and true to him (4:1).

Most pastors I talk to recognize the importance of good spiritual leadership in the church, but usually they do not feel they are responsible for the failure they see around them. Of course, God holds each person responsible for his or her own sins, but the Bible also puts accountability on the shoulders of spiritual leaders. The biblical prophets frequently condemn the false prophets and priests who think first of their own financial gain (Mic. 3:5–7, 9–11), and they criticize both priests and prophets who lead the people astray (Jer. 8:10–12; 23:9–40; Ezek. 13; Mal. 1:6–2:9).

Paul warned the church at Ephesus to beware of wicked leaders who would come from within and outside the church to destroy the flock by distorting the truth of God's Word (Acts 20:25–31). He urged Timothy to command certain men in Ephesus "not to teach false doctrines any longer nor to devote themselves to myths" (1 Tim. 1:3–4) because they promoted controversies and perverted the truth. J. MacArthur claims that "often a church that is failing to impact the world or that is experiencing strife and conflict among its members looks to new programming or other peripheral areas for answers, when the real problem may be that its leaders are spiritually unqualified for the task."[19] A question that every church should ask is: Do we have spiritual leaders who are qualified to lead us to know God and his will for our lives?

Although different pastoral roles involve different spiritual gifts and practical skills (i.e., a minister of music must have musical abilities), there are some fundamental requirements of all spiritual leaders. The key characteristic that Hosea pinpoints is the ability to communicate the Word of God (4:6). The spiritual leaders of his day were ignoring the law, even rejecting the knowledge of God that was found in their Scriptures (the Torah). In this way they "deserted the LORD" (4:10) to give themselves to other shameful deeds that led the nation further into sin.

Is this a problem today? Probably every pastor or church member can point to some other church in their town and say that they do not preach the gospel there. We usually perceive that we are doing fairly well ourselves—better than most churches, though with room for improvement. G. Barna's survey of 1,033 pastors found some claiming that the church was

---

19. J. MacArthur, *Church Leadership* (Chicago: Moody, 1989), 11. This fact was verified by one of my students, who was called to serve a church only to find out that half of his church council had little or no interest in spiritual things.

doing "tremendous, highly effective work" while others felt that the church was "failing miserably at every turn."[20] In another portion of this survey 85 percent of these pastors rated their knowledge of Scripture as superior.[21] But how dependable are these statistics, and what do they tell us about the theological message being taught in most churches?

While it is natural for people to make things look a little better than reality in any self-reporting survey, the major unknown in Barna's survey is the nature of what these pastors were preaching. I would like to know how many of these pastors preached from Amos, Hosea, or Micah in the last year. Are these people really preaching the whole counsel of God, or are they ignoring part of it? My own surveys of seminary students indicate that vast portions of the Bible are not being preached in many churches. How different is this from Hosea's accusation that the spiritual leaders of his day were "rejecting knowledge" and "ignoring the law of God"(4:6)?

Moreover, J. Hunter's study of the beliefs within evangelicalism demonstrates that the theological understanding of evangelical college and seminary students has shifted from some traditional positions, and these shifts are no doubt partially based on what these students heard from their pastor and teachers.[22] One can only wonder what these graduates are now teaching others as pastors throughout the world.

How will God react to spiritual leaders today who reject his revelation? Hosea is clear. They and their families will stumble, be destroyed, be rejected, be repaid for their deeds, and not have enough to eat. God's accountability is in direct relationship to the sins committed. These failures are not forgotten or ignored, because spiritual leaders in every age lead people either to glorify God or to act in a disgraceful way that does not glorify God (4:7). God's rejection of the spiritual leaders today will be in direct relationship to their rejection of him and his Word.

As Ezekiel heard about his role as a watchman (Ezek. 3:17–21), he came to understand that God would require the blood of the wicked from him, if he did not warn them when God spoke. As messengers of God's Word, we

---

20. G. Barna, *Today's Pastors* (Ventura, Calif.: Regal, 1993), 58. He also quotes one pastor from a church in Alabama who said, "I don't think any pastor truly committed to the gospel could look at America today and claim we've revolutionized this country."

21. Ibid., 71.

22. J. Hunter, *Evangelicalism* (Chicago: Univ. of Chicago Press, 1987), 19–50, deals with these theological changes. For example, only 66 percent of college students and 68 percent of seminary students agreed that "the only hope for heaven is through personal profession of faith in Jesus Christ" (35–36). The collection of essays edited by G. Marsden in *Evangelicalism and Modern America* (Grand Rapids: Eerdmans, 1984) also outlines some of the changes taking place within that movement.

dare not ignore what he says and allow our people to be destroyed because we are not communicating the knowledge God has revealed in Scripture. God cannot and will not reward those who fail to warn his people today. If he was willing to bring a curse on those spiritual leaders who were leading others astray in the Old Testament, and if Jesus condemned the hypocritical Pharisaic leaders of the New Testament, there is every reason to believe a similar fate awaits those who fail to teach God's Word in the church.

What kind of worship is unacceptable to God? Hosea describes a syncretistic kind of worship that was full of the culturally accepted practices common in Canaanite temples (4:11–14). Missionaries in some parts of the world will find a direct analogy with the idol worship that Hosea describes. But the points of application for most modern audiences must relate to the modern philosophies and cultural practices that the church has allowed to creep into the fabric of its theology and worship services. Some may point their finger at the upbeat choruses that many churches sing or the use of translations other than the old King James Version as signs of negative cultural influences on the church. Others may point to the decline in expository preaching and the increase of drama, especially in seeker-sensitive services.

It is difficult to say exactly what parallels Hosea's list of problems, but 4:11 seems to condemn anything that takes away the people's understanding of their relationship with God, 4:12a argues against looking to anything or anyone else than God for spiritual direction, and 4:12b forbids anything that leads to unfaithfulness to God. This even includes doing the right thing in the wrong way or at the wrong place (e.g., sacrifices, 4:13). Hosea also condemns any kind of sexually inappropriate behavior in 4:13–14.

Insofar as Hosea is calling Israel to evaluate the theological and cultural impact of Canaanite religious philosophy on Israelite worship, we too should call the church to be concerned about the influence of modern philosophical movements on our theology and worship. Although one could critique the New Age movement or existentialism, I will comment on a less recognized and more prevalent philosophical movement called pragmatism, an approach championed by W. James.[23] It focuses on what works or is useful, not on what is right or wrong. There are no absolutes, just ideas, explanations, or actions that have practical value.[24]

---

23. W. James, *Pragmatism: A New Name for Some Old Ways of Thinking* (New York: Meridian, 1955).

24. M. Erickson, *Christian Theology*, 1:43–44, quotes James as saying, "On pragmatic principles, if the hypothesis of God works satisfactorily in the widest sense of the word, it is 'true.'" This is not a strong or biblical endorsement of the foundation of all faith.

In many ways it makes sense to do what is practical and what works; after all, everyone wants to be pragmatic. But J. Piper says that the "recent lamentations over the drift of evangelicalism into pragmatism, doctrinally vague, audience-driven, culturally uncritical Christianity are, in my judgment, warranted and needed."[25] A. Fernando, a Youth for Christ leader in Sri Lanka, also has noticed that

> a major shift . . . has taken place in western evangelicalism where truth has been replaced by pragmatism . . . many evangelical leaders are so caught up in and blinded by this bondage to pragmatism that even though they may heartily endorse pleas to return to greater dependence on truth, endorsements make minimal inroads into their ministry styles and strategies.[26]

Scripture indicates that God does not do things just for their pragmatic value. Pragmatism cannot lead one to the truth, and it is a flawed method of discovering God's will.[27] Should we make changes in the church simply because people like it and it brings more in? Should we preach a pop-psychology message that touches people where they itch or employ popular marketing techniques because they get more people in the front door? Do leaders in the church make decisions on the basis of biblical doctrine or on the basis of what works the best?

Although things that work are not necessarily bad, utilitarianism is not a key biblical principle that helps people determine God's will. Any change that is motivated simply by what works puts biblical teachings, right and wrong, and following his will as secondary factors. Was it pragmatic for Jeremiah to preach the destruction of Jerusalem and get beaten and thrown in jail (Jer. 20:1–2; 37–38)? Was it pragmatism that drove Jesus to oppose the popular behavior of the Pharisees? Was John the Baptizer thinking in these terms when he declared that he must decrease while Jesus and his followers must increase? Was Paul thinking about what was practical or popular when he confronted the Corinthians about not taking a brother to court (1 Cor. 6:1–9) or their misuse of the Lord's Supper (11:17–34)?

Part of the problem of the church is that it has a "success" orientation borrowed from secular culture. Good is big, popular, exciting, growing, innovative, and on the cutting edge. For some, success is more power, more pres-

---

25. J. Piper, *God's Passion for His Glory: Living the Vision of Jonathan Edwards* (Wheaton: Crossway, 1998), 23, points to the criticisms by O. Guinness, *Fit Bodies, Fat Minds: Why Evangelicals Don't Think and What to Do About It* (Grand Rapids: Baker, 1994).

26. A. Fernando, *The Supremacy of Christ* (Wheaton: Crossway, 1998), 112–13.

27. J. MacArthur, *Ashamed of the Gospel* (Wheaton: Crossway, 1993), xii–xvii, sees many negative examples of pragmatism in the church.

---

tige, more money, and more popularity. But where does it say in the Bible that big is better, or that more is always what one should strive for? Note that Elijah and the seven thousand who had not bowed to Baal formed a minority in Israel (1 Kings 19). Success is doing the will of God, being faithful in what he has sent you to do, and committing yourself to glorify God rather than promoting yourself and your own agendas.

Is pragmatism any more pleasing to God than Baalism with its sexual prostitution? Both replace a dependence on God with a frame of reference that is more acceptable to the thinking of an average nonreligious person. Both reject the authority of God's words for a nonauthoritative perspective that changes with the whims of cultural change. If, however, the purpose of worship is centered around the glorification of God, all the prayers, singing, and preaching must focus attention on what God wants, not what makes pragmatic sense to a market strategist.[28] I doubt God will commend anyone on the day of judgment for being pragmatic. Paul recommends that the church not be conformed to the philosophies and patterns of this world, but that it be transformed by thinking differently (Rom. 12:2).

Is it ever too late? Hosea ends this section with the sad recognition that God's people are so stubborn and self-willed that it seems impossible for them to change (4:15–19). What does one do in such a situation? Hosea's words suggest practical steps.

(1) One can warn others (in Hosea's case, the people of Judah) to avoid the mistakes of those who have compromised their faith with their culture (4:15). One can do this by illustrating what has happened in other churches or in the lives of other people. Reading biographies of past saints and modern heroes provides a host of bad examples to avoid. Most newspapers carry an unending list of tragedies based on bad choices. *Christianity Today, Leadership,* and other such magazines discuss problems caused by people or churches that have bought into the philosophies of our age. A frank talk by a policeman at a kid's club, a testimony by a social worker at a youth meeting, or the honest assessment of life by Mom or Dad around the dinner table can go a long way toward making others aware of the consequences of wrong choices. Warning the innocent and naive of the danger of compromising with the subtle philosophies that pervade the world is an essential responsibility of every believer.

(2) The second thing one needs to do is communicate honestly with those who have already syncretized their faith with the philosophies of this world. Many of these people are unaware that their thinking is unbiblical

---

28. J. Piper, *The Supremacy of God in Preaching* (Grand Rapids: Baker, 1990), 17–26, deals with the goal of preaching.

because they do not see how pragmatism or any other "ism" contradicts biblical teaching. Sometimes a comment of concern about a decision is enough, but at other times a humble explanation of why this or that is not a good choice is needed. People who have fully bought into the worldview of the secular culture may need a sterner warning; they may need to know one's strong disapproval of their behavior (4:16). Confrontation is not wrong. If we truly love people, should we not care enough to warn them that they are in big trouble?

Hosea 5:1–14

¹"Hear this, you priests!
   Pay attention, you Israelites!
Listen, O royal house!
   This judgment is against you:
You have been a snare at Mizpah,
   a net spread out on Tabor.
²The rebels are deep in slaughter.
   I will discipline all of them.
³I know all about Ephraim;
   Israel is not hidden from me.
Ephraim, you have now turned to prostitution;
   Israel is corrupt.

⁴"Their deeds do not permit them
   to return to their God.
A spirit of prostitution is in their heart;
   they do not acknowledge the LORD.
⁵Israel's arrogance testifies against them;
   the Israelites, even Ephraim, stumble in their sin;
   Judah also stumbles with them.
⁶When they go with their flocks and herds
   to seek the LORD,
they will not find him;
   he has withdrawn himself from them.
⁷They are unfaithful to the LORD;
   they give birth to illegitimate children.
Now their New Moon festivals
   will devour them and their fields.

⁸"Sound the trumpet in Gibeah,
   the horn in Ramah.
Raise the battle cry in Beth Aven;
   lead on, O Benjamin.
⁹Ephraim will be laid waste
   on the day of reckoning.
Among the tribes of Israel
   I proclaim what is certain.

10 Judah's leaders are like those
    who move boundary stones.
I will pour out my wrath on them
    like a flood of water.
11 Ephraim is oppressed,
    trampled in judgment,
    intent on pursuing idols.
12 I am like a moth to Ephraim,
    like rot to the people of Judah.

13 "When Ephraim saw his sickness,
    and Judah his sores,
then Ephraim turned to Assyria,
    and sent to the great king for help.
But he is not able to cure you,
    not able to heal your sores.
14 For I will be like a lion to Ephraim,
    like a great lion to Judah.
I will tear them to pieces and go away;
    I will carry them off, with no one to rescue them."

THE STRUCTURAL MARKERS in Hosea's speech divide it into three paragraphs, each of which describes Israel's punishment. Verses 1–7 explain why God holds Israel's leaders accountable for the nation's promiscuous acts; verses 8–11 sound the alarm of war; and verses 12–14 draw symbolic pictures of God's destructive dealings with his people. The results of Israel's and Judah's promiscuous spirit will bear the fruit of death because God's people have been unfaithful and stubbornly refuse to acknowledge God as their Lord.

These paragraphs describe the consequences of the nation's sins. Continuing his judicial imagery from the courtroom, Hosea describes how God as judge will bring his verdict of "guilty" on the leaders of Israel (political and spiritual, see v. 1) because the people do not have a personal knowledge of God. This verdict includes an announcement of war (vv. 8–11) and a final series of bold images of God's judgment on his people. Within these judgments on Israel, Hosea indicates that God will also destroy the nation of Judah (vv. 5b, 10, 12b, 13, 14).

The alarms of impending war in 5:8–11 suggest that this message happened around 734–732 B.C., the time of the Syro-Ephraimite war (2 Kings

16; Isa. 7:1–9). At that time Rezin king of Syria joined Pekah king of Israel in attacking Ahaz king of Judah. They wanted to replace Ahaz (Isa. 7:6) or to force him to join their coalition against Tiglath-Pileser III and his Assyrian army. After Rezin and Pekah's forces killed 120,000 of Ahaz's troops and took 200,000 people captive (2 Chron. 28:6–8), Ahaz asked Tiglath-Pileser III to rescue him from his adversaries. After the Assyrian king defeated Syria and Israel, he required a heavy tax from Ahaz (2 Chron. 28:20–21).

These military events are pictured in the blowing of the trumpet (Hos. 5:8), while the results of this conflict are that "Ephraim [was] oppressed, trampled in judgment" (5:11). Hosea is not trying to give a detailed day-by-day reconstruction of these battles, but he does reflect the general military setting of this war within his message.[1]

Leaders Are Accountable for Israel's Promiscuity (5:1–7)

HOSEA BEGINS THE verdict by calling the priests and political leaders to hear what God is saying to them. They were responsible for the nation's decline, so they must now arise to hear what the judge will say about their leadership. The threefold summons to "hear ... pay attention ... listen" (5:1) indicates that an important statement is to follow.

The verdict ("judgment" in NIV) comes for several reasons. (1) The first is related to failures at Mizpah, Tabor, and probably Shittim (5:2, but NIV translates it "slaughter"[2]). Wolff hypothesizes that there were pagan cultic temples at these places, but perhaps these are random sites that demonstrate problems everywhere throughout the land.[3] Since the events Hosea refers to are lost to us, the only point to focus on is that the nation is snared, netted, or pitted through this experience (5:1b). These hunting images suggest an atmosphere of intrigue, deception, entrapment, and violence as individuals or groups try to control the political scene (note the assassinations in 2 Kings 15). God's verdict is to discipline the leadership for these acts (Hos. 5:2).

(2) Another reason for judgment is the religious prostitution the priests have encouraged (5:3). God knows about all their corrupt idolatrous

---

1. Garrett, *Hosea, Joel*, 149, rejects this hypothesis because it does not fit certain expectations. He objects to the idea in 5:10 that Judah is the aggressor, but it would not be odd for Judah to try to take back some of its territory after the Assyrians defeated her enemies. No one can date the appeal to avoid this conflict with Assyria in 5:13, but this may have happened anytime during these battles or at the end of the war, when Hoshea paid tribute to the Assyrians (2 Kings 17:3).

2. The Heb. text is not clear, so several educated guesses are possible. Several commentaries favor a reference to the town "Shittim," but no reading is without problems.

3. Wolff, *Hosea*, 98–99. One problem is that we do not know which city of Mizpah (in Gilead or Benjamin) Hosea is referring to.

behavior; Israel will not be able to hide her sins any longer. In contrast to God's intimate knowledge of the sins of Israel is Israel's lack of personal covenantal knowledge of God (5:4). The promiscuous deeds of the people have actually kept them from establishing a relationship with him. Without godly priests teaching and without godly worship at their temples, no change will take place. The situation is so bad that it is next to impossible for the people to return to God or know him as their covenant partner (5:4, 6).

(3) A third problem that Hosea raises is the nation's "arrogance" (5:5).[4] The people selfishly refuse to admit anything is wrong. Pride can lead to a hardened rebellion that refuses to change because it means an admission of guilt. Apparently all the people can talk about are their famous forefathers, the past wars they won, the glories of their cities, and all the good things of life. They are blind to the depravity of their present situation and do not want to face reality. They do not want to admit they have made mistakes or that the nation is in trouble. This pride is found in both Israel and Judah, and it will lead to their downfall.

(4) A final stumbling block to recovery is God's abandonment of the people (5:6). Although some may bring a sacrifice to a temple to worship, God will not be there. This reminds one of God's original prediction in the covenant that he "will hide [his] face from them" if they reject him (Deut. 31:17; 32:20). The people's unfaithful betrayal of God will not be tolerated forever (Hos. 5:7). They may think they can regain God's care and protection by offering a few additional gifts, but because of the uncleanness and debauchery at these temples, God will not hear them or answer their prayers (see Isa. 59:1−2). At this point it will be too late to make amends for their sinfulness.

These reasons justify God's verdict of guilty. Now is the time for "discipline"[5] and chastening (5:2), an idea that draws from the context of a teacher requiring accountability in order to instruct/discipline a student. This suggests that God's ultimate intention is to bring the people back to his way of thinking through a painful process of requiring accountability for every action. By disciplining the leadership, there is some hope for the rest of the people. If the evil leaders are not ensnaring the people, leading them in violence, directing their religious prostitution, and acting so arrogantly, then maybe the nation will not be stumbling so badly.

---

4. As McComiskey, *Minor Prophets*, 1:78, concludes, the "pride of Israel" in this context does not refer to God himself, but to things like the nation's history, wealth, territory, and institutions.

5. Stuart, *Hosea−Jonah*, 92, prefers to translate the word "shackles" rather than "discipline," which makes a nice contrast with snare and net in 5:1.

Warnings About the Impending War (5:8–11)

WITH GOD'S VERDICT legitimated (5:1–7), a terrorizing announcement of war is proclaimed by trumpet blasts around the countryside. Hosea encourages the warriors to prepare for battle, to warn the people that a military attack is about to happen (5:8). An unnamed enemy army is about to attack the land of Benjamin. P. M. Arnold does not see this verse as Judah's counterattack against Israel after Tiglath-Pileser III besieged Israel, as many suppose,[6] but believes it refers to Israel's earlier invasion of Judah in the Syro-Ephraimite war (734–732 B.C.).[7] This interpretation fits the historical allusions better.

If one accepts Arnold's view, Hosea is attempting to persuade Israel not to invade Judah in retaliation for Judah's errors. Why? Because this act will eventually lead to the disastrous situation where "Ephraim will be laid waste" (5:9). Its "day of reckoning" (lit., "chastening") did come soon after Israel and Syria invaded Judah because Ahaz called on the Assyrians to save them. Hosea knows that if the Israelites start this fight, they will certainly end up being losers.

This warning of Israel is interrupted by a condemnation of Judah because she has moved certain boundary stones that mark the border between Judah and Israel (5:10a). Wolff sees this as a quotation of certain Israelites who are trying to justify their attack on Judah.[8] Although there is no sign of a direct quotation, Hosea seems to be aware of this criticism of Judah. He is against those who want to turn Judah's stealing of Israelite land[9] into a pretense for war. He reveals that God will pour out his wrath on Judah for their sins and destroy their land like a flood (5:10b; see similar terminology in Isaiah's description of this war in Isa. 8:5–10). If God will exact justice for Judah's sins, there is no need for Israel to do so. The Israelites should worry about their own destiny, for they are in trouble themselves. The NIV connects Israel's troubles to the worship of "idols" in 5:11,[10] but a foolish war, not idolatry, is the theme of this paragraph.

---

6. Wolff, *Hosea*, 110–12, builds on, but adjusts various points in Alt's hypothesis of a counterattack. Stuart, *Hosea–Jonah*, 102–6, also sees this as Judah's counterattack, though there is no reference to any such attack in Kings or Chronicles.

7. P. M. Arnold, "Hosea and the Sin of Gibeah," *CBQ* 51 (1989): 447–60, includes a critique of Alt's views and proposes his own approach, based on a different geographic location of the cities in 5:8. Arnold believes both Hos. 5:8 and Isa. 10:27–32 trace the progress of this attack into Judah.

8. Wolff, *Hosea*, 114.

9. Deut. 19:14; 27:17 as well as Prov. 22:28; 23:10 warn against taking other people's land by moving boundary stones.

10. The word translated "idols" in NIV is unclear. *ṣw* could refer to something "worthless" (Wolff, *Hosea*, 104), "filth" (Andersen and Freedman, *Hosea*, 410), "command, policy" (Garrett,

Fearful Images of God (5:12–14)

HOSEA ENDS THIS section with several astonishing metaphors of God's future dealings with both of the guilty parties: Israel and Judah. He makes the shocking claim that God, their loving covenant partner, will be like "pus" in an open wound (NIV's "moth"[11]) and a "rot" to these people (5:12). These daring comparisons suggest that Israel and Judah will be like an injured soldier whose wounds are festering with terrible infection. Instead of cleaning, caring for, or healing these wounds of war so that his people can get better, God will be infecting them with more misery. Hosea is jarring his audience awake by showing that God will fight against them rather than for them if they continue with these war plans.

Realizing the vulnerability of their wounded situation, Israel is making things worse by seeking relief from Assyria rather than God (5:13). This may refer to Menahem's payment of tribute to the Assyrians (2 Kings 15:19–20) some years before the Syro-Ephraimite war.[12] Although Judah is not directly condemned for going to Assyria in this verse (possibly Ahaz has not yet made this fatal mistake), 2 Kings 16 records Ahaz's request for help from the Assyrians during the Syro-Ephraimite war. These human attempts to save themselves by depending on diplomatic manipulations and military conquests only bring more trouble for Israel and Judah rather than healing.

The second image pictures God as a destructive lion (5:14). He will tear his prey to pieces and carry off what remains, and no one will be able to stop him. Although Assyria was the means of bringing Israel and Judah to defeat, God proclaims that he is the real sovereign power who determines the future of both nations. From a human point of view it is natural for them to fear the mighty power of Assyria. Hosea warns that Israel and Judah should be more concerned with the power of God, for no one can do anything to resist the judgment of God's verdict.

Hosea., Joel, 152), "blah" (Stuart, *Hosea—Jonah,* 99). If the word carries the idea of something that is empty or worthless, Hosea is probably referring to Israel's policy to follow this path of war rather than to her sin of idolatry.

11. ʿš has been translated "moth, pus, maggot, decay, sickness." The parallelism argues against moth and for one of the other alternatives. See the discussion in Andersen and Freedman, *Hosea,* 412; Wolff, *Hosea,* 115.

12. Stuart, *Hosea—Jonah,* 105, thinks this verse may refer to Hoshea's submission and payment of tribute to Assyria immediately after the assassination of Pekah, the king who got Israel into this war (2 Kings 15:29–30; 17:3–4). But if Hosea is referring to events at the end of this war, it is surprising that he does not also mention Judah's mistake of calling on Assyria. McComiskey, *Minor Prophets,* 1:85, prefers a reference to Menahem in 5:13.

SINCE HOSEA 5:1–14 is tightly connected to specific events in the historical warfare between Israel and Judah, any attempt to apply this passage must be tied to the broad principles underlying God's message through Hosea, not to the events themselves. This section is an example of what any nation should not do if they want to avoid the wrath of God's judgment. Three bridging concepts support what Hosea announces in these verses.

God holds leaders responsible. God's verdict of guilty will be directed toward those spiritual and political leaders who mislead, deceive, and trap others with religious, political, and social ideas that do not come from God (5:1; see 4:6). Because of their trickery, Israel's leaders were able to "snare" people in their web; because of their rebellion against God, they defiled the people by encouraging their participation in the Baal religion. Through their military pride and lust for power, alliances, and revenge, the political leaders led the nation into a military situation that ended with tragic destruction and loss of life. Bad leadership was the basic problem in 4:4–10, and it emerges again as the primary cause for the nation's downfall in 5:1–7.

This issue is central to the history of Israel and the church in the New Testament. Saul failed to follow God's word in military matters (1 Sam. 13; 15), and Eli never trained his sons properly for their spiritual responsibilities (1 Sam. 2). Solomon, Ahab, and Manasseh became enticed by the worship of other gods (1 Kings 11:1–11; 16:29–33; 2 Kings 21).

By contrast, Hezekiah and Josiah sought the Lord and brought about great spiritual revivals in Judah (2 Kings 18; 22–23). Ezra, a great spiritual leader, interceded for those who had defiled the holy seed of Israel by marrying pagans and motivated people to return to God (Ezra 9). Although none of God's servants was perfect, God raised up leaders like John the Baptist, Peter, and Paul to challenge people to serve him. These few examples make it clear that leaders have an awesome responsibility to God and their followers, and that God holds them accountable for their words and actions.[13]

Sin separates people from God. God's verdict demonstrates that sin is rebellion against him (5:2) and cannot be hidden from him (5:3). Like prostitution, sin corrupts and destroys relationships between individuals and leads to a hardening of one's attitude against God (5:3). It keeps people from coming to God in repentance and perverts one's knowledge of God (5:4). Sin is caused by arrogance and results in selfish acts that ignore his will (5:5). Persistent sin can so harden the hearts of people that God will withdraw himself

---

13. J. R. Clinton, *Leaders, Leadership and the Bible* (Atlanta: Barnabas Resources, 1993), gives many examples of these and other biblical leaders.

and let them suffer the consequences of their sin (5:6). He will not accept worship from such people (5:7).

Hosea's message about the severity of sin in the lives of God's people is a sobering reminder that the "wages of sin is death" (Rom. 6:23). Saul's sin of disobeying God by not killing all the Amalekites resulted in God's rejection of him as king (1 Sam. 15), and Moses' sin of not treating God as holy meant he was not allowed to enter the Promised Land (Num. 20:1–13). David's sin with Bathsheba and against Uriah caused the death of his son (2 Sam. 12), and Gehazi's lie to Elisha resulted in his becoming a leper (2 Kings 5:20–27).

God rejected the sinful worship in Israel and Judah (Isa. 1:11–15; Amos 5:21–27) because sin had caused a separation between them and God (Isa. 59:1–2). By continually rejecting God, Pharaoh's own stubborn hardness separated him from repentance (Ex. 7–11). Paul indicates that such hardness is still possible for those who reject God's revelation (Rom. 1:18–32). As in the days of Ezekiel, sin can cause a holy God to abandon his people and withdraw his grace from their reach (Ezek. 8–12).

Sin had a devastating impact on the nation of Israel, and it will destroy every sinful individual and nation if it is not confessed and repented of. God's role as a lion who destroys or as pus that infects and kills (5:12, 14) is not limited to past events. The God who heals those who love him is also the God who attacks those who reject him. God was willing to destroy the whole nation of Israel when they worshiped the golden calf (Ex. 32) and actually did destroy the nation of Israel in 721 B.C. and of Judah in 586 B.C. According to Paul, "the wrath of God is being revealed from heaven against all the godlessness and wickedness of men who suppress the truth by their wickedness" (Rom. 1:18). Moreover, "because of your stubbornness and your unrepentant heart, you are storing up wrath against yourself for the day of God's wrath, when his righteous judgment will be revealed" (Rom. 2:5).

Military solutions do not solve spiritual problems. The final verses in this section contain Hosea's objections to the military answers that his contemporaries were proposing. Israel and Judah saw only two answers to the political crises: fight and kill the enemy, or make alliances so you can survive. Like Israel, many nations have used war as a means of righting minor wrongs against them, such as Judah's moving of boundaries (5:10a), but God is the One who will hold Judah accountable for her evil deeds (5:10b). Israel should be more concerned about her own spiritual failures, rebellion against God, and arrogance. The nation is corrupt and has turned to prostituting herself to Baal and to turning to other nations for help (5:3, 13).

Rather than depending on the unseen powerful God of heaven and earth, who controls all the military forces on the earth (Dan. 2:21; 4:17, 34–35),

God's people have all too often turned to man-made powerless gods and human armies for their security. They failed to realize that their military problems were caused by their own sinfulness and that God would heal their land and protect them from foreign dangers if they humbled themselves, confessed their sins, and turned from their evil ways (2 Chron. 7:14). The crossing of the Red Sea (Ex. 15), Gideon's defeat of the Midianites with three hundred men (Judg. 7), and David's defeat of Goliath (1 Sam. 17) all demonstrate that battles are won by the Lord, not by the military strength of a nation's army.

CAUSES OF CONFLICTS **and wars.** It would be entirely wrong for anyone to suggest that the events in Hosea 5 apply to military conflicts that exist today. Judah and Israel's problems cannot be identified with any nation today, and the Syro-Ephraimite war is not directly parallel to any war of modern times. The Assyrian conflict had its own historical characteristics, which we should not universalize.

Nevertheless, from this conflict one can learn why God judges nations, what nations need to do and not do in the midst of military conquests, and why every nation's military and spiritual leaders will be held accountable for their decisions. For those who are chaplains in the military or military commanders, it is especially important to pay close attention to what Hosea says. Political leaders who make decisions about national security and consider whether to declare war on other nations need to examine carefully their own motivations, the reasons why war seems so necessary, and to realize that God will hold them accountable for the way they lead their nation.

Citizens of countries likewise can exert political pressure on their leaders by approving or disapproving of military decisions; thus, they also play a vital role in encouraging or discouraging leaders to go to war. If every nation that wants to start a war would have a national day of self-examination and fasting before God, there may be fewer conflicts.

One of the first conclusions one sees in this passage is that sin causes conflicts and wars. Both sides of the conflict usually manifest sinful attitudes and action. Proud leaders refuse to back down on statements they have made lest they lose face in the eyes of their followers. Consequently, they make irrational attacks to demonstrate their toughness and strength. Leaders tend not to say "I was wrong" (much less, "I have sinned") or "I am sorry that I made that mistake." Although most leaders use religion to justify their deeds and call on God to bless their wars, one seldom sees a truly broken heart that turns to God (5:4) and acknowledges his will.

Following Hosea's example, every modern leader should ask: Is this conflict due to my failures? Is this God's punishment because of my sins (5:1)? Is this war God's way of punishing us for our corrupt ways (5:3)? Do we acknowledge God as the sovereign power over our nation, or are we so stuck in our sinful ways that God's ways are unimportant to us (5:4)? Are we motivated by our own pride and status rather than what God wants us to do (5:5)? Is God with us in all our actions, or has he forsaken us to our own devices (5:6)? Is the answer to our problems more fighting and war, or should we seek forgiveness to avoid God's judgment?

If we apply this section on a more personal level to conflict between people, we can ask these same questions. We will realize how sinful attitudes and actions separate us from God as well as from other people. Such separation leads to far greater misery and suffering through divine judgment, which God metes out so that we may turn from our wicked ways. The way to avoid this vicious circle of more and more judgment is to turn from these sins and ask God for forgiveness. Human efforts to get back at people only bring on more misery and do not address the fundamental problem of sin.

In searching for a way out of wars and conflict, one common tactic is to find support and strength through alliances with others (as the Israelites did with the Assyrians in 5:13). This solution assumes that resolution comes through the human manipulations of deal-making or annihilating the enemy with a superior combined force. Instead of looking for the spiritual problem, correcting the sinful source of the problem, or relying on the power of God for resolution, we tend to rely on human methods of conflict resolution. According to Hosea, God will not help those who ignore him.

If we avoid confronting the sin problem and the God solution, wars and interpersonal conflict will fester. Bitterness and hatred will seethe for months or even years until the offended party finds a new opportunity to open the wound and get revenge. Hosea suggests that when God is excluded from the solution process, he may actually exacerbate the problem rather than heal the situation (5:13—14). In fact, what people sometimes interpret as an earthly problem among humans may actually be a divine fight in which God himself is against us. The ultimate resolution to this kind of problem is to reject sin, seek God, and humbly plead for restoration.

Hosea 5:15–6:6

15 "Then I will go back to my place
   until they admit their guilt.
And they will seek my face;
   in their misery they will earnestly seek me."

6:1 "Come, let us return to the LORD.
   He has torn us to pieces
   but he will heal us;
he has injured us
   but he will bind up our wounds.
2 After two days he will revive us;
   on the third day he will restore us,
   that we may live in his presence.
3 Let us acknowledge the LORD;
   let us press on to acknowledge him.
As surely as the sun rises,
   he will appear;
he will come to us like the winter rains,
   like the spring rains that water the earth."

4 "What can I do with you, Ephraim?
   What can I do with you, Judah?
Your love is like the morning mist,
   like the early dew that disappears.
5 Therefore I cut you in pieces with my prophets,
   I killed you with the words of my mouth;
   my judgments flashed like lightning upon you.
6 For I desire mercy, not sacrifice,
   and acknowledgment of God rather than
      burnt offerings."

Original Meaning

THIS SECTION CONTAINS an invitation for the people to seek and acknowledge God (5:15–6:3), plus a divine response (6:4–6). Since several words repeat concepts found in chapters 4–5, this short section apparently serves as the conclusion to the first part of the prophet's covenant lawsuit (4:1–6:6). Like chapters 1–3, Hosea moves from accusations of sin (4:1–19), to God's punishment for their sin (5:1–14), to a concluding message of hope (5:15–6:6). God's response (6:4–6) suggests he is frustrated with the people's unwillingness to acknowledge his lordship.

Seek to Know God (5:15–6:3)

As J. L. Mays suggests, 5:15 is an "indispensable transition"[1] verse that connects what precedes with what follows. Although some include it with 5:1–14 because they see it continuing the lion imagery of 5:14,[2] there is no indication that God (the lion) will drag Israel (his prey) back to his lair in 5:15. Rather, the verse focuses on God's abandonment of his sinful people to their punishment (as emphasized in 5:6).[3] He will no longer come to his people's aid to rescue them. Instead, the divine chastening of destruction and captivity will cause them to accept responsibility for their sins (5:15) and to realize that their only hope is to seek God.

In the past God's people ignored his revelation and confused him with Baal, but in the future they will earnestly "seek my face." The duration of this period without God is limited only by their unwillingness to seek God. When they finally do come to recognize that their sins have driven God away, it will be possible for them to seek a personal and wholeheartedly devoted relationship with him.

The confession of 6:1–3, which expresses a desire to return to God, is the prophet's intercessory confession. He hopes his audience will accept this confession as their own decision to seek God.[4] Unfortunately, we do not know how many, if any, actually prayed these words. The prophet invites others to join in the process of returning to God, a typical Hebrew way of speaking of repentance (see 2:7b; 3:5; 5:4; 7:10, 16; 12:6). Such a commitment involves turning from past sinful ways and turning toward God. The people will have to reject Baalism and their dependence on military power and alliances and to trust in God alone.

One of the reasons for turning to God is the realization that he is sovereignly in control of life. Hosea confesses that the God who "has torn us to pieces" (6:1; cf. the lion metaphor in 5:14) is able to heal the people. God can also bind up the festering wounds full of pus (6:1b; see 5:12).

---

1. Mays, *Hosea*, 92, believes it stands apart from 5:10–14 as well as 6:1–3.

2. Wolff, *Hosea*, 116; and Andersen and Freedman, *Hosea*, 415, see the connection because of the repetition of the same verb "I will go" in 5:14 and 15.

3. Mays, *Hosea*, 92, follows this approach.

4. G. Yee, *Composition and Tradition in the Book of Hosea*, 157–58, does not believe Hosea wrote this section but assigns it to Redactor 2. Wolff, *Hosea*, 116–17, believes this penitential song was sung by the priests, not Hosea; but Stuart, *Hosea–Jonah*, 107, contends that its close literary connection to the preceding verses supports the idea that Hosea spoke these words.

These acts affirm Hosea's belief in God's power and dependability to respond to their repentance. This hope is based on his earlier promises to restore those who turn from their evil ways and repent (2:16–23; 3:4–5; cf. Deut. 4:25–31; 32:39).

Hosea is confident God will respond quickly to the people's turning to God—in two to three days (6:2).[5] Some see this as a national resurrection from the dead similar to Ezekiel 37, but the context of 6:1 suggests this is comparable to the reviving of a severely injured soldier.[6] Hosea also hopes to persuade the people to repent before they die from God's judgment. His desire is not just to see the nation revived (or resurrected) from its stricken state in the distant future, but to see the people "live in his presence" now.

It will take a mighty miracle of human confession and divine grace before God will revive this people and "restore" them, but it is possible. The people will have to "acknowledge the LORD" (6:3), a reversal of the present state of having no acknowledgment of God in the land (4:1, 6; 5:4). They will have to commit themselves to knowing their God in a personal covenant relationship. If they do this, God will respond to them.

Hosea motivates any doubters with the promise of the reliability of God (6:3). His appearance is not only 100 percent sure—like the positive experience of sunlight (a contrast to darkness) and rain (a contrast to drought). These comparisons are probably chosen because everyone knows that the sun and rain can be counted on and because these physical elements bring new life to dying plants. This hope also contrasts God's withdrawal from the nation (5:6, 15) with his gracious coming (6:3).

God's Frustration with Israel's Seeking of God (6:4–6)

GOD'S RESPONSE TO Hosea's invitation begins with a lament of disappointment. It is not that he does not know what to do; it is that he does not really want to do what he has to do. Somewhat like frustrated parents who are at their wits end on how to raise a deviant son, God wonders what he can do to bring about a real change in his people's hearts. The internal struggle suggests that he loves Israel and Judah dearly and does not want to punish them. But when they do not respond appropriately, what can he do? He has warned

5. "On the third day" is used in Luke 24:7 and 1 Cor. 15:4 in reference to the resurrection of Jesus, but it is hard to see any messianic reference in this verse. Some do suggest an analogy between the two situations (see H. K. McArthur, "On the Third Day," *NTS* 18 [1971–1972]: 81–86).

6. Andersen and Freedman, *Hosea*, 420; Stuart, *Hosea–Jonah*, 108; and Garrett, *Hosea, Joel*, 158, see a resurrection in 6:2, but Mays, *Hosea*, 92, and Wolff, *Hosea*, 117, prefer a revival from an injury. The New Testament and the early church fathers do not use this verse as a proof text for the resurrection of Jesus until Tertullian's *Against Marcion*.

them, chastened them to wake them up, and promised hope if they repent. What more can he do?

God's dissatisfaction with the devotion of his people is based on the fleeting nature of their covenant love for him (6:4b). Like dew, it disappears as quickly as a vapor. Commitments mean nothing; their consistency never lasts; they are positive one day and negative the next. They say they will seek God and worship him, but soon they are inquiring of Baal and depending on military power instead of on God. They do not seem to know what loyalty means. Because God's people do not consistently maintain their covenant relationship with him, he has sent prophets like Samuel, Elijah, Elisha, Micaiah, Amos, Isaiah, Micah, and others to declare in no uncertain terms what punishments God will send (6:5). These prophets declared God's intention to slay them for their sins if they did not love God with all their hearts.

These people know what they should do because God's "justice went forth as a light" (not NIV, "my judgments flashed like lightning upon you").[7] D. Stuart suggests that God's justice "functions like (sun)light, appearing daily and exposing what had been hidden,"[8] so that the darkness of their ways are known to him. In spite of this, all they can do is to mechanically bring their sacrificial gifts at their syncretistic temples to appease God (6:6). What God wants is their "consistent covenant devotion" (not "mercy," as in NIV). They need to know God by having a living relationship with him. Their worship at their temples does not satisfy the Lord because he wants them to love him, fear him, worship only him, serve him, and obey him (Deut. 10:12). Going through the religious motions will not cut it with God.

Bridging Contexts

GOD'S PLAN FOR REVIVAL. Hosea describes what God has done and will do to revive the spiritual vitality of his people. In order to bring them back to a personal relationship with himself, he has repeatedly revealed his will so that people may know what is expected. God's will has been made known in the Torah and through various prophets (6:5). This information is a light to their path because it explains in practical terms how God's justice works (6:5b). Without the power and wisdom of the words

---

7. The Hebrew *'or* means "light" except in those few cases where there is a thunderstorm. It that context lightning is being described (Job 37:3, 11, 15). "Upon you" in the NIV has been added and is not in the Hebrew.

8. Stuart, *Hosea–Jonah*, 110, sees God's justice as "inevitable and all-encompassing." It is what brought destruction on the nation in the Syro-Ephraimite war. Mays, *Hosea*, 97, interprets the sun positively. The prophets preached the light of God's way in all its clarity, but the people rejected the light of his Word.

of God, revival is impossible. These instructions will help people understand what they are to believe and do (6:6).

Just completing the prescribed ritual is not enough, however—not in Hosea's day or in Jesus' day. Jesus quoted Hosea 6:6 to show the Pharisees that God is more interested in the deeper principles like mercy, not just the keeping of the minor rules of Sabbath and sacrifice (Matt. 9:13; 12:7).

The basic principle established here is that rebelliousness often comes from rejecting the revelation of the Torah and the prophets. When this happens, it may be necessary for God to take more severe action to bring people back to himself. These initiatives may include severe warnings of judgment, possibly even the experience of a military defeat (5:8–14). If people continually fail to respond to these divine chastenings, God may choose to withdraw his grace and protection and to abandon his people (5:15).

Yet because of God's deep and abiding love, which does not desire that any should perish (Ezek. 18:23; 2 Peter 3:9), he does not give up in frustration on those he loves (Hos. 6:4a). He may withdraw for a while until people see the folly of their ways, but that withdrawal does not prevent people from seeking a new relationship with him. He will call his rebellious people to reject their sinful ways and return to him and will be quick to revive and heal those who respond. He will bind up their wounds, restore them, and let them live in his favored presence (6:1–2).

God's plan for revival is sure because he is the active power carrying out his plan. That plan is as sure as the cycles of nature, for he controls both. When he comes to those who respond to him, he will bring blessings with him (6:3). Although Hosea may not mention the work of the Spirit in revival (see Ezek. 11:17–21; 18:30–32; 36:26–27) and various other aspects of revival that appear in Acts, this picture in Hosea makes it clear that God is in charge and that he has a deep desire to renew his fellowship with his people.

People choose revival. God's persistence in calling his people back to himself is evident from the messages of all the prophets (6:5). But revival cannot happen unless people are willing to change their theology and behavior. Hosea makes it clear that his audience needs to respond to God's initiatives and transform their lives. Before revival can germinate and take root, people must "admit their guilt" and "earnestly seek me" (5:15). As the text indicates, this often happens when the misery of punishment and disappointment pushes people to look to God for some hope, after all human hope is gone.

Revival involves people choosing to return to God and believing he is able to heal them (6:1). This is a response to God, his character, and his promises. Although Hosea does not use the term *faith*, the confident statements that God "will revive us ... he will restore us" (6:2) represent a reliance and confidence that demonstrate trust in God. Such statements proclaim that deliverance is only through the gracious act of God and is not based on human abilities or worth. The choice of revival is not pictured as a single decision but as a pressing on to know God through an intimate covenant relationship (6:3).

True revival is not a transitory event with no lasting effect on a person's life. God will not accept a temporary change that disappears the next day (6:4). He wants people whose hearts are deeply devoted to loving him and who willingly acknowledge his lordship over their lives (6:6).

Participation in a few religious services will not satisfy God (cf. Jesus' reiteration of this principle in Matt. 9:13; 12:1–8), for only the evidence of a changed life verifies the presence of a revived spirit. Jesus and Hosea agree that merely participating in ritual or knowing the law does not make one a truly repentant believer. God wants the heart and soul, not just the lips and exterior facade. Life-transforming revival is the conscious choice to live in God's presence for the purpose of glorifying his name and reflecting his character in daily life.

THE PRINCIPLES OF revival are seen in churches throughout the world when God's Spirit moves to renew his work in people's lives. Before teaching this passage one should read several books on the revivals of the great preachers of the past to learn about God's marvelous work to revive the church.[9] Comparison of those experiences with Hosea's will be obvious.

All leaders of revival recognize that the change in people's lives is solely due to the powerful transformational moving of God. T. Phillips's account of the Welsh revival in 1859 states that the "best feature of all in the aspect of the present times . . . is the fact, now acknowledged even by the world, that there is a power at work in the hearts and conscience of people that is not to be accounted for by any human hypothesis. . . . These are 'times of refreshing from the PRESENCE OF THE LORD.'"[10] Later in the 1904 Welsh revival God used Evan Roberts initially to transform seventeen people;

9. R. M. Riss, *A Survey of 20th Century Revival Movements in North America* (Peabody, Mass.: Hendrickson, 1988), mentions revivals before the Reformation and during the Reformation (1515–1590), the Puritan revivals in England, the Great Awakening in America, and nineteenth-century revivals; the book also gives a detailed summary of twentieth-century revivals.

10. T. Phillips, *The Welsh Revival: Its Origin and Development* (Edinburgh: Banner of Truth, 1989), 2.

before God's work was done, over 37,000 people came forward to confess their sins.[11] H. Blackaby's study of experiencing God also emphasizes that "God always takes the initiative. He does not wait to see what we want to do for Him. After he has taken the initiative to come to us, He does wait until we respond to Him by adjusting ourselves to Him and making ourselves available to Him."[12]

Just as God sent prophets in the Old Testament to deliver God's word (6:5), God's modern means of revival is usually through fervent prayer and a renewed hunger for the teachings of the Bible. I. Murray puts it this way: "God works in accordance with his Word. Without Scripture there is no 'work of the Spirit.' The test whether experience is of the Spirit of God or of 'another spirit' is whether or not it brings greater understanding of the Bible and a closer obedience to it."[13]

As one reads the Scriptures and books on revival, the theology of Hosea jumps forth again and again. God is about the business of calling people to "admit their guilt" and "earnestly seek" him. Moses instructed the Israelites in Deuteronomy 4:29–31 to seek God in their day of distress and search for him with all their hearts. When they return to God, he will have compassion on them and will not fail to accomplish his will through them. In Solomon's great prayer at the dedication of God's holy temple in Jerusalem (1 Kings 8:31–39), he requests God to bring revival when the people confess their sins, pray, and turn to God.[14] Isaiah 55:6–7 encourages people to "seek the LORD while he may be found. . . . Let the wicked forsake his way, and the evil man his thought. Let him turn to the LORD." In all cases revival is a human response to God's call for fellowship.

Although some revivals may last a relatively short time, true revival in the heart thoroughly changes the individual forever. True transformation is not a transient affair. In the revivals led by David Morgan in Wales, the "effects were not transient. They left a deep impression on our minds, and have influenced our conduct for good. We feel more serious, more ready to speak about our religious life, more anxious as regards the salvation of the world, and more desirous that the Lord would dwell among us."[15]

---

11. J. Bright, *The Coming Revival: America's Call to Fast, Pray, and "Seek God's Face"* (Orlando: New Life, 1995), 79–80.

12. H. T. Blackaby and C. V. King, *Experiencing God: Knowing and Doing the Will of God* (Nashville: LifeWay, 1990), 33, illustrate this from the life of George Mueller.

13. I. H. Murray, *Revival and Revivalism* (Edinburgh: Banner of Truth Trust, 1994), 359.

14. Some calls to revival include fasting as well (e.g., 2 Chron. 20:3–4; Joel 2:15). Bright, *The Coming Revival*, 101ff., gives practical help on fasting, based on Bill Bright's own forty-day fast.

15. Phillips, *The Welsh Revival*, 13.

Revival enables a person to know and experience God as a real, living, powerful person. Those who dutifully mouth hymns about God, daydream through sermons, and drop in their obligatory offering are like the spiritually dead Israelites who followed the rules and regulations but did not truly know God (6:6). They are the modern Pharisees whom Jesus would condemn if he were here (Matt. 12:7). They are more interested in legalities and human traditions and are not as concerned about righteousness, mercy, and love for God. They are the people in the church who are spiritually dead and in need of revival.

Revival is not an optional course of action for a church. It needs to be a vital part of every church calendar and a prayer concern of every believer. Revival is about living for God and glorifying his name. It encourages people to be restored from a cold, deadened condition to a living state of joy and peace. Spiritual leaders in the church need to encourage people to return to God, to look to him for restoration, and to desire to live in his marvelous presence. If a spiritual leader rejects the path of revival, the church will die.

Hosea 6:7–7:16

⁷ Like Adam, they have broken the covenant—
    they were unfaithful to me there.
⁸ Gilead is a city of wicked men,
    stained with footprints of blood.
⁹ As marauders lie in ambush for a man,
    so do bands of priests;
  they murder on the road to Shechem,
    committing shameful crimes.
¹⁰ I have seen a horrible thing
    in the house of Israel.
  There Ephraim is given to prostitution
    and Israel is defiled.

¹¹ "Also for you, Judah,
    a harvest is appointed.

  "Whenever I would restore the fortunes of my people,
7:1   whenever I would heal Israel,
  the sins of Ephraim are exposed
    and the crimes of Samaria revealed.
  They practice deceit,
    thieves break into houses,
    bandits rob in the streets;
² but they do not realize
    that I remember all their evil deeds.
  Their sins engulf them;
    they are always before me.

³ "They delight the king with their wickedness,
    the princes with their lies.
⁴ They are all adulterers,
    burning like an oven
  whose fire the baker need not stir
    from the kneading of the dough till it rises.
⁵ On the day of the festival of our king
    the princes become inflamed with wine,
    and he joins hands with the mockers.
⁶ Their hearts are like an oven;
    they approach him with intrigue.

Their passion smolders all night;
    in the morning it blazes like a flaming fire.
⁷ All of them are hot as an oven;
    they devour their rulers.
All their kings fall,
    and none of them calls on me.

⁸ "Ephraim mixes with the nations;
    Ephraim is a flat cake not turned over.
⁹ Foreigners sap his strength,
    but he does not realize it.
His hair is sprinkled with gray,
    but he does not notice.
¹⁰ Israel's arrogance testifies against him,
    but despite all this
he does not return to the Lord his God
    or search for him.

¹¹ "Ephraim is like a dove,
    easily deceived and senseless—
now calling to Egypt,
    now turning to Assyria.
¹² When they go, I will throw my net over them;
    I will pull them down like birds of the air.
When I hear them flocking together,
    I will catch them.
¹³ Woe to them,
    because they have strayed from me!
Destruction to them,
    because they have rebelled against me!
I long to redeem them
    but they speak lies against me.
¹⁴ They do not cry out to me from their hearts
    but wail upon their beds.
They gather together for grain and new wine
    but turn away from me.
¹⁵ I trained them and strengthened them,
    but they plot evil against me.
¹⁶ They do not turn to the Most High;
    they are like a faulty bow.
Their leaders will fall by the sword
    because of their insolent words.
For this they will be ridiculed
    in the land of Egypt.

SINCE HOSEA CONTINUES his messages beyond 5:15–6:3, one must assume that many did not immediately repent and seek God. Some came to the temple to give their sacrifices, but they did not truly love God with all their hearts (6:6). Since God refused to give up on his people (6:4), he sent Hosea to present additional reasons (beyond the fact that they did not acknowledge God) why the people should admit their guilt and seek the Lord. The next section of the covenant lawsuit against Israel (6:7–11:11) focuses on a second major charge: The people are not steadfast in their loving devotion to God, as demonstrated by their sinful behavior at the golden calves and their alliances with other nations.

Hosea does not give the date of these messages, but the mention of a battle in 8:1 and of the assassination of kings in 7:3–7 suggests that they were given during or near the time of the Syro-Ephraimite war (734–732 B.C.), probably shortly after 4:1–6:6.[1] Although this gives a general dating for one portion of this long speech, it is impossible to securely date its many parts.

The structure of this second part of the covenant lawsuit fits the general pattern of the rest of Hosea, although it does not have any announcement of a case against Israel at the beginning, as in 4:1–3. These sermons include a series of accusations of sinfulness (6:7–7:16), a description of the punishment the nation will endure (8:1–9:17), another series of accusations (10:1–15), and a final message of hope (11:1–11). Hosea does not slavishly follow the lawsuit format throughout this section, but the broader framework of his approach draws on legal terminology and the punishment of people who fail to keep their covenant commitments.

In the first oracle of this new section (6:7–7:16) Hosea brings up additional examples to prove that the Israelites have broken their covenant with God. Their unfaithfulness includes a variety of sins. The priests (6:9) and political leaders (7:3–7) are singled out once again as those most to blame for the wickedness that is destroying the nation (see also 4:4–10; 5:1–2). They are evil people who selfishly do whatever they need to in order to get what they want. They rebel against God and do not turn to seek him.

This long series of accusations can be divided into several paragraphs: (1) 6:7–10 reveals how the sins of the priests have defiled the whole nation; (2) 6:11–7:2 explains that restoration is impossible because of Judah's and Israel's sins; (3) 7:3–7 deals with assassinations and corruption within Israel's political system; (4) 7:8–12 condemns dependence on other nations instead

---

1. Wolff, *Hosea*, 137; Stuart, *Hosea–Jonah*, 130; and Mays, *Hosea*, 114, date 8:1 to just after 733 B.C. and connect it with the attack by the Assyrian king Tiglath-Pileser III.

of on God; and (5) 7:13–16 is God's lament over Israel's coming destruction. Though it may be impossible to identify any of these accusations with specific incidents, the events surrounding the Syro-Ephraimite war from 734–732 B.C. provide the general background.

The Sins of the Priests (6:7–10)

ANDERSEN AND FREEDMAN have made the attractive hypothesis that this passage is describing one event rather than a random collection of different acts of violence in Israel.[2] If this is correct, the event took place in the territory of Gilead, on a road that goes to Shechem, and near the city of Adam. This city lies on the east bank of the Jordan River (Josh. 3:16) on the main road linking Shechem and Mahanaim.[3] Some hypothesize that this violence may relate to the assassination of King Shallum or Pekahiah (2 Kings 15:25 even implicates people from Gilead), but the text is not that specific.

The priests' violent action of shedding blood in some kind of ambush (6:9) on the road to Shechem is characterized as "unfaithful[ness] to me" (6:7) and a "shameful crime" (6:9) because these "wicked men" have "broken the covenant" (6:7). These descriptive phrases depict an act that goes contrary to the regulations of the covenant—a betrayal that violates the agreement between God and Israel. Hosea does not explain exactly why the priests were involved in this crime, but if the spiritual leaders were a gang of murderers who killed to get their way, one can only imagine how bad things were in Israel.

A second sin that implicates the spiritual leadership of the priests is the cultic prostitution that fills the land (6:10). God sees this "horrible thing" that defiles his holy land. It is not hidden from his sight, and he will not overlook it.

Restoration Is Impossible Because of Sin (6:11–7:2)

THE END OF the previous paragraph and the beginning of this paragraph are a matter of dispute. Some include 6:11a with the previous paragraph because the parallel constructions in 6:11b and 7:1a seem to bring 6:11b into the following paragraph.[4] But the brief comment about Judah's day of harvest in

---

2. Andersen and Freedman, *Hosea*, 433, 435, think this event was during the transition from Jeroboam II to Menahem, when several kings were assassinated (2 Kings 15).

3. Stuart, *Hosea–Jonah*, 111, interprets ʾdm as "dirt, soil," as does D. J. McCarthy, "Berit in Old Testament History and Theology," *Bib* 53 (1972): 110–21. Macintosh, *Hosea*, 236, list other views: Harper thinks this refers to "mankind," and Ridderbos prefers the person "Adam." Note that Gilead in 6:8 and Shechem in 6:9 are places.

4. McComiskey, *Minor Prophets*, 1:98–100, is one example of this division.

6:11a (i.e., its judgment, as in 10:13; Jer. 51:33) does not fit well with all the accusations against Israel in the rest of 6:7–10. Its inclusion with the previous section also leaves the temporal "when" clause in 6:11b without an independent clause to modify. Since 7:1 also has a temporal "when" clause modifying an independent clause, one should probably understand 6:11 in a similar way. Just as Israel's sins will be exposed when God comes to heal his people (7:1), so Judah's judgment will be necessary when God comes to restore his people to their covenant relationship (6:11).

These two verses are not primarily salvation promises[5] (although they recognize that healing will happen someday) because the main independent clauses (which are negative) determine the central emphasis of the sentence, not the subordinate "when" clauses. The focus is on the sinfulness of the people, which necessitates judgment. This sinful condition will delay God's gracious restoration of his people.

In 7:1b–2 Hosea lists some of the sins that God will expose. The people are characterized by deceit and falsehood instead of righteousness and justice. They steal from private residences and mug people in public on the streets, rather than loving their neighbors as themselves (Lev. 19:18). They have no respect for one another and do not treat each other as covenant members.

Most surprising is the utter callousness of the people toward these sinful acts. They do not seem to realize that these deeds are evil. Apparently these sins are normal, acceptable behavior in this society, since everyone seems to be doing them. They think nothing of these crimes and do not think God is paying any attention to them (7:2). Their Canaanite worldview has eliminated a holy God of justice, who sees, hates, and punishes sin. In contrast to their blindness to sin, the stench of their vile lives has come up to God because he sees everything they are doing. These sins destroy the people's covenant relationship with God.

Political Corruption in Government (7:3–7)

THE HEBREW TEXT of these verses is difficult,[6] but there is no doubt that God is critiquing the behavior of kings and officials of government who cause other kings to fall from power (7:3, 7). The historical description of the

---

5. Stuart, *Hosea–Jonah*, 112, interprets the harvest as a sign of God's abundant blessings. Garrett, *Hosea, Joel*, 166, sees the harvest as a punishment, but interprets 7:1–2 as a promise of restoration.

6. Commentators are forced to emend some words and make educated guesses concerning how these words fit together. The oven and baker images make an unusual and difficult comparison, but the burning heat of the oven seems to offer the central analogy for Hosea.

assassination of the Israelite kings Zechariah, Shallum, Pekahiah, and Pekah (2 Kings 15) provides the background to these accusations.[7] The subject of the verbs is undefined in 7:3–4,[8] so no specific group or person is identified at this point. Hosea is more interested in explaining what they do.

At first the people referred to here appear to be friends of the royal court (the king and his princes) because they delight the king by joining him in all kinds of evil deeds. Their deeds of deception may refer to conspiracies against an earlier king who was killed or to other unknown acts. This scheme to take political control through violence brings great joy to the victors in the royal court. Maybe the royal house is having a celebration marking the anniversary of the present king's rise to power.

Hosea describes these new rulers as "adulterers" (7:4), a word that refers to someone who is unfaithful to another person. He probably does not mean sexual infidelity[9] here but political unfaithfulness to the king (see similar uses in Jer. 9:2; 23:10–12). Like a hot oven these people burn in their passion for political power. They are compared to a baker because they do not carefully pay attention to their duties (a baker was supposed to stir the fire and knead the dough). Instead of protecting the king, they are in on the plot against this new king.

At a special royal celebration everyone becomes drunk (7:5), and scornful mockers join in the celebration. Instead of being guided by wise men with deep spiritual insight, like Daniel or Nathan, this king has surrounded himself with disrespectful fools. In their heated passion they wait all night to implement their ambush (NIV "intrigue") of the king in the morning (7:6). In a final blaze of irrational passion they viciously attack and kill their ruler (7:7).

This human tragedy takes place again and again (four kings are assassinated), but none of these violent people ever inquires of God about what they are doing. These murderers do not seek him to gain wisdom; they have the scoffing mockers to guide them. They do not wait for God to send a prophet to anoint the next king; they depend on cunning plots of deceit to remove and set up new kings. They are not concerned about doing what delights God because they are only concerned about what delights themselves. They do not even ask God for help because they slyly make alliances with one group or another to protect their interests. God's role of choosing each new king for the nation is usurped by vicious plots to grab power through violence.

---

7. Wolff, *Hosea*, 111; Mays, *Hosea*, 104; and Stuart, *Hosea–Jonah*, 117, think this section specifically describes the assassination of Pekah by Hoshea in 733 B.C. (see 2 Kings 15:30).

8. Andersen and Freedman, *Hosea*, 446, believe a group of priests (6:9) assassinate the king and his princes, but the text does not say this. They do not take the baker as a metaphor but think the king's baker is at the head of this plot (451).

9. McComiskey, *Minor Prophets*, 1:104, thinks Hosea refers to sexual unfaithfulness.

Political Dependence on Alliances (7:8–12)

INSTEAD OF DEPENDING on God to protect them and guide their political decisions, the new kings consolidate their power by forming alliances with other nations (7:8). When Hoshea became king, he dissolved the nation's political alliances with Syria, Philistia, and Egypt and created a new political alliance with the Assyrian king, Tiglath-Pileser III (7:11; see 2 Kings 15:30), and then turned around and made a secret alliance with Egypt (2 Kings 17:4). The "mixing" imagery (Hos. 7:8) draws on the bread metaphor in the previous verses, but in this case the king is so negligent that God views the nation as useless, unturned bread.[10]

These alliances are hurting the nation because they require payment of heavy tribute and encourage cultural and religious compromises to keep the peace with the Assyrians. This syncretistic trend drains the nation of its financial resources, its independence, and its moral strength (7:9). The surprising thing is that the people do not see how this creeping compromising (like the slow process of getting gray hair) is gradually undermining their identity. These are selfish acts of pride and self-determination that are not based on God's direction (7:10). Israel's leaders act independently and without reliance on God. Why should they bother mixing religion with their politics by asking God what he wants? Are they not able to handle things themselves through their alliances? How can God ever help the situation? Now that they have peace with Assyria, everything will be fine.

But Israel's situation changes, and soon there are attempts to make new alliances. Like a foolish dove Israel's foreign policy flips and flops back and forth without consistency or any lasting commitment (7:11). Although the specific event is unknown, the disloyalty of Israel is illustrated by King Hoshea's duplicity. First he paid tribute to Assyria, then a short time later he tried to make a new alliance with Egypt (2 Kings 17:3–4). God responds (Hos. 7:12) by capturing these senseless birds in his net and "disciplines" (see 5:9, not "hear them flocking together," as in NIV[11]) them when a certain report is received. The ambiguity of this line makes interpretation difficult, but T. McComiskey suggests that this refers to God's decision to destroy Israel once the news of her deceptive alliance with Egypt is known.[12]

---

10. This may refer to bread that is burnt on one side and not cooked on the other, or to bread that is not kneaded before it is placed in the oven. If the baker neglects the bread, it will be rejected as inedible.

11. The NIV repoints "like a report" to read "when I heard." Wolff, *Hosea*, 107, emends the last line to read "according to the report of their wickedness," while Stuart, *Hosea–Jonah*, 115–16, has "I will punish them sevenfold for their evil."

12. McComiskey, *Minor Prophets*, 1:111–12.

God Laments Israel's Coming Destruction (7:13–16)

THIS SERIES OF accusations reaches its climax with God's sorrowful lament over his hopelessly sinful people. This poem is similar to the cry of woe people mournfully express at the funeral of a loved one, or when they hear that a relative is about to die. God is singing his wailing lament over his people because it is now decided that they will soon die. He weeps because he has done so many good things for his people, but his people and their leaders have rejected him.

God's act of redemption in 7:13 is interpreted as a question by D. Stuart ("How can I redeem them?") and as a wish by most others (NASB; RSV; NIV). Andersen and Freedman, however, believe that God's two gracious deeds (7:13b, 15a) on behalf of his people refer to past events.[13] Long ago God graciously redeemed his people from Egyptian slavery (Ex. 3–15) to demonstrate his love and make them his own special people. Over the years since that time, God "trained" or instructed his people through divine revelation and the hard knocks of experience (7:15), in order to help them know what to avoid and to teach them the limitations of their covenant relationship. God also strengthened them in times of peace and war so that they would be able to defeat their enemies and defend themselves against oppressors (7:15). God did not fail to care for his people but faithfully demonstrated his steadfast covenant love for them. It is heart-breaking now when they do not appreciate or respond positively to such great acts of love.

The reactions of God's people to his great deeds of power and grace are lamentable. They have rebelled against his authority, strayed from his instruction, and lied about their love and loyalty to him (7:13). They do not cry out to God from a heart of love, but when they worship and bring their sacrifices to the temple, they worship other gods, using pagan methods (7:14).[14] That "they plot evil" against God may refer to political or religious actions that undermine the instructions and character of God (7:15). They are no longer loyal to God, their covenant partner; instead, they do whatever they want. The people are compared to a deceptive bow with defects. Like an arrow shot from a twisted bow, they miss the mark and serve other gods.

The consequence of Israel's action is "destruction" (7:13) and the military defeat of her leaders. All their deception will catch up with them, and then their former allies will laugh and "ridicule" them (7:16). Israel will get

---

13. Stuart, *Hosea–Jonah*, 123; Andersen and Freedman, *Hosea*, 473, who are followed by Garrett, *Hosea, Joel*, 172.

14. The "gather together" in 7:14 is possible, but "cut themselves" (cf. NIV note), a possible reference to a Baal ritual (I Kings 18:28), may be what Hosea is talking about (see Andersen and Freedman, *Hosea*, 475).

what it deserves from God and receive no sympathy from its former political partners. What a sad end for such a great people.

THIS SECTION DESCRIBES the sins of Israel. It is an ugly picture of rejection, violence, deceit, betrayal, robbery, and arrogance. These sins are primarily the work of the priests (6:7–10) and political leaders (7:3–13). In both cases these leaders have rejected God's standards of morality that govern the behavior of covenant partners. Both groups take control of their situation and enforce their will through violence. No one seems concerned about what God wants; in fact, Hosea observes a purposeful rejection of God's ways. Although the principles in this passage specifically apply to spiritual and political leaders, in the broader perspective God's condemnation of these sins relates to anyone who acts as these wicked Israelites do.

Who is a sinner? Hosea's main goal is to convince his audience that they are sinners who deserve God's judgment. He accomplishes this purpose by reciting the many sins of the spiritual and political leaders. The list is depressing and far too long:

6:7	break the covenant, unfaithful
6:8	wickedness, shedding blood
6:9	set ambushes, murder, shameful deeds
6:10	done horrible things, prostitution, defiled
7:1	crimes, deceit, thievery, banditry
7:2	evil deeds, sins
7:3	wickedness, lies
7:4	adulterers
7:5	inflamed with wine, joins with mockers
7:6	intrigue/deception, intense passion
7:7	destroy rulers, cause kings to fall, do not call on God
7:8	mix with the nations
7:9	do not realize how foreigners influence
7:10	arrogance, do not turn to God
7:11	deceived and senseless, depend on other nations
7:13	stray from God, rebelled against God, speak lies against God
7:14	do not cry to God from their hearts, sacrifice without turning to God
7:15	plot evil against God
7:16	do not turn to the Most High

Hosea uses every possible means to communicate that these people are sinners. Several sins stand out because they are repeated. God hates (1) deceit, plots, and lies; (2) violence and killing; and (3) not calling on or turning to God. Many in Hosea's audience do not realize these things are so bad. They foolishly think God will not remember their sins (7:2). But Hosea announces that God hates these sins. He will not treat them lightly because they destroy his covenant relationship with his people. He will punish, even destroy, those who do these things.

(1) One of the major sins that God will judge is deception. This was true in the Garden of Eden (Gen. 3), and it is true today. God had warned Israel not to be deceived by their prosperity in Palestine and turn to other gods (Deut. 11:16). He condemned Achan, who stole things sanctified to God and deceived the leaders by hiding what he took (Josh. 7:11). Jeremiah warned that the human heart is deceptive and desperately wicked (Jer. 17:9), and he announced that the arrogance of the Edomites had deceived them (49:16). Paul warns people not to deceive themselves because whatever one sows, that one will also reap (Gal. 6:7). John's final vision recognizes that the devil is the great deceiver (Rev. 20:10). When people lie and deceive, God is sure to judge. There is no such a thing as a harmless white lie. God desires truth.

(2) God's hatred for violence and murder is also found throughout the Bible. It was one of the main reasons for the Flood (Gen. 6:11, 13). It was the chief sin of the people of Nineveh (Jonah 3:8) and the complaint Micah brings against the rulers of Jerusalem (Mic. 3:10). The prophets complain of the violence of kings and princes who strut their power to gain status and financial rewards (Jer. 22:17; Ezek. 8:17; Hos. 4:2; Amos 3:10; Mic. 6:12; Hab. 1:2; Zeph. 1:9).

Although violence is not mentioned as often in the New Testament, the Roman rule of Nero spread a reign of terror in the area around Rome, which brought persecution to Christians. Hitler, Stalin, Pol Pot, and Idi Amin are modern examples of political leaders who have ruled by violence. The final days of this earth will be full of violence and tribulation for all people on earth (Dan. 7–8; 11; Rev. 6ff.), but God's new kingdom will bring about an era of peace.

(3) Not calling on God (7:7, 14) or not turning to him is the ultimate snub of defiance (7:10, 14, 16). These people act as if God does not exist. Whenever people ignore him, they assume that he has no power or sovereignty over this world. In other words, they deny his divinity by their actions. They do what they wish, somehow thinking that God does not know and does not see what they are doing (7:2). By this perverse conception of God they recreate a divine being that fits their own perspective on things. They present sacrifices to their made-up god, but they are turning away from the real God

when they worship. Such behavior attempts to put humanity as the creator of reality and demotes God into an inferior human construction of reality.

Although God wants to restore his people and bless them, this is impossible if they continually reject him and refuse to maintain their covenant relationship with him (6:11–7:1). Sin prevents God from pouring out his blessings and eliminates the possibility of healing. The negative themes of death, falling by the sword, destruction, and ridicule are the rewards of sin. It is a terrible thing to fall from God's grace and suffer the wrath of his punishment.

HOSEA'S SITUATION DURING the Syro-Ephraimite war is vastly different from the context of most readers today. Thus, the sins of people in the twenty-first century will not be identical to those of the Israelites in the time of Hosea. To create a parallel list of the ways people sin today, one could survey the newspaper or listen to one evening of TV, paying special attention to sins that overlap with those mentioned by Hosea. This list will demonstrate the pervasiveness of sin in society and raise the issue of God's attitude toward sin. We should also note whether these sins are presented as normal behavior or deviant acts that are wrong and deserve punishment.

Convincing people that they are sinners is the first step to getting right with God. This passage supports the broad principle that human sinfulness brings God's judgment. This is a basic idea that every evangelist must make in leading people to repentance. If people reject the concept that they have sinned against God, they will never turn to him for forgiveness. They must also accept the fact that God hates these sins and will judge sinners. Only then will people ask if there is some way of avoiding that deserved judgment and so turn to him for redemption. It all begins with an acknowledgment of sin.

In his excellent work on evangelism M. McCloskey says: "We must be ready to challenge all men and women with an accurate biblical analysis of their predicament before their creator. If evangelism is the cure to a terminally ill patient, we must help the patient realize the true nature of his disease."[15] McCloskey maintains that secularism is one of the main problems in our culture. By secularism, he means the concern for things in this present life and a consequent lack of concern about God and life after death.[16] As

---

15. M. McCloskey, *Tell It Often—Tell It Well* (San Bernardino, Calif.: Here's Life, 1985), 92, believes on biblical grounds that we must challenge the present philosophies that control the way many people think.

16. Ibid.

Michael Novack has said, "It is taken for granted in most intellectual circles that an intelligent person does not believe in God."[17]

Like the Israelites of Hosea's day, such people do not turn to or call on God (7:7, 14, 16). They believe that they can control their own future and determine what is right and wrong. They feel independent and self-sufficient enough to live without God. Jonathan Edwards faced this problem long ago, since many in his day deceived themselves into thinking that they could do whatever they wanted. They thought there was no life after death where they would be held accountable.[18]

It is easy for people to accept the educational propaganda drilled into their heads: "You can be whatever you want to be." Many teach that you are in control of your own destiny, with the result that God's design for a person's life is not even considered. Modern culture encourages self-reliance, worships individual freedom to do your own thing, and requires everyone to be tolerant and accept the lifestyle of others as legitimate. When cultures forget God, as Israel's did and ours does, sin becomes defined away. It becomes what I define it—abusing my rights or being intolerant of my chosen lifestyle.

In general in our society, sin is not defined by moral absolutes revealed in the Bible. When there are no higher moral principles, almost nothing is defined as a sin except a narrow-minded rejection of this permissive philosophy. When everything is permissible, the end justifies the means. In such a situation there is no need to tell the truth, no need to avoid violently killing unborn babies, and no need to depend on God. People learn that you can get what you want through skillful office politics, lies on the resume, or sleeping with the boss.

Such activities have become so accepted that people no longer look at them as sin. Instead, these evils are sensationalized in movies as exciting, the way to make the most of your opportunities. Go ahead and use your brain to advance yourself in whatever way you can. Like the priests and politicians in Hosea's day, people still believe the arrogant lie that self-determination through aggressive self-promotion and deceit is the way the system works.

Essentially, evangelism requires us to persuade people to reject the sinful philosophical underpinnings of a society that rejects God and removes the stigma of sin. Hosea calls these acts wickedness, injustice, crimes, deceit, arrogance, senselessness, straying from God, evil plots, a turning away from God, and rebellion against God. An evangelist today must likewise confront

---

17. Michael Novack, *Belief and Unbelief* (New York: MacMillan, 1965), 35.

18. J. Edwards, "Man's Natural Blindness in the Things of Religion," *The Works of President Edwards* (New York: Carter and Brothers, 1864), 4:26.

the immoral behavior of people and call it sin. A person of faith who loves God cannot condone or keep quiet about sin.

The Israelites were wrong to mix faith in God with dependence on Egypt and Assyria, and people today are in a similar danger when they try to mix Christianity with a "godless culture." Followers of God must reject all forms of sin and depend on God alone. This is not a rejection of any culture or modernity per se, but a repudiation of the godless beliefs and sinful behaviors that a secular society legitimates as appropriate, and sometimes even as virtuous.

God still hates sin, and the result of sin is still death. Destruction and ruin are part of his divine plan of justice in this world. Hosea makes it clear that God wants to and will eventually redeem his people and heal them (6:11–7:1), but restoration is impossible if people continue to sin. God laments the fact that when sin rules, death will be close behind (7:13–16). Evangelists must faithfully persuade their secular friends and neighbors that after death there will be a court of justice, where all people must give an account of their deeds (Rom. 14:10–12). The great hope for redemption from the penalty for sin has been provided through the death of Jesus Christ.

Hosea 8:1–9:17

⟨❦⟩

8:1 "Put the trumpet to your lips!
>   An eagle is over the house of the LORD
> because the people have broken my covenant
>   and rebelled against my law.
2 Israel cries out to me,
>   'O our God, we acknowledge you!'
3 But Israel has rejected what is good;
>   an enemy will pursue him.
4 They set up kings without my consent;
>   they choose princes without my approval.
> With their silver and gold
>   they make idols for themselves
>   to their own destruction.
5 Throw out your calf-idol, O Samaria!
>   My anger burns against them.
> How long will they be incapable of purity?
6   They are from Israel!
> This calf—a craftsman has made it;
>   it is not God.
> It will be broken in pieces,
>   that calf of Samaria.

7 "They sow the wind
>   and reap the whirlwind.
> The stalk has no head;
>   it will produce no flour.
> Were it to yield grain,
>   foreigners would swallow it up.
8 Israel is swallowed up;
>   now she is among the nations
>   like a worthless thing.
9 For they have gone up to Assyria
>   like a wild donkey wandering alone.
> Ephraim has sold herself to lovers.
10 Although they have sold themselves among the nations,
>   I will now gather them together.
> They will begin to waste away
>   under the oppression of the mighty king.

[11]"Though Ephraim built many altars for sin offerings,
  these have become altars for sinning.
[12]I wrote for them the many things of my law,
  but they regarded them as something alien.
[13]They offer sacrifices given to me
    and they eat the meat,
    but the LORD is not pleased with them.
  Now he will remember their wickedness
    and punish their sins:
    They will return to Egypt.
[14]Israel has forgotten his Maker
    and built palaces;
    Judah has fortified many towns.
  But I will send fire upon their cities
    that will consume their fortresses."

[9:1]Do not rejoice, O Israel;
    do not be jubilant like the other nations.
  For you have been unfaithful to your God;
    you love the wages of a prostitute
    at every threshing floor.
[2]Threshing floors and winepresses will not feed the people;
    the new wine will fail them.
[3]They will not remain in the LORD's land;
    Ephraim will return to Egypt
    and eat unclean food in Assyria.
[4]They will not pour out wine offerings to the LORD,
    nor will their sacrifices please him.
  Such sacrifices will be to them like the bread of mourners;
    all who eat them will be unclean.
  This food will be for themselves;
    it will not come into the temple of the LORD.

[5]What will you do on the day of your appointed feasts,
    on the festival days of the LORD?
[6]Even if they escape from destruction,
    Egypt will gather them,
    and Memphis will bury them.
  Their treasures of silver will be taken over by briers,
    and thorns will overrun their tents.
[7]The days of punishment are coming,
    the days of reckoning are at hand.
    Let Israel know this.

Because your sins are so many
    and your hostility so great,
the prophet is considered a fool,
    the inspired man a maniac.
⁸ The prophet, along with my God,
    is my watchman over Ephraim,
yet snares await him on all his paths,
    and hostility in the house of his God.
⁹ They have sunk deep into corruption,
    as in the days of Gibeah.
God will remember their wickedness
    and punish them for their sins.

¹⁰ "When I found Israel,
    it was like finding grapes in the desert;
when I saw your fathers,
    it was like seeing the early fruit on the fig tree.
But when they came to Baal Peor,
    they consecrated themselves to that shameful idol
    and became as vile as the thing they loved.
¹¹ Ephraim's glory will fly away like a bird—
    no birth, no pregnancy, no conception.
¹² Even if they rear children,
    I will bereave them of every one.
Woe to them
    when I turn away from them!
¹³ I have seen Ephraim, like Tyre,
    planted in a pleasant place.
But Ephraim will bring out
    their children to the slayer."

¹⁴ Give them, O LORD—
    what will you give them?
Give them wombs that miscarry
    and breasts that are dry.

¹⁵ "Because of all their wickedness in Gilgal,
    I hated them there.
Because of their sinful deeds,
    I will drive them out of my house.
I will no longer love them;
    all their leaders are rebellious.

¹⁶ Ephraim is blighted,
  their root is withered,
  they yield no fruit.
Even if they bear children,
  I will slay their cherished offspring."

¹⁷ My God will reject them
  because they have not obeyed him;
  they will be wanderers among the nations.

THIS LONG SECTION contains a series of explanations for, and warnings about, Israel's coming destruction and captivity. The reasons primarily relate to misguided political alliances and unacceptable worship. The consequences for these sins are painted in multicolored pictures of war, no food, wasting away, returning to Egypt, the burning of their fortresses, the end of feasting, a day of reckoning, no pregnancies, no divine love, and God's rejection. These breathtaking images jar the imagination with unthinkable punishments too horrible to contemplate.

Hosea's prophecies are purposely put into shocking images to force his Israelite listeners to evaluate the truthfulness of his divine message. Does God actually despise the golden calves at Bethel and Dan? Why is he not pleased with the sacrifices given to him? Why does he threaten that Israel will reap the whirlwind? Will God really destroy all of Israel's villages and fortresses and send his people into captivity? Why will there be no more festivals, no new children born, and no more love from God? Is the prophet Hosea totally crazy (9:7)?

The blowing of the trumpet in 8:1 fits the time of the Syro-Ephraimite war in 734–732 B.C. This war brought some reality to Hosea's words of God's judgment, for this defeat was one more step in Israel's decline and another fulfillment of Hosea's prophecies. This military loss should have opened the people's minds to the explanations of the prophet; God was chastening the Israelites for their sins. Things will get worse if they do not change. Destruction, captivity, and the end of Israel is at hand.

This section can be divided into three subsections: the destruction of gods and government (8:1–14), captivity that brings an end to Israel's festivals (9:1–9), and bereavement for Israel's sins (9:10–17). These verses persuasively explain and justify God's action. They present detailed arguments that tell people what they should not do. They legitimate God's plan to destroy them because they are following a course of action God rejects.

The Destruction of Gods and Government (8:1–14)

THE THEME OF destruction in 8:1–3 is implicit in Hosea's charge to sound the trumpet to warn the people about an approaching military threat (cf. 5:8). This war will produce the circling "vulture" (better than the NIV "eagle"),[1] who will devour the carcasses of the dead. The vulture's flight over "the house of the LORD" is a metaphorical way of describing God's judgment on the nation as a whole (see 9:8, 15 for a similar usage) rather than a prediction of death at a temple.[2]

The reason for this judgment is identical to the rationale in 6:7: The people have broken their covenant relationship with God by rebelling against his instructions in the Torah (8:1b). These covenant stipulations were supposed to guide the people so that they would know the meaning of loving God with all their hearts. The Mosaic statutes revealed what the people should and should not do in various civil, political, religious, and social situations so that they could maintain their favored relationship with God. The rebellion against these instructions (the "good" thing mentioned in 8:3) is thus a willful rejection of the authority of God and a repudiation of the unique relationship that has set them apart from all the other nations of the world.

In response to the impending disasters when Assyria (the "enemy," 8:3) attacks Israel, the people briefly call out to God for help, confessing he is their God (8:2). They claim with their lips to know God, but one cannot reject him on one day and call him "my God" on the next. Thus, God will allow their enemies to pursue and destroy them (8:3).

Verses 4–6 describe Israel's rebellion against God in the area of politics and worship. Referring back to his earlier discussion in 7:3–7, Hosea reminds his audience that they have removed one king and appointed another without asking God for direction or identifying his chosen leader (see 2 Kings 15). They have rejected God's sovereign control and "approval" of key decisions[3] and have taken over his role of directing the nation.

The people have also made idols of gold and silver, particularly the golden calves at Dan and Bethel (8:5–6; see 1 Kings 12). God's "anger burns against them" (8:5) because these bull images were quickly confused with the Canaanite god Baal, thus syncretizing perverse pagan ideas with the pure

---

1. McComiskey, *Minor Prophets*, 1:119, thinks Hosea is describing the enemy, who will swoop down like an eagle and destroy the people.

2. Garrett, *Hosea, Joel*, 181, prefers a reference to a temple because that is the meaning of "house of the LORD" in 9:4, but 9:8 and 15 demonstrate that Hosea can use this phrase in several different ways.

3. God chose earlier kings and sent prophets to anoint them (1 Sam. 10:1; 16:13; 1 Kings 11:29; 2 Kings 9:1).

revelation of God revealed in the Torah. God laments the impurity this has brought to the nation and yearns for the day when they will reject idols (8:5b). This hunk of metal in the form of a bull is just a man-made piece of art, not a divine being with almighty power. It is not the God of Israel. Therefore, God rejects this calf and will have it cut to pieces (8:4b, 6b).[4]

In verses 7–10 Hosea laments because Israel's sowing of friendly alliances with other nations will result in reaping the whirlwind of destruction. This agricultural proverb summarizes what every farmer knows: A harvest is directly related to what is planted. Since Israel will reap nothing good and the foreign Assyrians will take what little is harvested, one can assume that they have sown evil behaviors to produce these kinds of results (8:7). These comments can be understood literally of a famine or metaphorically for "Be sure your sins will find you out." Certainly the Israelites can understand this principle, for the nation is despised like a "cup that gives no pleasure" (NIV "a worthless thing"). Everything good in the cup (i.e., the nation's resources) has been swallowed or taken by their enemies (8:8).

This has happened because the nation willingly went "to sell herself" like a prostitute (8:9–10) through her alliance with the Assyrians—possibly a reference to Hoshea's submission to Assyria in 733 B.C.[5] In response, God will gather the nations together against Israel and send a "mighty king" (perhaps Tiglath-Pileser III) against them.

Verses 11–14 draw a logical connection between God's condemnation of Israel for giving unacceptable sacrifices and her rejection of God's instructions in the Torah. According to Leviticus, sacrifices were to be a sweet-smelling aroma that pleased God (Lev. 1:9, 13, 17; 2:9, 12; 3:5, 16; 4:31) because the people's worship and repentance brought forgiveness of sins. But in Hosea's time the people's "choice sacrifices"[6] (8:13) on the many pagan altars around the nation have brought greater sinning instead of expiation of sin and divine pleasure (8:11). This is due to the nation's rejection of the divine instructions God gave in the laws of Moses (Hosea blamed the priests for not teaching people these laws in 4:6).

---

4. Hosea 8:4b probably refers to the destruction of the idols made of silver and gold, not to the destruction of the Israelites. See Andersen and Freedman, *Hosea*, 481, 493, who translate the phrase "so that it will be cut off." This idea should not just be omitted as a gloss, as Mays, *Hosea*, 118, suggests.

5. Mays, *Hosea*, 120, believes this refers to Hoshea's payment of a large tribute to Tiglath-Pileser III. See *ANET*, 284, for the Assyrian record of Hoshea's tribute.

6. NIV has only "sacrifices." This is a difficult text but the word "loved" (which NIV translates "given to me") modifies the word "sacrifices." Andersen and Freedman, *Hosea*, 501, 510, suggest the translation "sacrifices of my loved ones they sacrificed," while Wolff, *Hosea*, 133, translates the clause, "sacrifices they love."

Since the people have adopted their theological understanding of sacrifices, dietary laws, the character of the divine, and appropriate social behavior from their Canaanite culture, God's instructions in the Torah seem strange and inapplicable in their setting (8:12). Since God's instructions do not fit in with the times, the people have rejected his covenant stipulations. They are like a spouse who has decided not to live by the marriage covenant any longer.

These actions give God few choices. He must punish the nation for her sins. The people are only pleasing themselves, not God, when they eat these sacrifices. They forget who God is, the One who originally made them into a nation (see Isa. 44:2; 51:13) and who can send them back to Egypt and nullify his redemptive acts (8:13). The leaders of the nation love the luxury of bigger homes and the security of stronger palaces and fortifications for themselves. But they forget that God protects cities, not walls. Therefore in the near future God will demonstrate his power and destroy these proud cities and the homes in them.

Captivity Will Bring an End to Israel's Festivals (9:1–9)

IN THE MIDST of a joyful harvest festival, Hosea boldly stands up and adamantly admonishes his listeners. Above the noise of joyful singing and dancing he shouts, as it were: "Stop the music! Stop celebrating! The party is over!" This must have seemed like a crazy thing to say since everyone is happy and having a good time. Certainly there cannot be anything wrong with celebrating the divine blessing of a good harvest, right? God has even instructed his people to rejoice (Lev. 23:39–43; Deut. 16:13–15) at the Feast of Booths. So what's the problem?

Hosea argues that the people should not be conducting their feasts like the pagans in other nations (9:1). Apparently this festival changed over the years into a pagan celebration by adding activities common in Baal festivals, such as sacred prostitution at their threshing floors. This paganization of Israel's faith (see 4:10–14) is an act of unfaithful prostitution against God. But the people love the rewards of a good harvest (the "prostitute's wages" in 9:1) more than they love God, so they have added Baal practices to ensure a better harvest.

In response, God will reverse their false theology and remove the fertility of the land, thus proving that Baalism does not work (9:2); he will also reverse the people's security by exiling them from God's holy land and putting them in some other countries (Egypt and Assyria). Because of their own uncleanness, they will eat unclean food in an unholy land. They will get exactly what they have wanted and exactly what they have chosen; they choose not to be the holy people of God.

In these pagan countries the Israelites will be unable to give to God their Levitical sacrifices (Lev. 1–5; 23:13; Num. 15:1–10), so it will be impossible to please him. By comparing their sacrifices to "the bread of mourners" (9:4), Hosea is saying that they will not sacrifice, for mourners who touch a dead body are unclean and cannot offer sacrifice to God (see Num. 19:11–16).

Will there be any more joyful festival days in the future (Hos. 9:5)? Will there be any way to please God? No, for "they will go from a desolate land" (9:6), meaning Israel (rather than NIV "even if they escape from destruction") will go down to Egypt, where many will die and be buried in Memphis, the graveyard of Egypt (9:6).[7] All the things they value (things of silver and gold) and the places where the people live will be desolate ruins overrun with weeds and briers.

In a final summary statement Hosea declares that the days of final reckoning and divine vengeance are close at hand (9:7). The day of God's judgment is going to come on Israel. This statement draws a strong reaction from Hosea's audience for they "know, perceive"[8] that the prophet is acting and talking like a ranting fool. He must be an insane maniac driven by an evil spirit, because he reacts so strongly to the sins of the nation.[9] Since they do not see their own action as sinful, Hosea is branded a radical reactionary, who makes such a big to-do about normal everyday things accepted in their culture. They scorn the prophet and call him bad names in order to dismiss his message, which does not fit their view of reality.

But Hosea sees himself differently. He speaks for God, for God is with him, and his Spirit inspires him with the words he speaks. He is God's "watchman," who warns the people of approaching danger to help them avoid destruction. The last line of verse 8 is difficult to interpret because there are no verbs, and it is unclear who the "his" refers to. If it is a continuation of 9:8a and is related to 9:9, the reference may be to hostilities against Israel about which Hosea warns the Israelites. But if this is seen as a contrast to 9:8a (the "yet" in NIV is not in the Hebrew), it may refer to the Israelites' hostility toward the prophet.[10] The first option seems best here.

---

7. Wolff, *Hosea*, 156.

8. The NIV's "Let Israel know this" (9:7b) is left as an unconnected independent sentence. It is perhaps better to see these words as an introduction to the rest of v. 7, which is a quotation of what other people think about Hosea.

9. Through several emendations Stuart, *Hosea–Jonah*, 139, 146, turns 9:8a into Hosea's question of his audience: "Is Ephraim a watchman? Is God's people a prophet?" This radical approach is unnecessary and ill-advised. The text makes good sense as the prophet's defense of himself.

10. Andersen and Freedman, *Hosea*, 534, and McComiskey, *Minor Prophets*, 1:145–46, think this refers to persecution of Hosea.

If so, then 9:9 gives a rationale for Hosea's claims of judgment on Ephraim in 9:8b. Their punishment is simply a natural consequence of their corruption and sin, which is similar to the godless corruption in the time of the judges (see the sin at Gibeah in Judg. 19−21), when "everyone did as he saw fit" (17:6; 21:25).

Bereavement for Israel's Sins (9:10−17)

THE FINAL PARAGRAPH is divided into two parallel segments: 9:10−14 and 9:15−17. Both draw on past sinful events in the history of Israel (Baalism at Baal Peor and Gilgal) to make comparisons with the situation in Hosea's time. Both portions end with a brief prophetic prayer and compare Israel's punishment to having no fruit or fertility.

The story of Israel starts with positive images of God's joy and excitement when he first entered into a covenant relationship with them (cf. Jer. 2:1−3; Ezek. 16:6−16). This experience compares to finding sweet, juicy grapes in a hot and dry desert, or to enjoying the first fruit from a fig tree (Hos. 9:10a). Both pictures contain a bit of surprise (since grapes do not grow wild in the desert) and remind the listener of how good fresh fruit tastes when you have not had any for a long time (cf. Isa. 28:4; Jer. 24:2). Hosea does not use traditional election traditions but creatively focuses on God's delight over this precious partner he found.

But this joy was abruptly turned into something shameful[11] when the people worshiped an idol at Baal Peor (9:10b; see Num. 25:1−5; Ps. 106:28−30). In these sins the people set themselves apart to an idol instead of God—presumably a reference to the vile sexual rituals that some Israelites participated in at Baal Peor (Num. 25:6−8). Although Hosea does not here connect these acts with the behavior of the Israelites in his day, his audience's present participation in the Baal cult gives them the same status as those who worshiped at Baal Peor.

God's curse on the nation for these detestable acts is described in 9:11−13. The nation's glory,[12] honor, power, resources, and people will disappear quickly into exile, like a bird flying away. Most Israelite women will no longer get pregnant or give birth, and the few who are born will soon die because God will turn against them. These warnings remind us of the covenant curses that predict the people will be bereaved and not have any children (Deut. 28:18, 41).

---

11. Mays, *Hosea*, 133, indicates that the word for "shame" (*bšt*) was used as a derogatory name for Baal. For example, note the change from Ish-baal to Ish-bosheth. The term translated "vile" is *šiqqusim*, another way of describing an idol as an "abomination, detestable thing."

12. Andersen and Freedman, *Hosea*, 542, and Garrett, *Hosea, Joel*, 200, think that the loss of glory refers to the loss of God because v. 11a is interpreted in light of v. 12b. I interpret v. 11a in light of v. 11b.

A final comparison of Israel with Tyre shows that both had great advantages ("planted in a pleasant place"), but now their children will be killed.[13] H. W. Wolff believes this refers to death through military conflicts, while D. Garrett thinks Hosea is describing the death of children through child sacrifice and war.[14] The clear point is that there is no doubt about the future of the nation because God will cut off the future generation.

Hosea interrupts this dire prediction of slaughter with a brief prayer in 9:14. Some see this as an intercessory merciful prayer that asks God to give one of his lesser punishments,[15] but this does not sound like the intercessory prayers of Abraham (Gen. 18:22–33), Moses (Ex. 32:11–14), Amos (Amos 7:2), or Jeremiah (Jer. 14:13–22). Hosea is not pleading for mercy or trying to keep back God's wrath.[16] He is sorrowfully agreeing with God's earlier statements: God should remove the fertility of the nation and curse their offspring (see Deut. 28:4, 11).

The final subparagraph (9:15–17) recalls Israel's sins at Gilgal. Hosea does not mention a specific sin at this city near the banks of the Jordan River, but there was a pagan temple there (4:15; 12:11; see also Josh. 4:19–5:12; Amos 5:5), and at this place Israel's first king was inaugurated (1 Sam. 11:15). God hated the present political system that sprang from this initial event and the worship practices that spread from Gilgal to infect the whole nation. As a result, he will drive them out of his land; he will love them no longer because there is no one to lead the people back to God. These are strong statements of rejection that express an unreserved finality. The results will be barrenness, fruitlessness, and premature death (9:16, see vv. 11–12).

Once again Hosea interrupts this prediction of judgment with a prayer (9:17) that agrees with God's conclusion. God should reject them as they have rejected God. They are no longer his people but will be fugitives, wandering homeless and aimless among the nations. Hosea may well be remembering God's earlier rejection of Saul at Gilgal (1 Sam. 15:23) and seeing how this rejection now extends to the whole nation. This truly is a depressing ending—without hope, without divine love, and without a prophet to intercede.

---

13. Hosea 9:13 is a difficult, cryptic text and widely emended in almost every translation.

14. Wolff, *Hosea*,166; Garrett, *Hosea, Joel*, 202, may pick this up from the reference to child sacrifice in Ps. 106:36–38.

15. Mays, *Hosea*, 134–35, and McComiskey, *Minor Prophets*, 152; but Andersen and Freedman, *Hosea*, 544, appropriately argue against this view.

16. See the discussion of this curse in D. Krause, "A Blessing Cursed: The Prophet's Prayer for Barren Womb and Dry Breasts in Hosea 9," *Reading Between the Texts: Intertextuality and the Hebrew Bible* (Louisville: Westminster/John Knox, 1992), 191–202, who connects this passage with Gen. 49:25.

THE PROPHECIES IN chapters 8–9 are about the sin and punishment of Israel many years ago, not about any nation or people group today. They do not predict anything about events in our day or in the future. Nevertheless, the history of God's dealings with Israel reveals the general principles of how a holy God deals with sinful people on the earth. These messages have been preserved to teach us how to live and what to avoid (Rom. 15:4). The present section describes a cycle of events that any group may experience if it acts as the children of Israel did. This cycle seems to follow a pattern that is played out again and again when people rebel against God.

Divine pleasure. Hosea begins by referring to times when God created this nation as his own people (8:14), when he had the surprising pleasure of finding them in the desert (9:10). At that time he revealed his divine instructions on Mount Sinai so that they would know how to maintain a covenant relationship with him and please him (8:12). This included instructions about rulers (Deut. 17), sacrifices (Lev. 1–6), and feasts (Ex. 23; Deut. 16), and warnings about not mixing with other nations (Deut. 7:1–9). Israel was graciously given a "pleasant place," flowing with milk and honey (Hos. 9:13). If they remained pure and followed God's instructions, they would please God and reap additional blessings.

Although these examples of divine favor are not part of the promises God extends to each people group or individual person, it is his pleasure to graciously bestow his blessings and truth on people in many different ways. He has created everyone in his own image and provided breath and strength for each day. He provides food to eat, rest from work, and purpose to life. God reveals himself and his ways through conscience, nature, and special revelation (Rom. 1–2) so that people can know how to have a covenantal relationship with him. All tribes and peoples sense that there is a connection between life on earth and divine favor and that they must please the divine being if they want to enjoy his blessings.

The New Testament provides specific guidelines on how to please God. Paul prayed that the believers in Colosse might "live a life worthy of the Lord and may please him in every way" (Col. 1:10). The book of Hebrews outlines essential internal qualities God looks for, such as the unambiguous declaration that "without faith it is impossible to please God" (Heb. 11:6). Broadly stated, pleasing God means following his will revealed in Scripture, living holy lives dedicated to worshiping and serving him, and avoiding the sinful practices of this world (1 Thess. 4:1–8).

Human displeasing of God. The picture of thousands of people rejoicing at a joyous fall harvest festival is a landscape of great pleasure (9:1–5).

The crops are in, an abundance of food has been stored for future use, and it is finally time to let one's hair down and enjoy the party. The people are enjoying food, their sacrificial offerings, wine, and sexual pleasures. But things that bring humans pleasure do not always please God. He is not fooled by all the joy because he notices that the people have "rebelled against my law" (8:1), doing things "without my approval" (8:4), being "incapable of purity" (8:5), selling themselves through alliances with other nations instead of trusting in God (8:8–9), "sinning" at the temple worship (8:11), viewing God's instructions as "something alien" (8:12), forgetting their "Maker" (8:14), being "unfaithful to your God" (9:1), rejecting his prophets (9:7), and doing other sinful hostilities (9:8). These failures make the political life of the nation and the worship of the people displeasing to God.

Such sins are a direct reversal of what pleases God. God wants the people to keep the covenant, but they have broken it (8:1). God was supposed to choose and anoint each new king; the people were not supposed to just appoint whoever might be the most powerful politician, yet that is what they are doing (8:4). God forbade the making of idols (Ex. 20:3–6), but the nation built the golden calves and other pagan idols (Hos. 8:6). Instead of worshiping God, the people have been sinning at their temple ceremonies (8:11). God revealed his will so the people could follow the stipulations of the covenant, but they have rejected them (8:12). They are more interested in pleasing themselves at temple events than pleasing God (8:13; 9:4). God has tried to call the people back to himself by sending prophets, but they consider the prophets fools (9:7). They love vile things (9:10) instead of God.

These accusations provide guidelines for any group of people who do not want to displease God. They warn us what we should and should not do. People in every generation need to ask if their behavior in worship and in the political sphere is pleasing to God. God is still displeased if people follow Israel's example rather than his instructions in the Scriptures.

Displeasing God reverses his grace. The tragedy of the situation for Israel is evident in the punishments God will bring on those who reject him. Instead of protecting the people, he will destroy the nation (8:3). Instead of receiving God's blessing and grace, the nation will suffer under his anger (8:5). God will remember the people's sins and punish them rather than forgive and forget them, for their worship does not please him (8:13). Instead of building up the nation, God will destroy their cities and fortified towns (8:14). There will be no more joyful feasts, no more coming to the temple, no glory to the nation, no children, no new births, no more divine love, and no more fruitfulness (9:15–16). God will hate them and reject them (9:15, 17).

These admonitions provide principles and illustrations that enable each person (or nation) to understand what will happen to it if he or she displeases

God. There is little mystery about what displeases God, and there is no doubt what God will do when people displease him. The future will bring disaster after disaster, and the nation will be destroyed.

THIS MESSAGE RAISES three fundamental questions: (1) What pleases God? (2) How can people please God? (3) How does pleasing or displeasing God affect people's lives today? The answers to these questions for modern Christians will not necessarily be identical to what Hosea told the people of Israel, but his basic principles do provide a framework that can be supplemented with additional information from the rest of the Bible.

A framework for pleasing God. (1) One can look at biblical narratives for individuals who pleased God and were used by him and contrast these with narratives of sinful people, who rebelled against God. Narratives sometimes explicitly condemn people for not doing what pleases God. For example, Israel's ancestor Abram made deceptive statements about Sarah being his sister (Gen. 12). Sodom and Gomorrah were boldly condemned for rebelling against God (Gen. 18). Pharaoh refused to accept God's will and let the Israelites go from Egypt (Ex. 7–12). Three thousand Israelites rebelled by worshiping a golden calf at Mount Sinai (Ex. 32), and Levi's sons died because they did not treat God as holy (Lev. 10:1–3).

After Joshua led the people into Canaan, a new generation grew up that did not know God and instead worshiped the pagan gods of their neighbors (Judg. 2:10–15). The people rejected God as their king and appointed a king like the other nations (1 Sam. 8), but King Saul did not obey the voice of the Lord (1 Sam. 15). David had sexual relations with someone who was not his wife (2 Sam. 11–12), and Solomon's wives turned his heart to worship foreign gods (1 Kings 11). Hosea emphasizes that Israel's worship did not please God (Hos. 8:13; 9:4) and that their political process did not take God into consideration (8:4, 8–10).

(2) By contrast, instructive literature (law, proverbs, beatitudes, exhortations) provides positive comments about what God wants people to do to please him and corrective passages on what displeases him. The apostle Paul summarizes a whole series of sinful deeds when he writes that "those controlled by the sinful nature cannot please God" (Rom. 8:8). Yet in spite of human sinfulness God is pleased to forgive, because he has committed himself to a people (1 Sam. 12:20–22). The people of Jerusalem were not better people or more deserving of God's grace; rather, it simply pleased God to prosper Zion according to his will (Ps. 51:18). God wills to choose and

to love, but not out of obligation or because it is deserved. He is just pleased to fulfill his plans, which are mysterious and beyond human understanding.

Amazingly, it even pleased God to crush the Suffering Servant and make him a guilt offering so that his offspring might live and the will of God be accomplished (Isa. 53:10). This is the One whom God said he loved and with whom he was well pleased (Matt. 3:17). Since the Bible reveals parts of God's plans for the future, one can discover some of the things he will be pleased to do in prophetic texts. God knows everything that has happened in the past and what is still to come, for he has said: "My purpose will stand, and I will do all that I please" (Isa. 46:10).

We can also find didactic instructions on what pleases God in the laws of the covenant, proverbial statements with advice on wise and righteous behavior, theological teachings that undergird practical applications in the letters, and pearls of truth in Jesus' teaching and parables. Hosea was particularly concerned about pleasing God in worship (8:13; 9:4) because the people he speaks to are worshiping before idols and are more interested in pleasing themselves than God. Although people often think that pleasing God in worship involves going to church, giving a tithe, and being baptized, the psalmist stresses that praising and glorifying God with thanksgiving please him more than any sacrifices or outward acts (Ps. 69:30–31). In David's confession of his sin with Bathsheba, he declares God's praise and realizes that God delights in a broken and contrite heart more than any sacrifices one might give (51:15–17).

Hebrews 13:15–16 encourages people to "continually offer to God a sacrifice of praise—the fruit of lips that confess his name. And do not forget to do good and to share with others, for with such sacrifices God is pleased." Micah 6:7–8 argues against trying to please God by impressing him with bigger and better gifts, for what God requires is justice, steadfast covenant love, and a circumspect walk with God. The author of Hebrews 11:6 indicates that faith in God is absolutely necessary to please him. Certainly loving the Lord with all our heart and soul delights God and should be the heart's emotional attitude in any act of worship (Deut. 6:5).

We could extend this list, but Paul's summary application in Galatians 6:8 makes a key connection between appropriate motivation to make the right choice with the results of that choice: "The one who sows to please his sinful nature, from that nature will reap destruction; the one who sows to please the Spirit, from the Spirit will reap eternal life." As in Hosea 8:7, Paul presents the consequences of pleasing God as a life-threatening or a life-giving decision. Thus, people need to carefully weigh the results before the wrong attitudes and responses are chosen.

Key areas for pleasing God. (1) God is fussy when it comes to worship; he will not accept worship from sinners who have not confessed their sins

(Isa. 59:1–2) and is not fooled by pious statements, flowery prayers, or hypocritical fasts (Amos 4:4–5; Matt. 6:5–18). Believers today should examine their own attitudes and actions to discover if they are worshiping God in a way consistent with Scripture. Would Hosea find anything to criticize in the worship of my church? How much do we focus on pleasing God? Have the modern trends in the key journals paid more attention to changing worship services to please the audience and make them comfortable, or have they placed a proper emphasis on pleasing God?

(2) Another area that did not please God in Hosea's day arose from inappropriate choices by politicians. The people did not consult God when they chose or appointed new rulers (8:2), sold their souls to other nations through treaties to escape defeat (8:8–9), and focused on building bigger and better fortifications to protect themselves (8:14). Similar government failures exist today across the globe. F. Schaeffer wrote that "God has ordained the State as a *delegated* authority; it is not autonomous"; nor should we "confuse the Kingdom of God with our country."[17]Although one hears presidents and prime ministers call on God to bless their country, the scandals in governments around the world testify that he is not nearly as important as the manipulation of the facts to gain political advantage and reduce negative fallout. After J. Ellul became convinced of the value of the writings of Marx, he had a meeting with Marxists in Paris. After the meeting he wrote, however: "I was deeply disappointed because I felt I was meeting people whose main concern was to 'make it' politically. Apart from that they had no interest in transforming society."[18] He learned that sinful leaders are the main problem of government; therefore, the problems with government are present in every political system.

The Watergate scandal in Washington, D.C.,[19] is one of the few cases where some of the details of sinful choices in government have become known, but similar systems of human manipulation are inside many governments today. I doubt that God was consulted before the Watergate break-in took place, and the filthy cursing on the president's Watergate tapes suggests that God was not part of the cover-up either. If government is for and by the people, the people need to be concerned about the moral character of their leaders and the extent of their trust in God, and not just their military experience and power.

---

17. F. Schaeffer, *Christian Manifesto* (Westchester, Ill.: Crossway, 1981), 91, 121.

18. J. Ellul, *Perspectives on Our Age* (New York: Seabury, 1981), 6, goes on to explain how the Moscow Trials of 1934–1937 totally turned him against communism because they showed that the government was a corrupt, totalitarian state.

19. See the brief treatment of it in C. Colson, *Loving God* (Grand Rapids: Zondervan, 1983), 61–70; or J. Dean, *Blind Ambition* (New York: Simon and Schuster, 1976).

Should God's people not be concerned if their rulers are unwilling to submit their decisions to the authority of God and his Word? It is not enough to go to annual prayer breakfasts, to be seen on television praying silently to remember the sacrifice of the dead in past wars, or to swear the oath of office on a Bible. People in nations around the world need to have leaders who humbly submit to God's will and trust in him for direction. A thorough study of R. D. Culver's book on the Bible's view of civil government may well serve as a basis for a serious look at how Christians can understand and relate to the political establishment in our day.[20]

If people do not please God with their worship and political leaders do not allow God to guide their decisions, how can God bless them with prosperity and children? Eventually these nations will end up like Israel. God will hate them because of their sinful deeds, no longer love them because of their rebellious leaders (9:15), and reject them because they have rejected him. If people do not put pleasing God as a priority, God will not be pleased with them.

---

20. R. D. Culver, *Toward a Biblical View of Civil Government* (Chicago: Moody, 1963).

Hosea 10:1–15

¹ Israel was a spreading vine;
    he brought forth fruit for himself.
As his fruit increased,
    he built more altars;
as his land prospered,
    he adorned his sacred stones.
² Their heart is deceitful,
    and now they must bear their guilt.
The LORD will demolish their altars
    and destroy their sacred stones.

³ Then they will say, "We have no king
    because we did not revere the LORD.
But even if we had a king,
    what could he do for us?"
⁴ They make many promises,
    take false oaths
    and make agreements;
therefore lawsuits spring up
    like poisonous weeds in a plowed field.
⁵ The people who live in Samaria fear
    for the calf-idol of Beth Aven.
Its people will mourn over it,
    and so will its idolatrous priests,
those who had rejoiced over its splendor,
    because it is taken from them into exile.
⁶ It will be carried to Assyria
    as tribute for the great king.
Ephraim will be disgraced;
    Israel will be ashamed of its wooden idols.
⁷ Samaria and its king will float away
    like a twig on the surface of the waters.
⁸ The high places of wickedness will be destroyed—
    it is the sin of Israel.
Thorns and thistles will grow up
    and cover their altars.
Then they will say to the mountains, "Cover us!"
    and to the hills, "Fall on us!"

⁹"Since the days of Gibeah, you have sinned, O Israel,
  and there you have remained.
Did not war overtake
  the evildoers in Gibeah?
¹⁰When I please, I will punish them;
  nations will be gathered against them
  to put them in bonds for their double sin.
¹¹Ephraim is a trained heifer
  that loves to thresh;
so I will put a yoke
  on her fair neck.
I will drive Ephraim,
  Judah must plow,
  And Jacob must break up the ground.
¹²Sow for yourselves righteousness,
  reap the fruit of unfailing love,
and break up your unplowed ground;
  for it is time to seek the LORD,
until he comes
  and showers righteousness on you.
¹³But you have planted wickedness,
  you have reaped evil,
  you have eaten the fruit of deception.
Because you have depended on your own strength
  and on your many warriors,
¹⁴the roar of battle will rise against your people,
  so that all your fortresses will be devastated—
as Shalman devastated Beth Arbel on the day of battle,
  when mothers were dashed to the ground with
    their children.
¹⁵Thus will it happen to you, O Bethel,
  because your wickedness is great.
When that day dawns,
  the king of Israel will be completely destroyed."

Original Meaning

THIS SECTION HAS a good deal of continuity with the previous one, since both condemn Israel's false worship at pagan temples and at the golden calves. The difference is seen in the absence of first-person speeches in chapter 10 (except 10:10–11) and in a greater emphasis on accusations rather than punishment statements. Like 9:10, 10:1 draws the analogy between grape vines and Israel; like 8:7, 10:12–13 uses the sowing and reaping metaphor. Both chapters refer to the sin at Gibeah (9:9; 10:9) and the slaughter of children in war (9:13; 10:14). The tragedy is that God has told his people what they must do, but they refuse to do it. God encourages them to seek him so that they may experience his steadfast covenant love (10:12), but they are wicked and deceptive (10:13).

The few historical references (10:4, 6, 14) probably refer to events at the end of the Syro-Ephraimite war (733 B.C.) or are prophetic statements about the coming fall of the nation in 721 B.C.[1] Since the second-person address is not used in 10:1–8, H. W. Wolff hypothesizes that Hosea was giving a "reflective or *didactic*" message to a closed gathering of his followers who are facing strong opposition,[2] but one would expect some words of support to his followers if this were actually the setting. The references to what the wicked people say and do (10:3–5, 8) imply that Hosea may be addressing their problems, not the problems of God's faithful followers.

The message of this chapter is structured into two large sections. The first (10:1–8) focuses on the detestable altars (10:1, 2, 8) where the Israelites worship, while the second (10:9–15) is centered around the wickedness that will bring war and destruction on the nation. Although the demise of Israel's king and the victory of a great Assyrian king are briefly mentioned (10:6–7, 15), this message is primarily concerned with the religious unfaithfulness at her temples.

Idols and Altars Will Be Destroyed (10:1–8)

THE IMAGERY OF the vine in 10:1 is complicated by the difficulty of interpreting the adjective modifying it. The word *bqq* is translated "spreading" in the NIV or "luxuriant" in the NASB, RSV, LXX, because it fits the context of fruitfulness in the rest of the verse, but all the other uses of this word carry the negative idea of something that is "laid waste."[3] Hosea's positive image of grapevines in 9:10, 13 has already been transformed into a tragic picture of fruitlessness in 9:16.

The negative view of the vine in 10:1 is based on a misuse of its abundance. Israel is like a destroyed vine because she has selfishly used its fruit

---

1. Wolff, *Hosea*, 173, believes Hoshea's revolt against Pekah at the end of this war provides the setting for this chapter.

2. Wolff, ibid., 172, does not explain who is opposing him and his followers.

3. BDB, 132, lists a separate root meaning "luxuriant," based on an Arabic word, but no other Hebrew usages of this root fit this meaning. Andersen and Freedman, *Hosea*, 549, think Hosea is describing what God did ("He made Israel, the vine luxuriant"), but this seems an impossible reconstruction.

for herself. This misuse took place at their many altars and before the pagan sacred pillars, which represented different gods.[4] They presumptuously use what God has given them and offer it to pagan fertility gods, hoping that these gods will bless them with even greater prosperity. Thus, God's blessings are causing them to sink further and further into sin at these pagan altars. In order to reveal the falseness and deceptiveness of their thinking, God will hold the people accountable, take away their abundance, and demolish the altars and sacred pillars (10:2). One should not confuse God with an idol or give an idol credit for God's rich blessings.

One way of understanding the quotation in 10:3 is to take it as a prediction of what the people of Israel will say after the fall of the nation in 721 B.C. The problem with this interpretation, however, is that we have no knowledge that these sinful people ever confessed a failure to fear God.[5] It is probably better to see "we [do] not revere the LORD" as parallel to "we have no king" and "even if we had a king, what could he do for us?" That is, the people reject God as their divine king and sovereign ruler. They do not fear or call on him for help because they do not think he can do anything to change their situation.[6] Instead of humbly confessing their failure to fear God, the people have made false promises and oaths to God and are unfaithful to their covenant with him (10:4).[7] Consequently, "justice" (not NIV's "lawsuits") is springing up like a poisonous weed instead of a beautiful grapevine (see Deut. 32:32–33; Amos 5:7; 6:12). Deception and lies poison their just relationship with God.

One of the main deceptions of their faith is the worship of the golden calf at Bethel (given the scornful nickname Beth Aven, "house of wickedness"). Verse 5 describes the people's deep commitment to this idol. They worship in fear and trembling before this and other false gods. They and the false priests will mourn before the splendor of the golden image of Baal in some sort of cultic ceremony. This may be their final act of worship as the gold of the idol is removed so that it can be used to pay the tribute required by Tiglath-Pileser III, "the great king" (10:6). This removal of the glory of the calf god will demonstrate to all that it has no power and cannot defend itself. The people will be ashamed and disgraced because the true colors of their ugly wooden idol will finally be known. They have been fools to trust it.

---

4. See Garrett, *Hosea, Joel*, 204–7, for a somewhat similar approach to interpreting this difficult verse.

5. Stuart, *Hosea–Jonah*, 160.

6. Andersen and Freedman, *Hosea*, 553.

7. I believe this relates primarily to Israel's relationship to God, but McComiskey, *Minor Prophets*, 1:164, thinks this refers to unfaithfulness to treaties with the Assyrians.

Not only will God emasculate the nation's gods, but he will destroy[8] its king and the people who live in Samaria (10:7). These captives will be like twigs floating down the river with no control over their fate, helpless to resist the force of the water that carries them along. Perhaps Hosea is reminded of a meandering river as he sees the flood of captives being swept down the road into exile by the momentum of the column of people. This loss of people and rulers has eliminated the nation's ability to defend itself and protect its "high places of wickedness" (10:8), a derogatory reference to the temple at Bethel (cf. "Beth Aven" in 10:5; see comments). This ungodly temple will be abandoned to weeds when Israel's enemies destroy it.

For good reasons Hosea calls the sins at this temple "the sin of Israel," for these sins have destroyed their understanding and steadfast covenant love for God. When Jeroboam I set up the golden calves after the death of Solomon (1 Kings 12:28–33), they were supposed to represent Israel's God Yahweh, who brought them up from Egypt (modeled on Aaron's calf in Ex. 32). But since Baalism pictured Baal as a bull calf, the common people thought Israel's calf and Baal's calf were the same god. This led to their acceptance of Canaanite religious and moral guidelines and a rejection of the holy God of the Bible. When the captive people finally see the impotence of Baal and the uselessness of faith in this idol, they will want to die (10:8b). It will seem better to be crushed by falling rocks dislodged from the side of a mountain by an earthquake than to suffer in captivity and be haunted with the stupidity of their belief in this false god.

A Devastating War Because of Wickedness (10:9–15)

HOSEA GOES BACK to the events at Gibeah (10:9) to remind his listeners of the civil war that took place in Judges 19–20 (see Hos. 9:9). Those events have blossomed into the sinful deeds surrounding the Syro-Ephraimite war, which also involved Gibeah (see 5:8). Hosea sees the spirit of violence and immorality that existed in Gibeah as continuing to haunt Israel in his time.

Verse 9b is difficult to understand because the negative "not" suggests that war will "not" overtake Gibeah. Historically, we know that war did come to Gibeah (5:8), so NIV makes this a rhetorical question about the past: "Did not war overtake . . . Gibeah?" H. W. Wolff solves this problem by taking the negative as an assertive ("surely") about the future: "Surely in Gibeah war shall overtake them."[9] These are possible interpretations, but simply reading

---

8. The main verb in the first line is "destroy," not "float away" (as in the NIV), so the line can be translated, "Samaria and her king are destroyed."

9. Wolff, *Hosea*, 178.

the imperfect verb as a rhetorical question about the future gives a translation, "Will not war against the evildoers overtake those in Gibeah?"

In other words, Hosea is removing any false hopes his audience may have. They will be chastened through military defeat by a much stronger army (the Assyrians) and put in bonds to go into captivity for two sins (10:10).[10] The "double sin" is not defined. Perhaps Hosea is referring to the two calves at Dan and Bethel, to the two times the people sinned at Gibeah, or to idol worship and trust in their army; these, however, are only educated guesses from the context.

Hosea quickly changes metaphors in 10:11 to draw on his audience's understanding of agriculture. He compares Israel to a good heifer, who was well trained and a hard worker at threshing time. God was impressed with this animal and wanted to make it his own (symbolic of his having a covenant relationship with the people). So he put his willing heifer to work plowing for him—an analogy that suggests God's election of his people to do his service. At that time God exhorted his people (the heifer) to sow righteousness so that they could reap the blessings (the "fruit") of God's steadfast covenant love (10:12). They needed to understand God's ways in the Torah, follow a path of justice, have unfailing love for him, and seek the Lord continually. God would then shower them with his righteousness. From the beginning he explained in the blessings and curses of the covenant that he would deal with them fairly and justly by giving them salvation if they would turn to him and seek to live according to the covenant relationship.

Unfortunately, Israel instead planted unrighteous seeds, and they will now reap a harvest of evil (10:13), just what they deserve. They have done exactly the opposite of what God has wanted, and the results are the opposite of what they want. Consequently, instead of eating the wonderful fruit of a righteous life, the people will have to swallow the poisonous fruit of their own deception. The lies and false beliefs they accept explain why the Israelites are being punished so severely by God. They have the opportunity to please God, they have the knowledge of what God expects of his covenant people, and they are aware of the consequences of their actions. God has chosen them, and all they need to do is to seek him and serve him with righteous living, but they reject God's way.

The first half of chapter 10 indicates that the worship of the Israelites at their many altars and before the golden calves is one of their main failures and deceptions; 10:13b–14 presents another major deceptive sin of the nation. They find it much easier to trust and depend on their own ways of

---

10. The written Hebrew text has "two eyes," which McComiskey, *Minor Prophets,* 1:173, keeps, but most others follow the spoken text, which has "two iniquities."

doing things (not "strength," as in NIV) instead of God's way, and on their own military power instead of God's power. What makes sense to them is not what God wants because the way that seems right to a person often leads to death and disappointment (Prov. 14:12). Self-dependence on what one can see seems to make more sense than trusting in the unseen power of God.

Because of Israel's trust in their army, God will destroy their military establishment and the fortifications that are designed to protect the army from attackers (10:14). The historical battle when Shalman devastated Beth Arbel is unrecorded elsewhere in history, though some suggest the Shalman is Shalmaneser V, the Assyrian king who ruled from 727–722 B.C., or Salamanu, a Moabite king.[11] This incident was a cruel and disastrous battle because some mothers and their children were thrown off a cliff onto rocks below. The heartless brutality and gross inhumanity of this battle will be replayed when God brings an enemy on the most evil city of Bethel, where its pagan temple with the golden calf dwells (10:15). Their enemies will have no mercy on the Israelites or their king. Nothing will protect them—neither their powerless gods nor their weak king. God will use this enemy to completely destroy them.

THIS CHAPTER DEALS with the issue of the proper worship of God (10:1–8). It gives examples of unacceptable worship and the consequences of failing to worship God in a proper manner. Although the specific factors that were a stumbling block to the Israelites may not be major factors today, they do exist in some parts of the world. To bridge these issues into the life of the church one must look at comparable problems and situations. For example, the sacred altars of that day were at temples, where people worshiped their gods; there are still sacred places, such as churches, where people come to have close communion with God.

Moreover, the key issues are related to what people do or do not do at these places of worship, not where they worship. This message explains that worship is based on a proper understanding of who God is and what he has done, and it inevitably involves what he will do for or against the worshiper.

What does God want from his worshipers? Hosea mentions several things that God expects of his worshipers and several things that are not permitted. First and foremost, God does not want people to worship anything or anyone other than himself. There is no room for other gods or other pri-

---

11. See Wolff, *Hosea*, 188, for these and other suggestions. Even if one of these identifications is correct, information about the battle is unknown.

orities. He will not permit false representations of God (the golden calf) or misconceptions of his true nature because they eventually lead to the worship of something other than God. He will not accept worship from people who have deceitful hearts (10:2), who do not keep their covenant promises but make false oaths of allegiance (10:4). He despises places where false religious ideas are taught, religious or political leaders who do not depend on God, and attitudes that question God's sovereign power (10:3, 13).

If people do not recognize the fundamental truth of God's kingship over this world, they will not understand God's sovereignty over their lives, will not fear him, and will not look to him for help (10:3). God wants his chosen people to serve him (his chosen heifer was to plow his fields in 10:11), to exhibit righteousness in all they do, and to seek the Lord with all their heart (10:11). They cannot do their own thing in their own way but must listen and follow God's way. This involves trust and dependence on God in times of difficulty rather than trust in human manipulation or military strength (10:13). Worship involves both the way people praise in his house and the way they live their daily lives.

Clearly, it is not enough to be sincere or to be involved with just any religious quest for spiritual meaning. God will not honor everyone who seeks a deeper religious experience because some will be responding to a sham that is nothing but a slick deception. Some gods are false, some methods of worship are inappropriate, some theological ideas are wrong, and some responses of worship are unacceptable. These principles are taught throughout the Old Testament. At Sinai God rejected the idea of Israel having a relationship with any other gods or idols (Ex. 20:3–6) and was angry when the people built a golden calf to represent him (Ex. 32). The essence of God's glory cannot be portrayed in a piece of wood or stone, and his almighty power cannot be captured by a lifeless object.

The revelation of God's will cannot proceed from something that cannot talk, and the presence of his nature everywhere on earth cannot be represented by a solid object located in just one place. Again and again the prophet Isaiah argued that the pagan gods are nothing but pieces of wood and stone that have no power (Isa. 41:21–24; 44:6–20; 46:1–13). The apostle Paul tried to convince the people in Athens that their "unknown god" was the only true God among all their idols (Acts 17:16–34). God is presented as the King of kings and Lord of lords, who created, controls, and will judge everyone on the earth (1 Tim. 6:15; Rev. 17:14). To misconceive the nature and character of God will result in the worship of a humanly created theological concept that bears no relationship to the glorious God of the Scriptures.

A central part of worship involves the worshiper's attitudes and actions before God. Moses emphasized the fundamental need to fear or revere God

(Deut. 6:2, 13, 24; 10:12), and wisdom literature sees fearing God as the first step in gaining true wisdom (Job 28:28; Prov. 1:7; 9:10; Eccl. 5:7; 8:12). Both Hosea 10:3 and Malachi 1:6 condemn God's people because they do not reverence him and treat him as holy. Hosea also mentions the demands of righteous living and seeking the Lord (Hos. 10:12).

Deuteronomy 12:5 exhorts the people to seek the Lord at the place God will later choose to have his temple built (Jerusalem) and implicitly warns about other high places where other gods might be worshiped. The psalm in 1 Chronicles 16:10–11 challenges people to "glory in his holy name; let the hearts of those who seek the LORD rejoice. Look to the LORD and his strength; seek his face always." God promises that if people seek him, humble themselves, and confess their sins, he will hear their prayers, forgive their sins, and heal their land (2 Chron. 7:14).

In the New Testament Jesus challenges his followers to seek first God's kingdom and his righteousness (Matt. 6:33). The righteousness of a true disciple must exceed the false piety of the Pharisees if a person wants to see the kingdom of God (5:20). Righteous living is not an option people can choose if they feel like it. Rather, it is outward proof that God's righteousness has transformed their deceptive and unrighteous hearts.

Another external evidence of people's internal relationship to God is their dependence on God's power and his revelation (Hos. 10:13). Rather than doing things the way everyone else does and rather than depending on money, status, military power, education, or any other human attribute, a worshiper of God must trust in God to provide wisdom and strength for everyday needs as well as for crisis situations.

What will happen to those who do not worship God? Failure to worship God in spirit and in truth (cf. John 4:24) has serious consequences in Hosea's theology and in the rest of Scripture. Hosea sees that this will lead to a perversion of one's theology (Hos. 10:1), deception (10:2), false worship (10:5), shame and disgrace (10:6), destruction of temples, exile of the people, and the death of their king (10:14). War will bring terror and such desperation that some will wish that they were dead (10:8, 14–15). This will not just be something that accidentally happens to them; it will be the purposeful execution of God's just plan. False worship, deceptive beliefs about God, a lack of trust in God, and not fearing him are serious failures for which people will be held accountable (10:2).

When people break their promises to God and put other things in his place, these poor substitutes will eventually disappoint and fail those who trust in them. Although no one can make specific predictions about how God will punish people today or in the future, his past dealing with these kinds of people sets a pattern that will probably be repeated in the future. God will show the uselessness of every false basis for trust and take away any supposed value gained through this misplaced trust.

People cannot get away from the old principle that they reap what they sow (10:12–13). If people trust in military power, God will destroy a nation's military strength. If they trust in money, financial resources will be removed. If they trust in a construal of God that is imaginary, those false aspects will eventually be shown to be delusions that have no substance in reality.

The cost of not worshiping God is enormous: shame, disappointment, suicidal tendencies, and the loss of contact with God. These people will lose everything—their families, abundance, freedom, nation, and even their lives. The cost is too great to make any mistakes about how we worship God.

WHAT ARE OUR deceptive beliefs and worship practices? What kind of deceptions or misunderstandings are present in churches today? Where have religious people twisted the truth and created theological beliefs and practices that pervert what God said? What worship activities are an abomination in his sight? In what ways do people put other things in place of God? One might think of some cult and a pagan theological perversion of what God's revelation says, but if we apply this passage in that way, it will not relate to our lives and what is going on in our churches. Such illustrations may be helpful to show that religious people can be seriously deceived or to make the point that God will hold them accountable for their beliefs and actions. But this would be like Hosea talking about the false beliefs of the Assyrians.

Instead, Hosea is critiquing the failures of his own people. Thus, one must apply this passage to what is happening among the "people of God" in the church. How will God evaluate our theological beliefs, our efforts to keep our promises, our reverence for God, and our trust in military power instead of him? Have deceptive ideas crept into the worship of the church? Will being baptized in a church automatically guarantee a place in heaven? Will attending church services and putting some money in the collection plate assure God's blessing? Will taking Communion magically produce forgiveness regardless of a person's true attitude? Will confirmation or church membership necessarily bring God's favor for the rest of a person's life? Are these wise maxims or deceptive myths? Unfortunately some people still attempt to comfort themselves by rationalizing deceptive ideas that contain a portion of the truth but miss the overall thrust of what is needed to please and glorify God.

Sociologists call this kind of self-deception a reification.[12] This happens when people think that some custom or belief is the only correct way of doing things. Thus, it takes on an ontological status that renders it fixed and unchangeable in different contexts. For example, a person may believe that a human social institution like the church must operate like the divinely designed pattern used by the early disciples in Acts 4:32–35. If one reifies this pattern as an absolute pattern, then no one can change any part of this formula.

If, however, the early church is seen as a human social institution guided by God to meet the needs of Jewish Christians during the famines in Jerusalem while the church was in its infancy, then the concept should not be reified, and it is open to change. People today are then free to ask how to conceptualize and organize the church to meet the needs of people today. The Amish have reified certain man-made cultural patterns of behavior and dress and have given them an absolute status. Other Christians look at the principles of modesty, humility, and simplicity and conclude that these ideas can be implemented without maintaining such a reified lifestyle.

The most serious reified self-deceptions are theological.[13] This happens when people give absolute divine authority and status to humanly created perceptions that do not fully represent what God has said or what he desires. The Scriptures teach about worshiping and glorifying God by singing his praise and giving testimony to his marvelous deeds (Ps. 95–99; 104–105). Unfortunately, some believe that this eliminates certain kinds of music (modern rhythmic choruses), certain musical instruments (drums), and certain kinds of behavior (lifting one's hands). This ignores the fact that every culture has its own indigenous and meaningful way of expressing worship.

To reify one cultural means of expressing praise to God into a universal, unchangeable norm is an erroneous approach to understanding the spirit of true worship. If a worship experience is not a meaningful way for me to express my love for God, then it is not my worship. At one time Gregorian chants were a meaningful means of praising God, but they are not meaningful to many today because they are not a part of the culture of most people.

Hosea is not just concerned with the outward presentation of worship; he is most concerned about the internal aspects of worship. Ultimately, these relate to people's view of God. Is God seen as the King of kings, who has all

---

12. Berger and Luckmann, *Social Construction of Reality*, 89–92.

13. R. Perkins, *Looking Both Ways: Exploring the Interface Between Christianity and Sociology* (Grand Rapids: Baker, 1987), 156–66, believes reification leads to exclusivity, parochialism, confrontationalism, pride, absolutism, and self-contradiction by modern Christians in the church. For example, not long ago Christians claimed that the Bible supported racism and slavery.

power, or have they reinvented him into someone less offensive, who gives them more rights and freedoms? If God is the sovereign ruler of this world and my life, I must revere him and worship in submission to him; but if God is perceived to be my daddy or my buddy, I will probably not revere him or his will as highly (10:3). The secularization of culture and the removal of God from everyday life has essentially left many professing church members saying the same thing as Hosea's audience: "What could he do for us?" (10:3). When God's power is diminished and his glory is no longer our chief end, God somehow seems less relevant. There is a need to ask: Do we actually worship God or some image we have created from our imagination?

An analogy can be drawn with human relationships. A son cannot go to just any father and expect him to pay for his food, provide spending money, give him a free ride through college, and let him use the family car. He must go to his own father, make an appropriate request, and respond to his father's gracious gifts with thanks. A son who does not respect his own father's authority, who does not think that his father can help him, and who does not seek to follow his father's will, will not receive the father's blessing. If a son misuses the father's abundant blessing (10:1), is deceptive in his dealings (10:2), does not keep his promises (10:4), and does not respect his father, the relationship will fall apart. If a son thinks his father loves and cares, that will encourage a growing relationship; but if a son thinks that his father does not care at all, the father will not play a significant role in his life.

The perception of the nature and character of God inevitably has an effect on the behavior of the average church member. Using Hosea's metaphor, God expects people to sow righteousness so that he can bless them with the matchless blessing of his unfailing love (10:12). He wants people to seek him and trust in him rather than in their own human abilities (10:12–13). These two objective and measurable criteria can be used as barometers that evaluate the spiritual temperature of the church. What examples of righteousness were exhibited in the past week? On what occasions did people seek to know and have a deeper relationship with God? When was God trusted?

Does proper worship matter? Probably everyone has heard it said that all religions are really the same and lead to the same results; they are just slightly different paths to help people get in touch with their spirituality. Behind these appeals for tolerance and acceptance is the postmodern conviction that my way is as good as yours, that there are no absolute right and wrong ways to get in touch with the divine. Too many today believe that God has not revealed only one way of doing things that everyone must follow. Like the Israelites, they syncretize what little they know about the Bible with various cultural trends and recreate a set of beliefs that comfortably fit their lifestyle. Little time is spent trying to figure out if this is really what the truth is or if this is actually what pleases God. It is not that important, they claim.

Hosea demolishes this baseless fantasy. The Israelites, the chosen people of God, can so pervert the truth of God's revelation that they totally miss God. Their worship at the Baal altars and before the golden calf at Bethel is unacceptable even though they are offering sacrifices and praying to a god. Even "good" forms of worship can be perverted when they are given to buy off God's favor or are offered to the wrong god.

If participation in a worship service does not honor God as sovereign King, what worship has taken place? If one does not believe God is all-powerful and can really help, then dependence, trust, and faith in him will be missing key ingredients. If the fruit of worship does not result in righteousness, then the source of people's actions comes from something other than true worship of God. God is just as fussy today about whom people honor and glorify when they worship in the church as he was in Israel's day.

The results are undeniable. A failure to worship God will result in our shame and death. God maintains that people "must bear their guilt" (10:2) when they accept false beliefs. God also removes his protecting hand and the abundance of his blessings. Eventually he will show the bankruptcy of these false religious systems, and people will receive their punishment. Israel lost her king, her land, her military strength, her people, her freedom, and her God. Will God deal with people today any differently?

Hosea 11:1–11

¹"When Israel was a child, I loved him,
   and out of Egypt I called my son.
²But the more I called Israel,
   the further they went from me.
 They sacrificed to the Baals
   and they burned incense to images.
³It was I who taught Ephraim to walk,
   taking them by the arms;
 but they did not realize
   it was I who healed them.
⁴I led them with cords of human kindness,
   with ties of love;
 I lifted the yoke from their neck
   and bent down to feed them.

⁵"Will they not return to Egypt
   and will not Assyria rule over them
   because they refuse to repent?
⁶Swords will flash in their cities,
   will destroy the bars of their gates
   and put an end to their plans.
⁷My people are determined to turn from me.
   Even if they call to the Most High,
   he will by no means exalt them.

⁸"How can I give you up, Ephraim?
   How can I hand you over, Israel?
 How can I treat you like Admah?
   How can I make you like Zeboiim?
 My heart is changed within me;
   all my compassion is aroused.
⁹I will not carry out my fierce anger,
   nor will I turn and devastate Ephraim.
 For I am God, and not man—
   the Holy One among you.
 I will not come in wrath.
¹⁰They will follow the LORD;
   he will roar like a lion.

When he roars,
>   his children will come trembling from the west.
11 They will come trembling
>   like birds from Egypt,
>   like doves from Assyria.
> I will settle them in their homes,"
>   declares the LORD.

THIS CHAPTER CONCLUDES Hosea's description of the second part (6:7–11:11) of God's covenant lawsuit against Israel. This section has similarities with the earlier conclusion in 5:15–6:6, which ended the first part of the covenant lawsuit (4:1–6:6), but there are a number of unique aspects in each concluding message. Similarities include: (1) God's past care and the nation's failure (6:5–6; 11:1–4); (2) God's internal struggle and lament over punishing his people (6:4; 11:8); and (3) the possibility of hope in the future (6:1–3; 11:10–11).

Two different impressions are left, however, after reading these parallel passages. (1) The first conclusion begins with the possibility of hope and ends with the nation's failure to worship God properly, while this second one begins with failure to worship God and ends with a divine promise of great hope. (2) The theme of seeking to know God is dominant in 5:15–6:6, while returning to their loving God is the emphasis in the second. In both cases God's heart of love for his people is evident, but they do not seem to reciprocate.

This concluding message has four brief subparagraphs. The prophet describes God's past loving care for his son and Israel's rebellion (11:1–4), his decision to punish his people (11:5–7), his loving lament that prevents the total destruction of Israel (11:8–9), and a final salvation oracle (11:10–11). We receive here a personal insight into God's internal struggles to deal with a rebellious son whom he loves deeply.[1]

God's Love for His Rebellious Son (11:1–4)

HOSEA PORTRAYS TWO contrasting images: God the loving Father and Israel the stubborn, unrepentant son (rather than the unfaithful wife).[2] The contrasts

---

1. Mays, *Hosea*, 152, thinks this message should be dated to Hoshea's rebellious act of going to Egypt for help (2 Kings 17:4), but there is little evidence in this chapter to allow one to date it.

2. D. A. Smith, "Kinship and Covenant in Hosea 11:1–4," *HBT* 16 (1994): 41–53, believes the kinship terminology of sonship was based on the idea of adoption into God's

are juxtaposed within the reciprocal responsibilities of a family context, for Israel was known as the "son/sons/children" of Israel since the Exodus (Ex. 4:22). Like Hosea 9:10, the prophet goes back to review the nature of God's early life with his people. When Israel was young and in need of tender care and guidance, God loved his people (11:1; see 2:1, 23). Deuteronomy connects this great event with God's gracious election of his people into his covenant family (Deut. 7:6–8).

God demonstrated this love supremely in his deliverance of a great multitude from Egypt. This experience established the father-son relationship and gave the Israelites a unique identity as "my son." As God raised his son, he continued to instruct him; but the son was independent and rebellious, so he responded when other gods called him (not as in NIV, "I called")[3] to follow them. The son rejected his father's love and foolishly sacrificed to Baal and to various other idols (11:2; see Ex. 32; Num. 25). Although these gods never loved them or miraculously delivered them from slavery, the ungrateful son went his own way.

Verse 2 emphasizes how quickly the nation fell into apostasy. But like a loving parent, God did not immediately give up on his son. In the midst of this rebellion, he taught him how to walk by holding his hands so that he would not fall or go astray (11:3). This verse may refer to how God showed the people where to walk in the desert or to his guidance through the giving of covenant instructions in the Torah. Although God was not given credit for it, he also healed his son—a possible allusion to his intervention at places like Marah in Exodus 15:26 (see also Hos. 14:5).

The metaphors in 11:4 are somewhat confusing because it appears as if God is dealing with an animal, not his son. The metaphors of cords, ropes, and yoke suggest aspects of control and servitude. But by defining these as "cords of human kindness, with ties of love," one gets a picture of gentle leading rather than abusive or forced labor. This kind leadership also involved lifting an abusive yoke—a reference to God's deliverance of the people from Egyptian slavery.

The final line in 11:4 describes God's tender care and provisions for his people. He "bent down" gently to feed them by graciously providing manna and quail for the forty years of wandering in the Sinai desert (see Ex. 16; Num. 11).

---

family. In Ezekiel 16 Israel is pictured as a young girl; many different analogies were usable to describe different aspects of God's relationship with his people.

3. Stuart, *Hosea–Jonah*, 175, and Wolff, *Hosea*, 190, plus NIV and RSV emend the Hebrew text "they called" to "I called," based on the LXX; others correctly keep the Hebrew text as it is. This change also requires a second change in the Hebrew from "them" to "me" at the end of the second line. McComiskey, *Minor Prophets*, 1:184, keeps the plural verb in 11:2a but thinks this refers to the prophets who called the people back to God.

No Repentance Leads to Punishment (11:5–7)

ONE WOULD EXPECT that a people receiving this kind of love and care would naturally follow God and enjoy the blessings of living in the Promised Land God gave them. Instead, Israel will end up losing their land and going back in bondage to Egypt and Assyria (11:5). Swords will be drawn, war will break out, and God will destroy the boasting of the "proud" people (not NIV "bar of the gate" in 11:6), who think they control the future of the nation. Israel's plans for greatness will vanish, and tragedy will overtake the nation as it falls apart.

Why will there be such a tragic reversal of fortunes for Israel? Why does God's tender care and love not keep the nation strong and powerful? These things do not happen by chance. The Israelites refuse to repent (11:5b) and turn back to the worship of God alone; instead, they stubbornly and consistently turn away from following him (11:7a). How can God exalt and empower people who reject the One who has done so much for them?[4] Eventually his patience will run out and his rebellious children must be judged. Although they may cry out for mercy, like a child about to receive a spanking, God's judgment will fall on Israel.

God's Lamenting Compassion for Israel (11:8–9)

THIS DECISION TO judge the people God loved was not a cold and heartless act. To make it more understandable to us, God is pictured as a father who has tried everything but has found that nothing works. God struggles with his decision and laments having to punish his people so severely. He cries out in the anguish of love: "How can I do this?" These words do not suggest God is confused or does not know what to do. Rather, they simply express the emotional intensity of God's love and anxiety in human terms that the audience can appreciate.[5]

God is not a cold computer or a philosophical abstract concept. He has an intimate relationship of commitment that involves him with his people's lives in more than a legal or contractual way. The husband-wife or father-son relationships help humans understand in an oblique way the personal caring involvement that a holy, mysterious God has with his people. In compassion God declares that he cannot totally give up on his people; he cannot totally annihilate Israel as he did Zeboiim and Admah—obscure cities that few

---

4. The Heb. text of 11:7b is problematic, with quite diverse renderings in different translations and commentaries. Is this calling on God or another god?

5. A. J. Heschel, *The Prophets*, 2 vols. (New York: Harper and Row, 1962), 1:48, sees Hosea as revealing the cardinal emotional pathos of God that is a fundamental part of his relationship with his people. See also J. L. McKenzie, "Divine Passion in Osee," *CBQ* 17 (1955): 287–99.

remember (two of the lesser-known cities destroyed by God along with Sodom and Gomorrah; see Gen. 19; Deut. 29:23).

God does not want the people he loves to become a mere footnote in world history. No, instead of overturning Israel as he "overturned" (*hpk*) Sodom, God's heart is "overturned" (NIV "changed") because his tender compassion for his people is aroused. What a marvelous expression of divine love and grace for sinful people!

Suddenly God announces that he will not annihilate Israel in his "fierce anger" (11:9);[6] he will not "turn and devastate Ephraim." Why not? What explains this sudden change of heart? Three factors reveal a slight crack that allows a peak at this mystery. (1) The arousing of God's compassion in 11:8 overtakes the execution of his justice. (2) He is God and not like humankind, so if God wants to, he has the ability to decide not to exact a just punishment in his fierce anger. (3) He is holy. He operates at a different level of action independent of human action and existence. He has chosen to fulfill his sovereign plan that is guided by his love as well as justice.

Although we may understand some aspects of God's just punishment of sin, we are much less able to comprehend the depths and extension of divine love and forgiveness to unworthy people. Holiness and compassion do not excuse seemingly irrational actions by God; they only reveal how the dynamics of the divine plan exceed the limitations of human rationality. The Holy One is so different, yet so compassionate.

God's Restoration Promise (11:10–11)

GOD'S SOVEREIGN PLAN includes restoration for his people. Thus, at some point in the future he will act like a lion and roar, calling his people to follow him and to return from the land of their captivity. Two important contrasts differentiate this passage from earlier lion passages. (1) The calling father of 11:1 will now call his children with a powerful voice to signal the beginning of a new age of restoration, rather than destroy his people by tearing them to pieces (5:14).

(2) The people will "follow the LORD" and "will come trembling," humbly fearing him and willingly responding to his call. This suggests a transformation of the rebellious house of Israel that used to act like a senseless dove (7:11; 8:8–10), trusting in other nations and worshiping pagan gods. At that time they will come back to their land in a new exodus and dwell in their own homes. God's love will accomplish his plan; human sinfulness will not triumph over his compassion. This is his promise.

---

6. Andersen and Freedman, *Hosea*, 574, 589, choose to interpret the negative "I will not" as an asseverative "certainly," which asserts God's determination to carry out his judgment; most other commentators reject this option.

Bridging Contexts

ASPECTS OF GOD'S love for his people. The prominent theme in Hosea 11 is God's love for his people. Although this chapter specifically relates to the divine plan for Israel, that plan is motivated by love and implemented through compassion that impacts every nation and every person on earth. The critical question is: Will God's just judgment determine the destiny of his sinful people, or will God's love? Put otherwise: Will God's plans hopelessly fail because sin has destroyed his people's relationship with God? Is God's hatred of sin greater than his love for them, or does love rule? The answer must unambiguously be: God is the Holy One, who justly punishes sinners and loves them. One cannot eliminate either divine justice or love because both play an important role in influencing the history of any group or individual.

Although this chapter pays more attention to the love and compassion of God, it does not eliminate the need for Hosea's audience to repent. Hosea never says that the nation will not be punished and exiled for its sins. He does not tell his audience they will not be held accountable for their sins. Their sacrificing to Baal and other gods (11:2) is a serious breaking of a committed covenant relationship with God. They will return to Egypt and Assyria because they have refused to repent (11:5). Their cities will experience the terrors of war (11:6).

But the core perspective of this chapter is that God has loved and will love sinful people. Being sinful and unworthy of his blessings does not automatically condemn you or me to a tomorrow without God. Tomorrow has been designed by God, and God can mysteriously choose to love any undeserving person or nation. His love has been demonstrated in a number of ways.

(1) God chose to love certain people and called them to be members of his covenant family (11:1; Eph. 1:4–5). He expressed his love by inviting them to become his children (Hos. 11:1). This election was according to God's chosen plan to love people and was not due to any human worth or value. God's love is beyond human understanding, although part of his plan is to bring glory to his name (Isa. 43:7; 44:23; Eph. 1:6, 12). All people can do is receive God's love and respond in praise and commitment to him.

Genesis 18:19 reports that God chose Abraham so that he could fulfill his plan. Deuteronomy 14:2 describes the people of Israel as a chosen treasured possession of God. Later God chose David to be king (2 Chron. 6:6) and Jerusalem as the place where his temple would be built (Ps. 132:13). At Jesus' baptism God called Jesus his chosen one (Luke 9:35). Believers today are a part of a "chosen people" (1 Peter 2:9). Being chosen is a great privilege, though it also carries great responsibility.

(2) God's love is expressed in his teaching and leading (Hos. 11:3–4). This involves the revelation of his will (the Torah and the rest of the Bible) to his children so they can understand the nature of their relationship with him. This teaching and guiding are not merely lectures on rules, but experiential caring appropriate to the circumstances of each person. Those young in the faith are helped to take their first steps (11:3); those who do not know what to do are guided with tender love. The laws in the Pentateuch, the moral lessons taught through historical narratives, the wisdom of the Proverbs, the exhortations in the Prophets, the lessons in Jesus' parables, and the didactic instruction in the New Testament letters are all gifts of God's love. They reveal to us the truth about God and provide guidance on how to live as his chosen people.

(3) God's love is shown in healing and delivering from trouble (11:3–4). In times of crisis, sickness, attack, or oppression, God sees us and miraculously delivers those unable to defend themselves. In our frail human condition in this sinful world, his love removes the threat and fear of death because he sovereignly controls each person's health and safety. He does not leave us to fend for ourselves in this hostile world but protects and delivers us from trouble. The ministry of Jesus is filled with examples where he lovingly heals the blind, lame, lepers, and demon-possessed. While these people did not deserve to be healed, Jesus performed his miracles in order that God's name would be glorified (John 9:1–4).

(4) God's love will not give up on people when they fail (Hos. 11:8). When his frail, sinful children yield to temptation, are led astray by others, or rebel against his will, God does not immediately reject all further contact and care for them. He does punish and chasten rebellious children because he loves them and wants to renew them to fellowship with himself. Repeated rejection of God will injure a relationship, but it will not destroy his deep love for people. He repeatedly promised that when Israelites were suffering in distress, he would not abandon them or fail to keep his covenant promises (Deut. 4:30–31; 31:6–8). Paul likewise teaches that real love "always protects ... [and] never fails" (1 Cor. 13:7–8).

(5) God's love will fulfill his promises (Hos. 11:10–11). Hosea 11 says nothing about forgiveness of sins or exactly how God will transform his people. It simply states that God will reveal his power (like a lion), and people will fear and follow him. This positive response assumes an end to rebellion against God and acceptance of his ways. The trembling suggests they have seen a new vision of their holy God and now fear and submit to him. The return from bondage to their own land assumes God has defeated their enemies and made restoration possible. God's gift of the land fulfills his original promises to Abraham and his seed. Being peacefully settled in their homes,

the people will experience the power of God's love. At that time God's children will follow him.

(6) The totality of divine love is not systematically explained in the limited context of Hosea 11, but one does learn that God's love is not totally quenched by human failures or disloyalties (11:8). God loved his people when they were few in number (Deut. 7:7–8), and he graciously gave them the land of Israel in spite of their stubbornness (9:4–6). God's acts of love were regulated by his choices (7:7), his promises (7:8; 9:5), and his faithfulness to his covenant (7:9); they were not based on Israel's goodness or acceptance of a few religious ceremonies. His love is a spontaneous force that has no justification or rationale; it is an inexplicable mystery whereby God relates his grace, compassion, and commitment to people. First John 4:16 summarizes this point by saying, "God is love."

Jesus as God's Son. We should also briefly examine the New Testament application of Hosea 11:1 ("Out of Egypt I called my son") to the life of Jesus in Matthew 2:15. This quotation is unexpected and unusual, since Hosea is not here giving a prophecy about the future; instead, he is referring to a past event when God delivered the nation of Israel out of Egyptian bondage. Matthew, however, sees an analogy between Israel and Jesus. Both are called "my son," and both came out of Egypt.

Yet some might think this new use of Hosea 11:1 in Matthew is a "distortion."[7] Certainly all interpreters admit to a partial change in meaning in Matthew's usage. But Matthew sees Jesus, God's Son, as the ideal Israelite. Note especially Psalm 2:7, 12 and Isaiah 9:6–7, both of which picture this future divine ruler as God's Son. Thus Matthew reads Hosea in light of the more specific messianic meaning of that ideal Israelite. I would not call this any kind of pesher interpretation or double fulfillment; rather, Matthew is simply noting that there are analogies (some call them typologies) between the way God works in different eras.

THE POWER OF **God's love.** In the Introduction to Hosea we looked at the definition of the Hebrew words for love. W. Eichrodt maintains that the Hebrew idea for love in Hosea 11 (ʾahab) "retains the passionate overtones of complete engagement of the will accompanied by strong emotion."[8] This kind of divine love is not based on covenant commitments but is a more "irrational power" that is unexplainable and para-

---

7. D. M. Beegle, *Scripture, Tradition, and Infallibility* (Grand Rapids: Eerdmans, 1973), 237.
8. Eichrodt, *Theology of the Old Testament,* 1:250.

doxical, since it is undeserved. It is a free giving of one's self to another to care for, forgive, and protect that person—without strings or conditions. Human language can never adequately define or surround the concept of divine love; it can only point to acts of God's love with amazement and respond either with disbelief or warm acceptance and peace.

Since it is difficult to comprehend the love of God, illustrations of human love can be powerful ways of illustrating some of the characteristics of divine love. Hosea uses the husband-wife and father-son relationships to describe the nature of divine love; these can help both believers and unbelievers understand some aspects of God's love. Hosea also uses the nation's past experience to legitimate his contention that God loves his people, and we can use similar examples from the New Testament and our own lives.

God's redemption of the nation Israel from Egyptian bondage is one of the greatest Old Testament examples of God's love, while Christ's death on the cross is the prime New Testament illustration. Yet for many people, the only real definition of love is impersonated in the attitudes and actions of some person they know today, not some event that took place thousands of years ago. Such experiences communicate the concept of love with a reality that goes beyond textbook definitions, rational formulas, secondhand experience, or lists of things to do or not to do.

Love needs to be experienced because it includes deep emotions that cannot be adequately expressed in a cold dictionary definition. Through experience people receive analogies that are partial and imperfect comparisons to God's love. Those who already have a relationship with him know something about this love and have the advantage of being able to comprehend some aspects of divine love based on their own personal encounter with it.

Unfortunately, many have never experienced this divine love, nor do they know what God has done for them. They picture God as a hateful judge, or their gods require people to earn love. Thus, we ought to follow the example of Hosea and simply tell people that God loves them. If people in the church have truly received the tremendous gift of God's love through salvation, "Christ's love compels us" (2 Cor. 5:14) to tell others that his death paid for their sins and the sins of the whole world. As M. McCloskey has put it: "Evangelism is grounded in love. It is the supreme act of love. . . . Love is action. Love is acting on another's behalf to meet his needs."[9]

If evangelism is a sign that believers have God's love in them and its transformational power compels them to tell others, one must wonder why there is such a small amount of the love of God exhibited in the life of so many

---

9. McCloskey, *Tell It Often—Tell It Well*, 144–45.

church members (in evangelism). Is it fair to say that a person who does not evangelize has never experienced the glories of God's love? Why does the love of God not compel more people to share their faith? Do people selfishly want God's love only for themselves? Do people not see his love in their election, salvation, guidance, protection, and hope for the future? Do they not realize the magnitude of the promise that nothing in this world or the next can ever separate them from the love of God (Rom. 8:35–39)?

The practical application of Hosea 11 gives reassurance to people today that God does graciously love his people even when they do not deserve it, even when he has to chasten them for their sins. Hosea is speaking of a situation where a lover (Israel) rejected the love from a partner (God). This forces us to ask the question: If people fall into sin and turn their backs on God, will God still love them? If people who have a relationship with God (like the Israelites) reject God's love and prostitute themselves by loving someone or something else more than God, will he reject them? Does God still love my college-age son who no longer goes to church and has drifted away from the faith he embraced as a child? How long does God's love last, and how much will he forgive?

Hosea's answer would be that *no one* has *ever* earned God's love; it is always a free gift to those who are unworthy. Neither the most holy saint nor the worst sinner deserves his love. Hosea 3:4–5 and 11:5–9 show that a husband's or father's abundant blessings are affected by unfaithful actions, but his overpowering love is not quenched by temporary rejection. God will not give up on the people he loves (11:8–9). Since God's love involves his emotional commitment of faithfulness to his people, his love is steadfastly loyal to those he loves.

God's love is overpoweringly persuasive and nearly irresistible; thus, it can soften and transform the hearts of his rebellious people hardened by years of rejection. His love provides the best for his people and energizes him to faithfully carry out all his promises (3:5; 11:10–11). The Scriptures assure us that God loves everyone in the world and does not want anyone to perish (2 Peter 3:9). Hosea 11:10–11 demonstrates that after a time of punishment the nation of Israel will be restored. God's love brings about the transformation of people and the fulfillment of his promises. Nothing can destroy or ultimately frustrate the plan of God to love people.

Hosea 11:12–13:3

^{11:12}Ephraim has surrounded me with lies,
    the house of Israel with deceit.
And Judah is unruly against God,
    even against the faithful Holy One.
^{12:1}Ephraim feeds on the wind;
    he pursues the east wind all day
    and multiplies lies and violence.
He makes a treaty with Assyria
    and sends olive oil to Egypt.
²The LORD has a charge to bring against Judah;
    he will punish Jacob according to his ways
    and repay him according to his deeds.
³In the womb he grasped his brother's heel;
    as a man he struggled with God.
⁴He struggled with the angel and overcame him;
    he wept and begged for his favor.
He found him at Bethel
    and talked with him there—
⁵the LORD God Almighty,
    the LORD is his name of renown!
⁶But you must return to your God;
    maintain love and justice,
    and wait for your God always.
⁷The merchant uses dishonest scales;
    he loves to defraud.
⁸Ephraim boasts,
    "I am very rich; I have become wealthy.
With all my wealth they will not find in me
    any iniquity or sin."

⁹"I am the LORD your God,
    ⌞who brought you⌟ out of Egypt;
I will make you live in tents again,
    as in the days of your appointed feasts.
¹⁰I spoke to the prophets,
    gave them many visions
    and told parables through them."

¹¹ Is Gilead wicked?
> Its people are worthless!
Do they sacrifice bulls in Gilgal?
> Their altars will be like piles of stones
> on a plowed field.
¹² Jacob fled to the country of Aram;
> Israel served to get a wife,
> and to pay for her he tended sheep.
¹³ The LORD used a prophet to bring Israel up from Egypt,
> by a prophet he cared for him.
¹⁴ But Ephraim has bitterly provoked him to anger;
> his Lord will leave upon him the guilt of his bloodshed
> and will repay him for his contempt.

¹³:¹ When Ephraim spoke, men trembled;
> he was exalted in Israel.
But he became guilty of Baal worship and died.
² Now they sin more and more;
> they make idols for themselves from their silver,
cleverly fashioned images,
> all of them the work of craftsmen.
It is said of these people,
> "They offer human sacrifice
> and kiss the calf-idols."
³ Therefore they will be like the morning mist,
> like the early dew that disappears,
> like chaff swirling from a threshing floor,
> like smoke escaping through a window.

THE FINAL SECTION of God's covenant lawsuit against his people (11:12–14:9) is centered around the charge that Israel is deceitful about her relationship with God. She lies (11:12–12:1), following the deceptive ways of Jacob (12:2). Merchants defraud people in business deals (12:7) instead of dealing honestly. God led the people and cared for their needs, but they have become proud and lack integrity with God (13:6). There is no truthfulness in their commitments to the covenant, for many worship Baal and other images (13:1).

Consequently, God again announces that he is bringing a covenant lawsuit against his people, both Judah and Israel (12:2). As earlier, this should not be seen as a literal court case but the creation of an analogy with a human lawsuit. Courtroom terminology and the broad use of accusations and punishments create the atmosphere of accountability for law-breaking as found in the courtroom (see Mic. 6 for another example of a lawsuit).

The threefold pattern of accusations (11:12–13:3), threats of punishment (13:4–16), and blessings for repentance (14:1–9) matches the structure of each major section of Hosea (4:1–6:6; 6:7–11:11; 11:12–14:9). Through these messages Hosea is persuading his audience that God will deal seriously with the problem of sin among his people. In the present section (11:12–14:9), the prophet attempts to convince the people that their behavior is sinful, that deceitfulness undermines their relationship with God, and that their only hope is to repent.

Hosea 11:12 in the English Bible is 12:1 in the Hebrew Bible. The common theme throughout 11:12–13:3 is the deceitfulness of Israel. Like an untruthful spouse who lies about her loyalty to her husband, Israel has been deceitful with God. To emphasize this deceit, Hosea contrasts the many gracious things that God has done for his people with their repeated unfaithfulness to him. These are marked by sudden changes, such as "but you" (12:6), "[but] I" (12:9), "but Ephraim" (12:14), and the "therefore" clauses in 13:3.

There is no clear evidence to suggest a date for this message, but it was likely spoken a few years before the fall of Israel in 721 B.C., during Hoshea's reign.[1] The fact that the nation is making alliances with various nations (12:1) fits Hoshea's final desperate attempts to save the nation from annihilation (2 Kings 17:1–4).

The structure of this unit follows the historical development of deception from Jacob to Hosea's time. It involves God's bringing a lawsuit for deceit (11:12–12:2); warnings to the Israelites not to follow Jacob, their deceitful forefather (12:3–6); forgetfulness on the part of Israel's deceitful merchants about what God has given them (12:7–10); Israel's choice of deception instead of God (12:11–14); and Israel's deceptive worship (13:1–3). This review demonstrates how God has graciously cared for his people in spite of their repeated deceptions. These accusations legitimate his decision to punish his people if they do not repent and deal honestly as a faithful covenant partner.

God's Charge of Deceit (11:12–12:2)

GOD BEGINS THIS new message by focusing on Israel's "lies ... deceit" (11:12). When God says that he is "surrounded" by this kind of people, he is

---

1. J. Limburg, *Hosea–Micah* (Interp.; Atlanta: John Knox, 1988), 43, thinks this chapter addresses people in Judah after the fall of Israel, but Stuart, *Hosea–Jonah*, 188, takes the references to alliances with Egypt and Assyria (12:1) to indicate this chapter should be dated to Hoshea's reign, when he sent for help from Egypt (2 Kings 17:3–4).

suggesting that untruthfulness characterizes their behavior; the Israelites do not fraudulently deceive God just once or twice. The prophet goes on to give illustrations of how the people have surrounded God[2] with lies. Judah is also condemned (not "approved," as in the RSV),[3] for God announces his case against both nations in 12:2. Their "unruly" behavior refers to the wandering and roaming of Judah "against the faithful Holy One" (NIV). Andersen and Freedman suggest that Israel "wanders with the gods, is faithful with the holy ones."[4] That is, Israel is trying to find meaning, support, and help in her present situation from gods who cannot fulfill her desires.

Israel is pursuing the wind (12:1). By going after something that is illusive and without substance, she shows her stupidity and the uselessness of her quest. Her devotion to futile hopes is strong (she does it "all day"), but in the process she only "multiplies lies." Another example of this futile action is Israel's pursuit of treaties with Assyria and at the same time giving expensive gifts to Egypt to confirm a political relationship with her (12:1b).[5] These nations will not give Israel protection and security; trusting them makes about as much sense as chasing the wind.

Because of these deceptive actions, God is bringing another charge in his lawsuit (12:2). Although it may seem odd to refer to Judah, since the rest of the chapter relates to Israel and is preached before an Israelite audience, God knows that Judah is involved in similar deceptions.[6] He intends to present legitimate arguments against his people that will demonstrate their guilt if they were tried in a courtroom. He wants the Israelites to understand why they are being punished; it is a direct consequence of their deceptive covenant relationship with God. What they have done will come back to haunt them; people reap what they sow.

Warning to Israel Not to Be Like Deceptive Jacob (12:3–6)

HOSEA BEGINS HIS case by going back in history to the story of Jacob, the founder of the nation of Israel. Using traditions from Genesis 25:21–26, Hosea describes Jacob's birth when he grasped his brother Esau's heel. The actual name "Jacob" (*ya'aqob*) means the heel "grasper," a play on the word

---

2. The image is comparable to the psalmist who laments that he is surrounded by enemies wanting to kill him (Ps. 22:12, 16; 118:10–12).

3. The RSV emends the text to say "Judah is still known by God," by using the LXX, Wolff, *Hosea*, 205, has "Judah still goes with God," while Mays, *Hosea*, 159, translates "Judah still roams with God" (a positive sense).

4. Andersen and Freedman, *Hosea*, 593, 603, believe Hosea is referring to the worship of the gods, while Wolff, *Hosea*, 210, rejects that position.

5. D. J. McCarthy, "Hosea XII.2: Covenant by Oil," *VT* 14 (1964): 215–21.

6. Wolff, *Hosea*, 206, removes the title Judah in 12:2 and replaces it with Israel.

"deceive" (ʿaqab). Later Jacob became known as a deceiver because of the deceptive way he stole Esau's blessing (Gen. 27:35–36). Jacob is pictured as one who spent his life using deceptive means to get ahead instead of trusting God—the same thing the people of Israel in Hosea's audience are doing.[7]

A second example from Jacob's life comes from his adult experience of wrestling with the angel of God by the river Jabbok (Gen. 32).[8] When Jacob was returning to Palestine from Laban's house, he was fearful about meeting his brother, Esau. He prayed for God's help but then deceptively sent a large gift to bribe Esau. That night God appeared to the patriarch "Israel" (yśrʾl), who "struggled" (yśr, from the verb śrh) with the angel of God. Jacob "overcame" or prevailed over the angel—not in the sense of defeating him[9] but in getting the blessing he wanted as he "wept and begged for his favor" (Hos. 12:4).[10]

Hosea does not draw a lesson from this incident, but he apparently wants to show how the Israelites struggle for their own way against God just like their forefather, and they will only prevail if they obtain God's blessing.[11] They should stop fighting God and start begging for his compassion. Maybe they can be transformed into a new nation, just as Jacob became a different man through these events.

The third incident draws from Jacob's meeting God at Bethel (see Gen. 28:10–22; 35:6–15). There is little for which to criticize Jacob when he met God on his journey to and from Laban's house. Garrett suggests this text implicitly criticizes what is going on at Bethel in Hosea's day.[12] That is, the prophet is criticizing the temple worship that mixes the golden calf with Baalism. Hosea's example is also a challenge for the people to go back to their roots to follow Jacob and meet Yahweh, the God of hosts (Hos. 12:5), and to truly listen to what he said at Bethel. At that time God promised to be their God, to care for them, and to give them the blessings of Abraham. This is Israel's promise and hope too, if they do not act like the younger Jacob, who tried to get everything through deception.

Hosea concludes this paragraph with an application to his listeners: "But you" or "But as for you." He tries to persuade his audience to "return to your

---

7. P. R. Ackroyd, "Hosea and Jacob," *VT* 10 (1960): 245–59.

8. Commentaries make an unusual amount of emendations in this verse and come up with quite different results because of these changes, which "correct" this problematic passage.

9. Wolff, *Hosea*, 206, thinks that the angel overcame Jacob in 12:4a. Since Jacob is the subject of the verbs in 12:4b, he must be the subject of the verbs in the first half of the verse.

10. W. Kaiser, "Inner Biblical Exegesis As a Model for Bridging the 'Then' and 'Now' Gap: Hos 12:1–6," *JETS* 28 (1985): 33–46, thinks the weeping is referring to Jacob and Esau weeping when they meet.

11. Mays, *Hosea*, 164, draws this lesson from the typology of Jacob.

12. Garrett, *Hosea, Joel*, 237.

God" as Jacob finally did, to have steadfast covenantal love for the God who made such great promises to Jacob, to follow the just practices outlined in the covenant stipulations in the Torah, and to earnestly wait for God in difficult times (12:6). Hope is possible if God's people follow his way, but not if they continue to follow the path of their ancestor Jacob. They cannot determine their own destiny through more manipulation and duplicity; they must listen to what God has said and learn from how he dealt with Jacob.

Forgetfulness by Israel's Merchants About God's Gifts to Them (12:7–10)

HOSEA NOW ANALYZES the contemporary economic situation where deceit rules instead of justice. The Israelite merchants are acting like their Canaanite neighbors[13] by using dishonest scales in their business dealings. By rigging two sets of weights for the scale, they can use one that is too heavy or too light. The merchant "defrauds" people by requiring that they put 110 percent of a shekel to balance his heavy weight. Or when the merchant sells, he weighs his product using a light weight so that he gives his customers only 90 percent of what they deserve.

This reminds one of Jacob's attempts to get ahead financially by taking advantage of Esau and Laban (Gen. 25:27–34; 30:30–43) as well as his attempt to bribe Esau with his wealth in order to escape responsibility for past mistreatment of his brother (Gen. 32). The people in Hosea's day continue this tradition. Those in the upper class boast about their illegally gained wealth (Hos. 12:8) and boldly flaunt their affluence with great houses that are richly decorated (cf. Amos 3:15). To make things worse, these same people think they are above the law, claiming that no one can ever make any charges stick against them (Hos. 12:8b).[14] They are trusting in their wealth to protect them, not the legal system or God. Like Mafia generals, they fix any court case so that they will never be held accountable for their deceptive financial dealings. They think they are above both the laws of God and the nation's legal system.

Now comes a strong contrast. They claim "I am very rich" (12:8), but in 12:9 God claims, "I am the LORD your God." He is the one who miraculously delivered them from Egyptian slavery. They owe their national freedom, existence, and identity to his gracious work on their behalf. They

---

13. The Hebrew word for "merchant" is a wordplay on "Canaan"; thus Hosea is suggesting that they act like Canaanite merchants.

14. Stuart, *Hosea–Jonah*, 193, turns the second half of 12:8 into a divine condemnation of the rich instead of their boast, but his emendations (based on the LXX) should not be accepted.

cannot determine their destiny through their wealth. Now God is going to bring an anti-exodus event and return them to the desert existence, where they will live in tents rather than rich homes. They already know something about this event because every year the Israelites celebrated the joy of the Exodus by living a few days in tents (on the Feast of Tabernacles; Ex. 23:16; Lev. 23:33–44; Deut. 16:13–17). But this time they will experience God's judgment. This refers to the uncomfortable life they will have after the nation is destroyed. Their wealth will not protect them from God's conclusion that they are guilty.

A second basis for determining guilt is the repeated warnings by the prophets God sent to deliver his words (Hos. 12:10). The people are not totally ignorant of what God wants. They have some idea that God does not approve of what they are doing. The prophecies, visions, and parables of Elijah, Elisha, and Amos taught the people God's will and warned of punishment if they did not repent (see cf. 6:5). They are therefore without excuse since they have stubbornly rejected God's will and refused to turn from their deceptive ways.

Israel's Choice of Deception Instead of God (12:11–14)

ANOTHER EXAMPLE OF deceit points to events that took place in Gilead and Gilgal. In this case Hosea mentions the sins of the present day first (12:11) and then draws on the history of Jacob (12:12). The syntax of 12:11 is not clear (the NIV makes two questions), but more likely the verse has two accusations and two punishment statements. The accusation against Gilead is that the people are guilty of wickedness and deceit at this location. This is a broad statement not supported by a description of any specific act or event. The sin at Gilgal is also ambiguous, for Hosea only charges that the people sacrificed there. Apparently the deceitful wickedness of Gilead was infamous (see 6:8) and Gilgal was a well-known place where people worshiped other gods (see 4:15; 9:15). The audience does not need explanation of all the details. It is like mentioning Las Vegas without describing what goes on there.

As punishment Gilead will be reduced to nothing, a "worthless" thing. Moreover, the stones on the altars at Gilgal will look like unorganized piles of rocks on a plowed field rather than a sacred altar for worship. Both images project a picture of destruction so severe that nothing of value is left. This once proud and prosperous people will end up having nothing and becoming nothing because of their deceptive ways.

A second illustration reminds Hosea's audience of Jacob's action of fleeing for his life to Laban in Aram and his work of tending Laban's sheep to pay the bride price for his wives (12:12; see Gen. 27–29). The purpose of bringing up this history is unclear. Hosea does not seem to condemn Jacob for going to Laban to find a wife and doing the demeaning work of tending sheep, nor does Hosea suggest Jacob should not have married Laban's daughters. Andersen and Freedman believe Hosea is contrasting Jacob's enslavement of "keeping/tending" sheep for a wife with the prophet Moses' "keeping/caring" for the Israelites (12:13) when they came up from Egypt to freedom.[15] Garrett finds other parallels between Jacob in Aram and Israel in Egypt: Both were in foreign lands; both worked in slavery for a time; both were delivered by God from enslavement; both had great wealth when they left.[16]

The similarity of "keeping/caring/tending" draws the experiences together, but the contrast between Jacob's experiences and those of Israel in Egypt is greater than the similarities. Through Jacob's own efforts he managed to survive Esau's hatred and worked for a wife, but the nation of Israel was freed from working as slaves by God's grace through Moses. The implication is that Hosea's audience should not follow the patterns of Jacob (self-effort and deception) but should allow God to care for them and bring them freedom through another prophet (Hosea).

Unfortunately, Israel has rejected God's grace and does not listen to God's prophets; consequently, they "provoke him to anger" (12:14). Therefore God, the Lord and master of Israel, will hold the nation accountable for its deeds. The verdict is guilty; they will have to pay the penalty for their sins.

Israel's Deceptive Worship (13:1–3)

THE CONTRASTS BETWEEN Israel's past (13:1), present (13:2), and future (13:3) continue to provide additional evidence of the nation's guilt and deception. The positive past depicts a time when Israel was a powerful nation and other nations feared when she threatened. This probably refers to the time of Jeroboam II, when Israel was prosperous and Assyria much weaker. Israel had a large army to defend itself and was one of the more important nations in the ancient Near East (see Amos 6:1–2). Although Israel had many things going for her at the time of Jeroboam II, the people turned away from God and deceptively synthesized the worship of Baal into their religious beliefs and practices. This led to the death of the nation rather than to fertility and life as Baalism promised. Mays connects this death with the state of the nation after their defeat by the Assyrians in the Syro-Ephraimite war (733 B.C.).[17] Many were killed, its army was decimated, some of its territory was taken away, and its viability as a military power ended.

---

15. Andersen and Freedman, *Hosea*, 621, see a strong contrast between these two events.

16. Garrett, *Hosea, Joel*, 246.

17. Mays, *Hosea*, 172, thinks Hosea attributes the terrible state of Israel at his time to God's death sentence.

As if things are not bad enough, the Israelites are continuing to build more and more idols (13:2). Some make their own idols, while others go to great expense to have skilled craftsmen fashion elaborate and beautiful idols of silver. Strangely, the people do not seem to realize that these idols of fertility that are supposed to bring life are actually the cause of their death. Making these idols is a direct rejection of God's commandment not to worship other gods or to make images of any gods (Ex. 20:3–4).

The last line of verse 2 is problematic, with all kinds of different translations. Although any translation is questionable,[18] what is clear is that some Israelites are encouraging others ("they say," not "it is said," in the NIV) to sacrifice and kiss the golden calf. First Kings 19:18 indicates that kissing the idol was a part of Baal worship, but this practice is now introduced into the worship of the golden calves at Bethel and Dan. Israel has become paganized by gradually joining the worship of Baal and God into one religious system.

The consequence (Hos. 13:3) of this deceptive idolatry is stated in another verdict: Israel will disappear! Hosea expresses this fate with three common metaphors from everyday life. (1) The mist or dew in the morning evaporates and disappears when the sun comes out. (2) The chaff in the grain disappears with the wind when the farmer throws the grain up in the air. (3) The thick smoke from a burning fire in the house suddenly disappears when it goes out the window. These images picture the great nation of Israel evaporating into thin air, quickly disappearing from sight. Hosea does not say here how this will happen or who will make Israel disappear. He simply makes the ominous statement: In a short time you will no longer exist. The exalted nation of 12:8 and 13:1 will be nothing.

Bridging Contexts

DECEPTION. The main theme in this section is the deceitfulness of God's people. From the very beginning Jacob tried to get ahead through his own cleverness and by manipulating his family and even God himself (12:3–4). The Israelites are still using deceit in Hosea's time to manage their political relationships with stronger nations (12:1). Hosea sees deception in the way merchants cheat their customers (12:7) and in how the people deceitfully mix the pure worship of God with Baalism and idols (13:1–2). Although God is the One who gave them the land of Israel, these people deceptively take the credit for themselves (12:8a).

---

18. Wolff, *Hosea*, 219, translates "those who sacrifice men kiss calves" and thinks this refers to human sacrifices. Andersen and Freedman, *Hosea*, 632, translate differently but also think this refers to human sacrifice. The syntax of this phrase does not support this interpretation.

They also deceive themselves into thinking that no one will be able to hold them accountable for their sins (12:8b).

When people use these kind of tactics, it is a sign they do not trust God to care for their needs and question whether he will accomplish what he has promised. To compensate for God's weakness and their own inability to deal with reality, these people lie, double-cross, pretend, and twist the truth so that they can get what they want. Honesty and integrity are not a part of their lifestyle. When people embrace this approach to life, they end up deceiving themselves into thinking they are not doing anything wrong.

Nor do the Israelites deal with God honestly and according to their covenant agreement. God has revealed himself to them as holy and faithful (11:12) and made known what he expects of his people. He exhorts them to return to him, maintain their covenant relationship of love with him, practice justice in their dealings with others, and put their hope and trust in God (12:6). The Lord does not deceive his people by telling them one thing in the law and the prophetic revelations and then doing another. His dealings are characterized by grace, faithfulness, and love. The contrast between God's action and Israel's response dramatically unfolds the full extent and true nature of Israel's deceptive dealings. They do not even worship him but honor man-made idols of silver (13:2).

Memory. Hosea links this idea of deception to that of forgetting God's grace (12:9–10, 13; see also Mic. 6:3–5). God's people should remember what he has graciously done for them so that they will have an appropriate response to him. God's grace is also evident in the many prophetic visions, parables, and prophecies that provide instructions on what to do and correct false ideas (Hos. 12:10). God's past blessing of greatness should not be taken for granted and his desire for justice and truth should not be forgotten.

It is dangerous to forget who God is, what he has said, and what he has done for us. As early as the giving of the law at Sinai, God called on the nation to remember "what I did to Egypt, and how I carried you on eagles' wings and brought you to myself" (Ex. 19:4) so that they would commit themselves to keeping the covenant stipulations. Childs concludes that memory indicates an active relationship to some object or person that exceeds a simple thought process.[19] It is a persistent and reflective examination of the implied meaning of an act so that its value is not lost to the people involved. Thus, a major function of worship ceremonies is to help people remember God's gracious deeds in the past.

In the covenant renewal ceremony in Joshua 24, the initial covenant deeds of God are traced back to his calling of Abraham out of Ur, guiding

---

19. B. Childs, *Memory and Tradition in Israel* (London: SCM, 1962), 17–30.

the lives of Isaac and Jacob, bringing the people up from Egypt, defeating King Sihon, frustrating Balaam's curses, crossing the Jordan, defeating the Canaanites, and finally receiving the land (Josh. 24:2–13). One of the key sources of Joshua's courage in entering the Promised Land was his remembering what God had done in the past and promised for the future.

When God's grace is ignored or forgotten, people soon lose any sense of connection with the past or responsibility to carry on the values of past generations. When people forget their history or take for granted all the wonderful things they have, they lose an essential ingredient of their identity and become something different from the ideals of their founders.

REMEMBER THE PAST **grace of God.** One way church members can ensure a proper relationship with God and avoid his condemnation is never to forget what God has done for them. The Psalms are rich with words of praise for what God has done for his people (see Ps. 103–106). Paul encourages the church at Corinth and us today to celebrate the Lord's Supper, based on the memory of what Jesus did at his Last Supper: "Do this in remembrance of me" (1 Cor. 11:24). He knew if believers forget that Jesus died for them, they will not live like people who are alive in Christ and dead to sin.

Of course, just remembering is not enough, for a dull hearer will not receive God's blessing, but only the active doer of what God has said (James 1:25). Although repeated remembering can turn into deadly boring repetition, values and beliefs are cemented in the minds of people by repeatedly reemphasizing them. Transformation comes when people's hearts are so touched by the past work of Christ that they are willing to take up their cross and follow him (Matt. 16:24).

The author of Hebrews reminds his audience not to forget the admonitions in the Old Testament books "that address you" (Heb. 12:5), for by this means God's people endure in faithfulness through the discipline of remembering the past. Peter also maintains that people who lose sight of the importance of moral discipline, self-control, the need for perseverance, and Christian love and godliness, do so because they do not remember the greatness of their purification from their past sins (2 Peter 1:5–9). Jesus called his audiences to "remember Lot's wife" (Luke 17:32) and not make the same mistake she did. In the Upper Room, Jesus also called his followers to remember his words (John 15:20; 16:4).

The apostle Paul asked the church at Ephesus to "remember that ... you who are Gentiles ... were separate from Christ ... without hope and without

God in the world" (Eph. 2:11–12). The angel of God called on the church of Sardis to "remember … what you have received and heard; obey it, and repent" (Rev. 3:3), lest judgment come on them like a thief in the night. Remembering the grace of God is not a useless attachment to old-fashioned ways; it is a central means of understanding and appreciating one's heritage and identity.

The educational function of the church is heavily related to edifying people about God's past dealings with his people. Through preaching and Bible study, people are reminded again and again what God has done for them. If we do not teach our children about the great deeds of God in the past, describe the teachings of Jesus, and drill into their minds the admonitions of Paul, how will they learn how to act in a Christian manner? A solid Christian education program is necessary if the church expects its members to maintain the integrity of the faith.

In the secular realm, every ethnic and national group knows that they must remind their young people about the history of that group to create identity and a connection with the ideals and struggles of the group. When any group, especially the church, forgets the suffering of the past and the many mistakes made, it is doomed to a loss of significance for the next generation and is in danger of extinction. If we as believers do not remember what God has done for us and said to us, how can we ever expect to maintain the church as a powerful force in society? As Hosea knows, a group that forgets what God has done for it will not act to please God.

What does God think of lies and deception? Hosea affirms that God holds everyone accountable for his or her acts of deception. If people forget what God has done or said, they are still accountable. Ignorance is not bliss. No one can really deceive a holy and just God. He sees all lies as lies and knows when our hearts are full of deceit. He is as much against deceitfulness today as he was in the time of Hosea. He will judge those who do not conduct their business dealings with others honestly and without deception or lies (see Amos 8:4–6; Mic. 6:9–12).

The Bible is full of admonitions about the importance of honest and ethical behavior in business (Deut. 25:13). Although many people today live outside the agricultural setting of selling grain that Hosea has in mind in this section, the trusting relationship between sellers and buyers is commonly experienced at farmers' markets as well as most other places of business or trade. All business and employment arrangements include written and unwritten expectations of both parties. The boss promises to provide certain benefits and rewards and the worker to perform certain required tasks. People can choose to keep their part of the agreement (to pay a full wage or to work a full eight hours) or to deceive their business partner and refuse to do faithfully what is expected of them.

One cannot be spiritual and have a close relationship to God while cheating another person out of his or her money. There is a direct relationship between people's acts and their heart. Those who consistently lie with their tongues and cheat others with their hands are people who do not love God. Those who claim to love God but worship something other than the holy God of revelation deceive themselves. If God is less important than financial gain, then there is not much question about what such a person is worshiping. He or she is not doing justice, returning to God, worshiping God, or hoping in God always (Hos. 12:6).

This theme of lies and deception is a troubling issue in every person's life. It is always easier to say something to please people when you really do not mean it. Just take care of a young child for a day and you will find that child not telling the truth about what he or she did.[20] Teenagers frequently lie about their homework, what they did with their friends, and when they will get home. Boys lie about their romantic conquests and their athletic skills, while girls lie about their boyfriends. Anyone involved with committing crime tries to cover his or her tracks with lies. Investigative TV programs repeatedly catch people doing something they should not be doing on a video camera, but such people usually lie about it when initially confronted. Even husbands and wives deceptively cheat on their partners.

The pervasiveness of lies and half-truths in interpersonal relationships was powerfully brought home to me some years back when I read about how the psychiatrist M. S. Peck tried to break through the massive web of deceit that people weave.[21] It seemed like a torturous task to uncover and understand what was actually happening because everyone was giving his or her own spin to the facts to cover self-interests and save face. Parents lied to a young boy named Roger and to his psychiatrist, and the young boy lied to protect himself. The parents wanted to keep what the doctor recommended and what they said to the doctor hidden from their son. How could they twist the truth if everyone knew what the other person really felt and said?[22]

Peck states that the parents told him "between one and two dozen lies.... Roger's parents lied to me repeatedly.... The process was very perverse."[23] Through all this Roger's parents were pretending that they were helping

---

20. A recent Candid Camera experiment showed 5 out of 6 kids not telling the truth about touching a real unloaded gun that was purposely left in their playroom with the other toys.

21. M. S. Peck, *People of the Lie: The Hope for Healing Human Evil* (New York: Simon and Schuster, 1983), tells many stories that illustrate this problem. I am thankful to my student Tom Rakow for giving me a copy of this book.

22. Ibid., 87–108.

23. Ibid., 106.

Roger, but actually they were more interested in preserving their own self-image. Most of us do not think our neighbors or friends are that kind of people; we think deceptions and lies are the tricks of criminals, lawyers on TV, and a few bad used-car salesmen. The fact is, even "good religious" people who go to church and sing beautiful songs of commitment and love to God sometimes use deceit in what they say. They lie to God and deceive other church members.

The problem of deception is not limited to what people say. It can also relate to the difference between what people say and what they do or what they believe. If one says that God is the sovereign ruler over the political affairs of the nations, one must trust in God to help solve political problems and not depend on underhanded political tricks (12:1). If people say they follow God's work in their business, it is deceptive to use shady practices to make an extra buck (12:7). If one claims to worship God as Savior and Lord, it is deceitful not to follow his revelation or listen to what his prophets have said (12:10). Why do so many unbelievers complain so much about hypocrisy in the church? For some it may be a lame excuse, but others know that deception is still a major problem among God's people in the church.

Hosea 13:4–16

4 "But I am the LORD your God,
    who brought you out of Egypt.
  You shall acknowledge no God but me,
    no Savior except me.
5 I cared for you in the desert,
    in the land of burning heat.
6 When I fed them, they were satisfied;
    when they were satisfied, they became proud;
    then they forgot me.
7 So I will come upon them like a lion,
    like a leopard I will lurk by the path.
8 Like a bear robbed of her cubs,
    I will attack them and rip them open.
  Like a lion I will devour them;
    a wild animal will tear them apart.

9 "You are destroyed, O Israel,
    because you are against me, against your helper.
10 Where is your king, that he may save you?
    Where are your rulers in all your towns,
  of whom you said,
    'Give me a king and princes'?
11 So in my anger I gave you a king,
    and in my wrath I took him away.
12 The guilt of Ephraim is stored up,
    his sins are kept on record.
13 Pains as of a woman in childbirth come to him,
    but he is a child without wisdom;
  when the time arrives,
    he does not come to the opening of the womb.

14 "I will ransom them from the power of the grave;
    I will redeem them from death.
  Where, O death, are your plagues?
    Where, O grave, is your destruction?

  "I will have no compassion,
15   even though he thrives among his brothers.
  An east wind from the Lord will come,
    blowing in from the desert;

> his spring will fail
> > and his well dry up.
> His storehouse will be plundered
> > of all its treasures.
> ¹⁶ The people of Samaria must bear their guilt,
> > because they have rebelled against their God.
> They will fall by the sword;
> > their little ones will be dashed to the ground,
> > their pregnant women ripped open."

Original Meaning

HOSEA MOVES HIS emphasis in this part of the lawsuit from accusations of sin (11:12–13:3) to the destruction of Israel. He begins 13:4–6a by rehearsing what God has graciously done for his people, briefly points to Israel's sins (13:6b), and then dwells on the future destruction of the nation (13:7–16). God, the Savior of the enslaved nation (13:4), will become a devouring lion (13:7–8). The nation will now be held accountable for its sins, and its punishment is inevitable. There will be no way to escape death and destruction (13:9–16).

This message comes late in the reign of Hoshea, the last king of Israel, but there is no evidence that the final battle has begun. The irresistible and unavoidable end is close at hand, and there is no longer any hope of escaping death. God is against his people and will not have any covenant love for those who reject him. As in 6:4 and 11:8 (near the end of each of the other parts of the lawsuit), at the last moment there is a caveat in 13:14. The people will experience death and destruction because God will not have compassion on them, but these forces will not have the final say. Instead, God's redemption of his people will (13:14).

God's Past Caring Will Turn to Tearing (13:4–8)

GOD'S CARE IS defined (13:4–6a) by who he is and by the relationships he has established through his great acts in salvation history. God's name is Yahweh ("the LORD"), the God of Israel (13:4). He is not Baal, he is not the golden calf, he is not some wooden image made by a skilled craftsman. He is the covenant-making God, who cared enough to deliver his people from Egyptian slavery. He expects exclusive worship from his people (Ex. 20:3). They are not to have a relationship with other gods or acknowledge any other divine beings in worship. Israel has only one Savior, God himself. He has given himself to them, and they are to give themselves to him.

A second demonstration of God's care was his provision for the nation while they were traveling for forty years in the hot and dry desert of Sinai (Hos. 13:5). God led them with the pillar of fire and the cloud, he daily gave them manna as food to eat and quail for meat, and he miraculously provided water again and again (see Ex. 15–17; Num. 11–16; Deut. 8). Anyone who has spent time in the Sinai desert in the dry summer months (as I have) will testify to the unbearable conditions in that stark and hot land. There is no doubt that God "knew" all about them and cared for their every need. If God had not cared, they would not have survived.

The third stage in God's relationship with his people was his abundant blessing of them in the Promised Land of milk and honey (Hos. 13:6a). God warned the people while they were in the desert to be careful not to forget what God did for them (Deut. 8:10–20). When they entered the land, he would provide brooks and fountains of abundant water, rich wheat and barley crops, a place where there would be no scarcity of food (8:6–9). But the danger was that in their fullness, they might forget it was God who gave all this to them. They might become proud and think that they accomplished all this by themselves, or figure that they did not need God's help any more (8:10–14). Hosea indicates that this is exactly what happened: The Israelites became proud and forgot that Yahweh their God had given them everything (Hos. 13:6).

This brief historical background sets the stage for the verdict of the lawsuit in the rest of this chapter. God will now turn against his people and tear them apart (13:7–8). He will no longer act in tender care but will deliberately act like a vicious lion or leopard, or like a mindless mad mother bear robbed of her cubs. Israel will be savagely ripped apart and torn limb from limb.[1] This is a horrifying picture of a merciless death at the hands of raging people who act like beasts.

Since Israel Rejects God's Leadership, God Rejects Israel's Leaders (13:9–11)

MANY TODAY WOULD probably object to the violent imagery of Hosea's announcement of judgment, but the destruction of Israel comes down to the simple fact that the people are against God their Savior (cf. 13:4).[2] There is

---

1. Hillers, *Treaty-Curses and the Old Testament* (Rome: Pontifical Biblical Institute, 1964), 54–56, demonstrates the common use of being attacked by a wild animal to express a curse (see also Deut. 32:24; Jer. 2:14–15; 48:40; Hos. 5:14).

2. The NIV passive "you are destroyed" in v. 9 catches the meaning but is not a literal translation ("it destroys/has destroyed you"), which Wolff, *Hosea*, 221, emends to "I will destroy you."

no mystery about God's plan, no hidden agenda that the people cannot figure out. They know what God desires, but they reject him.

Verses 10–11 seem almost as a taunting explanation of where the nation went wrong. They trusted in human leaders instead of God. God asks, as it were, "Where are your human kings, judges, and princes, who you thought would be your saviors?" God's surprising ironic response is that he will send the people of Israel what they want, a king. But this does not refer to a benevolent Israelite king who will save them; rather, it refers to an enemy king, whom God will send against them in his wrath.[3] If they will not submit and follow their true King and Savior, they will end up serving a human despot— their Assyrian conqueror.

Israel Will Die, But Death Will Not Overpower God's Plan (13:12−16)

THE FINAL PART of the verdict emphasizes the nation's death, using the analogy of abnormal childbirth, drought, and violent death in military conflicts. (1) The image of an abnormal childbirth (13:13) pictures Israel as a baby in the midst of the birthing process. The pressure of labor contractions is felt by this baby, but the child unwisely refuses to enter the birth canal. Apparently, Hosea sees Israel's upcoming suffering as analogous to the suffering of this baby. Like the child, Israel is not wise, but has made sinful choices. Although nothing is said about the fate of the breached baby, the implication is that the child (and Israel) will tragically die rather than live. Israel stubbornly rejects the path of life.[4]

(2) The metaphor of drought (13:15) pictures Israel as one of the thriving and successful nations in the ancient Near East.[5] But things change dramatically when God sends a hot desert wind from the east to dry up all sources of water. Pools of water are emptied by evaporation and overuse by people, and even the springs fail to produce fresh water. As a result, the nation will be stripped of its treasures and will die. This may be interpreted

---

3. Garrett, *Hosea, Joel*, 260–61, properly translates the verbs as futures (not as NIV, "I gave"). Stuart, *Hosea–Jonah*, 206, translates the verb similar to the NIV and thinks Hosea is thinking about God's past giving of Saul as king, even though it was against his desires.

4. Wolff, *Hosea*, 228, sees a divine promise of life in this verse, but this interpretation is unlikely. Garrett, *Hosea, Joel*, 263–64, ties this birth into the Baal fertility religion, but nothing is said of Baalism here.

5. There is much speculation about who the brothers are. Any other nation (Ammon, Moab, Edom, Judah) could be compared as a brother, particularly if there was a treaty relationship between Israel and that other nation. Wolff, *Hosea*, 222, changes the word "brothers" to "reeds" (the two spellings are close), while Andersen and Freedman, *Hosea*, 625, change "brothers" to "wild ass." The Hebrew text is fine as it is.

as the loss of agricultural wealth in its storehouses (they will have to eat it all during the drought) or to the Assyrians' raping of the land when the nation is conquered.[6]

(3) The third explanation of death is drawn from a military conflict (13:16b; 14:1 in the Hebrew text). Surprisingly, Hosea says nothing about the actual battles between the two armies; he simply reports the results of those battles. Three brief statements seal the fate of Israel. The people will die by the sword (probably referring to soldiers), children will be brutally killed, and the defenseless pregnant women will be savagely ripped open to kill their unborn children. It will be a horribly revolting slaughter that will show no mercy.

Why will this happen? Twice Hosea briefly reminds his audience that they must bear the guilt for their sins (13:12, 16a). Their evil deeds (11:12–13:6) are not forgotten but have been recorded for their day of punishment. They have rebelled against God, so now they are being held accountable for their action.

So far everything sounds like standard theology in Hosea, but in the middle of this announcement of judgment comes a caveat similar to 6:4 and 11:8–9. Although everyone translates 13:14b as questions ("Where, O death, are your plagues? Where, O grave, is your destruction?"), it is possible to view 13:14a as either questions or statements. Two very different interpretations derive from this decision. If these are statements (as in NIV, NASB), then God is promising to ransom his people from death. But if these are questions (as in RSV), then God is removing any hope of ransoming them from death.[7]

The argumentation in 13:4–16 is that Israel will die. Thus, if Hosea is consistent, one would think this verse is not offering hope. However, at the end of each of the other verdicts in this lawsuit (6:4; 11:8–9), God is overcome with love and refuses to totally destroy his people. This is the same passion that refused to give up on Israel and destroy them like Admah and Zeboiim (11:8). Hosea 13:14 seems to be a similar bold refusal on God's part to completely reject his people. This taunt of death is based on his redemptive power to overcome the curse of death (13:14a). Death will not defeat God's plans for his people.[8] One should not, of course, read into this passage personal or national resurrection as Ezekiel saw (Ezek. 37:1–14), although much later the apostle Paul saw the seeds of this idea in Hosea's words (1 Cor. 15:55).

---

6. Stuart, *Hosea–Jonah*, 208, believes it refers to agricultural wealth being lost, based on several curses in Deut. 28 and 32, while Mays, *Hosea*, 183, prefers the military explanation.

7. Mays, *Hosea*, 182, and Stuart, *Hosea–Jonah*, 207, interpret this as a hopeless statement.

8. McComiskey, *The Minor Prophets*, 1:223–24, and Andersen and Freedman, *Hosea*, 639, take this as a promise of hope.

The final clause in 13:14, "I will have no compassion," abruptly returns to the theme of judgment on Israel. How can such contradictory statements be set side by side? Can they both be true? How can God say they will die (13:12–13), then they will not die (13:14a-b), and then he will have no compassion on them and they will die (13:14c–16)? Hosea is not deceiving the people in verse 14 by telling them that God will not judge them. No, God will bring death on the nation soon, but death will not have final victory over God or his plans. In the midst of or after this judgment, he will ransom some from the power of death. In light of similar statements in Hosea 1:10–2:1 and 3:4–5, it appears that these people will make up part of that eschatological group that will again be called "my people," that is, the people of God.

GOD'S CARE BALANCED **with justice**. This verdict of judgment emphasizes God's care and judgment. God's past care was epitomized in his revelation of himself as God to his people, the Exodus experience where he delivered the nation from Egyptian bondage, his care for them during their long and hot desert journey, and his rich provision for all their needs in the Promised Land (13:4–6). God's present care is evident in sending the prophet Hosea to warn the people of God's impending judgment and to call the nation to repentance. God's future care will be known after the judgment, for God will ransom some of them from death.

God's care is a minor but important theme of hope in the midst of warnings of darkness and death. He does not just give up when the devastating power of sin ruins his plans. If God's acts of punishment are not understood in the light of his continual caring for his people, people may wrongly misinterpret his action. Judgment does not come because he is too weak to protect his people, because he does not really exist, or because he is a wrathful judge out for revenge. Punishment and death come because of a prideful, self-centered worldview (13:6b), because of trusting in a human king and forgetting about God's help (13:10), and because of accountability for sin that cannot be put off forever (13:12). That God still loves his people and will continue to care for them in the future (13:14) undermines any false claims about his love. That God has the ultimate power over life and death is a great assurance to believers in every age (see 1 Cor. 15).

God's care is balanced with his justice. God is not one or the other, but both. Since guilt for sin must be adjudicated before the bar of divine justice, a verdict of guilty is necessary when sinful rebellion against God exists (Hos. 13:16). The results of sin are astonishing and life-threatening; they produce the stench of death. Instead of care and help in times of need, God will take away the rain that brings life to crops and people. Instead of being a Savior from their enemies, God will bring new enemies to kill them with the sword. Sinners will be like defenseless animals ripped apart by a mad mother bear, people who suffer under a foreign king, babies dashed against the ground, and disemboweled pregnant women. People are helpless and hopeless in the grips of death. Only a caring God can ransom people from the deadly results of sin.

THIS PASSAGE IS about God's past grace to Israel and the death of the nation Israel, not any nation today. It is inappropriate to apply these predictions of national disaster and war to any group of people today. The value in such a passage is that it provides key insights into the way God works with people. He sees sin as a rejection of and ungratefulness for all of his gracious care in the past (13:4–6a). Any feeling of human self-sufficiency that does not give God credit for the marvelous things he has done is pride, which God hates (13:6b).

God keeps a record of sins, and people will eventually be held accountable for their guilt (13:12, 16a). No human rulers or leaders can protect people from the incredible power of God's wrath when the Judgment Day arrives (13:7–11, 15–16). Yet in spite of his wrath, death and destruction will not totally destroy all of God's plans. He will have the final victory (13:14).

Appreciate God's care; don't be proud. Hosea has already addressed the theme of not remembering God's grace in the past (11:1–4; 12:9–10), which can lead to pride and disobedience. The application in those passages is similar to this context because in all the examples given by Hosea, people got involved with sinful acts because they did not appreciate God's gracious care for them. This danger exists for people today as much as it did for the Israelites in the past, in that they may easily forget God's loving care.

How often do we think about God's care in the creation of this earth, his provision of just the right amount of oxygen in the air, or his power to keep the earth spinning around the sun at a consistent distance so that life can be preserved here? Usually only in a time of severe drought do people remember to thank God for past rains, or in a time of danger do they thankfully remember his protection in the past. We tend to take for granted God's care in providing relatively free democracies where we can make our own personal choices on where to live and what we will do to make a living. Because we have enjoyed religious freedom for so long, we often do not appreciate how God has sovereignly worked to cause many nations to give their citizens a considerable amount of freedom to worship God openly and without interference.

It is even possible to spend hours or days without consciously thinking about the wonderful gift of salvation God has provided through the death of his Son on the cross. Hosea's list of the gracious things God has done should remind us of the many wonderful things he has done for us. A periodic listing of the ways God has cared for us in the last week or month is one way to jog the memory and appreciate his grace.

When prosperity is abundant and the economy is going well, we tend to be self-sufficient and think we can handle things ourselves. We start to think that prosperity is a product of our own hard work and conclude that we are smart. People of some means look at themselves as better than others and become proud of what they have accomplished. God views these attitudes as filled with pride and despicable because he knows that people would have nothing if it were not given to them by him.

When the Israelites entered the Promised Land, they found wells dug and fields already planted, but the danger was that they would soon forget this was all a gift from God and not something they did or deserved (Deut. 8). In many parts of the world people today enjoy modern inventions like the airplane and air conditioning, drugs that kill bacteria and improve physical health, plus the ability to safely preserve food so that it can be eaten months later. These luxuries were unknown for thousands of years and are still beyond the reach of some people, but we in developed countries now tend to take these things for granted. Yet instead of being thankful for all God has given us, we complain about what we do not have. Instead of living today in full recognition of the multiple ways God graciously provides, we tend to proudly tell others about our accomplishments. God calls pride sin, and he will hold every person accountable for acts and attitudes of pride.

The unusual declaration of God's power over death in 13:14 will be one of God's final acts of grace. This promise is applicable to all believing Israelites and present-day followers of Christ. Paul used this promise in 1 Corinthians 15:55 to remind his audience that there is hope after death. Sin will not have the final victory over God's plan to redeem the world. Through his provision of salvation and forgiveness of sins, the sting of death is removed and eternal life with God is possible. This is just one more fantastic example of God's care for his people. The question that God's gracious care raises is: In light of God's past, present, and future care for us, how should we act today? Can we forget what God has done and proudly act as if we can take care of things ourselves?

Nothing can protect sinners from the wrath of God. Since God holds people accountable for their sins, all who have not received his forgiveness will experience his wrath (13:11). We may not like to think of God as wrathful and destructive, but the people of Israel, defeated by the Assyrians, came to understand that sin brought the consequence of God's wrath. The results of sin bring death because God is just and holy. Therefore, the images of God ripping and tearing people apart like a lion or a bear must be acknowledged as appropriate pictures of God's treatment of us if we do not reject sin.

The wrath of God will bring death, the destruction of everything we hold dear, and the removal of God's compassion (13:8, 15—16). Our political leaders (13:10), our resources, and our treasures will not protect us from that wrath (13:15). Those who reject God will suffer great indignities and violence.

These kinds of passages should persuade people in the church to take stock of their lives and evaluate what their future holds. Have we enjoyed the care of God? Have we rejected God in any way? Do we want to experience his wrath? Do we want God to remove the sting of death from our future? The answers to these questions help us know what our future will be—death and divine rejection, or victory over death.

Hosea 14:1–9

❧

¹ Return, O Israel, to the LORD your God.
　　Your sins have been your downfall!
² Take words with you
　　and return to the LORD.
　Say to him:
　　"Forgive all our sins
　and receive us graciously,
　　that we may offer the fruit of our lips.
³ Assyria cannot save us;
　　we will not mount war-horses.
　We will never again say 'Our gods'
　　to what our own hands have made,
　　for in you the fatherless find compassion."

⁴ "I will heal their waywardness
　　and love them freely,
　　for my anger has turned away from them.
⁵ I will be like the dew to Israel;
　　he will blossom like a lily.
　Like a cedar of Lebanon
　　he will send down his roots;
⁶ 　 his young shoots will grow.
　His splendor will be like an olive tree,
　　his fragrance like a cedar of Lebanon.
⁷ Men will dwell again in his shade.
　　He will flourish like the grain.
　He will blossom like a vine,
　　and his fame will be like the wine from Lebanon.
⁸ O Ephraim, what more have I to do with idols?
　　I will answer him and care for him.
　I am like a green pine tree;
　　your fruitfulness comes from me."

⁹ Who is wise? He will realize these things.
　　Who is discerning? He will understand them.
　The ways of the LORD are right;
　　the righteous walk in them,
　　but the rebellious stumble in them.

THE FINAL SECTION of this part of Hosea's lawsuit offers hope to Israel, just as the final sections of the earlier parts of the lawsuit did (5:15–6:6; 11:1–11). Although God will now judge his sinful people and send them into exile, this does not eliminate the possibility of restoration. People can choose to confess their failures and repent of their sins, and God can choose to forgive people's sins. Each generation and individual must choose between the way of rebellion and death or repentance and life. God offers these choices here to his people.

The structure of this message is: a call to repentance (14:1–3), God's promise of restoration (14:4–8), and an exhortation to choose wisely (14:9). The final exhortation in 14:9 seems to be a postscript, added at the time when Hosea's sermons were published in written form; it is not an integral part of this oral message.

The date and setting for this sermon is unknown. It was probably given sometime late in the reign of Hoshea but before the fall of Israel in 722/721 B.C.[1] At this time the people will finally realize that Assyria cannot save them and that their worship of man-made gods is of no help (14:3). Hosea is not offering a last-minute reprieve from Assyrian defeat but hope after the fall of the nation. God still has plans for those who faithfully serve him and do not trust in the idols of other nations. We do not know how the audience responded to this final word of hope.

A Call to Repentance (14:1–3)

THE FINAL WORDS from the Lord are not hopeless ideas of death and disaster. God wants to give life and blessing to his people, but this will only be possible if the problem of sin is dealt with and removed. Parallel to the model prayer of confession and commitment to God in 6:1–3, Hosea again exhorts his listeners to "repent, turn, or return" (*šwb*) from "your sins" to God. Sin has brought the "downfall" (lit., "stumbling," as in 4:5; 5:5; 14:9) of the nation. Once they take the step of turning to God instead of sinning, they will be able to speak to him about the choice they have made. Although it is an argument from silence, it seems significant that Hosea asks only for a change of the heart's relationship to God, not some act of sacrifice.

The people's prayer to God (14:2b–3) should involve confession of sins, rejection of past deceptive faith, and recognition of hope based on the

---

1. Wolff, *Hosea*, 234, thinks the disastrous fall of Samaria has already happened, but Mays, *Hosea*, 185, seems to be closer to the date when he suggests that it was spoken "in the final months of the northern kingdom's defeat by Shalmaneser V."

character of God. This simple but profound prayer asks for forgiveness, then openly and honestly admits the failures that broke fellowship with God. The first step in renewing any relationship is a humble admission of one's mistakes.

The prayer goes on to ask God to "accept the good" (not NASB, NIV, "receive us graciously").[2] This phrase is connected to the last line in the verse, for it gives the basis for the subsequent words of praise and worship. Hosea is not suggesting that the people's "good works" will earn them the right to worship God in the future. Instead, the repentant person is requesting God to accept the "good thing" they are doing, namely, their prayer to return to him. They are conveying to God their utter dependence on his response to their prayers and are not presumptuously assuming his grace. They are accepting responsibility to present a true and good confession before they will be able to praise God from a heart of joy.

The people's rejection of past deceptive sources of faith and hope is an integral part of any authentic act of repentance (14:3a). The two main areas of sin were the nation's failures to trust in God for political guidance and protection and the worship of pagan gods. Now that they have turned to God, there is no longer any need to look to Assyria or Egypt for political survival.

In the final analysis, political alliances cannot save people, provide true independence, or bring prosperity. Foreign nations are fickle and undependable, the military strength of kings rises and wanes, and such associations require payment of heavy taxes. There is a better way. Having turned to their covenant God, the people now vow to trust in his power, not warhorses, to control political affairs. God's power is made complete through human weakness. His name is glorified when he brings the victory.

A second vow renounces all relationships with other gods (14:3b). It is absurd to think any man-made object can actually be a god. It is a pagan deception to suppose that Baal or any other idol can help anyone. This revival will cause the people to confess that Yahweh, the God of Israel, is their God.

The reason why the people will make these vows is that they will finally come to know and experience the character of their God (14:3c). They will acknowledge that he is supremely motivated by his compassionate love for people. Equally important is the remembrance that God's compassion (Ex. 34:6; Lev. 26:42–45; Deut. 4:31; Neh. 9; Ps. 68:5; Hos. 3:5; 6:1–3; 11:8–11) extends to the weak, the lowly, and the powerless. This brings great comfort to those praying, for they know there is no hope except in God's deep love for helpless, undeserving people.

---

2. Wolff, *Hosea*, 231, follows R. Gordis, "The Text and Meaning of Hosea 14:3," *VT* 5 (1955): 88–90, who thinks "good" means "word."

God's Promise of Restoration (14:4–8)

THE TEXT DOES not indicate if anyone actually prayed Hosea's model prayer of confession in 14:1–3, but Hosea clearly reveals how God will respond when people do turn to him and worship only him: He will heal their sinful waywardness[3] (14:4), since they do not seem to be able to resist the temptation to turn away from God. This suggests that people are weak and unable to do what they want or should do (see Rom. 7). It also may imply that sinning is not just a simple act of the will, but that past choices influence the pattern of later choices.

Under such negative forces, people need a miraculous act of God's healing grace to enable them to respond to his gifts of restoration. This is nothing less than his marvelous love offered freely, voluntarily, and spontaneously. This love is unearned; it is a free expression of divine commitment and deep emotional care for undeserving people. God's past anger will "turn" away from his people because he will heal and remove their sins.

Once the problem of sin is dealt with, God will bless his people (14:5–7; see 2:16–23). He is pictured as the dew that brings life-giving moisture to the plant life in Israel in the dry summer months. This divine life will transform the people. They will look like a beautiful blossoming lily and be as enduring as the towering cedars of Lebanon (or the lilies of Lebanon).[4] The Israelites will be like a plant with deep roots so that they cannot be easily destroyed.

The splendorous looks and fragrant smell of the nation will be like a luxurious olive tree in full bloom, even the large olive trees in Lebanon.[5] The fruitfulness of the nation is also compared to a bountiful grain field, a blossoming grapevine, and the famous wine from Lebanon (14:7). These are all pictures of God's rich blessing on the nation. Instead of bringing drought and death, God will lovingly give his returning people the covenant blessings he promised long ago (cf. Jer. 33:13; Joel 3:18; Amos 9:13–14).

An additional promise of people living "in his/its shade" (14:7a) is unclear.[6] Does this refer to God's shade, Israel's shade, or the shade of the olive tree

---

3. Literally, their "turning" from God, a wordplay off the word "return" in 14:1.

4. The Hebrew text does not have "cedar" (as in NIV "cedar of Lebanon"), just "Lebanon," but the reference to the deep roots suggests that Hosea is perhaps thinking of the famous "cedars of Lebanon." Andersen and Freedman, *Hosea*, 646, maintain Hosea is thinking of the crocus and olive trees of Lebanon. This is an acceptable, if not better alternative to the NIV.

5. The word "cedar" in NIV is also missing in 14:6. Here it makes more sense to think of the fragrance from Lebanon olive trees.

6. The NIV "again" apparently represents the word "return," which appears again in this verse. It would be better to translate the first line, "The ones who dwell in his/its shade will return."

in 14:6?[7] Since Israel is the olive tree in verse 6, this must refer to the return of people to live again in the land.[8] The fruitfulness of the land will make it an attractive place. God's rich blessings will abundantly support a great multitude of people.

This paragraph ends with a contrast between God and the fertility gods of Baalism (14:8). God is the One who produces fertility through his blessing of the earth (see 2:16–23). He proclaims, "I am like a green pine tree; your fruitfulness comes from me." God takes for himself the right, the responsibility, and the joy of giving his people everything they need. The people see his good, perfect, and abundant gifts and cement their relationship with him alone.

God will no longer need to talk about the deceptiveness of idol worship because at this time the nation will serve God, and he will bless them. The whole idea of consulting idols will be a thing of past history. As Hosea predicted in 2:21, he again promises that God will respond to his people by caring for (lit., "watching over") them. God will not be far away or inattentive to the people he loves so dearly. Since the word "watch over him" sounds like the word "Assyria," T. McComiskey sees a second implied message that God will watch over them, not Assyria.[9]

Exhortation to Choose Wisely (14:9)

THIS FINAL ADMONITION was added to Hosea's collection of sermons to encourage every reader to be wise and respond to God's words appropriately. Just because it refers to wisdom and discernment does not mean it was written by someone from a wisdom school rather than the prophet.

The first half of verse 9 uses questions, while the second half has a series of statements. The exhortation is to not follow the path of Israel and act unwisely. The danger is that people will read what Hosea has said and not understand it, miss the subtle nuances of his bold analogies, or be offended by his metaphors. The reader must not let the difficulty of his poetry, the theology of judgment for sins, or the hopeful passages close his or her mind to the message of this book.

Although misinterpretation is always a danger, a more common problem is to understand the words but be unmoved by their meaning. Hosea exhorts

---

7. Mays, *Hosea*, 184,189, emends the text to "my shade," meaning God's shade, since God does compare himself to a tree in 14:8.

8. Garrett, *Hosea, Joel*, 275, suggests that this may refer to the Gentiles, who will come to Israel in the *eschaton* (cf. Gen. 12:1–3), but Hosea has made no reference to this idea in the context of this passage.

9. McComiskey, *Minor Prophets*, 1:236.

the wise person to realize and fully comprehend the implications and significance of what God has revealed. Internalizing the truth of God's Word is one of the wisest things anyone can do. People must be open to the convicting power of the Spirit and be constantly asking how Hosea's words apply to their lives.

Some readers may have had a question about the necessity of paying attention to what Hosea has said. Those people need to remember three basic principles. What the Lord says is just and "right." If you want to be considered an upright or "righteous" person in God's eyes, you must follow what he has said. If, however, you reject what God has said or refuse to apply his Word, you will "stumble" and be ruined. You cannot rebelliously reject God's way and be righteous. You cannot be wise and continue to refuse to submit to God's will.

THE ACT OF REPENTANCE. Both Old and New Testament proclaim that the only way to come to God is through repentance for sin. The problem of sin must be dealt with and the curse of sin be removed if a person wants to have a relationship with God. Repentance precedes forgiveness, conversion, restoration, and regeneration into a new person.[10] Repentance involves a "turning to" God and "turning away" from sin (14:1–2). It results in God's "turning away" his anger (14:4) and his people's "turning" to enjoy God's blessings once again (14:7).

Repentance is an act of the heart and voice. It involves a decision to respond to God's call to turn to him (14:1) and to trust him completely (14:3). Once the heart decision has been made, people need to open a personal relationship with God by confessing their sin and humbly asking for forgiveness (14:2). The confession should also express the new direction of life. This will involve a vow not to have a relationship of dependence or trust in human power or any other deceptive substitutes for God (14:3a). Trust will be based on the compassionate love of God (14:3b), which has overcome the power of sin through atonement.

John the Baptist preached repentance as a prerequisite for entering the kingdom of God and associated this with confession of sins (Matt. 3:2, 6). After repentance it was expected that people would be baptized and produce good fruit (3:6–10). Jesus connects repentance to faith (Mark 1:15) and

---

10. W. Eichrodt, *Theology of the Old Testament*, 2:465, believes that seeking God, humility, softening the heart, acknowledgement of sin, and turning from sin must come before forgiveness is possible.

shows that it leads to forgiveness (Luke 17:4). Paul knew that repentance involved a total change of direction for he preached that people "should repent and turn to God and prove their repentance by their deeds" (Acts 26:20). He warns the Romans that those who have stubborn and unrepentant hearts will have to face God's wrath on the Day of Judgment (Rom. 2:4–5). John's letters to the seven churches demonstrate they will suffer God's judgment if they do not turn from their sins and repent (Rev. 2:5, 16, 22; 3:3, 19).

In all these cases repentance is the fundamental act that signals the person's intention to change thinking and behavior. It involves rejecting the deceptive and selfish interpretation of what is meaningful and appropriate and accepting a God-centered perspective.

God's love makes repentance possible. In spite of the human tendency to sin and not to follow God's way, God freely chooses to love sinful people (Hos. 14:4; see Rom. 5:8). His love impacts people in several ways. It extends a call to the unrepentant, invites them to turn to him (Hos. 14:1), and accepts the good choices of those who respond to that call (14:2). God's compassion for those who are weak and helpless motivates them to trust in him rather than their own human abilities or the power of other stronger people (14:3).

God's love for those who repent changes not only them but also the environment they live in. The presence of God's blessings and removal of his curse demonstrate his love (14:5–6). He can change anger to love, drought to fertility, death to growth, desolation to flourishing abundance (14:6–7). All this happens when God responds in love to those who reject sin and any other gods (14:8).

If one puts together all the promises of God's love in Hosea 1:9–2:1; 2:14–23; 11:9–11; and 14:6–8, a fantastic picture of a new world arises. At the end of time God will bring in his kingdom and renew his relationship with his people. This world will change, and in its place will be a new paradise on earth. God's original plan for humanity will be accomplished through his great acts of love. In spite of sinful rebellion in this present world, God still is committed to transform it through his love.

The way of wisdom. The final verse encourages the reader of Hosea to understand what God has said in these messages of judgment and hope. The prophet exhorts us to respond wisely to God's offer of love and his call for repentance (14:9). If we refuse to internalize these words and continue in our sinful rebellion, we will stumble and suffer under God's judgment. But if we wisely accept God's offer of repentance and walk in his ways, we will enjoy the blessings of his love. God is just and his ways are right, so it is best to submit and follow him. Only a fool chooses to reject God's way and scoffs at his justice.

The book of Proverbs gives an expanded discussion of the way of the wise person and the fool. It would be inappropriate to imply all of that discussion into what Hosea is saying in these verses. Although Hosea probably knew about Solomon's proverbs, those texts had not yet been collected into the Hebrew canon. But a prophet does not have to be a member of a wisdom school or well versed in wisdom literature to know that it is wise to repent and follow God. Hosea is simply saying: Read what God has revealed to you and understand the choices he offers. Make a wise decision based on his character and take into consideration his past and future dealings with humankind.

SHOULD WE PREACH REPENTANCE? Genuine repentance is not bringing a gift in order to bribe or appease God, nor is it a feeling of sorrow or shame about getting caught for doing something wrong. It is not making a deceptive speech about turning over a new leaf when a complete change of priorities and loyalties is not planned. It is genuinely turning from a life of sin to serve the living and true God. True repentance is an essential part of God's plan to change this world and bring in his kingdom.

Why, then, are there so few sermons on repentance? It is impossible to generalize and explain why individual pastors shy away from this touchy topic, but we should answer that question for ourselves. How often was this topic the central theme in sermons in the past year? If it seldom appears, it is worth taking the time to ask why. Perhaps certain cultural factors discourage people from making repentance a central issue.

(1) Repentance often gets a bad press because it was used in the past to beat people over the head. Too often these negative attacks pronounced people guilty when they were actually trying to live in obedience to God. Preachers with this message were presenting the bad news of the gospel instead of the good news. A constant reminder of failures makes people think they are unworthy and hopeless, that God does not love them. Who wants to be told you are no good?

(2) The present cultural acceptance of pluralism means that people can "do their own thing" and everyone is supposed to accept them. This approach rejects any acts and attitudes as inherently sinful and rejected by God. In this kind of context people do not want others telling them what to do. Bigots and intolerant people are sinners, not those who are tolerant. Moreover, if people do have problems, they tend to exonerate themselves by blaming parents, schools, prejudice, or some other convenient scapegoat, like Adam in the Garden of Eden (Gen. 3). People do not want to take

responsibility for their choices and reject the message that they are sinners who need to change.

(3) Modern culture makes light of sin. It is not seen as prostitution, as rebellion against God, as something God hates. When so many politicians and business people lie, cheat, and get involved in improper relationships, such behavior becomes acceptable. To preach a strong message of repentance goes against this cultural downplaying of sin. It is more acceptable to label sin as an unwise or inopportune act, not as something God hates. Or perhaps we can plead innocence on the basis of a misunderstanding in communication. If, then, there is no sin, repentance is unnecessary.

The people in Hosea's time were just as averse to admitting their wrongs as people today, and they did not enjoy hearing negative messages that defined their activities as sin. Nevertheless, Hosea faithfully gave people the choice of judgment for sin or hope through repentance. Preaching repentance is necessary since there is no other way to begin a relationship with God. Repentance is not just a negative theme of rejecting or "turning from"; it also has a positive theme of "turning toward." If the abundance, joy, and hope of Hosea's presentation of repentance are contrasted with the hopelessness of the status quo, suddenly repentance becomes a positive change that has appeal. If God calls people to repent and follow him, then repentance must be preached today. It is his way of entering a relationship with people.

The sufficiency of God. Part of the reason why people do not want to repent and follow God is that they think that they can do a better job of directing their lives than God. They are self-sufficient, self-directed, self-motivated, and self-assured. They can handle the problems of life in the future and do not need to depend on God. They have their own man-made ways of coping with life's problems and can call on their friends to get things done (cf. 14:3). Because they can handle things quite well themselves, God is replaced.

These people have usually not faced situations beyond their control. They blindly maintain their deceptive worldview as long as it lasts. Hosea indicates people must turn from themselves and their self-made world and find their sufficiency in God. He has sufficient power to destroy sinners and sufficient love to forgive those who repent. He has compassion to help those in need, to heal those who have rejected him, and to love those who do not deserve his forgiveness (14:3−4). God alone can turn death into life, a dry field into a flourishing garden of olives and grain. Only his powerful love is sufficient to change people and this world.

What is the best choice? Hosea's final words exhort his readers to make the best choice by walking in God's ways (14:9)—a choice based on a wise understanding of all the facts God has revealed. A discerning mind can distinguish among a bad choice, a choice with pluses and minuses, and a good choice. The last is the best option because it is supported by God himself. Since his character directs his actions, one can be assured that God's ways are just. Since God rejects sin and honors holiness, choosing to be one of his disciples presents limitations on human behavior. Nevertheless, these are the good choices of the righteous person.

This challenge raises questions about the choices we make. How wise are we? Do we understand the issues? Are we well acquainted with what God has said so that we can include his way in the decision-making process? Do we carefully discern the strengths and consequences of each choice available? Do we believe God's way is always the best? Do we realize the results of rebelling against him? May God give us the wisdom and courage to follow him.

Introduction to Amos

FAILURE IS TERRIBLE. Most people do not want to face the fact that they have failed in life, and even fewer enjoy having others remind them about their past mistakes. Kids do not like to be told that they are not skilled enough to avoid being cut from the sports club. College students dread getting back an exam they have failed, and older adults hate to admit that a business venture was not a financial success.

It is also hard to tell people that, in spite of all their good intentions and efforts, they have failed in some way. It is easier to ignore a soured romantic relationship than to face the music and end it with an honest talk. It is easier not to inform people or to send an impersonal form letter telling them that they will not be hired, than to confront them with a character flaw that their references mention. Giving bad news is not an enjoyable task, and finding the right words to say is always a struggle. Because of this, many are left to guess at what the problem is. This can leave people confused and angry, because no one warned them ahead of time or advised them on things they could do to avoid failure.

It is also not easy to tell people that they have failed to meet God's requirements and will not enjoy his blessing. How does one break the news to religious people that their good lives, deeds, behavior, and theology do not please God? How does one tell others that God will judge them for behavior they see as ethical? What is the right way of exposing deceptive theology or of undermining one's security in useless acts of worship? Such difficulties cause many not to bother addressing the issues of spiritual failures in others. This has the advantage of minimizing interpersonal conflict for the moment, but it does not change the eternal destiny of those who are not in a right relationship with God. If a person really cares about another person, will there not be some effort to point out that a problem exists, to warn that person of the dire consequences of inaction, and to convince him or her to accept a different way of thinking and acting?

The prophet Amos faced some of these issues when he was called to warn the Israelites about a great punishment God was going to bring on them because of their failures. This prosperous and strong nation would soon be defeated and sent into exile. The palaces that the rich lived in would be reduced to rubble, and a strong foreign military force would humiliate the elite troops in Israel's army. Amos called the nation back to their ancient religious traditions in the Torah[1] and introduced new ideas that called for a transformation of the way his audience thought about God and their relationship to him.

But Amos communicated a revelation from God that was based on standards that were in conflict with the norms that many people were living by at that time. His words included criticisms of inadequate worship, misguided priorities, oppressive acts against the weak, and a lack of holiness. His messages were not given to degrade or ostracize the listeners, but to help people understand God's view of reality, to warn them of the judgment God would bring on the nation, and to cause a remnant of the people to change their behavior and turn to God. Amos wanted people to love God with all their heart and to live like God's people in his chosen land, but they would not be able to do this if they continued in their sinful ways.

Amos's message was a call to recognize the deceptive nature of some of the people's failures. The prophet earnestly prayed for his listeners, lamented, and wept over what he saw coming on the land of Israel. He tried to motivate his brothers and sisters to transform their theology and personal behavior to avoid God's hand of punishment.

When we read what Amos said and wrote, it is clear that he was speaking to an ancient people group who lived over twenty-five hundred years ago in a different part of the world. Their culture was very different from the jet age we live in, and they spoke in a Hebrew dialect. Thus this commentary, and any interpreter who wishes to communicate what God was saying through the prophet, must pay careful attention to their world of ideas. What did the prophet's message mean to his audience at the capital city of Samaria? What was the economic, political, social, and religious situation in the northern nation of Israel? How did these people construct their view of reality?[2] What was the nature of the theological problems being addressed in each of his sermons? How did he communicate to convince people to change their thinking and behavior?

In revisiting the world of the prophets we must try to imagine their setting so that we can relate the principles in the prophet's message to our cul-

---

1. The Heb. word *torah* has frequently been translated "law" and consequently the idea is sometimes viewed in a legalistic way. Although it can have this connotation, the idea is drawn from the concept of the "teachings, instructions" that were given by God in the first five books of the Hebrew Bible. These revelatory teachings formed the foundation for all of Israel's theology, so Ps. 119:97 can talk about the psalmist's love for God's instructions and Paul (Rom. 7:14) refers to God's "law" as spiritual.

2. P. Berger and T. Luckmann, *The Social Construction of Reality* (New York: Doubleday, 1966), recognize that each group's view of reality is socially constructed by the traditions, experiences, and culture of that group.

ture and our own personal lives. What can we learn from the failures of the Israelites during these years? Do the sermons of the prophet address basic issues that people still struggle with today? Can we discover something about effective strategies for sharing the truth God gave with audiences that fail to serve him? Does the spiritual life of the prophet and his view of ministry set an example for me in some area of my ministry? What areas of thinking is God trying to transform in my life? In order to do this we must go back to the time of Amos and gain some appreciation of the world in which he lived.

Israelite Society During Amos's Ministry

Worship in Bethel

IF ONE WERE able to ask Amos what happened when he went to preach at the city of Bethel, he might tell about his experiences at the temple. Bethel, meaning "house of God," received its name because Jacob saw a vision of angels going up and down a great stairway, with God himself at the top. At this place God declared that Jacob would receive the great promise of Abraham (Gen. 28:10–22).[3] But this sacred place where God appeared had changed dramatically since Jacob's day. The northern nation of Israel had separated from Judah after the death of Solomon (1 Kings 11–12). Jeroboam son of Nebat, commonly called Jeroboam I, became the ruler of the new nation of Israel. In order to maintain national loyalty, he built new temples at the northern end of his kingdom (at Dan) and at the southern end (at Bethel). He put a golden calf in each temple to represent the God who brought them up from the land of Egypt (cf. Ex. 32), anointed non-Levitical priests to serve in these temples, and instituted new feasts that replaced those celebrated in Solomon's temple in Jerusalem.

New pagan innovations were introduced some years later by King Ahab and his wife Jezebel, when they built a temple in honor of the Canaanite god Baal in the capital city of Samaria (1 Kings 16:29–34). During these years the prophets of God were murdered and the prophets of Baal and Asherah were accepted by the common people and in the king's palace (18:13, 19). The prophet Elijah fought against the influential Baal prophets, and King Jehu tried to eradicate this pagan worship from Israel by destroying the temple in Samaria. But many people continued to embrace it (only seven thousand rejected Baalism in Elijah's day; see 1 Kings 19:18; 2 Kings 10:18–28).

This legacy of perverted syncretism, which mixed the worship of Baal, the golden calf, and Yahweh together, still existed when Amos spoke at the

---

3. V. P. Hamilton, *The Book of Genesis 18–50* (NICOT; Grand Rapids: Eerdmans, 1995), 236–49, traces Jacob's experiences at Bethel, the former city of Luz.

temple in Bethel in 765–760 B.C. (Amos 7:10–17). Amos not only condemned the worship of other gods (5:26; 8:14) but also questioned the motivations of those who claimed to be worshiping Israel's God. They seemed to give their tithes in order to be noticed for their generosity, not to turn truly to God in repentance with their whole heart. They would sing and sacrifice at the temple without any sense that their theology should influence the way they treated people after the worship service (4:4–13; 5:21–24). Amos believed there was a need for the Israelites to transform both their worship and daily behavior. He wanted them to seek God so that they could live (5:4).

Politics in Samaria

WHILE AMOS WAS in Israel preaching, he was confronted by Amaziah, the temple priest (7:10–17). The priest not only kicked Amos out of the temple but sent a message about Amos's treasonous words to Jeroboam, the king of Israel (commonly called Jeroboam II). Politics determined what was politically correct in "the king's sanctuary and the temple of the kingdom" (7:13); any words against the king or official practices at his temple were strictly forbidden.

There is no evidence that Amos ever met Jeroboam II or condemned him personally, but he knew of his military fame and predicted the end of his reign in the near future. Thus, it seems best to date Amos's ministry in the second half of the reign of this king (around 765–760 B.C.), after he defeated the neighboring nations and was able to establish Israel as a wealthy nation.[4]

Many people supported Jeroboam II because he brought freedom from oppression and prosperity to the nation. Before his reign, Israel had suffered under the weight of Syrian domination (2 Kings 10:32; 13:3, 7), but God was gracious to Israel and did not completely destroy the nation (13:22–23). Jeroboam II gained considerable political and military power in the region because Syria was defeated around 800 B.C., and Assyria had a series of weak kings who were more concerned about threats on their northern borders.[5] This allowed Uzziah, king of Judah, to equip an army of 307,500 elite troops and gain great prosperity through military victories

---

4. J. H. Hayes, *Amos, The Eighth-Century Prophet: His Times and His Preaching* (Nashville: Abingdon, 1960), 16–27, places Amos later, around 750 or later. H. W. Wolff, *Joel and Amos* (Hermeneia; Philadelphia: Fortress, 1977), 274–75, dates 6:2 after Tiglath-Pileser III defeated Hamath in 738 B.C., but this text can be explained without supposing that Amos (or a redactor) preached (or edited) this message in Judah at this late date. J. D. W. Watts, "The Origin of Amos," *ExpT* 66 (1954–55): 109, speculated that Amos 8–9 were written by Amos in Judah after the fall of Samaria in 722/721 B.C., but the background of Amos does not fit such a late date.

5. S. H. Paul, *A Commentary on the Book of Amos* (Hermeneia; Minneapolis: Fortress, 1991), 1–2.

(2 Chron. 26:1–15; Isa. 2:6–7). Jeroboam II was just as powerful, extending the borders of Israel to Hamath in the north, as Jonah the prophet predicted (2 Kings 14:25; Amos 6:14).

The military and political strength of Israel under Jeroboam II was a source of great pride and resulted in a smug feeling of complacency by the wealthy (6:1–2). This attitude of superiority created a stumbling block that prevented people from taking Amos's messages of God's future destruction of the nation seriously (2:13–16). The weak political status of Syria and Assyria made his claim that Israel would go into exile beyond Damascus seem preposterous (5:27). They thought that Israel's army would have no trouble defeating the "superpowers" of that day.

Economics in Israel

SINCE AMOS WAS a businessman before he became a prophet (a manager of shepherds and a grower of figs, 7:14), he was interested in the dynamics of Israel's national economic system. He saw how the geographic expansion of Israel's borders led to a new supply of tribute from defeated enemies and a demand for expanded trade for expensive items by the wealthy. As financial resources grew, a new affluent class of merchants and government officials gained economic control of Israel. Amos was overwhelmed by their wasteful and luxurious lifestyle and ashamed of their magnificent palace fortresses and winter homes full of the finest ivory furniture (3:15; 5:11).[6] Amos even visited one of their opulent funeral banquets, where he saw the prime meat they ate, the expensive wines they drank, the wild music they played, the imported oils they used, and the ivory inlays on the furniture they lounged on (6:4–6).

Amos also met individuals on the other side of the economic scale. He saw the poor, oppressed by merchants who cheated them with dishonest scales and mistreated by wealthy landlords who charged high rents for the use of farm land (5:11; 8:4).[7] The poor were especially hard pressed because God had sent various plagues on the land, which devastated their agricultural means of making a living (4:4–10). Much of what the poor had was taken from them by the upper class, and no one pitied them.

---

6. N. Avigad, "Samaria (City)," *The New Encyclopedia of Archaeological Excavations in the Holy Land*, 4 vols. (Jerusalem: Israel Exploration Society & Carta, 1993), 4:1300–10; J. D. Purvis, "Samaria," *ABD*, 5:914–21; G. E. Wright, "Samaria," *The Biblical Archeologist Reader*, vol. 2, ed. E. F. Campbell and D. N. Friedman (Garden City, N.Y.: Doubleday, 1964), 248–57.

7. B. Lang, "Social Organization of Peasant Poverty in Biblical Israel," *JSOT* 24 (1982): 48–58, believes that rent capitalism was the primary system that led to the problem Amos condemned. The urban property owners apportioned land to peasants at such high rents that the poor farmer was kept in continual poverty.

Amos did not preach political revolution or lead the poor on economic boycotts. One might assume that the poor appreciated his criticisms of the injustices against them, but there is no indication in his sermons of any support from among the poor. His main purpose was not to lobby for economic revolt by the poor; he was sent to announce God's judgment on Israel and to call for spiritual transformation that would influence economic, social, and religious behavior.

Social Relations in Israel

PERHAPS AMOS PREACHED in Israel for only a year, but he observed what was happening to people in Bethel, Samaria, and the little villages and farmsteads he visited. Amos found that the social relationships among people were no longer governed by principles found in the Mosaic covenant instructions. Society changed from following the principles of justice and care for the weak to a much more selfish and aggressive approach.

Amos was most disturbed by the pervasive oppressive behavior against the poor and disadvantaged people in the ancient Near Eastern world. This violence was seen in the cruel ways nations treated innocent civilians during wars (1:3–2:3) and in the way Israelites took advantage of one another. One could go to the temple in the evening at Bethel and see the rich wearing the clothes of the poor. These garments were given to assure that the debtor would repay his debt, but they were not returned in the evening as they were supposed to be (2:8). If you went to a court proceeding, you might see someone bribing a judge to win a case against another person who was actually innocent (5:12). The wealthy upper class was guilty of violence so that they could maintain their lifestyle. It almost seemed as if they did not know the difference between right and wrong (3:9–10).

Amos's Ministry in Israel

Amos's Background

AMOS CAME TO Israel from the small city of Tekoa, a village in Judah about ten miles south of Jerusalem. This was close enough to Jerusalem to permit visits to the temple on feast days and Sabbaths, but far enough away not to be directly influenced by many of the political events taking place there. Amos's worldview developed in this small rural city that had a military fortification to protect Judah's southern flank (2 Chron. 11:5–12). It provided him with the opportunity to learn information about earlier military battles and to hear a war oracle before the local troops headed out for battle (cf. 1:3–2:16).

The topography around Tekoa was dry and uninhabitable to the east by the Dead Sea. To the west were the rocky rolling hills that were suitable for grazing sheep and goats. Before Amos became a prophet, he was a shepherd and one who cared for sycamore figs—these grew in the lower elevations of the Shephelah to the west (1 Chron. 27:28) and in the Jordan Valley north of the Dead Sea (Amos 1:1; 7:14). The word for shepherd (*nqd*) is a relatively rare word, which refers to one who manages shepherds, so Amos probably had a middle-class job and was not a poor, ignorant peasant.[8] God called him from his secular responsibilities to be a prophet to the neighboring nation of Israel (7:14–15). From a modern perspective, some might consider him one of the earliest foreign missionaries. This event transformed his life and required him temporarily to leave his way of life and travel north to Israel to speak for God.

In Israel, Amos had to communicate with people who thought differently from him, who had cultural and religious practices that were inconsistent with his worldview, and whose behavior was based on theological principles he could not accept. As a prophet, he knew that God spoke to him and that he was responsible to speak what God communicated to him (3:7–8).

But Amos's purpose was not just to say the words he was supposed to say and go home. He needed to communicate God's intention to destroy Israel with clarity and power, but he also wanted to change the thinking and behavior of some in his Israelite audience. If he was going to speak to their needs and present God's thoughts in the most persuasive manner, he would need a thorough background in the culture of his Israelite audience. He would want to listen to what people were saying, observe what they did, talk to people in many different occupations to find out how they thought, go to the temple with them, watch them worship, and learn their way of looking at life.

There is evidence that Amos did all this, for he visited the temple in Bethel (7:10–17), attended a funeral banquet in Samaria (6:1–7),[9] and observed how the wealthy treated the poor and practiced violence in their homes (2:6–8; 3:9–10). He also used literary forms of speech like the war oracle (1:3–2:16) that the people were familiar with from military speeches. If Amos hoped to change his audience through his preaching, he would need to argue his case in terms that made sense to the listener and depend on the Spirit's power to transform the people's hearts.

Amos's Preaching

AMOS'S MINISTRY COVERS less than two years (1:1), somewhere between 765–760 B.C.; in fact, it is probably only several months long. He gives his sermons

---

8. P. Craigie, "Amos the *nōqēd* in Light of Ugaritic," *Studies in Religion* 2 (1982): 29–32.
9. Paul, *Amos*, 212.

at two key cities: Samaria, the capital and center of Israelite government (probably 1:3–6:14), and Bethel, a center of Israelite religion (7:1–9:15). He spoke two years before a great earthquake hit the nation and devastated many government buildings, temples, and private homes.[10] The solar eclipse recorded in Assyrian annals in 763 B.C. may have helped Amos to describe the cosmic events that await the nation (4:13; 5:8; 8:9). This general date fits the second half of the reign of Jeroboam II, who was involved in the military expansion of the nation's borders in earlier years. By 765–760 B.C. these battles were over, and the upper class in Israel was enjoying the fruits of military victories and living in great prosperity.

The sermons preserved from Amos's preaching demonstrate a familiarity with events recorded in the Pentateuch, especially God's covenant with his chosen people. The prophet condemns them for not following God's stipulations in the covenant (2:4), such as not returning a garment taken in pledge (2:8; see Ex. 22:26–27; Deut. 24:12–13). He sees the powerful crushing the weak into the dust (Amos 2:7) rather than sharing with them (as required by Ex. 22:21–23; Deut. 16:11, 14). He reminds the nation of the Exodus traditions, God's care for them in the desert journey, and his destruction of the tall and strong Amorites in the land (Amos 2:9–11; see Ex. 14–18; Num. 13–14; Deut. 1; 29). He refers to the creation of the earth (Amos 4:13), the destruction of Sodom and Gomorrah (4:11), the plagues in Egypt (4:10), and the Nazirite vow (2:11).

Amos connects natural disasters with covenant curses (4:6–11), reviews the Day of the Lord traditions (5:18–20), and recalls the Davidic promises (9:11–14). He is therefore deeply steeped in the religious traditions of Israel, which suggests that his audience has at least some knowledge of and appreciation for these sacred traditions. These traditions remind the listeners of what God has done for them and point out false and deceptive interpretations that some people give to their traditions. They legitimate the prophet's claims that God will punish them for failure to follow previous instructions. Amos firmly grounds his sermons on what God has said earlier so that his messages will have maximum persuasive power.

Amos's preaching is highlighted with literary devices that give rhetorical punch to what he is saying. With irony he puts some sting into his words to the wealthy women, who boss around their husbands and oppress the needy. He irreverently compares them to the well-fed "cows of Bashan" (4:1). He characterizes the wealthy merchants as people who can hardly wait till the Sabbath is over, so they can get to the market to cheat more people with

---

10. Y. Yadin, *Hazor II: An Account of the Second Season of Excavation, 1956* (Jerusalem: Magnes, 1960), 24–26, 36–37.

deceptive weights (8:4–6). He spices up his visions with wordplays between *qayiṣ* (summer fruit) and *qeṣ* (the end, 8:2). By repeatedly using the word "first" in "the foremost nation" (6:1), "the finest lotions" (6:6), and "the first to go into exile" (6:7), Amos ironically shows that those who are first in privilege will be the first to experience the degradation of defeat. It is only poetic justice that they should suffer first. Another technique Amos uses is that of quoting what others think (e.g., 9:10).[11]

Finally, Amos loves to surprise people, to throw them a curve ball that will force them to rethink their theology. He does this by reversing the way they usually look at something. This technique of preaching is illustrated in 3:1–2, where Amos quotes the positive theological themes that God miraculously delivered Israel from Egypt and called them to be God's special people from among all the families of the earth. What a wonderful, affirming message of God's grace. Many Israelites thought that this automatically assured them of God's continued protection and favor in the coming years, for they are God's people.

But then Amos takes this same idea and reverses its message by reminding his audience that great privilege requires accountability before God's blessing can be received. God does not automatically supply an unending guarantee of blessing to those who reject him. The covenant relationship is a mutual commitment of love, with reciprocal devotion that cannot be turned into an absolute and eternal promise that has no connection to the emotional or behavioral responses of the people of Israel.[12] This idea is somewhat revolutionary and unwelcome.

Consequently, Amos comes back to this idea near the end of the book (9:7–10), when he claims that other nations like Philistia and Aram (Syria) have also had exodus experiences. If God has done this for other nations, is Israel really that special? Does having an exodus experience guarantee a nation a special place in God's eyes? No, but one key is the sinfulness of a nation, for God will eventually destroy all sinful kingdoms (9:8). These surprising ways of looking at reality are the prophet's wake-up call to his audience. They must change their culture's way of thinking and get in touch with God's perspective.

---

11. G. V. Smith, *Amos* (Fearn, Scotland: Christian Focus, 1998), 18–27, contains additional information on the nature of the Hebrew text and Greek translation of Amos, its style, and various structural methods of arranging the oracles in the book.

12. Berger and Luckmann, *Social Construction*, 89–91. This process of absolutizing conditional promises is a reification. Reification happens when people do not see parts of social reality as human creations based on social relationships, but give them an independent status separate from human relationships. Thus the blessings of the covenant are seen as an absolute fact, not based on one's relationship to God.

Amos's Purpose

THE BOOK OF Amos never states the purpose for writing down the prophecies Amos spoke in Israel; in fact, the book never clearly states who actually did write down these oracles. Since print media is so common today, we tend to look at this as a natural thing to do and assume that all prophets recorded their messages. This is not the case, for Amos may be the first written text of a Hebrew prophet's messages. He started a new trend, which became the standard practice for later prophets. There is no record that God told him to write out his sermons, but the dramatic earthquake that took place two years after his sermons (1:1) may have given his prophetic words about a coming earthquake (possibly in 2:13; 8:8; 9:5) such stature that people wanted to know exactly what Amos said. Although some critical scholars question whether Amos wrote all of the sermons contained in this book, I do not believe the evidence supports the view that there was a long editorial history for the composition of these sermons.[13]

Since we do not have much information about the writing of this book, it is important to understand what Amos's purpose is in preaching these sermons in Israel. His mission or commission is to "go, prophesy to my people Israel" (7:15), but the key themes in his sermons suggest that his central responsibility is to warn the people about God's roaring attack that will bring the nation to an end (2:13–16; 3:8, 11; 5:2, 18, 27; 6:7, 14; 7:9, 11, 17; 8:3). This is astonishing news, for the people of God think that God loves them and will protect them from foreign threats. This news of the demise of the nation seems an impossibility for a rich and powerful nation like Israel. It runs contrary to everything the people have been taught and everything they are presently experiencing. This message seems out of touch with reality.

Amos wants people to rethink their theology and change their view of God's dealings with Israel. Thus, he has several themes or strategies in his preaching. (1) Amos questions the prevalent view that Israel has a sacred, untouchable, and indestructible status based on ancient covenant and Day of the Lord traditions (3:1–2; 5:18–20).

(2) He probes the true nature of the people's worship of God. Is it a genuine turning to God or something different (4:4–5; 5:21–26)?

(3) He draws the attention of the wealthy in the land to the violence and injustices that they perpetrate (2:6–12; 4:1–3; 5:11–14; 8:4–6). If they see

---

13. H. W. Wolff, *Joel and Amos*, 106–13, traces the redactional history of the book through six editorial stages that stretch from 750 to 450 B.C. Paul, *Amos*, 16–24, and G. V. Smith, *Amos*, 25–27, 65–68, 110–14, 357–58, present evidence to support the unity and authenticity of Amos's oracles. G. F. Hasel, *Understanding the Book of Amos* (Grand Rapids: Baker, 1991), 91–99, surveys the different views on this issue.

this behavior as unacceptable to God, maybe they will "hate evil, love good; maintain justice in the courts" (5:15).

(4) He attempts to destroy the upper classes' trust in their wealth, pride in their military achievements, and security in their grand homes (6:1–14). These cannot save anyone, and each will be taken away if the nation does not change.

(5) He reminds everyone that the coming destruction of the nation of Israel does not mean that God's covenant promises will never be fulfilled. The promised time of peace and prosperity will come in the future, sometime after Israel's destruction (9:11–15).

Each of these issues raises questions about God's intention to end the nation of Israel. Through these strategic approaches, Amos is able to communicate in a persuasive manner what God will do and why he is doing it. This provides the audience with information on God's future plans for Israel and gives them an opportunity to change their theology and behavior.

Amos's Intercession

IN ADDITION TO his sermons, Amos receives five visions (7:1–9:4) that graphically portray the coming end of Israel. In the first two visions (7:1–6) he delays God's judgment of a locust plague and huge fire by interceding for the people of Israel. Amos prays, "Sovereign LORD, I beg you, stop! How can Jacob survive? He is so small!" (7:5). In both cases Amos knows that the people of Israel do not deserve God's mercy. He is aware of God's intention to end this wicked people. They have not repented of their sins and fully deserve God's wrath. In spite of this, his heart goes out to the people. He cares about them; he wants to see them change their lives and avoid these terrible judgments.

Like the prophet of old, Moses, who interceded for the children of Israel at the golden calf (Ex. 32–33), Amos identifies with these people and moves God to relent concerning these plagues. Amos stands in the gap and extends God's mercy twice so that his audience will have another chance to respond to God. In the third vision God reveals that he will spare them no longer (7:8), so Amos knows the possibility of holding back God's hand is now past.[14]

Amos's Theology

THE THEOLOGY IN these sermons is a practical theology that interacts with what the audience thinks and how they relate to other people. Amos's theological methodology is to intertwine the common things of life with the

---

14. See B. K. Smith, "Amos," *Amos, Obadiah, Jonah* (NAC; Nashville: Broadman and Holman, 1995), 128–30, for a discussion of Amos's intercession.

listener's larger theological framework. He sees a theological connection between the things his audience knows about (wars, homes, furniture, banquets, selling grain, sacrifices, the courts, temples, kings, water, crops, and locusts) and what God is doing in relationship to their lives.

Broad theological principles can be identified, such as God as the One who formed the mountains and created the winds (4:13). These, however, are not so much theological doctrines about creation as practical statements of God's power. Amos warns that the sinful people of Israel will face the mighty power of the Creator when this judgment comes on them. Thus, his theology is a description of God's relationships with people in all aspects of their world.

God is at the center of Amos's theology. Theology is about what God does to, for, against, or with his created world. He may interact with individuals, nations, animals, places, or parts of nature. All of his relationships are affected by the fundamental belief that he is the sovereign Lord, who controls all nations on the earth; thus, Israel and all her neighbors are under his rule. Because he is in charge of everyone, he can move nations from one geographic area to another and raise up one nation to destroy another—yes, even to destroy the people of Israel, the nation he promised to bless many years earlier (3:11; 4:2–3; 5:27; 6:14; 7:17).

But God does not do this without a reason, for a basic determiner of God's relationship to a nation is that nation's sinfulness (9:8). God sees all violent behavior, and those responsible are held accountable for their sinful deeds (1:3–2:16). Although all people are dear to God (even the distant Ethiopians), some (like the Philistines, Syrians, and Israelites) are given special treatment by God (9:7). These factors suggest that Amos sees God as acting with justice on some occasions and in loving creative freedom at other times. Although God's justice is understandable because it is related to obedience or disobedience, there does not seem to be a human way to explain his gracious deeds that are undeserved.

Some of these theological beliefs are not accepted by Amos's audience, while others are applied to other nations but not to themselves (i.e., God's judgment on the Day of the Lord is for the nations but not Israel). Therefore Amos has to argue his case persuasively to show both the commonalities and differences between God's treatment of Israel and the other nations. God's special covenant relationship to Israel resulted in this people being chosen as his people (3:1–2). In great power and grace God delivered these people from Egyptian slavery and defeated their enemies so that they could possess the land of Palestine (2:8–10).

But this great privilege meant that Israel has the responsibilities to act like holy people and not like the other nations (Ex. 19:4–6). The Israelites are to treat even the weak and helpless with justice and mercy and not take advantage of them. They must worship God alone, and worship him with a transformed heart that turns toward him in praise and love (Amos 5:21–24). This meant that they are not to be conformed to the ways of their contemporaries, but must pattern their behavior after God's instructions in the Torah and his revelations through his prophets.

Amos's theology classifies people (both Gentiles and Jews) who treat others with injustice and violence as sinful people who will be judged by God (1:3–2:16). His theology will not let him approvingly smile at bribery in the courts, the rent-gouging of wealthy landlords, or the deceptive scales of the merchants. These people have sinful relationships that God despises. If they do not restore their worshipful relationship with God and consequently change their daily relationship with others, God's continued blessing on them will cease (4:6–12). They can "seek God and live" so that God may be gracious to them (5:4–6, 14–15), or they can suffer God's judgment on the Day of the Lord with the other pagans (5:18–20).

Unfortunately, most in Amos's audience are theologically blind to God's way of dealing with people because they do not have a living and dynamic relationship with God. They have a deceptive "religious" sense of well-being because of their faith heritage, but they have no mature faith development and thus are shocked by Amos's radical analysis of their faith relationships.

Amos also sees that God works through nature to accomplish his will in people's lives. God can use a locust plague, a great fire, a drought, a blight, mildew on the crops, and even an earthquake to warn people of his coming judgment (4:6–11; 8:8; 9:1). These are some of the covenant curses God said he would send if his people did not obey him (Deut. 27–28). But in the distant future, when God sets up his kingdom, the covenant blessing will be poured out on the earth so fully that wine will flow down the mountains and the reapers will not be able to keep ahead of the planters (9:11–15).

Unfortunately, some Israelites do not make the connection between their sinfulness and God's cursing of nature; thus, they do not have the spiritual insight to understand his warnings. Consequently, God reveals his secrets to Amos and sends him to warn the people. In spite of this, some Israelites reject his words and refuse to let God's prophet speak (2:11–12; 3:7–8; 7:12–13).

Amos's theology also affects the way he acts, for God has instituted a new relationship with him. When God called Amos to be a prophet, Amos responded by giving up his secular employment and going across the border to Israel (7:14–15). When God spoke, Amos felt he had to speak; he could not avoid this burning obligation (3:8). When God gives visions of destruction, a true messenger of God must communicate the message to the intended audience with accuracy and power; there can be no distortion of the truth or its implications.

The Heart of Amos's Message

HOW DOES ONE move from the experiences and theology of Amos to relate what he says to audiences and experiences in our modern context? To develop a contemporary significance of what Amos says, it is necessary to look beyond the specifics of what is being done—the bribing of officials, charging high rents, selling people into slavery for small debts, and cheating people by using two sets of weights for a scale. These sinful acts represent the moral values of the community that these individuals represent.

(1) Moral principles or ethical values guide people in Amos's audience to conclude that certain attitudes and actions are (a) acceptable in the community that establishes these mores, (b) consistent with the moral absolutes God requires, or (c) the kind of behavior that will promote the welfare of an interest group. But when circumstances change in a society, pressure is exerted on one's values, for there may be no predetermined norms that identify the proper response in a new context. People will then argue over what is the best, ideal, or right behavior. It is not always clear how one should react to the gray areas presented in some situations. In these settings people honestly struggle to know what is best.

At other times, however, there is no gray area involved, and the community is not facing a new situation where the proper moral reaction is still being debated. People sometimes purposely reject or pervert what is known to be right; they are no longer concerned about ideals such as the good of the whole, the stipulations of God, or sanctions from the community. Values like pride, greed, self-interests, gaining wealth at any cost, maintaining one's status regardless of the pain it causes others, military might as more important than what is right, and deceitfulness can replace moral commitments widely accepted by others in the society. These broader principles are behind the accusations Amos brings against his audience. Such issues allow us to search our contemporary context today to find analogous settings where we can address the values that govern on the societal level as well as in individual relationships.

(2) Another area where the preaching of Amos presents principles that can be developed into issues for application to contemporary situations relates to the deceptive understanding that people develop to justify their worldview. In Amos's context the issues arose from: (a) a deceptive way of looking at God's earlier promises of peace and prosperity as an absolute blessing unrelated to the people's covenant behavior (3:1–2; 9:7–10); (b) their notion that they will be guaranteed the rewards of God's kingdom on the Day of the Lord regardless of their present action (5:18–20); (c) their deceptive view that their present wealth and military power will secure their future against

destruction (6:1–14); and (d) the false view that one can actually worship God by going through the ritual and not turning oneself fully to God (4:1–13).

The heart's ability to deceive is legendary (Jer. 17:9), and this fundamental problem will permit us to inquire about deceptions that parade around as truth in our culture. Some false perceptions may exist in our understanding of Scripture (like the Israelites' misunderstanding of the covenant relationship) as well as in our estimation of how God views what we do and say. Honesty can be painful, and facing the tricky process of evaluating our emotions, motivations, and deeply held assumptions can be difficult. Nevertheless, two of the most important things we can do is (a) to commit ourselves to the lifelong task of transforming our minds from conformity to the secular culture, and (b) to insulate ourselves from the false security of the quasi-Christian subculture that can ensnare us.

(3) A third area where principles can be developed comes from Amos's theological and rhetorical method of persuasively interacting with the thinking of his audience.[15] How does he attempt to transform their practical theology of living their daily lives? How does one address the underlying failures and sins that beset the church today? What rhetorical skills and communication practices will enable the Spirit to penetrate the hearts of listeners who may be defensive, uninterested, offended, threatened, or openly hostile to our application of God's Word to their situation? How does spiritual transformation take place, and what is our role in encouraging it? Can general principles of persuasion used by Amos be used to bring about change in our settings?

Challenges for the Modern Church

CONTEMPORARY ANALOGIES THAT allow the application of broader principles in these three areas are present in the settings of most churches. Such applications will vary from community to community, but if we carefully analyze the culture of our communities and reexamine our exegesis of the Bible, transformation may be possible. Kosuke Koyama suggests in his *Water Buffalo Theology*[16] that effective change is unlikely in our world if there is no commitment to these two tasks. We must first think about how Amos's questions about Israel's moral values and deceptive beliefs relate to our culture. Then, following Amos's example of questioning whether Israelite ways were consistent with the expectations in the Mosaic covenant, we must compare the behavior

---

15. G. V. Smith, *An Introduction to the Hebrew Prophets: The Prophets as Preachers* (Nashville: Broadman and Holman, 1994), 5–24, discusses the rhetorical aspects of communication theory illustrated in prophetic preaching.

16. K. Koyama, *Water Buffalo Theology* (Maryknoll, N.Y.: Orbis, 19), 91.

and beliefs of people today with biblical principles. Once we know what is needed, a strategy for persuasion can be developed and implemented.

What Are Our Values?

SOME YEARS AGO John Naisbitt's study of *Megatrends* described ten factors that will lead to the restructuring of American society.[17] Most of these related to technology, globalization, and political changes. On the surface they seem to have little to do with a major change in values. Yet under each of these reorienting movements is an underlying change in principles that people find important. The movement to a more technological sophistication is not motivated simply by the fact that someone invented it. Innovations are accepted because they have the value of making life more enjoyable, productive, and cost-efficient, or they make products or services more attractive to consumers.

Some employers have found that it is advantageous (they value higher productivity), for example, to move to a more participatory relationship with employees because they know that workers value privacy, free speech, due-process procedures, equal pay for equal work arrangements, and other worker-rights agreements. It does not matter whether the issue is economic, political, or religious; values are implicitly an important part underlying almost every change we make. Although we may not consciously identify how the restructuring of some part of our life will affect our moral values, there is no way to prevent the transformations of our world from having an impact on what is valued.

Like Amos, we must stop and examine what values are determining decisions that impact our lives. What principles support each new suggestion or policy? What ethical values are being promoted, and what is of secondary importance? Are these changes consistent with the divine values that God has provided in Scripture? What changes can be made in what we are doing to make our actions more consistent with scriptural values?

Changes in moral values are evident in many secular magazines and television, and we as Christians confront them no matter where we live or work. George Barna's surveys of over one thousand Americans (825 claimed to be Christians) uncovered some disturbing facts about their view of absolute truth. He found that 28 percent of those interviewed "strongly agreed" with the statement that "there is no such thing as absolute truth," while another 38 percent said they "agreed" (a total of 66 percent in all). Surprisingly, 23 percent of those who claimed to be "born again" Christians "strongly agreed" that there is no absolute truth. Within the Christian and non-

---

17. J. Naisbitt, *Megatrends: Ten New Directions Transforming Our Lives* (New York: Warner, 1982).

Christian Baby Busters age group, 73 percent "agreed" with this statement. This view has infiltrated the church at large (59 percent agree) and society as a whole (81 percent agree).[18]

These statistics can be used to suggest a reason why people's values are mixed up and not based on biblical guidelines, yet 70 percent of the adults questioned "agreed" or "strongly agreed" that "the Bible is the written word of God and is totally accurate in all it teaches."[19] This paradox suggests an unwillingness by many of these "Christian" people to let the totally accurate word of God function in their lives as absolute truth in determining the values and choices they make. This is perhaps not dissimilar to Amos's situation. He is addressing Israelites from the chosen nation of Israel who know about earlier Pentateuchal guidelines that identify what is ethically acceptable, yet they are not living according to these principles.

In recent years there has been a deluge of authors decrying the moral decline in values. William Bennett of the Heritage Foundation reported a 560 percent increase in violent crimes and a 400 percent increase in illegitimate births in the United States from 1960–1993. Educational achievement in schools is not keeping up with other nations, and "there is a coarseness, a callousness, a cynicism, a banality and a vulgarity to our time. There are too many signs of a civilization gone rotten."[20]

Richard Eckersley's research into drug abuse, crime, unemployment, suicide, and child-abuse problems in American culture concludes that these are signs that the culture has "failed to provide a sense of meaning, belonging, and purpose in our lives, as well as a framework of values. People have to have something to believe in and live for, to feel they are a part of a community and a valued member of society, to have a sense of spiritual fulfillment."[21] When values get cut loose from a solid foundation and become the free choice of each person, it is not hard to predict what will happen. Soon the thoughts and attitudes that motivate people will be based on what is important to them at that moment. Inevitably some will value themselves over others, pleasure over work, spending money instead of saving it, and freedom to do their own thing in place of commitment.

Values such as these breed the worst kind of relativism, the kind in which everyone has an equal right to determine his or her own moral preferences without regard to the welfare of others or the good of the community. When there are no rules, when relationships do not count, when there is no

18. G. Barna, *The Barna Report: What Americans Believe* (Ventura, Calif.: Regal, 1991), 83–85.
19. Ibid., 292.
20. W. J. Bennett, "Commuter Massacre, Our Warning," *Wall Street Journal* (Dec. 10, 1993).
21. R. Eckersley, "The West's Deepening Cultural Crisis," *The Futurist* (Nov./Dec. 1993), 10.

imaginative vision of what the future could be, life can become hopeless, valueless, and meaningless.

Amos argues that certain values in Israel are wrong and are producing behaviors that are unacceptable. Even irreligious people can see the wrong motivations in the behavior of others and criticize the shortcomings of another person. Everyone has a conscience and a basic sense of right and wrong that object when powerful people take advantage of weaker people. It is not hard to recognize when a boss or fellow employee does not treat customers fairly by selling them a defective product. Most conclude that promotions to elderly people that promise prizes if a large entrance and processing fee is paid are nothing but rip-offs.[22]

Most people think of their medical doctor as an honest and trustworthy person, who knows the importance of good interpersonal relations and operates on the basis of ethical principles that cause people to trust him or her. One would not expect the family doctor to make deceptive claims on a résumé about doing research in an area that was never studied. No one would want that doctor to perform surgery on them if he or she had not actually done the studies to become an expert in that area. Yet a University of Pittsburgh School of Medicine study found that 20 percent of the applicants for a medical fellowship lied about their research credentials and 30 percent fabricated information about articles published in professional medical journals. Dr. Gail Sekas, the coauthor of this study in the *Annuals of Internal Medicine*, said, "I guess I'm a little naive, but I thought doctors were a bit more honorable."[23]

We need to look not only at the inadequacies in the value system of our culture, but ask what positive values need to be emphasized. What virtues can we promote to prevent similar problems in our society and in our churches? What passages in the Old and New Testament can we find to help us develop principles for a biblical value system? Are the virtues we practice just based on personal choice, or are there virtues that have universal and eternal value? Can each person decide for himself or herself what he or she wants to value, or do some other criteria regulate behavior? Can society exist if everyone individually chooses a personal set of values? Is God not the true source of values for a Christian?

Deceptive Theology

IT WOULD NOT be hard to find a Baptist who might say that his Presbyterian brother in the church down the street was misguided on his view of baptism

---

22. M. J. Harris, "Elder Fraud," *Money* (Nov. 1995), 145–50.

23. R. Winslow, "Hypocritical Oath: Study Finds Doctors Lied on Resumes," *Wall Street Journal* (July 3, 1995), B8.

(and the feeling would probably be mutual). But usually people are charitable and do not say that the other person has a deceptive or false theology, just a lack of insight into the full meaning of several passages. We can allow for differences of opinion on some issues and still maintain a certain level of Christian fellowship with one another. Amos probably makes the same exceptions for people who do not vocalize every Hebrew word in the Bible just as he does.

But when Amos deals with his audiences at Samaria and Bethel, he realizes that certain theological beliefs have caused his listeners to so misconstrue the truth that false theological conclusions are reached. Somehow the hermeneutical process of understanding or applying what God said has missed a proper step. To Amos, a particular interpretation is definitely not the meaning God intended if the whole context of Scripture is studied.

For example, the covenant blessings God promised were real and part of the great hope of the Hebrew people, but it is false to conclude that these blessings promised to Abraham and his successors are unconditionally granted to every Israelite regardless of his or her beliefs and behavior. That view may sound good to some, but it is not based on what God said. Thus, God's final plan is to destroy all his enemies on the Day of the Lord and to bring in his kingdom for the benefit of his people. But this great hope does not ensure the future for Israelites who do not love and serve God.

Theological misconceptions and cultural blind spots in our understanding are a thorn in the side of every generation of believers. How can we be sure that we have not misconstrued the faith in some way? I imagine that there will be many people in heaven who will have to eat humble pie and admit that they were wrong about some of their interpretations. The tragedy is that some who use the Lord's name and have good intentions in their service to the church will be so deceived that they will not enjoy the pleasure of entering the kingdom (Matt. 7:22–23).

Jesus and Paul faced similar problems. Jesus condemns the Pharisees who deceptively think they can please God by tithing everything to the exact penny. This is a false belief about what God wants, for in the process they ignore justice, mercy, and faithfulness, which are far more important to God (Matt. 23:23). Paul strongly condemns those who are teaching the Galatians that certain legal requirements, plus trust in Christ, are necessary for salvation. This is a false and deceptive gospel that rips the heart out of the idea that grace is an undeserved free gift (Gal. 1–2). It is another gospel, which Paul considers anathema.

Dietrich Bonhoeffer, that great resister of Hitler's political designs, spoke out against that evil ideology, but he knew the heart of the gospel was being justified by faith, being free from sin through forgiveness, and leaving all to follow Christ. He was not impressed by some who called themselves

Christians, for "those who try to use this grace as a dispensation from following Christ are simply deceiving themselves."[24] This gets at the heart of the matter. Are we actually following Christ, or are we justifying some political or social ideology? Many times our deceptions are so much a part of who we are that only the grace of God can bring clarity and transformation.

What are some of the deceptions that parade as truth today? It is a deception to call drug use and sexually transmitted diseases mere health problems. It is deceptive for the National Association for the Education of Young People to teach children from their "Anti-Biased Curriculum" that witches have nothing to do with evil; they just use herbal remedies to help people.[25] It is a deception for the ACLU to twist the First Amendment statement that "Congress shall make no law respecting an establishment of religion or prohibiting the free exercise thereof" into "a wall of separation of church and state," which in effect creates some sort of secular state. It is significant that on the same day this amendment was passed, this same congress also passed a bill to have a national day of prayer.

Thomas Jefferson, the author of that famous "separation of church and state" phrase, was not intending to outlaw manger scenes on government property at Christmas by this law, for he later approved the use of federal funds to send missionaries to the Native Americans.[26] These deceptions that slyly change the truth into a lie today are different from the deceptions that fooled Amos's audiences, but the same fundamental problem exists. People today cannot transform their minds and behavior if someone does not open their blind eyes to the subtle lies that parade around as what is "politically correct."

Persuasive Interaction to Transform

AMOS KNOWS ABOUT the dismal state of moral values in Israel, and he is aware of some of the deceptive lies that the Israelites have easily swallowed (i.e., the false idea that Israel is too strong and God will never destroy his chosen people). In order to transform the thinking of some of his listeners, Amos knows he will have to present his ideas in such a persuasive way that his audience will reject their present understandings and accept a new way of looking at reality. Through his persuasive interaction and the Spirit's convicting and enlightening work, change is possible. Some may accept his news that God is going to destroy Israel.

---

24. D. Bonhoeffer, *The Cost of Discipleship*, trans. R. H. Fuller (New York: Macmillan, 1963), 57.

25. C. Colson, *A Dance with Deception: Revealing the Truth Behind the Headlines* (Dallas: Word, 1993), 27.

26. Ibid., 67.

As Christians interact with people at work, in their neighborhoods, or in their local school districts, they will meet some people who follow a deceptive worldview and others who support an approach that opposes biblical values. How does one interact with these people? They can be confronted and condemned, but probably this will not cause them to change their minds. There is a place for this kind of direct condemnation of those who continually refuse to listen or consider other views (Jesus did speak strongly to the Pharisees), but no one should ostracize people who can be persuaded to change their views. Change and transformation are a key goal of all preachers; we do not want to harden people in their opposition to biblical principles.

Four practical applications are evident in Amos's ministry. (1) He takes the time to understand what his audience believes. We, like Amos, must walk and talk with those we hope to reach to find out why they accept a deceptive lie. Have they thought about the implications of these positions? Have they questioned the accuracy of statements and the authority of their sources? What do they read, whom do they trust, and what is their attitude to the Bible? If we do not care enough about our audiences to find out what they believe and why they believe these things, we will probably not have much of an effect on their lives. Persuasion requires us to show the weakness in one's present way of thinking and to present a more logical or authoritative alternative. The only way one can do this is to get to know what our audience thinks.

(2) Amos cares enough about his listeners to pray for God's mercy on them, to weep when the news comes that God is going to punish them. We also must examine our heart's attitude toward those with whom we speak. Are we more interested in their condemnation and defeat? Do we not only pray for them, but even intercede on their behalf before God—even when they do not deserve God's grace? Have we wept for them? Do we care for their eternal souls, or do we just want to be proven right?

Growing up in a conservative country church, I heard that God would someday destroy the evils of the ungodly Soviet Union, but I never heard anyone praying for the salvation of their souls. Indeed, God has destroyed some of the power of the former Soviet Union, and the gospel is now preached there with great freedom, but I doubt that God's transformation of this evil empire was accomplished because of the prayers for mercy from his people. To our shame, we wanted them killed, not saved. But this is not the attitude of Amos, and it should not be part of our approach to people in our culture. They need to have someone graciously share the truth in a way that they can understand.

(3) Amos legitimates his point of view from the sacred tradition of his audience, their experience, and God's new words to him about the future. We also must give a reason for our beliefs that is understandable and supportable

by the evidence of historical experience and by the witness of clearly laid-out scriptural principles. Some people will be gullible and accept ideas that are unreasonable, but most people want to have good evidence presented to them before they will change their opinion on an issue.

For example, several years ago one of my students found himself serving a congregation that did not accept several theological positions that he found essential to biblical faith. Later he discovered that the people in his congregation had a deep respect for the writings of Wesley, so he wisely used Wesley's ideas as support for these theological positions. Such practices do not lower the value of Scripture but take people from where they are to a deeper understanding of God's eternal truth. People's minds were changed because the historical experiences of a great man of God were a powerful testimony to what God desires in the heart of a believer.

We must use the testimony of Scripture and whatever other evidence we can muster to convince people to change their thinking. Although we may draw some people closer to a better understanding of what God wants, we must always be aware that it is not our rhetoric that changes a person's will; rather, it is the work of the Spirit within them.

(4) Amos speaks with a rhetorical skill that forces people to consider the truthfulness of his case. Amos, or any person today, can speak a word of truth about an issue, but that does not mean it will be accepted. We can point out deceptive thinking or failures in moral values, or we can give solid reasons why people should change, but all too frequently nothing happens. Why? Why are people not persuaded? Because people can choose to say no to the prompting of the Spirit, the devil can steal the seed that is sown and prevent it from taking root, or the listeners may foolishly harden their hearts against change because of social embarrassment. We cannot force people to transform their lives.

Nevertheless, we can improve the receptivity of our audience by skillfully presenting our material. We can avoid putting unnecessary stumbling blocks in front of people that make it harder for them to accept a new idea. All of us have heard effective speakers and boring duds. All of us have seriously considered changing our opinion on a topic and then suddenly decided not to when the speaker foolishly said something that just does not fit. Honing one's rhetorical skills does not minimize the work of the Spirit any more than memorizing your testimony limits the Spirit's power in a witnessing context. Developing solid communication skills makes good sense if we are really interested in persuading people to change.

Outline of Amos

I. Introduction (1:1–2)

II. A War Oracle Against the Nations (1:3–2:16)
   A. Oracles Against the Foreign Nations (1:3–2:3)
   B. Oracles Against Judah and Israel (2:4–16)

III. The Verification of God's Judgment on Israel (3:1–6:14)
   A. The Relationship Between Cause and Effect (3:1–8)
   B. The Confirmation of Israel's Punishment (3:9–4:3)
   C. Israel's Worship Is Not Acceptable (4:4–13)
   D. A Lament over Israel, the Dead Nation (5:1–17)
   E. Woe Oracle Concerning False Hopes (5:18–27)
   F. Woe Oracle Concerning False Security (6:1–14)

IV. Visions and Exhortations of the End (7:1–9:15)
   A. Compassion in Visions of Judgment (7:1–6)
   B. Visions of Destruction Cause Conflict (7:7–17)
   C. Wailing at the End, Not Forgiveness (8:1–14)
   D. No Sinner Can Escape from God's Hand (9:1–10)
   E. The Restoration After God's Judgment (9:11–15)

Annotated Bibliography on Amos

The following brief collection of books provides helpful discussions of the key issues in interpreting Amos's preaching. A fairly complete listing of articles and commentaries is found in the books by G. F. Hasel and S. M. Paul, or in A. van der Wal, *Amos: A Classified Bibliography*, 3d ed. (Amsterdam: Free University Press, 1986).

Andersen, F. I., and D. N. Freedman, *Amos: A New Translation with Introduction and Commentary*. AB. New York: Doubleday, 1989. A long and technical study of the final form of the Hebrew text, which emphasizes rhetorical factors.

Finley, T. J. *Joel, Amos, Obadiah*. WEC. Chicago: Moody, 1990. A solid exposition with Hebrew notes at the end of each section.

Gowan, D. E. "Amos." *New Interpreter's Bible*. Pages 339–431 in vol. 7. Nashville: Abingdon, 1996. A commentary followed by pastoral reflections after each section of text.

Harper, W. R. *A Critical and Exegetical Commentary on Amos and Hosea*. ICC. Edinburgh: T. & T. Clark, 1905. A classical explanation of the higher-critical approach.

Hasel, G. F. *Understanding the Book of Amos*. Grand Rapids: Baker, 1991. A survey of eleven controversial areas of critical, historical, and theological research. It interacts with all sides of each topic.

Hubbard, D. A. *Joel and Amos: An Introduction and Commentary*. TOTC. Downers Grove: InterVarsity, 1989. A brief treatment with a good introduction.

Jeremias, J. *The Book of Amos*. Translated by D. W. Stott. OTL. Louisville: Westminster/John Knox, 1998. A higher critical examination of the composition of Amos through several redactional stages.

Mays, J. L. *Amos: A Commentary*. OTL. Philadelphia: Westminster, 1969. A short but solid treatment that attributes some portions to later writers.

Niehaus, J. "Amos." Pages 315–494 in *The Minor Prophets*, vol. 1. Ed. T. McComiskey (Grand Rapids: Baker, 1992). An exposition that heavily draws on covert covenant connections in Amos.

Paul, S. M. *Amos: A Commentary on the Book of Amos*. Hermeneia. Minneapolis: Fortress, 1991. Probably the best detailed and technical commentary.

Smith, B. K. "Amos." *Amos, Obadiah, Jonah*. Pages 23–170. NAC. Nashville: Broadman and Holman, 1995. A good survey of various interpretations of Amos.

Smith, G. V. *Amos*. Fearn, Scotland: Christian Focus, 1998. For each portion there is a discussion of the background, structure, unity, meaning, and theology.

Soggin, J. A. *The Prophet Amos*. London: SCM, 1987. A brief but detailed discussion that reports what many others have said about each section in Amos.

Stuart, D. *Hosea–Jonah*. WBC. Waco, Tex.: Word, 1987. A balanced presentation of what Amos taught, with special emphasis on Amos's use of covenant curses.

Wolff, H. W. *Joel and Amos*. Hermeneia. Philadelphia: Fortress, 1977. A detailed critical commentary that finds six redactional stages and sees Amos heavily influenced by the style and thinking of clan wisdom.

Amos 1:1–2

❧

THE WORDS OF Amos, one of the shepherds of
Tekoa—what he saw concerning Israel two years
before the earthquake, when Uzziah was king of
Judah and Jeroboam son of Joash was king of Israel.
²He said:

"The LORD roars from Zion
  and thunders from Jerusalem;
the pastures of the shepherds dry up,
  and the top of Carmel withers."

THE HEADING TO this scroll of sermons (1:1) introduces the readers to the person God uses to
deliver his message, the general audience this
message addresses, and the time when Amos
interacts with his audience. It also contains a brief thematic statement about
his message (1:2).

These two verses are not part of the message Amos spoke in Israel but have
likely been added to his sermons when they were put in written form. They
orient readers to what follows and prepare them to interpret these messages
in light of their original context. "Two years before the earthquake" places this
written document at least two years after their original proclamation. The
large earthquake mentioned has already happened and is a reminder of Amos's
predictions that God will shake the earth (2:13; 8:8; 9:1–2, 5). It verifies the
authority and truthfulness of this prophet's claims and gives people a reason
to preserve and publish his sermons.[1]

Structurally these two verses are independent of each other and are held
together only by their common interest in "the words of Amos" and in how
these words relate to the "LORD's roaring" that Amos "saw'" or perceived from
a divine source. The narrative style of verse 1 is traditional in all prophetic
superscriptions, while the poetic format of the thematic summary in verse 2
fits the form of the prophet's other messages. These two verses serve as an
introduction to the whole book.

---

1. Paul, *Amos*, 36, believes this earthquake "was interpreted as a fulfillment of some of
his prophetic oracles, and authenticated his being accepted as a true prophet."

The Superscription (1:1)

THE FIRST VERSE of most prophetic books introduces the reader to the prophet and his occupation, residence, call, audience, and general date of preaching. Each author has his own way of putting these things together. Since this is likely the earliest prophetic book, this superscription has several unique characteristics.

The first thing that catches one a little off guard is the claim that "Amos" is the one who speaks "the words." Although this is a natural way of identifying a speaker, it is not the way many later prophetic books start. They tend to focus on "the word/vision of the LORD" (Zeph. 1:1; Hag. 1:1; Zech. 1:1) rather than the human author of the words.

In this introduction the original divine source of Amos's sermonic material is emphasized by the verb "he saw" (*ḥazah*). His words have been based on the insight of divine revelation. The noun form of this root refers to "visions," but the semantic field of the verb includes both the idea of spoken and visual ideas received by prophets (cf. Isa. 1:1; 2:1).[2] The frequent introductory messenger formulas throughout these sermons verify that "this is what the LORD says," and the concluding "says the LORD your God" (9:15) reemphasizes this fundamental belief about the source of Amos's ideas.

Amos is largely unknown except for these sermons. The text says nothing about his family of origin or whether he has a wife and children (the father and family of Hosea are known to us in Hos. 1−3). He comes from Tekoa, a small rural Judean (not Israelite) village about ten miles south of Jerusalem, and we assume that he was born there. This village is located on the edge of the rugged desert area that extends to the east down to the Dead Sea. The area to the west is rocky and hilly and suitable for grazing sheep; thus, it is not unusual for Amos to be identified as one of the shepherds in this village.

The Hebrew word for "shepherd" used here (*nqd*) is a rare word in the Hebrew Bible,[3] but the word is used in Akkadian and Ugaritic texts to refer to a person of status who is in charge of a group of shepherds. This implies that Amos is not a poor, uneducated shepherd, who spends his day leading a group of sheep. He probably is a manager of shepherds, possibly for a wealthy family or the government. This pastoral background explains why he uses illustrations about birds (3:5), lions (3:12), and the separation of the grain from other foreign material (9:9). These are all a part of his daily life in his natural surroundings. His involvement in the business world before going

---

2. D. Stuart, *Hosea–Jonah* (WBC; Waco, Tex.: Word, 1987), 298, believes that Amos "perceived a revelation" that had no hint of visual content.

3. In the Old Testament, it is only used one other time—to describe Mesha, king of the Moabites, who had to pay a large tribute of sheep to the Israelites (2 Kings 3:4).

from Judah to Israel gives him insight into the way people sometimes unjustly treat others and makes him sensitive to the abuses he will observe later.

Amos's ministry is in the northern kingdom of Israel, not in his homeland, Judah. These two nations have been separate now for almost two hundred years. They have fought wars against each other and have a clear sense of their own political and religious identity. Although the Israelites still speak Hebrew, there are many cultural differences between Amos and his audience in the key cities of Samaria and Bethel.

Amos's ministry in Israel takes place during the prosperous days of the Israelite king Jeroboam II, who reigned at the same time as Uzziah in Jerusalem. The only exact date within this period is the earthquake, which took place two years after Amos preached in Israel. If this event can be connected with signs of an earthquake in the archaeological excavation of stratum VI at Hazor,[4] then a date just before 760 B.C. is a likely time for his ministry. This is well after Jeroboam's successful military campaigns to expand the borders of Israel as far north as the entrance of Hamath (6:14). These conquests have enriched the nation with tribute and trade, exactly the situation Amos observes when he visits Israel some years later.

The Theme (1:2)

THE POETIC PART of the introduction announces God's roaring revelation from Zion in what appears to be a hymnic description of a theophany[5] (possibly quoting from a well-known hymn of that time). This hymn emphasizes God's roaring voice, his thunderous appeal from Zion[6] (i.e., the temple in Jerusalem, where he resides). The imagery of roaring describes the bellowing warning that foreshadows an attack by a lion (3:4, 8). God's roaring communicates his intention to attack. This warning is equated with the words Amos speaks both here and in 3:8.

The source of this warning is the Lord God, not Baal. The prophet reveals here his Judean theological position, namely, that God speaks from his temple in Jerusalem, not from the Israelite temples in Bethel and Dan. Since Amos does not use specific Judean theological issues to argue his case elsewhere, one can probably conclude that this verse was not part of his preaching in Israel, but has been put here after his ministry was completed, when these sermons were collected in written form. Thus, this verse is not an

---

4. Y. Yadin, *Hazor II: An Account of the Second Season of Excavations, 1956* (Jerusalem: Magnes, 1960), 24–26, 36–37, dates this earthquake to 760 B.C.

5. A. Bentzen, "The Ritual Background of Amos I.2-II.16," *OtSt* 8 (1950): 85–99.

6. This statement relies on traditions about David's bringing the ark to Jerusalem (2 Sam. 6–7), Solomon's dedication of the temple (1 Kings 8), and various psalms (Ps. 46; 47; 48; 99).

attempt by Amos to convert Israelites to a Judean ideological point of view during his ministry in Israel. His warnings have a more serious intent: He is proclaiming the approaching end of the nation of Israel.

The second half of this hymnic poem focuses on the nature and extent of the prophet's warning. The thundering voice of God will not bring rain and blessing, but the curse of drought and disaster, signs of his punishment (Deut. 28:22–24; Isa. 5:6; 19:7; 42:15). God, not the Canaanite fertility god Baal, controls the land. His curse will affect even the forested hills of Mount Carmel in Israel and the pasturelands of their shepherds. What does a shepherd like Amos think when there is no grass for his sheep? When the grass is gone and the vineyards and trees of Carmel turn brown for lack of water, one must ask why. Is this not the hand of God? Is God not trying to say something to us?

FOUR PRINCIPLES. Few principles can usually be derived from the introduction of a book. The issues discussed in verse 1 are unique to this time period and this historic situation. In other words, we should not try to draw any principle for application from the fact that Amos is a shepherd and then spiritualize this into an application suggesting that everyone who shares God's word must have a shepherd's heart. Although one may find other passages that encourage people to be good shepherds of God's flock (John 21:15–16; Acts 20:28; 1 Peter 5:1–4), this is not the principle found in this passage. I propose four general principles here.

(1) Verse 1 illustrates the broad principle that God chooses regular people with common jobs, and sometimes foreigners who have to travel to a foreign land, to communicate his words to others. Amos is not a prince, the son of a priest, a well-known orator of international standing, or a person who is already well-respected in Israel. If we could ask the people in Tekoa about this fellow named Amos, they might describe him as a hard worker with a good reputation, but they would probably not suggest he is likely to become a prophet like Elijah or Nathan. God calls common people such as Amos to be his servants, and these people are not always the most qualified; they are simply people willing to speak God's words.

(2) The brief reference to the earthquake is a powerful reminder that God does what he says. Amos warns of this earthquake in his preaching, but some probably took it as prophetic hyperbole—scare tactics designed to strike the fear of God into the heart—or perhaps just an empty threat. When it does not happen immediately, many simply forget about this warning. God is patient in not bringing this judgment immediately on the people of Israel. But eventually the land does tremble dramatically, moving up and down like the Nile (8:8; 9:5).

God's words do come true. Everything he has predicted will come to pass on the day he has chosen. The prophet Isaiah makes the same point, for God says that his word will "accomplish what I desire and achieve the purpose for which I sent it" (Isa. 55:11). Jesus himself knows that everything in the Law will be accomplished, down to the smallest letter (Matt. 5:18).

(3) Verse 2 announces God's ability to control the forces of nature.[7] He is not just a God of history who marvelously redeems people from superior armies; he is also the God who has created and continues to control every aspect of this world. "The earth is the LORD's, and everything in it" (Ps. 24:1); thus, he sends both the blessing of rain and fertility and the curse of drought and death. By implication, Amos's claims devastate the Israelites' belief in the fertility and power of Baal, for he is powerless, not even worthy of mention next to the mighty power of Yahweh. God's daily providential care of nature and his unusual intrusion into the regular patterns of nature to create miracles are two primary ways of controlling the lives of people and accomplishing his will on earth.

(4) These two verses also picture God as one who reveals himself to humankind. His Word and will are known and are not a dark secret. He is near enough to communicate his wishes as well as his disappointment with his people. He can speak in many ways—from a still small voice (1 Kings 19:12-13) to sounding like a roaring lion. The analogy employed usually gives insight into the purpose of the message and lends support to the intensity of the message.

GOD'S USE OF **common people.** Many of the great men and women of God in our time started out much like Amos. They were common people who had no special status and limited potential in the eyes of their friends and family. Yet God chose them to demonstrate his power through their weakness (1 Cor. 1:27). When God chose the young shepherd boy David, his father and brothers appeared surprised. When Samuel asked to see Jesse's sons that he might anoint one as king, Jesse did not even bother to bring David in from the field. But Samuel was told that God does not look on the outward appearance, he looks on the heart (1 Sam. 16:1-10). Therefore, it did not matter that David was a common shepherd of a relatively young age.

It is easy to forget that Moses was originally a slave's son, destined to die in the Nile to reduce the number of Hebrews in Egypt. But God miraculously

---

7. R. A. Simkins, *Creator and Creation* (Peabody, Mass.: Hendrickson, 1994), traces both the biblical and ancient Near Eastern people's view of how the gods/God controls nature.

saved him from certain death when he was a helpless child (Ex. 2). Later he became a fugitive from Egypt and wandered in the Sinai desert, taking care of sheep (Ex. 3). He was not an eloquent speaker, was somewhat unwilling to be used by God, questioned if any of the Hebrews in Egyptian bondage would believe him, and feared for his life (Ex. 4−6). Nevertheless, God called him to speak his words to the Egyptian king and to lead the people of Israel out of slavery.

The famous church father Augustine, bishop of Hippo, wrote numerous foundational theological works, including *The City of God.* He defended the faith against certain teachings of Pelagius. His theology so influenced Martin Luther that he quoted him over a hundred times in his revolutionary commentary on Galatians. But Augustine did not live for God in his early years. Before he became a Christian and dedicated himself to the lifestyle of a monk, he was heavily involved with pagan philosophy, addicted to sexual gratification, and pursued worldly success. For thirteen years he lived with a woman he was not married to and later lived with another woman to satisfy his addictions.[8] Yet God delivered Augustine through the preaching of Ambrose, bishop of Milan, and he was dramatically freed from his former bondages. God took this unlikely person and changed his life.

These examples are not intended to suggest that God rejects people of status, power, and wealth. Rather, they simply demonstrate that he can use common people who do not have these characteristics. God does not seem to be as interested in our past successes or failures as in our present willingness to respond positively to his call.

The reliability of God's Word. The reference to the earthquake in 1:1 illustrates that God reveals his will to humankind and does what he says he will do (2:13; 8:8; 9:1−2, 5). This principle is seen throughout the Old and New Testaments. God said he would give Israel a land, and he did (Ex. 3; Josh. 1−14). He told Micaiah ben Imlah that King Ahab would be killed in the battle for Ramoth Gilead, and he was (1 Kings 22:1−39). Through Jeremiah God revealed that Jerusalem would be destroyed by the Babylonians, and it happened (Jer. 34:2; 39:1−10).

Do we ourselves believe and accept what Scripture says about God? No one can make another person accept something he or she is unwilling to believe, but an underlying theme of almost every sermon should be the foundational emphasis that God does what he says. It makes a difference whether you reject what God says. People who ignore God's warnings pay a heavy price. God is trustworthy and does not deceive people with empty threats.

---

8. M. R. Miles, "Augustine," *Encyclopedia of Early Christianity,* ed. E. Furguson (New York: Garland, 1990), 121−26.

Our hope is based on the belief that he will fulfill all his wonderful promises for the future.

This principle often is left as an unstated assumption that we think everyone accepts. Yet many ignore what God says and do not believe that he will actually do what he has said. Even some who call themselves Christians ignore verses to avoid facing reality, hermeneutically twist clear statements into culturally relative options that they can apply as they wish, and refuse to believe because a certain verse does not fit their mental reconstruction of who God is. Christians should allow for different interpretations of difficult verses, but they should not allow this to compromise their acceptance of what God has said. It will happen whether we believe it or not.

God's control of nature. The short thematic statement in 1:2 suggests another principle: God controls nature. Today we know that high pressure systems, the jet stream, humidity, and temperature affect atmospheric conditions to produce the weather we enjoy. Consequently, many do not see God as the power controlling these events; science has demystified the unknown and removed our need to see his sovereign power. The same thing has happened in the medical field, where doctors have explored the mysteries of how the human body works and how genetic factors influence health. When people had no understanding of these things, they left them in the hand of God. But as science began to explain them, suddenly God disappeared from the picture.

This approach to weather and medicine suggests that natural laws can explain everything. But one must ask: Who thought up all these natural laws? Who instilled them in nature centuries ago? Who regulates them? No one would look at a baseball game and say it just happened in the regular course of nature. Too many things happen the same way. There must be someone who has designed the game, there must be rules controlling what people do and there must be a coach who is advising the players to work cooperatively to win.

God is in control of nature today, just as he was in Amos's day. People may not recognize his hand or they may deny his power over certain things, but the One who made the world and owns it as his possession is still in control. Although this may seem like a primitive way of thinking to some, it is the consistent testimony of the Old and New Testaments.

This teaching requires us to recognize our true relationship to God—he is the Creator and we are creatures—and to be sensitive to his warnings. In the book of Amos God spoke volumes through the devastating droughts he sent on the land (1:2; 4:6–8), but most Israelites did not see this as his attempt to get them to repent (4:6–13). By ignoring God's working through the "accidents" of nature, we too may fail to see his subtle messages intended to wake us up.

235

Amos 1:3–2:3

❦

³This is what the LORD says:

"For three sins of Damascus,
  even for four, I will not turn back ⌐my wrath⌐.
Because she threshed Gilead
  with sledges having iron teeth,
⁴I will send fire upon the house of Hazael
  that will consume the fortresses of Ben-Hadad.
⁵I will break down the gate of Damascus;
  I will destroy the king who is in the Valley of Aven
and the one who holds the scepter in Beth Eden.
  The people of Aram will go into exile to Kir,"
                                    says the LORD.

⁶This is what the LORD says:

"For three sins of Gaza,
  even for four, I will not turn back ⌐my wrath⌐.
Because she took captive whole communities
  and sold them to Edom,
⁷I will send fire upon the walls of Gaza
  that will consume her fortress.
⁸I will destroy the king of Ashdod
  and the one who holds the scepter in Ashkelon.
I will turn my hand against Ekron
  till the last of the Philistines is dead,"
                          says the Sovereign LORD.

⁹This is what the LORD says:

"For three sins of Tyre,
  even for four, I will not turn back ⌐my wrath⌐.
Because she sold whole communities of captives to Edom,
  disregarding a treaty of brotherhood,
¹⁰I will send fire upon the walls of Tyre
  that will consume her fortresses."

¹¹This is what the LORD says:

"For three sins of Edom,
  even for four, I will not turn back ⌐my wrath⌐.
Because he pursued his brother with a sword,
  stifling all compassion,

because his anger raged continually,
and his fury flamed unchecked,
¹²I will send fire upon Teman
that will consume the fortresses of Bozrah."

¹³This is what the LORD says:

"For three sins of Ammon,
even for four, I will not turn back ⌐my wrath⌐.
Because he ripped open the pregnant women of Gilead
in order to extend his borders,
¹⁴I will set fire to the walls of Rabbah
that will consume her fortresses
amid war cries on the day of battle,
amid violent winds on a stormy day.
¹⁵Her king will go into exile,
he and his officials together,"

says the LORD.

^{2:1}This is what the LORD says:

"For three sins of Moab,
even for four, I will not turn back ⌐my wrath⌐.
Because he burned, as if to lime,
the bones of Edom's king,
²I will send fire upon Moab
that will consume the fortresses of Kerioth.
Moab will go down in great tumult
amid war cries and the blast of the trumpet.
³I will destroy her ruler
and kill all her officials with him,"

says the LORD.

THE WAR ORACLE Against the Nations (1:3−2:16) describes the sins and punishment of eight nations. It can be logically divided into two parts: six oracles against the foreign nations (1:3−2:3) and two final oracles against Judah and Israel (2:4−16). This series of highly repetitive oracles is grouped in pairs based on three elements.

(1) Family connection: Ammon and Moab came from the children of Lot (Gen. 19:30−38), while Judah and Israel were the two Hebrew nations

(2) Repeated words: "I will destroy the king . . . and the one who holds the scepter" in 1:5 and 8; offenses against one's "brother" in 1:9 and 11; and "war cries" plus the death of the king and his officials in 1:14–15 and 2:2–3[1]

(3) The stylistic construction of each pair[2]

These characteristics argue that these oracles fit together as a well-planned rhetorical argument aimed to change the Israelites' view of their future political status.[3]

Oracles against the nations are found in later prophetic books (Isa. 13–23; Jer. 46–51; Ezek. 25–32; Nahum; Obadiah), but they are primarily given to encourage a Hebrew audience to trust in God's sovereign ability to destroy the nations that threaten them or to encourage political leaders to trust God and not in alliances with these nations. Amos's oracles are related to the first purpose, but he twists what his audience thinks is a message of salvation from foreign domination into a judgment message by ending his oracle with words of Israel's demise (2:6–16).

This unique approach suggests that Amos may have patterned his words after a war oracle that prophets would give before a nation went to war (similar to the war oracles he has probably heard in the military camp at Tekoa). Before an army would march off to battle, a priest or prophet was usually asked to inquire if this was God's will (cf. Judg. 1:1–2; 20:23–28; 1 Sam. 14:18–19). The answer promised the defeat of their enemies and Israel's victory (Judg. 7:9–14; 1 Sam. 23:2, 4, 9–12). The prophets would then charge up the troops with this news so that they could face the violence of war with confidence, knowing they would win (Josh. 6:1–5; 8:1–8). Such pep talks inspired the enthusiasm of the troops as they agreed with the news of their impending victory and shouted out their approval.[4]

The setting of Amos's oracles is not identified. We assume they are given in the capital city of Samaria like all the other oracles in 1:3–6:14. Andersen and Freedman maintain that this message is given later in Amos's career and not at the beginning, but we see more evidence for treating the messages

---

1. S. H. Paul, "Amos 1:3–2:3: A Concatenous Literary Pattern," *JBL* 90 (1971): 401–3.

2. G. V. Smith, *Amos*, 64–65, outlines this stylistic pattern of short accusations, lengthy punishment clauses, and a final messenger formula in oracles 1 and 2, 5 and 6. Oracles 3 and 4, plus 7 have a long accusation, short punishment, and no final messenger clause. Oracle 8 is unique.

3. Wolff, *Joel and Amos*, 140–43, does not see this as a unified rhetorical piece but finds later redactional additions. Paul, *Amos*, 16–26, presents strong arguments against this position.

4. D. Christensen, *Transformations of the War Oracle in Old Testament Prophecy* (Missoula, Mont.: Scholars, 1975), 1–15.

in Amos as chronological.[5] The event at which Amos delivers these messages is not stated and the audience is not identified. The military nature of the war oracles and the final prediction concerning Israel's army suggest that some military officials are in the crowd. It would be ironic if Amos actually gives this to some troops before they go out to war.

Oracle Against Syria (1:3–5)

AS THE AUDIENCE listens to Amos begin his prophecy, they hear a word about the past atrocities of a Syrian military battle and that nation's future punishment for these deeds. Since his listeners know the circumstances surrounding these battles across the Jordan in Gilead and have heard about the horrendous barbarity of the Syrian troops, most would agree with what this new prophet from Judah is saying.

Amos begins by claiming to declare the word of Yahweh ("this is what the LORD says"), a credentialing formula that legitimates his message. The regular charge against each of the nations in this list is that they have sinned ($pš^c$), a word that refers to willful rebellious acts against an authority in a political (1 Kings 8:50; 2 Kings 3:5) or religious context (Isa. 1:28; Jer. 2:29). This rebellion is heightened by its continued occurrence on three or four occasions.[6] This is a pattern of detestable behavior, and God will not overlook it any longer. Because the offense is so great, his wrath[7] against them will not cease to burn against Damascus until it accomplishes justice.

The rebellious act of the Syrians that Amos mentions is undated, but it probably happened years earlier, either when Hazael took the Israelite territory around Ramoth Gilead (2 Kings 8:28–29; 10:32–33) or when Ben-Hadad conquered Jehoahaz (2 Kings 13:1–7)—or perhaps at both of these defeats! The atrocity involved the threshing of people in Gilead like grain (possibly a metaphorical statement). It was as if they ran over the people with threshing planks that had iron teeth protruding out of them to separate the grain from the stalk. What this symbolism refers to is unclear, but the

---

5. F. I. Andersen and D. N. Freedman, *Amos* (AB; New York: Doubleday, 1989), 6–8, believe the first four visions (7:1–9:10) plus chs. 4–6 were spoken before this war oracle. I see chs. 4–6 as the prophet's attempt to legitimate his claims in chs. 1–2, and I do not connect the visions with his original calling.

6. D. Stuart, *Hosea–Jonah*, 310, believes the numbered sequence simply refers to many sins while M. Weiss, "The Pattern of Numerical Sequence in Amos 1–2: A Reconsideration," *JBL* 86 (1967): 416–23, believes Amos is referring to seven sins, a typological number of completeness.

7. The word "wrath" is not in the Hebrew (it merely reads "I will not turn it back"), but the parallel terminology in Isa. 9:8–10:4 and Jer. 23:20 explains that "it" refers to God's anger. In a similar phrase God says that he "will spare them [Israel] no longer" (Amos 7:8; 8:2).

graphic imagery represents a most inhumane humiliation (treating people like stalks of grain) and harsh cruelty to people made in the image of God.

Finally, although many of these people in Gilead are Israelites, this uncivilized act by the Syrians was probably not committed against the people Amos is talking to at this time. Nevertheless, their blood boils when they are reminded of these evil deeds against other Israelites; they too see these as acts that should arouse God's anger.

The punishment Amos announces involves the destruction of the king's house and military fortresses that have given him security and protection from reprisal. The king ordered the assault; he was the commander ultimately responsible for these evil deeds. Thus, he is pinpointed as the guilty party. Fire from military conquest will destroy the protective gates of Damascus, Syria's capital. With the defeat of the king and his army, the fall of the surrounding Syrian city-states like Beth Eden is sure (Bit Adini is about two hundred miles north of Damascus on the Euphrates River).[8] Those captured in the defeat of Syria will go into exile in Kir, the place where the Arameans (Syrians) came from (see 9:7). Amos closes this brief oracle with a reminder that these are the words of the Lord for Syria—a claim that Amos's audience surely accepts, based on the content of his message and their own hatred of the Syrians.

Oracle Against Philistia (1:6–8)

LIKE ANY GOOD rhetorical sermon that wants to emphasize certain points, Amos builds on the patterns and theological support he has developed in his first oracle. The Lord has spoken again; he has seen the rebellious acts of the Philistines and will act in wrath against them for their many sins. These identical statements create a link between the speaker and the audience, because the latter now can anticipate what the speaker will say and say it with him. What is true of God's dealings with Syria is also true of his handling of Philistia.

The Philistine rebellious acts against God's authority involve capturing whole communities. Since both foreign and Israelite law allowed for taking prisoners of war (Deut. 20:10–11; 2 Chron. 28:8), the crime cannot refer to a military action in war.[9] Instead, this is a wholesale kidnapping of peaceful people for the purpose of turning a profit. These slave raids set gangs of armed thugs against defenseless rural villages, who had no one to protect

---

8. Archaeologists have found correspondence from Shamshi-ilu, the ruler of Bit-Adini from 780–752 B.C. (see Paul, *Amos*, 53). The Valley of Aven, probably the Lebanon Valley, represents the southern part of Syria while Beth Eden represents the north, so Amos is saying the whole country will fall, from south to north.

9. I. Mendelsohn, *Slavery in the Ancient Near East* (New York: Oxford, 1949).

them. These innocent people are suddenly deprived of all rights, treated like cattle, and sold to the highest bidder. The size of this atrocity and the motive for doing it condemn the Philistines. Their desire for wealth has led them to dismiss the basic value of human dignity for every person, and to repudiate the people's deep ancestral connection to the land of their ancestors. When it comes to making a buck, they seem to have no problem sacrificing moral principles to get what they want.

With a main trade route from Gaza to Beer Sheba and on to Edom, it was easy to ship these people off to other nations and collect a handsome financial reward. We can probably assume that these poor people who have been captured and sold are Israelites, though Amos does not say that, nor does his case depend on that assumption. Regardless of who they are, it is wrong to sell free people into bondage.

Philistia's punishment is similar to Syria's. God will cause the walls of its five major cities to fall; their strong military fortresses will crumble. The various kings who reign in these cities have apparently approved of these slave raids; thus, they carry a heavy responsibility and are picked out as special recipients of God's wrath. The final end of the Philistines is complete; annihilation will greet even the common people, and no one will be left.

Amos ends this oracle with a reminder that this is the message of the Lord for Philistia—a claim that Amos's audience surely accepts, based on its content and their own hatred of the Philistines.

Oracle Against Phoenicia (1:9–10)

THIS ORACLE FOLLOWS the same initial pattern as the two previous messages: God has spoken; Tyre, the leading city of Phoenicia, has rebelled many times; God will act in wrath against them. Their sin seems to be similar to the crimes of Philistia, and one wonders if Tyre, Philistia, and Edom were not in some sort of organized business of trafficking slaves. The difference between Tyre and Philistia is that Tyre is only accused of selling whole communities, not of capturing them. Thus Tyre may have primarily functioned as a middleman, brokering captured people from various nations to the highest bidder—and particularly to the Edomites.[10]

The more limited involvement of Tyre does not lessen their guilt, however, for they evidence the same callous disregard for human rights and allow their business profits to override basic moral convictions about the dignity of human life. Their sin is presented as a betrayal of friends, for the very people they have political treaties with are being sold as slaves. They are

---

10. The cooperation among these nations in selling slaves is also mentioned 150 years later in Joel 3:4–8.

"disregarding a treaty of brotherhood" with these nations. Amos does not specify which nations have this treaty with Tyre, but we know that in the preceding century Ahab's marriage with Jezebel, daughter of the king of Tyre, established a significant cooperative relationship between Phoenicia and Israel.

Although Amos does not fill us in on the details or the reasons for Tyre's action, Jehu's violent purging of Ahab and Jezebel's heirs (2 Kings 10:1–11) may have provided an excuse for Tyre to retaliate against Israel. Although this is one possible explanation, the date and the name of the people who have been enslaved are not Amos's main interest. He emphasizes the betrayal of those who have trusted in Tyre's loyal observance of her covenant relationships. Everyone hates a traitor, and Amos's Israelite audience would say "Amen" to his accusations.

The punishment statement is brief and is not followed by a final formula like the earlier oracles, but the point is clear. God will go into action against the people of Tyre, bring down the thick walls of the city, and cause its strongly fortified palace-fortresses to go up in flames. Amos's audience would certainly agree with God's decision to punish them for their sins.

Oracle Against Edom (1:11–12)

THIS MESSAGE STARTS the same as the preceding oracles: God has spoken to Amos about the rebellious deeds of the Edomites and will not reverse his determination to act against them. These people were related to the Hebrews because Esau, the father of the Edomites, was Jacob's brother (Gen. 25:21–26). This brotherhood between Hebrews and Edomites should not be seen as a political treaty relationship, for no treaty is mentioned.[11] They have a deeper, blood brotherhood with kinship obligations that demands support and love for one another.

But no love was lost between these peoples. Edom's rebellious acts involve chasing his brother with a sword, having no compassion, and exhibiting a continuous attitude of rage that flames out in an uncontrollable manner. One gets the picture that Amos is describing a mad beast with rabies that foams at the mouth in a senseless, destructive lust for blood and revenge. The deep emotional ties between brothers has turned bitter, and the familial connection has been replaced with vehement attacks of relentlessly inhumane rage.

The incidents that Amos refers to are not specified, but Scripture describes years of animosity between these two brothers. It should be noted that the Hebrews did not treat the Edomites as brothers either (2 Sam. 8:11–14;

---

11. M. Fishbane, "The Treaty Background of Amos 1:11 and Related Matters," *JBL* 89 (1970): 313–18, believes this does refer to a political treaty, but this seems unlikely.

1 Kings 11:15–16; 2 Kings 8:20–22; 14:7; 16:6). The people that the Edomites have lashed out against are not specified, but since Edom is situated east and south of the Dead Sea, its evil deeds are probably committed against Judeans from Amos's home country and not the Israelites in his audience in Samaria. Nevertheless, the Israelite listeners would agree with God's displeasure with Edom's rebellion.

The punishment clauses are brief and devastating announcements of God's intention to end the terror that Edom has unleashed on its neighbors. The key cities of Teman and Bozrah are targeted for destruction, thus removing the Edomites' prime military and economic centers. Nothing is said about who will conquer Edom or about the possibility of survivors.

Oracle Against Ammon (1:13–15)

THE FOURTH AND fifth oracles against the two tribes that descended from Lot return to the formal structure of the first two messages. This oracle announces God's word about Ammon's rebellious acts, which deserve his wrath. The Ammonites have carried out military campaigns to take control of Gilead on the east side of the Jordan but in the process have massacred innocent and defenseless pregnant women. These women are of no military value, and their slaughter is a heartless and savage act of cold-blooded murder. These acts have terrorized other people living in Gilead, causing them to leave the area so that the Ammonites can expand their borders. Such merciless inhumanity to both mother and unborn child outrages Amos and his listeners; these people deserve God's judgment.[12]

God's judgment on Ammon involves the destruction of their capital, Rabbah (modern Amman, Jordan), and the military fortresses in it. Amos foresees a great battle with blasting trumpets, shouting troops, ferocious primal yells as the battle progresses, and a great slaughter of Ammonites. It will be like a great storm, an image frequently associated with a theophany when God himself appears on the Day of the Lord to execute his wrath (Isa. 29:6; Nah. 1:3). God will enter the stream of history and change Ammon's future. Her king and officials responsible for Ammon's military policies will go into exile. Now they will suffer humiliation and know what it means to be powerless and at the mercy of others. Certainly Amos's audience would wholeheartedly approve of God's word about Ammon.

---

12. Earlier the Ammonites agreed to let the Israelites live in Jabesh-Gilead, but the Ammonites demanded that the Israelites had to let them gouge out their right eyes first (1 Sam. 11:1–2). In one text the Assyrian king Tiglath-Pileser III brags that "he slit the wombs of the pregnant women, he gouged out the eye of the infants, he cut the throats of their strong men" (see M. Cogan, " 'Ripping Open Pregnant Women' in Light of an Assyrian Analogue," *JAOS* 103 [1983]: 755–57).

Oracle Against Moab (2:1–3)

THE LAST FOREIGN nation mentioned is Moab, the sister nation of Ammon. The Moabites live just south of Ammon and just north of Edom, on the east side of the Dead Sea. Their willful rebellious act has been to burn the bones of the king of Edom, an act that did not involve any Israelites. This dese-cration of the buried bones of a royal figure was bad enough, but the Moabites have gone one step further by using the king's remains as lime, possibly to plaster the walls of a house. This was an act of total disrespect for the dead, something that no one would want to happen to anyone in their family. In the ancient Near Eastern world there was a strong sense of con-nectedness between the living and the dead who occupied the family tomb. This act broke that bond, but also the connection between a people and their political leader.[13]

God's judgment of Moab is similar to what will happen to Ammon. The military fortress at Kerioth (which also has a temple for Chemosh, their god)[14] will burn with fire, and God will defeat the Moabites in a great bat-tle. When the trumpet blows, they will yell as they charge, but God will destroy their ruler and key officials. The final "says the LORD" emphasizes again that God has spoken and thus it will happen.

Bridging Contexts

THESE POWERFUL ORACLES about the specific sins of foreign nations do not apply to any modern Middle Eastern nation today, but they do help the ancient and modern reader with insights con-cerning the broad principles that guide God's evaluation of government poli-cies that are oppressive and inhumane. The very fact that God knows exactly what each nation has done and is involved with their histories shows that he is the Lord of all nations. One might be tempted to restrict God's work and concerns to his chosen people Israel and ignore non-Israelite nations in the Hebrew Bible. Yet God reveals himself to Amos as the One who controls all nations.

These speeches suggest two primary principles that we will develop more fully below; one relates to the content of what Amos said, and the other relates to the way he said it. These oracles demonstrate that (1) God holds all nations accountable for their acts of inhumanity to individuals, and

---

13. The Greek translation could not make sense of this passage and thought Amos was condemning the Moabites for offering sacrifices to a demon, but this translation cannot be trusted here.

14. The Mesha Stone, lines 12–13, refers to this temple.

(2) Amos first identifies with the facets of his audience's theological world-view in a nonthreatening setting, so that he can later show how these theological beliefs should impact their own self-evaluation.

Nations being held accountable. Kings, presidents, prime ministers, military generals, and other persons with political and economic power have a tremendous responsibility to use their power sparingly, wisely, and with equity. Their actions show whether they value personal riches and status or service to the needs of those under them. These oracles against several ancient Near Eastern countries describe how certain leaders and officials did not judiciously set wise policies concerning the treatment of weak or innocent people. They did not wisely control the behavior of generals, troops, or gangs of lawless thugs who had the power to take advantage of other people.

Although we are still shocked when we hear about it, everyone knows that heinous acts of violence like these are committed by crazy people somewhere in this world in almost every century. But Amos is not referring to a rare deranged act of insanity by an individual. He describes national governments that support, legitimate, and foster such violence as acceptable behavior. God sees what these nations are doing and will hold them accountable for their actions. He knows what they value and put first.

Accountability is usually based on knowingly breaking a law, principle, or social expectation that a group of people has accepted as a norm for their behavior. In Amos's speech, God holds six foreign nations responsible for the barbarous treatment of defenseless people, but the prophet never mentions what laws have been broken. On the basis of terms like "treaty of brotherhood" (1:9), G. E. Wright has proposed that these nations were guilty of breaking their covenant relationship, since they were once united by covenant with Israel and a part of the larger Israelite empire during the time of David and Solomon.[15] D. Stuart has a similar view, though he assumes that God has a covenant relationship with these nations.[16]

This reasoning seems inadequate for several reasons. (1) Amos himself speaks of Israel as the only family God has chosen (3:1–2); (2) several of the nations mentioned have not committed sins against the northern nation of Israel; (3) none of these nations are condemned for their rejection of a unified Davidic empire; and (4) Tyre was never a part of David or Solomon's kingdom. It is better to follow J. Barton's suggestion that these nations are guilty of breaking laws of right and wrong that were based on conscience,

---

15. G. E. Wright, "The Nations in Hebrew Prophecy," *Enc* 26 (1965): 225–37; also J. Mauchline, "Implicit Signs of a Persistent Belief in the Davidic Empire," *VT* 20 (1970): 288–90.

16. Stuart, *Hosea–Jonah*, 290, 308.

national law codes in their own countries, international treaties, and common-sense principles of morality.[17]

Archaeologists have found Sumerian and Assyrian law codes, Hittite and Egyptian treaties, plus wisdom texts containing laws and moral principles that guided the behavior of people in these foreign nations.[18] They knew right from wrong—for example, that both ripping open pregnant women and selling innocent free people as slaves just to make extra money were unacceptable acts toward people within their own village.

Romans 2:12–16 indicates that no one has an excuse before God; those who do not specifically know the law of God will be judged based on what they do know because it has been written on their hearts as human beings made in the image of God. They have a conscience that intuitively warns them about wrong behavior, they have social laws that govern the proper way to treat other people in society, and they know that they should keep the agreements (business, political, and personal) they have made. Not one of these nations would have said it is morally right for another nation to come into their territory and desecrate their king's grave or thresh their defenseless citizens after a war.

It may seem as if nations today and in the past have acted as if they had no conscience, but this is only possible because they have numbed their conscience through repeated senseless atrocities. Every heathen and Christian nation is responsible for its actions; every big and little nation will need to give an account of what it has done. The Lord of all nations is attentive to the way people treat one another. Acting on the appropriate values does make a difference.

When God finds a nation repeatedly misusing its power against others, he considers this a rebellious and willful act of defiance. Human beings have the freedom to choose to do what is legally, religiously, or socially ethical, or they can rebel and forcibly assert their power over other people. Perverted human values are not exempt from responsibility and will not escape God's hand of justice. God can forgive if a nation is repentant (see the story of Nineveh in the book of Jonah), but persistent violations of acceptable patterns of behavior require some kind of punishment. God is the moral standard of right and wrong, and he will not cool his wrath until it is spent to remove the evil that defiles the earth.

Sins of other nations. These principles underpin everything Amos says, but one wonders why he is telling the Israelites about the sins of other nations.

---

17. J. Barton, *Amos's Oracles Against the Nations* (Cambridge: Cambridge Univ. Press, 1980), 42–61; see also G. H. Jones, "An Examination of Some Leading Motifs in the Prophetic Oracles Against the Nations," an unpublished Ph.D. dissertation at the University College of North Wales, Bangor, 1970.

18. *ANET*, 34–36, 159–210, 217–21, 412–26.

What is the purpose of having his audience agree that these foreign nations should be punished? Amos is not just concerned about what will happen to Tyre; he is trying to persuade his audience that these principles apply to *every* sinful nation. If Amos is going to convince his Israelite audience to change their own oppressive and violent behavior in a later oracle, and if he wants them to believe that God is actually going to destroy them for their rebellious acts, he knows he must base his arguments on clear theological principles acceptable to his audience.

Do they accept the idea that God reveals his will to prophets like Amos? Do they believe that God sees the rebellious deeds of nations? Do they believe that God will judge nations who have committed atrocities against others? If so, then they will be hard-pressed not to accept the same principles if the prophet happens to hear a word from God about the Israelites. They know the difference between right and wrong and abhor these barbarous deeds. They are happy to accept these principles and apply them to other nations.

Amos wisely establishes these basic theological agreements with his audience on noncontroversial issues about other nations in the first half of his sermon so that he can use the force of these arguments when he begins to talk about how God views the Israelites in his audience. Amos is not too different from the apostle Paul, who went to Mars Hill in Athens and waxed eloquent about the altar to the unknown God (Acts 17:16–31), or Jesus, who talked to the woman at Jacob's well near Sychar about drawing living water that will quench one's thirst forever (John 4). In each case the speaker knows the thought framework of the audience, uses the context of their setting as an aid to emphasizing a principle, and then brings a theological conclusion to bear on the principle already accepted. A speaker cannot be held accountable for how people respond to God, but these messengers do everything in their power to persuade some to accept the truth of their divine messages.

HOW DOES GOD view inhumane violence? If one is looking for situations to apply the principle that God holds every nation accountable for its acts of inhumanity against people, one can look for atrocities in peaceful foreign nations that have a poor record on human rights, discover how military personnel treat innocent civilians in war time, or move away from the national focus to examine the way individual people use their power to abuse others.

The United Nations adopted the Universal Declaration of Human Rights on December 10, 1948. Article 1 states: "All human beings are born free and equal in dignity and rights. They are endowed with reason and conscience and should act towards one another in the spirit of brotherhood."[19] In 1948 the United States Secretary of State George Marshall condemned the widespread modern denial of basic human values where "millions of men and women live in daily terror, subject to seizure, imprisonment and forced labor without cause and without fair trial."[20] Although great progress has been made since 1948, this is still a problem today and should be a concern of all believers who take Amos's warnings seriously.

Foreign immigrants are still treated with hatred, racial and ethnic minorities are killed to maintain majority rule (so-called "ethnic cleansing"), and economic enslavement is still a reality for many. Even in peaceful times nations abuse their own citizens by degrading human dignity. Yuri Orlov, a Russian doctor who started a human-rights group in Moscow, found himself in jail less than nine months later. Yelena Bonner and Dr. Scharov, fellow members of Orlov's group, were exiled against their wills to Gorki, while Anatoly Scharansky was jailed for nine years. The Soviets were uncomfortable with the claims of human-rights abuses made by this group and violated their freedoms to remove the embarrassment they were causing.

Worse crimes of torture are chronicled in Jacobo Timmerman's *Prisoner Without a Name, Cell Without a Number*. This respected Argentine journalist and editor of the newspaper *La Opinion* was arrested, tortured, and left to rot in a forgotten maze of totalitarian political abuse. In India ancient attitudes toward people in the lower caste and women still linger. Thousands of female babies are killed each year because families value male children. Ancient Indian tradition maintains that "to educate a woman is like placing a knife in the hands of a monkey.... Woman, thou hast three good qualities (to sing, to burn as a *sati* [cremation at the death of her husband], to produce sons) and 400,000 bad."[21] These attitudes and acts of inhumanity to other human beings can be multiplied over and over.

Although it is somewhat natural for ethnic tribes, nations, races, and interest groups to act in their own political or economic interest and show a favoritism or loyalty to members of their own group, acts of torture, unreasonable seizure and imprisonment, and murder deny people even the most basic respect and dignity. Government systems can get out of control, official policy can be discriminatory, and even religious tradition can be marshaled to support cultural practices that deny value to another person's human

---

19. R. F. Drinan, *Cry of the Oppressed: The History and Hope of the Human Rights Revolution* (New York: Harper and Row, 1987), 23.

20. Ibid.

21. C. Lacy, *The Conscience of India* (New York: Holt, Rinehart and Winston, 1965), 231.

freedom. God hates these inhumane acts and considers them a rebellion against his plan for good social relations.

Another arena of application is found in the way the military conducts war. It is relatively rare that a person will have an opportunity to address national figures about the weaknesses of a nation's military policies or the way soldiers should treat prisoners of war. Nevertheless, citizens of every country need to be informed about the military policies of various candidates for office so that they can vote intelligently and protest illegitimate actions their government has approved. Military chaplains have a special opportunity to apply what Amos says to the troops in their care so that each soldier can ethically take full responsibilities for his or her actions in battle. In addition, individual enlisted men and women who may fight in future wars need to hear from God's Word about the dangers of misusing one's power over those defeated.

Some Christians believe all war is inhumane because of its violent killing of individuals. Mennonites and Quakers, for example, believe that we are to fight only spiritual battles, to love our enemies, and not to resist one who is evil (Matt. 5:38–48).[22] Others maintain that "just wars" are a legitimate means God uses to rid the world of evil. Thus, it was not wrong to oppose Hitler's philosophy of eliminating the Jewish race; the war effort against the Third Reich was a vindication of the divine standard of justice. Those who have entered military service undoubtedly hold to the second position, and most of their concerns relate to the just conduct of war, particularly the proper treatment of prisoners and innocent noncombatant civilians.[23]

Military people believe that they can uphold the virtues of loyalty, courage, selflessness, and justice by fighting a war against an evil oppressor who rejects peace and the process of free self-determination through normal political means. S. P. Huntington maintains that military people believe that (1) people are selfish and prone to seek greater power and wealth, fighting for what they want; (2) in the uncertain times of war an organized and disciplined group approach to conflict helps control the fears of the combatants and more efficiently accomplish the task of the group; (3) selfless subordination of the individual to the purpose of the unit produces the best results; and (4) when military orders conflict with the moral conscience of the individual, a person can make the difficult choice of disobedience.[24]

---

22. J. J. Davis, *Evangelical Ethics: Issues Facing the Church Today*, 2d ed. (Phillipsburg, N.J.: Presbyterian and Reformed, 1993), 207–28.

23. R. L. Holmes, *On War and Morality* (Princeton: Princeton Univ. Press, 1989), 183–213, has a whole chapter on the topic of "The Killing of Innocent Persons in Wartime."

24. S. P. Huntington, "The Military Mind: Conservative Realism of the Professional Military Ethic," *War, Morality, and the Military Profession*, ed. M. M. Wakin (London: Westview, 1986), 35–56.

These principles sound good, but what happens in the heat of battle? Should one torture a prisoner to obtain information that could prevent the bombing of an innocent village, pinpoint the real location of the enemy, and save the lives of some troops? Is there an absolute rule that applies to every ethical dilemma, or should a soldier take a utilitarian approach that is more concerned about the final better outcome than the slightly questionable method of achieving it? Although the utilitarian answer seems to compromise ethically the highest standards, it seems in a nonmilitary setting, for example, that any good husband will lie about his wife's being in the house to protect her from being unethically killed or raped by a burglar.

But utilitarianism has its limits. The massacres of large civilian populations seems to have no ethical justification; the indiscriminate destruction of noncombatant women, children, and the harmless elderly citizens is senseless violence that must be condemned.[25]

In the end the military person must also ask what God thinks of his or her act. A superior commander may order it, the deed may have some possible utilitarian benefit, and other soldiers may favor it. Yet as Amos maintains, God sees and will judge those who illegitimately violate the dignity of other human beings.

If we move beyond the obvious military settings that are the context of Amos's statements, we can raise general questions: What value does society or do we as individuals put on human life? Do we let people take advantage of others and do nothing to stop them? Are we concerned about the ethical treatment of the "worthless" people in society? Do the unborn have a right to life and protection from the selfish desires of a parent? What political laws need to be changed and what additional social services need to be provided to ensure the sacred status and dignity of each person?

Improving your power in persuasion. Amos identifies with the facets of his audience's theological worldview in oracles about other nations so that he can later show how these theological beliefs should impact their own self-evaluation. He is probably listening for their reaction to see if they believe that God is speaking through him. He wants to know if they also think that these nations deserve God's judgment for their willful rebellion against God.

Amos needs to know whether his listeners oppose inhumane atrocities against innocent people. If they do not agree with Amos, then his later words about Israel will not be particularly convincing. But if they agree with Amos, his listeners cannot logically deny these theological beliefs when they are

---

25. J. G. Murphy, "The Killing of the Innocent," *War, Morality, and the Military Profession*, ed. M. M. Wakin (London: Westview, 1986), 341–64.

applied to their own situation. Amos is not just preaching; he wants to change the way people think about their own relationship to God. Because of the military power and prosperity of Israel, Amos knows it will not be easy to convince people that God will judge them, so he carefully plans his entire sermon for the maximum possible persuasive effect.[26]

Amos's sermon raises questions about how to preach for results. It stresses the importance of preparing our audience to receive what God is saying. We need to do more thinking about how to present the truth of God's Word so that listeners will be grabbed by the force of the argument and find it logical to agree. Aristotle's rhetorical studies emphasized the need for logical argumentation, where what is said is supported by solid evidence. If sermons make a statement that God is going to do this or that, it is important to present real-life examples and biblical evidence that justify the conclusion one proposes. Loosely arranged random thoughts on a passage rarely provide a solid base for people to make a significant commitment.

Hermeneutical tricks that do not treat the biblical witness honestly but wring out of it thoughts that are not really there do not convince most people. If you are preaching to the choir about things they already believe, you do not have to worry about having a persuasive argument. But if you dare to preach things that the audience does not believe, then persuasive effort must be put into constructing the logic of the sermon in such a way that it convinces the skeptic.[27]

This sermon also demonstrates the need to talk about God in concrete ways that people understand. Although Amos could have talked about God's universal sovereignty, he has chosen instead to describe his dealings with many nations. Amos could have raved on about God's wrath against atrocities and inhumane treatment of defenseless people, but instead he simply describes known historical cases where other people have treated innocent people in a barbaric fashion. This does not suggest that the preacher should water down the sermon with a multitude of illustrations (certainly some are needed), but it argues for using terminology that is understood and avoiding theological babble that does not communicate clearly.

Finally, a convincing sermon engages the emotions. Amos's audience is undoubtedly enraged by the atrocities of the neighboring states. It is terrible, inexcusable, sadistic, animal behavior! They are angry and want God to bring judgment now! As Amos goes through nation after nation, the crowd's enthusiastic support for Amos's message of judgment grows stronger and

---

26. G. V. Smith, *The Prophets As Preachers*, 19–22, discusses aspects of persuasion in the prophets.

27. S. Toulmin, *The Use of Argument* (Cambridge: Cambridge Univ. Press, 1958), 97–104.

stronger. Today most preachers tend to favor a more thoughtful approach. But rationality and emotions are not opposites. Emotions move people to action and motivate the will to act.[28] One should never manipulate people's emotions, but the strength of a listener's determination and the level of commitment should involve a change in both the mental and emotional aspects of a person's being. Powerful persuasion interacts with the whole person so that the Spirit's work in his or her heart will produce lasting results.

28. Motivational theory is discussed in D. McClelland, *Human Motivations* (Glenview: Scott, Foresman, 1985).

Amos 2:4–16

❧

4This is what the LORD says:

"For three sins of Judah,
　　even for four, I will not turn back ˌmy wrathˌ.
Because they have rejected the law of the LORD
　　and have not kept his decrees,
because they have been lead astray by false gods,
　　the gods their ancestors followed,
⁵I will send fire upon Judah
　　that will consume the fortresses of Jerusalem."

⁶This is what the LORD says:

"For three sins of Israel,
　　even for four, I will not turn back ˌmy wrathˌ.
They sell the righteous for silver,
　　and the needy for a pair of sandals.
⁷They trample on the heads of the poor
　　as upon the dust of the ground
　　and deny justice to the oppressed.
Father and son use the same girl
　　and so profane my holy name.
⁸They lie down beside every altar
　　on garments taken in pledge.
In the house of their god
　　they drink wine taken as fines.

⁹"I destroyed the Amorite before them,
　　though he was tall as the cedars
　　and strong as the oaks.
I destroyed his fruit above
　　and his roots below.

¹⁰"I brought you up out of Egypt,
　　and I led you forty years in the desert
　　to give you the land of the Amorites.
¹¹I also raised up prophets from among your sons
　　and Nazirites from among your young men.
Is this not true, people of Israel?"
　　　　　　　　　　　　　　　　declares the LORD.

¹²"But you made the Nazirites drink wine
>   and commanded the prophets not to prophesy.

¹³"Now then, I will crush you
>   as a cart crushes when loaded with grain.

¹⁴The swift will not escape,
>   the strong will not muster their strength,
>   and the warrior will not save his life.

¹⁶The archer will not stand his ground,
>   the fleet-footed soldier will not get away,
>   and the horseman will not save his life.

¹⁶Even the bravest warriors
>   will flee naked on that day,"

declares the LORD.

AMOS 2:4–16 TREATS the final pair of nations, Judah and Israel. These oracles bring the sermon to a climax by applying the theological principles developed in 1:3–2:3 to Amos's own countrymen in Judah and then to his Israelite audience in Samaria. Since this is merely a continuation of the preceding section, the same date, background, and structure are maintained.

The surprising reversal of the usual positive ending of the war oracle gives this section a dramatic conclusion. Instead of ending his message with the expected promise of victory, saying that Israel will be saved by God's strong hand and defeat all her enemies, Amos predicts the unparalleled defeat of Israel's army. This shocking conclusion probably catches most of his listeners off guard and forces them to imagine what was previously thought to be impossible. How could God ever destroy his own people whom he earlier promised to bless? How could Israel's strong army actually be annihilated? Is God speaking to Amos? Has Israel rebelled against God, and will they be punished for their sins of oppression just like the other nations?

Oracle Against Judah (2:4–5)

WHEN AMOS MENTIONS the rebellion of Judah, some people in his audience are likely surprised that he attacks his own countrymen.[1] Yet God has given

---

1. Wolff, *Amos,* 140, and J. L. Mays, *Amos: A Commentary* (OTL; Philadelphia: Westminster, 1969), 41, do not believe the Judah oracle was originally included in Amos's speech, but think a later redactor has added it. Hayes, *Amos,* 101–3, and Paul, *Amos,* 20–24, reject this perspective.

him a message about Judah, and Amos knows the people in Judah are sinful. He may have also assumed that his credibility will be weakened if he shows any favoritism toward his own people. Thus he follows the same structural pattern that he has employed earlier. Nothing has changed: God speaks against another people, they rebel again and again, and God will judge them severely.

The willful sin of Judah is not described as an oppressive act against some foreign nation that has ignored the ethical standards of the Judeans' conscience, but a direct refusal to follow God's stipulations and instructions in the Torah. They are breaching covenant responsibilities with God. Moses warned the people not to forget what God did for them in the past and what God said to them at Sinai. If they did forget, they might soon become proud and self-sufficient, thinking that they really did not need God (Deut. 8:1– 20). This presents a high standard for Judah, for they have been given the full revealed truth of what God wants them to do; they do not have to wonder what is right and wrong based on their conscience.

In spite of such privileges and extraordinary knowledge of God's will, many Judean people have turned to follow "lies," which leads them astray from God. Some translations suggests that these lies are actually "false gods," but this interprets the Hebrew too specifically.[2] The Hebrew root *kzb* (falsehood, lie) is used in other prophetic oracles to describe the lies that the false prophets and political leaders tell the people (Isa. 3:12; 9:15–16; 28:15; Mic. 3:5). Although the deceptions of these leaders and prophets may have included encouraging people to worship other gods, they lead the people astray in other ways too. They have adopted social, economic, and political principles from the neighboring cultures and pervert the moral, ceremonial, civil, and economic guidelines in the covenant. These leaders have a clear understanding of what God wants from them, but they still fail to lead the people to follow after God. Who should be followed, God or these liars?

Because of this direct refusal to accept what God has said, God will treat Judah just like every other nation. No special mercy will come and no second chance is mentioned. The people of Judah have sinned; they will have their secure fortresses destroyed and the capital city of Jerusalem devoured with flames. The political and religious leaders living in Jerusalem will be punished for leading the nation astray.

Amos's Israelite audience probably agrees that Judah deserves this judgment, but when they do this, they are admitting that God's law is a legitimate standard to judge a nation's morality. If so, it may then serve as a scale for

---

2. T. J. Finley, *Joel, Amos, Obadiah* (WEC; Chicago: Moody, 1990), 159, believes this is the only case where this word means idols, but Andersen and Freedman, *Amos*, 302, maintain that there is no case where *kzb* means "idol, god." In most cases it refers to the teachings of the false prophets.

evaluating Israel's behavior as well. Many in Israel are somewhat aware of what God demands in the covenant stipulations. By supporting God's punishment of Judah, the listeners recognize the authority that will spell out their own shortcomings.

Oracle Against Israel (2:6–16)

NOW AMOS TURNS toward his audience in Samaria and addresses them directly. Although the Israelites are likely expecting Amos to give a salvation oracle that describes their defeat of the surrounding nations (like other war oracles), he surprises them with an announcement of their own demise. Suddenly the cheering stops and no one shouts "Amen." By using the same terminology used against the other nations, Amos communicates that Israel is no different in God's eyes. God does speak to Amos about Israel, they rebel repeatedly just like the other nations, and they will suffer defeat like everyone else.

The specific accusations against Israel are grouped into two paragraphs: Verses 6–8 describe how Israel oppresses the weak, and verses 9–12 make the point that God graciously cared for Israel when they were oppressed. Amos does not mention just one rebellious act of Israel, as in the earlier oracles against the foreign nations, but seven ways that the Israelites have taken advantage of the powerless. Their sin is made even more inexcusable by the fact that they are oppressing members of Israelite society, their own brothers and sisters, not unknown foreigners after a war. Those doing the oppressing are state officials and upper-class merchants with money to loan for a business or agricultural need, judges in the court, and wealthy people who can afford to have servants.

Israel's oppression of the weak (2:6–8). The first accusations in 2:6 involve the unnecessary foreclosure on small loans by money lenders. This process, which may be technically legal, deprives the "righteous" (i.e., legally innocent, or guiltless) debtors of the possibility of getting clear of their debt. If debtors cannot pay up on demand, the lender may confiscate their land and tie them up in court proceedings they cannot afford. Some have probably even been driven into human slavery for an insignificant debt ("a pair of sandals").[3]

This accusation is not pinpointing any illegal court action, but the merciless selling of destitute people who could likely remove their debt if given just a bit more time.[4] This is a blatant case where wealthy Israelites do not

---

3. It is unlikely that the giving of a single sandal in Ruth 4 to confirm a transaction has anything to do with the pair of sandals mentioned in this verse.

4. Andersen and Freedman, *Amos,* 308–10, connect these sins to illegal court activity, but people were not "sold" in court. Selling is used in the context of collecting unpaid debts that were promised and did not usually require separate court action.

care for the poor as the covenant stipulations required (Ex. 21:2–11; Deut. 15:12–18). Israelites were not to take interest, but were to have an open hand to share with those in need and to have mercy on the needy, for God's covenant people were freed from slavery at the time of the Exodus from Egypt (Ex. 22:25–27).

The accusations in 2:7 emphasize the physical abuse of the helpless and weak. The strong metaphorically trample or crush the powerless into the ground.[5] The NIV adds a comparative "as" to the clause "upon the dust of the ground," but this seems unnecessary. Thus we prefer the translation "they trample the heads of the weak in the dust." This is a metaphor of power for one group and utter humiliation for the other. Isaiah also questions the powerful in Judah by asking, "What do you mean by crushing my people and grinding the faces of the poor?" (Isa. 3:15). Amos does not say what the stronger are doing specifically to crush the weak, for there probably are several methods of accomplishing their devious ends.[6]

Another abuse is literally the "turning aside of the afflicted," a phrase that refers to illegal action in a court context in 5:12; thus, the NIV refers to "deny[ing] justice." Again it appears that interpreters have been too anxious to specify an identifiable setting for this abuse. When this phrase refers to a court setting in other passages, there is always an additional word to indicate that court justice is in mind; but Amos omits any additional modifiers in this case.[7] Therefore, he is simply referring to powerful people who contemptuously manipulate the weak and afflicted, push them around, control their lives, and deprive them of the rights that every free human being deserves. When a person has no power, others can whip you around, make you jump through their hoops, force you to do things you do not want to do, and make life miserable.

The third rebellious act in 2:7 is the sexual abuse of a servant woman by both a father and son. This probably has nothing to do with the sacred prostitution practiced at Baal temples, nor an attempt by fathers to have sexual relations with their daughters-in-laws.[8] Instead, it refers to sexual mistreatment

---

5. Most commentators conclude that the Hebrew *š'p*, which can mean to be eager, pant, is an alternate spelling of *šwp*, to trample, crush, which makes better sense.

6. In light of the next phrase D. Hubbard, *Joel and Amos* (TOTC; Downers Grove: Inter-Varsity, 1989), 142, thinks the rich are treating the poor like dirt in the court, but that may be too specific.

7. G. V. Smith, *Amos*, 120–21, and Paul, *Amos*, 81, both find inadequate information to suggest a judicial interpretation because a word like "judgment, justice" is not found here as it is in 5:12 (cf. also Deut. 16:19; Prov. 17:23; Isa. 10:2).

8. Hubbard, *Joel and Amos*, 142, thinks these women are daughters-in-laws but *naʿarah* usually refers to a servant.

of a hard-working household employee. Fathers and sons were not to have sex with the same woman (Lev. 18:8, 15, 17; 20:10–20). The law provided some protection for female slaves because they were so vulnerable to mistreatment by their masters (Ex. 21:7–11; Lev. 19:20–22). In spite of this, powerful men could intimidate them with dire financial consequences if they did not cooperate with their deviant immoral desires. The emphasis is still on the strong-armed oppression of defenseless people.

The powerful probably look at these things as small indiscretions, as minor issues that everyone does. If one does business in the real world, some win and others lose; that is the way life is. But God looks at these oppressive acts as rebellious acts that "profane my holy name." They are polluting the morals of God's holy nation, desecrating his reputation, and defiling their sacred covenant relationship. God sets himself apart from sin and has set holy standards for his people to follow. He is holy, and they should be holy (Lev. 19:2). Their sins are a repudiation of God's honor and glory and a shameful rejection of their holy covenant relationship.

The final accusations of oppression in 2:8 chronicle additional ways the powerful exploit the destitute. Wealthy people who were owed money could legally collect the last thing their debtors owned, their outer garments, to ensure that payment would be made (Ex. 22:25–27; Deut. 24:12–13). This usually happened when people defaulted on their loans. But these legal formulas also demanded that the garments be returned to their destitute owners at night so that they could at least keep warm.[9] Amos not only condemns those who break these laws, but points out their shameful practice of wearing these same garments to a temple for a festival or worship event. Will God be pleased to see these well-dressed worshipers sitting on stolen clothes at the temple?

A similar irony is found in the behavior of certain judges who collect legal civil fines for breaking the law. If the guilty party pays the fine with a container of wine, it becomes the property of the state or city. But some of the selfish judges in Israel take the wine to their temples and consume it or give it as a drink offering. Besides taking advantage of the destitute, they are hypocrites and give something that really does not belong to them. It is clear from Amos's condemnation that God is not impressed with their gifts or how they got them.

God graciously cared for Israel when they were oppressed (2:9–12). Amos now changes his approach to describing Israel's rebelliousness. He

---

9. Paul, *Amos*, 83–85, provides ancient Near Eastern examples of the same abuse in cultures surrounding Israel, so apparently this was a common practice that the Israelites adopted. See J. Naveh, "A Hebrew Letter from the Seventh Century BC," *IEJ* 10 (1960): 129–39.

emphasizes what God[10] did for Israel in the past by rescuing them when they were oppressed by stronger nations. One would expect Israel to be thankful to God and obey his covenant stipulations because of his grace. One would also assume that the Israelites would understand from their past history that God consistently fights against oppressors and on behalf of the oppressed. This view of God's ways puts the present Israelite oppressors in a dangerous position as God's potential enemies. Their failure to appreciate his gracious deeds in the past and their rejection of his attempts to warn them through the prophets and Nazirites put the nation on a collision course with God.

Initially Amos recites the well-known tradition about God's great acts of salvation, which were part of the nation's sacred history (Ex. 15; 20:1−2; Deut. 32; Josh. 24). These contain warning not to forget God's grace (Deut. 32:15−29; Josh 24:14−24), but most of the prophets point to this as one of Israel's main failures and the cause of their rebellion (Hos. 2:13; 4:6; 8:14; 13:6; Jer. 2:6−8). The Exodus story was such a tremendous demonstration of God's sovereign power over oppressors and such a wonderful story of freedom from enslavement that one would think that it would never be forgotten. But traditions that get told again and again get old. If they are not my personal experiences and my story, they do not seem as real or as earth-shaking.

In 2:9 Amos reminds his audience that God destroyed the many Amorite cities, states, and tribes that controlled Canaan back at the time of Joshua. Some of the Amorites were giants, who seemed to be as "tall as the cedars and strong as the oaks." This is reminiscent of the spies' report that claimed that the Nephilim were men of great stature who lived in cities with high walls. This made the spies feel like grasshoppers (Num. 13:31−33). Yet God destroyed every last vestige of these enemies (both "his fruit above and his roots below") when the Israelites conquered the land, because these supermen were nothing before God's power.

In 2:10 Amos recalls how God delivered the people from Egyptian bondage (Ex. 14−15), led them through the Sinai desert for forty years (Deut. 8:1−5), and gave them a wonderful land (8:6−10). These events were at the heart of Israel's identity; they were the people God powerfully delivered from Egypt. Their oppressive power over others was not key to their success; God's grace provided for all their needs. Oppressors are the enemies of God.

How should Israel be responding to God's grace? One would think they would respond in gratitude and service to the One who has done all these things for them. Amos's Israelite audience is rejecting God and the spiritual

---

10. The emphatic Hebrew personal pronoun *ʾanoki* (I myself) appears twice to focus on what God did. This contrasts with the third person plural verbs that emphasize what the Israelites are doing in 2:6−8.

leaders he has sent. In the years since the Exodus God graciously sent various prophets (Samuel, Nathan, Gad, Ahijah, Elijah, Elisha) to communicate messages from God, to encourage the people to maintain their covenant relationship with him, and to call them back from their sinful ways. God also raised up Nazirites (Samson in Judg. 13; Samuel in 1 Sam. 1) to be examples of holy living.[11] They followed a disciplined manner of life, dedicated themselves to live in an especially close relationship to God, and strictly observed the promises of their vows. They were illustrations of godly living. They were so thankful for God's grace to them that they purposely changed their lifestyle to show their gratitude.

But some Israelites in Amos's audience apparently oppose the Nazirites and prophets. In 2:12 he reports that these Israelites coerce people who have taken a Nazirite vow into drinking wine and thus force them to break their vows of abstinence. This is in direct conflict with what God required and is a blatant attempt to substitute their own cultural rules for God's expectations. Maybe less spiritual people are embarrassed by the dedication of the Nazirites, or perhaps they consider the Nazirite rules as old-fashioned cultural remains from a bygone era. The fact that they make the Nazirites do these things suggests a dictatorial atmosphere in which people feel obligated by social pressure or priestly demands to do something they do not want.

The prophets are also oppressed and rejected. People are telling some of them to stop prophesying. Amos may have been thinking of Jezebel's killing of many prophets (1 Kings 18:4; 19:2, 10), Ahab's silencing of Micaiah ben Imlah (22:26–27), or Joram's attempt to kill Elisha (2 Kings 6:31). Amos later experiences this kind of repression himself (Amos 7:10–17). But this offense is not just the oppression of the revolutionary voice of the prophets; it is the silencing of God's voice. They are muzzling God's ability to communicate with them and in the process frustrating his attempts to warn the people of his plans to judge them.

The defeat of Israel's army (2:13–16). The punishment statement against Israel does not begin like the judgments on the kings and the fortified cities of the foreign nations. Instead, it focuses on the utter annihilation of Israel's army. God intends to take away the very source of the people's security— the power they depend on and are so proud of. Once Israel's strong army is out of the way, the rest of the nation will crumble to pieces.

---

11. Some like Samuel were Nazirites for life, but others were Nazirites only for a specified period of time. The Nazirites would not touch the fruit of the vine, a dead body, or cut their hair (Num. 6:1–8). See M. Weiss, "'And I Raised Up Prophets from Amongst Your Sons': A Note About the History and Character of Israelite Prophecy," *I. L. Seeligmann Volume: Essays in the Bible and Ancient World*, ed. A. Rofé and Y. Zakovitch, 3 vols. (Jerusalem: E. Rubenstein, 1983), 1:257–74.

Verse 13 announces what God will do, while verses 14–16 describe what will happen to Israel's troops. There is confusion surrounding the translation of the key verb in verse 13. It is clear that God is somehow compared to an agricultural cart or wagon loaded with grain. The metaphor is unique to Amos and both surprising and confusing. Since there are a number of meanings to various related Semitic roots (ʿqq, ʿwq, ʿyq), some suggest that the verb describes God's "cutting, splitting open" like a full cart cuts into the ground, his "groaning," his "pressing, crushing" (NIV), or his "hindering."[12]

Amos draws his imagery from a common agricultural setting so people can understand it easily. I prefer to interpret this verb as referring to God's splitting open the ground and think it is Amos's first prediction of the earthquake that comes about two years later (see other predictions in 6:11; 8:8; 9:1–2, 5).[13] Regardless of the specific nature of God's judgment, what is clear is that God will do it, and his powerful action will be aimed at Amos's Israelite audience.

The results of God's action are astonishing. God will shake up the troops in Israel's army so badly that they will not be able to escape in an upcoming battle. The fast runners will find that they are not swift enough and cannot escape defeat. The strongest and bravest will have no fortitude for battle and will be unable to save even themselves from death. The archers will not stand their ground in the face of the enemy's charge, and horsemen (probably charioteers) will unsuccessfully try to run away.

In other words, Israel's strong military force will collapse and run, and none will escape death. This will be an awesome demonstration of God's power! As Amos's audience in Samaria hears these words, they must have been astonished and petrified. How can such a thing happen? Will God actually do this? What will happen to them if such a disaster does take place?

THESE CONCLUDING ORACLES continue to build on Amos's basic principles in 1:5–2:3 that (1) every nation is accountable for its inhumane acts of rebellion against God, and (2) if one can identify some common theological agreement with the worldview of an audience, those points can be used to evaluate the behavior of the listeners. But Amos goes beyond these two points in 2:4–16 to suggest that (3) those who have received greater revelation of divine truth will be evaluated on the basis of what they know; (4) God holds people accountable if they reject

---

12. Paul, *Amos*, 94, has a full listing of options, but none are without problems. He rejects the earthquake interpretation, which we prefer.
13. G. V. Smith, *Amos*, 108, 129.

his gracious deliverance of them from oppression and start oppressing others; (5) rebellion against God's design for healthy human relationships erodes his holy reputation; and (6) God fights on behalf of the oppressed.

Greater revelation means greater accountability. A change is evident in the level of accountability in these oracles because both Judah and Israel have received the covenant stipulations in the Torah and are not just dependent on conscience to develop their sense of right and wrong. God does not judge the foreign nations for not keeping his law because it was not revealed to them. According to Paul, the Gentiles will receive God's wrath if they suppress the truth they understand from viewing the creation, pursue futile speculations rather than honoring God, follow their lusts by abandoning their natural functions, and do not follow the instructions written on their conscience (Rom. 1:18–27; 2:14–15). But the Jews have received the oracles of God (Rom. 3:1–2), and they will be judged based on his law (Rom. 2:12).[14]

The cost of defying the Lord is high. Moses reminded the children born in the desert of their parents' failure to enter the land at Kadesh Barnea (Num. 13–14) and described them as "unwilling to go up; you rebelled against the command of the LORD your God. You grumbled in your tents and said, 'The LORD hates us . . .'" (Deut. 1:26–27). After God said that this generation would die in the desert, they decided to go up and fight the Amorites even though God warned them against it since he would not go with them. Nevertheless in arrogance they rebelled against the command of God and were defeated (Deut. 1:41–44).

This principle should not be reversed to suggest that people are better off if they do not know the truth, insofar as they will not be held accountable if they do not know. Unfortunately, many of us have received traffic tickets even when we did not know what the speed limit was, even when we thought it was okay to park in a certain spot. Ignorance may be an explanation, but a police officer will seldom take it as sufficient to excuse guilt. Paul did not consider those without the law to be free from guilt. They have no excuse, though they will be judged guilty on the basis of a different standard.

In the Judah oracle Amos condemns the prophets and politicians of leading the people astray with their lies. They know what God wants in the covenant relationship, but they deceptively guide the nation in another direction. In the Israelite oracle Amos points to judges, moneylenders, employers, and people in power, who probably know about the covenant

---

14. This correlation between unintended and intended sins is represented in the difference between the law for dealing with unintentional homicide and premeditated murder (Ex. 21:12–14). The offering laws also distinguish between what is required of the one who unintentionally sins and the one who rebels against God (Num. 15:27–31).

traditions that should govern their behavior but who choose to reject these divine instructions. People in power are especially warned about the high level of accountability they have. God has entrusted them with special privileges. Their failures not only assure their own demise but may cause others to stray from the narrow path. In the New Testament James uses this principle to warn teachers that they will be judged more strictly (James 3:1).

The purpose of God's past actions of grace. God also holds people accountable if they reject his grace in delivering them from oppression and start oppressing others. God's grace in delivering Israel from Egypt, guiding them in the desert, and defeating the strong Amorites should have brought a response of gratitude and obedience from the Israelites. While God does not give grace conditionally on the basis of a promise of praise and worship, no one should ignore or forget his grace. If a person does not let a past act of grace guide his or her future beliefs or actions, that very act will guide God's responses. In other words, grace is not given to be wasted but is provided to encourage a positive response of thankfulness and service.

Another act of grace happens when a person is warned of danger and is saved from certain destruction. The sending of the prophet, the apostles, and missionaries to spread the good news of God's love is an act of his grace. Accepting the warning might mean deliverance from judgment and hope for the future. Rejecting the messenger and denying the importance of the message would be a slap in the face of one who put forth the effort to make the warning. Restoration is possible only if people are open to God's gracious attempts to convict them of sin and his gentle prodding to discipline those who need correction. If people are not affected by God's grace, they will one day stand accountable before his face.

Human rebellion against God erodes his holy reputation. Amos describes multiple ways in which the Israelites are inhumanely treating one another. They use their economic advantage of having money to loan to their financial advantage, their political status as judges or officials to show partiality in judgments, their power as employers to intimidate, and their ability to manipulate others' lives to oppress the weak and powerless. This has produced a shameful reputation in the community. Their values are an embarrassment to God. Since most outsiders know God through the lives of those who follow him, God's holy reputation is ruined by this kind of behavior.

The honor of God's name is a concern Moses had on Mount Sinai when God wanted to destroy those who worshiped the golden calf (Ex. 32:12). What would the Egyptians say if God destroyed Israel? They would conclude that God had no power and was no better than their own Egyptian gods, who could not protect them. The Israelites were not to worship other gods or follow the abhorrent customs of the nations, because God is holy and his people were to be holy (Lev. 20:22–26). If the Israelites did not separate themselves from the ungodly practices of the Canaanites, how would people ever know about the holy God of Israel?

God's holy reputation is also a key theme in Ezekiel's prophecies. The people had defiled God's holy temple so much that he left it so that it could be destroyed (Ezek. 8–11). Judah profaned God's holy name by their evil; thus, out of concern for his holy reputation, God would vindicate the holiness of his great name so that all would see who he really was (36:20–23). He would do this by restoring his people to the land, cleansing them from their filth, and giving them a new heart. Then the nations would know that his name is holy (36:23–36).

God fights on behalf of the oppressed. In Amos 1:3–2:3 the prophet emphasized God's desire to fight against the oppressors of this world, but Amos never predicted deliverance for the oppressed. In 2:9–10 the prophet reminds his audience that God has acted on behalf of his people in the past by delivering them from bondage, leading them, and providing them a promised land. One should not assume, of course, that God fights for the winning side in every case, for some battles were meant to accomplish his will of destroying a nation, not of building up another. Hezekiah's victory over Sennacherib, for example, was not designed to bring territory or glory to Judah's king but to bring glory to God (Isa. 37). Assyria's earlier victory over Ahaz, Pekah, and Rezin was not an endorsement of the Assyrian king (Isa. 7:1–10:19).

God does care for the defenseless widows and orphans (Isa. 1:17, 23; Jer. 5:28; Ezek. 22:7). His eyes see the oppression, and he will restore the afflicted, help the lame to walk, and gather the outcasts to establish a remnant for himself when he sets up his eternal kingdom (Mic. 4:6–8). Although this present sinful world may have much oppression and it may seem at times as if God does not care about those who have no power or riches, his grace is sufficient for each trial and his strength can help one through testing. His reasons for allowing problems and oppression are usually beyond human comprehension, but we can always be sure of God's sympathies and his eventual deliverance.

THE PRIMARY PRINCIPLES enumerated above seem especially relevant to the church today. (1) We who have received the most revelation from God (both Old and New Testaments) will be evaluated on the basis of what we know. (2) The church will be held accountable if it rejects God's grace and supports oppression. (3) Rebellion against God's design for healthy human relationships erodes God's holy reputation and the church's testimony in the world. (4) The idea that God fights on behalf of the oppressed should be both a warning to those who are tempted to abuse others and a hope to Christians in difficult situations.

Living in a post-Christian age. In a sense, Amos is living in a postcovenant moral era for most Israelites and a precovenant era for the pagan population in and around Israel. If one looks at the cultures around the world today, one could suggest that some countries are in a pre-Christian era, while others (especially Western) appear to be in a post-Christian era. As far back as 1949 T. S. Eliot examined the culture of England and discovered that the rhythm, structure, and principles of the Christian faith no longer had a pervasive influence on social behavior: "Prosperity in this world for the individual or for the group ... [was] the sole conscious aim."[15]

The church should be less concerned about its loss of status in influencing the general values of society and concentrate more on getting its own house in order. If we hope to influence people in our culture, we cannot hide in a "church ghetto." We are called to be a light to the world (Matt. 5:14–16)— but we will do so only if we walk in the light of the revelation we have received. Those who ignore or reject what God has made known about his will for humankind in Scripture will be responsible for their decisions and behavior.

Accountability is based on the assumption that people have the ability to make choices to do or not to do something. If they have this ability, a choice will be made on the basis of some reasoning, an emotional process, a traditional belief, or possibly social pressure. If people knowingly and purposely choose to act in arrogance or in defiant rebellion against what they know God desires, the full weight of responsibility falls on the accountable persons. There is a direct relationship between the knowledge one has, the leadership position held, and the responsibility that is expected.

The problem is not that the world and the church have not received any knowledge from God. Although some have never heard the good news about the coming of Christ, the last two hundred years have witnessed a great expansion in the missionary efforts to share the gospel with unreached tribes and nations. Israel's and the church's problem is that many people ignore the revelation that is given and do not treat it as authoritative in determining their values or behavior.

Why is this so? One reason is that people have not been clearly exposed to the importance of the authority of the biblical witness. W. Stringfellow believes that

---

15. T. S. Eliot, "The Idea of a Christian Society," *Culture and Christianity* (New York: Harcourt, Brace & World, 1949), 10.

the weirdest corruption of contemporary American Protestantism is its virtual abandonment of the Word of God in the Bible.... The Bible has been discarded in Sunday School in favor of baby-sitting, group dynamics, religious gibberish, moralistic counselling, sectarian indoctrination, romantic versions of church history, and stories about the Bible which are, more often than not, editorially biased, badly drafted, and unbiblical anyway.... Protestants in America are neither intimate with or reliant upon the Word of God in the Bible, whether in preaching, in services in the sanctuaries, or in education or nurture.[16]

One might get defensive and claim that Stringfellow surely has not attended a church in my denomination, but for this to exist in any group of churches is a tragedy. Barna's 1990s survey found that only 58 percent of the Christian adults claimed to read something from the Bible each week.[17] My own experience gives some support to these findings, for every year I have seminary students in my class on the prophets who confess that they are having trouble internalizing the material because they had never read the books of Nahum, Zephaniah, Obadiah, or Ezekiel, never heard a sermon on these texts, and never had a Sunday school lesson on them.

These few examples suggest there is a need for more direct exposure to what God has said in Scripture, but there is probably just as great a demand for closing the gap between what people know and what they actually do. Many Israelites probably had a general knowledge of the covenant stipulations in the books of Moses. They knew that it was wrong to oppress others, that injustices in court proceedings were unethical, and that sexual abuse of employees was not something God would approve of. Yet some did just the opposite anyway.

In an age of relativism, Baby Boomers tend to accept everyone's point of view.[18] It is less important to be logically consistent because an argument could be made to suggest that a certain activity is not an absolute wrong in every situation. Others are motivated simply by a desire for status, economic gain, or pleasure and do not worry about whether their actions are right or wrong. They want to enjoy the good life and will do whatever it takes to achieve their goals—stealing, lying, cheating, sexual harassment, hiding evidence from the court, and racial prejudice. The biblical prohibitions against such actions can be rationalized or relativized, or a person may just choose to refuse to be governed by biblical ethics. Some people

---

16. W. Stringfellow, "The Church's Neglect of the Word of God," *Sojourners* 15 (1986): 36–39.

17. G. Barna, *The Barna Report: What Americans Believe* (Ventura, Calif.: Regal, 1991), 289.

18. M. Bellah, *Baby Boom Believers* (Wheaton: Tyndale, 1988), 55.

connect sin and wrong more with getting caught than with doing something displeasing to God.

The cost of such willful rebellion against God is high for the individual, for the fellowship of Christians, and for the reputation of God. Individuals can allow sinful rebellion to so control their lives that they have no spiritual walk with God. The testimony of the congregation in the larger community is blemished with a cloud of hypocrisy and distrust. None of this glorifies God and magnifies his holy name. Through such events God's reputation is stained and his kingdom is hindered.

Sexual sin. As Amos knows (2:7), one of the most damning instances of this happens in sexual misconduct. In recent years, the most celebrated and devastating examples of sin in the church have been the plague of sexual infidelity by church members and their pastoral leaders. B. Moeller notes that a survey of 3,432 Americans in the early 1990s showed that only 50.5 percent of those who called themselves conservative Protestants maintained that their religious beliefs concerning the sinfulness of sex outside of marriage always guide their sexual behavior. Approximately 17 percent of conservative Protestants and 15 percent of mainline Protestants had slept with more than one person in the last year.[19]

This problem in Catholic circles is heightened by the requirement of priestly celibacy. D. Rice reported that "almost one quarter of the active priests in the world" have left the ministry for sexual reasons,[20] while A. W. R. Sipe concluded that "about 20 percent of priests vowed to celibacy ... are at one time involved either in a more or less stable sexual relationship with a woman or, alternatively, with sequential women.... An additional 8 to 10 percent of priests are at a stage of heterosexual exploration."[21]

Although some of the above-mentioned people are lonely, have a disappointing sexual relationship with a spouse, or come from a dysfunctional family background, these excuses do not absolve guilt. Other acts of sexual misconduct are perpetrated by predators who use their power (as in Amos's example) to take advantage of others. All acts of oppression are wrong, but this one seems to have an overwhelming effect on people.

This sin will usually end the pastoral career of a priest or minister and devastate the trust level between clergy and congregation. It arouses the anger of the congregation, who thought so highly of the one who supposedly

19. B. Moeller, "The Sex Life of America's Christians," *Leadership* 16 (Summer, 1995): 30–31, based this information on the findings in the book *Sex in America: A Definitive Study* by R. Michel, J. Ganon, E. Laumann, and G. Kolata in 1994.

20. D. Rice, *Shattered Vows: Exodus from the Priesthood* (Belfast: Blackfast, 1990), 3.

21. A. W. R. Sipe, *A Secret World: Sexuality and the Search for Celibacy* (New York: Brunner/Mazel, 1990), 74.

preached with such conviction, and ruins the reputation of the church in the neighborhood. Families are broken apart and children's lives scarred, but one of the greatest tragedies is the lasting shame this will bring to God's glory. The message of other ministers will have less credibility, cynicism will increase, and calls for holy living will be taken less seriously. This is a betrayal of God. Consequently, God's holy name is profaned.

All those who might be tempted to oppress others should remember that God is against every type of abuse or oppression and graciously fights for the deliverance of the innocent who are oppressed. Believers must not make the mistake of the Israelites and misuse their power, nor should they forget that God has graciously delivered them from oppression and the power of sin (Rom. 8). As Amos says, the battle will not be won by the swift, the brave, or the mighty (2:14—16). The battle belongs to the Lord, and he will not strengthen the legs of those who oppress others.

Amos 3:1–8

HEAR THIS WORD the LORD has spoken against you,
O people of Israel—against the whole family I
brought out of Egypt:

2 "You only have I chosen
    of all the families of the earth;
therefore I will punish you
    for all your sins."

3 Do two walk together
    unless they have agreed to do so?
4 Does a lion roar in the thicket
    when he has no prey?
Does he growl in his den
    when he has caught nothing?
5 Does a bird fall into a trap on the ground
    where no snare has been set?
Does a trap spring from the ground
    when there is nothing to catch?
6 When a trumpet sounds in a city,
    do not the people tremble?
When disaster comes to a city,
    has not the LORD caused it?

7 Surely the Sovereign LORD does nothing
    without revealing his plan
    to his servants the prophets.

8 The lion has roared—
    who will not fear?
The Sovereign LORD has spoken—
    who can but prophesy?

Original Meaning

THIS PARAGRAPH BEGINS the second series of oracles (3:1−6:14).[1] In these messages Amos attempts to persuade his audience to believe the disastrous news that he just announced in 2:6−16. God will indeed defeat Israel, his chosen people, because of their rebellious acts.

Since Israel is a strong nation at this time, it would be natural for his listeners in Samaria not to believe what Amos is saying. Some perhaps think that their minor acts of oppression are not really that bad; it is culturally acceptable behavior in that day. Others may be doubting whether the punishment will really be as bad as Amos pictures. Can an enemy actually destroy their strong fortresses? Israel is, after all, a strong nation, a winner, a rich people with a powerful army. A few probably think that this will never happen because the people still do worship God at the temple at Bethel. Moreover, God had blessed them with freedom and prosperity. How could anyone believe this crazy foreign prophet from Judah?

Amos attempts to convince his audience of the truthfulness of his words from God by verifying what God has said to him: The nation will be destroyed. Chapters 3−6 are introduced by a unique series of rhetorical questions drawn from nature and the logic of everyday experience. Amos argues that there is a cause behind everything that happens.

The people listening to Amos can hardly help but agree with the examples he gives in these first few verses, for they are obvious. A trap jumps because some animal has tried to eat the bait; there is a cause behind the result. If people know this to be true regarding the things they see happening in the natural world, then certainly it is true in the spiritual world. There is a reason for God's plan to punish Israel; such things do not happen by chance. It is logical to believe that nations fall because God wills it. It is reasonable to think that Amos is prophesying because God has revealed the future to him. It is logical to fear when you hear these divine warnings.

Some commentators associate this first paragraph with a wisdom disputational speech; others think it is similar to a covenant lawsuit. But it does not seem to follow the complete structure of either.[2] Amos uniquely joins covenant concerns in 3:1−2 with a disputational style of arguing in 3:3−8 in order to break the logic of the faulty reasoning patterns of his listeners. The first five questions in the disputation move from results back to the cause, but

---

1. See the outline of the book in the Introduction to Amos.

2. Wolff, *Amos*, 93, 183, makes the wisdom connection, while Finley, *Amos*, 177, follows the covenant-lawsuit approach of M. O'Rouke Boyle, "The Covenant Lawsuit of the Prophet Amos: III.1−IV.13," *VT* 21 (1971): 338−62.

in 3:6 the cause precedes the results.[3] This change is also consistent with the topical movement from the animal world to the realm of God's involvement in human history.[4]

A Chosen, Covenantal Status
Does Not Guarantee Blessing (3:1–2)

AMOS IS PROBABLY responding to the expressed or expected objections of people in Israel to what he has said about them in chapter 2. Although their opinions are not quoted directly, in his answer he quotes from the traditions they accept about their election and Exodus experiences (Deut. 7:6–8; 10:15).

God has treated the Israelites as a special people, for they are the only people he has intimately known (*ydᶜ*, know, choose) and chosen to be his covenant people.[5] Amos uses the rare formula that they were picked out of all the families of the "earth" (*ʾadamah*, see Gen. 12:3; 28:14), thus representing the patriarchal promise when Israel's ancestors were initially identified as God's people. Moses also referred to this promise and to the Exodus of the nation from Egypt in his prayer after the golden calf incident, hoping to persuade God to have mercy on the people who sinned (Ex. 32:11; Deut. 9:26). Many Israelites still believe these experiences (their election and Exodus) will somehow protect them from God's wrath and guarantee his continued favor.

Amos surprisingly expresses a different understanding of God's relationship to Israel.[6] He does not deny their special status but suggests that this status carries with it an extraordinary responsibility. If the Israelites are God's people, they are to be "a kingdom of priests and a holy nation" (Ex. 19:6). Like their father Abraham, they must "walk before me and be blameless. I will confirm my covenant between me and you" (Gen. 17:1–2). As at the time of the golden calf, God is still "compassionate and gracious . . . slow to anger, abounding in love and faithfulness, maintaining love to thousands, and forgiving wickedness, rebellion and sin. Yet he does not leave the guilty unpunished" (Ex. 34:6–7).

The people were led out of Egypt to be God's people, not a people who followed their own whims and worshiped Baal. They must love the Lord their God with all their hearts, fear him, and serve him alone (Deut. 6:5, 13; 10:12,

---

3. Andersen and Freedman, *Amos*, 387, provide a grammatical outline and comparison of each line of 3:3–8 to show both the similarities and differences in this section.

4. Paul, *Amos*, 106–7.

5. B. K. Smith, "Amos," 70–71, emphasizes that election involves choice and an intimate relationship.

6. G. V. Smith, *Amos*, 143–46, and Paul, *Amos*, 102, see this as an unexpected and surprising answer.

20; 11:1, 13). These requirements are integrally connected to following God's covenant stipulations so that his blessing may be enjoyed. If the Israelites forget what God did for them and do not live as his people, the curses of the covenant are inevitable (Deut. 27–28). Since the oppression of the Israelites (Amos 2:6–8) demonstrates covenant unfaithfulness, Amos announces God's intention to punish them according to that covenant agreement.

This argument supports Amos's conclusion in 2:13–16 and removes a deceptive theology of the nation that God will never punish his chosen people. Privilege comes with the heavy weight of responsibility; these advantages do not provide a guaranteed free ride with no strings attached. The Israelites must listen to God's warning and fear him if they are truly his covenant people.

There Is a Reason for Everything (3:3–8)

THE LOGIC OF 3:1–2 probably surprises and shocks the people in Samaria. It does not make any sense to some of them. Therefore, God directs Amos to draw an unmistakable connection between cause and effect to legitimate what God will do to Israel. He begins with uncomplicated examples that everyone accepts. Each question in 3:3–5 expects the answer No. Everyone knows that two people do not enjoy the results of walking somewhere together unless there is the preceding cause that they agree with one another.[7] Enemies do not walk together. This question does not refer to making an appointment to meet (NIV "have agreed to do so"), for many people met and walked together by chance in the ancient Near Eastern world. They did not have telephones to make appointments, but when they were on the road, they naturally found it more comfortable to walk with a person they agreed with on political, economic, or religious issues.

Amos's second illustration comes from nature. People are acquainted with the habits of lions (3:4), who roar (the result) because they are attacking their prey (the cause). Do lions foolishly roar before their attack and give the prey a premature warning to run? The young lion in the second half of the verse also hunts from his "hiding place" (not his "den" as in NIV) and growls at the appropriate time.[8]

---

7. Stuart, *Hosea–Jonah*, 324, and Paul, *Amos*, 109, translate the verb "meet" rather than "agree." It seems that people must surely meet before they walk together, but the togetherness idea suggests agreement. People who meet often do not agree and thus do not walk together. Both of these commentaries also reject the view that this is referring to an appointment.

8. Many commentaries (J. Niehaus, "Amos," 1:378) translate *meʿonah* as "den," but it is the "dwelling place," likely the hiding place in the forest, based on the analogy of God's description of the lion in Job 38:39–40. Animals do not hunt from their dens but from a favorite hiding place.

A similar logic fits the behavior of traps (3:5). A bird does not get caught in a snare (the result), unless someone has set the trap (the cause). Likewise, a trap does not jump shut (the result), unless some animal has been around and sprung the trigger mechanism (the cause). As in chapter 1, Amos uses illustrations that his audience can easily accept. His rhetorical skill of persuasion is nonthreatening so that he can use these principles to prove his point later.

In 3:6–8 Amos lists the cause before the result. Amos begins by asking if a watchman's trumpet blast from the city wall will have the effect of causing the people in the city to fear for their lives and make preparations to fight the approaching enemy.[9] The natural answer is Yes; only a stupid person ignores a watchman's signal. Amos does not name a city, but in light of what he has said earlier, the audience can hardly help but wonder if he was talking about their city, Samaria.

The second half of 3:6 expands the questioning to ask who causes cities to fall. Most Israelites would agree that cities are destroyed by divine action. Soldiers and generals may do the fighting, but in the end these things are determined by the sovereign power of God. But if this is true, God is also the one who has the power to cause the destruction of Samaria, as Amos hints in 3:2. If one compares these ideas with what he has just said about the roar of the lion, the similarity is astonishing.

The flow of this long series of questions is broken in 3:7 by the bold, parenthetical explanation of what God does before he brings disaster on a city (3:6). God does not just destroy cities or nations on a whim. He does not take any pleasure in the death of the wicked but instead desires that they turn from their evil ways (Ezek. 18:23). Consequently, God will send a natural disaster or a plague to wake people up and cause them to turn to him for help (Amos 4:6–11). Or perhaps he will reveal his plans to one of his prophets and send him to warn a city of those plans (Jonah 1:2). God's secret plans about the Flood were revealed to Noah (Gen. 6:13–21), and his plans to destroy Sodom were made known to Abraham (18:17–21). Like Amos 3:7, each of these examples has the result (God's action) preceded by the cause (God's plan), which is explained to a prophetic messenger.

The implications are too obvious to miss. Why has Amos given this news about God's plan to destroy Israel? He has not dreamed these ideas up out of the blue. God has revealed them to the prophet because he intends to act in the near future, and he desires to have one of his servants warn those he will judge.[10]

---

9. Ezek. 33:3 illustrates the role of the watchman.

10. Hayes, *Amos*, 126, and Hubbard, *Joel and Amos*, 148, think the main purpose of this verse is to defend the prophet's status and credibility before a protesting audience. Certainly this verse legitimates what Amos says, but I believe Amos is more concerned about persuading his audience that the message is God's plan, rather than defending his own authority.

The final verse (3:8) is the conclusion, and it calls for action. It encourages the listener to be aware of the cause (God's roar) and to accomplish the intended results (fear God). Amos is repeating God's roaring words to persuade the Israelites that God is roaring against them. They must realize that God can and will destroy Israel.

Amos calls for a personal decision to respond appropriately (with fear) to God's revelation of his plans. The Israelites are failing to live responsibly and to follow covenant values. The prophet integrates his earlier references to the lion's roaring just before it attacks its prey (3:4) with his comments about the need for people to fear when God destroys a city (3:6). His prophecy is God's roaring warning of his impending attack; it is that trumpet blast that warns of an approaching danger. Amos's words (the results) are based on what God said (the cause). He cannot keep quiet, because he also wants his audience to heed the warning and respond with fear.

THIS PASSAGE PROMOTES the principle of thinking logically and basing beliefs and behavior on God's revelation. So often disagreements among believers center on emotional feelings, debatable reasoning, cultural traditions, or differences in procedural methods, not on the teaching of the Bible. These minor debates are best solved by examining the evidence for both sides of a question and by avoiding the trap of turning these differences into major divisions through personality conflicts. On some of these issues there is more than one way of understanding things. A Christian spirit of tolerance should rule wherever possible, saving serious disagreements for correcting deceptive interpretations or false applications of biblical passages.

Two theological principles arise from these verses. (1) God's revelation should not be turned into deceptive lies that make conditional promises into absolute guarantees of blessing. (2) When people hear an unpopular word of criticism or judgment, they should ask two questions: What might cause these results (the criticism or judgment by others), and what results should this lead to (how should I respond)? Both of these issues relate to dealing with conflicts that may arise when one person is trying to change the values or worldview of another person.

Self-deception among believers. Amos addresses a problem within the theology of Israel, the people of God. The question relates to the fundamental relationship between God and his people. Is it purely a one-sided commitment, where Israel will eternally enjoy God's grace and experience only the fulfillment of promised covenant blessings?

Certainly every believer's relationship to God is based on his grace. No one would deny its central role. Amos reminds his audience of God's grace in calling only this one family of the earth to be his special people—a nation whom God graciously delivered from Egyptian bondage (3:1–2). Many years later Paul similarly reminded the Ephesians that their relationship to God is based on grace received through faith in Christ, not on their own works of righteousness (Eph. 2:8–10). Any attempt to add any other requirements to the gospel turns it into a contrary and deceptive gospel (Gal. 1:6–10).

But Amos is not arguing with his audience about how Israel received God's favor when they first became his people. This nation clearly did not deserve or earn those blessings (Deut. 7:6–8; 9:1–8), and there is no reason to believe Amos and his audience disagree on this point. Neither is the issue whether Israel can still receive more blessings in the future when God establishes his eternal kingdom.[11] The discussion is over what God's people can expect from him right now, and what he can expect from his people. Will God only deliver blessings? Will he test some with a trial or sickness? Will he absolutely guarantee blessing regardless of the behavior of the recipients? Is not the covenant relationship a two-way street with both blessings and cursings promised (Deut. 27–28)?

The early history of the nation shows that they did not always receive blessings. The account of the Israelite judges contains cycles of the people rejecting God, being persecuted by an enemy, and then being delivered by a judge sent by God (see Judg. 3). How can Amos's audience think they will be blessed regardless of their behavior? This is a deceptive theology.

In the New Testament Paul states that unbelievers have suppressed the truth and deceived themselves (Rom. 1:18–22),[12] but it is surprising to learn that the Hebrew people in Amos's time and again later on in Jeremiah's day deceived themselves into believing that they were innocent of sin (Jer. 2:35). Even though Israel had already gone into exile by Jeremiah's time, people in his day were still deceiving themselves into thinking that God would not destroy Judah (6:13–15; 14:13–14). Jeremiah saw the temple as a source of deception because some thought it would automatically protect them from destruction no matter what they did (7:1–14).

Being born a Hebrew does not guarantee God's blessing (see Hos. 1:4–9), offering a sacrifice does not guarantee God will forgive one's sins (Isa. 1:10–15), and proclaiming you believe but not showing it in your life does not impress God since even demons believe (James 2:14–19). Self-deceptions

---

11. This issue of Israel's eschatological hope is addressed in Amos 9:11–15.

12. G. L. Bahnsen, "The Concept of Self-Deception in Presuppositional Apologetics," *WTJ* 57 (1995): 1–31.

may become so severe that people will actually think they are believers when they are not (Matt. 7:21–23).

For a while, self-deceptions make life easier, happier, less disciplined, and less demanding. They often turn hard questions that people need to struggle with into meaningless, pat answers. An absolute "because God said so" is an appropriate answer to some questions, but it can hide an unwillingness to deal with the complex hermeneutical challenges of making the Bible meaningful today. Many self-deceptions arise when people do not weigh the whole counsel of God together, but inappropriately give undue attention to a few verses that may be taken out of context. Making conditional promises into unconditional guarantees may make people feel good, but they have no authority and will ultimately fail the disappointed victims of deceit.

Understanding causes and results. When people look at events that happen to them, some deny God a place in their lives and conclude that he is uninvolved with their world, that he does not cause anything. Others limit the input of scientific rationalism and believe that God is actively influencing them and leading them to the truth through the power of the Holy Spirit, who dwells in them (John 16:7–13). They know God sovereignly controls nature and can bring either blessing or harm to people (Amos 4:6–11). God raises up nations and destroys others as he brings about his master plan for all peoples (Dan. 2:20–21; 4:28–37). These facts do not obliterate free choice and the participation of humankind in influencing events, for God is not playing games but maturing believers and developing relationships with people (Jer. 18:1–12).

Many people get obsessed with one theological brand of understanding the degree of human freedom or the degree of divine enforcement of his will, but Amos seems unconcerned about these theoretical debates. He simply makes the point that people need to recognize God's hand in their lives. He puts forth three principles in 3:6–8: (1) On the national level, God is involved with the process of bringing sinful nations (a status they have willfully chosen) to an end; (2) God warns people, often by sending a messenger, to give them an opportunity to influence the results (a choice can then be made by those warned) of his plans to judge them; (3) the appropriate response to God's warning (the cause) is to turn to him in repentance and to fear him (the results).

These principles are illustrated in God's plan to destroy the wicked Assyrian capital of Nineveh (Jonah 1:2). God warned the Ninevites through the prophet Jonah (Jonah 3:1–4), and the people responded positively by believing God, fasting, and ending their violent behavior (3:5–10). Both positive and negative causes produced results that went far beyond anything Jonah expected. The Ninevites originally did not think their violence would bring their downfall; instead, they thought it was their ticket to power and riches.

Jonah did not expect that getting on a boat to Tarshish would endanger his life and the lives of many other sailors. But free choices can produce disastrous results when a wrong choice is made. God's sovereign plan to send Jonah to Nineveh was not destroyed by his sinful choice, because God persuaded Jonah to change his opinion about going to Nineveh. The result of his message was the repentance of Nineveh, and this in turn led God to be compassionate and not judge the Assyrians.

In the Jonah story God was actively involved with causing people to choose to do his will so that the results would bring him glory. The results did not happen by accident, the causes were not accidental, and the choices were not trivial. People who realized the importance of God's plan (even though they did not understand its breadth and complete significance) knew that their choice to be involved with the fulfillment of God's plan produced results that outweighed any objections—even the ridiculous one of Jonah that God was too compassionate (Jonah 4:1–2).

DEALING WITH DECEPTIONS. Does being baptized in a church automatically guarantee a place in heaven? Does taking Communion magically produce forgiveness regardless of a person's true attitude? Does confirmation or church membership necessarily bring God's favor for the rest of a person's life? Does keeping the Golden Rule guarantee a person will be treated kindly by God? Are these wise maxims or deceptive myths? Are these foolish ideas or rules to live by that are widely believed by religious people? Unfortunately, some people attempt to comfort themselves by rationalizing deceptive ideas that contain a portion of the truth but miss the overall thrust of what is needed to please and glorify God.

Sociologists call this kind of self-deception a reification.[13] This happens when people view a social phenomenon in the world as fixed and unchangeable, thus giving it an ontological status. They may believe that a human social institution like the church must operate like the divinely designed pattern used by the early disciples in Acts 4:32–35. If one reifies this pattern as an absolute one, then no one may change any part of this formula. If the church service is a divine pattern of social relationships to be used by all cultures, then it is not possible to adapt it to different situations or cultures.

If, however, the early church was a human social institution guided by God to meet the needs of Jewish people during the famine in Jerusalem while the church was in its infancy, then its structure in the early pages of Acts

---

13. Berger and Luckmann, *Social Construction of Reality,* 89–92.

should not be reified but is open to change. People today are then free to ask how to conceptualize and organize the church to meet the needs of people today in different cultures, such as in China, Brazil, Kenya, and Sweden.

Many in the Amish community, for example, have reified certain cultural patterns of behavior and dress. They have given a certain dress code an absolute status, but other Christians look at the principles of modesty, humility, and separation from the world and conclude that these ideas can be implemented without maintaining such a fixed, reified dress code.

The most serious reified self-deceptions are theological.[14] This happens when people give absolute divine authority and status to humanly created perceptions that do not fully represent what God has said or what he desires. The Scriptures teach about worshiping and glorifying God by singing his praise and giving testimony to his marvelous deeds (Ps. 95–99; 104–105). But some people believe that this eliminates certain kinds of music (modern rhythmic choruses), of musical instruments (drums), and of worshiping behavior (lifting your hands). This ignores the fact that every culture has its own indigenous meaningful way of expressing worship.

To reify one cultural means of expressing praise to God is an erroneous approach to understanding the spirit of true worship. If a worship experience is not a meaningful way for people in each culture to express their love for God, then it is not worship that can naturally flow from the inner being of that people group. At one time, for example, Gregorian chants were a meaningful means of praising God, but today they are seldom heard since for most people they are not a part of their culture.

Some people suffer under the delusions of television pastors who promise health and wealth if one gives money to the work of that ministry. Oral Roberts, A. A. Allen, Gordon Lindsay, Kenneth Hagin, and a host of lesser known preachers have published and preached the prosperity message, claiming that God promises wealth and prosperity to those who claim his promises.[15] This teaching is based on the King James translation of verses like 3 John 2, "I wish above all things that thou mayest prosper and be in health," Old Testament covenant blessings of wealth for those who remain faithful (Deut. 7:13–15; 8:18; 28:1–14), and God's promise to Joshua that he would

---

14. R. Perkins, *Looking Both Ways: Exploring the Interface Between Christianity and Sociology* (Grand Rapids: Baker, 1987), 156–66, believes reification leads to exclusivity, parochialism, confrontationalism, pride, absolutism, and self-contradiction by modern Christians in the church. For example, not long ago Christians claimed that the Bible supported racism and slavery.

15. See books like O. Roberts, *God's Formula for Success* (Tulsa: Healing Waters, 1955); Gordon Lindsay, *God's Master Key to Prosperity* (Dallas: Christ for the Nations, 1960); or K. Hagin, *How God Taught Me About Prosperity* (Tulsa: Kenneth Hagin Ministries, 1985).

prosper and be successful if he meditated on God's law (Josh. 1:8). Through Christ, Abraham's blessing are considered to be available to Christians today.

These preachers also teach that Christ's atonement has delivered believers from the curse of the law and the three major enemies of the Christian: poverty, sickness, and death.[16] Such deliverance and consequent prosperity are usually presented as conditioned by a believer's willingness to plant a financial seed, so that it can bear fruit a hundredfold. Of course, each of these preachers strongly encourages, and at times badgers, people to give that seed money to their ministries, not to their local church.

Is this a deceptive theology that twists the truth of Scripture? Many think so. Is God primarily interested in developing a wealthy social class of believers? Can one take the specific promise given to Joshua and directly apply it to our modern situation? Was not Joshua's prospering more related to successfully conquering the Canaanites rather than becoming a rich man? Are believers today still under the covenant stipulations and the blessings that applied to Abraham or Moses? Are we not under the new covenant through Christ? And is not the statement in 3 John 2 the author's own specific wish for Gaius, the recipient of John's letter, not God's promise to all Christians?

Gordon Fee says that "to extend John's wish for Gaius to refer to financial and material prosperity for all Christians of all times is *totally foreign* to the text"[17] (emphasis his), for this was just a common greeting. How does this health and wealth teaching coincide with Paul's warning to Timothy (1 Tim. 6:9–19) about the evil of loving money? Why were not Jesus, the disciples, and the early church wealthy if this is really God's will for all believers? Even people within this movement have criticized the excesses and abuses this movement has generated.[18]

Overemphasis on these theological beliefs can also lead to materialism, "the idolatrous elevation of money and material possessions it will buy as the goal of life."[19] Hebrews 13:5 warns believers: "Keep your lives free from the love of money and be content with what you have." Jesus himself warned a wealthy man to "be on your guard against all kinds of greed; a man's life does not consist of the abundance of his possessions" (Luke 12:15). In a parable Jesus saw a strong negative side to wealth because "the worries of this life, the deceitfulness of wealth and the desires for other things come in and choke the word, making it unfruitful" (Mark 4:19). First John 2:15 also warns:

16. B. Barron, *The Health and Wealth Gospel* (Downers Grove, Ill.: InterVarsity, 1987), 66–67.

17. Gordon Fee, *The Disease of the Health and Wealth Gospels* (Costa Mesa: The Word for Today, 1979), 4.

18. Jerry Savelle, *Living in Divine Prosperity* (Tulsa: Harrison House, 1982), 27, 91–92, 178–79.

19. H. Schlossberg, *Idols of Destruction* (Nashville: Nelson, 1983), 88.

"Do not love the world or anything in the world. If anyone loves the world, the love of the Father is not in him." Among the many proverbs about the dangers of wealth is: "Better a little with the fear of the LORD than great wealth with turmoil" (Prov. 15:16).

These verses suggest that the health and wealth gospel has selectively emphasized a few key verses but ignored the broader teachings of Scripture on wealth. They have deceptively interpreted verses that do not directly apply to anyone today and engendered a spirit of materialism and greed, rather than the wise stewardship of whatever amount of money God allows each person to use to bring glory to his name.[20] Jesus encouraged his disciples to seek first the kingdom of God, and all the other things we need will follow later (Matt. 6:33).

Cause and effect. Each spring when my father let the cattle on our farm out to start eating the new fresh grass, some cows had to relearn the cause-and-effect principle related to electric fences. Some just sniffed at the wire and remembered the painful effect of the electric jolt they received the previous year when they touched it with their wet noses. Others approached the flimsy fence for the first time and received the shock of their life, but somehow they did not fully realize what was causing this terrible pain. Since they did not perceive the relationship between the single strand of barbed wire and this strong electrical jolt, they foolishly ignored their earlier warning and attempted to eat grass on the other side of the fence. Usually it only took a couple tries and all the animals feared (the effect) the thin wire (the cause) and stayed far away from it.

Sometimes people learn by trial and error too, but we have the advantage of having friends and family who can tell us what causes bad results. Parents naturally make the connection between cause and effect to teach their children about the dangers of fire (it will burn you), the nearby river (you may drown), and playing in the street (a car may hit you). Drivers realize that speeding may result in an expensive ticket, and airplane pilots know that gravity will cause a disaster if the airplane does not maintain sufficient speed.

Many times it is not hard to see the connection between cause and effect, but at other times this relationship is mysterious. Many sick patients wonder what is the real cause of their discomfort. Sometimes medical doctors agonize over unclear or confusing symptoms. Is the medical problem in the nervous system caused by a virus, a psychological problem, a cancerous bone disorder, or a little known chemical in the environment producing strange changes in neural responses?

---

20. For a more balanced and healthy view of wealth, see J. Barnett, *Wealth and Wisdom: A Biblical Perspective on Possessions* (Colorado Springs: NavPress, 1987).

When people deal with the spiritual realm, a similar situation exists. Spiritually sensitive people know some of the moral laws of God and see them as clearly as the effect of gravity in nature. Other causes and results are as mysterious as Job's trials—beyond human comprehension. Though believers in Christ must freely admit that they will never understand every cause and effect, God has not left people totally in the dark. There are things we can understand. Amos 3:1–8 suggests some questions that people can ask themselves: What are God's plans and the spiritual principles that govern life (3:6)? Has God sent a message to warn about his impending plans (3:7)? What is the best way of responding to God's admonitions (3:8)?

It is not hard to see that nations who are strong and wealthy and who have deceived themselves into thinking that disaster will never strike them (9:10) are in the great danger of not understanding the planned relationship God has made between their sins (the cause) and their punishment (the effect). Individuals who are proud and do not want to be involved with God (the cause) often find out the hard way (the effect) that God wants to have a relationship with them. Surprisingly, people who are usually oriented in the natural world can be blind when it comes to God's participation with national events as well as each person's individual pilgrimage. The modern culture's overemphasis on individual freedom and self-determination has idealized the value of free choice and reacted against the thought that anyone, even God, will sovereignly bring about an effect (his plan) for their lives.

This dilemma addresses the essence of faith and the Christian life, for those who willingly submit their will to the plan of God and entrust themselves to his care recognize that he directs the results and believe that his plan is best (Eccl. 3:12–14). This process still involves a choice, but it purposely limits other choices to those proposed by God. The effect of becoming mature in Christ, of using spiritual gifts, and of fulfilling God's calling cannot be achieved without repeatedly choosing to accept God's plan.

Thus, as Amos suggests, believers must continuously inquire about God's plan (since we know he has one), listen for warnings from divine messengers that raise questions about the plan that the believer is following (since we know he sends people to warn us), respond to that warning with fear, and change (we know God accepts this response). To ignore the relationship between cause and effect is as silly as saying that a trap was sprung, but nothing caused it (Amos 3:5).

Amos 3:9–4:3

3:9 Proclaim to the fortresses of Ashdod
    and to the fortresses of Egypt:
"Assemble yourselves on the mountains of Samaria;
    see the great unrest within her
    and the oppression among her people."

10 "They do not know how to do right," declares the LORD,
    "who hoard plunder and loot in their fortresses."

11 Therefore this is what the Sovereign LORD says:

"An enemy will overrun the land;
    he will pull down your strongholds
    and plunder your fortresses."

12 This is what the LORD says:
"As a shepherd saves from the lion's mouth
    only two leg bones or a piece of an ear,
    so will the Israelites be saved,
those who sit in Samaria
    on the edge of their beds
    and in Damascus on their couches."

13 "Hear this and testify against the house of Jacob,"
declares the Lord, the LORD God Almighty.

14 "On the day I punish Israel for her sins,
    I will destroy the altars of Bethel;
the horns of the altar will be cut off
    and fall to the ground.
15 I will tear down the winter house
    along with the summer house;
the houses adorned with ivory will be destroyed
    and the mansions will be demolished,"
                                  declares the LORD.

4:1 Hear this word, you cows of Bashan on Mount Samaria,
    you women who oppress the poor and crush the needy
    and say to your husbands, "Bring us some drinks!"
2 The Sovereign LORD has sworn by his holiness:
    "The time will surely come

when you will be taken away with hooks,
   the last of you with fishhooks.
³ You will each go straight out
   through breaks in the wall,
   and you will be cast out toward Harmon,"
                                    declares the LORD.

IN THIS SECOND part of the section 3:1–6:14, Amos attempts to convince his listeners of the reality of his threats by expanding the basis of his earlier statements. The evidence supports his claim that they have sinned by oppressing others. As a result, an enemy will come and destroy their objects of security. Their richly decorated and strong palace fortresses, as well as the altar in their temple at the city of Bethel, will protect them no longer.

The setting of these oracles is the city of Samaria (3:9, 12; 4:1), but the exact occasion is unknown.[1] The audience appears to include some wealthy people who have opulent summer and winter homes (3:15). These upper-class citizens have everything anyone could ever want, but the moral values of this elite group are most despicable. There is so much oppression and violence in their homes that it looks as if they do not know right from wrong (3:10).

These verses are grouped into three short paragraphs (3:9–12; 3:13–15; 4:1–3), each of which begins with an imperative form of the same verb (šm᷾, to hear) and includes accusations and punishments, typical characteristics of a prophetic judgment speech. Some find evidence of a covenant lawsuit here, but most of the structure of a lawsuit is not present.[2]

An Enemy Will Destroy the Places of Violence (3:9–12)

AMOS BEGINS THE first paragraph with a call for the wealthy people (they live in fortresses) in two foreign nations to serve as witnesses to the violence in Samaria.[3] This will verify his earlier claims of oppressive acts in 2:6–8 and legitimate the need for Israel's judgment. It is ironic that Amos calls two oppressive pagan nations to serve as impartial expert witnesses. This summons

---

1. Andersen and Freedman, *Amos*, 402–3, see a progression from the destruction of the shrine at Bethel (3:14) and their homes (3:15), and then the exile of the people (4:2–3)—the similar structure of accusation and punishment uniting these oracles.

2. M. O'Rouke Boyle, "The Covenant Lawsuit of the Prophet Amos," 338–62.

3. Hebrew law requires two witnesses in capital cases before a case can be prosecuted (Deut. 17:6; 19:15).

is probably intended to have a dramatic effect on his audience because the Israelites would abhor the thought of people from Egypt and Ashdod[4] watching what they are doing inside the city walls of Samaria and then condemning them for improper behavior.

This summons is probably a rhetorical device to make a point since there is never any report of what these people see.[5] Amos's own experience in Samaria has informed him what these witnesses would see inside the fortresses in Israel. The Israelites are full of "unrest" and "oppression" (3:9), which characterize the lifestyle of the rich and famous. The two Hebrew words used here point to confusion, violence, and panic. The nobles and royal families have produced a disorientation to what a secure way of life should be. The exploitation and intimidation of the poor and powerless have allowed the upper class to live in luxury. Their lust for power and status have led to violence and a disrespect for human values. These two activities are the opposite of God's peace (2 Chron. 15:5) and the state of joy he can give (Ezek. 7:7).[6]

Amos concludes that those who live in these palace fortresses have developed a culture of accepting this kind of violence as a normal pattern of behavior. Consequently, they seem not to know the difference between right and wrong (3:10). They do not value the ideals of justice, honesty, and proper interpersonal relationships that are foundational to the covenant and part of every person's conscience. Common sense and fair play, humanitarianism and mutual respect are foreign to their thinking. Presumably the Israelites have adopted the moral standards of the secular culture around them and are behaving like Canaanites, though Amos never makes that explicit connection. The Israelites have the sin problem, which cannot be sidestepped by blaming others or by rationalizing their actions with the excuse that everyone else is doing it.

The upper class is consumed with amassing more possessions. The NIV's "who hoard plunder and loot" is an interpretation of the literal metaphor of "who hoard violence and destruction." The first term usually describes bloodshed and the assaulting of other people, while the second Hebrew root relates to the way one treats property. In this case the Israelites' violence against the others allows them to hoard their furniture and personal belong-

---

4. The LXX has "Assyria" instead of "Ashdod," but Ashdod is a more difficult reading and likely the original reading.

5. G. V. Smith, *Amos*, 163; Paul, *Amos*, 115.

6. Finley, *Joel, Amos, Obadiah*, 188, notes that the second word can refer more specifically to "extortion, bribery," but the context here seems to point to a more general semantic range of meaning like "oppression," which may have involved several different methods of gaining financial advantage over others.

ings. This probably includes both the taking of belongings as a result of wars the Israelites have won and the semilegal robbery of poor people in Israel.[7] It enables the rich to furnish their homes with great splendor; in fact, they are even stockpiling some of these treasures. In God's eyes the results of these cruel acts are living proof of guilt.[8] It seems surprising that these people have the audacity to proudly display such things openly, feeling no shame for what they have done (cf. 2:8).

Since Amos wants to convince his audience that God will actually judge them, he must not only remind them of their sins and failures but also warn them that the acts listed in 3:9–10 will produce disastrous consequences for the nation (see 3:11–12).[9] God will bring an unnamed enemy nation to oppress the royal and noble inhabitants of Samaria, and they will receive the same treatment they have given to others.

This will be a three-step process (3:11). First, an army will surround the land of Israel so that there will be no escape, then the walls of the secure fortified cities will be pulled down, and finally the enemy will help themselves to the lavish assortment of plunder from the homes of the upper class.[10] Note that Amos does not talk in general third-person terms about some unnamed people who will experience these things, but he uses the second person to emphasize that these things will happen to "you who are now listening to me" (cf. "*your* strongholds . . . *your* fortresses").

The extent of the destruction in Samaria is illustrated by a common analogy known from the experience of shepherds who care for sheep belonging to someone else. Everyone knew it was impossible to protect every sheep and lamb from every wild animal that roamed the hills around Samaria. If a sheep was killed, Israelite law required the shepherd to "recover" (not "save," as in the NIV) whatever remained and bring those few scraps to the owner to prove he did not steal the animal (Ex. 22:10–13). Although God miraculously enabled David to rescue sheep from both a lion and bear (see 1 Sam. 17:34–37), most shepherds had to wait until the sheep was eaten and then pick up the remains (e.g., "two leg bones or a piece of an ear"), to demonstrate how the animal was killed (Amos 3:12).

---

7. Finley, ibid., 189, does not believe these possessions came from warfare, while Andersen and Freedman, *Amos*, 407, think that part of it may have come from military victories.

8. Stuart, *Hosea–Jonah*, 330.

9. Ibid, 331. Stuart connects these punishments to covenant curses in Deut. 28:31, 43, 52 and Lev. 26:19.

10. Archaeological excavations of Samaria have discovered both large and small homes, many pieces of ivory from these wealthy homes, and a five-foot-wide inner wall and thirty-foot-wide outer casemate wall. See J. Crowfoot, K. Kenyon, and E. Sukenik, *Samaria-Sabaste I: The Buildings of Samaria* (London: Palestine Exploration Fund, 1942), 9–20.

Amos saw a parallel between this imagined scene and what will happen when Samaria is destroyed, but the interpretation of some words in the second half of 3:12 is difficult. Amos does not say who is like the lion (probably God, based on 3:8), but the destroyed sheep are compared to the people of Samaria. The two small parts left of the dead sheep are like the two small pieces of wood left after the destruction of Samaria. The word *ubdmšq* is unclear, and it has been interpreted to refer to (1) people in the city of "Damascus" (as in the NIV), (2) "damask" silk that might be put on a bed, or (3) "a part of a leg" of a bed. This last suggestion is preferable and is based on the idea that *ubdmšq* was originally two words that somehow mistakenly became joined by a scribe as one word.[11] A final problem relates to whether *yšb* refers to those who "sit" on their couches (as in NIV) or is describing those who "dwell" in Samaria.[12]

In spite of the technical problems with interpreting this verse, all agree Amos is using a powerful metaphor to communicate the total destruction of Samaria by an enemy army.

God Will Destroy Their Places of Security (3:13–15)

THIS BRIEF PARAGRAPH begins with two imperatives that call for someone to "hear . . . and testify against" or solemnly warn (cf. 3:9) this Israelite audience of coming judgments. This oracle has no formal accusation section like a usual judgment speech, but the reference to God's plan to "punish Israel for her sins" connects this speech with the prophet's earlier accusations in 2:6 and 3:2. There is no mention of an enemy army here as in 3:11; God himself is the real power that will bring destruction on Israel's "day" of divine visitation. This day is undefined, but it probably refers to the "day of the LORD," the day of God's terrible visitation of wrath on Israel (mentioned more explicitly in 5:18–20).

To drive home God's main point, Amos describes the removal of two of Israel's sources of security: the altars where they worship and their strongly fortified mansions. The altars of Bethel include those in the king's state temple (7:13), where the golden calf was located (see 1 Kings 12:28–32). The mention of the horns of the altar points to the removal of two important functions. (1) The people will no longer be able to put some of the blood from their sacrifices on the horns of the altar (Lev. 4:7; 16:18), so that the possi-

---

11. Hayes, *Amos*, 134–35, prefers Damascus, but the Hebrew word has an š rather than a ś, which is normal for the name Damascus; moreover, Damascus usually has a double *m* sound, which is not the case here. And since there is no evidence that "damask" silk was made at this time, the best solution is to accept the third alternative.

12. Paul, *Amos*, 120, and G. V. Smith, *Amos*, 166–69, prefer this approach.

bility of making atonement for their sins is being removed. (2) Nor will they be able to grasp the horns of the altar to gain protection from punishment (Ex. 21:12–14; 1 Kings 1:50; 2:28). These images forewarn the impending end of Israel's religious security. They will have no cultic way of protecting themselves from God's wrath when he visits the nation on that fateful day. Their last security blanket will be removed.

God will also remove the royal court and the wealthy's social status, financial security, and physical protection (3:15) when he tears down their homes (see also 6:8, 11). These palace fortresses were elaborately furnished with expensive furniture with rare carved ivory inlays imported from both Assyria and Africa.[13] These fine pieces in elegant style filled their winter homes (at warmer lower elevations) and summer homes (at cooler high elevations).[14] The demolition of these luxurious villas will remove all the economic advantages of the rich and vaporize any sense of physical security.

God Will Exile the Oppressors (4:1–3)

LIKE THE EARLIER two oracles, this final one also begins with the imperative "hear this word." Amos now addresses a specific group of people in Samaria— its wealthiest citizens. A few have understood the "cows of Bashan" as a symbol of the leaders of Samaria or a reference to the Baal fertility cult, but most conclude that this imagery is a cutting reference to the rich women in Samaria.[15] The feminine gender of cows and the fact that these "cows" ask their husbands to wait on them (4:1) imply that Amos is addressing women.

"Cows of Bashan" is a fitting symbol for these wealthy women, because the area north of the Yarmuk river in Transjordan was known for its fertile fields and its well-fed cattle (Deut. 32:14; Ps. 22:12; Ezek. 39:18). These pampered, self-indulgent, and bossy ladies maintain their lifestyle by exploiting the poor, crushing the needy, and speaking demandingly to those around them. The exact method of doing this is not explicitly described, but the result is the subjugation and impoverishment of many poor people to produce

---

13. J. Crowfoot and G. Crowfoot, *Samaria-Sebaste II: Early Ivories from Samaria* (London: Palestine Exploration Fund, 1938), contains photographs and a description of these ivories. Some are displayed in the *New Encyclopedia of Archaeological Excavations in the Holy Land*, ed. E. Stein, 4 vols. (Jerusalem: Israel Exploration Society, 1993), 4:1305.

14. S. Paul, "Amos III:15—Winter and Summer Mansions," *VT* 28 (1978): 358–60, refers to the summer and winter homes of Barrakkab. Ahab also had two homes (at Jezreel in 1 Kings 21:1 and at Samaria in 21:18; 22:39).

15. The Targum and Calvin thought the cows refer to leaders, while J. Williams, "A Further Suggestion About Amos IV:1–3," *VT* 29 (1979): 206–11, and J. D. W. Watts, "A Critical Analysis of Amos 4:1ff.," *SBL Seminar Papers, 1972*, 2 vols. (n.p., 1972), 489–500, relate this term to pagan cultic practices.

greater wealth for those who are already rich. There is no concern, compassion, or care for the weak, only further crushing demands and more injustice. These women also treat their husbands (lit., "lords") the same way, demanding that they wait on them hand and foot so they can indulge themselves in satisfying their pleasures.

Verses 2–3 are God's irrevocable oath of judgment against these women. He swears on the basis of his own "holiness" to emphasize the irrefutability of his decision. When God says something, it will happen; but when God swears an oath, it is impossible to imagine anything less that 100 percent accuracy. When God's holy character is invoked in an oath, he is putting his divine character at stake. Through this terminology Amos communicates in the most powerful way possible the unalterable will of God.

The oath itself warns of "coming days" (hidden by the NIV's "the time") that will signal the beginning of a new era for Israel. It may be an eschatological day (9:13) or just a new period in the near future (Jer. 7:32; 16:14). The general picture in Amos 4:2–3 is that the walls of the city will be destroyed and the people of Samaria will go into exile.

Although this much is clear, the meaning of several words is difficult to understand. The word *ṣinnot* means "shields" elsewhere in the Old Testament (1 Kings 10:16; Ezek. 23:24), but that does not fit here. It is better to follow either the common suggestion that this refers to the idea that people will be taken from Samaria with "hooks" or "fishhooks" (NIV, NASB, RSV)[16] or, using another fishing analogy, like "baskets" or "pots."[17] This may suggest a situation similar to that pictured in Assyrian reliefs, which show captives marching off into exile with each prisoner being connected to a rope through a hook in his or her nose or lip.[18] Those who have treated other people like animals will reap what they have sown. These symbols of defeat and humiliation will put an end to the luxurious living and oppressive behavior of the "cows of Bashan."

This will happen when an enemy nation, or possibly an earthquake, creates several breaches in the strong walls of Samaria (4:3) so that the population can be removed from the city at many places. The people's opulent homes, wealth, and power over others will not save them. They will be unceremoniously thrown out of this secure environment and left in "Harmon" (NIV), a possible geographic reference to the area of Mount Hermon. This is generally parallel to the later announcement that the people will be exiled

---

16. S. M. Paul, "Fishing Imagery in Amos 4:2," *JBL* 97 (1978): 183–86.

17. For a full discussion of the various proposals that have been made, see Paul, *Amos*, 130–34.

18. J. B. Pritchard, ed., *The Ancient Near East in Pictures Relating to the Old Testament* (Princeton: Princeton Univ. Press, 1954), 152, fig. 440.

"beyond Damascus"(5:27). The tragic end of Israel will include both the disgraceful treatment of its finest citizens and their deportation to an unknown life of captivity and abuse by others.

With this kind of abrasive vocabulary and straightforward confrontation, Amos is not so much trying to persuade people to believe what God has said he will do; rather, he is simply telling them that this severe destruction will happen. Sometimes honest confrontation will harden the heart of the listener, but at other times an offensive means of communicating a message actually helps to get the seriousness of the point across.

THE MESSAGE AMOS communicates to the people in Samaria is a specific message from God that applies to the people living at that time. Although the destructive punishment in each of the paragraphs is primarily related to the ancient audience Amos encounters, each oracle in this sermon does address fundamental issues not limited to his time. Several enduring theological principles help us relate these ideas to modern situations today.

God cannot bless those who use violence to gain possessions and power. All three oracles are addressed to people who put a high value on possessions, wealth, pleasure, and their own personal security. These are the upper income earners of society, who have many of the material things that common people yearn to have. Although wealth, pleasure, and possessions are not forbidden and security from danger is a good feeling, Amos's audience obtains these worldly advantages in an immoral way and gives them inordinate status far beyond their true value. Thus, the real problem is not that wealthy people exist in Israel; rather, it is the way they live and how they have gotten their wealth—they are unjust.[19]

In 3:9–10 and 4:1 God condemns a lifestyle of violence, oppression, anarchy, selfishness, and injustice toward others. Violence and oppression characterize the aggressive actions of the powerful toward those who are weak and poor (4:1, possibly poor peasants who work the land of these rich Israelites), and this attitude is a major behavioral characteristic even within their grand homes (3:9–10, possibly in relationships to servants). God has rejected violence as an acceptable behavior pattern as far back as the Flood (Gen. 6:11–13). He judged the Egyptians for their oppression of the Hebrews (Ex. 3:7–9; 5:14–16) and determined to destroy the Assyrian empire and its capital of Nineveh because of its excessive military savagery (Jonah 3:4–10).

---

19. D. Gowan, "The Book of Amos," 378, believes that every society will be held accountable for oppression and how it deals with the poor and needy.

The legal traditions in the covenant stipulations present a strong case for the just treatment of others and specifically forbid the oppression of the poor (Lev. 25:35–43; Deut. 15:7–18; 24:15). God warns against hardening one's heart against the needy and encourages people to give generously to them, just as he had generously provided for his people in their time of affliction. To behave oppressively is a sign that one does not fear God (Lev. 25:43). People who act this way have either thoroughly rejected God's instructions about justice in earlier tradition or are so perverted by their selfishness and rationalization of improper behavior that they no longer fully comprehend the distinction between right and wrong (3:10). In such a state, selfish goals and desires are given the highest value.

This sometimes evidences itself in the hoarding of unneeded expensive possessions (furniture with ivory inlays in 3:15) or multiple homes (3:15), which have no utilitarian purpose or necessary function. These patterns of greed and power may be based on the perverted values of the secular culture, but often these acts run contrary to the religious ideals of society as well as the consciences of most moral people. God sees how people treat one another and will hold each generation accountable for their acts of violence and their attitudes toward wealth.

Possessions and even religious institutions provide only a deceptive security. Once people begin to amass expensive homes, power over other people, and a big income, it is easy for them to find their identity and value in these things. If a person's reputation and hope for the future is invested in these material values, there is a natural tendency to place one's security in them. When possessions take on this kind of importance, people will go to great extremes to protect their power. Moreover, when anything seriously threatens their status, they will sometimes act in illegal or immoral ways to maintain their affluent lifestyle. Amos views these as false sources of security that God will remove.

A more legitimate source of security is the people's worship of God at the temple. If appropriate sacrifices are presented at the altar, God promises to forgive people of their sins, and they will be protected from his wrath (Lev. 4–5). The altar also provided temporary security if a crime was accidentally committed (cf. Lev. 4:22–26). But Amos envisions a time when all religious symbols of security will be removed (Amos 3:14). If the people coming to the altar are guilty of deliberate crimes of violence and oppression, neither the horns of the altar nor any other religious ritual can save them. If there is no genuine confession of sin and commitment to change their behavior, any sense of security gained from being at the temple is false.

This oracle thus provides a warning for everyone to avoid false assumptions based on the existence of temple buildings or the observance of required rituals. God wants people in every culture and time to depend on him alone. We cannot substitute some cheap religious counterfeit that produces a false source of security. When religious institutions get in the way of our relationship with God, they have lost all value and need to be eliminated.

On God's day of judgment, he will remove all sources of false security. The "day of the LORD," his great day of judgment, is introduced as the ominous time when God will take sovereign control of his people's history and bring it to a temporary end. He will direct nations to attack his own people to remove their possessions, wealth, expensive furniture, and secure homes. Nothing will stand—not the thick walls that protect their cities, nor even their temples and the altars where God is worshiped. God's day will destroy the worldview of the wealthy Israelites by eliminating the props that support it. The wealthy will no longer have grand, luxurious homes, power to boss others around, or altars where they can seek God's mercy. The nation of Israel will be in ruins, and the upper class will be led into captivity.

Power, wealth, and religious symbols do not provide eternal security. God's intervention to remove these false sources of security is sometimes the only way he can teach people that these factors have limited value. When human sources of security become stumbling blocks to a trusting relationship with God, they may need to be removed. Such events will force people to reevaluate their thinking about God and their possessions: Why has God allowed this judgment on me? Did I do something wrong? How can I change so as to remove God's curse and be assured of his blessing in the future?

HOW SHOULD CHRISTIANS **today deal with possessions and wealth?** Are possessions and wealth evils that God hates, or can people have possessions if they do not let them become a source of security? Are large homes and expensive furniture forbidden, or is God mainly concerned with how people value these objects? What can believers say to the materialistic society of today concerning the gaining and maintaining of wealth? While Amos mainly focuses on implications related to the last part of this question, he assumes some basic conclusions related to a theology of possessions.

It is not hard to find passages outside the Old Testament prophets that condemn people who are wealthy. In John's message to the church at Laodicea, he says: "You say, 'I am rich; I have acquired wealth and do not need a thing.' But you do not realize that you are wretched, pitiful, poor, blind and naked" (Rev. 3:17). Similarly the apostle Paul encourages Timothy: "Command those who are rich in this present world not to be arrogant nor to put their hope in wealth, which is so uncertain, but to put their hope in God, who richly provides us with everything for our enjoyment" (1 Tim. 6:17). Paul also warns that "people who want to get rich fall into temptation and a trap and into many foolish and harmful desires that plunge men into ruin and destruction" (6:9).

In these cases wealth can became a stumbling block to a person's trust in God, a source of temptation to sin, and may lead to a false perception of reality. James 5:3—6 also confirms that God will judge those who have

> hoarded wealth in the last days. Look! The wages you failed to pay the workmen who mowed your fields are crying out against you.... You have lived on earth in luxury and self-indulgence. You have fattened yourselves in the day of slaughter. You have condemned and murdered innocent men, who were not opposing you.[20]

In light of these dire warnings, it may seem somewhat surprising to learn that God is the One who gives people the possessions they have and also the ability to gain wealth (Deut. 8:17—18). God's original intention was that people be fruitful and multiply (Gen. 1:26—28), and he promised the patriarchs fruitfulness and blessings (12:1—3). God gave the Israelites possession of the land of Canaan with homes, wells, vineyards, and fields full of grain for them to inherit (Deut. 8:6—9). In these and other cases it is clear that possessions and wealth are not inherently inappropriate for believers. Yet these passages tend to conflict with Jesus' demand to the rich young ruler to sell everything (Luke 18:22) and the early church's practice of renouncing personal property and holding everything in common (Acts 2:44—45). Jesus also taught his disciples to go out and spread the good news of the kingdom without a purse, extra sandals, staff, or money (Luke 9:1—5).

If there is one thing we learn from this variety of viewpoints, it is to be careful about making blanket applications about possessions based on one verse. Each of these teachings makes sense in its context, but not all people are in these same contexts. In each case the interpreter must deal with the attitude a person has toward wealth and material things. As L. Johnson says, "The way we use, own, acquire, and disperse material things symbolizes and expresses our attitudes and responses to ourselves, the world around us, other people, and, most of all, God."[21]

One can read one text and come to the conclusion that God hates the rich and loves the poor (e.g., Luke 16:14—31), but we must go beyond this surface impression to ask why God relates to these different groups in such dif-

---

20. For a survey of biblical statements about possessions see, G. A. Getz, *A Biblical Theology of Material Possessions* (Chicago: Moody, 1990).

21. L. T. Johnson, *Sharing Possessions: Mandate and Symbol of Faith* (Philadelphia: Fortress, 1981), 40.

ferent ways. "Is wealth determined by the quantity of material things I have or the degree of my attachment to them?"[22] If this second point is true, then the love of money, greed, and focus on gaining more possessions may be as much of a problem for the poor as the moderately well-to-do. The broader principles of Scripture condemn anyone (rich and poor) who centers attention on gaining possessions, finds ultimate value and self-esteem in wealth, is preoccupied and motivated only by expanding material security, and places hope and satisfaction in money. But if the heart is centered on God and possessions are seen as gifts from God, then contentment can be found in enjoying whatever God has given.

In God's wisdom he has not given the same amount of material possessions to everyone. Those without abundance must be content, and those with abundance must be content and generous with what they have (Phil. 4:12; 1 Tim. 6:17–18). If people take what God has given to another or obtain goods stolen through the slave labor of another, God will correct the injustice by removing the unjust gains. God's opposition to inappropriate means of accumulating wealth through oppression of weaker people is a central emphasis in Amos's message. This is a prophetic message that the church must live by and proclaim to the world today. According to Bonhoeffer, "Our being Christian today will be limited to two things: prayer and doing justice among men."[23] Such statements should not be taken lightly, for a people's devotion to prayer and justice reveals the essentials of their relationship to God and others.

Where does true security come from? A biblical attitude toward possessions is directly related to the issue of security. But earthly possessions are not the only source of deceptive security. One way of developing false hopes is by turning religious institutions, ceremonies, or symbols into something more than what they really are. The altar, sacrifices, ark, and temple were important parts of Israel's worship environment designed by God. Each had a positive meaning that helped people understand how they could be forgiven of their sins and renew fellowship with him. But each was also open to many misunderstandings and deceptive perceptions.

The ark, for example, was the holy furnishing associated with God's presence in the Most Holy Place (Ex. 25:22), but it was not a magical wand or security blanket that would protect the Israelites at all times. When they brashly "brought back the ark of the covenant of the LORD Almighty" into battle to gain power over their enemies (1 Sam. 4:3–4), God did not give them victory over the Philistines. Instead, Israel was defeated, and the ark was

---

22. Ibid., 15.
23. D. Bonhoeffer, *Letters and Prayers from Prison* (London: Collins, 1959), 300.

taken into the temple of Dagon (4:10–5:12). Later in Jeremiah's day, the prophet accused the people of falsely trusting in God's presence in the temple in Jerusalem (Jer. 7:4). He claimed that the temple would not protect them when God destroyed Jerusalem. If one trusts in a building, even a special religious structure dedicated to God, there will be disappointment. The key to our security is to be found in stopping forbidden behaviors that displease God and in amending our ways (7:3–9).

Likewise, Luther preached against the false teaching of the Roman church of his day because it led people astray into false securities not based on grace. He claimed:

> Every teacher of works-righteousness is a trouble-maker . . . the pope, cardinals, bishops, monks, and that whole synagogue of Satan are trouble-makers . . . they are worse than false apostles. The false apostles [in Galatia] taught that in addition to faith in Christ the works of the Law of God were necessary unto salvation. But the papist omit faith altogether and teach self-devised traditions and works that are not commanded of God.[24]

After seeing the light of God's grace from Paul's letter to the Galatians, Luther knew he had to give up the false security of his old ways. He confessed, "I was much in fasting, watching, praying, saying of masses, and the like. Yet under the cloak of my outward respectability I continually mistrusted, doubted, feared, hated, and blasphemed God. My righteousness was a filthy puddle. Satan loves such saints."[25]

Are there people in our churches today who need to come to the same realization about their spiritual condition? What kind of religious or theological securities do we depend on? What beliefs or practices assure us that everything is right between us and God? Naturally, the answers will vary on the religious traditions practiced and the spiritual maturity of the person. I have spoken to people who believe they will be treated kindly by God because they have kept the Golden Rule of "treating others as they want to be treated." Others feel their baptism as a child or their partaking of Communion recently will please God. Others depend on a ritual prayer or the repetition of some formula. There seems to be a widespread feeling that if I do certain things, God will repay me with his favor. This is based on a general belief in the justice of God and biblical passages that connect God's covenantal blessings to human obedience (Deut. 27–28).

---

24. M. Luther, *A Commentary on St. Paul's Epistle to the Galatians*, trans. T. Graebner (Grand Rapids: Zondervan, n.d.), 32.
25. Ibid., 43.

Three problems surface with these kinds of expectations. (1) Human experience demonstrates that good people sometimes suffer unexpected tragedies. This has happened in my own family and in the families of two of our friends. It is a deceptive security to depend on your good behavior to automatically bring material blessings. This is much like the case of God's righteous servant Job, who suddenly had God's blessings removed and his health destroyed (Job 1–3). When these things happen, it is not unusual for people to question God (much as Job did) because they live with the false security that bad things will not happen to good people.

Such incidents do not mean that God does not exist or that he is unjust; rather, they point to the fact that there is not always a one-to-one relationship between a person's actions and God's response in this world. People may try to limit what God can and should do, but such positive formulations only make the reality of life more bitter when God does not follow these plans.

(2) The Bible describes the harsh treatment of his servants the prophets (Jer. 15:10–21; 20:1–6; 28; 37–38), Paul's many persecutions (2 Cor. 12:10), and Peter's advice that his audience should not be surprised if they suffer rejection (1 Peter 4:12–19). Yet most people today have a false security that they will not suffer persecution. But note that many Christians today are being persecuted *because* they are believers. Their lives are anything but peace and prosperity, in spite of the fact that they are living in a way pleasing to God.

(3) It is all too apparent that many false securities are not based on a fundamental belief that every good thing a person has received is an act of God's grace (they somehow think they have earned it). It is a perversion to conclude that we get what we deserve. If that were true, there would be no basis for any security, for everyone falls short of holiness and deserves God's judgment.

The common element these examples have with Amos's message is that people create false expectations and develop an empty security based on inappropriate religious grounds. At this point in Amos's sermons (3:9–4:3), the prophet does not attempt to create a positive set of criteria for authentic security. His purpose is to remove those factors that have caused the people to develop a false sense of security. On God's day of judgment he will allow Israel's enemies to destroy their temples and sacred altars. There is no reason to believe God will be any less severe in removing modern securities that parade in religious or material dress. We must also warn people about imaginary securities that have no basis in Scripture and twisted biblical teachings that create false impressions of an easy way to earn God's approval. We must confess that it is all by God's grace.

Amos 4:4–13

4 "Go to Bethel and sin;
  go to Gilgal and sin yet more.
Bring your sacrifices every morning,
  your tithe every three years.
5 Burn leavened bread as a thank offering
  and brag about your freewill offerings—
boast about them, you Israelites,
  for this is what you love to do,"
                    declares the sovereign LORD.

6 "I gave you empty stomachs in every city
  and lack of bread in every town,
  yet you have not returned to me,"
                    declares the LORD.

7 "I also withheld rain from you
  when the harvest was still three months away.
I sent rain on one town,
  but withheld it from another.
One field had rain;
  another had none and dried up.
8 People staggered from town to town for water
  but did not get enough to drink,
  yet you have not returned to me,"
                    declares the LORD.

9 "Many times I struck your gardens and vineyards,
  I struck them with blight and mildew.
Locusts devoured your fig and olive trees,
  yet you have not returned to me,"
                    declares the LORD.

10 "I sent plagues among you
  as I did to Egypt.
I killed your young men with the sword,
  along with your captured horses.
I filled your nostrils with the stench of your camps,
  yet you have not returned to me,"
                    declares the LORD.

¹¹"I overthrew some of you
    as I overthrew Sodom and Gomorrah.
You were like a burning stick snatched from the fire,
    yet you have not returned to me,"
declares the LORD.

¹²"Therefore this is what I will do to you, Israel,
    and because I will do this to you,
    prepare to meet your God, O Israel."

¹³He who forms the mountains,
    creates the wind,
    and reveals his thoughts to man,
he who turns dawn to darkness,
    and treads the high places of the earth—
    the LORD God Almighty is his name.

ALTHOUGH AMOS DOES not record how his audience responded to his message about the destruction of Israel's temples and altars in 3:14, one can assume that some of his listeners (if not the majority of them) do not appreciate or agree with his prophecy. How would you and I respond if someone announced that God was going to destroy our church or synagogue? We would probably object by telling that person all the good things that are happening at our holy place of worship. Likewise, the Israelites probably think it is unbelievable that God will actually destroy a temple where his people have been bringing sacrifices and tithes to honor him. Amos's sermon in 4:4−13 seems an attempt to answer mental or spoken objections to this prospect.

This section has three interrelated paragraphs. First, the prophet sarcastically calls for more sinful worship at Israel's temples (4:4−5), an obvious put-down of what has been happening in their "wonderful" worship services. He next gives a brief history lesson, describing how God brought a series of covenant curses on the people because they never truly turned to meet God in their worship (4:6−11). Finally, Amos thunders an ominous warning that the people should prepare themselves now, because God will soon come to meet them (4:12−13). If the people can reconceptualize worship from God's perspective, they can begin to evaluate if they are truly turning to God in their worship.

A Sarcastic Call to Worship (4:4−5)

IN OTHER WORSHIP contexts the priests call God's people to the sacred assemblies (Lev. 23:2, 4): "Enter his gates with thanksgiving and his courts with praise" (Ps. 100:4); "Come, let us sing for joy to the LORD" (95:1); and, "Sing to the LORD a new song" (96:1). The prophet Joel calls out to the priests:

> Put on sackcloth, O priests, and mourn;
>> wail, you who minister before the altar.
> Come, spend the night in sackcloth,
>> you who minister before my God. . . .
> Declare a holy fast;
>> call a sacred assembly.
> Summons the elders
>> and all who live in the land
> to the house of the LORD your God,
>> and cry out to the LORD. (Joel 1:13−14)

Amos follows this traditional pattern by mimicking a call to worship,[1] but he twists it in dramatic ways by changing the vocabulary. He does not just encourage people to go to the temples in Bethel and Gilgal;[2] in 4:4a he sarcastically exhorts them to multiply their "rebellious acts" (*pš᷾*, NIV "sin . . . sin yet more") of worship. This paradoxical statement reveals the value of the people's useless praise. Their sacrifices do not bring forgiveness of sin but add to the people's sinfulness before God.

Amos's second encouragement (4:4b) mocks the people's overemphasis on the repeated bringing of sacrifices (every morning) and tithes (every three days, not every "three years" as in NIV). Although God commanded the people to bring regular sacrifices for atonement of sins, for dedication of themselves to God, and for fellowship with God (Lev. 1−5), the normal practice was for families to bring their sacrifices once a year, not every day (1 Sam 1:3, 7, 21). In addition, Moses spoke of the tithe of the produce of the land being paid in the third year (Deut. 14:22, 28; 26:12), not every third day. Amos cynically urges them to continue their multitude of useless acts that will not appease God. He wants his audience to ask themselves whether God is primarily impressed with the number of religious acts his people do, or is it something else?

The third exhortation involves offering up or burning a thank offering of leavened bread (Amos 4:5). Although leavened bread was specifically forbidden in the instructions on some blood sacrifices (Ex. 23:18; 34:25; Lev. 2:11), the Levitical regulations did allow for thank offerings of leav-

---

1. Paul, *Amos*, 138, thinks Amos is adapting a "priestly Torah."

2. Gilgal was near Jericho, at the north end of the Dead Sea. It was the place where Joshua set up the twelve stones taken by the children of Israel from the Jordan River when they crossed into the Promised Land (Josh. 4:19−20; 5:1−10).

---

ened bread (Lev. 7:13), but there is no instruction to burn this bread.[3] Thus, the problem Amos is pinpointing here relates to the pious person's bragging about his or her thank and freewill gifts. Their motivation for sacrificing is a selfish desire to be seen by others. The prophet focuses on the Israelites' love to boast about the greatness of their gifts. Their worship has little to do with glorifying God; they are far more concerned about honoring themselves.

Amos's rhetorical twisting of this call to worship turns it into an accusation of sin. No one can miss the irony of his call to sin or his strong criticism of their motivations for worship. This kind of worship will not please God or keep him from destroying their temples and altars.

No One Turns to God,
Even After Chastening (4:6–11)

THIS PARAGRAPH IS divided into five short sections by the concluding phrase, "'yet you have not returned to me,' declares the LORD" (4:6, 8, 9, 10, 11). By the repetition of this phrase, Amos hammers home the central message that the Israelites do not have a proper relationship with God. The paragraph is also unified by the recitation of five different curses God has already brought on the nation (no food, no rain, no crops, no life, and his overthrowing of them). These are the covenant curses God said he would bring on the nation if they disobeyed him (see Lev. 26; Deut. 27–28).[4]

These judgments can be understood in two ways. They are perhaps God's punishment for the people's unacceptable worship in 4:4–5, or they may be seen as trials sent by him to humble the nation and encourage them to turn to God for help. Throughout these formulaic curses is the powerful theme that God himself is the One who brought all the natural disasters into Israel's history to transform their lives. Amos's repeated use of this pattern of "a curse, but no response" shows that the people are responsible for their own fate and thus deserving of God's judgment.

The first three curses affected nature, while the last two fell directly on the people. (1) God gave the people "cleanness of teeth" (lit. trans. of the Heb. in 4:6; see NIV note), which resulted in "empty stomachs" because of a nationwide famine ("in every city"). Although the date of this famine is unknown, it is probably one the audience has experienced and not the much earlier famine in the time of Elijah (1 Kings 17:1). God sent this disaster to

---

3. J. Niehaus, "Amos," 396–97, indicates the bread was to be eaten by the priests, though unleavened bread was burned in the thank offering (Lev. 2:11; 6:17).

4. Stuart, *Hosea–Jonah*, xxxii–xl, and Wolff, *Joel and Amos*, 213, describe these covenant curses.

bring the nation to its knees before him, but the people showed a stubborn unwillingness to turn to him. Turning *from* implies a change of direction and repentance, but the context suggests that Amos is simply describing a refusal to turn *to* God—no true worship of God. This is surprising, for one would think that in times of crisis people would naturally turn to God for help. Sure, they were going to the temple and repeating ritual, but God did not see any real heartfelt turning to him. A intimate personal relationship—the thing God desired most—was missing.

(2) One reason for this lack of food was God's withholding the normal spring rain (February–April) so that the barley harvest in May and June was virtually nil (4:7–8). Although some fields received a little rain, others received nothing. The drought grew so bad that in desperation people traveled from one village to another looking for someone who still had fresh water in a deep well or even a little stagnant water at the bottom of a large cistern. They desperately needed water in order to stay alive. In spite of all this the people remained unmoved and did not turn to God. These punishments were intended to bring restoration and a revitalized relationship with God, but the Israelites failed to respond to this chastening.

(3) Another reason for the famine was that God sent hot winds and mildew on the grain crops, plus locusts on the family gardens, vineyards, and fruit trees (4:9). Leaves and branches turned a sickly yellow-brown, and what was left was eaten by insects. This was an enormous blow to the agricultural economy, which threatened the existence of many poor farmers. What would they eat, where would they get seed to plant for the next year, and how could they cook food and light their lamps if they had no oil? One would think that people would cry out to God for help in such circumstances, but Israel did not learn from these bitter experiences.

(4) God allowed the strong army of Israel to be defeated, killing many young men (4:10). He also brought plagues similar to those experienced by the Egyptians when Moses led the people out of bondage (Ex. 7–12), though Amos does not specify the exact nature of these plagues. The key factor to notice is that God is now treating his own people as he previously treated his enemy Egypt. The nation that fought against Israel in these wars is not identified, but a few years earlier King Hazael of Syria defeated Israel and killed many of her horses (2 Kings 13:7). Amos reminds the people of the stench of rotting horse flesh and the terrible loss of life that affected so many families. How could they forget these events and not learn from them? These were acts of God against his people, yet the people did not transform their lives and turn to God in true confession and worship. Israel's stubborn unwillingness to change was almost unbelievable.

(5) In his final curse of this series Amos describes how God overthrew the people as he overthrew Sodom and Gomorrah (4:11). Yes, the Israelites are as evil and stubborn as Sodom was and deserve to be treated similarly. It is not clear what the word "overthrow" (also used in Deut. 29:23 concerning Sodom and Gomorrah) refers to. Some have suggested an earthquake,[5] but the comparison may be a more general comment about the suddenness and completeness of both destructions.

Whatever the source of this disaster, Amos mentions that only a few survived; they were like smoldering sticks pulled out of a fire. Yet amazingly, they still did not turn to God. The way to grace was provided through each trial, but the people did not see these as opportunities to turn to the Lord. They ignored what he was doing in their lives, as well as the prophet's theological interpretation of these events as God's curses.

God Will Meet Israel with Judgment (4:12–13)

THIS SERMON COMES to a climax with a final warning that the people of Israel must "prepare to meet ... God." They can no longer avoid God because he is coming to meet them. In an almost oath-like formula (cf. 1 Kings 2:23) the Lord declares what he will do to them. His patience has ended, and he will no longer chasten them with additional curses in hopes of bringing them into a dynamic covenant relationship.

In earlier times the people prepared to meet God and to confirm the covenant on Mount Sinai by purifying themselves for three days (Ex. 19:11, 15, 17). They also prepared themselves before going into holy war (Josh. 3:5) and prepared for worship at the temple, where God's glory dwelt (2 Chron. 30:19; 35:4). In this worship context Amos calls these unwilling and unresponsive people to prepare to enter the threatening divine presence of their holy God.

The hymnic fragment in 4:13 describes this God as the Creator of the earth, the One who reveals his thoughts—whose judgment can turn day into night and whose name is "the LORD God Almighty." This doxology[6] celebrates the glorious power of Israel's God. No one can stand upright before a God with this power or survive his almighty judgment. Amos may have quoted a popular hymn that the people regularly sang but never thought much about. Indeed, it is a fearful thing to fall into the hands of an angry God.

---

5. Paul, *Amos*, 149.

6. J. L. Crenshaw, *Hymnic Affirmations of Divine Justice* (Missoula: Scholars, 1975), attributes this hymn to a later editor, but Stuart, *Hosea–Jonah*, 286, and G. V. Smith, *Amos*, 190–92, argue that Amos is quoting a hymn from his own time.

Bridging Contexts

TRUE WORSHIP. This message evaluates Israelite forms of worship at semipagan Israelite temples, but the focus of attention is on the nature of true worship, not on the forms of ancient Israelite worship (sacrifices or the presence of the golden calf at Bethel), which are different from our methods of worship. Amos challenges the nation's view of worshiping God and claims it is inadequate, even sinful. The central principle that forms the basis of this critique is that their worship is not based on a personal relationship with God. Their worship is unacceptable because:

(1) People cannot please God in their worship simply by increasing the quantity of gifts or confessions (4:4);
(2) they cannot honor God with praise if they end up putting most of their attention on themselves (4:5);
(3) they cannot develop a relationship with God by ignoring his chastening or by being unwilling to turn to and depend on him in times of trouble (4:6–11); and
(4) it is necessary for everyone to begin preparing for the day when they will meet the Creator of the universe face to face (4:12–13).

Worship traditionally is defined as the act of attributing worth to something. When people worship God, they give him the praise and glory that is due the holy and sovereign King of the universe (Ps. 96:7–8; Rev. 5:12). Throughout the years God has provided his people with information on different ways of worshiping, and they have developed cultural variations (in liturgy, music, and ritual)[7] that are meaningful to them.

Since some ancient Israelite and New Testament church worship was rejected by God (e.g., Isa. 1:10–15; Rom. 14:16–18; Heb. 12:28), we know that God finds certain attitudes and activities unacceptable. As D. Peterson says, "acceptable worship under both covenants is a matter of responding to God's initiative in salvation and revelation, and doing so in the way that he requires."[8] This means that worthwhile acts of prayer, praise, or ritual must be directed toward God and not be something that just makes people feel good. Worship is based on a willful turning to God in dependence for salvation and daily life. It gives glory to him through continual steadfast devotion of the heart rather than frequent performance of external obligations. Worship may "be judged by the degree in which it leads to Holiness"[9] and a relationship to God.

---

7. H. J. Kraus, *Theology of the Psalms* (Minneapolis: Augsburg, 1986), 94–97.
8. D. Peterson, *Engaging with God: A Biblical Theology of Worship* (Grand Rapids: Eerdmans, 1992), 19.
9. E. Underhill, *Worship* (New York: Harper, 1936), 77.

Looking at examples of worship in Israel's past history, we find a stark difference between true worship and what the people in Amos's audience are doing. Abraham worshiped after God appeared to him (Gen. 12:7–8), Jacob made an oath of devotion to God after he saw a vision of God in a dream (28:12–22), and Moses bowed his head to the ground when God spoke to him from the burning bush (Ex. 3:1–6). The Hebrews worshiped God at the desert tabernacle and the Jerusalem temple, where God's glory dwelt (Ex. 40:34; 1 Kings 8:10–11). In each case, worship was a humble response to the presence of Israel's holy God.

Worship does not gain something that people can earn from God; it is a loving response to what God has already freely given. Amos's audience does not please God since they are indifferent to his presence (they do not turn to him), nor are they focused on what he is doing. Even when God reveals his presence through several chastenings, they do not recognize his hand at work in their lives or submit to his will.

Biblical history includes comparable situations where God confronted a group unwilling to worship him appropriately. The people of Sodom ignored God, the Canaanites refused to turn to him, and the nation of Judah strayed far from him (Amos 2:4–5). All of these groups eventually had to face God and submit to his powerful judgment.

Israel's prophets held the same expectation for future nations unwilling to turn to God (Isa. 24–27; Dan. 7–8). When God comes to this earth in power and glory, some will be prepared to meet the sovereign King of the universe and others will not. Those who worship God in Spirit and truth will bow before him and enjoy his kingdom, while others will be destroyed (Zech. 14; Rev. 19). Someday every knee will bow and every tongue will confess God's praise (Isa. 45:23; Rom. 14:11; Phil. 2:10–11). In the end God's people will give him praise while those who hate him will be put to shame (Isa. 45:24–25). There is no other way, so each individual and every people group need to prepare for the day they meet the Lord face to face.

Contemporary Significance

HOW CAN THIS passage have an impact on the daily private worship of individual believers in the church? What principles need to be observed by those who plan and direct church worship each week? How can a believer use this passage to evaluate worship in order to discover if it is pleasing to God? One must realize, of course, that this passage is not a complete systematic treatment of worship or a full list of things to do or not to do. Nevertheless, it does give practical guidelines that can help the church and its leaders focus on what God sees as important.

Avoiding cultural stumbling blocks. We must first be careful not to get distracted by the Hebrew forms of worship that are so different from modern worship practices. We no longer offer burnt offerings or thank offerings with leavened bread in churches today (4:4–5), but we do have a variety of symbolic rituals that represent spiritual truths. Our prayers, songs, liturgies, and repeated acts can become just as dead as the meaningless offerings that some offered in Israel.

The interpreter must also beware of focusing on issues not raised by Amos. For example, the prophet does not mention the golden calf at the temple in Bethel in this sermon. Rather, he focuses attention primarily on the people's misunderstanding of the nature of true worship. This does not mean that Amos approves of the golden calf; it just means that the prophet chooses to challenge the people on a different level.

In modern terms this is comparable to talking to a Catholic friend about worship without getting involved with an argument over her view of Communion. Maybe I do not agree with her theological interpretation of Communion, but I can choose to discuss worship based on her relationship with God rather than her understanding of ritual practices. Either approach is legitimate, but it is important that one not read into or add arguments that are not a part of the reasoning of the text. It is vital that believers today learn to discuss theological differences on several levels. Thus, I may get further in dealing with the spiritual life of my neighbor by focusing on her view of the death and resurrection of Christ rather than by bringing up the touchy issue of her interpretation of the Eucharist.

Amos also does not condemn sacrifice as a meaningless way of worshiping God. He assumes that this is a good way of relating to God, even though he is aware that some misconceive the nature and meaning of rituals or do not perceive how this ritual symbolizes the nature of their relationship to God. Nevertheless, worship should not just "be identified with a special sense of the presence of God,"[10] as if its essence is associated solely with a feeling or with a prescribed experience one has. Such definitions can lead to deceptive subjective feelings that are self-defined rather than biblically defined and can lead people to make claims that are exclusive of other legitimate expressions.

In spite of this caution, worship is experiential in nature because it engages the worshiper in a relationship with God. This relationship is based on his self-revelation in words through Scripture and in deeds through a person's encounter with God. The natural response of a believer to the glorious and fearful presence of a holy and all-powerful God is humble submission, reverence, and praise. This is part of what Amos has in mind when he talks

---

10. Peterson, *Engaging with God*, 16.

about "turning to God." If people are self-centered or unwilling to turn to God (4:6–11), worship is missing.

Evaluating our worship. What impact should Amos's warnings have on worship services in churches today? Worship leaders should first evaluate what is happening in their churches to discover if true worship or sinful rebellion (4:4) is taking place. These contrasting alternatives provide an intimidating challenge that discourages careful analysis because God provides no in-between option. Worship is either good and honoring to God or it is sinful. If we are honest with ourselves, many would have to admit that they have been in worship services where they are preoccupied with other things and not focused on worshiping God, attended church with unconfessed sin, spoken words of praise without any real meaning behind them, or gotten involved in leading worship for personal recognition.

Although most people tend to look at such situations as inappropriate or unfortunate, we usually do not emphasize them as sin and rebellion against God. Maybe I have lived a sheltered life, but I seldom hear anyone confess the sin of not truly worshiping God when they go to church. In contrast, when the prophet Malachi observes useless ritual that does not honor God, he challenges the spiritual leaders to close the temple rather than continue unacceptable worship (Mal. 1:5–10). Jesus himself condemns the hypocritical Pharisees who love to stand in the synagogue or on the street corner to gain attention to themselves when they pray to God (Matt. 6:5–7). Maybe it is time for churches to be more concerned about the quality of their worship and less focused on the particular style that each age group prefers.

Amos provides at least two criteria to help believers and worship leaders assess the quality of worship. (1) Do God's people place special value in the quantity of worship acts or their frequent repetition, an attitude that can easily develop into an approach of trying to earn God's favor (4:4)? (2) Do people love those acts of worship that draw attention to themselves or display their piety before others (4:5)?

These criteria should not be just used as negative factors that condemn; they can also be positively employed to plan and encourage meaningful worship of God. Worship naturally involves doing the same kind of things week after week. Worship is a verb that describes what people do to honor God; it is not just a passive activity where people are entertained by performers.[11] This repeated activity of honoring God takes place when people sing of his glory, rehearse his great deeds, and glorify his holy name.

But this activity of repeatedly doing similar things automatically raises two dangers. (1) First is the danger of vain repetitions. While there is nothing

---

11. R. E. Webber, *Worship Is a Verb* (Waco, Tex.: Word, 1985), 19–20.

wrong with repeating a prayer or song if it is a meaningful expression of the heart, there is a strong possibility that too much of the same thing will result in habit-forming repetitions that are unconsciously mouthed because they are not fresh and full of dynamic significance. This suggests that one should not plan to sing the same worship chorus week after week. It also raises questions about the same liturgical phrases that so easily flow through the sanctuary. Certainly a new approach will require more work in preparation. This may shake up some people who thrive on the security of what is familiar, but the result may be some real mental involvement in the worship of God.

(2) A second danger is the subtle feeling that I myself have done something that deserves attention. If I have demonstrated my spirituality by doing something, God will reward my devotion and faithfulness to him. Although God does desire faithfulness, praising him is not a means for a person to gain his favor. The purpose of worship is not to earn points with God. Worship is focused outwardly to God and not inwardly on the worshiper. There is no place for declaring to others what we have done or how much we have given (4:5).

Why does God send troubles? When one hears about people losing their business in a tornado, farmers having their crops destroyed by a flood, or the burning of homes in a wild forest fire, it is hard to understand why these things happen. In the end, few people in the church today can ever fully know the reasons for these kinds of events. But Amos records five cases (4:6–11) where God himself planned and brought disasters on his people for a specific purpose. These verses emphasize that God was and still is sovereignly in control over nature (rain, wind, and heat), animals (locusts), and historical events (wars). These "natural disasters" are really "acts of God" that do not just happen by the chance blowing of high-pressure weather systems or accidental political mistakes.

Believers need to see the presence of God's hand in the circumstances that surround them. This does not mean that every problem is caused by God, for Job 1–2 indicates that Satan is hard at work trying to tear down believers, and evil people have freedom to sin. Nevertheless, God can use evil deeds to bring glory to himself and growth in the hearts of his people. His purposes may sometimes be unknown, but his acts can be a means of bringing people to their knees.

In Amos's case God brought these difficulties on the Israelites in order to cause them to turn from their sinful worship and come back to him (4:6–11). God wanted his people to approach their worship with a fresh vitality and turn to him for mercy and help. Since we usually do not know what God's reasoning is in sending problems into people's lives today, it is impossible to suggest that difficulties have come into a person's life because of sin. Yet in spite of our limited knowledge, it is always appropriate for us to examine our lives and to turn to God for wisdom, strength, and grace. If we refuse to do so, he will probably deal with us in the same way he dealt with the Israelites.

If the church and its members are repeatedly unwilling to respond positively to God, he has only two options available: send another plague to wake us up and motivate us to turn to God, or give up on the possibility of change and bring judgment. The book of Jonah is an example of how God pursues a rebellious prophet to transform his behavior, while Romans 1:18—32 describes how God gives some people over to their evil desires and depraved minds because they purposely reject the revelation they have received. A stubborn unwillingness to listen to God will inevitably lead to judgment.

Preparing to meet God. Amos ends his sermon with the challenge to prepare to meet God. This is an issue the church cannot ignore, even if it makes people uncomfortable. Isaiah 45:23 predicts that "before me every knee will bow," and Paul warned that "we will all stand before God's judgment seat . . . each of us will give an account of himself to God" (Rom. 14:10, 12). Although the challenge is not often heard today, it is not inappropriate to ask if people are prepared to meet the almighty Creator and Judge of this world face to face (cf. Amos 4:12—13). Fire and brimstone preaching may be a thing of the past, but the facts remain the same. Everyone must prepare for that eventual meeting with the sovereign Creator of the universe, the King of kings.

On July 8, 1741, Jonathan Edwards preached his most famous sermon, "Sinners in the Hands of an Angry God." Edwards was generally more pastoral in his sermons and was not one of the legendary hellfire preachers like George Whitefield; yet in this sermon he focused on the vengeance of God on a people unprepared to meet him. He claimed that "there is nothing that keeps men at any one moment out of hell, but the pleasure of God."[12] God has the power to throw rebellious sinners into hell, they deserve God's divine justice, their sins condemn them, and God is angry at sinners. Thus, Edwards saw people on the brink of hell, walking over the pit of hell on a rotten cloth. Human wisdom gives no security, and many unprepared sinners will say:

No, I never intended to come here: I had laid out matters otherwise in my mind; I thought I should contrive well for myself; I thought my scheme good; but it came upon me unexpectedly . . . death outwitted me. . . . O my cursed foolishness! I was flattering myself, and pleasing myself with vain dreams of what I would do hereafter.

---

12. H. P. Simonson, ed., *Selected Writings of Jonathan Edwards* (New York: F. Unger, 1970), 97.

Edwards called his audience to consider their dangerous position, the suffering that goes on in the fiery pit of hell, and the terrors of the wrath of an almighty Creator. This is what Jesus meant when he said in Matthew 25:31–32, 41:

> When the Son of Man comes in his glory, and all the angels with him, he will sit on his throne in heavenly glory. All the nations will be gathered before him, and he will separate the people one from another.... He will say to those on his left, "Depart from me, you who are cursed, into the eternal fire prepared for the devil and his angels."

If Amos and Jesus accepted the task of warning people about their eternal destiny, should we not take on the responsibility of persuading people to evaluate whether they are ready to meet God? Our only hope is to prepare to face God before that fateful day, to repent of our sins, and throw ourselves on his mercy.

No anxious bride would go to her wedding without hours of careful thought and preparation for the wedding day. No serious politician would come to an election without months of campaigning so that victory will be possible. No successful business person would purchase a new company without weeks of examining the market for its products and due diligence in evaluating the company's financial records. In everyday life people know that preparation is required in all aspects of life if one hopes to accomplish any significant goals.

People also know that the amount of preparation is directly tied to the importance of the decision. The higher the goal or the more important the person you are meeting, the greater the amount of money spent and the more one prepares. Certainly there can be no more important issue, no more powerful person, no more significant decision than the question of your eternal relationship to God.

Amos 5:1–17

HEAR THIS WORD, O house of Israel, this lament I take up concerning you:

2 "Fallen is Virgin Israel,
    never to rise again,
deserted in her own land,
    with no one to lift her up."

3 This is what the Sovereign LORD says:

"The city that marches out a thousand strong for Israel
    will have only a hundred left;
the town that marches out a hundred
    will have only ten left."

4 This is what the LORD says to the house of Israel:

"Seek me and live;
5   do not seek Bethel,
do not go to Gilgal,
    do not journey to Beersheba.
For Gilgal will surely go into exile,
    and Bethel will be reduced to nothing."
6 Seek the LORD and live,
    or he will sweep through the house of Joseph like a fire;
it will devour,
    and Bethel will have no one to quench it.

7 You who turn justice into bitterness
    and cast righteousness to the ground
8 (he who made the Pleiades and Orion,
    who turns blackness into dawn
    and darkens day into night,
who calls for the waters of the sea
    and pours them out over the face of the land—
    the LORD is his name—
9 he flashes destruction on the stronghold
    and brings the fortified city to ruins),

¹⁰ you hate the one who reproves in court
and despise him who tells the truth.
¹¹ You trample on the poor
and force him to give you grain.
Therefore, though you have built stone mansions,
you will not live in them;
though you have planted lush vineyards,
you will not drink their wine.
¹² For I know how many are your offenses
and how great your sins.

You oppress the righteous and take bribes
and you deprive the poor of justice in the courts.
¹³ Therefore, the prudent man keeps quiet in such times,
for the times are evil.

¹⁴ Seek good, not evil,
that you may live.
Then the LORD God Almighty will be with you,
just as you say he is.
¹⁵ Hate evil, love good;
maintain justice in the courts.
Perhaps the LORD God Almighty will have mercy
on the remnant of Joseph.

¹⁶ Therefore, this is what the Lord, the LORD God
Almighty, says:

"There will be wailing in all the streets
and cries of anguish in every public square.
The farmers will be summoned to weep
and the mourners to wail.
¹⁷ There will be wailing in all the vineyards,
for I will pass through your midst,"

says the LORD.

Original Meaning

THE LAMENT NATURE of this message is introduced in verse 1. In other texts a mourning theme like this is connected to the death or funeral of a loved one (Gen. 23:2; 50:1–4; 2 Sam. 1:17–27) or a nation (Lam. 1–4). People also lamented the approaching threat of death of a person because of sickness, oppression, or injustice (Ps. 6; 13; Jer. 11:18–23), or the impending demise of a nation (Isa. 15:1–9; Jer. 48:36–44; Ezek. 27:1–36).[1] When people in ancient times mourned, they often shaved their hair, wore sackcloth, sat in ashes, wept, and sometimes employed professional mourners.[2]

Since these were the normal cultural behaviors for people giving laments, it is safe to assume that Amos follows at least some of these practices. He may be weeping as he sings this dirge. If his stern condemnations in earlier sermons have not softened any hearts, perhaps his plaintive cries will cause some to listen with a sympathetic ear. This sad dirge, which reveals the agony of the prophet's heart, may cause them to change their thinking.

The presence of the *qinah* dirge in 5:2–3, which is characteristic of laments, and the repeated mourning vocabulary in 5:16–17 demonstrate that this is indeed a lament. But why is Amos expressing grief over the end of the nation of Israel when it is in fact a strong military power in the ancient Near East during the reign of Jeroboam II? Amos is prophesying the approaching doom of the nation, which he foresees in the near future. His wailing chant is designed to send shock waves through the nearly "dead" nation of Israel to bring them back to reality. This is the prophet's dramatic rhetorical attempt to convince the people of their true status before God.[3] Although they think everything is great, in actuality they are enjoying their final few days of the good life.

This sermon is arranged in a chiastic structure of conflicting themes (death in vv. 1–3, 16–17; life in vv. 4–6, 14–15; note also accusations in vv. 7, 10–13),[4] with the central emphasis placed on the pivotal doxological hymn that commemorates the name and power of Yahweh (5:8–9), the almighty God who determines the future of the nation.

---

1. C. Westermann, *Praise and Lament in the Psalms*, trans. K. R. Crim and R. H. Soulen (Atlanta: John Knox, 1981), 261, describes the different kinds of laments.

2. G. Stahlin, "κοπετός," *TDNT*, 3:836–41.

3. G. V. Smith, *Amos*, 206–9.

4. J. de Waard, "The Chiastic Structure of Amos 5:1–17," *VT* 27 (1977): 170–77 and N. J. Tromp, "Amos 5:1–17: Toward a Stylistic and Rhetorical Anaysis," *OtSt* 23 (1984): 72–73, identify the parts of the chiasm but neither were able to integrate 5:13 into this structure.

> A Lament the death of the nation (vv. 1–3)
>   B Call to seek God and live (vv. 4–6)
>   C Accusations of no justice (v. 7)
>   D Hymn to Yahweh (vv. 8–9)
>   C' Accusations of no justice (vv. 10–13)
>   B' Call to seek God and live (vv. 14–15)
> A' Lament the death of the nation (vv. 16–17)

Commentators have derived different emphases in 5:1–17. (1) Some make the call to seek God and repent the main emphasis, treating the laments as mere warnings to bring the people back to God. (2) Others make the laments predominant and treat the calls to seek God as empty offers of hope because the nation's destruction is already determined. (3) Still others refer the laments to the nation as a whole but apply the calls to seek God to the righteous remnant that will respond to the prophet's message (5:14–15). This last alternative seems the best way to understand this passage because it maintains the validity of both the lament and the call to seek God.[5] The prophet's purpose is to convince the nation that things are so bad that God will soon bury its memory, but in the process he persuades a few responsive people to seek God and live.

Lamenting the Death of the Nation (5:1–3, 16–17)

THIS FUNERAL SONG begins and ends by emphasizing the horror of the death of the nation of Israel.[6] Amos's emotional dirge pictures Israel (or the city of Samaria)[7] as a virgin, which implies that she is like a young girl in the prime of life, about ready to enter the most exciting and fulfilling time of her life: being a wife and mother. But tragedy strikes and wastes her potential; her untimely death brings to an end her great hopes and dreams, as well as God's wonderful plans for her.

Amos personifies the nation as already fallen (a perfect verb describing completed action), a phrase that is used in other laments as a euphemism for death (2 Sam. 1:19, 25, 27; Lam. 2:21). This once vibrant virgin now lies totally helpless without hope of revival. She has been deserted by

---

5. A. V. Hunter, *Seek the Lord: A Study of the Meaning and Function of the Exhortations in Amos, Hosea, Micah, and Zephaniah* (Baltimore: St. Mary's Seminary, 1982), 61–65, surveys these alternative approaches.

6. Hayes, *Amos*, 155, believes Samaria is the addressed because the virgin terminology is elsewhere used of cities (Jer. 18:13; 31:4, 21) not countries, but most think that Amos is addressing the whole nation of Israel.

7. See J. J. Schmitt, "The Virgin of Israel: Referent and Use in Amos and Jeremiah," *CBQ* 53 (1991): 365–87.

friends, family, and God. Using the analogy of dead troops left to rot on the battlefield, she is alone without anyone to care for her or to bury her. The bitterness of the prophet's grief is evident and the finality of Israel's destruction is clear.

Verse 3 points out why the nation has no hope: Its army has been decimated (90 percent of the troops have been killed),[8] exactly as Amos predicted in 2:13–16. The existence of a small remnant of these troops should not be seen as a sign of hope from the prophet, for who would gain hope from hearing the news that three of your four children were killed in a car accident?[9]

When the army is defeated, the rest of the nation will go into mourning, following the example of Amos (5:16–17). Everyone will mourn because death will touch every family. People will wail in the streets, in the town square, and in the vineyard; the nation will be in shock. The magnitude of the weeping will be enormous. When death comes, it is natural to ask why, but on this occasion people will already know the answer. Amos has told them that this death will come about when God "pass[es] through your midst," a phrase borrowed from the Exodus and Passover events (Ex. 11:4; 12:12). The difference is that now God is not passing *over* his people and judging an evil foreign nation; instead, he is destroying the families in Israel. What a reversal of fortunes! God has turned the great Exodus themes into death threats.

A Call to Seek God and Live (5:4–6, 14–15)

NEXT TO THESE devastating lamentations is what appears to be a prophetic call of hope. It is confusing to find such final statements about the death of the nation beside these exhortations to seek God and live. How can they both be true? S. Paul believes this is one final offer of hope if the people will only repent; thus, he does not take seriously Amos's statement that the nation is dead. Their repentance can cancel God's plan to judge them, just as Nineveh's repentance caused God to have compassion and not destroy the city (Jonah 3:3–10).[10]

I have difficulty in seeing this as a real offer of hope for the whole nation. It seems more likely that it functions rhetorically in two ways: (1) as a partial explanation for why God is judging the wicked—they are not seeking God but wasting their time at various temples; and (2) as an encouragement

---

8. Stuart, *Hosea–Jonah*, 345, connects this consequence to the curse in Deut. 28:62: "You who were as numerous as the stars in the sky will be left but few in number."

9. Hubbard, *Joel and Amos*, 165, also finds no message of hope in this passage.

10. Paul, *Amos*, 161–62, finds this approach justified by Jeremiah's explanation that God will have compassion and change his plans if people repent of their evil (Jer. 18).

to a small "remnant" of seekers (5:15) to respond positively to God and not get fooled by all the religious activity at Israel's temples.

Both of these audiences in the crowd that listens to Amos must understand there is a difference between going to the temples at Bethel, Gilgal (Hos. 4:15), or Beersheba and truly seeking God. One obvious reason why these religious shrines will be of no help is because they will be destroyed and the people living there will go into exile. There will be no protection or security gained from worshiping there. The fire of military destruction will sweep through "the house of Joseph" (the northern nation of Israel), and no one will be able to stop it (Amos 5:6). Elsewhere (4:4–11; 5:21–27; 8:14) Amos suggests that people are not truly seeking or worshiping God at these temples; therefore, God is not willing to accept their sacrifices or their wild music. Yet there is no indication that Amos is trying to argue here in favor of worshiping only at Jerusalem.

Amos's exhortation to the small remnant that desires to please God is that they should seek to know him, turn to him for forgiveness, follow the divine patterns of hating evil and loving good, establish justice in the courts (5:14–15), and call on God for mercy and protection. They also should not be fooled by the syncretistic worship and pious words they hear at the various temples around the country. God searches the heart and knows the true intentions of the thoughts. Seeking God requires an attitude of dependence, a love for God, a humble submission, faith that affects behavior, and a willingness to follow his covenant stipulations.

The results of this vital relationship with God will be life (5:6), the Lord's presence with them (5:14), and the possibility of his mercy (5:15). This is no guarantee that everything will be okay if a few people seek God, but there is no possibility of God's abiding presence with them if they refuse to seek him with all their heart.

Accusations of No Justice (5:7, 10–13)

IN THE MIDST of this wailing lament song is a series of accusations that seem to function as another reason for God's plan to destroy the nation of Israel. Perhaps some are wondering why God would want to destroy his people. The straightforward answer goes back to the way these people treat others. Some in Israel have perverted the central religious and social ideals of righteousness and justice. Their moral values are not governed by relationships of justice in the courts, honesty, fairness, equality (5:10, 12), and respect for the norms of the covenant.

Justice is an outworking of God's character of holiness, but the nation does not emulate him. They have changed the sweet experience of dealing with people based on righteousness into a bitter and evil thing through their mistreatment of those who are poorer or less powerful. By manipulating the courts through bribery, supplying false witnesses, and intimidating judges, the powerful political and business leaders are able to maintain their lifestyles and insulate themselves from accusations of unfairness. Amos laments these unbearable injustices. These rich people make life miserable for the poor, who suffer under them.

As a result, God will not allow the wealthy to enjoy the fruits of their crimes. They will not be able to live in their fine mansions built of expensively cut stones or appreciate the wine that comes from their well-groomed vineyards (5:11). They make others poor and homeless; now the same will be done to them.

Verse 13 also contains a condemnation of these "prosperous" (*śkl*) people in Israel (not the poor "prudent" person, as in NIV). This understanding of *śkl* creates a parallelism with the people condemned in 5:11–12. The judgment clause after the word "therefore" in verse 11 is then parallel to the "therefore" judgment in verse 13. God will cause these prosperous and unjust leaders to "be silent," a euphemism for death (cf. Jer. 6:2; 47:5; 48:2; 50:30),[11] when he destroys the nation on the day of their judgment. Amos sorrowfully proclaims their crimes of injustice will not pay rich dividends any longer, for they will soon be dead.

Hymn to Yahweh (5:8–9)[12]

THE CENTRAL PART of this chiastic dirge appropriately focuses on God, the One who will bring about the death of Israel. Using a series of participles ("he who ..."), which is typical of other hymns, Amos reminds his audience that he is not talking about a weak power or a pantheistic personification of nature. In this muted polemic against the pagan astral gods,[13] Yahweh is seen as the One who created the magnificent spectacle of nature that people see every night in the heavens—the constellations of Pleiades and Orion (see also Job 9:9; 38:31; Isa. 40:26). The prophet is using positive traditions to support

---

11. For a defense of this translation, see G. V. Smith, "Amos 5:13: The Deadly Silence of the Prosperous," *JBL* 107 (1988): 289–91.

12. Mays, *Amos*, 83, 95; Wolff, *Joel and Amos*, 215–17; and Crenshaw, *Hymnic Affirmations of Divine Justice*, 5–24, suggest that these verses have been added by a later editor because of their advanced theology; but T. McComiskey, "The Hymnic Elements of the Prophecy of Amos: A Study of Form Critical Methodologies," in *A Tribute to G. Archer*, ed. W. C. Kaiser and R. Youngblood (Chicago: Moody, 1986), 105–28, defends the position that this hymn has been put here by Amos.

13. Hubbard, *Joel and Amos*, 170, sees this as a secondary purpose of this passage, but it is just as likely that Amos is contrasting a true biblical view of God with a humanly created and socially constructed image of God.

his view of God; he may even be quoting from a well-known hymn that the people sing in their temple worship services.[14]

The middle of this hymn emphasizes God's sovereign power to change the course of nature. While the people of Israel "turn [change] justice into bitterness" (5:7), God can change night into day or day into night. "Those who are guilty of social inversion will now witness and suffer cosmic inversion."[15] God can bring both the security and blessing of the day as well as the dangers and threats of darkness.

This hymn is particularly interested in the negative changes as characterized in the flooding of water over the face of the earth (5:8c), a haunting illusion to God's destruction of the whole earth at the time of Noah's flood (Gen. 6–8). These examples not only illustrate the potential of God's power, but they dramatically make the point that no person or nation can hope to withstand the awesome power of God. Yahweh, the God of Israel, is the God who can and will do these things (5:8d).

In the second part of the hymn (5:9), Amos focuses on the application of God's power over the wealthy people in his audience. Today they may live securely in expensive mansions in strongly fortified cities, but soon God will flash destruction over these places and leave them in ruins (see 3:11, 14; 4:3–4; 5:11).[16] This hymn supports Amos's persuasive attempt to convince the people that their relationship to God is central to their future. God has the power over life and death, and death will soon bring mourning and wailing to the nation of Israel.

THE ALTERNATIVES OF **life or death**. Amos's dirge draws a line of connection between Almighty God (life and death, justice and righteousness) and the people. Life for people is not guaranteed, but it is a possibility for those who seek God and hate injustice. Since God is the sovereign power over nature and humanity, he is the One who establishes standards of justice for all people. He administers judgment to those who practice injustice. Blessing, joy, security, and success are not inalienable rights or something everyone deserves; they are gifts of God's mercy. Human appreciation of life is usually heightened to the extent that a person understands the preciousness and precariousness of life.

---

14. Andersen and Freedman, *Amos*, 453–54, suggest that all the hymns in 4:13; 5:8–9; 9:5–6 may have come from a single, well-known hymn.

15. Paul, *Amos*, 168.

16. J. Niehaus, "Amos," 419, illustrates the common tendency to trust in strong walls from the *Annals of the Kings of Assyria*, 35–36 (by Tiglath-Pileser III) and 293 (by Ashurbanipal II).

Some have no thought or fear of death, believing they are indestructible. Others value life because they know that the withdrawal of God's presence with them could bring death (5:14). God's power can suddenly change day into night, life into death (5:8). He can bring destruction on the whole earth or on individual homes and cities (5:9). No military power or high social position can protect a person from death. God's administration of death is particularly focused against those who do not seek him and who pervert his standard of justice.

These connections are not new with Amos but go back to the basic choice that Moses presented to the Israelites when they were getting ready to enter the Promised Land:

> See, I set before you today life and prosperity, death and destruction. For I command you today to love the LORD your God, to walk in his ways....
>
> This day I call heaven and earth as witness against you that I have set before you life and death, blessings and curses. Now choose life, so that you and your children may live and that you may love the LORD your God, listen to his voice, and hold fast to him. For the LORD is your life, and he will give you many years in the land...." (Deut. 30:15–16a, 19–20)

In the New Testament life is associated with the Father and especially the Son of Man, who has received the authority to judge the world (John 5:26–27). Although the wages of sin is death (Rom. 6:23), those who believe in Christ will have life (John 6:25–26). These passages demonstrate a pervasive and consistent theological position on God's control of life and death. Can a more convincing argument be developed to support the exhortation that people should seek God if they want to live? How can anyone who refuses to seek God think he or she has any hope for the future? Only those who foolishly think that they (rather than God) control their own lives would make such a mistake.

Is there a reason to lament? Lamentation and wailing seem a normative practice in the Hebrew culture of the Old Testament, and it is mentioned from time to time in the New Testament. Many of these examples relate to the death of someone, but better parallels to this passage in Amos are those examples where someone weeps because God's people have not responded to a prophet's ministry and will be judged. The prophet Jeremiah laments his own personal trials and failures (Jer. 11:18–23; 15:10–21; 20:7–18), but he also mourns and intercedes with God when he hears that God is going to judge his covenant people and send them into exile (8:18–9:2; 14:17–15:2). Jeremiah cries out in anguish and asks for mercy:

> Have you rejected Judah completely?
>   Do you despise Zion?
> Why have you afflicted us
>   so that we cannot be healed? . . .
> For the sake of your name do not despise us;
>   do not dishonor your glorious throne.
> Remember your covenant with us
>   and do not break it.[17] (14:19, 21)

Although Jesus weeps when Lazarus dies (John 11:33–35), much more significant is his weeping over Jerusalem because he wants to gather these people together into his kingdom (Matt. 23:37). Paul also seems to be in mourning and in anguish over the stubborn resistance of his Jewish brothers and sisters, who refuse to respond positively to the messianic claims of Christ (Rom. 9:1–3).

In each case a messenger of God declares his message, an audience rejects this revelation, and a deep sorrow over the coming divine judgment arises. The first two factors are common to many forms of prophetic speech, but the third is unique to the lament. In the process of persuasion, the lament is a powerful alternative to accusation and condemnation. It expresses an attitude of identification and sympathy rather than opposition and conflict. In the lament the speaker takes the side of the audience and expresses regret (and sometimes uncomfortableness or disagreement) for what is about to happen.

This perspective leads the audience to react appreciatively because of the support offered rather than defensively because of the speaker's severe condemnation. The lament builds a bridge of commonality with the one who suffers, but it does not deny the truth that God will bring judgment. In many ways the lament may be a more effective persuasive tool than the judgment speech because the listeners finally realize the emotional depth of the speaker's concern for them.

The reason for giving a lament must arise from the inner agony of the messenger and not from a desire to manipulate the emotional response of the audience. The apostle Paul was willing to have himself "cursed and cut off from Christ for the sake of my brothers" (Rom. 9:3), and Moses was willing to have his name blotted from God's book for the sake of the nation of Israel (Ex. 32:32).[18]

---

17. See A. R. Diamond, *The Confessions of Jeremiah in Context: Scenes of Prophetic Drama* (Sheffield: JSOT, 1986); M. S. Smith, *The Laments of Jeremiah and Their Contexts: A Literary and Redactional Study of Jeremiah 11–20* (Atlanta: Scholars, 1990).

18. J. I. Durham, *Exodus* (WBC; Waco, Tex.: Word, 1987), 432–33, makes the point that Moses goes through the emotional responses of pleading for mercy, anger, reasoning, taking control of the situation, and seeking forgiveness for the people.

Jesus expressed deep sorrow for the stubborn and unresponsive people of Jerusalem, and surprisingly for the hypocritical Pharisees (see Matt. 23).

It is essential to notice that in moving to a lament form of expression, a speaker does not modify his or her theological beliefs. Moses and Paul did not all of a sudden change their minds about the sinfulness of their audience and take a mushy position that God's love will somehow overlook all their evil. Laments are not a sign of weakness or pastoral compromise, a denial of responsibility, or a softening of a belief in God's justice. Rather, they are personal expressions of real sorrow that people are so set in their sinful ways that the Lord must end his long-suffering patience and mercy and bring severe judgment on them.

GRIEF AND LAMENT. When I hear of a life-or-death situation, my mind remembers my mother-in-law, Dorothy, who died twenty some years ago of Amytrophic Lateral Sclerosis (Lou Gehrig's Disease), or Glen, a close friend who died this past year of a rare incurable cancer called Multiple Myeloma. If a friend or relative has one of these diseases, there is usually little hope of survival unless God provides a miracle. In these contexts there seems to be little choice; one must learn to accept the inevitable, center one's energies on whatever medical treatment is available, enjoy the pleasures of each day, try to keep the spirits up, and hang on to trust in God's sovereign plan. Although one can easily slip into denial and try to avoid discussion of death, the disease and its emotional consequences cannot be managed by refusing to acknowledge it.

Most visitors feel uncomfortable talking to people with incurable diseases because there is little hope and no explanation as to why this is happening. In private there is plenty of lamenting and mourning, but a public expression of sorrow is usually silenced by social pressure.

It is instructive to see the way people deal with the threat of physical death. Lamenting may be rejected because it is seen as blaming God; it is not a mature way of faith but a surrender to the negative instincts of giving up all hope. Others with good intentions may object, asking:

> Haven't the New Testament and resurrection morning effectively eliminated the need for lament? Aren't the Old Testament cries of anguish superseded, rendered unnecessary? Might they even be a sign of unbelief now that God has raised Jesus from the dead? ... If Jesus' followers really believed in the resurrection, if they really believed in the power of God to overcome evil and provide joy and comfort in his

Spirit, the lament wouldn't be needed. Maybe laments are for those who can't really believe as they ought.[19]

This kind of reasoning may sound like good theology, but it seems to imply that the coming age is here already and that this present evil age of suffering is past. In one sense death was defeated by Christ's death and resurrection, but the final elimination of death and sorrow is yet to be fulfilled at some future time (Isa. 26:19; 1 Cor. 15:24−26). Death still does have power over believers and unbelievers. Those who want to eliminate grief usually fail to bring any comfort by their pious remarks and only increase the weight of guilt and grief for those who need to mourn. Criticisms of mourning should not be centered on the sufferer's unbelief or on belief in the resurrection, because the lament is simply an honest confrontation of God with questions and struggles that are not understood and emotions that are overwhelmed with sorrow and confusion.

A. Resner suggests that part of the reason for this dilemma about grief is that the church has lost the legitimate use of the Old Testament lament tradition.[20] R. Davidson suggests that our truncated canon, our lopsided liturgy, and our incomplete preaching of the whole counsel of God have created a need for psychotherapy and self-help groups.[21] He quotes a therapist who says that "churches have not learned that the best way to pass from defensive rationalizations to secure faith is to let doubt, inconsistencies, confusion and rebellion come out in the open instead of using various forms of spiritual coercion to keep them hidden."[22]

The believer does not need to deny feelings of pain and loss, for God was willing to listen to the groaning and weeping of his people in the past. He repeatedly responded to the cry of his people, comforted them, and helped them. Those who do not cry out to God make him irrelevant to their lives and delay healing by not embracing the pain they experience. The Old Testament believers did not exclude God as part of the solution to their misery but openly expressed their exasperation and grief over the calamities of life.

Amos, Job, and the psalmists allow us to face our deepest fears and sorrows simply because they voice their grief. They do not face this pain alone but bring it to God, who can do something about it. Underlying the sorrow is a faith that believes God is trustworthy and understanding; he is a resource who can change the lament orientation into assurance and praise.[23] The

---

19. A. Resner, "Lament: Faith's Response to Loss," *Restoration Quarterly* 32 (1990): 129.
20. Ibid., 132.
21. R. Davidson, *The Courage to Doubt* (London: SCM, 1983), 16.
22. Ibid., 17.
23. W. M. Soll, "The Israelite Lament: Faith Seeking Understanding," *Quarterly Review* 8 (1988): 79−85.

effort to eliminate human laments to God has the effect of making God impotent to change our sorrows or understanding and unable to bring comfort to our spirits. It also eliminates the question of theodicy and related questions about the purpose, meaning, and justice of human life with God.[24] It discourages honest and open interaction with God based on what people really feel.

Those who discourage lamenting take away a canonical form of expression that is an accepted and meaningful way in which past saints dealt with their grief.[25] The church should not teach people to suppress their deepest feelings and to pretend that we are big enough to handle the trials of life on our own without God. E. Kubler-Ross's study of the five stages of grief suggests that acceptance of death is only possible if we stop our denial and isolation, deal with anger and depression, and gain the loving support of others.[26] Although she does not employ biblical laments, it seems that Old Testament laments are the Hebrew culture's way of handling this issue in a constructive way.

If the church can come to the place where it will allow laments, then Amos's lament in 5:1–17 begs us to ask a second, more difficult question. Should Christians or the church community, like Amos, be involved with lamenting God's legitimate punishment of people and nations? This raises all kinds of disturbing thoughts. Do not rebellious people deserve God's wrath? Should we feel sorry for those who have freely chosen to reject God and his Word? These questions reveal some of our deepest attitudes toward ungodly sinners in this world. Should we pray against them or for God's mercy on them? Do we love them enough to have a theodicy crisis when God judges them? Do we just tell them a few Bible verses, or do we cry out to God in intercession for their lives? Do we show them our deep emotional hurt (assuming we do feel it) that they have chosen to reject God's way?

We know that Moses, Paul, and Jesus lamented over those who rejected God, and I have seen a mother lament her son's depraved life of sin, but the church seldom follows these examples by mournfully expressing its profound grieving love for the lost. Have we just lost our ability to lament, or have we also lost our compassion on those who will die and experience God's judgment?

---

24. W. Brueggemann, "The Costly Loss of Lament," *JSOT* 36 (1986): 60–63.

25. S. P. McCutchan, "Illuminating the Dark: Using Psalms of Lament," *The Christian Ministry* 24 (1993): 14.

26. E. Kubler-Ross, *On Death and Dying* (New York: Macmillan, 1969), 38–88. W. Brueggemann, "The Formfulness of Grief," *Int* 31 (1977): 267–74, makes positive and negative comparison between laments and Ross's approach.

Amos 5:18–27

¹⁸ Woe to you who long
     for the day of the LORD!
Why do you long for the day of the LORD?
     That day will be darkness, not light.
¹⁹ It will be as though a man fled from a lion
     only to meet a bear,
as though he entered his house
     and rested his hand on the wall
     only to have a snake bite him.
²⁰ Will not the day of the LORD be darkness, not light—
     pitch-dark, without a ray of brightness?

²¹ "I hate, I despise your religious feasts;
     I cannot stand your assemblies.
²² Even though you bring me burnt offerings and
         grain offerings,
     I will not accept them.
Though you bring choice fellowship offerings,
     I will have no regard for them.
²³ Away with the noise of your songs!
     I will not listen to the music of your harps.
²⁴ But let justice roll on like a river,
     righteousness like a never-failing stream!

²⁵ "Did you bring me sacrifices and offerings
     forty years in the desert, O house of Israel?
²⁶ You have lifted up the shrine of your king,
     the pedestal of your idols,
     the star of your god—
     which you made for yourselves.
²⁷ Therefore I will send you into exile beyond Damascus,"
     says the LORD, whose name is God Almighty.

THIS SECTION IS divided into three paragraphs:
5:18–20 addresses the sad state of Israel's deceptive theology concerning the Day of the Lord,
5:21–24 undermines the people's false hopes in
their unacceptable worship, and 5:25–27 predicts their exile because some

Israelites worship false gods. These sections question the people's basic beliefs about their relationship to God.

This questioning does not raise doubts concerning the Israelites' knowledge of temple worship or eschatological events but inquires about their deceptive approach to these topics. They have turned worship into something worthless and eschatology into escapism. It is a tragedy to hear that someone is tricked into believing in a baseless illusion, but it is especially regrettable to find out that religious people, who know biblical traditions and participate in religious services, have deceived themselves by constructing a theological perspective that twists God's truth into a nonexistent mirage.

Since there is no sign of a positive response to Amos's lament in 5:1–17 and the book continues with additional warnings, one can assume that most people have not internalized the prophet's call to seek God. Some in the prophet's audience could have defended themselves by claiming that Amos is all mixed up in his theology. The day of God's judgment will bring the destruction of their enemies, not Israel. The Day of the Lord will be a glorious day of victory over these enemies, not Israel's demise. In response, Amos's woe oracle (5:18–20) attempts to destroy these false hopes of security and divine blessing by reversing the people's expectations concerning the Day of the Lord. Although most long to see that great day, it will in fact be a day of darkness and humiliation for Israel.

Several woe oracles in the Old Testament are associated with a lament for the dead (1 Kings 13:30; Jer. 22:12–13; 34:5),[1] so one should hear this message as sorrowful words, similar to the lament in the preceding section. Amos's lament (5:1–17) and these woe messages (5:18–27) are tied together because both relate to upcoming divine judgments that will obliterate false hopes. Both condemn the people for their inattention to justice and righteousness (5:7, 10–13, 24). Since God does not accept the people's worship, how can they expect to escape God's judgment on the Day of the Lord?

The Day of the Lord Will Bring No Hope (5:18–20)

THE CONCEPT OF "the day of the LORD" was likely used in Israel before Amos spoke,[2] but Amos has the earliest reference to this as a technical term describing God's future victory over his enemies. Amos seems to have several themes in common with later prophetic references to this day. The Day of the Lord

---

1. See G. V. Smith, *Amos*, 238–40, for other possible views on the background of the woe oracle and several proposals about the origin of the Day of the Lord concept.

2. The "day of the LORD" is any time God miraculously intervenes in the course of history, particularly when God gives marvelous victories over enemies in holy war (Judg. 7; Isa. 9:4).

is often associated with the military defeat of a nation (Isa. 13; 34; Ezek. 30; Joel 2), various symbols (such as darkness and gloom), and a theophany appearance by God.[3] The preceding sermons of Amos also tell of God's plan to fight against Israel (2:13—16; 3:11—15; 4:2—3; 5:2—3) and destroy it when he passes through her midst (5:17).

Amos describes his audience as people longing for or yearning for the coming Day of the Lord (5:18). At first this sounds positive because this was seen as the day when God would vindicate himself and destroy his enemies. Why would the Israelites not long to see that day? Amos's audience views this day as the time when they will have a guaranteed victory over their enemies. They also have great expectations concerning what God will do for them when he establishes his divine kingdom on earth on that day.

When Amos, however, laments over those who want this day to come, many of his listeners probably wonder what is wrong with this crazy prophet. Why would anyone not look forward to the time when God will bless his people and defeat their enemies? Amos's answer to his rhetorical "why" question in 5:18b reveals that he has a different conception of this day. He reverses his audience's understanding because he sees it as a day of darkness for Israel. Israel will suffer God's judgment with the ungodly because they are a sinful people, just like the foreign nations. They will experience the gloom and darkness of political defeat. Darkness symbolizes danger, hidden things that one cannot see, an absence of safety, and no divine protection (Job 18:6; Ps. 27:1; Isa. 9:1—2; Lam. 3:2; Joel 2:10). This must have seemed like a heretical statement. Will God judge his own people?

To help persuade his listeners of their misunderstanding, Amos illustrates the danger of this day with a rural example showing that the disastrous consequences of this day are inevitable (5:19). A person fleeing from one danger (a lion) will run into another (a bear). Those who finally reach the safety of home will not escape either, because something there will get them when they least expect it (a snake will bite them as they relax, leaning against a wall). There will be, in other words, no place to run or hide.

To emphasize this point Amos ends this short message with the reminder that this will be a very black day, without a single ray of bright hope for the future (5:20). The reality of this day will be horrible; it will not be the day the people are longing for. Thus, Israel's theology is right (on the Day of the Lord God will defeat his enemies), but their theological expectations of what God will do for them are false (he will judge *all* sinners—in Israel and the nations).

---

3. G. von Rad, "The Origin of the Concept of the Day of Yahweh," *JSS* 4 (1959): 97–108, emphasized the military setting and A. J. Everson, "The Day of the Lord," *JBL* 93 (1974): 329–337, noted the emphasis on the theophany.

God Rejects the People's
Ritualistic Worship (5:21–24)

THE PRESENT TEXT makes no overt causal connection between the Day of the Lord (5:18–20) and Israel's unacceptable worship (5:21–24), but their juxtaposition suggests that Israel's unacceptable worship is a main reason why the people will suffer under God's powerful hand on the Day of the Lord.[4]

Amos reintroduces his critique of the nation's sacrifices and singing (see also 4:4–5) with powerful persuasive clauses that claim God's vehement opposition to what is happening at Israel's temples. "I hate, I despise … I cannot stand … I will not accept … I will not listen" are emphatic statements of God's unmovable disposition toward Israel's worship. These statements bristle with force and deep resolve; this is not politically correct or tolerant language. The verbs carry the intense emotions of rejection and repudiation. They reverse God's normal and expected attitude toward those who worship at Israel's temples. Although God asked the people to offer burnt offerings, grain offerings, and fellowship (peace) offerings in Leviticus 1–4 and exhorted them to sing his praises (Ps. 92:1; 95:1–2; 96:1; 98:1, 4–6; 100:1–2), he does not accept mechanical offerings and rote songs that do not come from a heart of love and a commitment to act in righteousness.[5]

Verse 24 exhorts the people to pay close attention to the implications of what it means to worship God. If you worship him, you must walk in his ways. If worship does not further the development of spiritual character, it may just be empty emotions. When worshipers offered sacrifices to God, they were supposed to confess their sins as they put their hands on the head of the animal being sacrificed (Lev. 1–4), turn away from their past failures, and commit themselves to keep his guidelines for daily behavior. Since the Israelites are not doing these things, their sacrifices have no value. What should be a sweet-smelling aroma to God (3:5, 16) is becoming a putrid stench he cannot stand. The beautiful harmony of their singing and the trumpet blasts of their music are turned into obnoxious noises. Their sin separates them from God (Isa. 59:1–2).

Justice among individuals should have been a hallmark distinguishing Israel from her neighbors, but God does not see this moral value in the lives of many Israelites. Amos exhorts the people to let righteousness and justice

---

4. Hubbard, *Joel and Amos*, 179, follows Everson and makes this connection by suggesting that the worship is at an event celebrating that coming Day of the Lord. J. Hayes, *Amos*, 171, goes to the extreme of suggesting this was the third day of the Feast of Booths. Such suggestions hypothesize more than is necessary to interpret the text.

5. H. H. Rowley, *Worship in Ancient Israel: Its Forms and Meaning* (London: SPCK, 1965), 144–75, surveys various ways of interpreting the prophets' reaction to temple worship but concludes that this was not rejection of all ritual.

characterize all their activities. Justice should flow continually like a year-round river, not like an undependable *wadi* that has water in it only when it rains. Justice is not an optional trait that one can choose to practice; it is a key value that must characterize the behavior patterns of those who claim to love and follow God.[6] If these people would let justice govern their action, God would look at their worship in a different way. They are not deceiving him with their meaningless worship; rather, they are only fooling themselves.

False Worship Will Bring Exile (5:25–27)

THERE IS A fair bit of confusion among translators and commentators about the text and interpretation of these verses. Everyone agrees that Amos is predicting a future exile of Israel beyond Damascus because they are worshiping other gods (5:27), but the details in verses 25–26 are not clear. There are two main problems. (1) How does one interpret the question concerning sacrifices when the Israelites were wandering in the desert in 5:25 (or should this verse even be translated as a question)? (2) Should one follow the New Testament translation of 5:26 found in Acts 7:43 (which is heavily dependent on the LXX) or keep with the Hebrew text and relate these terms to Assyrian gods the Israelites worshiped?

(1) Verse 25 can be read (a) as a question whether God gave Israel any laws about sacrificing while they were in the desert of Sinai; (b) as a suggestion that people did not sacrifice during the desert years because they did not have many sheep (cf. Jer. 7:21–23); (c) as a claim that the desert generation offered sacrifices to other gods and "did not bring them to me [Yahweh]"; or (d) as a question whether the people only brought sacrifices and nothing else to God.[7]

Since the Pentateuch records God's instructions concerning sacrifices and many examples of the people sacrificing (Ex. 20:5, 22–26; 23:14–19; 24:4–6; 29; 32:6–8; 34:13–20; 40:29), interpretations (a) and (b) seem unlikely.[8] Except for the golden calf incident (Ex. 32 and Num. 25), there are few indications that the Israelites regularly worshiped other gods during the desert period, as option (c) suggests. Thus, Amos is probably asking whether the central aspect of Israel's relationship to God is based *only* on their sacrificing (interpretation [d]). The assumed response to this questions is negative. In other words, Amos is hinting that the people's relationship with God is not primarily based on

---

6. M. Weinfield, *Social Justice in Israel and the Ancient Near East* (Philadelphia: Fortress, 1995).

7. Harper, *Amos*, 136–37, and Andersen and Freedman, *Amos*, 531–32, survey numerous approaches to this verse.

8. Stuart, *Hosea–Jonah*, 352–53, and B. K. Smith, "Amos," 114, believe that the Israelites did not offer regular sacrifices in the desert.

sacrifices, but on their covenant love with God. This is supposed to be the central feature of their relationship (Deut. 6:5), and it is missing.

(2) Verse 26 is even more controversial. The NIV refers the time of the verb to past events (like v. 25),[9] but S. Paul and others translate the perfect consecutive verbs in the future tense and connect them to the exilic experiences in verse 27.[10] Either translation is possible, but it seems that verse 26 is not part of Israel's exilic experience ("therefore" in v. 27 begins a new subparagraph about their exilic judgment). There are also major differences on how to translate some of the nouns in verses 26–27. The Hebrew text did not originally have written vowels, so it was possible for people to pronounce words in different ways and thus give different meanings to the same series of consonants (e.g., if you drop out the vowels in English, *bt* could refer to *bet, bit, bat, bait, boot, but,* or *beet*). Different vocalizations (and some editorial shifts) produce the following variations:

Masoretic Hebrew	*Acts 7:43*
Sakkuth/Sikkut	tabernacle
king	Molech
Kaiwan/Kiyyun	Rephan
Damascus	Babylon

The Masoretic Hebrew vocalization makes the first word the name of an Assyrian god Sakkuth/Sikkut (Ninurta or Ninib), which was identified with the planet Saturn. The third word Kaiwan/Kiyyun is another name for this same astral deity (a star god). This pronunciation of these words suggests that Amos is condemning the people for worshiping pagan Mesopotamian gods. If the Greek translators who lived many years later did not know the names of these gods, it would be natural for them to read the words with a pronunciation that would make sense to them. The Greek translators thought that *sikkut* could refer to a tent in which a god would be placed and *malkekem* ("your king") could be taken as a reference to the Ammonite god Molech (1 Kings 11:7; 2 Kings 23:10).[11] A scribal confusion between *k* and *r* accounts for some of the confusion with the third word, while the change from Damascus to Babylon seems to be a later historical revision.

We believe that Amos is talking about the people's worship of Assyrian astral gods and that the Greek translators misunderstood the meaning of several words here. Even though there is some level of misunderstanding of

---

9. Stuart, *Hosea–Jonah*, 352, also translates the verb in a past tense.
10. Paul, *Amos*, 188, 194; Andersen and Freedman, *Amos*, 529.
11. R. de Vaux, *Ancient Israel: Religious Institutions* (New York: McGraw-Hill, 1965), 444–46, provides background on the worship of Molech.

this text, the Greek translation also condemns pagan worship, so it has not missed the central thrust of the original. These conclusions are totally opposite those who suggest that "Amos is here not depicting and condemning pagan deities nor criticizing Israel for apostasy. The items noted should be seen as traditional elements of the Yahwistic cult."[12]

Finally, it is not clear if the verb *ns'* refers to the "transporting, carrying" of an idol or the "lifting up" of the idol for purposes of worship.[13] The second interpretation seems to fit the context better if verse 26 is an accusation of improper worship.

This message ends with a concluding statement of punishment that outlines the consequences of improper worship of God. There is no doubt about what will happen, who will do this, or where the people will go. God will exile the Israelites into some nation far away, into an unknown land beyond Damascus. Later records in 2 Kings 17:23–24 verify that God did send these people into Assyria about forty years after Amos's prophecy (721 B.C.).

THIS PROPHECY MAKES specific accusations about Israelite misconceptions concerning God, worship, and his future plans for Israel. We cannot directly translate his warnings about Mesopotamian astral idolatry or the unacceptable sacrificing of burnt offerings into many modern cultures. Missionaries living in countries where pagan idols are still worshiped with sacrifices will have a more direct application to their setting. But regardless of the contextual setting where we minister, each paragraph focuses around a central problem that has parallels in the lives of people who attend worship services in our settings.

True theological ideas can be turned into deceptive lies. Although people may be put off by the forcefulness of the terminology Amos uses, humanly created interpretations of biblical ideas can sometimes miss the intention of the text so much that they should properly be called deceptive lies. This is true of some interpretations of human depravity, Christ's deity, and events at the end of time. Throughout history a few individuals have claimed special knowledge about things that will happen to destroy the world and begin God's kingdom. Groups have reinterpreted numbers and symbols, found secret insights into God's plan through extrabiblical revelations (e.g., the Mormons), and used their special knowledge for creating their own little

---

12. Hayes, *Amos*, 178, accepts this view and believes Amos is describing a procession celebrating the enthronement of Yahweh.

13. See G. V. Smith, *Amos*, 245, 255, or Paul, *Amos*, 194–97, for a further discussion of these issues.

kingdom. Too often this special knowledge is employed for the purpose of scaring people into their group.

Eccentric approaches are usually characterized by bizarre hermeneutics and suspect methods of interpretation. Although most Christians are not deceived by these movements, we have our own hermeneutical idiosyncrasies that blind us. All believers need to search for the truth, realizing that they too can fall victim to deceptive teachings not completely consistent with God's point of view.

A fundamental hermeneutical problem for all deceptive theological reconstructions is one's view of God. Some approaches seem to be based on the premise that God is trying to keep secret truths from the common-sense interpretations of devoted believers. These leaders claim that God reveals the deep mysteries of his ways only to a few insightful leaders and is still in the process of giving new "canonical" revelations through them. Others have taught that God is such a wonderful God of love and compassion that everyone will go to heaven (Amos's audience seems to think that God will favor them on the Day of the Lord). Of course God is a God of love, but his holiness and justice will result in the merciless destruction of rebellious sinners who refuse to love him and deal justly with others.

One characteristic of God that underlies the Day of the Lord idea in 5:18−20 is that God is a divine warrior who will execute holy war against his enemies. Although this is not a popular part of our picture of God, the all-powerful Lord praised by Moses and the children of Israel after the crossing of the Reed Sea is a divine "warrior" (Ex. 15:3), who "shattered the enemy" (15:6) and consumed them with the majestic presence of his holiness.[14] The battle for the possession of Canaan was God's holy war to destroy the sinful people in the land and keep his holy chosen people separate (Deut. 7:1−6). Battles by Joshua, the judges, and David were really the Lord's battles because he gave the wicked nations into their hands (Josh. 2:24; 6:2; 8:1; 10:8; Judg. 3:28; 5:4−5; 1 Sam. 23:4) and fought for his people (Deut. 1:30; Josh. 10:14; 1 Sam. 17:45−46).[15]

The prophets describe God's final battle with Gog and Magog (Ezek. 38−39), God's plan to destroy all the evil kingdoms of the earth (Hag. 2:21−22; Isa. 24; Dan. 2; 7), and God's victory over the nations that will attack Jerusalem (Zech. 14).[16] T. Longman and D. Reid extend this theme into the

---

14. P. D. Miller, *The Divine Warrior in Early Israel* (Cambridge, Mass.: Harvard Univ. Press, 1973), 113−17, notes the standard distinction between God's love and deliverance of his people and the warrior's destruction of his enemies.

15. G. von Rad, *Holy War in Ancient Israel*, trans. M. J. Dawn (Grand Rapids: Eerdmans, 1991), 41−49.

16. C. Sherlock, *The God Who Fights: The War Tradition in the Holy Scriptures* (Lewistown, N.Y.: Mellen, 1993), 141−225, has an extensive treatment of the key prophetic texts on holy war.

New Testament's treatment of Jesus, the slain warrior who is finally triumphant over sin, Satan, and his evil kingdom (Matt. 12:28; Luke 10:18–20).[17] Jesus had twelve legions of angels at his disposal (Matt. 26:53) and spoke of the future coming of the Son of Man in the clouds in power (Matt. 24:29–31; Mark 13:24–27; Luke 21:25–28). Paul also referred to Christ's battle against the power of sin, the defeat of his enemies at the cross (Col. 2:14–15), and the victory over his final enemy, death (1 Cor. 15:24–27). The New Testament ends with a symbolic description of Jesus as the divine Warrior coming on a white horse with the armies of heaven in one final victorious battle (Rev. 19: 11–21).

A complete biblical view of God must avoid the illusory tendency of focusing mainly or only on God's love, while downplaying his role as a divine warrior. Amos is against any slanted view of God that deceptively reimagines God as a loving power who will pour out his blessings on his people regardless of their behavior. God is a warrior who will wipe out all evil—both the abhorrent idolatry of pagans and the rebellious sinfulness of his own people. This concept of God provides us with clear criteria to evaluate various hypothetical predictions of what his future action will be. False reconstructions about God's action on the Day of the Lord existed in Amos's day and still do today, but the biblical record demonstrates what God has done and will do to destroy sin from the world. False notions about God can turn worship into nothing more than playing church.

Does God accept all worship? The second and third paragraphs (5:21–27) deal with two kinds of unacceptable worship: Proper forms of worship are rejected because the worshiper's life is not characterized by justice or righteous action, and deceptive forms of worship are rejected because the worshiper does not distinguish between proper and improper conceptions of God. Both errors happen to religious people concerned about their relationship with God, not to atheists who have no interest in spiritual things.

Although Amos does not explain how God's people have strayed from doing what pleases him, it appears that these worshipers have made two mistakes. (1) They have not paid close attention to the biblical warnings about accepting other notions of God common in the culture in which they live. These include prohibitions against making images of God that other religious groups use (Ex. 20:1–5; Deut. 4:9–20), against following the ideas of spiritual leaders who claim to do miracles in the names of other gods (Deut. 13:1–18), against bringing anything other than one's best to God (Lev. 22:17–33; Mal. 1:6–14), and against accepting cultural forms of worship (mediums, necromancy, astrology) that defile a person's holiness (Lev. 20:1–6).

---

17. T. Longman and D. Reid, *God Is a Warrior* (Grand Rapids: Zondervan, 1995), 91–135.

(2) The Israelites think that the primary way of pleasing God is to get involved in the ritual acts of worship. This misconception ignores his emphasis on holiness throughout the Levitical instructions (Lev. 11:44–45; 19:2; 20:26). Psalm 15 indicates that God requires worshipers to have a blameless walk, do what is righteous, speak the truth, honor those who fear God, keep their oaths, and do not accept bribes, while Psalm 24:4 requires the worshiper to have holy hands and a pure heart, reject idols, and commit oneself to tell the truth.

Samuel reminds Saul that obedience is more important than sacrifices (1 Sam. 15:21–22; Hos. 6:6), and David realizes that the main thing God desires is a pure and contrite heart (Ps. 51:16–17). After Amos, Isaiah condemns the sacrifices given by sinful people in the temple (Isa. 1:11–15), and Jesus rejects the tithe of the Pharisees because they ignore the most important things—justice, mercy, and faithfulness (Matt. 23:23). Both Isaiah and Jesus find people who "honor me with their lips, but their hearts are far from me" (Isa. 29:13; Matt. 15:8–9).

DECEPTIVE THEOLOGICAL ISSUES in the church. In light of the strength and pervasiveness of the theme of God's role as a divine warrior, it is important for believers to balance this important theme with other key ideas about God. This is no time for Christians to live securely in their fortresses, thinking they have won the victory. People in the church cannot afford to forget that they are in a battle to influence the minds and hearts of people in this world. This war is not primarily "against flesh and blood, but against the rulers, against the authorities, against the powers of this dark world and against the spiritual forces of evil in the heavenly realms" (Eph. 6:12). The battle requires defensive armor as well as offensive tools (6:13–18).

When believers come prepared to fight and bathe their efforts to share the mysteries of the gospel in prayer, they are able fearlessly to communicate their faith in a persuasive manner. Paul describes the struggle between the power of sin and the words of God within himself as a war between two conflicting ways (Rom. 7:23). He exhorts believers to "fight the good fight" as he had (1 Tim. 1:18; 6:12; 2 Tim. 4:7).

If people picture God only as a kind, loving Father who is merciful and forgiving of all human mistakes, they will probably not expect him to hate sin, reject unacceptable worship, or judge his own unfaithful people at the end of time. A slanted view of God that does not recognize his holy and just nature is an illusion that will produce a false perception of what God expects of people today. Jesus warns about the people who will say "Lord, Lord" and think they should be allowed into his kingdom, but he will reject them because they have not done the will of the Father and because he never knew them (Matt. 7:21–23).

The audiences of Amos and Jesus have the same deceptive beliefs: They think they will automatically be included in God's kingdom on the Day of the Lord because they have been involved with "appropriate religious activities." A true understanding of who God is and what he desires will eliminate false expectations and destroy theories of cheap grace.

As Amos persuasively lays out the truth to his deluded audience, people must be honest with the teachings of Scripture about God and faithful to give a full picture of his character and roles. When God's promises become more important to people than his character and presence, a deceptive hope can easily arise.[18] A slanted and incomplete understanding of God is no better than none at all. A popular presentation that guts the truth and eliminates any correspondence with God's actual plans for the Day of the Lord is worse than no knowledge at all. Those teachers and preachers who lead people astray with false information will be held accountable to a higher standard (James 3:1). It is hard to imagine the bitterness some will feel toward spiritual leaders who have distorted God's character and twisted his revelation in Scripture.

What does it mean to worship God? The prophet Amos addresses two kinds of unacceptable worship (5:21–27) that are still a problem in the church. (1) Although many churches are struggling with people's preferences for different styles of worship format (seeker, contemporary, or traditional), a much deeper and more serious issue is the lifestyle people follow after the worship service is over. As E. Underhill suggests:

> A ceaseless moral striving, a steady effort to please God—must be part ... of worship ... therefore he [the worshiper] cannot divorce faith from works, or adoration from ethics. To worship well is to live well.... This idea of the sanctification of life, as the creative goal toward which Christian worship must tend, is found under different forms of expression in all types of Christianity.[19]

Several key phrases emphasize the same theological point made in Amos's message. The ethics of a worshiper matter. If the lives of church members do not overflow with justice and righteousness, one must ask if the "creative goal of worship" has been achieved and if God will in any way be pleased. True and acceptable worship is not so much about issues of the style adopted

---

18. G. V. Smith, *Amos*, 256–57.
19. E. Underhill, *Worship*, 79.

by a particular congregation, but the extent to which the worshiper's life is transformed by being in the presence of a holy God. That transformation should result in adoration of the Almighty, praise of the Father, Son, and Holy Spirit, thankfulness for God's grace and mercy, and a recommitment to walk in his ways.

(2) A second application flows from this first principle. God hates, despises, rejects, and abhors deceptive worship that draws no connection between worship and ethics. No one can be neutral before God. The ethics of justice and righteousness are not optional characteristics that would be nice to see in a few worshipers. The text makes its case without reservation or qualification: God will not accept certain kinds of Hebrew or Christian worship. He does not say that anything goes, or do the best you can, or do what makes people feel good about themselves so that they will have a high self-esteem.

God does not, of course, demand that a certain style of worship be instituted in every culture or every setting. Paul himself seems to suggest that the hour or day of the week is not the most important thing about worship (Rom. 14:5–8). He concludes that "the kingdom of God is not a matter of eating and drinking, but of righteousness, peace and joy in the Holy Spirit" (14:17). That is, the way we carry out our worship practices (eating and drinking) is not as important as the change God brings about in our lives through worship. Times and cultures will create new and effective ways of worshiping God that are meaningful to believers, but there is no room for compromising justice and righteousness. God hates fake worship.

Who should we worship? In the final section of this passage (5:25–27) Amos describes deceptive forms of worship that are rejected because the worshiper does not distinguish between proper and improper conceptions of God. Missionaries must contend with people who actually have images of gods in their homes or places of worship. This passage gives practical support to a missionary's exhortations to remove all idols because God will judge people who worship false gods. More sophisticated Western intellectuals may not worship any kind of idols in their homes, but they may believe there is truth in the predictions of the horoscopes, so they trust in the alignment of the stars and planets instead of the Creator of the stars.

A contemporary area where the church may need to apply lessons from this passage is seen in the new interest in Sophia, the goddess figure that some feminist groups have deified. *Sophia*, the Greek word for wisdom, describes the wisdom of God (Rom. 11:33; 1 Cor. 1:24; Eph. 3:10). The strong connection between God and wisdom is especially prominent in Proverbs 8–9, where wisdom says, "I was appointed from eternity, from the beginning, before the world began" (Prov. 8:23). Wisdom is personified as a female figure, yet is closely identified with God himself. Although some authors may use the term as just another name for God,[20] others have crossed far beyond that threshold and introduced a foreign female goddess.

Those attending the "Re-Imagining" conference heard about a "Second Reformation" for the church. S. Cyre reported that "working from a basis in feminist theology, conference participants looked to pantheistic religions and the heritage of the Gnostic gospels to 'reimagine' a new god and a new road to salvation. The attendees blessed, thanked, and praised Sophia as a deity."[21] Mack B. Stokes viewed the conference as "theologically ignorant . . . ontologically superstitious . . . Christologically blasphemous . . . ecclesiastically irresponsible."[22]

T. Finger takes a less confrontational approach to the subject, but clearly recognizes wisdom in Proverbs 8–9 as "a personification of one of Yahweh's attributes."[23] Finger finds traces of the idea of wisdom in Proverbs 8–9 and Wisdom of Solomon 7:24–26, where *sophia* "pervades and penetrates all things. For she is the breath of the power of God, and a pure emanation of the glory of the Almighty . . . a reflection of the eternal light, a spotless mirror of the working of God."

Finger also sees a connection between "wisdom" and Jesus as the "Word" in the Gospel of John (both were with God at creation and both manifest God's glory). The wisdom connection with Jesus is also evident in 1 Corinthians 1:24, where Jesus is called the "wisdom of God" (cf. also Col. 1:15–17).[24] Finger does not object to the use of "Wisdom" as a name for God to enrich our appreciation and understanding of him, but he does object to the current trend because "much current Sophia worship . . . is so focused on an immanent divine presence, and seems to regard Jesus as so little different from us."[25]

L. Lafebure has traced the history of Sophia in the church and finds that Catholics have often identified Sophia with Mary while Russian Orthodox thinkers have developed a mystical tradition around reflection on Sophia.[26] Second-century gnostic heretics developed elaborate mythologies about Sophia,

---

20. E. Schüssler Fiorenza, *In Memory of Her: A Feminist Theological Reconstruction of Christian Origins* (New York: Crossroad, 1983), 130–33, identifies feminine images of God with Sophia but later speaks positively of the integration of Egyptian Isis goddess language into Jewish monotheism. In spite of this she warns of "ditheism" and says that "goddess-language is employed to speak about the *one*-God of Israel."

21. S. Cyre, "Fallout Escalates Over 'Goddess' Sophia Worship," *CT* 38 (April 1994): 74.

22. Ibid.

23. T. Finger, "In the Name of Sophia: Seeking a Biblical Understanding of Holy Wisdom," *CT* 38 (November 1994): 44.

24. Ibid.

25. Ibid., 45.

26. L. D. Lafebure, "The Wisdom of God: Sophia and Christian Theology," *Christian Century* 111 (October 1994): 951.

while the early church tended to follow the lead of Philo of Alexandria, who made a connection between Sophia and the Logos.[27] Origen saw that Christ was called wisdom and suggested that Sophia was "begotten beyond the limits of any beginnings that we can speak of or understand."[28] Irenaeus, by contrast, identified Sophia with the Spirit rather than with Jesus.[29] This desire for a female goddess by some women has and will continue to challenge the limits of church tolerance and inclusiveness. Although there is nothing wrong with imagining God as a mother caring for a child, a failure to distinguish between metaphor and reality can lead the church into further strife.

Many people are not even aware of the Sophia movement, but everyone is involved with reimagining God based on scriptural metaphors, church traditions, and meaningful cultural models. Thus, there is a danger that anyone can imagine God in a way that is so far from the truth that a false god is created in the mind of the worshiper. Drawing the line between heresy and an unbalanced picture is not our concern at this point. The main need is for each person to evaluate his or her own conception of God (as Amos is encouraging his audience), and for pastors and teachers to make sure that their representations of God are not out of focus or lopsided pictures of the fullness of the mystery and majesty of God.

Do we use the term *Father* too much and thus give a male gender to God? Do we emphasize God's love, grace, and mercy but ignore the fact that he can hate and despise evil? In a world of democracy and individual rights, do we ever picture God as the all-powerful King of kings, who is to be absolutely obeyed? Have we caused people to be afraid of God by making him a stern judge who is sitting in heaven and watching us so that he can catch us in some small mistake? Or has God become so much a friend and buddy that there is no majesty or fear? What emphasis is placed on his holiness? Do we emphasize the justice of God and thus encourage justice in relationships between genders, races, employees and employers, and nations?

How we imagine God does make a difference. People tend to develop their worldviews (including religious images) from their social relationships, so the church has an awesome responsibility to give the world an accurate picture of the sovereign God that is biblically, rather than culturally, based. God's decision to destroy Israel because they misconceived who he is demonstrates that the way one reimages God does matter to him. In Amos's time the nation adopted a popular cultural model (an Assyrian image). But this mistake is an issue each generation faces—the threat of allowing our culture to remold God into its own image.

---

27. Ibid., 954.
28. Origen, *On First Principles* 1.2.1–2.
29. Irenaeus, *Against Heresies* 4.20.3.

Amos 6:1–14

¹ Woe to you who are complacent in Zion,
  and to you who feel secure on Mount Samaria,
you notable men of the foremost nation,
  to whom the people of Israel come!
² Go to Calneh and look at it;
  go from there to great Hamath,
  and then go down to Gath in Philistia.
Are they better than your two kingdoms?
  Is their land larger than yours?
³ You put off the evil day
  and bring near a reign of terror.
⁴ You lie on beds inlaid with ivory
  and lounge on your couches.
You dine on choice lambs
  and fattened calves.
⁵ You strum away on your harps like David
  and improvise on musical instruments.
⁶ You drink wine by the bowlful
  and use the finest lotions,
  but you do not grieve over the ruin of Joseph.
⁷ Therefore you will be among the first to go into exile;
  your feasting and lounging will end.

⁸ The Sovereign LORD has sworn by himself—the LORD
God Almighty declares:

  "I abhor the pride of Jacob
    and detest his fortresses;
  I will deliver up the city
    and everything in it."

⁹ If ten men are left in one house, they too will die. ¹⁰ And if
a relative who is to burn the bodies comes to carry them out
of the house and asks anyone still hiding there, " Is anyone
with you?" and he says, "No," then he will say, "Hush! We
must not mention the name of the LORD."

  ¹¹ For the LORD has given the command,
    and he will smash the great house into pieces
    and the small house into bits.

¹²Do horses run on the rocky crags?
>   Does one plow there with oxen?
>   But you have turned justice into poison
>   and the fruit of righteousness into bitterness—
¹³you who rejoice in the conquest of Lo Debar
>   and say, "Did we not take Karnaim by our
>   own strength?"

¹⁴For the LORD God Almighty declares,
>   "I will stir up a nation against you, O house of Israel,
>   that will oppress you all the way
>   from Lebo Hamath to the valley of the Arabah."

THIS WOE ORACLE is closely connected to the lament in 5:1–17 and the woe oracle in 5:18–27. All of these refer to injustice (5:7, 24; 6:12), end with an announcement of punishment, and are set in a weeping or lamenting setting. Perhaps Amos dresses in sackcloth and sits in ashes as he gives these woeful dirges. By lamenting the bad things that come on his audience, Amos is identifying with the pain his listeners experience. He knows that the people in Israel will more likely listen to what he has to say if he sympathizes with the nation's difficult plight in the future.

Amos 6:1–14 is divided into two paragraphs: 6:1–7 laments for the people because their complacency and affluence will bring destruction, while in 6:8–14 Amos repeats God's oath to exile Israel because of its pride. Complacency, affluence, strong cities, huge military fortresses, and military victories in the past have created a spirit of invincibility and false security that God hates. The upper-class leaders think that they do not need God for anything, for they have everything anyone could ever want. Amos's woe oracle bursts this bubble of deceptive security; things are not what they appear. Israel will soon suffer a death blow.

The setting of this sad woe oracle is a funeral banquet (*mirzaḥ*). These upper-class banquets are mentioned in Jeremiah 16:5–9 (Jeremiah is not to go to these banquets) as well as in Ugaritic, Phoenician, Nabatean, rabbinic, and later texts.[1] Since many of these texts come from non-Israelite cultures or from periods long after the time of Amos, it is difficult to reconstruct what

---

1. See Paul, *Amos*, 210–12, for a survey and full bibliography of texts and articles on these funeral banquets.

such a banquet is actually like in Amos's day.[2] At a minimum, it is known that there is a large banquet where mourning and feasting take place after someone has died. Amos finds that the wealthy people at these funeral banquets in Samaria are not doing much grieving; instead, they are carefree and happy, putting all their efforts into enjoying their sumptuous feasts.

Consequently, Amos offers his own lamenting woe oracle about the coming death and exile of these Israelites, who should be mourning the death of others in their nation. These opulent funeral feasts will cease, and the nation of Israel will be exiled.

Lament, for Complacency and Affluence Will Bring Destruction (6:1–7)

THE FIRST PART of this woe oracle laments the nation's false sense of security (6:1–3). It is unified by the repeated use of participles and the key word "head, first" (*roʾš*) in 6:1, 6, and 7. Amos sorrowfully remembers that the people in Zion,[3] the capital of Judah, as well as the people in Samaria, the capital of Israel, have a deceptive feeling of well-being and security (6:1). At this time in the reign of Jeroboam II, Israel was one of the most powerful nations in the ancient Near Eastern world.[4] They were not worried about military threats or the state of the economy. The days of the wealthy and distinguished leaders were carefree. Amos, however, sees this worldview as an illusory perception that ignores the true state of the nation. These leaders feel important because people come to them for advice and help, but their significance is greatly exaggerated.

The people in Samaria are no better than those in surrounding cities (6:2). A person can go north of Israel to Calneh, the capital city of Hattin (cf. Isa. 10:9), or to great city of Hamath on the northern border of Israel (Amos 6:14), or to the Philistine city of Gath and find the same thing. Some com-

---

2. H. M. Barstad, *The Religious Polemics of Amos: Studies in the Preaching of Amos 2,7B–8; 4,1–13; 5,1–27; 6,4–7; 8,14* (VTSup 34; Leiden: Brill, 1984), 127–42, imports (through his comparative studies) the worship of the dead and pagan deities into Israelite funeral feasts, but Jeremiah and Amos say nothing about these. M. Pope, *Song of Songs* (AB; Garden City, N.Y.: Doubleday, 1977), 210–29, hypothesizes all kinds of bizarre sexual behavior, but the prophets never attack that kind of behavior when they mention these funeral banquets.

3. Wolff, *Amos*, 270, objects to this reference to Zion and thinks it was added later, but there is no reason why Amos should not critique his own people, demonstrating that they are no better than the people in the northern kingdom, where he is ministering (see 2:4–5).

4. Hayes, *Amos*, 183, concludes that Amos is referring to the Assyrians because he dates Amos later in a period when Israel is weak and Assyria is strong. Since the book of Amos pictures Israel as strong, I do not accept Hayes's dating. It is better to apply all of the second half of 6:1 to Israel, not Assyria.

mentators think Amos is referring to the defeat of these places when Tiglath-Pileser III conquered much of this territory in 738 B.C.; but Amos is writing long before these events (between 765 and 760), so he cannot be warning people that the same kind of thing may easily happen to Israel.[5] Perhaps Amos wants people to see the effects of earlier conquests at 800 B.C. (though most of these ruins were rebuilt by 765), or he is quoting the proud opinions of the leaders of Israel.[6] It seems best, however, to conclude that he is just contrasting the lack of complacency and illegitimate optimism in these cities with the excessive complacency in Samaria. These cities understand that they are vulnerable to attack and must be prepared to defend themselves at all times. They are not the biggest or the best, so there is no illusion about their security.

Because of Israel's misperception of its political situation, there is a real possibility that they may be defeated (6:3). The interpretation of verse 3 is complicated by the fact that there are two paradoxical phrases about both the "bringing near" and the "putting off" of evil terror in the near future. Since one cannot both put off and bring near the same thing, some interpreters conclude that the people imagine they are putting off the evil day but are actually bringing it near.[7] Another suggestion is to continue the comparison from 6:2 into 6:3 so that the first line describes "these nations"[8] (6:2) as "putting off the evil day" because they feel overly secure. They are contrasted (similar to the contrast in v. 2) with "you ... bring near" this terror; that is, the secure Israelites bring it near. This reading enhances the prophet's rhetorical arguments against those who are foolishly resting secure.

The second half of the woe (vv. 4–7) laments the people's careless ease and security derived from their wealth. These rich people have everything anyone can imagine, so they eat and drink the best that money can buy at their opulent funeral banquets. They lounge (lit., sprawl out; *seruḥim*) on expensive couches that have ivory inlays on the wood frame of the furniture (6:4).[9] The

---

5. Wolff, *Amos*, 274–75, but Paul, *Amos*, 203, shows that this timing just does not fit.

6. Hubbard, *Joel and Amos*, 190. This runs contrary to Amos's habit elsewhere because he normally introduces the speakers (see 4:1; 5:14; 6:13; 8:5; 9:10).

7. Stuart, *Hosea–Jonah*, 357–59, connects these verbs to the idea of divination, but this does not fit here.

8. The participle in the first part of 6:3 could refer to "you" but more likely to "they, those who," since the subject is undefined. The finite verb in the second half of 6:3 is a second-person verb and must be translated "you." The subjects of the participles in 6:4–6 are also undefined and best translated as a relative clause "the ones who ...," not "you" as NIV. For details, see G. V. Smith, *Amos*, 273.

9. J. B. Pritchard, ed., *The Ancient Near East: An Anthology of Texts and Pictures* (Princeton: Princeton Univ. Press, 1958), fig. 122, has a picture of a mural where the Assyrian king Ashurbanipal is banqueting on a couch with ivory inlays at the junctions of the legs.

existence of these ivories was confirmed when archaeologists found over sixty pieces of ivory in the excavation of the city of Samaria.[10]

These rich people eat grade A tender beef from prime fattened calves and choice lambs (not old or mature sheep). Although most people can rarely afford to eat any kind of meat, these people waste precious animals on their fleshly desires. This is a shocking display of inexcusable waste and hedonism in the eyes of a humble shepherd.

The people also enjoy the finest music at these banquets; they even "esteem themselves to be like David [not 'improvise,' as in NIV] on musical instruments" (6:5).[11] How arrogant they are to openly compare themselves to the godly man David, who sang his songs to glorify God (1 Sam. 16:16, 23). The final physical aspect of these sumptuous banquets that catches Amos's eye is the huge bowls of wine in front of each plate (they prefer to drink from punch bowls rather than tiny goblets) and the expensive imported body oils, lotions, and perfumes that people rub into their skin (see Deut. 28:40; Song 1:3; 4:10).

All these excesses are contradictory and extraneous to the real purpose of lamenting the death of a friend at a funeral banquet, but the rich relish their money and what it can buy. These people are so busy enjoying themselves that they do not notice their nation is falling apart; they "do not grieve over the ruin of Joseph" (i.e., the nation of Israel, 6:6). They are not upset that people are being oppressed, that the moral and economic fiber of the nation is crumbling, or that its military power is about to be decimated. With their money and power they have everything they want. They are happy, so they ignore and deny the true status of their sick and dying nation.

Amos is in grief over the blindness of the revelers at this funeral banquet, so he ends his sorrowful lament with a dire warning of exile for the upper class. He ironically announces that these people—the "first" citizens of the "first" nation in the Near East (6:1)—will be the "first" to go into captivity (6:7). All luxurious eating, fine dining, and sprawling feasts will end. The party is over; the end has come! What a lamentable ending for God's chosen people.

God's Oath of Destruction for Pride (6:8–14)

THIS PARAGRAPH CONTAINS two parts: 6:8–11 is God's oath and a description of the effects this oath will have on the nation, while 6:12–14 describes the absurdity of Israel's military pride. These verses have prose sections that

---

10. J. and G. Crowfoot's *Samaria–Sebaste II: Early Ivories from Samaria* contains photographs of these ivories, while the *Encyclopedia of Archaeological Excavations in the Holy Land*, 4:1039, has a plate of a few ivories.

11. G. V. Smith, *Amos*, 204, interprets ḥšb in its most frequent sense of "to think, consider." See also D. N. Freedman, "But Did King David Invent Musical Instruments?" *BR* 1 (Summer 1985): 50–51.

---

include dialogues and a series of questions—grammatical characteristics not found in 6:1–7. The conclusion to both of these subsections (6:11, 14) begins with *ky-hnh* ("For behold, truly" or "So it will be"; NIV "For").

In verse 8 the prophet utters a powerful sworn oath. "The oath is of particular importance because it conveys to the listener the finality of the judgment and the authority of the word of God. It express the assurance that God is speaking the truth."[12] In the ancient Near East, oaths were taken seriously. A person was required to carry out an oath no matter how painful it might be. Oaths were used to finalize covenants to demonstrate that the covenant could not be broken (Gen. 26:28–31). When God swears an oath, it will happen. He cannot go back on his word because it will be contradictory to the character of deity and his commitment to accomplish his irrevocable decisions. By communicating these words of judgment in an oath form, Amos leaves no doubt about what God will do, for his very existence as God is behind this statement. This is his final, solemn, unalterable decree.

The oath expresses God's deep feelings of abhorrence for Israel's trust in her strong, fortified cities (6:8, 11). The powerful palace-fortresses are the status symbols of the rich and famous. The Israelites take great pride in these monuments of security. In one sense these buildings of rock replace God. The people do not need to trust him for protection because the people are already protected. They do not need to depend on God to deliver them from warring enemies or to humble themselves and pray for help since their mighty fortresses are their gods. They already have everything they need to be successful and safe. Because of such arrogance, God detests these fortresses and has decided to destroy them. He will smash these great houses to bits (6:11).

In 6:9–10 Amos illustrates what will happen to the people who live in these fortresses. There may be a house where a small remnant of ten men will be left, but they too will die. The graphic death scene in this house is described in verse 10. Some relatives (maybe from a different village) or someone assigned to burn the decaying bodies[13] will come to see what has happened. One of the first things the person will do is to search the house for any survivors. The question, "Is anyone with you?" is a circumlocution for "Is anyone alive?" This question is answered with the disappointing "No" and an exhortation to "not mention the name of the LORD."

This prohibition is puzzling. Wolff sees undertones of a magical fear that pronouncing the name of Yahweh may cause the curse of death to return,[14]

---

12. G. V. Smith, *Amos*, 262.

13. Usually the Israelites burned only the bodies of criminals (Lev. 20:14; 21:9; Josh. 7:15, 25). But if in a large battle or a plague after a battle many died, it might be necessary to burn the remains for sanitation purposes.

14. Wolff, *Joel and Amos*, 283.

but Stuart suggests that "since the speaker already uses Yahweh's name, the issue cannot be prohibition of mere oral formulation, but must concern calling on Yahweh ... in prayers of lamentation or the like.... Survivors will want him to stay away, not come back"[15] A slightly different but preferable approach interprets this prohhibition as a modal use of the verb; thus, silence is suggested by the relatives because "it is no longer possible to call on the name of the LORD."[16] Since they are all dead, it will not do any good to call on God to save someone. In a similar context David ceased praying for his son once he knew the boy was dead (2 Sam. 12:16–23).

The final subsection (6:12–14) abruptly begins with a series of absurd questions. Would anyone do anything as absurd as to run a horse on a rocky cliff? It would be crazy to do so, because it would be almost impossible for the horse to run without tripping or breaking a leg. Would anyone try to plow a rocky cliff with a pair of oxen?[17] How could any plow ever manage to actually go through these rocks, and how could any plants actually grow there?

By using these ridiculous rhetorical questions, Amos gets his listeners to agree with him. This makes it easier for them to see the absurdity of their own action of turning righteousness into something vile, bitter, or poisonous. This type of injustice is as absurd as riding a horse over a rocky field; it makes no sense. In this verse "righteousness" is not defined by a specific context (social relationships, religious, or a worship context), but it is frequently used in relationship to social justice in other contexts in Amos (5:10–15, 21–24). At the least, it indicates that people are not living according to the standards of God's law or demonstrating just behavior or pure heart attitudes in their relationships with God and other people.

A final absurdity is the proud claim that Israel has won great military battles at the Transjordan cities of Lo Debar (a pun on the name of this city, which means "no-thing") and Karnaim (a pun on "horns, strength"), which they took with "our own strength." In God's eye there is no reason to rejoice over "nothing." They are bragging about this great victory, but it amounts to nothing significant; it is mostly just military propaganda with little substance. Equally ridiculous is the audacity to boast about the strength that won the battle at Karnaim. Who do they think they are? God is the One who gives

---

15. Stuart, *Hosea–Jonah*, 364.

16. The Hebrew modal use is discussed in GKC, 112m, x, or B. K. Waltke and M. O'Connor, *An Introduction to Biblical Hebrew Syntax* (Winnona Lake, Ind.: Eisenbrauns, 1990), 508, par. 31.4e.

17. Andersen and Freedman, *Amos*, 577, divide the Hebrew word "with oxen" into two separate words "with oxen the sea," while the NIV implies that the oxen are plowing on the cliff mentioned in the first line.

enemies into the hands of an opposing army. Amos's sarcasm transforms these military victories into absurd boasts because the people claim the power to do what only God can do. No wonder God hates their pride and absurd arrogance.

This paragraph ends with two predictions: God himself will raise up an unnamed nation against Israel, and this nation will oppress Israel from the northern tip (Hamath) to the southern tip (the valley of the Arabah). No glory is given to the nation that will defeat Israel, for they will be given power by God. No place will be safe or unaffected when the divine warrior goes to battle against his people. Although the nation is unknown, the reference to "beyond Damascus" in 5:27 hints at the Assyrians.

SECURITY. This lament deals with the problem of false security (6:1). Everyone naturally wants security from robbers, hunger, financial ruin, medical malpractice, and misrepresentation of products. Security results in the removal of feelings of anxiety, doubt, and fear. When one is secure, there is no danger, apprehensive feelings, or threat that will ruin the pleasant life one now enjoys. Security relates to being sure of your situation and certain about the future.

But security can lead to feelings of overconfidence and carelessness. When situations change, people can sometimes maintain their old attitudes of security and have a false perception of reality. The broad question Amos asks the Israelites is: Why do you feel so secure? This is a question that individuals in the church need to address because it is easy to rest blindly in inappropriate sources of security. A person can easily take on the modern cultural definitions of security and ignore God's role in providing freedom from anxiety and fear.

Amos addresses the issue of security by analyzing the basis of Israel's security. After a person can verbalize the reasons why he or she feels secure, then it is possible to ask if it is wise to trust in these factors. Have situations changed that require a new appraisal of one's confidence, or was a certain factor never a secure basis for hope? People can also compare their own confidence with that of others to see if there is some inconsistency between their attitudes and behaviors. Another avenue one can pursue is to discover what sacred traditions have to say about placing security in various objects or people. Should people, armies, and finances be the basis of a believer's confidence and security? Although no one can totally ignore these human factors of security, people need to think about the role God plays in providing security.

When Isaac went to Gerar, he was insecure about his safety, so he lied about his wife and claimed she was his sister. He did this because he thought "the men of this place might kill me on account of Rebekah, because she is beautiful" (Gen. 26:7). By contrast, the Hebrew midwives in Exodus 1:17, 21 feared God and were not persuaded to follow the Egyptian pharaoh's command to kill all the male children at birth. Their personal security was threatened by their disobedience, but they did not allow this danger to prevent them from doing what was right and honoring to God.[18]

King Saul responded quite differently when God commanded him to destroy utterly the Amalekites (1 Sam. 15). Because he feared the people (15:24), he allowed the troops to take the best of the spoil. This was a sign of a weak king with poor leadership abilities, who felt he was in an insecure political position.

When King Hezekiah was attacked by the Assyrian king Sennacherib, there was great fear and little security in Judah (2 Kings 18–19; Isa. 36–37; 2 Chron. 32). Some officials wanted to trust in the Egyptian army for help and security (Isa. 30:1–3; 31:1–5), but Isaiah condemned those who relied on horses and chariots. The Assyrians tried to convince Hezekiah to surrender without a fight and reminded him of his insecurity by questioning his confidence (2 Kings 18:19), his dependence on God (18:22), and the ability of God to deliver him (18:29–30, 35). In the midst of all this Hezekiah encouraged his troops: "Do not be afraid or discouraged because of the king of Assyria and the vast army with him, for there is a greater power with us than with him. With him is only the arm of flesh, but with us is the LORD our God to help us and to fight our battles" (2 Chron. 32:7–8). As a result, "the people gained confidence from what Hezekiah the king of Judah said" (32:8).

In each of these examples there was a situation that lacked security because of threats of danger. The people were pushed to decide what they would depend on. In some cases they chose to depend on God; in others they relied on the human might or their own wisdom. Those who chose sinful rebellion against God found they did not have a solid foundation for trust in the Lord. For Amos's audience, the sources of trust are based on a deceptive comparison of their size with other nations (6:2), their wealth and ability to enjoy all the good things of life (6:4–6), their pride in huge and strong palace fortresses (6:8), and their military victories (6:13). These are false sources for confidence.

People in any culture are tempted to rest their confidence in things they

---

18. T. E. Fretheim, *Exodus* (Interp; Louisville: John Knox, 1991), 32–35, draws out the ironic contrasts between Pharaoh's fears, which are alleviated by killing innocent male babies, and the midwives' fear, which is alleviated by their fear of God and their commitment to preserving life.

can see and to depend on financial and military plans that make sense in that setting. This is a materialistic approach, which places the highest value on material well-being and material progress rather than on spiritual things. Western materialism, just like Israelite materialism, tends to place higher regard and trust in material things than in God.[19] We cannot, of course, totally remove ourselves from the physical aspects of living in this world; thus, there is both a good and controlled use of material things and an overemphasis on having things to gain fulfillment.

Amos connects a false sense of security to riches, pride, and military achievements. These dangers were included in the warning to kings in Deuteronomy 17:14–17. The king must not be a foreigner, must not acquire great numbers of horses that he might trust in, must not take many wives by making astute political alliances, and must not accumulate large quantities of silver and gold. Instead, he is to make his own personal copy of God's revelation in the Torah and read it daily so that he will revere God and follow his instructions.[20] The king is to avoid pride and not think of himself as better than his brothers (17:18–20).

King Solomon failed to follow many of these instructions (1 Kings 11), and Isaiah condemned Judah during the prosperous days of Uzziah because the land was full of horses and chariots as well as gold and silver (Isa. 2:7). Anyone who has riches and a position of power is susceptible to the dangers of pride. The people who believe that these things give security have deceived themselves. One can only lament that so many people over the centuries have foolishly bought into this illusionary vision that has no substance.

 HOW CAN BELIEVERS today live and work in a materialistic world that places a high value on possessions, political power, and pride in a person's accomplishments and yet avoid the trap of depending on these things for security? Should Christians try to avoid the problems of having a false sense of security by turning down salary increases, refusing to run for high political office, or deciding not to own a home or any fine furniture? If pride and a deceptive security tend to develop inevitably

19. J. White, *The Golden Cow* (Downer's Grove, Ill.: InterVarsity, 1979), 25.
20. E. H. Merrill, *Deuteronomy* (NAC; Nashville: Broadman and Holman, 1994), 264–66, sees these instructions for Israel's kings as a contrast to the sources of security that were so important to the other kings that surrounded Israel. The threat of such influences on Israelite thinking is evident in the people's request for a king like the other nations (1 Sam. 8:5).

from things like these, then it might be good to avoid anything that could lead a person astray.

By using an exaggerated example that called for dismemberment of parts of a person's body, Jesus encouraged people to do everything in their power to avoid falling into sin (Matt. 5:30). Nevertheless, many people can handle salary increases without becoming proud or dependent on money for their security. Some politicians are not out to make a name for themselves and run the world but view a political appointment as an opportunity to serve others and employ biblical principles in the governing of society. Some people can live in a nice home with quality furniture and not derive their sense of importance from these possessions. Stereotypical judgments of others should be avoided; instead, each person should honestly analyze his or her own sources of pride and security. The four sources of false security that Amos mentions are still common to many people today.

Making comparisons. Amos refers to the tendency to compare oneself or one's country with others for the purpose of building up a sense of security and self-confidence. Almost everyone can find someone or some other nearby country that is smaller or not as powerful. Once that weaker one is identified, it is easy to develop a rational basis for suggesting I am better. Russia can look down its nose at the small country of Lithuania, China can easily see that it is far more advanced than Burma, Mexico is far bigger than El Salvador, and the United States has more people than Canada.

At work or in a person's neighborhood, there are people who have less expensive homes or cars or lower paying jobs and who do not have as much education or social status as others. Comparisons can lead to pride if one is bigger or better, or to discouragement and resentment if one does not have the things others have. Pride can lead to a carefree lifestyle that is driven by the pursuit of pleasure and a complacent life that ignores the plight of others less fortunate.

This problem does not exist just for the superrich or only among those with great power. There is probably not a country, culture, or neighborhood where the attitude that I am bigger or better is not a problem. It is evident already in the behavior of small children who brag about how much better their bicycle is, high school students who claim superiority in some sport, or adults who put others down because they do not measure up to some imagined standard. As C. S. Lewis claimed, pride means that I am more clever, richer, or more good-looking than you.[21]

Competition is not all bad, but it can engender a comparative pride that gives a false sense of reality. Such attitudes can cause nations to think that

---

21. Cited in K. Lysons, "The Seven Deadly Sins Today: vii. Pride," *ExpT* (98 (1987): 178.

they are better off than they really are, companies to lose their motivation to maintain excellence, or individuals to become stuck up and unconcerned about the problems others have. When people think they have it made, they must watch out, because their demise is not far away.

The story is told about how the famous missionary doctor Albert Schweitzer, who held several doctorates, one day asked an African bystander to help him move some planks in French West Africa. The person declined and said, "I don't do manual work. I'm an intellectual." Schweitzer, who willingly helped with manual labor, humbly responded: "I too tried to be an intellectual, but I didn't make it."[22] Pride is not based on who we are, but on what we think about ourselves.

Paul calls believers to have sober judgment about themselves rather than a prideful attitude (Rom. 12:3) and to be humble like Christ (Phil. 2:1–11). B. Mitchell concludes that the sin of pride is fundamentally "to take credit to oneself for one's accomplishments and to forget the grace of God."[23] This can result in "a truly satanic pride, in which individuals or groups are no longer answerable to the laws of God or to the demands of truth."[24] Such pride can come from a person's conclusion about his or her own superior intellect, racial characteristics, economic power, social status, or theological superiority. A true picture of God, as well as of human depravity, is essential if one is to combat this pervasive human tendency.

Riches and wealth. Amos saw how riches and wealth cause the upper-class people to spend their time in selfish indulgences, to find fulfillment in opulent, wasteful feasting, and to base their security in having the best money could buy. This wealth assures that they will be invited to the most exclusive parties and will have the most expensive clothes. They are the important people, like the movers and the shakers of our day who can afford to have the best furniture, the finest wine, the most popular live bands at their parties, and a French chef in their kitchens. These people get security from their money, which can buy things to impress people.

Does this mean that believers today must buy old pine furniture instead of new oak pieces, or that a wedding party for your daughter should serve only crackers and cheese plus a wedding cake? Is it wrong to have a Christian Businessmen's luncheon at an expensive hotel, or is it an immoral demonstration of dependence on wealth to buy your wife a larger diamond ring for your fiftieth wedding anniversary? There is no single answer to questions on

---

22. Ibid., 179.

23. B. Mitchell, "The Sin of Pride," *Theology* 90 (1987): 426, emphasizes both the horizontal and vertical aspects of pride.

24. Ibid., 429. This is evident in 2 Thess. 2:4, where the Antichrist exalts himself to take the seat of God.

wealth because so much depends on the attitude people have toward the way they use their money.[25]

I know a wealthy family in the trucking business in Winnipeg, Canada, who live in a nice home but do not flaunt their wealth in any way. They generously give many thousands of dollars to missions, Christian schools, and their local church. They never talk about money and purposely give God the glory for what he has entrusted to them. Christendom needs rich Christians like this to extend the work of the kingdom of God. Churches would not get built and some missionaries might give up trying to raise their support if Christians did not have excess funds to give to God's work. The problem is not that God entrusts some people with a lot of money; it is with wanting more or misusing what one has.

It seems that many people with only moderate incomes are not able to handle the temptation to display their wealth. Although they may not admit it, many middle-class people are subtly addicted to getting rich. Their life centers around both spouses working, and for some it even involves going to the casino in order to hit the big one or getting a lucky pick at the horse track. No matter what a person's economic level, the love of money can lead to great evil (1 Tim. 6:10). No one would want to suggest that it is wrong to have money, or that money always corrupts, or that people do not need money. Money is not the problem; we are.

Security in things. God particularly despises and loathes the security that the great palace-fortresses provide for the wealthy (6:8–11). Deuteronomy 28:52 warns of putting your security in big walls. The opposition is not to home ownership or to having a security system on your house, for it is the responsibility of parents to provide shelter and protection from harsh weather and evil people that might harm family members. The application must focus on what meaning people give to their homes and how they value or use them, and not just their size.

It may be true that people with larger homes will have more temptations to define their worth based on their possessions, but this can also be a problem for a teenage boy who gets his first car or the grade school student who gets a new pair of tennis shoes autographed by a sports hero. Whatever the material object is, if people use it to support their pride and allow it to insulate themselves from the problems of others around them, God will be against it.

We could raise the question whether there is any justification for a Christian to buy a half-million-dollar home. Is this not a waste of God's money that he has entrusted to his servants to use for his glory? These questions are not

---

25. D. E. Gowan, "Amos," 400, reflects on the attitudes of wealthy people today.

directly answered by our passage, but an expensive home may be the only kind of home available in Tokyo or Los Angeles. The price is not the main point; it is the pride and security people can derive from having a large home. Pride comes when people in Israel in Amos's day, and people around the world today, who can afford to live in what amounts to "a king's palace" do not need God to protect them or provide for their security. They are in control of their fate, not God. A. C. Lane concludes with Augustine that pride is a "false estimation of our capacity, the conception that we do not need to rest in God's grace because we think that we can find rest and contentment in temporal things."[26]

Military pride. Finally, Amos pinpoints the security from military pride (6:12–13). It is only natural for generals as well as the people who live in countries that have strong armies to feel a sense of pride when a battle is won. But the Bible has story after story where an inferior power wins over a larger army because God decides who will win each war. Israel escaped from the powerful armies of Egypt at the Reed Sea at the time of the Exodus without even lifting up a sword (Ex. 14–15), and Gideon defeated the larger Midianite forces with only three hundred men (Judg. 7). David defeated Goliath with one small stone (1 Sam. 17), and the angel of God killed 185,000 Assyrians surrounding Jerusalem at the time of Hezekiah (Isa. 36–37).

Jeremiah warns that people should not boast in their wealth, wisdom, or might but should boast in their knowledge of the Lord (Jer. 9:23–24). God judged Babylon for its arrogance (Isa. 13:11; 14:4–21), Moab for its pride (16:6), and Assyria for its haughtiness (10:5–16). The Edomites were condemned for pride (Obad. 3). Pride can come from many things, but military forces are a major source of government spending even in poor Third World countries. There will always be armies, and some will be large, but size and pride do not win wars. God raises up kings and removes them (Dan. 2:21); he determines who will win each war.

The application of this section is not limited to warnings about pride. It also includes a warning not to let pride, riches, and power blind one to the suffering of others (Amos 6:7). When everything is going fine for me, it is easy to ignore the plight of others. My preoccupation with my house, my social calendar, and my successes can lead to a lack of understanding of another person's problems and an unsympathetic and intolerant attitude. Individualism is not just a modern disease; there has always been a temptation to give charity at home first. An attitude of no compassion, this behavior of doing nothing to help others, is an abomination to God.

---

26. A. C. Lane, "Sin, Pride, and Shame: A Short Historical Response to Douglas Thorpe," *Koinonia* 3 (1991): 67.

Each believer must walk the streets of his or her neighborhood with an eye open and a heart ready to give God's love and a cup of cold water. A warm smile, a compliment, a helping hand, or a few dollars are the least we can do to support other human beings in need. James claims that true religion that God accepts includes looking after the orphan and widow in their distress (James 1:26–27). As R. Sider laments, "So often the Christian Right has rightly championed the family and the sanctity of life but neglected to work for equal opportunity for the poor ... and neglected the struggle against racism."[27] God's will is that we love one another by sharing and caring for the spiritual and physical needs of others.

---

27. R. Sider, "Our Selective Rage," *CT* 40 (August 12, 1996): 14.

Amos 7:1–6

❧

THIS IS WHAT the Sovereign LORD showed me: He was preparing swarms of locusts after the king's share had been harvested and just as the second crop was coming up. ²When they had stripped the land clean, I cried out, "Sovereign LORD, forgive! How can Jacob survive? He is so small?"

³So the LORD relented.

"This will not happen," the LORD said.

⁴This is what the Sovereign LORD showed me: The Sovereign LORD was calling for judgment by fire; it dried up the great deep and devoured the land. ⁵Then I cried out, "Sovereign LORD, I beg you, stop! How can Jacob survive? He is so small!"

⁶So the LORD relented.

"This will not happen either," the Sovereign LORD said.

THESE VISION REPORTS in Amos 7 begin the third major section of the book. Five visions are described (7:1–3, 4–6, 7–9; 8:1–3; 9:1–4), with the first two having a common structure: an introductory formula, a description of the vision (introduced with the particle *hinneh*, "behold," not trans. in NIV), the intercession of the prophet, and God's decision. The almost identical wording of the prophet's prayer and God's response draws the two visions together as a pair. The autobiographical nature of the language of the dialogue testifies to the personal nature of the prophet's involvement in the process and his deep concern for his audience.

In light of the contextual arrangement of these visions with the conflict that arose at the temple at Bethel (7:10–17), one can assume that Amos is at Bethel when he communicates these visions to his audience. If one assumes that the book is chronologically arranged (as I do), then between chapters 6 and 7, the prophet travels from the capital city of Samaria to the temple in Bethel. The text gives no hint about when or where Amos is when he receives the visions, but it is most natural to assume that he receives them at the place where he gives them.

Numerous authors have tried to classify the different kinds of visions in the Old Testament in order to better understand their cultural origin and use. J. Lindblom has divided visions into pictorial and dramatic groups and connected them to wisdom schools in Israel. Long offers the categories of oracle visions that focus on a proclamation (e.g., 7:7–8; 8:1–2), dramatic word visions (Amos's other visions), and revelatory or mystery visions with bizarre images (e.g., Zech. 1–6).[1]

Visions and dreams were common in the Old Testament and in the ancient Near East. Jacob had a vision at Bethel (Gen. 28:12–22), and an Egyptian pharaoh had visions about an upcoming famine that Joseph interpreted (ch. 41). Likewise, Nebuchadnezzar, the Babylonian king, and Daniel had visions (Dan. 2; 4; 7–8). In ancient Near Eastern texts a whole variety of people had visions.[2]

News and information were primarily communicated orally at this time. Since few had a copy of Scripture, God often chose to communicate through visions or dreams. People believed these visions were divine revelations by the gods/God, so they took them seriously. There is no indication that visions were more important than oral means of communicating with a prophet. But the graphic nature of visions allowed the prophet to see God's intentions, thus bringing out a more powerful understanding and feeling about what he said he would do. Amos's visions move him to cry out for mercy and to intercede for those who will suffer, a reaction that is not aroused by the earlier spoken words by God in chapters 1–6.

The Vision of Locusts (7:1–3)

IN THE INTRODUCTORY formula, the Hebrew word meaning to see, show (Hiphil of *r'h*), indicates that this new divine message is received in a unique way. It includes both words and images to dramatically portray the action that God will take. There is no indication that this vision is based on anything happening in nature (e.g., a plague of locusts; 4:9), nor is there any hint of an ecstatic experience associated with this vision. God is the author, who causes Amos to see something that will devastate the land.

Amos thus sees God forming a huge swarm of locusts that can devour every green plant (cf. Joel 1). The timing of this plague is critical, for two chronological indicators appear in this vision. The locusts are being formed after the king's share of the crop has been harvested (probably grass for his horses; see 1 Kings 4:26–28; 18:5) and just as the young tender spring crops

---

1. J. Lindblom, *Prophecy in Ancient Israel* (Philadelphia: Fortress, 1962), 122–239, also refers to minor categories of "symbolic perception" and "literary visions." See also B. O. Long, "Reports of Visions Among the Prophets," *JBL* 95 (1976): 353–65.

2. Pritchard, *ANET*, 76, 109–10, 560–63, 624–31.

are sprouting (probably in April).[3] This suggests that the royal needs have been met but that the average peasant farmer will be in serious trouble. If the locusts had come a few weeks earlier, there would not yet be any sprouting grain and thus no harm to Israel's farmers. If it had come later, the crops would be set back by the locusts but not totally destroyed. This heightens Amos's compassion for the poor farmers, who will be left in a hopeless situation.

The action in 7:1 sets the plot, but nothing has actually happened yet. Some translations of 7:2 picture the crops already eaten by the locusts (RSV, NASB, NIV). This raises the difficult situation of having the prophet intercede after the danger is past and of God's stopping the punishment after it has already happened. This makes no sense and is not required by the Hebrew text. Since the word used here (*klh*) can mean to determine, decide, complete a plan (1 Sam. 20:7, 9, 33; Est. 7:7; Prov. 16:30), the text can read, "when he determined to destroy the vegetation."[4] With this translation, Amos's intercession comes when he realizes God has finally determined to release the locusts on the land.

At that point the prophet prays for compassion. Much like Moses at the golden calf, Amos relies on the long-suffering, patient, and forgiving nature of God (Ex. 34:6). But unlike Moses, there is no reasoning with God about the impression this will have on Israel's neighbors or any appeal to some promise to the forefathers (32:11−14). The prophet's prayer seems more like a lament (a lament often asks how long or why; see Ps. 13:1−2; 42:5, 11; 79:5), which is full of deep sympathy for the poor farmers who will suffer the most misery. They have already suffered under the oppression of the wealthy landowners. Why will God make them the object of his anger?

Amos boldly calls for God's forgiveness, though usually forgiveness is based on a previous response of repentance (1 Kings 8:30−39, 48−50; 2 Chron. 7:14). When sin is confessed, God no longer holds the sinner accountable, and the punishment is removed. Since there is no sign of any repentance by Israel, Amos is asking for an act of pure grace that was undeserved. He requests God's compassion because some in Israel will not be able to survive; they are just too small and insignificant. These were the little people, like the orphan and widow, with whom God is especially concerned (Ex. 22:22; Deut. 10:18; 24:17−22; Isa. 1:17). Jeroboam's army is strong and his horses have plenty of hay, but the poor people will have nothing without God's mercy.

---

3. B. K. Smith, "Amos," 128, points out that the Gezer Calender lists the third and fourth months of the year as the "second crop," similar to this passage.

4. Andersen and Freedman, *Amos*, 739; G. V. Smith, *Amos*, 300.

God's response is immediate and somewhat surprising. The plague is stopped before it begins, and without any prerequisites. God does not make his decision to stop the locusts if the people first do this or that—a condition that would make his decision understandable (see Jer. 18:1–12). It is an act of pure grace on a people who have been rebelling against him for centuries. God's relenting (*niham*) on his plans is an anthropomorphic way of explaining his personal interaction with the prophet and his people. Compassion for the people is not inconsistent with God's character; rather, it reveals the depth of his patience and his openness to hearing the prayers of righteous intercessors (James 5:13–18).

God is not a mindless abstract principle of philosophy who rules by some set of mechanical computer formulas. He is a personal caring ruler who does not enjoy the punishment of the wicked (Ezek. 18:23). He richly pours out his love to those who do not deserve it. The removal of the locust plague postpones God's wrath for another day.

The Vision of the Fire (7:4–6)

THE SECOND VISION has a structure parallel to the first vision. God shows Amos a great fire[5] that can destroy the sea and land. A ferocious and powerful fire that can devour both matter and the water in the depths of the ocean is a divine fire of enormous size. Deuteronomy 32:22 also refers to a fire that burns to the lowest part of Sheol, that consumes the earth, and that sets on fire the foundations of the mountains. This seems to be either a huge volcanic eruption or a burning star that hits the earth.

Whatever the source of the fire, Amos intercedes with a prayer for God to stop the fire before it destroys the land of Israel.[6] Amos laments the fate of the nation, but unlike the first vision, there is no request for forgiveness in this second one. The basis for this request is the same as his earlier rational: Israel is so small, and it cannot last under this great judgment. God's response is the same as his earlier decision. He stops the fire, for no one can survive the onslaught of his wrath. More time is provided for the Israelites to respond before his judgment. Indeed, God is long-suffering and surprisingly patient; his grace extends to undeserving people again and again.

---

5. *rib baʾēš* is translated "judgment of fire" in the NIV, but D. R. Hillers, "Amos 7:4 and Ancient Parallels," *CBQ* 26 (1964): 222–23, divides the Hebrew consonants differently (*rbb ʾš*) and gets a better reading of "rain of fire" (see Gen. 19:24; Ezek. 38:22). Stuart, *Hosea–Jonah*, 370, and Andersen and Freedman, *Amos*, 745, follow Hillers's suggestion.

6. The NIV translates the verbs as past, "dried up the great deep and devoured the land," but it is too late to intercede if the land has already been devoured. It seems better to translate "dried up the great deep and was about to devour the land."

Bridging Contexts

VISIONS. These visions are a special means of revelation to the prophet. God communicated earlier through the use of words in a war oracle (1:3–2:16) and in woe oracles (5:18–27; 6:1–14), but the visions provide a more stark and realistic view of the tragedy that will happen to the Hebrew people where Amos is prophesying. A vision allows the receiver to imagine the human suffering that will take place when God acts in wrath, to dialogue with God concerning his plans for the future, and to identify with the people who will die.

There is no theological principle that can explain when or why God sometimes chooses to reveal his will at one time in words and in another context through visions. Both methods are equally valid, and one is not superior to the other. The purpose of a vision is to give clear information, not to hide things or confuse the one receiving the vision.

Joel 2:28–32 refers to a future time when many people will see visions and dream dreams, so it is clear that God will reveal his will in this way in the future. While this is not necessarily totally fulfilled in Acts 2, it at least begins to be fulfilled when the Holy Spirit comes on the first members of the church. John's great vision of the future in Revelation is also a partial fulfillment of what God said through Joel. Since false prophets in the Old Testament also claimed to see visions from God (Jer. 23:9–40), it is always important for people to carefully evaluate any claims (visionary or vocal) of a divine revelation.

The role of intercession. In the midst of this dynamic interaction Amos sets an example to all believers with his intercession for those whom God plans to judge. Intercession involves mediation for the sake of someone else to alleviate a conflict between two parties. Labor disputes sometimes are solved by mediators who intercede and help the parties come to wage or contract agreement. Although people know that a person can often bargain for better benefits at work, at first it seems a little paradoxical to think that someone can get almighty God to listen to human ideas about his plans.

Those who believe in intercession do so because of certain theological attitudes or beliefs about God's relationship with people. (1) They believe that God hears a person's prayers on behalf of others and will consider requests made by sincere people. Hezekiah interceded for deliverance of his nation from the destructive hand of the Assyrian king Sennacherib (Isa. 37:14–20): "Give ear, O LORD, and hear ... [and] listen to all the words [spoken by the evil king] Sennacherib." The Psalms frequently have such requests as "O LORD, hear my prayer, listen to my cry for mercy" (Ps. 143:1).

In fact, God promises that "if my people, who are called by my name, will humble themselves and pray and seek my face and turn from their wicked ways, then will I hear from heaven and will forgive their sins and will heal their land" (2 Chron. 7:14). The prophet Isaiah reminded his audience that God's "ear [is not] too dull to hear. But your iniquities have separated you from your God; your sins have hidden his face from you, so that he will not hear" (Isa. 59:1–2). Prayer is a conversation with a God who hears our words and knows our thoughts.[7]

(2) Those who intercede care deeply about the ones for whom they are praying. Amos prays for God to stop the locusts because the poor farmers will not be able to survive these tragic events (7:2). Moses cared so much for the Israelites who sinned by worshiping the golden calf that he pleaded with God to "blot me out of the book you have written" (Ex. 32:32). "Such a total commitment ... is a central feature of his role as mediator and intercessor."[8] The prophet Jeremiah, the weeping prophet, interceded with words like the following:

> Since my people are crushed, I am crushed;
>   I mourn, and horror grips me.
> Is there no balm in Gilead?
>   Is there no physician there?
> Why then is there no healing
>   for the wound of my people?
> Oh, that my head were a spring of water
>   and my eyes a fountain of tears!
> I would weep day and night
>   for the slain of my people. (Jer. 8:21–9:1)

Jesus sets an example with his care for little children (Matt. 19:13), love for his disciples, and concern for their unity after he would leave them (John 17). Paul's care for his new churches is evident in his intercessory prayers for enlightenment of believers (Eph. 1:18), strength and good theological roots (3:16–17), knowledge of God's will and spiritual wisdom (Col. 1:9–10), and a worthy walk that glorifies God (2 Thess. 1:11–12). Paul exhorts the church at Ephesus to "be alert and always keep on praying for all the saints" (Eph. 6:18). James encourages people to intercede for the healing of others (James 5:16).

God himself cares about what might happen to these people. His love for his people is evident in 2 Chronicles 7:15–16, where he promises that "my eyes will be open and my ears attentive to the prayers offered in this

---

7. For a discussion of prayer in the Old Testament, see S. E. Balentine, *Prayer in the Hebrew Bible: The Drama of Divine-Human Dialogue* (Minneapolis: Fortress, 1993); P. D. Miller, *They Cried to the Lord: The Form and Theology of Biblical Prayers* (Minneapolis: Fortress, 1994); or K. N. Jung "Prayer in the Psalms," *Teach Us to Pray*, ed. D. A. Carson (Grand Rapids: Baker, 1990), 19–57.

8. R. W. L. Moberly, *At the Mountain of God* (Sheffield: JSOT, 1983), 57.

place ... my heart will always be there." According to Romans 8:34, Jesus is "at the right hand of God and is also interceding for us" (cf. Heb. 7:25), and "the Spirit himself intercedes for us with groans that words cannot express" (Rom. 8:26).[9]

What are we to conclude about people who do not intercede for others? It is hard to make generalizations, but busyness, other priorities, a fatalistic approach to life, a low view of God's ability to transform a situation, and a lack of compassion may result in no intercession. When someone does not care about what happens to others, that person usually does not take the time to intercede for them. If people are focused on their own desires, they will spend little time to pray for the needs of others.

(3) Those who pray and intercede for others do so because they think that it will make a difference regarding the future. Some prayers focus on changing what people will do (repent and come to God), while others request a different response from God (forgive, heal, or guide). The one praying serves as a mediator to modify the results of a seemingly inevitable outcome.

Samuel, for example, not only promised to teach Saul to do what is right so that he would fear and serve God faithfully with all his heart, but also assured the new king that he would pray for him (1 Sam. 12:22–23). Both the instruction and the prayer were central to modifying Saul's behavior away from evil and God's consequent judgment. In a quite different series of events, Nehemiah's prayers of intercession for his brothers back in the unwalled city of Jerusalem moved him to the place where he was willing to be personally involved with changing the situation in Jerusalem (Neh. 1) and asked the Persian king to give him time off to go to Jerusalem (2:1–10). Later Nehemiah interceded for God to take action against Sanballat, Tobiah, and their associates, who were mocking the meager efforts of those rebuilding the walls (4:1–5).

Does God change his mind or repent? It is not hard to understand how God can influence people to bring changes in their lives, but does prayer just change people? This question is raised by English translations that render the Hebrew verb *nḥm* (7:3, 6) with words like God "repented" (KJV), "changed his mind" (NASB), or "relented" (NIV). If God is in charge of this world and knows everything about it, does he not carry out his perfect purposes without hesitation or human interference? Since God knows much more than any human being about each situation, it seems that people should leave things in his hands and not try to tell him what should or should not be done in each

---

9. For a specific treatment of prayers in different sections of the New Testament, see M. M. B. Turner, "Prayer in the Gospels and Acts," D. C. Peterson, "Prayer in Paul's Epistles," and "Prayer in the General Epistles," plus E. Y. L. Ng, "Prayer in Revelation," in *Teach Us to Pray*, 58–135.

instance. Even Scripture states that we do not know how to pray as we should and need the Holy Spirit to intercede for us (Rom. 8:26).

If these points are true, then it seems rather presumptuous for any human being to try to get God to "repent" or "change his mind," and rather contradictory to his nature for him ever to change his mind. Who would presume to put themselves above God and suggest that their way of dealing with a situation is better than God's way? Although Job initially was confused about God's action and questioned God's justice toward himself, his final responses to the divine revelation of wisdom and power was a humble attitude of submission. He admitted he did not know the plans and reasons for God's actions; God's ways are too wondrous and marvelous for any person to understand (Job 40:4–5; 42:1–6).

Because it seems illogical for a perfect, all-wise, transcendent God to change, some solve this dilemma by concluding that this is just anthropomorphic and anthropopathic talk about God to help humans refer to the mystery of divine activity. They believe these human descriptions are misleading and inadequate to represent accurately the true nature of God.[10]

In spite of the theological problems raised by this metaphorical language, clearly God's people in the Bible and today have repeatedly interceded for others and encouraged him to respond in grace and mercy rather than in wrath and judgment. Prayer to God is based on the view that God has and desires a relationship with people; it is not an obnoxious intrusion that he abhors. Prayers are a continuation of the relationship God has already established with people.

Consequently, some prayers of intercession, such as Exodus 32 (where God wanted to destroy the nation and start over so that the covenant promises would be fulfilled through Moses' children), discuss the nature of the covenant relationship in which God previously gave his people promises about their future (Gen. 12:1–3). If there appears to be some new initiative in the relationship or if one partner in the relationship does not understand what the other person is doing (God viewed the worship of the golden calf as a rejection of himself and the covenant relationship), questions are asked, requests are presented, and appropriate actions are taken.

Frequently intercession is a request for undeserved mercy from God that goes beyond the normal understanding of the covenant relationship, thus avoiding an immediate execution of God's justice. Amos's intercessory cry for forgiveness and the stopping of God's destruction of Israel (Amos 7:1–6) is a request for God to patiently suspend his just judgment for a time so that his people will have further opportunities to repent of their evil and continue

---

10. L. J. Kuyper, "The Suffering and Repentance of God," *SJT* 22 (1969): 258.

a healthy relationship with God. God is addressed out of human weakness and a need for compassion.

A person could conceive of God as a giant computer that keeps track of the deeds and thoughts of every person in order to automatically and impersonally carry out just commands according to the preset rules designed by the mind of the divine programmer. In this scenario, no one could communicate with the computer and no one could adjust the timing or nature of the computer's response to human behavior except the programmer himself. Everything would be predetermined by the code inserted into the operating system. This conceptualization of the divine/human setting is nonrelational, impersonal, and, most important, inconsistent with the biblical description of the way God is involved with the world he created.

Part of the problem is our inability to understand how God can know the end from the beginning and still be open to the influence of human prayer. One aspect of the explanation is that God's plans include the necessity of prayers for things to go as planned. It is also clear from numerous texts that some of God's plans are given conditionally, based on the behavior of some specific group of people (Deut. 27–28; Jer. 18:1–12).

But even these two facets do not fully explain God's repentance or changing his mind. Some of the problem here is based on a misunderstanding of the Hebrew verb *nhm*. Wolff thinks the term "designates a change of mind prompted by the emotions,"[11] while Willis suggests that this metaphor means that God "experienced a reversal or change with respect to some past statement of action."[12]

Parunak's extensive survey of the semantic fields of this root has identified four primary senses of *nhm*: (1) comfort, have compassion; (2) suffer emotional pain; (3) relief of emotional tension by performing declared action; and (4) release of emotional tension by detracting a declared action.[13] In each case *nhm* describes an emotional response (usually a compassionate one) to human behavior—sometimes to establish justice, at other times to show compassion instead of justice. In the process change takes place, but the meaning of this word is not a synonym for change; this word focuses on relieving emotional tension. Thus God's compassion to Israel in Amos 7:3 and 6 removes the tension of destroying the nation. This picture of God turns the strict, unattached, computer-driven judge into a compassionate and caring covenant partner.

God is not unaware of what will happen, nor is he fooled and surprised by what does happen, but his gift of compassion awaits the intercessor's

---

11. Wolff, *Joel and Amos*, 298.

12. J. T. Willis, "The 'Repentance' of God in the Books of Samuel, Jeremiah, and Jonah," *HBT* 16 (1994): 158.

13. H. Van Dyke Parunak, "A Semantic Survey of NHM," *Bib* 56 (1975): 512–32.

request for it. The human intercession is, therefore, essential and effective in moving God to respond compassionately to situations where his emotional distribution of wrath would normally be expected.

PRAYING FOR SINNERS. If Abraham interceded for the few righteous people in the ungodly cities of Sodom and Gomorrah (Gen. 18:22–33), if Moses interceded for the sinful Israelites who worshiped the golden calf just a few days after they had seen the glory of God on top of Mount Sinai (Ex. 32), if Amos interceded for the pagan Israelites who worshiped the golden calf at the temple in Bethel (Amos 7:1–6), if Moses interceded for the wicked people of Israel after their rebellion against him (Num. 14:10–25), if Jesus interceded for the Roman soldiers crucifying him (Luke 23:34), and if Paul repeatedly interceded for the Jewish people who were not saved (Rom. 9:1–5; 10:1), it seems only reasonable to conclude that God expects believers to intercede for his mercy on the wicked today. When the church does not pray and ask, it is legitimate to wonder whether God will respond in compassion. When the church does not have time or energy to intercede, it is legitimate to wonder if people still care for others. When the church does not come to God for answers to problems, it is legitimate to wonder if his people still think that this God is interested enough or powerful enough to respond with life-transforming grace. The practical question that must be asked is: When was the last time I followed the examples in Scripture by deeply interceding for an undeserving sinner in this world?

Clearly some believers do pray fervently, consistently, and effectively for the ungodly people of this world (the Billy Graham organization is characterized by this concern), but in the local church I hear many more prayers of intercession for the health needs of the saints than the eternal needs of sinners. It often appears as if the church is more interested in God's compassion and strength for the physical needs of church members than anything else (play back the tapes of the worship services for the last month to check this out from the pastoral prayers in your church). Why does the church not take more time and put more effort into praying for the condemned people of this world, who do not know God or Jesus as their Savior?

Does the church still realize that God takes no pleasure in the punishment of the wicked (Ezek. 18:23) and that he desires that no one should perish but that all will come to a knowledge of the truth (2 Peter 3:9)? Do Christians not care enough to pray, or is the problem more related to the fact that they have not taken the time to get personally involved with unbelievers? Any single answer would be an overgeneralization, not true of many Christians or churches. But it would not surprise me if we will be asked one day: Who were the sinners you prayed for?

One answer to the problem is for pastors and leaders to set a positive example in their lives and in their public ministry. E. Bradford boldly states that the "judgment is inescapable that the minister who does not pray for those to whom he is called to minister, is indeed, no minister at all. He is proud, conducting his labors as though he can succeed without God's power. He is cold and lacking in compassion."[14] This sounds good, but do church leaders think of the phrase "those to whom he is called to minister" as including non-Christians?

The "Directory for Worship of the Orthodox Presbyterian Church" states that the duty of the minister is to include "offerings of prayer to the Lord on behalf of the congregation" (6.A.2), for this follows the example of the leaders of the early church, who devoted themselves to prayer and the ministry of the Word (Acts 6:4). In contrast, John Calvin found that "it was the duty of a prophet, not only to comfort the afflicted by the word of the Lord, but also to offer prayers for their salvation."[15] Paul exhorted the young pastor Timothy that "requests, prayers, intercession and thanksgiving be made for everyone. . . . God our Savior . . . wants all men to be saved and to come to a knowledge of the truth" (1 Tim. 2:1–4).

Intercession should include prayers for the bad people of our world, the foul-mouthed laborer, the undeserving criminals, and the obsessed molester. Intercessors should plead with God that their neighbors will be saved and not just limit their prayers to the wants of the church. Because of neglect or unbelief, "many have been given up who were still within the reach of grace. There have been many who have been put into the spiritual burial shroud even by Christians, given up to damnation even by ministers. . . . Oh, give up on nobody! Pray still! Lay none out for spiritual dead until they are laid out naturally dead."[16]

Prayers of intercession should not be aimed so much at those who want or even deserve a better life but should focus the burden of our hearts on those who deserve eternal damnation under the wrath of God. They have no hope but the intercessory prayers of saints. Perhaps we can stay God's hand of judgment for a brief time so that there will be additional opportunities to respond to God's grace.

---

14. E. Bradford, *Intercessory Prayer: A Ministerial Task* (Boonton, N.J.: Simpson, 1991), 17.

15. J. Calvin, "Commentary on the Book of the Prophet Isaiah," *Calvin's Commentaries* 8 (Edinburgh: Calvin Translation Society, 1850), 111.

16. A. Murray and C. H. Spurgeon, *The Believer's Secret of Intercession*, ed. L. G. Parkhurst (Minneapolis: Bethany, 1988), 38.

God and human prayers. Of course, to offer such prayers assumes that intercessory prayer can influence God, that God can choose to be more compassionate and delay the execution of his judgment (cf. Amos 7:3, 6). This raises the ancient and modern question of the "openness of God" to human requests.[17] Supporters of an "open God" approach believe that "when we address God in prayer . . . we are entering into a genuine dialogue and . . . the future is not settled."[18] God has intentions or plans, but these "are not iron-clad decrees that cannot be changed . . . consequently, God can reformulate his plans, or alter his intentions, in response to developments."[19] This thinking explains the references to God's repenting of what he had planned to do (e.g., his plans about Nineveh in Jonah 3) or his sorrow over something done earlier that did not work out (e.g., choosing Saul to be king in 1 Sam. 15). These scholars picture a God of feelings, who listens to intercessory petitions, and they criticize those who define the sovereign predestination of God so tightly that real human freedom does not exist and real human-divine interaction is compromised.

This approach does provide a dynamic interplay between the various metaphors of divine activity with humankind, but it has been severely criticized by more traditional theologians because it radically changes most conceptions of God's immutability, transcendence, and foreknowledge. R. Olson applauds many of the emphases of this new approach but is uncomfortable with the position that "God does not know future free decisions and actions of his creatures."[20] D. Bloesch also has difficulty with this idea but prefers the mystery explanation of all this because he feels there is really no "rationally satisfying answer to this problem."[21]

Although this discussion may sometimes seem like an intellectual struggle between classical and open theology, at the heart of its debate is the practical question of the nature of God and how he relates to people. If God only has "present knowledge" and no foreknowledge of what will happen in the future, and if he allows people complete freedom of choice between a variety of options, then his power to control and direct a positive outcome to this world and his ability to answer our prayers is relatively limited. I would argue that the open view of God has overreacted to a Greek philosophical view of the divine and an extreme view of divine sovereignty that makes God into some distant, uncaring, untouchable, and unloving

17. *The Openness of God: A Biblical Challenge to the Traditional Understanding of God*, ed. C. Pinnock et al. (Downers Grove, Ill.: InterVarsity, 1994).
18. Ibid., 7.
19. Ibid., 26.
20. R. Olson, "Has God Been Held Hostage by Philosophy?" *CT* 39 (Jan. 9, 1995): 30–31.
21. D. G. Bloesch, *God the Almighty* (Downers Grove, Ill.: InterVarsity, 1995), 257.

monarch. Few people would identify with this straw man that the "open view of God" rejects.

Classical theology puts together a God who is both a loving Father and the powerful King of the universe. God's power is not undermined and his foreknowledge is not put in question when he responds to the repentant people of Nineveh (Jonah 3) with compassion. God's justice is established by judgment if the people do not repent and his justice is established with compassion if the people do repent. God's character or nature has not changed, his personal relationship to people is maintained, and his power to control the future history of a great empire is not compromised. The Bible never has represented a deistic God wholly unrelated to the world in some sort of abstract transcendent realm. Moreover, it is a myth to suppose that humans are completely free to choose (even sociologists and psychologists know this) and to suppose that God is somehow not in control, but merely reacts to free human decisions.

Nevertheless, this new view of God has given positive emphasis to the existence of real emotions within God's relationship, to God's responsiveness to human prayers and actions, and to the existence of human freedom/responsibility to intercede with God for the sake of others. People intercede because God's power is not limited, because he knows what will happen, and because he has the ability to influence the self-destructive choices people sometimes make. A mother could not pray with much confidence for her drug-obsessed son if she thought that God did not have the power to change her son's life. A husband could not pray with much confidence about his unfair treatment at work if he believed that the boss was totally free to make his own choices and that God could not influence his decisions.

Human freedom sounds nice and a limited God with less control over us gives us more power, but in this world we need fewer powerful people making sinful choices and a greater demonstration of the divine power to change people's lives. All prayers of intercession depend on a God who can and does overpower the forces of evil within us, who can powerfully transform us into new creatures in Christ. God has the power to release people from slavery to sin (not the freedom to sin) to become servants of and brothers with Christ.

Having an impact. One final lesson needs to be emphasized. If Christians do practice intercession, if they believe that their prayers can influence the compassion of God, if they believe that God has the power to intervene in the lives of people, then they will find that they themselves can have an impact on the situations they are praying about by simply telling others about their intercession.

True, Amos's intercession was effective without ever telling anyone about it, and our intercession is also to be practiced in our closets with God. But a powerful impact can be achieved by humbly describing our intercession in a way that focuses on God's grace. Amos's retelling of his experience to his audience has the rhetorical effect of identifying the prophet with the audience's need. An intercessor does not condemn those in need but stands with them to help them avoid punishment. The sharing of a personal experience always has greater persuasive power than mere negative declarations or statements of facts.

Intercessors experience the agony of the potential situation with the sufferers, and consequently their mediation on behalf of the listeners speaks volumes about the care and deep concern of the intercessor. The rhetorical nature of intercessory visions, or any type of intercessory role, enables the message of judgment to be communicated clearly but puts it in a third-person context (God said). This allows the intercessor to take the first-person role (I prayed) on behalf of the listener. Such approaches cause the listener to be more accepting of the intercessor because he or she is not the source of bad news, but of good news.

Set in our day, this means that parents might accomplish more by telling a child that they are praying for them to find good Christian friends, rather than constantly complaining or giving speeches about what they should be doing. A pastor who identifies with his congregation and shares the burdens of his heart for them may gain more acceptance than the one who condemns a congregation. At the same time, no pastor should use such intercession as a mechanism of manipulation, for people can quickly see through the fog of hype.

Amos 7:7–17

THIS IS WHAT he showed me: The Lord was standing by a wall that had been built true to plumb, with a plumb line in his hand. ⁸And the LORD asked me, "What do you see, Amos?"

"A plumb line," I replied.

Then the Lord said, "Look, I am setting a plumb line among my people Israel; I will spare them no longer.

⁹"The high places of Isaac will be destroyed
    and the sanctuaries of Israel will be ruined;
    with my sword I will rise against the house
      of Jeroboam."

¹⁰Then Amaziah the priest of Bethel sent a message to Jeroboam king of Israel: "Amos is raising a conspiracy against you in the very heart of Israel. The land cannot bear all his words. ¹¹For this is what Amos is saying:

" 'Jeroboam will die by the sword,
    and Israel will surely go into exile,
    away from their native land.' "

¹²Then Amaziah said to Amos, "Get out, you seer! Go back to the land of Judah. Earn your bread there and do your prophesying there. ¹³Don't prophesy anymore at Bethel, because this is the king's sanctuary and the temple of the kingdom."

¹⁴Amos answered Amaziah, "I was neither a prophet nor a prophet's son, but I was a shepherd, and I also took care of sycamore-fig trees. ¹⁵But the LORD took me from tending the flock and said to me, 'Go, prophesy to my people Israel.' ¹⁶Now then, hear the word of the LORD. You say,

" 'Do not prophesy against Israel,
    and stop preaching against the house of Isaac.'

¹⁷"Therefore this is what the LORD says:

" 'Your wife will become a prostitute in the city,
    and your sons and daughters will fall by the sword.

Your land will be measured and divided up,
    and you yourself will die in a pagan country.
And Israel will certainly go into exile,
    away from their native land.' "

THIS SECTION IS divided into two subparagraphs: the plumb line vision of destruction for the king and the temple in Bethel (7:7–9), and the conflict over this vision of destruction (7:10–17). The structure of the vision is different from the two visions in 7:1–3 and 7:4–6, and also different from the confrontation in 7:10–17. This third vision is parallel in structure to the fourth vision in 8:1–3 (making them a pair like the first two visions). Both visions have appendixes added to them (7:10–17 and 8:4–14) and identical clauses that demonstrate a parallelism between them.[1] Although these visions are paired, each one and its appendix will be treated separately because of its length and unique characteristics.

The structure of the third and fourth visions includes (1) an introductory formula, (2) a description of the vision, beginning with "behold" (*hinneh*, not trans. in NIV), (3) a dialogue between God and Amos in the vision, and (4) an explanation of the vision. There is no prophetic intercession or divine answer to the prophet's prayer in these visions. The first vision is held together by related themes and the word *ʾnk*, "plumb line, plumb, tin," and is connected to its pair in 8:1–3 by the repeated phrase, "I will spare them no longer."

The autobiographical disputational conflict in 7:10–17 is closely tied to the vision in 7:7–9 through the partial repetition of similar phrases from 7:9 in 7:11. This disputation can be divided into two parts according to the main speakers and theme. Amos 7:10–13 describes Amaziah's rejection of God's word and of Amos's calling to preach in the northern nation of Israel, while 7:14–17 is Amos's confirmation of his calling from God to prophesy in Israel and a confirmation of God's word. The worldviews of Amos and Amaziah are completely in conflict, and both try to persuade the other of the authoritative value of their perspective.

The absence of a conclusion that resolves the tension suggests that neither person accepts the argument of the other. It may appear that Amos's prophetic career is over at this time because of Amaziah's authoritative state-

---

1. Hayes, *Amos*, 199, does not see 7:7–17 as a unit but puts 7:1–9 together with 8:1–9:15, while Stuart, *Hosea–Jonah*, 368–69, more understandably puts 7:1–8:3 together, but this disconnects 8:4–14 from the vision in 8:1–3.

ments, but Amaziah's authority probably only relates to the temple area, not the rest of the city of Bethel or the rest of the nation of Israel (that is why he has to send a letter to King Jeroboam II). The total rejection of God's word in this conflict may partially explain why God "will spare them no longer" and why the prophet does not try to intercede in the third and fourth visions.

Vision of the Plumb Line (7:7–9)

THE INTRODUCTORY CLAUSE, "This is what the Lord showed me," demonstrates that the prophet receives another vision from God, in which Amos sees God "standing" (*nṣb*) beside a wall (presumably a large city wall of an important place), holding something. In this initial description of the vision (7:7) the word *ʾanak* is used twice—once modifying the wall and once specifying what God has in his hand.

Since this is the only time this word is found in the Bible, there is some guesswork involved in defining it. Landsberger and Holladay believe the comparable Akkadian term *annaku* refers to "tin" rather than lead or a plumb line.[2] Some commentators change the word to *ʾeben* (stone) to make better sense, drop this word as a dittography with the next line, or suggest the word refers to a metal instrument like a pickax that might be used to destroy a wall.[3] Those who prefer the interpretation "tin" see it as a metal of weakness showing that Israel is extremely weak, while others admit that the imagery makes no sense but must symbolize a metal of strength and be comparable to the "bronze wall" in Jeremiah 1:18; 15:20.[4] Given the primitive metallurgical methods at that time, this metal may not have been pure tin and much closer to lead,[5] but the decisive issue is the use of this lead/tin in the vision.

In spite of all the difficulties left, the traditional interpretation that this is lead used to plumb a wall makes the most sense. Just as a builder tests the

---

2. B. Landsberger, "Tin and Lead: The Adventures of Two Vocables, *JNES* 24 (1965): 285–96, and W. Holladay, "Once More *ʾanak* = TIN,' Amos 7:7–8," *VT* 20 (1970): 292–94. More recently Paul, *Amos*, 234, and Gowan, "Amos," 406, prefer the translation "tin."

3. Paul, *Amos*, 234, catalogues several different ways people have tried to solve this enigma. It is unclear why Amos does not use the usual term for plumb line, which symbolizes God's testing of his people in 2 Kings 21:13; Isa. 28:17; 34:11; Lam. 2:8, but maybe the technical vocabulary for instruments used in building in Israel is different from the vocabulary used in Judah.

4. Paul, *Amos*, 234, sees it as a metal of softness and perishability, while Hayes, *Amos*, 205, compares this wall to the analogy in Jeremiah. After considering all the possibilities, H. G. M. Williamson, "The Prophet and the Plumb-line: A Redactional-Critical Study of Amos vii," *OtSt* 26 (1990): 121, concludes that God had a plumb line in his hand.

5. R. J. Forbes, *Studies in Ancient Technologies* (Leiden: Brill, 1964), 124–70, thinks this term refers to tin, but admits it can easily be confused with lead.

straightness of a wall with a plumb line, God exposes the true state of his people's moral character and covenant faithfulness with his plumb line. In the earlier visions guilt is implied, but this testing procedure legitimates the conclusion that it is no longer possible to delay the judgment of Israel.

The dialogue in 7:8 begins to point toward the meaning of this symbolism. God will put this plumb line[6] in the midst of Israel, and because of that action he has decided to spare "my people Israel" no longer. Those closely connected to God through a covenant relationship, whom God loved and chose to be his special people (Deut. 7:1–7), will not be pardoned again. God's patience has been exhausted; he will not "spare" or "pass over" their sins any longer but "will pass through [their] midst" (5:17); his punishment will not be delayed.

The final part of the vision (7:9) explains specifically what this symbolism means to the audience Amos addresses. The application is surprisingly specific: God will destroy both the religious places of false worship and the dynasty of the king of Israel. Both the local high places and the state temple at Bethel will end up in a heap of ruins. Surprisingly, perhaps, there is no specific condemnation of pagan gods or illegitimate worship at these places.

The prophet Hosea spent a great deal of his ministry describing and condemning the open-air sanctuaries with their wood-carved poles and stone pillars, but Amos's method of delegitimating these places of worship is very different. He tries to persuade people to believe that God can and will take away their two great social institutions that control and order much of their social life. Without any place of worship, how will they relate to the divine powers? Without any king, how will they preserve order and maintain their secure and prosperous lifestyle? Without the powerful house of Jeroboam II, the nation will come to nothing.

The means by which God will accomplish this is not stated. Elsewhere God mentioned an army (3:11–12; 6:14), the destruction of the walls and cities (4:3; 6:11), and going into exile (5:27; 7:17), but here the focus is on God himself as the force bringing about the tragic destruction of his own beloved people. The vision abruptly ends without any prayer of intercession or any message of hope for Amos's audience. Will this vision persuade them to change their perception of the future, or will they stubbornly reject God's words through Amos?

---

6. Stuart, *Hosea–Jonah*, 373, interprets "I will set a plumb line" as a wordplay between ʾanak (tin) and ʾanaq (mourning) because there is a need for a wordplay here, since there is a wordplay in the fourth vision. This increases the parallelism between the two visions, but there is little to support his suggestion.

Conflict over God's Words (7:10–17)

AN AUTOBIOGRAPHICAL NARRATIVE that records a disputation between the priest Amaziah and Amos develops as a direct reaction to Amos's third vision. There is nothing in this brief encounter that enables the interpreter to specify an exact date or occasion.[7] The incident focuses on two factors: (1) the authority of Amos's vision about the future destruction of Israel's temples and ruling family, and (2) the nature of Amos's prophetic calling. Amos and Amaziah have conflicting points of view on both issues and dispute the validity of Amos's words from the Lord.

Amaziah's authoritative tone and strong statements suggest that he is the high priest at the Bethel temple. He seems to be an important government official with the power to regulate and supervise what happens at this sanctuary and to protect it from foreign ideologies that might undermine its state-approved religious activities. Amaziah's strong accusations (7:10–13) that Amos's words are a "conspiracy" (*qšr*, falsehood, treasonous act) suggest an organized plot to overthrow the government. This would be considered rebellion, sedition, or subversion by those in authority. No wonder Amaziah thinks the land cannot possibly allow him to speak like this in Israel (7:10). As a loyal political appointee and protector of the status quo of that culture, Amaziah communicates his concern over Amos's words to King Jeroboam II.

His quotation of Amos (7:11) is not exact. He slightly changes the prophet's warning about the end of the "house of Jeroboam" (7:9) into a direct attack on Jeroboam II himself, then adds the idea about going into exile, and omits any reference to the destruction of the temple. It seems odd that the priest does not mention the destruction of the temple. Possibly Amaziah wants Amos to appear like a political threat and not just a diverse theological opinion that the king might be willing to tolerate. Amaziah seems to reinvent Amos as a dangerous dissident who might stir up support from the poor people of the land or political rivals of the king. His hyperbole is a fear tactic to quiet any opposition to the king and himself. Finally, Amaziah significantly omits anything about what "God" is going to do to Israel or that these are the "words of God." Yes, Amaziah rejects Amos, but more important, he rejects what God says. Amos would not be rejected as a traitor if it were not for the message of God that he has spoken.

Amaziah's solution to his and Amos's conflict is for them to separate peaceably. Amos should just back off and return to Judah before he causes

---

7. Hayes, *Amos*, 231–32, guesses that this takes place at the fall festival when the king is present at the temple, but this is just speculation.

any more problems. Amaziah tells Amos what he should do (go home in v. 12) and what he should not do (continue to prophesy in the Bethel temple in v. 13). In his words he designates Amos as filling the social role of a "seer." Some conclude that "seer" is not a derogatory term[8] and is chosen simply because Amos is reporting visions he has seen (see 7:1–9; also 1:1). Others believe it has a negative connotation because it describes someone who is prophesying for money, while a third group thinks it is just a technical term for a southern prophet from Judah.[9]

One would expect Amaziah to have a negative view of Amos, so he probably does not use a neutral term in describing a traitor. Amaziah's threat to Amos requires him to flee back to Judah, suggesting a quick movement away from potential persecution. The motivation that Amaziah provides to encourage a positive response is that Amos can make money in Judah. This comment imputes negative financial goals (he is a professional prophet who wants to get rich off the people of Israel with his wild prophecies) as Amos's primary reason for prophesying. Finally, Amaziah legitimates his own authority by stating that this is a state temple that is controlled by the king; thus, he has the power to deny permission for anyone to make negative political statements about the king in the temple area.

Although this confrontation probably ends Amos's preaching in the Bethel temple, there is no statement about regulating his activities outside the temple. It is interesting to observe that in all of Amaziah's objections, he never claims that Amos is not a prophet or that he has not received a word from God. He just rejects the message and the messenger.

Amos's response to Amaziah's threats (7:14–17) includes a confirmation of his calling (vv. 14–15) and a confirmation of the words of the Lord that exile is coming to Israel (vv. 16–17). Contrary to Amaziah's suggestion, Amos claims that he is not a professional prophet or the son of a professional prophet who is in business to get rich in Israel. Commentators have struggled over the translation and meaning of verse 14. Since Amos was sent to prophesy, his statement that he is not a prophet (7:14) can make sense only if *nby’* (prophet) is interpreted to mean a professional prophet who makes his living by being paid for prophesying.[10] Some prefer to take another alternative, suggesting the negative in verse 14 is an absolute nega-

---

8. E.g., Mays, *Amos*, 136, since Gad is called both a prophet and seer of David (2 Sam. 24:11).

9. H. H. Rowley, "The Nature of Old Testament Prophecy in Light of Recent Studies," *The Servant of the Lord* (Oxford: Blackwell, 1965), 120–201, holds that the term is negative, while D. Petersen, *The Roles of Israel's Prophets* (JSOTSup 17; Sheffield: JSOT, 1981), 56–57, believes this is a technical term for a Judean court prophet.

10. Rowley, "The Nature of Old Testament Prophecy," 120–21.

---

tion and thus translate the phrase "No, I am a prophet, I am the son of a prophet."[11]

Since there is an emphasis on how Amos makes his money in Amaziah's critique (7:12) and in Amos's reply (7:14), the first option fits the context better.[12] Amos makes his living by employment in the sheep business and by caring for fig-bearing sycamore trees. He is not prophesying to get rich, so that is not a legitimate issue to raise to try and get rid of him. The exact nature of Amos's work with the fig trees is unclear because the Hebrew word *bls* is found only here in the Hebrew Bible. Since some figs had to be slit open to give them a sweeter taste, Amos may have been occupied with this task, but Wright's investigation has shown that some Egyptian and Palestinian figs did not need this operation.[13]

Although no entirely satisfactory solution exists for this problem, the main point is still evident. Amos makes his living by secular employment and is not motivated to come to Israel to prophesy for money. The motivation for his prophecies is the call of God that has instructed him to prophesy in Israel (7:15). He is under divine compulsion to do what Amaziah says he may not do. Amaziah is in rebellion against God's plan and opposes God's power. His command to Amos is a conspiracy against the divine command and God's obedient servant. Amaziah's rejection of both the message and the messenger of God puts him in opposition to God.

Amos demonstrates this by contrasting what God says to him ("Go, prophesy to my people Israel," 7:15) and what Amaziah says to him ("Do not prophesy against [in] Israel" in 7:16). Like Amaziah's quote of Amos earlier (7:11), Amos does not exactly quote what Amaziah has said in 7:12–13. This juxtaposition of Amaziah against God demonstrates the true nature of the conflict described in these verses. This is not just an argument about where Amos can speak; this is a spiritual battle about accepting the message of the Lord or rejecting it.

This conflict demonstrates Amaziah's guilt before God and his unworthiness to be the spiritual priestly leader of the nation of Israel. Such action justifies God's judgment on Amaziah and shows the bankruptcy of the religious beliefs and practices promulgated at the temple at Bethel. If the priest rebels against the words of God, there is little chance that the people worshiping at the temple will listen to what God has said. No wonder the third

---

11. S. Cohen, "Amos Was a Navi," *HUCA* 32 (1962): 175–78; in an odd variation of this Stuart, *Hosea–Jonah*, 376, translates, "No, I am a prophet though I am not a professional prophet," by taking the first negative as an absolute denial, but not the second parallel negative.

12. For a full discussion of the many different proposals for interpreting 7:14, see G. V. Smith, *Amos*, 322–25, or Paul, *Amos*, 244–47.

13. T. J. Wright, "Amos and the Sycamore Fig," *VT* 26 (1976): 362–68.

and fourth visions include the hopeless formula "I will spare them no longer" (7:8; 8:2).

God's decision is to bring five curses on Amaziah and the nation of Israel (7:17):

- His wife will become a prostitute (cf. the curse in Deut. 28:30).
- His children will be killed (see the curses in Deut. 28:32, 41; 32:25).
- His personal property will be given to others (see Deut. 28:30; also Lev. 26:32).
- He will die in a pagan land (see Lev. 26:38–39).[14]
- The nation will go into exile, as Amos earlier announced (Amos 5:27; 7:11).

These may seem severe at first and particularly focused on the priest, but a religious leader like Amaziah is God's representative to the congregation that gathers each Sabbath. He is to teach what God says to the people who come to sacrifice and sing his praises at the temple. How can he intercede for them if he rejects what God says?

Bridging Contexts

THESE TWO SECTIONS are related to specific people and situations in the northern nation of Israel; thus, the modern interpreter must be careful not to suggest that the exact same results will fall on any church group today. It is necessary to look behind the individuals in the vision and biographical story of conflict to determine if there are broader issues or principles presented within these texts. Thus, it is not appropriate for spiritual leaders to announce to people who will not listen to them (cf. what Amos does here) that "God will spare you no longer."

This sorrowful consequence is always true at some point just before God's judgment falls, but most of the time spiritual leaders do not know the exact timing of that judgment. It is tempting for leaders to be too impatient with people they dislike and too easy to allow personal feelings to interfere with God's will for each person's life. Like Amos, all people in leadership positions have a responsibility to humbly discipline the flock in love (Matt. 18:15–17), but they should primarily be concerned with making God's people aware of their sin and bringing restoration where this is possible.

Church discipline. In the area of church discipline there are two extremes in the church today. (1) Some churches have a limited theological backbone

---

14. Paul, *Amos*, 251, emphasizes the "uncleanness" of the land where Amaziah will die. He will become contaminated and polluted by living and dying in an "unclean" place. This was a great indignity for a priest.

and fail to stand up against diverse opinions or heretical behavior, even when these run directly contrary to explicit statements in the Bible. They want to be loving and inclusive, to reach out to people who are searching and struggling to find truth in their own way. Accepting people as they are is a central part of their approach, and they are committed to an individual's right to construct one's theology without harassment from others. They recognize that everyone is on a journey and that people are to be loved and accepted even though they are at different places in their own quest.

(2) By contrast, other churches have very strict standards of conduct and dress and require everyone to accept a fine-tuned set of beliefs. They are confrontational in weeding out heresy and limit a person's individual freedom to have alternate opinions on minor issues that are not clear in the biblical text. Acceptance is given to those who submit to these standards, and even the slightest deviations are excluded. Responsibility and truth are stressed rather than freedom and struggling on a person's personal journey. Discipline for mistaken behavior or beliefs can be swift and strict.

I have seen firsthand the tragedy this latter approach can bring because our family purchased a rural home from members of a conservative Mennonite group that had shunned a family and driven them from the community after the father worked at a secular job off the farm. This is not that far from the Montanists of earlier church history, who "practiced hyper-rigorist ecclesial discipline on the extreme assumption that the church is actually within history a purified and holy community not solely by grace but in actual behavioral practice."[15]

Neither of the above-mentioned alternatives is satisfactory, and many churches try to avoid these extremes. Nevertheless, because of a fear of lawsuits and the desire to increase the size of churches, there is a growing hesitancy, even among those who call themselves conservatives, evangelicals, or orthodox, to practice church discipline. Sometimes this even extends to a hesitancy to discipline pastoral leaders or board members. Amos stands out as a person of boldness, who speaks strongly about the issue of confronting leaders of spiritual institutions who do not accept the teachings of the Bible.

Although the news media has played up examples of sexual failures by ministers, Amos is more concerned with the core spiritual issue of submission to God's revelation. This is the central criteria that all churches and all church members should hold up as their standard. If a spiritual leader (or, for that matter, any person in the church) rejects God's will and denies his power to correct and guide through the divine revelation of his will, that person

---

15. T. C. Oden, *Corrective Love: The Power of Communion Discipline* (St. Louis: Concordia, 1995), 58.

should be strongly confronted, gently exhorted, and persuaded to change his or her view. After repeated refusals to change, strong confrontations must follow. Note how the apostle Paul encouraged the Christians in Corinth to remove the arrogant man who was unwilling to end an immoral relationship with his father's wife (1 Cor. 5:5), warned Timothy not to accept Alexander the metalworker because he opposed Paul's teaching (2 Tim. 4:14–16), and delivered the blasphemers Hymenaeus and Alexander over to Satan (1 Tim. 1:19–20).

Amos's confrontation with Amaziah and his unbending prediction of the fall of Israel and the Bethel temple suggest that there is a place for bold confrontation of unbelief when all other avenues of persuasion are rejected. Christians do have a responsibility to warn those who repeatedly reject all loving warnings and consistently ignore all faithful witnesses to the truth in Scripture. They need to know what God has said, what action God will take, why God will act this way, and what they have done wrong.

I WILL DEVELOP two applications out of these principles. One relates to how churches should deal with situations of conflict where a leader (like the priest Amaziah) is unwilling to accept biblical teachings, and the other relates to how a Christian should understand and react to opposition or persecution. This passage is not a complete primer on facing opposition or a well-organized pastoral letter on how churches should handle conflict situations, but it does raise practical questions that we should process before a crisis breaks out.

How should churches deal with leaders who reject God's Word? It is inappropriate to develop a full range of suggestions on how to handle all kinds of conflicts in the church from this passage. It specifically deals with a spiritual leader, the high priest Amaziah, who rejects God's negative words of judgment about the destruction of the Bethel temple, the end of Jeroboam's dynasty, and the exile of Judah (7:9–13). It is also inappropriate to draw a direct analogy between the destruction of the Bethel temple and the end of the church in some country, or to compare the coming exile of Israel with the modern exile of some nation.

This passage does, however, support several theological principles that can be applied to situations in the life of the church today. (1) Godly leaders and spiritually minded laypeople, like Amos, must boldly address issues where God's people (and the leaders that guide them) do not measure up to God's standards and warn them of God's future judgment of such action (see 7:7–9). (2) In prayerfully evaluating the legitimacy of acts and beliefs of leaders, the key criteria is: Do these people accept what God says, and do they submit to it? (3) Those who reject the Spirit's convicting power should be warned (cf. Amos's earlier prophecies and Matt. 18:15–18). If they are unwilling to change, they should be boldly condemned and not given approval for positions of leadership in the church. Since leaders carry a greater responsibility for directing God's people, they will be judged more severely if they fail to listen to what God says (cf. James 3:1).

Many have recognized that the church's failure to institute these basic principles of church discipline has led to serious problems. E. Brunner sadly concluded that the "absence of any kind of church discipline inevitably gives the impression that to belong or not to belong to the church comes to the same thing in the end, and makes no difference in practical life."[16] Thus, church "discipline that takes sin seriously is almost extinct."[17] Like the plumb line in the Lord's hand that evaluates the straightness of Israel's walls, churches need not only to have a theological statement of their beliefs in their constitution in order to evaluate teachings that are excluded, but also biblical teaching and doctrinal preaching that explains and justifies these core beliefs.

In this modern era, where it has become accepted dogma for pastors and teachers to focus on the practical places where people itch, there is too little knowledge of the church's theological foundations. Thus, it is not surprising that strange ideas often pop up or that people import a great deal of their secular cultural values into forming theological opinions. As a result, the first practical thing churches can do to prevent the need for church discipline is to teach theology, to provide a theological framework for people so that they themselves will be able to evaluate error and reject it. If no criteria of theological orthodoxy are taught or known by a congregation, how can people spot unbiblical ideas? This process of preparing for and teaching the congregation will keep church leaders from straying from the truth and needing church discipline.

In this process of establishing a standard for a congregation or a minister in a denomination, focus should be on the essentials of faith rather than on issues where there are legitimate differences of opinion over unclear passages. The key criterion for membership in a group is that each person agrees that the foundation doctrines of the church reflect the teaching of the Bible and that they will guide their thinking and behavior. Acceptance of what God says is of central importance, not acceptance of a catechism or creedal statement.

This is not to say that man-made creeds are bad or that they should not be used; it is merely an attempt to keep the focus on what God says in

---

16. E. Brunner, *The Divine Imperative* (Philadelphia: Westminster, 1947), 558–59.

17. J. White and R. Blue, *Healing the Wounded: The Costly Love of Church Discipline* (Downers Grove, Ill.: InterVarsity, 1985), 21.

Scripture. It is one thing for pastors to fudge on the exact wording or meaning of a denomination's doctrinal formulation, but it is unacceptable if a church leader will not accept what God has said in his revelation. A heart unsubmissive to God's will has put itself above God and should not be entrusted with leadership. The process of discipline can be a positive experience if there is a spirit of humility that considers others highly, an attitude of gentleness and patience, a spirit of love and unity (see Phil. 2:1–11), and a desire to submit to God's will.

In situations where discipline is necessary, the New Testament provides guidelines that describe an appropriate process (Matt. 18). The prophet Amos sets an example by balancing intercession for undeserving people with bold confrontation against those who repeatedly reject God's will. The New Testament process eventually comes to the same point of confrontation and rejection if there is no repentance. This is a frightful circumstance to be in, yet both denominational leaders and congregations must discipline leaders who reject what God says.

Of course, even in this context, there is the hope that the ultimate step of rejection will bring transformation and renewal of fellowship. Rejection and dismissal of a leader through church discipline is not an attempt to exclude someone for life from the kingdom. If leaders repent, they are to be welcomed back. Although most biblical examples are not fully parallel to the process of church discipline we are discussing here, God did not totally reject Abram when he lied about his wife (Gen. 12), Moses when he murdered the Egyptian (Ex. 2), David when he had Uriah killed and slept with Bathsheba (2 Sam. 11–12), or Peter when he betrayed Christ (Luke 22:54–62).[18]

Each of those involved in the discipline process should also remember Paul's words that "if someone is caught in a sin, you who are spiritual should restore him gently. But watch yourself, or you also may be tempted" (Gal. 6:1). Confrontation of spiritual leaders is not easy, but the future vitality of the church is dependent on the preservation of a faithful witness to the authority of the Scriptures and each person's submission to the God who speaks through them.

How should people handle opposition against them? Throughout the Old and New Testament are incidents where godly people are opposed or persecuted—for example, the Israelites in Egyptian slavery and the various attempts by the pharaoh to reduce their numbers (Ex. 1). When it comes to the oppression of spiritual leaders like Amos, one is reminded of attempts to kill Moses when the people heard the spies' report of the giants in Palestine

---

18. T. LaHaye, *If Ministers Fall, Can They Be Restored?* (Grand Rapids: Zondervan, 1990), 111–19.

(Num. 14), Saul's attempts to kill David (1 Sam. 18; 24), Jeremiah's being beaten and rejected by other prophets and priests and their attempts to kill him (Jer. 20:2; 26; 28), the stoning of Stephen (Acts 7:54–60), and the many trials of Paul (Acts 13:50; 14:5, 19; 2 Cor. 11:24–27).

Opposition to God and his messengers is not a thing of the past. Hussein Qambar Ali, an Iranian convert to Christianity, faced the threat of death because he became an apostate from Islam. Sudanese Christians have been crucified, and a Filipino pastor leading an underground church in Saudi Arabia barely escaped execution.[19] Muslim extremists in Egypt, Pakistan, Algeria, Sudan, and Bangladesh are particularly guilty of forcing their ideologies on governments and intimidating individuals with threats. Unfortunately, as W. Wong states, "There is a lack of recognition that Christians are still facing severe persecution in many places."[20]

Amos 7:10–17 teaches that God does call people from their present line of work (Amos was a "second-career minister") to deliver God's words to people who need to be taught about him and warned of his impending action. These called people may face strong opposition to their teaching and suffer persecution. Paul recognized that "everyone who wants to live a godly life in Christ Jesus will be persecuted" (2 Tim. 3:12). When these times of opposition come, it will surprisingly often come from other religious leaders rather than pagans (cf. the Pharisees' plots to kill Jesus, reflected in John 11:45–53; 15:18–25). When such conflicts come, God's messengers will find great reassurance and comfort in their memories of God's original calling to service, especially when their persecutors question the legitimacy of both their message and their call to ministry (Amos 7:12–14).

In times of conflict, God's messengers must always go back to his promises for strength and use them as a basis for confronting opposition. In this process God's messengers should not try to make things more acceptable to opponents by compromising his demands for purity and obedience. If people choose to reject God's way, they will eventually suffer his judgment.

Although life-threatening persecution is not unusual in some countries, Christians in democratic countries by and large do not need to worry about severe persecution. Instead, they face situations more like that of Amos. Someone expresses an idea or belief, and sooner or later someone else disagrees. When these disagreements reach a certain level, a person can choose to go to a different church and find new friends (as Amaziah encourages

---

19. K. A. Lawton, "The Suffering Church," *CT* 40 (July 15, 1996): 54–59, catalogs numerous modern examples of persecution of church members and their leaders.

20. Cited in ibid., 59. For a full but disturbing account of some examples of martyrdom, see J. Hefley and M. Hefley, *By Their Blood: Christian Martyrs of the Twentieth Century* (Grand Rapids: Baker, 1960).

Amos to go somewhere else). But Amos does not take the path of least resistance to avoid conflict, nor should we.

If differences of opinion are based on a misperception of a person's motivations (Amaziah thought Amos was motivated by money), we must clarify any misunderstandings. One can also seize an opportunity to give a testimony concerning one's personal faith and obedience to God and one's strong commitment to God's calling. Assuming the issue of conflict is not a peripheral point where legitimate differences of opinion should be permitted, a clear explanation of what God has said in Scripture must be provided (Amos reports to Amaziah what God has said). Finally, one should always "make every effort to keep the unity of the Spirit through the bond of peace" (Eph. 4:3) because there is only one body, one faith, and one Lord.

Nevertheless, as Amos and Paul found out, there are times when people must take a strong stand against those who reject true doctrine and who oppose what God is trying to accomplish. Each person should be aware that such confrontations (like confronting an alcoholic parent) may be difficult emotional experiences, but people should not let fear prevent them from taking responsibility to oppose the spiritual forces of evil in this world. This may not reduce persecution or conflict, but it will establish the truthfulness and authority of what God has said. It is the foundation of our faith, and it is worth fighting for.

Amos 8:1–14

❦

T HIS IS WHAT the Sovereign LORD showed me: a basket of ripe fruit. ²"What do you see, Amos?" he asked.

"A basket of ripe fruit," I answered.

Then the LORD said to me, "The time is ripe for my people Israel; I will spare them no longer."

³"In that day," declares the Sovereign LORD, "the songs in the temple will turn to wailing. Many, many bodies—flung everywhere! Silence!"

⁴Hear this, you who trample the needy
      and do away with the poor of the land,

⁵saying,

"When will the New Moon be over
      that we may sell grain,
and the Sabbath be ended
      that we may market wheat?—
skimping the measure,
      boosting the price
      and cheating with dishonest scales,
⁶buying the poor with silver
      and the needy for a pair of sandals,
      selling even the sweepings with the wheat.

⁷The LORD has sworn by the Pride of Jacob: "I will never forget anything they have done.

⁸"Will not the land tremble for this,
      and all who live in it mourn?
The whole land will rise like the Nile;
      it will be stirred up and then sink
      like the river of Egypt.

⁹"In that day," declares the Sovereign LORD,

"I will make the sun go down at noon
      and darken the earth in broad daylight.
¹⁰I will turn your religious feasts into mourning
      and all your singing into weeping.

I will make all of you wear sackcloth
    and shave your heads.
I will make that time like mourning for an only son
    and the end of it like a bitter day.

¹¹"The days are coming," declares the Sovereign LORD,
    "when I will send a famine through the land—
not a famine of food or a thirst for water,
    but a famine of hearing the words of the LORD.
¹²Men will stagger from sea to sea
    and wander from north to east,
searching for the word of the LORD,
    and they will not find it.

¹³"In that day

"the lovely young women and strong young men
    will faint because of thirst.
¹⁴They who swear by the shame of Samaria,
    or say, 'As surely as your god lives, O Dan,'
    or, 'As surely as the god of Beersheba lives'—
they will fall,
    never to rise again."

THESE VERSES ARE divided into two main sections: (1) the fourth vision of summer fruit that symbolizes the end of Israel (8:1–3), and (2) a message about how the end of Israel will bring wailing and no revelation from God (8:4–14). The vision itself is connected to the plumb-line vision in 7:7–9 because both have the same structure and the same conclusion that God "will spare them no longer" (7:8; 8:2). This continuity suggests that the fourth vision is also given at the city of Bethel, shortly after Amos's confrontation with Amaziah (7:10–17).

This vision is also closely connected to the verses that are appended to it (8:4–14). Both sections describe a future time of mourning and wailing (8:3, 8, 10) and death (8:3, 14), which will take place on "that day" (8:3, 13; cf. 8:11), at the "end" (8:2, 10).[1] The repetition of these ideas has the rhetorical

---

1. The NIV does not use the word "end" in 8:2 but translates the Hebrew word *qeṣ* (end time) as "ripe" to help clarify the wordplay with the vision of "ripe fruit" in 8:1 (see comments on 8:1–3). This has the negative effect of showing less connection with the idea of "the end" in 8:10.

effect of confirming the point and sealing the matter in the mind of the listener. While the appended material after the third vision discusses the disaster that will happen because of the rejection of God's words from the prophet (7:10–17), the material appended to the fourth vision refers to a time when people will want to hear a revelation from God but will find it is unavailable (8:11–12). Indeed, God will spare his beloved people no longer.

Within the judgment speech in 8:4–14 Amos raises some issues discussed earlier in the book. Especially repetitious are the accusations concerning the poor (2:6b–7a and 8:4), but these new accusations are put in the new context of explaining how the merchant class cheats the poor (8:5–6). The theme of mourning (8:3, 8, 10) draws from similar ideas in 5:16–17 and 6:9–10, falling and never rising again in 8:14 is related to 5:2, and the "day" is probably the same as the "day of the LORD" in 5:19–20.

Such repetition shows the unity of Amos's messages as well as the creative way in which he is able to repackage the same motifs to different audiences. Such repetition is probably needed because in chapters 7–9 he is in Bethel, speaking to a new audience that has not heard his earlier prophecies at Samaria (chs. 1–6).[2] Without the repetition of this information, Amos's new audience at Bethel will not be able to understand fully the basis for God's judgment and Amos's understanding of what God will do on the Day of the Lord. References to temple songs (8:3), Sabbaths, New Moon festivals (8:5), and swearing by the name of some god (8:14) reveal a shift of application to a temple audience, probably a group of people just outside the Bethel temple.

Vision of the Ripe Summer Fruit (8:1–3)

THE FOURTH VISION begins with the key introductory notice that God has given Amos another new revelation. The ripe summer fruit in the vision involves a wordplay between *qys* (summer, summer fruit) in the visionary images and *qs* (end) in the explanation of the vision (8:1–2).[3] This is a dramatic picturing of future events that reemphasizes the finality of God's decision to destroy "my people Israel" and "spare them no longer." What a tragedy! Not only will the king and temple be destroyed (7:9), but God's own special covenant people will cease to exist in the near future. This is not a temporary separation for a trial period, but the end—the end of the nation. This

---

2. G. V. Smith, *Amos*, 245, supports this understanding.

3. See B. D. Rahtjan, "A Critical Note on Amos 8:1–2," *JBL* 83 (1964): 416–17. The Gezer Calendar, a secular ninth-century B.C. agricultural calendar, refers to the summer with the spelling *qs*, which suggests the possibility that the two words may have been spelled and pronounced exactly the same at Amos's time. Paul, *Amos*, 254, draws on the spellings of words on ostraca found at the city of Samaria to confirm this point. See *ANET*, 320, for a translation of the Gezer Calendar.

prophecy is unqualified by any "if" or "when" phraseology; there is no escape clause or hint of hope at this point (see 5:14–15 for the hope of a remnant). If the compassion of God is no longer available, there is nothing to stop this disaster from happening.

The final part of this vision explains the implications of this great event for worship at the temple (8:3). On "that day" of judgment, events at the Bethel temple in Israel will be quite different from the day when Amos visited it.[4] The contrasts are striking. Now there is joyous singing, but these songs will turn into wailing. There will be "an inarticulate, shattering scream"[5] because of disaster. Now there is life and many people, but there soon will be dead bodies lying everywhere.[6] The military defeat will be complete, and the dead bodies will remain in a disgraceful unburied state, available for vultures and wild animals to eat. All one can do is gasp in horror at the enormity of the slaughter, turn one's eyes away from the mutilated carnage and bloated bodies, and flee from the unbearable stench of death and rotting flesh.

This scene will be so tragic and so far beyond belief that a deathly silence will fill the temple (cf. 6:10). No enemy is named, nor is there any explanation as to how this will happen. These are insignificant details in comparison to the immediate emotional reaction to the presence of so much death at the temple. It is clear that the Bethel temple will not protect the worshipers, for God will bring mass destruction.

The End Will Bring Wailing but No Word from God (8:4–14)

THIS MATERIAL APPENDED to the fourth vision is made up of three short paragraphs. We assume that these words are given right after the vision, to the same audience in the city of Bethel. It answers the natural questions that many in the audience have: Why will this happen? Who will do this? Will God or any other god come to our aid and give us some word of hope to help us through this time of mourning?

The answers found in this judgment speech begin with an accusation of oppression of the poor (8:4–6), which gives one reason why God will judge the nation. Verses 7–10 describe who will bring this disaster on the nation (God himself) and how people will react to his attack on them (they will

---

4. There is some ambiguity about the place where this disaster will take place. Andersen and Freedman, *Amos*, 798, believe the language could refer to either the king's palace or the temple; Paul, *Amos*, 254, prefers the palace; while Stuart, *Hosea–Jonah*, 379, suggests the temple.

5. A. Baumann, "ילל," *TDOT*, 6:82.

6. Andersen and Freedman, *Amos*, 799, suggest that the scattering of bodies implies the desecration of graves and the scattering of bones, but this is not necessary.

mourn). The final declaration informs the listeners that the people will not get any words of hope from any God/gods on that day (8:11–14).

Earlier when Amos was in Samaria, he accused the "cows of Bashan" (4:1) of oppressing the poor and the wealthy people living in palace fortresses of mistreating the innocent and weak (2:6–8; 3:9–10; 5:1–13). Now he focuses on the merchants, who trample all over the needy. Thus, it is not just one group of people who mistreat weaker members of society; every group seems tempted to mistreat the group below it. Huffmon thinks the oppressors in 8:4–6 are middle-class merchants who sell or loan wheat to poor farmers for planting in times of famine, while Lang derives these abuses from a rent-capitalism system of farming.[7] Whatever the exact nature of the economic system for these shady business deals, Amos focuses on the acts of the oppressors in verse 4, and their motives and methods in verses 5–6.

The acts of oppression (8:4) include "trampling on the needy" and "doing away with the poor of the land." Those who need help and cannot make it on their own receive no compassion or assistance but are taken advantage of. In their weak and defenseless position, they cannot protect themselves from those more economically powerful. There were manageable ways outlined in God's law for the poor to regain their self-respect and begin to stand on their own two feet. Israel's tradition encouraged people to help and share freely with the needy (Ex. 22:21–23; Deut. 16:11, 14; 24:17–21). In the present situation, however, those with the economic ability to help refuse to assist them; in fact, they purposely exacerbate the problems by manipulating things to their own advantage. In this way they "do away with" the poor. Such deeds, in other words, result in their annihilation, probably through starvation, poor health, or slavery.[8]

Amos quotes what these evil people say to one another about their methods of oppression and their true motivations (Amos 8:5–6). These are not pagans who reject or refuse to observe Hebrew customs. Rather, they are religious or practicing Hebrews in Israel who go to the New Moon festivals (cf. Lev. 23:23–25; Num. 10:10; 28:11–15). They observe the Sabbath as a holy day to worship God (Ex. 20:8–11; Deut. 5:12–15), where there is to be no selling or work (Neh. 13:15–22; Jer. 17:21–27). They maintain a semblance of orthodoxy in their outward observances of religious holidays.

Their formal piety, however, is betrayed by their true inner desires. They can hardly wait until these nonworking and nonprofit-making days are over.

---

7. H. B. Huffmon, "The Social Role of Amos' Message," *The Quest for the Kingdom of God: Studies in Honor of George E. Mendenhall*, ed. H. B. Huffman, F. A. Spina, and A. R. W. Green (Winona Lake, Ind.: Eisenbrauns, 1983), 109–16; B. Lang, "The Social Organization of Peasant Poverty in Biblical Israel," *JSOT* 24 (1982): 58–59.

8. Stuart, *Hosea–Jonah*, 384.

Their hearts are not enthralled by these special days off work, for their real desire is to sell and buy, to make a profit from having the marketplace open. If such people spend their hours thinking about their business while at a worship service, their religious facade does not bring pleasure to God's heart. It is not hard to identify the inner values that motivate their behavior.

The method of oppression these merchants have chosen is the age-old trick of short-changing both the buyer and the seller so that the middle-man always wins (8:5). By having two sets of weights and different sizes of measuring containers, the wheelers and dealers can outfox anyone. If someone comes wanting to sell grain, they use an oversized container (e.g., a bushel basket that is larger than the standard) so that it takes more grain to fill the basket. When the merchants then sell the grain, they use an undersized bushel so that the customer will not get the full amount he or she deserves.

Another way to skim extra profit is to have two sets of weights for their scales, one that weighs things heavy and the other that weighs light. If all else fails, the merchants can include a little dirt, chaff, or other useless fillers in a sack of grain so that it will not cost so much to fill it with "grade A" wheat. In his law, God required merchants to use just weights and measures (Lev. 19:35−36; Deut. 25:13−15; Prov. 20:10) and despised those who would stoop to using false scales (Prov. 11:1; 16:11).

Through these dishonest methods the wealthy merchants end up "buying the poor with silver" (Amos 8:6). As debts mount up for the poor through these schemes, people are forced to sell themselves or their children into slavery to cover their debts. This is not just a descriptive statement of what is happening but is part of the quotation of what the merchants say. The tragedy is that on Sabbath days, the merchants want to get back to work so that they can end up driving more people into debt in order to own these people.

God is angry over this greed and these injustices, so he swears an oath that he "will never forget anything they have done" (8:7). By this oath God binds himself to a specific, unalterable course of action. He will not change or pass over this brutality against the poor for any reason. Accountability will be demanded for every single act; nothing will be forgotten.

Earlier Amos reported God's oath as based on his holiness (4:2) and on himself (6:8); here it is based on "the Pride of Jacob" (8:7). Elsewhere in the Old Testament the phrase "the pride of Jacob" refers to the land of Israel (Ps. 47:4; cf. Isa. 58:14), but since this passage is not describing the land, "the Pride of Jacob" here must be a title for God himself. This understanding makes this oath formula comparable to the two earlier ones.[9] Since *ga'on* can mean

---

9. Less likely are the suggestions by Paul, *Amos*, 260, who prefers to interpret this verse in light of 6:8, where God abhors the pride of Jacob, or Andersen and Freedman, *Amos*, 808,

"pride, glory, majestic one," this usage seems to be an ironic condemnation of his listeners. They do not demonstrate any pride or glory in God, so God will swear on the basis of his truly glorious and majestic name to defend his real character (Ezek. 38:16, 23; 37:7, 21). If there is one thing the people can count on, it is that the Majestic One will act on the basis of his character.

The next verses (8:8–10) say that mourning will take place on the day of God's judgment "for [on account of] this" (8:8a). That is, God will act because of the oppression of the poor in 8:4–6. This section focuses on two issues: God will judge the land, and the people of Israel will mourn. The mourning theme is repeatedly emphasized at the beginning of verse 8 and throughout verse 10 (continuing the emphasis in 8:3).

In a rather hymnic fashion (repeated in 9:5) Amos describes how the land will tremble and mourn. When God comes in theophanic power, the land will quake and melt before him (Ps. 97:4–5; Isa. 24:4; 64:1–3; Mic. 1:4; Nah. 1:5). Amos appears to be describing an earthquake (see also Amos 2:13; 9:1, 5) and an eclipse in these verses. The convulsions of the land during this earth-quake are compared to the rising and sinking of the Nile River, a theme found in other accounts of God's judgment of the earth (see Isa. 24:1–4, 18–20). This demonstrates both the majestic power of God over nature and the total help-lessness of humankind, for when the ground gives way, people have no sure footing and nothing to depend on. The violent movement of solid ground is terrifying. The report of an earthquake two years after Amos's prophecy in 1:1 is apparently seen as the beginning of the fulfillment of this warning.

In addition, there will be unusual signs of God's power over the heavens. The sun's light will cease in the middle of the day (probably an eclipse),[10] sym-bolically representing the earlier warning that the Day of the Lord will be a day of darkness and not light (5:18–20). This removal of light was predicted in earlier curses (e.g., Deut. 28:29)[11] and continued to be an important theme in later prophets like Joel (see Joel 2:10, 30–31; 3:15). But Amos is not pre-dicting the final end of the world as Isaiah 24 does; rather, he is predicting the approaching Day of the Lord for Israel when the religious, political, and social status quo will end (fulfilled in 722 B.C., when the Assyrians captured Samaria).

This great disaster for Israel will lead to great mourning, weeping, wear-ing of sackcloth, shaving of heads, and bitter lamenting (Amos 8:10, con-tinuing the theme of 8:3, 8). A great transformation will occur, which will turn

---

who suggest that this is a shortened form of the full oath where God swears by himself against the pride of Jacob.

10. This may have been fulfilled in the eclipse on June 15, 763 B.C., which is recorded in ancient Near Eastern documents (see Paul, *Amos*, 262–63).

11. Stuart, *Hosea–Jonah*, 385.

the happy and optimistic oppressors in Israel into a deep depression. Joyous festivals and feast days will be filled with the sorrow of death and the hopelessness of bitter weeping. This change will come about because God causes it. "I will turn" and "I will make" are central to understanding the disaster about to encompass the people at the Bethel temple. Their God will turn against them and bring the nation to a final end (8:10; cf. 8:3). They think that the God they worship will protect them; but instead, he will annihilate them from the face of the earth.

The final paragraph (8:11–14) warns the people that on that final day there will be no word of help or comfort from God or from any of the pagan gods they worship. These two statements about what will happen on that fateful day are introduced with the clauses "the days are coming" (vv. 11–12) and "in that day" (vv. 13–14).

In the midst of this death and mourning, the Israelites will remember that the Creator is all-powerful, and they will look to him for help in their deep distress. But when they go to a temple or inquire of a prophet for a word of hope from God, there will be nothing. When they have lost all power and there is nowhere else to find hope, they will thirst for news from God. In their deepest moment of need, they will finally turn to God for some response and explanation (cf. 4:6–12, where they were unwilling to turn to God). But at that point God will abandon his people (cf. a similar situation in Judah in Ezek. 9:9; 11:22–23), refuse to listen to their prayers, or respond with a prophetic word of reassurance (Isa. 59:1–2; Lam. 2:9; Ezek. 7:26).

The severity of this famine for God's words is illustrated by the extensiveness of the search. Like a desperate and confused traveler who does not know where to find water, these confused people will be unable to find any message from God. Their deep desire is evident in their extensive and thorough search throughout the land, but their efforts will produce nothing. They will stagger around, roaming in misguided steps based on ignorance. It is as if the people have lost contact with God for so long that they do not know how to find him any more. The tragedy of this blind groping after an answer is shocking, but God will not be found (see Ps. 32:6; Isa. 55:6). The final verses (Amos 8:13–14) deepen the hopelessness of "that day" by noting that the strongest members of society will grow faint and end up resorting to other gods.

The Israelites were to fear God and swear by his name (Deut. 6:13; 10:20) and not swear by the names of other gods (Jer. 12:16; Zeph. 1:4–5). But when God abandons them, these people will swear oaths of loyalty to other gods to try to get an answer from them (Amos 8:14). The translation of verse 14 is difficult, but there appears to be three oath formulas used in reference to deities at three different places: Samaria, Dan, and Beersheba.

The oath related to Dan is not that difficult because 1 Kings 12 refers to the setting up of one of the golden calves at Dan many years earlier, in the time of Jeroboam I. Amos does not identify this god, but in light of Hosea's strong condemnation of Baalism in Israel, it is unlikely that any kind of pure worship of Israel's God still existed at Dan. Archaeologists have uncovered the sanctuary area in Dan, and a horn was found from the large altar there, but this does not explain the religious beliefs of the worshipers at this temple.[12] At best, there is a syncretistic worship of Yahweh, Israel's God, along with other gods.

The references to the "shame of Samaria"[13] and the "god of Beersheba" are less clear, though 1 Kings 16:26–34 indicates that Ahab did build a Baal temple at Samaria. Amos appears to be making a negative judgment on the worship going on at this temple, for certainly the people going there would not use this kind of negative terminology. Although other passages refer to worship at Beersheba (Amos 5:5), little is known about the God/gods worshiped there or what it means to swear "by the life of the way of Beersheba" (which the NIV translates as "the god of Beersheba").[14] This translation is possible because the Ugaritic *drkt* (which means dominion, strength, might) may also be an epithet for a deity. If this is accepted, then all three phrases in verse 14 refer to attempts by Israelites in their day of distress to gain words of hope and consolation from gods other than Yahweh.

Yet in spite of all their efforts, there will be no answer of protection or salvation from any of these gods. The nation of Israel will suffer defeat, and the people will die. Amos ends this section with a brief and unequivocating conclusion: These people will "fall, never to rise again" (8:14). The earlier vision (8:1–3) and this final statement emphasize that death will bring an end to the nation of Israel.

Bridging Contexts

EARLIER BRIDGING CONTEXTS sections have discussed several of the theological themes that appear in the present passage. These include Amos's treatment of the idea that God will judge those who oppress the poor (2:6–8; 4:1–3; 5:10–13), God will spare his people no longer (7:7–9), and the end of the Israelites is at hand and their

---

12. A. Biram, *Biblical Dan* (Jerusalem: IES, 1994); "An Israelite Altar at Dan," *BA* 37 (1974): 106–7.

13. Some have played with the idea that *ʾšmt* (in construct form), "shame, guilt," may refer to Ashima or Asherah. See the full discussion of these options in Paul, *Amos*, 269.

14. In the excavation at Beer Sheba, stones that belonged to an altar have been found. See Ze'ev Herzog, "Tel Beersheba," *The New Encyclopedia of Archaeological Excavations in the Holy Land*, 1:167–73, which shows a reconstruction of this altar.

lives will be filled with mourning (5:1–17). Therefore, we will deal here only with the unique features of this section: the consequence of being rejected by God, the oppressive business ethics of the merchants, and the nation's famine for a revelation from God.

The theology of divine rejection. Most people do not like to consider the possibility of divine rejection. The Lord is known as "the compassionate and gracious God, slow to anger, abounding in love and faithfulness, maintaining love to thousands, and forgiving wickedness, rebellion and sin" (Ex. 34:6–7a). Since nothing can separate us from God's love (Rom. 8:38–39), how can he ever come to the point where he says to his own chosen people: "I will spare them no longer" (Amos 8:2)? How can God purposely turn joy into wailing? If he could graciously have compassion on the violent people of Nineveh (Jonah 3:9–10) and forgive the vile king Manasseh (2 Chron. 33:12–19), why is he not willing to be compassionate to Amos's audience in Israel?

One should not compromise or in any way diminish the magnitude or breadth of God's compassion, for it is a clear and indisputable aspect of his relationship to humankind. But immediately next to Exodus 34:6–7a, which trumpets God's grace, are the sober words of 34:7b: "He does not leave the guilty unpunished." Paul's letter to the Romans also tells us that "the wrath of God is being revealed from heaven against all the godlessness and wickedness of men who suppress the truth by their wickedness" (Rom. 1:18).

This condemnation is especially appropriate for those who know about God's will but choose to reject what he says. The Jews have no excuse for they know God's righteous decree but do not practice it (Rom. 2:17–29). Amos and Paul know that the stubborn and unrepentant hearts of the people in their audiences will bring on them God's wrath because God gives to each person according to his or her deeds (Amos 8:7; Rom. 2:5–6). Paul states that for "those who are self-seeking and who reject the truth and follow evil, there will be wrath and anger" (Rom. 2:8).

If God is a holy God, who is just in his relationships, then there is a solid basis for believing in his wrath. If people stubbornly reject and willfully rebel against his will, there are consequences once the long-suffering patience of God runs out. God provided Israel with numerous trials to bring them to repentance, but they repeatedly were unwilling to turn to him (Amos 4:6–11). God graciously held back their punishment in two visions of destruction (7:1–6), but there has been no hint of Israel's repentance or humility before God. What can God do with these people? In this context his wrath seems unavoidable.

The only other possible way of resolving the broken relationship between God and the human race is either to deny the holiness and justice of God or to deny the sinfulness of humankind. Although no one would ever want to fall under the curse of God's anger, it is a reality that cannot be removed by the clever wishfulness of human imagination, for the Bible states that everyone will have to bow before God some day.

Simply put, God's wrath is his administration of justice. When this cold, abstract statement is implemented in the lives of people and nature, the consequences are enormous. There will be death, wailing, mourning, bitterness, and astonishment among human beings (8:3, 10). The earth will tremble and quake at God's awesome presence, and the normal functioning of the heavenly bodies will be disrupted (8:8–10). Since the time when Adam and Eve sinned in the Garden of Eden, the earth has groaned under the curse of sin (Gen. 3:17–18; Rom. 8:20–25). The covenant curses in Leviticus 26 and Deuteronomy 27–28 expand the connection between human disobedience and divine judgment. The prophets and Paul maintain this tradition of future divine judgment on the world but also look forward to a future kingdom when the effects of the curse will be lifted from humankind and nature (Isa. 11:6–9; Hos. 2:16–23; Amos 9:11–15).

Business ethics. Amos's messages about God's justice interact with and respond to real-life issues that permeate the lives of people in Israelite society. This means Amos is taking the time to know what is happening in the everyday lives of people as they try to make a living. He has to mix with the average farmers, go to the marketplace, watch the sellers and traders, listen to people's complaints, hear the merchant's side of the story, and investigate claims and counterclaims. He does not spend his evenings going to meetings, nor does he focus his energies on administrating a complex organization. He spends much of his time mingling with the rich and the poor so that he will have a message that deals with the reality his audience faces and that penetrates below the surface to the essential struggles in society. Everyone who wishes to apply God's revelation to people's lives needs to get to know the real-life issues people face so that the Scriptures can powerfully influence the process of resolving their dilemmas.

Making a living, feeding one's family, and providing the basic necessities of life are central issues vital to every person. When any messenger of God sees people struggling with these problems, he or she will have an opportunity to minister to ears looking for answers. Sometimes the answer will come in the form of a cup of cold water in the name of Christ, helping someone find medical treatment, or giving a financial gift of charity to meet an economic need. These needs are not isolated problems but are related to the basic problem of needing good-paying jobs and the wise use of financial resources.

Although the church is not a business, an employment agency, a legal-aid society, a human-rights organization, or a food bank, God's people work in these places and must assist people in need if the church hopes to have any credibility in this world. Amos and other prophets interfere in the business ethics of their day because they care about the people who are suffering and repudiate the dishonesty they observe. Amos's sermons suggest that these kinds of ethical issues are of interest to God and should be of prime importance to all his people, particularly to preachers and teachers who lead churches.

The world of business is not just a secular opportunity to get rich; it is a theological task God cares about. We do not have the power to produce wealth on our own; God is the One who gives every person the ability to make a financial gain (Deut. 8:17–18). Thus, he has an interest in how people carry out their activities of making money. He knows that the implementation of ethical principles in daily business affairs will frequently be an accurate barometer of the true transformational impact that spiritual ideas have on the life of a religious person.

Amos does not provide a formal series of principles that can be copied by any existing or start-up business to assure that they institute the best moral practices into their company. But his critique of the business ethics of his day does include a few fundamental principles that must be a part of the economic endeavor that desires to please God with its involvement in the marketplace.

Motivations. Amos's accusations (8:4–6) refer to motivations of business people and their conduct of business activity. Motivations are often revealed in a company's mission statement as well as in the attitudes that the owners and employees develop in the process of carrying out their responsibilities (often termed *the company's culture*). One of these attitudes relates to the conflict between business opportunities to be at work to make a profit and a person's religious responsibilities to take time away from work to worship God. Two questions surface from an analysis of this passage:

(1) Is it more important to be open for business on Sunday or to worship God (and think about what God has done) and observe one day of rest from work?

(2) If one does set aside one day of the week for worship and rest, is there a contentment and joy in this celebration, or is there a mental preoccupation with work and planning how to make money even on this nonwork day?

These are questions of motivation, separate from the ethical questions about how one goes about making money. They relate to the values people place on business and the temptation to allow work to be the top priority for one's time, energy, and thinking. Several years ago a person suggested that if all church people quit shopping on Sundays and shut down their businesses on Sunday, few people would be breaking the Sabbath. This may not be an accurate reading of many "post-Christian" communities any more, but it raises the question about how those who claim to be Christians treat the Sabbath day of rest. Has the desire to earn more money in modern culture been accepted as a legitimate value that is higher than the value God places on the observance of a day of rest and worship? The author of Ecclesiastes states that the person who "loves money never has money enough," for "as goods increase, so do those who consume them. And what benefit are they to the owner except to feast his eyes on them?" (Eccl. 5:10–11).

Business operations. Another issue is the way business people make money in their operation. Amos addresses the fundamental issue of honesty and fairness. Are products sold for what they are worth, or are customers tricked by deceptive claims, insupportable promises, or false information? Is it appropriate to claim "no fat" on the label of a product that is incapable of including fat? It would be ridiculous to advertise "no fat paper" for your computer, but businesses will sometimes include erroneous information on labels just to sell products. A label of "new," "improved," or "super" can be nothing but hype, and a "going-out-of-business" sign on an oriental rug store may mean absolutely nothing about the closing of that business.

It is unethical to sell cars that were in accidents as new cars and dishonest to twist the numbers in a car lease to make it look like a person is getting a better deal than he or she really is. Those who shortchange the seller and overcharge the buyer may be clever, and some may make a great deal of dirty money, but they are the enemies of God. Those who discover such dishonesty need to stand up like Amos and denounce such practices.

The famine for a revelation from God. Amos realizes that when God destroys Israel, there will be a new desire to turn to him in the midst of this tragedy. People without any hope will naturally look to God for help and deliverance when they see no human way of solving their problems. Unfortunately, these people—who have until now rejected the message of God that is available to them—will find no revelation from God when they finally come to the point where they want to hear his message of comfort and hope.

Isaiah's encouragement that his listeners should "seek the LORD while he may be found; call on him while he is near" (Isa. 55:6) suggests that if people do not respond now, it may be impossible to receive forgiveness from him at some later date; the Day of Judgment may arrive first. In some texts the problem is not that God is so far away that he cannot hear or help; he is still near and available. But people feel his absence when sin has caused a separation between them and God (Isa. 59:1–3). When things do not go as people expect, they wonder whether God is absent or whether he has noticed their acts of devotion (58:3).

Job felt abandoned by God and deeply desired to hear a word from him to clear him of the false accusations made by his so-called comforters (Job

13:24; 19:7–8).[15] When people in the Bible refer to God as hiding, this may indicate his wrath and rejection of them (Deut. 31:17–18) or a fearfulness and loneliness because God is not actively answering a prayer right now (Ps. 13:1; 44:24). The prophet Ezekiel describes God's literal abandonment of the temple in Jerusalem because of the sinfulness of the nation (Ezek. 8–11).[16] In other words, the absence of God may be real and literal at times.

This sense that God is absent and not to be found is complementary to the idea that God's power and words of assurance are unavailable. When God speaks, he is present; when he is silent in word or deed, he is absent or hidden from people's perception. When people are in trouble, a verse from God can give an explanation of the cause of a problem, offer a word of hope, or make one aware of the need for remedial action. If God would just speak, at least the listeners would know why circumstances are so difficult, would not be in the dark about the future, and would not sense an isolation from God.

Communication of God's words opens the door for understanding, acceptance, and the possibility of change. God's silence offers no explanation but results in frustration, confusion, and hopelessness. It is always better to hear some news, even if it is bad news. At least there is communication and the possibility to understand and move forward.

ISSUES RELATED TO the application of just relationships between people have already been addressed in the discussion of 2:6–8; 3:8–9; 4:1–3; and 5:10–13, 15; thus, the focus here will be limited to the new areas of application that Amos raises. It is inappropriate to assume that all merchants in contemporary culture behave like those Amos describes in 8:4–6 or to project that most people in business have these same attitudes in our day and age. One major difference is that many merchants at that time still kept the Sabbath as a day of rest. Another is that few people today have anything to do with selling agricultural commodities. Nevertheless, the church does need to instruct its members on how to conduct themselves in the business world in a way that pleases God.

How does God impact our business? In order to make a sale, a seller must induce a buyer to think he or she is getting a quality product and a good deal on its price. But the seller's motivation of making a profit requires that the selling price be larger than what it cost. Thus, one must naturally include a

---

15. D. J. A. Clines, *Job 1–29* (WBC; Dallas: Word, 1989), 319.

16. See S. E. Balentine, *The Hidden God: The Hiding of the Face of God in the Old Testament* (Oxford: Oxford Univ. Press, 1983).

reasonable markup. Everyone understands that bulk purchases come cheaper and that for the sake of the convenience of smaller amounts, people are willing to pay a little more. The danger comes when merchants mark up products but add no value, motivate customers to buy with false information, or mislead customers by misrepresenting their product through deceptive claims. Sometimes there is more show than substance to advertisements because unproved statements that appeal to buyers are used to hide the true value of a product.

Although many people live outside the agricultural setting of selling grain as Amos describes it, the trusting relationship between sellers and buyers is commonly experienced at the grocery story. The dishonesty of fooling customers by keeping the same size box while reducing the weight of the product inside is a part of the present cereal wars. The company that brags about the hefty weight of its hamburgers usually has a small-print disclaimer admitting that this weight is connected to the produce before it is cooked, thus allowing the company to include inexpensive and disappearing water and fat as part of their quarter-pounders.

Misrepresentation of products can come in all forms, but all of it is motivated by the desire to show a product in a way that will encourage customers to buy. Although some business people might respond that "everyone else is making similar deceptive claims," most books on business ethics maintain that "customs, conventions, and the accepted courtesies of a society are not the foundation of ethics."[17] Deep convictions of right and wrong should undergird ethical principles, and respect for the personal dignity of each person gives root to the honest treatment of others.[18]

Since buyers usually do not have enough information about the expenses of producing a product, the actual fair-market value plus a reasonable markup is usually unknown. This lack of information can lead to unethical price fixing by collusion among sellers. Charging whatever the market will bear is not an appropriate ethical pricing policy, though a few sellers in ancient Israel up to today periodically attempt to implement schemes that give the customer inflated costs for doing business or deflated rewards for producing goods.[19] Illustrations of ethical problems in doing business abound in business textbooks;[20]

---

17. T. Garrett and R. Klonoski, *Business Ethics* (Englewood Cliffs, N.J.: Prentice-Hall, 1986), 1, claims that laws describe only the minimal regulations necessary for public order.

18. Ibid., 3

19. See ibid., 100—108, where the authors discuss the issue of price fixing and the alternatives of government controls on prices.

20. M. Velasquez, *Business Ethics* (Englewood Cliffs, N.J.: Prentice-Hall, 1988), discusses Union Carbide's problem (p. 3), Johns-Mansville's problems over asbestos (p. 47), Ford and Chrysler (pp. 118, 168), plus General Electric (p. 205).

these can function as case studies for ethical analysis and the development of appropriate moral responses to business situations.

Although some may think of "business ethics" as an oxymoron as unthinkable as "military intelligence," this perception should be understood as a sign of the society's desperate need for principled and trustworthy business practices. Because so many scandals have been uncovered in the last twenty years (often much worse than Amos's example of having two different sets of weights), an examination of business ethics needs to be addressed by churches in order to enable Christians to avoid the pitfalls of "business as usual." Ethical theories of egotism, relativism, utilitarianism, religious ethics, and ethics determined by conscience should be examined for strengths and weaknesses.[21] Since as people often get uncomfortable when preachers start talking about money, perhaps an interactive seminar on business ethics could open the door to a more comfortable discussion about God's concern with all financial matters.

Part of any discussion on business ethics must deal with attitudes and motivations people have toward their business activities. Amos identifies an attitude of impatience with a Sabbath observance of no work and an internal drive to end religious duty and get back to making money (8:5). This accusation pushes the reader to ask: What are my motives? Are my actions heavily based on motivations related to making more and more money? How does my fear of the Lord motivate me to conduct myself in business settings (2 Cor. 5:9−11)? How does my servant attitude shape my interrelationship with customers (Phil. 2:1−11)? How does the love of Christ constrain me to not live selfishly (2 Cor. 5:14−17)?[22]

Believers need to be motivated by basic convictions of honesty and truthfulness, the challenge of fulfilling their God-given purpose in life, accepting responsibility for their choices, and honoring God in what they do.[23] When the worship day is preoccupied with thoughts of getting back to work, there are problems both with an obsessive motivation to make money and with a lack of motivation to rejoice, remember, and enjoy the blessings of a divinely appointed day of rest. These two motivations may cause the grocery-store

---

21. R. Green, *The Ethical Manager* (New York: Macmillan, 1994), 56−65, surveys these approaches to ethics.

22. S. Briscoe, *How to be a Motivated Christian* (Wheaton: Victor, 1987), addresses a number of other factors that should motivate Christians (gratitude, duty, a sense of privilege, compassion, and a team spirit).

23. K. D. Bruner, *Responsible Living in an Age of Excuses* (Chicago: Moody, 1992), 83−190, focuses on the need to be responsible and therefore to take control of life. The desire to avoid pitfalls, make wise choices, and enjoy the benefits of success are a few of the motivators that cause people to act responsibly.

clerk or the manager of a department store to work on Sunday, but there are probably many Sunday workers (and Sunday shoppers) who never think much about whether they should work (or cause others to work).

Although some may feel they have to work on Sunday because they may lose their jobs, many others never think about their motivations for working. The church seldom addresses this issue today; thus, people accept the cultural norms that business has dictated a life of not honoring God on his day of rest. When there is no motivation to honor God, Amos's warning and condemnations suddenly seem applicable.

Is there really going to be a day of judgment? Some people do not believe that God's justice will cause the curse of his wrath to fall on anyone. In an age where religious pluralism is rampant, many feel it is wrong to claim that there is only one way to heaven and that everyone must accept Christ as Savior or suffer judgment. With so many new immigrants and foreigners going to university, it is no longer unusual to see a family or fellow employee who comes from a different cultural and religious tradition. Many of these people are hard-working, moral people, who are responsible neighbors and colleagues.

Religious pluralism believes that each person has a right to make his or her own choice of religious beliefs and that one cannot say that one is right and the other is wrong.[24] This quickly leads to a relativism that compromises the uniqueness of the Christian faith,[25] denying that Christ is the sole mediator between God and humankind. Although this pluralistic approach used to sharply divide evangelical Christianity from radical liberalism, in recent years a group of writers have tried to develop a middle ground between these two camps. In all these discussions, one important topic that arises is: What will happen to the good religious people who take a pluralistic view on these issues, and what will happen to the unevangelized after death?[26] Will God's wrath fall on them?

Concerning the unevangelized, E. Trueblood concludes that the simple solution that sends them all to hell "is neat and simple, but it is morally shocking and consequently not a live option of belief for truly thoughtful or sensitive persons of any faith."[27] J. A. T. Robinson believes that the strong love of

---

24. C. H. Pinnock, *A Wideness in God's Mercy* (Grand Rapids: Zondervan, 1992), 9–10, notes that to many people today, everything is to be tolerated except intolerance.

25. J. Hick and P. F. Knittner, eds., *The Myth of Christian Uniqueness: Toward a Pluralistic Theology of Religions* (Maryknoll, N.Y.: Orbis, 1987).

26. Pinnock, *A Wideness in God's Mercy*, 149–80, gives a whole chapter to the latter question.

27. E. Trueblood, *Philosophy of Religion* (New York: Harper and Row, 1957), 221, feels God would be irrationally punishing these people simply on the basis of the accident of where they were born, which was beyond their control.

God will not give up on any sinner; thus, he concludes that there will be universal salvation for all and no one in hell.[28] Some popular literature ridicules Christian doctrine with snappy titles like "Soft-Selling Hell: Don't Worry Says a Catholic Theologian, It's Really No Worse Than a Three-Star Motel."[29]

L. Dixon has reviewed these theories and demonstrates from the mouth of Jesus that the future judgment of those who reject Christ is real.[30] God's judgment, of course, is not limited to what will happen in the future, nor is it aimed at the unevangelized. The shocking and almost unbelievable truth is that even God's own chosen people will suffer under his wrath if they do not repent and turn to him. A holy and just God does not play favorites but will judge those who know of his love more severely if they willfully reject his sovereign grace and salvation.

Yes, there will be a day of judgment, as Amos predicts. Although Amos never focuses on the existence of hell, his words of impending disaster are meant to warn his fellow Israelites of the curse of God's wrath on their nation. Human death and natural disasters will bring an end to life as normal in Israel. The Israelites can ignore Amos's teaching, doubt that God will ever do this to them, espouse a doctrine of universal salvation for the seed of Abraham, or claim that Amos is insensitive, but none of these solutions will change the historical fact that God did in fact destroy the nation of Israel in 722/721 B.C. History has proved that Amos was right, and the future will show which view of divine justice is correct for our age.

Amos's audience is deceiving itself with false hopes, and some follow that path today. Soft-selling judgment and hell may be popular in a modern pluralistic and relativistic culture, but it never has or never will have much of an effect on what God does to establish his version of justice on earth. If people do not change their thinking about the fundamental character of God, the agonizing effect of his wrath will come on all who reject the teaching of God's Word.

Where is the Word of God? Amos 8:11—14 focuses on the nation's inability to find God or receive a word of comfort or encouragement from him in the midst of their punishment. The most common situation where this attitude is expressed today is when a tragedy strikes a family. Almost everyone knows of someone who has died of cancer at a relatively young age, who has

---

28. J. A. T. Robinson, *In the End, God* (London: Clarke, 1950); see esp. the discussion in ch. 9. Those interested in seeing the historical development of many of these ideas back in the early church and through the centuries can read D. P. Walker, *Hell in Decline* (Chicago: Univ. of Chicago Press, 1964).

29. *Western Report* (July 8, 1991).

30. L. Dixon, *The Other Side of the Good News: Confronting the Contemporary Challenges to Jesus' Teaching on Hell* (Wheaton: Victor, 1992), 121—87.

---

had a child die of a mysterious sudden death syndrome, or who has had a family member killed in a car accident.

I recently read the story of a woman from Rose Lake, Minnesota, who experienced the death of two relatives in childhood, the near-death of her firstborn son shortly after birth because of pneumonia, the sad discovery that this child was autistic, and the misguided comments of friends and "comforters."[31] Later when this autistic child was badly burned on his legs, together they went through the agonizing process of skin grafts, including some that did not take. Yes, in these situations God seems to have had his hands in his pockets and to be looking the other way. Where was this all-powerful God, and why did he not choose to intervene?

Although more theological and philosophical, Philip Yancey's book *Where Is God When It Hurts?* deals with the problem of pain and attempts to provide some general answers. Yet in the end, no one can fill the emptiness of that feeling when God seems absent.[32] When God is absent, there is no word of explanation, no hope of change, and no meaning derived from a terrible experience. People cry out for a good word from God, but real trust involves faith in the things that people cannot see.

Although this passage does not say anything about the absence of prophets or the prophetic word since it focuses on the impotence of Israel's pagan gods (8:14), it seems that the famine for a divine message must partially be due to the fact that there will be no prophetic figures who can deliver or are willing to deliver God's revelation. In spite of strong oaths of commitment on the part of the seeker and desperate searching at various locations, the prophetic and priestly mediators have lost contact with the divine and are unable to satisfy the needs of their worshipers.

The question of application then comes: Are there people today who desire a message from God but who cannot find it, because their pastor or spiritual mentor has no real relationship with God? It is easy to point to some other church across town where the gospel is not preached, but each congregation and each pastor probably could conduct an unbiased analysis of what they are doing. E. Achtemeier asks why "three million Americans now practice transcendental meditation, five million engage in yoga, three million have turned to eastern religions, nine million belong to healing groups."[33] If the church was providing the truth of Scripture, would these people be searching for some meaning to life in these strange ways?

---

31. P. Giesbrecht, *Where Is God When a Child Suffers?* (Hannibal: Hannibal Books, 1988), 11–66.

32. P. Yancey, *Where Is God When It Hurts?* (Grand Rapids: Zondervan, 1990), makes some logical sense, but most people want more than that when tragedy strikes.

33. E. Achtemeier, "The Famine for the Word," *Faith and Mission* 2 (1985): 64.

Achtemeier recognizes that we often blame the secular materialistic culture for leading people astray, but she concludes that the real reason for the famine in our land is "precisely because we church leaders have failed to proclaim the message. Could it be that people come to us week after week, searching for the word of God, and go away unfed and hungry?"[34] So many churches are torn apart by the type of hymns or choruses they sing, the purchase of Sunday school supplies, denominational bureaucracy, and a million other trivial and asinine issues of little eternal significance. No wonder hurting people who want to hear God never hear his voice.

Sometimes God seems absent and far away to outsiders because the insiders are so busy squabbling that the voice of God is drowned out. Other congregations are so fearful of offending outsiders in their seeker-sensitive services that they have gutted the service of God-talk and replaced it with group counseling sessions that appeal to the material, social, and psychological needs of people. The famine is sometimes simply due to an unwillingness to have a prophetic voice in a lost world.

The final situation where God is absent is in the presence of sin. When people repeatedly and consistently refuse to recognize his will, God literally rejects and removes himself from them so that justice can be carried out. After the golden calf God had to remove his presence from the rebellious people lest he destroy them all (Ex. 33:1–3). Ultimately, this will happen at the end of time, when the wicked are judged and thrown into the lake of fire (Rev. 20:7–15).

---

34. Ibid., 65

Amos 9:1–10

I SAW THE Lord standing by the altar, and he said:

"Strike the tops of the pillars
    so that the thresholds shake.
Bring them down on the heads of all the people;
    those who are left I will kill with the sword.
Not one will get away,
    none will escape.
² Though they dig down to the depths of the grave,
    from there my hand will take them.
Though they climb up to the heavens,
    from there I will bring them down.
³ Though they hide themselves on the top of Carmel,
    there I will hunt them down and seize them.
Though they hide from me at the bottom of the sea,
    there I will command the serpent to bite them.
⁴ Though they are driven into exile by their enemies,
    there I will command the sword to slay them.
I will fix my eyes upon them
    for evil and not for good."

⁵ The Lord, the LORD Almighty,
    he who touches the earth and it melts,
    and all who live in it mourn—
the whole land rises like the Nile,
    then sinks like the river of Egypt—
⁶ he who builds his lofty palace in the heavens
    and sets its foundation on the earth,
who calls for the waters of the sea
    and pours them out over the face of the land—
the LORD is his name.

⁷ "Are not you Israelites
    the same to me as the Cushites?"

                                declares the LORD.

"Did I not bring Israel up from Egypt,
    the Philistines from Caphtor
    and the Arameans from Kir?

8 "Surely the eyes of the Sovereign LORD
    are on the sinful kingdom.
I will destroy it
    from the face of the earth—
Yet I will not totally destroy
    the house of Jacob,"

                                  declares the LORD.

9 "For I will give the command,
    and I will shake the house of Israel
    among all the nations
as grain is shaken in a sieve,
    and not a pebble will reach the ground.
10 All the sinners among my people
    will die by the sword,
all those who say,
    'Disaster will not overtake or meet us.'"

THE THREE PARAGRAPHS in this section remove any remaining false hopes that Amos's audience may still have. His final persuasive arguments are contained in a vision emphasizing that no one can escape God's judgment (9:1–4), in a hymnic fragment about the overwhelming power of God (9:5–6), and in a disputation against Israel's false belief that its special status will prevent it from being overcome by any enemy (9:7–10).

This fifth and final vision has no paired element, unlike the previous four visions, but is balanced by the dispute in 9:7–10 (similar to the dispute in 7:10–17, which comes after the vision in 7:7–9). One reason why there is no parallel vision is because God actually executes his final judgment in this vision, and no one is allowed to escape. Thus, there is nothing left to warn the people about.

The hymn that follows the vision (9:5–6) emphasizes the power of the God who will bring an end to the nation of Israel. Parts of the hymn are identical to the hymnic fragments in 5:8 and 8:8; thus, the prophet reemphasizes the unavoidable and overpowering strength of God's controlling hand. God's sovereignty is legitimated by claims that he is the One who has control over the heavens, the land, and the sea.

The dispute (9:7–10) further undermines the audience's confidence by attacking the theological basis of their false hopes. Does their elect status and their past Exodus experience guarantee God's favor forever? No, God relates to people primarily on the basis of either their sins against him or their love for him.

The Vision: No One Can Escape (9:1–4)

THIS VISION HAS a shortened version of the introductory formula found in the earlier visions, a description of the visionary action, and an application of the vision to the audience. The introductory "I saw" may be brief because Amos sees the Lord himself rather than something else (like the locusts or a plumb line). The Lord is standing by an altar in the temple, an association that fits with Israelite tradition. Although the temple is not identified and one would usually connect God with the Most Holy Place in the temple in Jerusalem, almost everyone agrees that the temple being destroyed in this vision is the one with the golden calf at Bethel.[1] In other words, Amos is not primarily interested in getting his audience to accept a Judean theological construction of orthodox theology (it would limit God's presence to the temple in Jerusalem) but communicates the truth in Israelite theological categories that are more acceptable to his audience.

The action within the vision involves an unknown power (some suggest an angel)[2] shattering the columns that hold the roof of the temple. If this structural damage to the columns and the shaking of the foundations of the building are connected to Amos's other predictions of an earthquake, then it is unnecessary to hypothesize any other power at work. God himself is behind this enormous earthquake, which happened about two years after Amos spoke (1:1).

Once the earthquake begins, the building crumbles on the heads of those gathered for worship. Instead of providing security and hope, this temple will bring deadly panic. Its destruction is a direct sign of divine disapproval. These events lead to the divine determination to kill the remaining Israelites "with the sword" of an enemy army (9:1; cf. 2:14–16; 3:11–12; 4:2–3; 5:2–3, 27; 6:7–11; 7:17). No one will escape God's judgment. This vision removes all hope and security;[3] no exceptions are noted until we get to 9:8.

This message of total annihilation is probably rejected by many of Amos's listeners because Israel has a strong military at this time and feels secure (cf. 6:1). To convince the audience of the impossibility of any hope of survival, a series of five conditional clauses are presented (9:2–4). Each gives a possible way one might try to escape from God's mighty hand of judgment, but each is a useless waste of effort because there are no limits to the power of God's eyes or hands. The extreme effort of digging down to Sheol (NIV "the

---

1. Paul, *Amos*, 274. He guesses this event took place on a Hebrew holiday because the place is full of worshipers, but this is not required.

2. Wolff, *Joel and Amos*, 334, changes the vocalization of the verb to "he smote," while Harper, *Amos and Hosea*, 188, prefers "I smote," but the text does not need to be changed.

3. Gowan, "Amos," 421, sees a loss of security because they cannot go to the temple.

grave") to hide in the inaccessible abode of the dead is as useless as the attempt to climb up into heaven and dwell in God's place. God will find anyone who tries this and will deal with those who attempt to escape. No matter what the distance, God is present (cf. Ps. 139:7–9), for neither height nor depth can separate us from his love (Rom. 8:38–39) or hide us from his justice.

The second set of comparisons contrasts the many good hiding spots in the thick forests and caves of Mount Carmel[4] and the unexplored coral reefs in the dark, uninhabitable depths of the ocean. Those who imagine that they can hide from God in these places will not escape either, for God will hunt them down or send a divinely controlled sea serpent to find them. Even if a few remain alive and go into exile after the nation is conquered, God will intently fix his gaze on them so that they do not escape (9:4). There is simply no geographical place in heaven or on earth in which to hide from God or escape his power.

The Hymn: God Has All Power over the Heavens and the Earth (9:5–6)

SINCE AMOS HAS inserted hymnic fragments at key points in other sermons to emphasize the power of God, who will judge Israel (4:13; 5:8–9; 8:8), the abrupt change here to hymnic words of praise is not unexpected.[5] Amos probably uses the words of a familiar hymn because the audience knows it well and accepts its theological picture of God. The hymn celebrates the power of God over the heavens and the earth (the theological key to the vision in 9:1–4) and supports the conclusion that one cannot escape from the power of this kind of God. This good news about God's power becomes a terrifying and fearful truth in this context.

The hymn is a picture of a theophany appearance of the majestic glory of God on earth, of his glorious dwelling place in the heavens, and of his powerful deeds of judgment on the earth. His name is appropriate; he is "the LORD Almighty," Lord of the hosts of heaven, the heavenly warrior. The power of his touch dissolves nature and makes the earth shake. The hard and solid land rises and falls like the unstable water in the Nile River. The people who see this awesome demonstration of his power will "mourn" in fear and grief.

---

4. Obadiah, the person in charge of Ahab's house, hid a hundred prophets of God in caves in the Carmel ridge because Jezebel was trying to kill all the good prophets (1 Kings 18:4).

5. Although some think the hymn was added by a later redactor and is out of place in this section, the consistent use of hymns in Amos in order to remind the listener about the true nature of God seems appropriate and a fitting means of supporting the prophet's claims about future judgment. See Hayes, *Amos,* 218.

Yes, this is the God who lives in a lofty and exalted "palace in the heavens" (9:6), who formed and established the very foundations on which the land rests. He is able to set limits on the sea and to remove those limits and let the waters flood the land (Gen. 6–9). Truly, Yahweh, the God of Israel, is all-powerful. Amos uses this hymn of praise to God, which probably celebrates God's power over Israel's enemies, to support his claim that this omnipotent God will judge Israel. There is no way to avoid him or escape his wrath.

The Dispute: Does Israel Have a Special Protected Status? (9:7–10)

THE FINAL PARAGRAPH refutes an implied or real objection by the audience. They question Amos's conclusion that Israel will actually be destroyed by God. They argue instead that "disaster will not overtake . . . us" (9:10), basing their confidence in God on what he has done in the past and the promises he made to their forefathers. God's promise to Abraham gives them eternal possession of the land (Gen. 13:14–18), his election of them out of all the families of the earth gives them special status as his chosen people (Deut. 7:6–7), and his great act of deliverance from Egypt at the Exodus proves what he will do to fulfill his promises and deliver his people from their enemies (Ex. 14–15). How can God now reject his own people?

Amos does not dispute any of these facts of history but raises questions about how the Israelites have theologically interpreted these events. They have reified these ideas into absolute guarantees (focusing only on God's promises in his covenant relationship), thus disconnecting the nation's future from their daily covenantal relationship with him. They have not connected God's blessings to their righteous behavior; they think he will care for them no matter what. But the covenant conditions state that if God's people do not follow him or maintain their covenant relationship with him, he will not automatically bless them. Blessings are not a right to be claimed, but the fruitful outworking of a godly life.

Amos wisely approaches this subject by inviting his listeners to consider the broader aspects of God's behavior in order to discover what principles direct his activity. This questioning method of persuasion invites dialogue and avoids the defensive response of people who are accused of misunderstanding what God will do. When Amos asks if the Israelites are not the same to God as the Cushites in Ethiopia (9:7), many would have wondered what Amos is talking about. What does God have to do with this black African tribe in the God-forsaken fringes of a distant continent?

Some listeners would no doubt scoff at this ridiculous comparison. Are not the Israelites God's chosen people? The Cushites mean nothing to God. Others probably wonder what point Amos is trying to make. The point becomes clearer in the second comparisons at the end of 9:7, where Amos refers to the common exodus experiences by the Syrians, Philistines, and Israelites. This comparison clearly puts Israel on the same level as two of her bitterest enemies. Certainly no Israelite would believe that the exodus experiences of the Syrians and Philistines guarantees them eternal protection from God's judgment.

But this conclusion means that Israel also has no automatic protection based on God's past grace on them. The Israelite audience cannot argue against Amos to the effect that God is not the sovereign Ruler who has delivered all of these other countries from difficult situations and given them a new land. They can, however, argue that they have a special covenantal relationship with God, which makes their experience unique. That is precisely Amos's point: Blessings are not based on a person's identity or past deeds of grace but on a nation's loving covenant relationship with God now. Thus, if the Israelites do not maintain their relationship with God, their future destruction is just as possible as Philistia's. Past election (3:1–2) and past acts of divine grace (2:9–10) do not rule out the possibility of future punishment.

God judged Achan when he stole the booty from Jericho (Josh. 7) and Solomon when he began to follow the pagan gods of his wives (1 Kings 11–12). In other words, God's protection in the future is not simply based on his grace in the past. If anything, God's grace in the past puts a nation under greater obligations in the future. This broader perception of God's action with other nations should keep the listeners from jumping to false conclusions based on a limited amount of information and a narrow theological perspective.

One of the keys to understanding God's sovereign plan is the conclusion that he sees what the people in every nation do and will hold each nation accountable for its sins (9:8). This has been a consistent emphasis throughout Amos's sermons: God judges sinful, oppressive people and sinful, oppressive nations. If the Syrians, Philistines, or Israelites sin, all God's past grace will not prevent his future judgment (see 1:3–2:16).

But this principle is not a blanket condemnation of every person in a sinful nation. It is true that sometimes the innocent suffer as God judges the guilty, but God confirms through Amos that not every person in Israel will be killed (9:8): "I will not totally destroy" is God's commitment that sin makes a difference in determining who will be destroyed and who will be spared. There is hope for the remnant who seeks God (5:14–15). This clause clarifies the message of no escape in 9:1–4 and maintains God's mercy in the midst of judgment.[6] It also explains how God will finally fulfill his past promises to his people in the distant future, when he establishes his kingdom (9:11–15).

---

6. G. V. Smith, *Amos*, 366.

To illustrate what will happen when the righteous are distinguished from the wicked, Amos draws from the harvesting process of separating good grain from the chaff and straw by the use of a sieve (9:8–9). An agricultural society such as Israel readily understands this metaphor of shaking the nation as one shakes grain to separate the good grain from the useless trash.[7] The surrounding nations will shake the nation of Israel so that sinners can be punished with the sword. How foolish some people are when they proudly suppose that God will never allow them to be overtaken by any enemy.

THE AWESOME POWER **of God.** God's power to rule the world is described with great vividness in this section, and it forms the fundamental theological basis for fearing, loving, and honoring God. Since his power universally reaches to the heights of heaven and the depths of Sheol, and since he has designed the earth and the far reaches of the heavens, there is nothing outside of his frame of influence or knowledge. He not only has complete knowledge about the creation of all the diverse parts of the earth; he also has eyes and hands that control the expanse of the universe.

The magnificence of what God has created relates to its size, its beauty, and the way it works together as a unified whole. The breadth of God's control far outstretches anything we can imagine or hypothesize, for humankind has never even seen the vast majority of what God has created. Even our ability to control a minor part of this creation is limited. Although we can dig a ditch and change the course of a stream in order to irrigate a field, God has the ability to set boundaries for oceans and then change those boundaries. People can shake a flimsy man-made wagon so that someone cannot stand up in it, but God can move the solid ground up and down so violently that it destroys strong buildings made by human beings. Truly, God is powerful, and his creative ability extends far above what people can imagine. We can only praise him and stand in wonder and amazement at what he has made.

Whenever we meet any natural force that has overwhelming power (a tornado, a forest fire, or bitter freezing cold), we must quickly recognize our own limited ability in the face of such overpowering forces. We may try to hide to protect ourselves from the brute destructive energy of such experiences, yet nature's power consistently leaves us surprised and awestruck by the enormous damage that can come in a matter of a few seconds.

---

7. Commentators are not sure if the good grain falls through the sieve in this example and the straw and stones are thrown away, or if the good grain remains in the sieve with the dirt and chaff falling through. Stuart, *Hosea–Jonah*, 394, and others argue for the first interpretation.

Yet nature's force in these incidences is but a tiny representation of God's awesome power. His creative ability enables him to make and place in orbit millions of burning stars brighter than our sun. If he wishes, the earth will melt at his touch or be destroyed by water at his command. Hiding from God is the ridiculous thought of proud persons who imagine they have primary control of themselves and their surroundings. Adam could not hide from God (Gen. 3), and we can be sure that our sins will find us out (Num. 32:23). Trying to hide or escape from God is an impossible reality, because he is not deceived by human plans. He knows every place and sees everything that we do. If these theological constructs of reality are understood, there should be no room for creating false conceptions of unrealistic hope based on human wisdom.

How foolish it is to believe that nothing will ever happen to me because I happen to think God will protect me (Amos 9:10). It is a delusion to conclude that I am somehow so special or important to God that he will deal with me in a unique manner different from all others. It is stupid to rest securely on the positive experiences of the past and assume that nothing will ever go wrong in the future.

Yet these are precisely the mistakes that the Israelites in Amos's audience are making. They believe that God's grace in the past (the Exodus events) assures them of special treatment in the future and unusual protection from harm. They assume their status as his chosen people is the only basis for their relationship with him. Too often their hope from past experiences is substituted for a present dynamic, living fellowship with God. The elite status of having the title "Israel, the people of God" is of no significance unless these people identify themselves with God, have a relationship with him, and demonstrate their commitment to him in their daily walk.

Sin destroys a person's relationship with God. Thus, if there is no confession of sin, there is no continuing relationship with God. His protection is not a question of title but of the heart's love and fear of God and of forgiveness of sins. God cannot overlook sin, for no one can hide from its consequences unless he or she is forgiven by God. God is always gracious and ready to forgive sin, but sin cannot be ignored.

THE DECEPTION OF misunderstanding the seriousness of sin. It is not hard for people today to fall into the same deceptive trap that twisted the thinking of the Israelites. Although they were the special chosen people of God, who had been miraculously and graciously delivered from Egyptian bondage, their response to God's grace would have a direct effect on their relationship with God. If the people rejected God and sinned against him, he would not bless them but would bring judgment on them.

People who have grown up in the church, been baptized, been approved through confirmation, or been accepted as members have a similar reason to expect God's approval and blessing. They may think that they have the right to God's protection and blessing because of their past experience with God. People who go through the church rituals of identification with Christianity can follow up their religious experience either by continually walking closely with God in a dynamic faith relationship or by ignoring their identification with Christ and living self-sufficiently sinful lives, separated from any conscious dependence on God.

Amos 9:7–10 suggests that sin is the poison that keeps people and nations from receiving God's blessing. The question is not which sins have been committed (they are identified elsewhere in Amos, though not here); rather, the central point is that sin seriously changes and determines a person's relationship with God. To ignore the presence of sin or its destructive power is to live in a world of delusions, far from God.

Some people tend to look at the good things God has done for them in the past and to assume he is still on their side. They also remember the good things they have done for God in the past and assume that they are still on his side. In both cases, such people make the fatal and deceptive mistake of basing a relationship on past experiences and ignoring present realities. They focus on the good things and assume that a positive relationship continues. In neither of these approaches do people admit failures or deal with the issue of sin. Yet the presence of sin is the key reason why people do not have a living relationship with God. God's grace makes a relationship with him possible, but sin makes it impossible.

Is sin more important than grace? No, grace is essential for a relationship with God, but God's grace is abundantly poured out on all people. God graciously moved the Syrians, the Philistines, and the Israelites to new lands. God's power and grace are evident in the creation, which richly produces food for all people around the world. Grace is God's love that draws people to himself. Of course, God's most precious act of love and grace was given to all people when Christ died for our sins (even for the Cushites or Ethiopians in 9:7). Truly, the abundance of God's grace is overwhelming.

Nevertheless, earthly and heavenly relationships are not established simply by one party graciously doing something for another party. Relationships involve the mutual response of both parties. We know this is true in friendships and in marriage, but it is also true of a relationship with God. If one spouse, for example, ignores the other partner or does not appreciate what has been done for him or her, no lasting relationship can be established.

Even more devastating are those situations where a gracious act brings about an initial positive response, but this is followed by rejection and offensive acts that interrupt normal fellowship.

Can we apply this passage to the church today? What past acts of God's grace function as deceptions in the church today, and how can we cause people to recognize that the devastating power of sin breaks our relationship with God? It would be inappropriate to suggest that there is one primary deception. For one denomination it may be too much dependence on the significance of baptism; for another it may be a particular gift of the Spirit. The deceptions can even be varied within a church, in that the kind of things that give one person problems may not affect another.

Sensitivity to the way people express their thoughts about their relationship to God should give some clues. Testimonies that always relate to God's past acts of grace without any reference to a present living, dynamic relationship may indicate a problem. Refusing to confess sin may also be a sign that a person does not see sin as something that destroys one's relationship with God. A third signal might be an overly optimistic view of God's protection from danger (see 9:10), or the naive view that believers will always be abundantly blessed by God.

Another serious source of deception is through incomplete teachings of true statements of Christian doctrine. No one should falsely think that all God requires is for us to be baptized or to join the church, though some do believe this because the truth of Scripture has not been adequately explained. Strong Bible teaching is necessary to ground people firmly so that they are not led astray with deceptions.

Removing deceptions. To undermine the false views of the Israelites, Amos emphasizes two themes: No one can escape God's judgment (9:1–4), and God is the all-powerful One who controls the universe (9:5–6). It is clear from the deceptive statement "Disaster will not overtake . . . us" (9:10) that some Israelites believed they would escape any judgment. To combat those who still hold this falsehood in the church, the messenger of God today must demonstrate that no one has the ability to escape from God. Some may try to reduce him to something that has no relationship to his real character, while others will ignore him. D. Turner describes one kind of escapism as "the general disposition of people . . . is to look straight into the face of God, or else turn away after seeing what is plainly there in His eyes."[8]

Anthropologists and historians have found that a high percentage of people believe there is a God, but all too many run their lives as if he does not

---

8. D. Turner, *Escape from God: The Use of Religion and Philosophy to Evade Responsibility* (Pasadena, Calif.: Hope, 1991), 4.

exist. Even some respected modern sociologists and psychologists assume that God is not important if you want to understand how people think or why they act the way they do. Philosophers like B. Russell have tried to escape from God by saying that "the whole conception of God is quite unworthy of free men,"[9] but his philosophical pronouncements do not absolve him of responsibility before God.

Today people may not try to escape from God by going to some distant geographic location (cf. 9:2–4), but many still imagine that they can eliminate the problems God raises in their lives by simply not believing that he exists. Others foolishly believe they will never be held accountable for their beliefs and actions. Some even blindly think that God will ignore their bad deeds because they have done some good things in their lives. They do not understand the terrible consequences of sin against a holy God.

In order to remove deception, one must first find out what subtle false beliefs a friend, relative, or congregation might have. Once they are identified, God's messenger must use every tool possible to persuade people of the truth. One can make comparisons with other peoples, as Amos does (9:7), develop striking illustrations that make the facts evident (9:9), identify the deceptive beliefs in a clear and succinct way (9:10), and counter the illusion with the unmistakable truth that: (1) God is an all-powerful, holy God; (2) sin separates us from him; and (3) no sinner can escape from his justice. Like Amos, we must state, repeat, and reemphasize these basic principles again and again. The eternal destiny of each person is dependent on accepting these truths.

---

9. B. Russell, cited in ibid., 110.

Amos 9:11-15

11 "In that day I will restore
 David's fallen tent.
 I will repair its broken places,
  restore its ruins,
  and build it as it used to be,
12 so that they may possess the remnant of Edom
  and all the nations that bear my name,"
  declares the LORD,
  who will do these things.

13 "The days are coming," declares the LORD,

 "when the reaper will be overtaken by the plowman
  and the planter by the one treading grapes.
 New wine will drip from the mountains
  and flow from all the hills.
14 I will bring back my exiled people Israel;
  they will rebuild the ruined cities and live in them.
 They will plant vineyards and drink their wine;
  they will make gardens and eat their fruit.
15 I will plant Israel in their own land,
  never again to be uprooted
  from the land I have given them,"
  says the LORD your God.

THIS FINAL PROMISE of hope contains two salvation oracles that introduce positive promises about Israel's "day" of restoration: Verses 11–12 discuss the coming day when the kingdom of David is restored, while verses 13–15 deal with the restoration of the land. The first paragraph focuses on first-person action that God will do, while the second describes what will happen to the fertility of the land when God pours out his abundant blessing on it. Ruins, desolation, and breaches are replaced by building, planting, and possessing the land to demonstrate the great reversal that will take place in the future.

If these events are to happen "in that day" (9:11; cf. 9:13), they are clearly after the destructive events described "in that day" of chapter 8 (8:3, 9, 11,

13). There is also a contrast between the destruction that will happen to the sinful nation (9:8) and the blessings that will come to all who identify with the Lord (9:12). God's judgment before these events will cause the nation to be "overtaken" by other nations (in spite of their denial in 9:10) and be shaken like a sieve among the nations (9:9–10); but in the future kingdom the enormity of God's blessings will "overtake" them (9:13).

This short message informs the deceived people in Amos's audience of what they will miss and gives a short word of encouragement to that faithful remnant that still exists among the people (5:15; 9:8). At some point in the future God's covenant promises through Moses (Lev. 26) and to David (2 Sam. 7) will be fulfilled so that this faithful remnant may enjoy them. Thus, no one should think that the destruction of Israel implies that God has given up on his people or abandoned his original plans or promises. The righteous people in Israel should not give up hope in the midst of judgment, for God will establish his eternal kingdom.

Numerous commentaries have trouble seeing Amos as a preacher of these positive words of hope after he has given so many negative messages. They hold that these hopeful words have been added by a later deuteronomic or exilic editor[1] because (1) this picture of restoration is contradictory to Amos's message of destruction in the rest of the book; (2) a positive attitude toward Judah and Jerusalem is not appropriate for an Israelite audience but fits a later Judean audience; (3) the historical background presupposes the fall of Jerusalem; and (4) the emphasis on material blessings is contrary to Amos's strong focus on ethical behavior elsewhere.[2]

In contrast to this conclusion are the recent works by Hayes, Hubbard, Stuart, Andersen and Freedman, Finley, Smith, and Paul,[3] who conclude that 9:11–15 is a part of Amos's preaching. They offer various reasons. (1) Amos is not being inconsistent with his earlier messages of destruction, for he is offering hope only to a small remnant of people after the destruction of Israel, not to the nation as a whole.

(2) The message about the restoration of the Davidic empire is not just a Judean hope, for the Israelite nation too had a special place for David because of his revenge of the death of Saul (2 Sam 1:11–16), his lament for Saul and Jonathan (1:17–27), and his covenant with the northern nation of Israel (5:1–3). In fact, the people of Israel at one time believed they had a

---

1. W. A. G. Nel, "Amos 9:11–15—An Unconditional Prophecy of Salvation During the Period of the Exile," *OtSt* 2 (1984): 81–97, believes this section was added in the exilic period.

2. Harper, *Amos*, 194, raises linguistic arguments as well, but Paul, *Amos*, 289, has demonstrated the weakness of this kind of evidence.

3. G. Hasel, *Understanding the Book of Amos* (Grand Rapids: Baker, 1991), 116–20, provides a list of authors on each side of these arguments.

greater claim on David than the people of Judah (19:43), and God did promise to build the eternal house of David through Israel's king Jeroboam I if he would follow God (1 Kings 11:30—38).[4]

(3) Most of the prophets see through their gift of prophecy that God's judgment will be followed by the establishment of his kingdom (cf. Hos. 14; Joel 3:17—21; Zeph. 3). Thus, it is not necessary to postdate the words of Amos or any of the prophets; in fact, if the "David's fallen tent" refers to the breakup of the Davidic kingdom in 930 B.C. rather than the fall of Jerusalem in 586 B.C.,[5] there is no need to date these verses in the exilic period.

(4) Amos's promise of blessing falls only on those who associate with the name of the Lord. Thus, the key theological and ethical dimension of his preaching is maintained; he does not throw the doors of the kingdom open to the ungodly and unethical Israelites whom he condemns elsewhere in the book.

The Coming Day Will Bring the Restoration of the Davidic Kingdom (9:11–12)

THE COMING DAY of hope is set somewhere in the unknown future. It points to that ideal day when the Lord will take direct control of his people's destiny and graciously act on their behalf. In a series of first-person unconditional promises, God announces: "I will restore/raise up David's fallen tent/booth."[6] Usually the dynasty of David is described as the "house [*bet*]" of David (2 Sam. 7:11, 27); only Isaiah refers to the city of Jerusalem as a lonely "shelter" or "booth" (Isa. 1:8) and to a Davidic judge who will be on the throne in the "tent of David" (16:5, see NIV text note).[7] Amos is probably referring back to the "fallen" family rule of David and Solomon, which was continually destroying the vitality of both nations since the kingdoms were divided into the

---

4. G. V. Smith, *Amos*, 279—80, expands this line of argumentation to show that Israel did have a Davidic hope. See, e.g., Hosea's promise to the Israelites of one king in the tradition of David (Hos. 1:11 and 3:5).

5. Andersen and Freedman, *Amos*, 916—17, believe David's dynasty fell when the kingdoms were divided in 930 B.C. after the death of Solomon (see 1 Kings 11—12).

6. J. Mauchline, "Implicit Signs of Persistent Belief in the Davidic Empire," *VT* 20 (1970): 291, takes the "booth" to be royal imagery that refers to the Lord's presence in the city, but this seems unlikely. Stuart, *Hosea–Jonah*, 398, and H. N. Richardson, *"Skt* (Amos 9:11): 'Booth' or 'Succoth'?" *JBL* 92 (1973), 375—81, suggest that this word refers to the city of Succoth, but most reject this hypothesis.

7. G. B. Gray, *The Book of Isaiah* (ICC; Edinburgh: T. & T. Clark, 1912), 289, takes this to be a messianic text, but Amos is less specific, for he does not mention a throne or the one sitting on the throne (as Isaiah does).

northern country of Israel and the southern country of Judah after Jeroboam I refused to submit to Rehoboam (see 1 Kings 12).

Amos's prophecy does not refer to the fall of Jerusalem and her exile, for later prophecies that do mention this are much more specific and graphic (Jer. 7; Ezek. 4–5).[8] This text does not explain how this Davidic rule will be restored or clarify details about the ruler; it merely states that God himself will bring it about. The fallen nature of this little tent shows how insignificant and powerless God views these Hebrew nations at the present time.[9]

The second thing God promises is that "I will repair its broken places [lit., breaches] [and] restore its ruins." In military passages breaches and ruins usually refer to the destroyed walls of a city (1 Kings 11:27; Isa. 14:17). Earlier Amos predicted that destruction would come to many cities in David's old empire (2:5; 4:3). The breaches[10] of these cities will then be restored and "its [David's kingdom's] ruins" will be rebuilt so that the ideal empire of old can be restored. These glorious promises must have quickened the heartbeats of the righteous remnant.

The consequences of this Davidic revival will impact other nations so that they may gain inclusion into this future kingdom (9:12). The reference to the "remnant of Edom" may stem from Uzziah's restoration of parts of Edom to Judean control (2 Kings 14:22; 2 Chron. 26:2) during the time of Amos. The final rebuilt empire will not only include the remaining portion of Edom but many other nations that God will control (these are the people who will be called by his name). If they go by God's name, they are part of his possession and his people. Amos here foresees the conversion of many Gentile people groups to God, an insight that helped the New Testament church decide to include Gentile converts into their fellowship in Acts 15.[11]

---

8. Andersen and Freedman, *Amos*, 916, support this interpretation.

9. This small temporary tent (God's perspective of the nation) is in stark contrast to the palace-fortresses that the people of Israel were so proud of elsewhere in Amos.

10. W. Kaiser, "The Davidic Promise and the Inclusion of the Gentiles (Amos 9:9–15 and Acts 15:13–18): A Test Passage for Theological Systems," *JETS* 20 (1977): 97–112, pays special attention to the variations between the pronouns in "*their* breaches/broken places" and "*his* ruins." For an alternate view that takes the pronouns seriously, see Hayes, *Amos*, 224–25, who believes "their breaches" refers to breaches in the Davidic alliance by rebellious cities and "his ruins" refers to those who oppose "his authority," i.e., that of the new Davidic king.

11. The application of this passage to the New Testament situation was made easier because the early church leaders were following the LXX in reading "humankind" rather than "Edom."

The Coming Day Will Bring the Restoration
of the Land (9:13–15)

ONCE THE POLITICAL status of the new kingdom is explained, Amos focuses on God's transformation of the fertility of the land. God will replace his curse of destruction on the land. It will truly overflow with milk and honey. Using hyperbolic language, the prophet describes how those plowing the fields in October through November will overtake those harvesting the crops. The abundance of the crops will be beyond everyone's imagination and exceed human ability to collect them. The grapes that are harvested around August and September will be so numerous that they will still not be finished at planting time in November. In fact, the grapes will be so full that there will be streams of grape juice flowing down the hillsides.

This is an astonishing picture, for if one visits the Holy Land today in the summer, a primary impression of that rocky and dry land is not one of fertility. In places where there is no modern irrigation, one sees the exact opposite of fertility and no overwhelming abundance of crops. The contrast between the agricultural fertility in Amos's day and that future time of divine blessing on that coming day is dramatic—an obvious sign that God is blessing his people (cf. Lev. 26:42; Deut. 30:9). It is almost like a rebirth of the Garden of Eden (see Ezek. 36:35).

God will also return his people to the land (Amos 9:14) after the destruction and exile (5:27; 7:17). When they return, they will rebuild its cities, plant new crops, and enjoy the produce of the land. This sharply contrasts with Amos's earlier prediction that they will build homes but not dwell in them, and plant vineyards but not enjoy their fruit (5:11). This miraculous change is instituted by God's action of returning the people to the land and the people's action of settling and working the land. There is no conditional phraseology to limit the fulfillment of this transformed situation. It will happen; God will see to it.

This salvation oracle ends with an unending covenantal promise of God's eternal granting of the land to his people (9:15). They will permanently possess this land and will never be driven from it again. This reverses the immediate destiny of the nation (5:2), which will soon be uprooted and sent into exile. They will no longer be sojourners but landed citizens, deeply rooted in the place God has given them.

These final promises convey a powerful message of hope in God. It may have persuaded some listeners to join the small remnant of Israelites who still trusted in God. This message of restoration demonstrates that God is still sovereign over the affairs of his people and will faithfully fulfill everything he has promised to their forefathers. It will happen in spite of the failures of the people in Amos's day and in spite of the failures of the church today. God's love is gracious beyond measure and his power to transform is unlimited.

RESTORATION OF BLESSINGS. The primary theological theme of this section is that God will one day restore his blessings on all who are called by his name. Although this is his specific promise to bring hope to the people of Israel, it has much in common with the eschatological vision for Judah that God inspired in the hearts of Isaiah, Jeremiah, and Ezekiel. It is, of course, inappropriate to read into Amos's message all the things these later prophets describe—such as the cleansing of the sins of the nation (e.g., Ezek. 36:25, 29, 33), God's transformation of the hearts of the people through his Spirit (36:26–27; 37:14), the leadership of a Davidic servant king (34:23–24; 37:24–25), the eternal covenant of peace (34:25; 37:26), and the future place of worship where God will dwell (chs. 40–43)—but the full weight of Amos's promises is not diminished by their simplicity or incompleteness.

It is possible that Amos has a much fuller eschatological understanding than what is presented in this passage. But the present level of detail is what God wants the prophet to share with his Israelite audience. Thus, a fundamental principle of interpretation of prophecy is to discover the meaning of the words spoken[12] and not to put in the prophet's mouth ideas and issues of fulfillment not based on the text. What the later prophet Isaiah says has little impact on interpreting Amos because Amos does not go into the detail Isaiah does. Biblical teaching on Amos must derive from this text; otherwise, we could import anything into this text and twist it to our own ends (many complain about the cults doing this but practice their own brand of the same thing). Amos does not mention many eschatological details,[13] but he does claim that God will restore his blessings on all who are called by his name. That is his powerful message.

Amos draws a connection between God's past promises in the covenant (the blessings and curses in Lev. 26 and Deut. 27–28) and his promises to David (2 Sam. 7; Ps. 89), and the future events in the coming days. Although there is general reference within these promises to the material benefits that will be enjoyed by humankind, the focus of attention falls on the work of God. "I will" is the power behind all this transformation. This passage exalts the faithfulness and power of God to bring restoration out of a cursed nation.

---

12. R. H. Stein, *Playing by the Rules* (Grand Rapids: Baker, 1994), 17–60, gives an understandable explanation of the basic rules of interpretation, following the approach of E. D. Hirsch.

13. Finley, *Joel, Amos, Obadiah*, 324, identifies this as the "millennial kingdom," but that information is totally unknown to Amos and all the other Old Testament prophets (the thousand-year reign is only mentioned specifically in Rev. 20).

He will bring about a great change in Israel, but his original plans have not changed. He has always intended to make Abraham's seed into a great nation, to use them to bring his blessing on the Gentiles from other nations, and to give them a land flowing with milk and honey (Gen. 12:1–3; 17:1–8; 26:1–3; 28:14).

The tragedy of this whole plan is that God's chosen people then and today resist his grace and authority so much that it is impossible for the plan to be enacted. As at Pentecost, God will one day powerfully intervene again and through his Spirit bring about the completion of his original plan. God has not been confused by the intervening years, nor has he had to go to Plan B because the first one did not work. This plan included curses and blessings (Gen. 12:3), so that the Israel of Amos's day will feel the brunt of God's wrath but those in the future will experience his gracious restoration.

Finally, this text assures listeners that God has not left humanity without any hope. Today may be terrible, and tomorrow may bring more sorrow than any one person should have to bear, but there is hope because God exists and has a plan to bring this world to a wonderful end. If more unconditional grace is available, restoration for a failed world exists. If people are not stripped of all hope, faith and trust are possible. If people desire to participate in the transformation God offers, a new world can be born. No matter how severe God's judgment is, he does not leave people without hope.

PREACHING HONEST ESCHATOLOGICAL **messages.** Amos's eschatological presentation of hope and restoration may not include all that he knows and does not include many of the details that later prophets mention, but it does include the primary message that God will transform both people and nature when he brings about the fulfillment of his plans. Amos speaks what God has instructed him to say, and one must assume that this limited amount of information is adequate for the needs of the audience.

Amos simply reveals what God will do, but the plan is vague on when it will happen (cf. "in that day" in 9:11). Nor is the prophet overly concerned with explaining who will be in this kingdom (surprisingly he never even mentions the people of Judah and does not specify who the "nations" are who will be called by "my name" in 9:12). This leads one to wonder about the need for this information. Is our faith to be centered on what God will do, or on when it will happen, and on who it will happen to? Does speculation about what a prophet might have meant increase our ability to believe it? Does reading between the lines or adding things from the New Testament provide a sure foundation for what Amos is teaching?

No, the challenge is to preach and teach what God has revealed through Amos, not what I want to explain from the wealth of my eschatological knowledge. If faithfulness to the words that Amos speaks is forsaken, there is a real danger that people will miss the main point God and Amos are making in this passage. Limiting oneself to the biblical revelation of a text is a hard discipline that every interpreter needs to learn.

How did the church in Acts apply this text? If one wants to look at the interpretation and application of Amos 9:12 in the early church in Acts 15:16–18, one is initially faced with the interpretive problem that the New Testament text has "men" rather than "Edom." But the significance of this fact is reduced once one realizes that Edom sometimes stands as a symbol for all the nations.[14] The key question of application in the Jerusalem council is this: How does this verse help the church decide whether Gentiles should be included with Jews in the kingdom of God? Would God concern himself with taking from the Gentiles a people who are called by his name (Acts 15:14)? James, the apostles and elders, and the whole church at Jerusalem are led by the Spirit (Acts 15:28) to apply Amos 9:12 to their situation and conclude that it is God's plan to call out Gentiles to himself.

True, the Jerusalem council does not pay much attention to the time specifications in Amos 9:11–12, nor do they focus on who these Gentile nations are that Amos is speaking about. They go instead to the heart of the issue: God's plan is to include "Gentiles who bear my name" (Acts 15:17). This lesson in application turns accepted church polity upside down (after this council meeting the church will never again be an exclusive Jewish fellowship); its application opens the door to Gentile acceptance and the evangelism of the world.

If this one verse had been misinterpreted or misapplied, the Western world might still be in pagan darkness. In the new policy accepted at the Jerusalem council, additional requirements are placed on the Gentiles to maintain moral and social unity between peoples from different cultures (Acts 15:19–20). This is not derived from Amos 9 but from the early church leaders' knowledge of other passages. They apply common cultural sensibilities to their situation in order to enable this culturally diverse church to be pure (following the known will of God revealed in the past), free from unnecessary cultural restraints, and unified together as one (Acts 15:28–29).

It seems that missionaries who spread the gospel in foreign cultures must make similar judgments of application to protect the purity, cultural freedom,

---

14. See Isa. 34:1–8; 63:1–6; possibly Obad. 15–21. Note M. W. Woudstra, "Edom and Israel in Ezekiel," *CTJ* 3 (1968): 21–35, who offers examples of passages where Edom seems to stand for all the nations.

and unity of the church. Similar insights should characterize the fellowship among African American, American Indian, Hispanic, and white churches today. We all worship the same Lord and will be with one another for eternity in heaven, but it seems as if cultural and denominational distinctives are so strong that it is easier for each group to do its own thing and not associate with other groups. But a church divided is not a church united, and unity was one of Jesus' main concerns before he left his disciples (John 17). Certainly Gentiles needed the Jerusalem church to send out missionaries, and the Jerusalem church needed assistance from the Gentile churches during the famine in Jerusalem. Do we not still need the fellowship of the whole church today?

Is there any hope? The final words of Amos offer hope to the faithful remnant who will suffer with the wicked when God brings destruction on the nation of Israel. It also challenges unbelievers with the choices they can make: Reject God and suffer his curse, or turn to God and accept this offer of hope. Everyone needs to have some hope in his or her life. Hope is not based on an eschatological chart or eliminated by difficult circumstances. God is the One who offers hope to those who will believe in him. Therefore, he must be at the center of all eschatological teaching.

Introduction to Micah

PEOPLE IN EVERY AGE suffer injustices at the hands of the strong. In every neighborhood and business there are strong and arrogant individuals who feel that they deserve to spend more money or have greater political clout than anyone else. Some companies want an exclusive monopoly on their product so they can make a larger profit, some bosses want control over the social behavior of others, and some commercial farms want to farm more land and control the market on a product. In order to make their dreams come true, such people often end up forcibly imposing their wills on the lives of others.

This process usually involves treating some people in an unjust way. Right and wrong are forgotten so that the selfish goals of the powerful can be achieved more quickly. Ethics are ignored, and decisions are not made on the basis of the best interests of all involved. No matter what the reason or what the situation, the Bible consistently pictures God as One who hates injustice and who fights to establish justice.

In every age God's people need to encourage and support civic, military, social, religious, political, and family leaders who are bold enough to lead them in just ways that please God. Israel needed this kind of capable leadership in the time of Micah, and the church needs people in all walks of life to stand up and challenge others to let principles of justice influence all their relationships. Since the Creator's dealings with his created world are based on people's loving God and their neighbors (the two great commandments in Deut. 6:5 and Lev. 19:18, respectively, which Jesus repeated in Matt. 22:37–39), there is no other way to please God.

In a similar manner, Micah summarizes what God requires of people into three basic principles: to act justly toward others, to love steadfast covenant loyalty with God, and to walk humbly and circumspectly with him (6:8). These are essential qualities that should stand out as bright lights for everyone to see. Without spiritual development in these areas there is little hope of pleasing God in worship, of fulfilling one's leadership responsibilities, of becoming a transformational influence in society, or of being a role model in family life.

When people fail to lead others in just and loving ways, disorder and chaos reign. That is one of the reasons why the perversity in the modern world seems to get worse and worse. But similar problems were also present in Israelite society long ago. No matter where one lives, if justice is ignored, those in power can use their privileged position to take possessions and property from people

(2:8–9), to treat others inhumanely (3:1–3), and to selectively interpret God's mercy to enhance their own financial gain (3:5). Rulers may not always value fairness and may eventually get to the place where they abhor justice. Judges may be approached to accept bribes, and spiritual leaders may start being primarily concerned about how much they are paid. At the same time, many of these same people will deceptively profess to be servants of God who are protected and blessed by his presence (3:8–11).

Without love, justice, and a trust in God, nations put their confidence in horses and chariots to win wars, large cities for security, and perverse theological understandings of reality (5:11–13). Before long these people forget what God really requires of them when they worship (6:6–8), and families lose all sense of confidence and trust in other family members (7:5–6). Eventually persecution, fighting, and war will turn life into a bitter experience.

When one looks at the daily newspaper, *Time* magazine, or *Christianity Today*, it is not unusual to read about injustices that pervade the lives of people in our own hometown or in nations around the world. Palestinians have land taken from them, Korean labor disputes turn violent, African Tutsis are murdered by Hutus and vise versa, and a young American girl is abused by her mother's boyfriend. In these situations there is a crying need for Christian moral leadership from those who can have a positive impact by standing up for justice. Unfortunately, the holy grail of "separation of church and state" has so permeated education and civic institutions that many people are quiet and afraid to express their Christian convictions.

Moreover, many problems appear so complex and insurmountable that one gets the idea that the answer of loving God and dealing with others justly will not solve the world's problems. Although these fears are not totally unfounded, families and communities throughout our world need people who will fight for the basic principles of acting justly, loving mercy, and walking humbly with God. Leadership can be shown in talking to our boss at work about the way individuals are being mistreated, by intervening in the way children play together, or by making positive suggestions about the way a congregation of believers might help people of different races and cultures.

Like Micah, people today can still look to God in their hour of darkness, wait on his salvation, and be confident that God hears all they ask him (7:7). People should confess their own failing and plead for God to shepherd his flock in power (7:9, 14). God will pardon those who confess their sins, for he delights in forgiving sins and showing mercy (7:18–19). But if no leaders step forward to guide people back to a right relationship with God and with their neighbors, God will eventually come in power to deal with the situation himself, as he did at the time of Micah (1:2–7).

The challenge that Micah faces is not that different from the context of our modern world. Believers must be in the forefront of guiding their communities toward eliminating the injustices that so seriously plague the social, economic, and political life of cultures in every corner of the world. That kind of biblical leadership starts with the transformation of each person's own desires and actions. Then it can infiltrate into the very fiber of the relationships people have in their homes, their churches, their work, and their play. Loving mercy, acting justly, and walking circumspectly with God are not just possible options that a person may want to think about; they are the heart and soul of pleasing or displeasing God.

Judean Social Context During Micah's Ministry
The Worship of God

IN CONTRAST TO the context of Amos (Amos 7:10–17), there is no explicit indication in the writings of Micah that the prophet preached any of his sermons in a temple. Perhaps some were originally given or repeated on visits to the temple area, but the prophet never mentions this. Nevertheless, in his conversations with his listeners, Micah brings threatening words against the high places of Jerusalem and compares them with the idol worship in the temple at Samaria (Mic. 1:5–7). This suggests that he has visited both places of worship and has seen the illegitimate worship of the people in both these capital cities.

Micah writes about the sorcerers, fortune tellers, Asherim idols, and carved images present in the nation's temples (5:12–14). The connection made between these practices and "Ahab's house" (6:16) shows how pagan worship in the northern nation of Israel has negatively impacted the worship in the southern nation of Judah. Micah observes that some of the prophets accept payment for prophecies while the priests instruct for a price (3:5, 11). Thus, he vigorously condemns the religious leaders who control the theology and worship practices at the temple. God is displeased with their unjust behavior, their spiritual blindness caused by a lust for financial gain, and their unwillingness to identify the sins of their audience (3:8, 11).

These people have the outer trappings of religious people and even claim to trust God for their protection because he is in their midst (3:11), but their unjust behavior reveals their true character and will determine their future destruction (3:12). Micah's covenant lawsuit is against those who do not understand how to come to God with sacrifices (6:1–8). They are primarily concerned with the size of their gifts, not the state of their relationship with God. The prophet's main concern is to deliver God's message in such a manner that the blind eyes of worshipers will be opened. He wants to persuade them of their need to transform their unjust behavior so that God will not have to destroy the nation of Judah.[1]

Micah does have some insights about the worship in Jerusalem in the coming years, for his warnings refer to a day in the near future when there will be no worship because the temple area will be overgrown like a forest and the city of Jerusalem will be in ruins (3:12). He also sees a time in the distant eschatological era when God himself will dwell in Zion and all nations will come to learn of God's ways and worship him (4:1–8). This is a picture of the ideal kingdom of God. Added to this is the great hope that the Ruler of Israel (the Messiah) will arise from Bethlehem and shepherd the flock of God in strength (5:2–4). Finally at the end of time, God's people will have good leaders, and they will be transformed by the teaching of God himself. Even the foreign nations will come to worship God in that day.

Additional assistance for understanding worship in Judah is provided by Isaiah, whose ministry overlaps with Micah. He refers to the people's pagan practices (Isa. 8:19), the insincerity of their worship (29:13), and their struggle to trust in God (30:1–3; 36:1–22). The authors of 2 Kings (chs. 16, 18–21) and 2 Chronicles (chs. 28–33) include extensive accounts of Ahaz's acceptance of pagan worship practices, Hezekiah's great spiritual awakening and celebration of the Passover, and Manasseh's tragic reversal of Hezekiah's temple reforms. The periods of these three kings have different kinds of worship, which can be identified in Micah's writings:

(1) extensive Baalism and unacceptable worship of God in the reign of Ahaz (Mic. 1–2) and into the first few years of Hezekiah (Mic. 3);
(2) Hezekiah's reform movement, which brings many people back to a true worship of God (Mic. 4–5);
(3) a return to Baalism and various pagan religions in the time of Manasseh (Mic. 6–7; cf. 2 Kings 21).

It is important to recognize these changes because the prophet is speaking in different settings. Micah's sermons dramatically change according to the needs of his audience in each period. In spite of external trials and personal disappointments, he lives through these turbulent political and religious times and remains a faithful leader of this sinful group of people.

The Political Situation

THE PROPHET MICAH lived in Judah during a volatile and insecure political period. In one sense his preaching should have been easy to believe because

---

1. G. V. Smith, "Persuasive Rhetoric in Divine Inspiration," *Didaskalia* 8 (1997): 60–74, pays special attention to the persuasive qualities of Micah 3. Jeremiah 26:17–19 testifies that this sermon caused Hezekiah to change his ways and fear God.

his warnings of military defeat occurred during a period of Assyrian strength when that empire was lead by powerful military kings who made several campaigns into Judah: Tiglath-Pileser III, Shalmaneser V, Sargon II, and Sennacherib. These great Assyrian kings used their large armies to control the ancient Near Eastern world during the reigns of the Judean kings Jotham, Ahaz, Hezekiah, and Manasseh (1:1).[2] Although Micah did not refer specifically to any of these kings by name in his sermons, his appeals to the "leaders of Jacob [and] rulers of the house of Israel" (3:1, 9) demonstrate his concerns for the way the Judean politicians were leading the people.

A later reference to Micah's preaching by some elders in Jerusalem confirms that Judah's famous king Hezekiah did hear Micah's warnings and was persuaded to fear God and trust him for deliverance from Sennacherib (Jer. 26:17–19; cf. Isa. 36–37; Mic. 3:12). The other Judean kings during Micah's time were not known for their spiritual commitment to God, the enforcement of justice in society, or their wise political leadership. If these historical events are correlated with the sermons Micah preaches, it will help the interpreter see why God inspired Micah to give such different messages in each historical period.

The first Judean king in Micah's days was Jotham (742–735 B.C.). He is classified as a good king, although he had only a brief and insignificant reign in Judah (2 Kings 15:32–38). During these years Tiglath-Pileser III brought the northern nation of Israel under his control and taxed it heavily (during the reign of Menahem in 738 B.C.; 2 Kings 15:19–20). Micah does not refer to these events. He probably grew up in this period, though he did not prophesy at this time.[3]

The second Judean king was the evil king Ahaz (735–715 B.C.). During his reign Judah was attacked by a coalition of Israel (lead by Pekah) and Syria (lead by Rezin) because these nations wanted Judah to join them as a united front against the might of Assyria (2 Kings 16:1–5).[4] This Syro-Ephraimite war (734–732 B.C.) resulted in the death of over 120,000 Judean soldiers and the capture of over 200,000 men, women, and children (2 Chron. 28:4–8). In addition, the Edomites attacked Judah from the southeast, and the Philistines successfully took some cities of Judah in their vicinity (28:17–19). Jerusalem was not conquered because in panic Ahaz called on the Assyrian king Tiglath-

---

2. Manasseh is not mentioned by name in 1:1, probably because Hezekiah had not died. The setting of Micah 6–7 seems to reflect an evil period after Hezekiah's reform when the prophet was very disappointed about the fruits of his own ministry.

3. Micah's first message (1:2–7) came sometime before 722/721 B.C. and the fall of the northern nation of Israel. This prophecy was probably during the time of Ahaz in Judah, close in time to the fall of Israel.

4. J. H. Hayes and J. M. Miller, *Israelite and Judean History* (Philadelphia: Westminster, 1977), 421–33, discuss this war and its ramifications in great detail.

Pileser III to deliver him, instead of trusting in God—as the prophet Isaiah suggested (Isa. 7:1–13). The Assyrians delivered Judah from their enemies but also required heavy tribute from them (2 Chron. 28:20–21).

While Ahaz was struggling in Judah, Hoshea king of Israel refused to pay tribute to the Assyrian king Shalmaneser V (who succeeded Tiglath-Pileser III) and sought to defend himself by making alliances with Egypt. (2 Kings 17:4). But Samaria was captured, and the people were exiled by the next Assyrian king, Sargon II, in 722/721 B.C.[5] This fulfilled Micah's prophecy that Samaria would be destroyed (1:2–7). Following this conquest the Assyrians put down revolts in southern Palestine at Gaza, an area close to Micah's hometown of Moresheth.[6]

A few years later, in the reign of Hezekiah (715–687 B.C.), Ashdod revolted, but Isaiah warned Hezekiah not to join this movement (Isa. 20:1–6). Sargon II put down this uprising and took control of this area in 711 B.C. This conquest in the Philistine plain may have caused Micah to take up his lament for the cities in that area and warn of the future demise of Jerusalem (1:8–16).[7] When Sargon II died and the new king Sennacherib came to the throne (704 B.C.), Hezekiah made some political contacts with Egypt and Babylon (2 Kings 19:9; 20:12) and refused to bow to Assyrian authority. During these years Micah also criticized the inadequate political and religious leaders in Jerusalem (Mic. 3). Eventually Hezekiah responded positively to Micah's persuasive sermon (Jer. 26:17–19).

Isaiah also challenged Hezekiah not to trust in foreign troops (Isa. 30:1–3; 31:1–3) or fear the Assyrians (ch. 36), but to trust God. Because of Hezekiah's rebellion against the Assyrians, Sennacherib attacked Jerusalem in 701 B.C., but God miraculously delivered him when an angel killed 185,000 Assyrian troops in one night (2 Kings 18–19; Isa. 36–37).[8] During this siege

---

5. *ANET*, 284, gives Sargon's boastful account of his conquest of Israel.

6. J. Bright, *A History of Israel*, 3d ed. (Philadelphia: Westminster, 1981), 286–88, describes some of the problems with untangling these events.

7. C. S. Shaw, *The Speeches of Micah: A Rhetorical-Historical Analysis* (Sheffield: JSOT, 1993), 56–67, reviews various theories about the date of 1:8–16 (701, 711, and 734 B.C.) and then proposes an early date at the beginning of Jotham's reign. R. L. Smith, *Micah–Malachi* (WBC; Waco, Tex.: Word, 1984), 5, dates 1:10–16 with Sennacherib's march to Jerusalem in 701 B.C., but it seems better to interpret this as a reference to earlier military conflicts in the Shephelah (the low Judean hills) in 720 or 711, and a warning about a future threat to Jerusalem (fulfilled in 701 B.C. and finally 586 B.C.).

8. Bright, *History of Israel*, 298–309, hypothesizes two campaigns by Sennacherib, but this view is widely questioned. See B. Childs, *Isaiah and the Assyrian Crisis* (London: SCM, 1967), R. E. Clements, *Isaiah and the Deliverance of Jerusalem* (Sheffield: JSOT, 1980), or D. Redford, *Egypt, Canaan, and Israel in Ancient Times* (Princeton: Princeton Univ. Press, 1992), 351–58, for a full explanation of the problem and possible solutions.

Micah gave Hezekiah and the people in Jerusalem some much-needed words of hope that God would establish his kingdom in spite of the present difficulties his people were having with their enemies (Mic. 4–5).

At the end of Micah's ministry (Mic. 6–7), Hezekiah was old, and his evil son Manasseh took control of the nation. Manasseh did not trust God but submitted to the Assyrians and turned the nation away from God. These political, religious, and social changes may be the reasons for Micah's condemnation of pagan practices borrowed from Ahab in 6:16 and for Micah's deep despair over the seeming failure of his ministry in 7:1–6, 10.[9] It must have been heart-breaking to see all the people who had earlier rallied around the political and religious reforms of Hezekiah suddenly return to their former unjust and ungodly ways.

Social and Economic Conditions

MICAH DOES NOT give a full explanation of the socioeconomic situation in his messages, but if one puts together his limited information with comments in Isaiah, Kings, and Chronicles, the general picture becomes clearer.

The Syro-Ephraimite war (734–732 B.C.) and the conquest of the nation of Israel by Sargon II (722/721 B.C.) in the days of Ahaz, plus Sennacherib's attack (701 B.C.) in the time of Hezekiah, brought about major destruction of property, the loss of many lives, the exile of talented business people and politicians, and the displacement of thousands of people who were trying to escape the Assyrian onslaught. The destruction of key civic institutions, the fracturing of families, the pillaging of farms and cities, and heavy taxation after these wars left the remaining people in a crisis situation. One only has to read about the social and economic consequences of wars today to get a little insight into the lasting tragedy war brings to a community.

A large increase in poor immigrants into Judah when the northern nation of Israel was defeated only added to the social upheaval and economic pressure in Judah.[10] Even though Sennacherib did not defeat the city of Jerusalem in 701 B.C., the rest of the nation suffered an enormous social and economic blow to its vitality because his soldiers pillaged the country, taking whatever they wanted. After each war families had to start over from scratch, and many of these families were now without a son or father to do some of the heavy work.

---

9. Some prefer to place these chapters in the time of Ahaz, while others put part or all of this section into an exilic setting (esp. 7:8–20). See L. C. Allen, *The Books of Joel, Obadiah, Jonah and Micah* (NICOT; Grand Rapids: Eerdmans, 1976), 250–52, for a survey of opinions.

10. M. Broski, "The Expansion of Jerusalem in the Reign of Hezekiah and Manasseh," *IEJ* 24 (1974): 21–26.

In times of great social and economic change, special responsibility is placed on governments to help the weak. A complicating factor is the added pressure war places on the wealthy, who now struggle to maintain their lifestyles. Consequently, in the days of Ahaz the powerful attempted to seize land from the weak (2:1–2). People robbed defenseless war refugees on the road after the fall of the nation of Israel (2:8), and took advantage of vulnerable widows who lost their husbands in the war (2:9). Even in the early years of Hezekiah politicians did not stand up for justice (3:1–2, 9), judges were swayed by bribes (3:11), and lives were sacrificed to get government building projects done quickly (3:10). Micah despised these abuses and tried to persuade the leaders in his audiences to restore justice in the land of Judah.

Later in the reign of Manasseh, Micah complained about the violence and deceitfulness of the wealthy and the use of improper scales by businessmen cheating their clients (6:10–12). Politicians, judges, and the powerful in society were again shedding innocent blood, taking bribes, and scheming to take advantage of others (7:2–4). Social distrust grew so bad that one had to be careful what one said to a friend, and even to a spouse or children (7:5–6). This was not a pleasant time to live in Judah, and it was especially difficult to be a prophet of God.

The Ministry of the Prophet Micah

Micah's Background

MICAH WRITES LITTLE about his own personal life, his occupation before becoming a prophet, or his family of origin. He grew up in Moresheth (see 1:1; it is probably the Moresheth Gath of 1:14), a country village in the Philistine plain about six miles north of the major fortress at Lachish. He does not tell us why he left Moresheth, but apparently he gave most if not all of his sermons in the capital city of Jerusalem. Even though his ministry took him away from home, much of his thinking and theology were formed while he was growing up in a rural setting.

H. W. Wolff has suggested that Micah was one of the leading elders of Moresheth and that his strong criticisms of social injustices by large landowners is part of his defense of the rights of his constituents before the authorities in Jerusalem. This approach, however, is at odds with Micah's primary focus of condemning the leaders in Jerusalem, not in Moresheth (3:9–12).[11] A. S. Kapelrud thinks Micah was a cult prophet, and W. Rudolph calls him a

---

11. H. W. Wolff, *Micah the Prophet* (Philadelphia: Fortress, 1981), 17–25. Wolff also considers it significant that one of the elders of Israel remembered Micah's words (since he was thought to be one of them) at the time of Jeremiah.

landowner, but these educated guesses mainly illustrate the breadth of Micah's knowledge of his world and his ability to interact with the worldview of people at various levels within his society. His own confession of his self-understanding reveals that he believed he was a prophet sent by God; thus, the source of his power and the basis for his identity is the filling of God's Spirit (3:8). He has the prophetic responsibility of telling people about their sins.

There is some evidence that Micah was persecuted and opposed by some in his audience (2:6–7). This was no doubt a result of his strong words of condemnation about what was happening in Jerusalem, as well as his deviant theological ideas (deviant from the widely accepted views of other religious and political leaders in Jerusalem). Most likely Micah was seen as a problem person in the reigns of Ahaz and Manasseh (Micah functioned as a peripheral prophet), though he did receive support from the reformer Hezekiah (as a central prophet)[12] after the king chose to trust God as Micah and Isaiah encouraged him.

If chapter 7 is interpreted as a personal lament by the prophet,[13] Micah apparently becomes discouraged after so many people abandon Hezekiah's reform movement in the time of Manasseh. Although he pours out his heart in disappointment over what he sees happening in his society (7:1–7), this lament also shows how Micah draws strength from God and earlier sacred traditions to overcome his exasperation. This more personal lament and his earlier lament for the cities that will be destroyed (1:8–16) demonstrate that Micah is a caring person who is deeply hurt by what he sees happening in Judah. Consequently, he intercedes with God and encourages his listeners to humble themselves before him and ask for his mercy.

Micah's Preaching

THERE IS NO way to know exactly how long Micah functioned as a prophet in Israel. Although he probably preached other messages in his lifetime (and repeats these on several occasions), the evidence from the sermons in his book suggests a ministry that stretched from about 725 B.C. to 690 B.C. Since Jotham is mentioned in 1:1, Micah may have started preaching as early as 735 B.C., but little is known about these early days or the prophet's age at this time.

The sermons that are preserved demonstrate a knowledge of Exodus traditions (Mic. 6:4, based on events in Exodus), God's deliverance of the people

---

12. See R. R. Wilson, *Prophecy and Society in Ancient Israel* (Philadelphia: Fortress, 1980), 32–51, 58–59, for a description of these terms. Peripheral prophets did not support the people in power, argued for radical change in society, and emphasized the injustices in the present political and social system.

13. See comments on chapter 7 for this and other interpretations of the first-person references in that lament.

from the plans of Balaam and Balak, the king of Moab (Mic. 6:5, drawing on Num. 22–24), God's opposition to bribery (Mic. 3:11, based on Ex. 23:8) and false weights (Mic. 6:11; see Lev. 19:36), God's characteristics of being forgiving, loving, and compassionate (Mic. 7:18–20; cf. Ex. 34:6), God's requirements of his people (Mic. 6:8; from Deut. 10:12; Hos. 6:6), and themes from various psalms.[14] These references indicate something of Micah's religious training and his deep respect for the authority of God's past revelation. They legitimate his accusations and point his audience toward the truth found in the people's own ancient traditions. This gives him greater persuasive power as he confronts the deceptive understandings of his listeners (see Mic. 2:6–7; 3:11; 6:6–7; 7:10).

Micah uses forms of literature common to the people of that day. He communicates effectively by using a theophany (1:2–4), laments (1:8–16; 7:1–6), a covenant lawsuit (6:1–16), a hymn (7:18–20), judgment oracles (2:1–4; 3:1–4), and salvation oracles (2:12–13; 4:1–8). This variety enables him to address many different people and topics with a variety of approaches. The listener also realizes that this prophet is not tediously playing the same tune over and over but is addressing the key needs of his audiences in unique ways. The Word of God applies to each new setting, and it is the prophet's responsibility to transmit God's message in as persuasive a form as possible so that the Spirit's work in the hearts of the audience will bring transformation.

Micah's cleverness at preaching and writing is seen in his puns on the names of the towns he mentions in 1:10–15 (e.g., the town of Aczib [deception] will prove to be a deception [1:14]). Micah repeats words to gain focus ("prophesy/drip" in 2:6, 11), to structure parallel sayings ("and now" in 4:9, 11; 5:1), and to organize what he says ("in the last/that day" in 4:1, 6). Another technique that gives authenticity to his messages is his practice of quoting what others are saying. Some suggest that Micah should be quiet (2:6) and that God's presence in the temple is all they need (3:11). At one point they question what they should give to God (6:6–7); others mock Micah's trust in God (7:10). Micah knows his audience and is thus able to address their real needs.

Micah's role as a preacher is to speak God's words with courage and to emphasize the theme of God's justice (3:8). Although courage is found in the heart of the speaker and evident in the oral delivery of the message, it cannot be seen in the written words in the text. Nevertheless, one cannot downplay this primary characteristic of his preaching. Those who hear him are undoubtedly surprised at his boldness and impressed with the dynamic way in which he addresses them. He has received messages from God, and it is his obligation to confront the serious injustices in his society. Fear must be

---

14. See 4:1–5 for a discussion of its relationship with Isa. 2:1–4.

overcome, unpopularity must be ignored, and the practices of other prophets and priests must be rejected. If Micah is going to do what God wants, he has to speak the truth in love. He must have courage to reach his goal of causing people to recognize their own sinfulness. Only then will he be able to lead them to the point where they will allow God to transform their lives.

Micah's Purpose

MICAH'S PREACHING HAS different purposes based on the audience he is addressing. Since there is no record of his call to explain why God is sending him to be a prophet, we must depend on Micah's own confession that one of his purposes is to declare the sins of the people (3:8). The failures of the nation and its leaders can no longer be swept under the rug. Sinful rebellion against God must be identified for what it really is. This explains the purpose of his judgment speeches and his covenant lawsuit. Within these messages Micah makes a clear connection between the earlier sins of Ahab, Samaria, and the northern nation of Israel and the present sins he sees in the nation of Judah (1:5–7; 6:16).[15] Since similar sins brought the downfall of Judah's northern neighbors, the threat to Judah's existence should be real to his listeners.

Micah's threats are accompanied by laments and instructions that urge the audience to recognize the seriousness of the situation and turn to God (1:8–16; 6:8). His own behavior of lamenting and looking to God for hope (7:7–9) is an example of what the listeners should do. Although the news of the possible demise of Judah seems foreign to the theology of many in his audience (3:11), we know that Hezekiah takes these warnings seriously and transforms his thinking by trusting in God when Sennacherib attacks Jerusalem in 701 B.C. (3:12; see Jer. 26:17–19; also Isa. 36–37). This brings about a great revival in Judah.

The authenticity and purpose of the positive words of hope are more difficult to discover.[16] Some scholars suggest that later writers in a different situation have added them. L. Allen objects to the use of so-called "late" theological terms like "the remnant" in 4:6–8, J. Limburg dates 7:8–20 late because he thinks 7:11 refers to the fall of Jerusalem in 587 B.C., while J. L. Mays takes all of chapters 4–5 as an encouragement to the small remnant that

---

15. Baalism was strong in Judah during the reigns of Ahaz and Manasseh.

16. W. Rudolph, *Micha-Nahum-Habakuk-Zephanja* (KAT; Gutersloh: Mohn, 1975), 25, and Allen, *Joel, Obadiah, Jonah and Micah*, 241–52, believe that Micah did not write the positive passages in 4:1–8; 5:6–8; 7:8–20. J. L. Mays, *Micah: A Commentary* (OTL; Philadelphia: Westminster, 1976), 23–33, attributes the positive statements in 2:12–13 and all of chs. 4–7 to someone other than Micah. Both of these approaches ignore many of the factors that bring coherence to the book. For a detailed study of points of coherence, see D. G. Hagstrom, *The Coherence of the Book of Micah: A Literary Analysis* (Atlanta: Scholars, 1988).

stays in Jerusalem after its destruction in 587 B.C.[17] These approaches strip Micah of any words of hope and make him into a negative prophet of doom. They also do not explain how or why some later person would want to, or would be allowed to, misrepresent the words God spoke to Micah. If most of the other prophets balance their messages of judgment with words of salvation, why is this strange in the book of Micah?

One would naturally expect Micah to give words of warning (as Isaiah does in Isa. 30–31) to Hezekiah and the people in Jerusalem before they transform their thinking and trust only in God (Mic. 3:1–12). Is it then not natural to give words of encouragement and hope (as Isaiah does in Isa. 37), once Hezekiah puts his trust in God (Mic. 4:1–8)? These passages promise a restoration of the nation in the future in order to strengthen the righteous in their resolve to trust God in difficult times. Similar words are needed in the evil days of Manasseh to remind God's prophet (7:11–20) that God's earlier promises will not fail, that his character has not changed, and that he will restore his people one day in spite of the evil of the present day.

His Theology: The Heart of Micah's Ministry

THE THEOLOGY OF the prophet derives from who God is and what he has done in the past. Growing from these fundamental concepts is an understanding of how God will act in relationship to the different groups addressed in Micah's ministry. Thus the focus of his theology is on the practical ways God will impact the world of his listeners. If his audience knows what God is going to do in certain situations and why he is responding to the people in this way, they will be able to change their behavior to avoid negative consequences.

Micah's picture of God emphasizes his power over the whole world, both the military powers that control the destiny of the people (1:15; 2:12; 3:12; 4:3, 10, 13; 5:6; 7:16) and the powers of nature (1:4; 4:4; 6:15). He is able to destroy his own people as well as their enemies who have gathered at Jerusalem to destroy it (4:12). He is also able to restore nations that have been exiled and to bring peace among all the nations when he sets up his kingdom (4:3). His ability to determine the future military strength of each nation and the economic prosperity of each nation means that no people should be deceived about their ability to determine their own fate. Unfortunately, Micah's audience and Judah's enemies do not understand much about the sovereign plans of God (4:12; 6:6–8; 7:10).

Micah reveals that God is not some far-off nebulous concept or an idol that does not affect people's daily life. His character is known, and he acts

17. Allen, *Joel, Obadiah, Jonah and Micah*, 244–45; J. Limburg, *Hosea–Micah* (Interp; Atlanta: John Knox, 1988), 162; Mays, *Micah*, 26.

in ways consistent with his nature. He is the holy God, who will come in power to judge sinners on the earth (1:2–7); yes, Judah's disastrous destruction will come from God because of their sins (1:12). This theological perspective conflicts with the popular view that God's Spirit will not be angry with them (2:7) because God is present in Jerusalem to protect them (3:11). But Micah knows that because God is holy, he must act in justice against those enemies of his who act unjustly (2:1–4, 8; 3:9–12; 6:9–16). This must even apply to God's unjust covenant people ("my people" in 2:8–9; 6:2–3) whom he graciously brought up from Egypt. Particularly at fault are the unjust leaders: the rulers, priests, prophets, and judges who take advantage of others for their own financial gain (3:1–12).

God is also known as a forgiving, compassionate, and merciful God, who will keep his oath to Abraham (7:18–20). In compassion he delivered his people in the past as he shepherded them from Egypt, and he will also graciously shepherd his people again, defeat their enemies, and restore them (5:2–9; 7:11–16). He will raise up a ruler over his people who will be a good leader (5:2–4 is in contrast to Judah's bad leaders), a picture that has clear messianic implications. God's grace will be fully seen when he sets up his kingdom in Zion, teaches the nations his righteous ways, and brings in peace and prosperity (4:1–4). At that time God will restore all his oppressed people and reign in power from Zion forever (2:12–13; 4:6–8). This kind of gracious and powerful God is one whom Micah's audience can choose to trust, for he will bring the ultimate victory for his people and subdue all nations under his feet.

Micah's theology works itself out into a practical appeal for people in Judah to recognize what God will do to those who reject him. This possibility causes him to lament at the thought of such a disaster (1:8–16). If God's people do not rid themselves of their deceptive theology and if their leaders do not rule justly, there will be no hope. Micah's theology is principled by God's character and applied to bring about change. The leaders in the days of Ahaz and Manasseh reject God's ways, but Hezekiah transforms his theology and God answers his prayers (Isa. 37:14–20). Indeed, acting on the basis of good theology changes everything.

Challenges for the Modern Church

THE ANALOGY BETWEEN the nation of Israel and the church is not a one-to-one comparison. In other words, "God's people" cannot be identified with any one nation today, for believers exist as a small part of many nations. Therefore, it is important for people in every nation to look for the basic principles Micah is applying to his audiences to see if some of the same problems he deals with still exist. Although there is a good deal of discontinuity between comparisons on the national level (between Judah and any nation today), there is a great deal of continuity on the individual level. Judges in every culture and in every era should make judicial decisions with fairness and equity. Although sentencing may vary in different contexts, all judges should seek to uphold an equitable moral order by their just decisions.

In teaching or preaching about justice it is always easier to see the evil in the behavior of others. Many can recount a situation where they personally were cheated or unfairly treated or stories about injustices they have heard about on TV or from friends. As a messenger of God's Word, one usually does not know what issues of fairness and justice are most important to a modern audience, so it is important to listen carefully to the issues that are crucial in each setting.

Retired employees may be most concerned about the injustice of being told by a former employer that their benefit package will be reduced because the costs of doing business in today's competitive environment have risen too much. A taxpayer may be enraged at the injustice of government policies that allow huge amounts of money to be spent on researching the life cycle of the mosquito but refusing to fund Head Start programs. Divorced mothers may be discouraged over the injustices that allow their ex-husbands to get away without paying child support. Employers may be angry about the stealing of company products by employees. A school teacher may be concerned about the unjust way the school board dismisses a fellow teacher on the basis of nothing more than the questionable criticism of a few vocal parents. An African-American teenager may be upset over being unjustly accused of something just because of the color of his skin. A person may be angry at a local HMO for not covering the cost of a needed treatment for an elderly parent, while a retired person may be concerned about the unjust treatment by a broker who did not follow the investment instructions they agreed on. These are only a few possible places where the issue of justice arises in the lives of people in the church.

It is not hard to get people to agree that the injustices against them are wrong, for they personally feel the sting of being unfairly treated. It is more difficult to get people interested in the broader issue of God's view of the proper relationships between the rich and powerful and the poor and powerless. This is partially because most people compare themselves to others around them and do not feel as if they are rich or powerful. Also, some feel that a good portion of the poor are lazy and prefer to just collect money from the government. In spite of prejudice or misunderstanding, people do need to think about the broad roles government should play in regulating fair economic activity, caring for the poor, and protecting the rights of all people.

This can be a fruitful area to investigate if national, state, or community leaders are present in the congregation, because these people set policies in these areas. Even beyond the importance of these discussions to key social and political leaders, the voters who elect government officials to administer programs that address these issues should be concerned about justice in public policy. The broad issues of justice are not some impersonal problem that unnamed people in government should correct; they must be dealt with at every level of political and economic decision making. These policies affect people's welfare and should be the interest of every citizen.

For the Christian this issue is doubly important because the Bible repeatedly places God on the side of the poor and against the wealthy and powerful.[18] God fought against the Egyptians and delivered his people from oppression in Egypt (Ex. 6:5–7). He destroyed his own people who crushed the heads of the poor into the ground (Amos 2:7). He promised to punish those who turned away the needy and robbed the poor of what little they had (Isa. 10:1–2). Proverbs 14:31 claims that "he who oppresses the poor shows contempt for their Maker, but whoever is kind to the needy honors God."

God is particularly concerned about the disadvantaged widows, orphans, and strangers, all of whom can easily be cheated (Ex. 22:21–24). Jesus showed his concern for the poor by encouraging people not to invite their friends over for diner but to invite the lame, blind, and poor (Luke 14:12–14). A. Kuyper said that "when the rich and the poor oppose each other ... both the Christ, and also just as much His apostles after Him as the prophets before Him, invariably took sides *against* those who were powerful and living in luxury, and *for* the suffering and oppressed."[19]

John Calvin warned the wealthy in his congregation: "If the poor souls that have bestowed their labor and travail and spent their sweat and blood for you be not paid their wages as they ought to be ... if they ask vengeance against you at God's hand, who shall be your spokesman or advocate to rid you out of his hands?"[20] N. Wolterstorff claims that the problems are even deeper because they are inherent with the modern capitalistic system that disadvantages one group of people to the advantage of another.[21] Although this is not the place for a debate of economic theory,[22] every social and economic system can be improved to make it more just.

---

18. R. Sider, *Rich Christians in an Age of Hunger*, 3d ed. (Dallas: Word, 1990), 39–64, has a whole chapter dealing with Scripture passages on this topic.

19. A. Kuyper, *Christianity and the Class Struggle* (Grand Rapids: Piet Hein, 1950), 27, 50.

20. J. Calvin, *The Sermons of M. Iohn Calvin upon the Fifth Booke of Moses Called Deuteronomie*, (London: Middleton, 1583), 770, from a sermon on Deut. 22:1–4.

21. N. Wolterstorff, *Until Justice and Peace Embrace* (Grand Rapids: Eerdmans, 1983), 23–42. He identifies a high degree of differentiation and value generalization as aids to the development of an ethos of self-sufficiency that employs peripheral people to gather surplus for the core wealthy people.

22. R. C. Chewning, *Biblical Principles and Economics* (Colorado Springs: NavPress, 1989), has edited a series of papers and responses that are helpful.

Our concern is not solely the arrangement of order in a society, but the evil people who twist and pervert even the finest system of ensuring just relationships among people. The Bible does not reject a system that allows for the ownership of property or claim that the wealthy are an evil consequence of a certain economic system.[23] Fair, respectful, and appropriate measures are available in most societies to deal with justice issues, but all too often individuals willfully misuse, ignore, or reject these social mechanisms to further their own selfish interests. In this process the natural human rights of others are trampled underfoot and oppression takes place.

The Bible does give some broad principles of relationships that may help correct some of our thinking. Concerning economic factors, there are two fundamental principles that Christians must remember. (1) God is the real owner of the land, all property, and all possessions (Lev. 25:23; Job 41:11; Ps. 24:1–2; Hag. 2:8), not the earthly person using what God owns. These are gifts from God to us, not earned rewards or rights that we deserve and can control in any way we wish (Ex. 6:8–9; Job 1:21; Eccl. 5:19–6:2). God even gives people the ability to earn wealth (Deut. 8:17–18). (2) In Bible times God was much involved in putting limits on economic activity and gave regulations as guidelines for ordering the social and economic relationships between people (see the laws in Ex. 21–23 and the prophets, who saw these laws being ignored).

These ideas are too often foreign to modern approaches that separate God from social and economic relationships. Work is often thought of as a secular activity, and hard-nosed labor negotiations are not perceived as anything God is interested in. The Bible suggests that God is much involved and interested in all human relationship. He is especially careful to notice where people treat others unjustly. "Justice for all" is a banner that the church should raise high as well as a motto we should live by.

---

23. D. C. Jones, "Economics in Theological Perspective," *Biblical Principles and Economics,* 111.

Outline of Micah

I. **God Is Coming in Power to Establish Justice** (1:1–2:13)
   A. God Is Coming to Destroy His People (1:1–16)
      1. God's Judgment on Judah Is Like Israel's (1:1–7)
      2. Lament Because Disaster Is Coming to Jerusalem (1:8–16)
   B. The Reason Why Judah Is God's Enemy (2:1–11)
      1. The Powerful Covet and Steal Property (2:1–5)
      2. The Powerful Reject God's Word (2:6–11)
   C. God Will Gather a Remnant (2:12–13)
II. **Just Leadership Will Come to Zion** (3:1–5:15)
   A. Evil Leaders Will Be Removed (3:1–12)
   B. God Will Establish Justice in Zion (4:1–8)
   C. Jerusalem Will Be Afflicted and Delivered (4:9–5:9)
   D. God's Removal of All False Hopes (5:10–15)
III. **Coming to God in Justice, Covenant Loyalty, and Hope** (6:1–7:20)
   A. A Covenant Lawsuit for Not Coming to God Properly (6:1–16)
   B. Trusting in God for Hope in a Time of Despair (7:1–20)
      1. A Lament of Hopelessness (7:1–6)
      2. Hope Is Found in God's Promises and Love (7:7–20)

Annotated Bibliography
on Micah

Andersen, F. I., and D. N. Freedman. *Micah*. AB. Garden City, N.Y.: Doubleday, 2000. A solid and detailed discussion of Micah's ministry and message.

Allen, L. C. *The Books of Joel, Obadiah, Jonah and Micah*. NICOT. Grand Rapids: Eerdmans, 1976. A good discussion of each chapter of Micah with a detailed introduction to the book (especially on the structure of the message), which concludes that a few sections of the book were later additions.

Barker, K. L. "Micah." In *Micah, Nahum, Habakkuk, Zephaniah*. NAC. Nashville: Broadman and Holman, 1998. A nice exposition of key interpretive issues.

Hillers, D. R. *Micah*. Hermeneia. Philadelphia: Fortress, 1984. Hillers has extensive textual notations on variant readings with a short commentary that uses Hebrew.

Kaiser, W. *Micah–Malachi*. Mastering the Old Testament. Dallas: Word, 1992. A good, practical, conservative exposition of the meaning of the prophet's message.

Limburg, J. *Hosea-Micah*. Interpretation. Atlanta: John Knox, 1988. A brief discussion of Micah's messages with some preaching suggestions. Limburg believes later editors added passages to Micah's message.

Mays, J. L. *Micah: A Commentary*. OTL. Philadelphia: Westminster, 1976. An extensive discussion of the long process of composing these messages (and their later additions) with a critical exegetical discussion of the text.

McComisky, T. E. "Micah." Pages 395–445 in *The Expositor's Bible Commentary*. Ed. F. E. Gaebelein. Grand Rapids: Zondervan, 1985. A good discussion of Micah's message with some Hebrew notes added for each section.

Rudolph, W. *Micha–Nahum–Habakuk–Zephanja*. KAT. Gutersloh: Mohn, 1975. A detailed critical German exposition of Micah.

Shaw, C. S. *The Speeches of Micah: A Rhetorical-Historical Analysis*. Sheffield: JSOT, 1993. This work focuses on identifying rhetorical markers and the setting of each message in the book.

Simundson, D. J. "Micah." In *The New Interpreter's Bible*, vol. 7. Nashville: Abingdon, 1996. A brief commentary with pastoral reflections on the text.

Smith, J. M. P. *A Critical and Exegetical Commentary on the Books of Micah, Zephaniah, and Nahum*. ICC. Edinburgh: T. & T. Clark, 1911. A detailed critical discussion of Micah that concludes that Micah did not write parts of the book.

Smith, R. L. *Micah–Malachi*. WBC. Waco, Tex.: Word, 1984. A somewhat brief study of this prophet with minimal exegetical comments.

Waltke, B. "Micah." In *Obadiah, Jonah, Micah*. TOTC. Downers Grove: Inter-Varsity, 1988. A conservative treatment of the message of Micah.

_____. "Micah." Pages 591–764 in *The Minor Prophets: Obadiah, Jonah, Micah, Nahum and Habakkuk*. Ed. T. McComiskey. Grand Rapids: Baker, 1993. A detailed study of Micah that makes excellent use of Hebrew syntax and semantics.

Wolff, H. W. *Micah: A Commentary*. CC. Minneapolis: Augsburg, 1990. A form-critical and detailed analysis of Micah with many textual notes (using a lot of Hebrew) and a thorough bibliography of books and articles on Micah.

_____. *Micah the Prophet*. Philadelphia: Fortress, 1978. Discussion of Micah's background as an elder in Judah, the main message of each section, and some sermons on several portions.

Micah 1:1–7

THE WORD OF the LORD that came to Micah of Moresheth during the reigns of Jotham, Ahaz and Hezekiah, kings of Judah—the vision he saw concerning Samaria and Jerusalem.

²Hear, O peoples, all of you,
   listen, O earth and all who are in it,
  that the Sovereign LORD may witness against you,
   the Lord from his holy temple.

³Look! The LORD is coming from his place;
   he comes down and treads the high places of the earth.
⁴The mountains melt beneath him
   and the valleys split apart,
  like wax before the fire,
   like water rushing down a slope.
⁵All this is because of Jacob's transgression,
   because of the sins of the house of Israel.
  What is Jacob's transgression?
   Is it not Samaria?
  What is Judah's high place?
   Is it not Jerusalem?

⁶"Therefore I will make Samaria a heap of rubble,
   a place for planting vineyards.
  I will pour her stones into the valley
   and lay bare her foundations.
⁷All her idols will be broken to pieces;
   all her temple gifts will be burned with fire;
   I will destroy all her images.
  Since she gathered her gifts from the wages of prostitutes,
   as the wages of prostitutes they will again be used."

THIS INTRODUCTORY MESSAGE sets the tone for the first section (1:1–2:13), which deals with God's coming to earth to establish justice through his judgment. The section is organized into several negative messages and a brief concluding promise of hope at the end.[1]

After a superscription that identifies the source, time period, and topic of the book (1:1), a series of short paragraphs focus on the sins of Jerusalem, which will lead to its destruction. These messages come from the early ministry of Micah before the time of Hezekiah. The initial judgment oracle (1:2–7) must come before the fall of the northern nation of Israel in 722/721 B.C., the lament (1:8–16) predates Sennacherib's attack in 701 B.C., and the series of oracles against the powerful leaders in Judah (2:1–11) probably refers to the wicked leaders in the time of Ahaz. The common theme uniting the section is that Judah's sin will cause God to destroy Jerusalem.

The Lord is coming against Samaria and Jerusalem (1:3); a wound will come to Jerusalem (1:9), and God will cause a disaster to strike this city (1:12). The structure of 1:2–7 includes a theophany report of God's powerful appearance on the earth (1:2–4) and a judgment speech against Israel and Judah (1:5–7). Since there is no record of Micah's preaching in the northern nation of Israel, the rhetorical situation must be an audience in Jerusalem that needs to learn from the situation facing Samaria.[2] If they observe the similarities between what is happening in these two countries, they will realize that a similar fate awaits Jerusalem. This warning should lead them to transform their behavior so that they can avoid God's judgment.

The Superscription (1:1)

THIS PROPHETIC BOOK begins in the usual manner: announcement of the divine source of the words that follow, the identification of the prophet who receives these words, the time periods when the prophet preaches, and a

---

1. See the extensive discussion of the structure in Allen, *Joel, Obadiah, Jonah and Micah,* 257–64, and his review of the way others deal with these issues; also J. T. Willis, "The Structure of the Book of Micah," *SEÅ* 34 (1969): 5–42; Hagstrom, *Coherence of the Book of Micah,* 45–59.

2. Mays, *Micah,* 25, 28, 42, 47, and Wolff, *Micah,* 46, 51, eliminate this problem by concluding that the universal statements (1:2) and some of the references to Samaria (1:5b–7) are later additions (because Micah is not concerned with idolatry in his other messages). But J. Willis, "Some Suggestions on the Interpretation of Micah i.2," *VT* 18 (1968): 378–79, shows how 1:2 fits in this context. Though some question his words about Samaria in 1:5b–7, they are consistent with the preaching of Hosea, who wrote before Micah. Even if one excludes any knowledge of Hosea, Micah was an adult when Samaria fell and certainly he knew about the idolatry there.

brief comment about the subject of the prophecies. This information is not part of the preaching of the prophet but was attached to these sermons when they were organized in a written form. The supernatural messages that the prophet "sees [perceives]" (*ḥzh*)[3] carry authority; they are not just the imaginations of a human being. The divine source of these words makes them important to preserve in Micah's day, and we too must seriously consider whether they have application to our lives in the church today. When God speaks, people must listen and learn.

The prophet Micah is from Moresheth[4] (probably "Moresheth Gath" in 1:14), a city about twenty-five miles southwest of Jerusalem in the Philistine Plain, between the major southern fortresses of Azekah and Lachish. Micah's ministry extends from the days of the Judean king Jotham, through the reigns of Ahaz, Hezekiah, and into the years of Manasseh's coregency with his father. This overlaps with the ministry of Isaiah, so additional background information about these kings and the situation in Judah can be gleaned from his preaching.[5]

God Will Come to Judge the Earth (1:2–4)

MICAH BEGINS BY describing the Lord's appearance in a theophany. This evokes not only a sense of awe and fear but also a sense of joy in his Hebrew listeners. The awe and fear arise because the power and glory of the majesty of God are seen coming to earth. The joy arises because of the Hebrew expectation that God is coming to defend his people and defeat their enemies as he did in earlier appearances (e.g., the Exodus events).

The initial call to attention that opens this section ("Hear") is surprisingly addressed to all the nations of the earth.[6] Everyone needs to see what God is doing and saying, not just the Hebrews in Jerusalem; his words have universal application because they have lessons for all people. God appears as King of the earth, who comes from his holy "temple" (the *hekal*, or kingly

---

3. D. Vetter, "חזה," *THAT*, 1:400–403, believes this verb is used to describe prophetic revelations.

4. Archaeologists think Tell el-Judeideh, just a short distance from Mareshah, is the site of this town.

5. J. Oswalt, *Isaiah 1–39* (NICOT; Grand Rapids: Eerdmans, 1986), 5–13.

6. This is not a new universal eschatological theme introduced in the Exile, as Wolff (*Micah*, 41, 51) suggests, for theopany language and events go back to God's appearance at Sinai in Ex. 19; historical events in Judg. 5:4; 2 Sam. 22:8–16; hymnic literature in Ps. 77:17–20; 114:3–8; and the prophets Nahum (1:2–6) and Habakkuk (3:3–15). J. T. Willis, "Some Suggestions on the Interpretation of Micah i.2," 377, believes that the references to the nations are actually the Hebrews listening to Micah. B. Waltke, "Micah," *The Minor Prophets*, 617, seems to agree with Willis.

---

palace) in heaven (Ps. 18:10; Isa. 26:21; Jer. 25:30) to dispense justice. God, who rules the earth from his throne, is holy; therefore, all his acts are just. God will not only judge his enemies, but he will also be a witness against all unjust defendants[7] (cf. Jer. 29:23; Mal. 3:5).

The focus of attention in 1:3–4 is on the wonder of the Lord's appearance and how it affects nature.[8] The language may be borrowed from a well-known hymn that his audience recognizes and appreciates.[9] By using a hymn, Micah gains his listeners' acceptance, which would improve the persuasiveness of his sermon and the possibility that they will follow the theological logic of his presentation.[10]

As God reaches the high mountains[11] of the earth, everything is torn from its foundation. This is perhaps the imagery of an earthquake or volcanic eruption. The rocky mountains melt like wax (Ps. 97:5), and the level plains split apart. Nothing can remain unmoved and unshaken in God's powerful presence. If the solid ground and mighty mountains are dissolved before God's power, surely no nation can stand before a God with this kind of awesome might.

Up to here Micah's audience probably identifies positively with what he has said. The dramatic nature of the metaphors and the dynamic messages of this speech grab their attention. It is a popular message because the Hebrews looked forward to the day when God would come in power and judge the nations—particularly the strong nation of Assyria, which is threatening their future. But the following section contains some rhetorical surprises, for God's awesome coming is an expression of his anger over the sins of Judah, the people listening to Micah.[12]

---

7. Sometimes the heavens and the earth are witnesses (Deut. 31:28; 32:1) but not in this case.

8. W. Kaiser, *Micah–Malachi*, 31–32, notes similarities between the response of nature here and at Mount Sinai in Ex. 20:18–21.

9. Mays, *Micah*, 42, connects this to the hymn used in Nahum 1 (see Judg. 5:4; 2 Sam. 22:10; Ps. 68:8 as possible sources). It is likely that Nahum and Micah used the same earlier tradition from one of these texts. G. Stansell, *Micah and Isaiah: A Form and Tradition Comparison* (Atlanta: Scholars, 1988), 9–34, compares the use of the theophany in Mic. 1:2–4 in a negative context, with the use in positive contexts in Isa. 3:13–15; 30:27–33; 31:4.

10. See G. V. Smith, *An Introduction to the Hebrew Prophets: The Prophets As Preachers* (Nashville: Broadman and Holman, 1994), 5–46, for a discussion of various aspects of the process of persuading people to transform their thinking and behavior.

11. Not the pagan high places where false gods were worshiped.

12. Micah uses the "rhetoric of entrapment," similar to Amos 1–2, to set his audience up before he brings the bad news to them in Mic 1:5–6. See R. Alter, *The Art of Biblical Poetry* (New York: Basic Books, 1985), 142–46, or the discussion of Amos's method of entrapment in G. V. Smith, *Amos* (Fearn, Scotland: Christian Focus, 1998), 52–132.

God Will Judge Israel and Judah (1:5−7)

NOW MICAH EXPLAINS why ("all this is because") God is coming in power to judge.[13] First, God accuses the northern nation of Israel of insurrection or rebellion (*pš^c*) against himself, an idea that the people in Micah's Jerusalem audience readily support. Since Judah has recently suffered severely when Israel and Syria attacked them during the Syro-Ephraimite war (734−732 B.C.), Judah feels little love for the Israelites living in Samaria. But Micah goes on to raise two questions, comparing Israel's sin in its capital city of Samaria with Judah's sins in Jerusalem at its high places of worship (1:5; see 2 Kings 16 on idolatry at the time of Ahaz). This is a shocking comparison! How can anyone suggest that worship in Jerusalem is as bad as the corrupt religion practiced in Samaria?

God predicts the total destruction of the northern nation of Israel. The stones of her city walls and houses will be removed down to their foundations (1:6), and her idols will be destroyed (1:7). The land will then revert back to its original use of being a vineyard, a fate that began to be fulfilled when Sargon II destroyed the city a few years later (721 B.C.). This curse was finally completed when John Hyrcanus devastated the place in 107 B.C.[14] God is especially interested in the destruction of the idols of the fertility religion of Baalism in Israel, the real cause of his anger.

The "temple gifts" (*'etnan*, 1:7) are in fact the "wages [also *'etnan*] of prostitutes,"[15] the chief source of income for these houses of prostitution. These will all be either burned (1:7a) or given to others. This strange imagery suggests that the people of Israel will not profit from the money they spend on the gold to make their idols or their sacrificial gifts to Baal. Instead, the conquering soldiers will use this gold—possibly a reference to the soldiers spending this money to hire prostitutes for themselves and further their own depraved idol worship.[16] Verses 6−7 powerfully communicate God's verdict for Israel in first-person verbs ("I will"). By focusing on Israel, Micah alleviates

---

13. Verse 5 begins with a Heb. phrase that shows a connection between the sins in 1:5−6 and the theophany in 1:2−4.

14. Josephus wrote: "And when Hyrcanus had taken that city, which was not done til after a year's siege . . . he demolished it entirely . . . he took away the very marks that there had ever been such a city there" (Flavius Josephus, *Antiquities of the Jews* 13.10.3, in *The Works of F. Josephus*, trans. W. Whiston [Philadelphia: Winston, n.d.]).

15. On the meaning of this word, see J. P. van der Westhuisen, "The Term *'etnan* in Micah," *OTWSA* (1973): 54−61.

16. Hillers, *Micah*, 20−21, has this interpretation. Kaiser, *Micah−Malachi*, 33, and Barker, "Micah," 53, believe the money was used to pay for cult prostitutes and that it will have that use again. Also see W. G. E. Watson, "Allusion, Irony and Wordplay in Micah 1,7," *Bib* 65 (1984): 103−5, for a discussion of the meaning of some of the difficult words in 1:7.

---

some of the tension created by his earlier reference to the sins of Judah, but any thinking listener in Jerusalem will not have a hard time seeing the unstated negative implications for Judah, based on the initial comparisons in verse 5. What will keep Judah from suffering a similar fate? Has not Ahaz brought similar religious abominations into the temple in Jerusalem? Will God come after Judah next?

THE SPECIFIC CONTEXT of this message to the Hebrew people in Judah limits any direct application to the church, for it applies to the past destruction of Israel and Judah. But the theological truths it contains about God's relationship to humankind and nature provide a basis for raising questions about its implications for us today. Just as Micah's audience in Judah could draw lessons for themselves from what the prophet said about Israel, so we can learn things from this sermon.

The nature of God and his ways. Micah emphasizes that God is a universal God, who rules all nations and peoples (1:2); there is no person or thing outside his control. God is holy (1:2), so his rule is characterized by a just administration that is applied to everyone. God is a witness to the actions of the people in every nation (1:2), so nothing can escape his notice or his just response. God's power is also so great that it overwhelms even the most solid and permanent aspects of nature (1:3–4); therefore, there is nothing any nation or person can do to avoid the enforcement of his just decisions.[17] God's judgment of sinful and rebellious people will result in an overwhelming and complete destruction of all they hold dear and trust in, particularly those things that replace or stand in the way of the true worship of God (1:5–7).

These principles were manifest when God delivered his people from Egypt many years earlier. God ruled over all the earth, including Egypt (Ex. 9:29; 15:18). He was a holy and righteous God, who ruled from his heavenly habitation (9:27; 15:11, 13), and in his overwhelming power he brought ten plagues of nature and separated the sea so that his people could escape (chs. 7–12; 14–15). There was nothing that Pharaoh or his people could do to escape God's powerful judgment of their sins (9:27; 15:1–10). Egypt and the gods they trusted were destroyed (8:24; 9:6, 15; 10:7; 12:12); no other god could compare to Israel's God (9:14).[18]

---

17. See similar reflections in D. J. Simundson, "Micah," 7:544–45.

18. See J. I. Durham, *Exodus* (WBC; Waco, Tex.: Word, 1987), 89–210, for a discussion of some of these themes in the Exodus events.

These same principles will be seen in the future when God establishes his final kingdom. God will again take control of the fate of all nations in his seven bowls of wrath (Rev. 15–16). In his holiness (15:4) he will bring more plagues of nature on the earth (chs. 15–16) so that no one who blasphemes the name of God can escape from his hand (16:19). The resulting destruction will bring about the final defeat of the nations and the fall of Satan and his false prophets (16:17–21; 18:1–19:21). Then the King of kings will reign triumphantly in Zion forever (chs. 21–22).

These theological truths, which formed the basis for God's relationship to Egypt during the Exodus and his dealings with Israel and Jerusalem in the time of Micah, are still the foundation blocks for understanding God's relationship in our present era, and they will continue to be valid until the final days of humankind. It is essential that every person understands the nature of God and his ways, so that the mistakes and misunderstandings that existed in Micah's audience do not persist.

THIS SECTION DOES not directly address the problems in the capital city of any nation today (based on an analogy of what was happening in Jerusalem). Thus, one should not try to apply this passage to what is going on in London, Amman, or Washington, D.C., but try to focus on the timeless principles found within this time-bound message. But there are similarities between what God was doing in Judah at the time of Micah and what he is doing now and will do in the future. Consequently, the truth of God's divine revelation still has the ability to teach and convict women and men in quite different historical circumstances. Jesus himself said that if people are unwilling to listen to Moses and the Prophets, they will not be convinced even if one should rise from the dead (Luke 16:31). Through this he was implying that we must listen to what Moses and the prophets have said because their words are applicable to us.

Dealing with sin. Micah 1:2–4 asks all people on the earth, now as well as then, to hear or pay attention to what God is doing and what he is going to do. Just as God witnessed the acts of people in Micah's lifetime (1:2), the great evil in Sodom and Gomorrah (Gen. 18:20–21), and the violence of Nineveh (Jonah 1:2–3), he sees the evil going on in our world. He knows what is happening in the smallest tribes hidden from civilization among the jungles of the Amazon River, in the boardrooms of the major corporations that control the economies of the world, and in the bedroom of a tiny European baby.

Psalm 139 celebrates the fact that no matter where we go (heaven, Sheol, or the remotest parts of the earth), God's Spirit is present to lead and protects us. Amos 9:2−4 takes this same truth and shows that God's all-seeing presence makes it impossible for anyone to hide from his punishment. It is a sobering thing to imagine that God is a witness to everything we do, yet it is also a point of comfort when times are difficult.

These thoughts can lead people to respond in several ways. If we have dishonored God or rebelled against his guidance, God's constant watching is an unwelcome concept because it convicts us of wrong. We cannot fool him—an uncomfortable situation if we try to put on a good front at church on Sunday while secretly living another life during the rest of the week. The holy God has proof of our past failures, a record of incriminating evidence, and the inside story on what really happens. In light of his complete knowledge of our lives, we cannot shrink from our responsibility, blame others for our sins, or pretend ignorance. Each person must deal seriously with the problem of sin in his or her life or be ready to accept the consequences. Yet God is willing to forgive every sin and desires that no sinner should perish (Ezek. 18:23, 32; 2 Peter 3:9); thus, fear of his judgment can be removed through the grace of his forgiving love.

Micah offers a second factor that can motivate us to deal seriously with the problem of sin. He focuses on the overwhelming and irresistible power of God, pictured as an unstoppable force that melts even the permanent fixtures of nature (1:4). People need to realize that no military power, presidential decree, law, or personal wish can stand in the presence of a holy God when judgment is determined. If mountains melt like wax before his power, can people oppose him or defend themselves against his powerful hand?

Such a thought is not even voiced by Micah since it is so ridiculous. It would be like suggesting that people can stop the shaking of the ground in an earthquake or hold back the wind of a typhoon. No, when faced with these natural disasters, people run for cover and pray for mercy because the power of natural disasters can be enormously destructive. Yet 1:4 suggests that nature has no power when compared to the power of the God of heaven and earth. Since the Lord has this kind of might, we should all consider what we will say when we meet him and have to take responsibility for our deeds. No human being can hope to survive his anger. The only hope for us as sinners is to turn from the sin that enrages God and rest in the power of his grace, which brings forgiveness.

What God witnesses. No application of this passage would be complete without an explanation of what God has witnessed and why it makes him come in power to destroy parts of the earth. God witnessed rebellion and sin (1:5) among his chosen people, who were supposed to be a holy people, separated from the sinful ways of other people in the world (Ex. 19:4−6). God is equally displeased when he witnesses sinful attitudes and rebellion against his revealed will in his people today. Sin is especially disturbing to God when it involves the worship of anything or anyone other than God alone. The act of bowing to our own ambitions, serving ourselves, putting ourselves first, and loving our desires more than God's is nothing less than a veiled denial of God's lordship and divinity. If we put anything before God, he will witness that fact, and judgment will be forthcoming.

God is a witness to the sinful deeds of every individual and nation. The international chaos caused by evil choices of leaders in nations throughout the world may bring death to innocent people, but God knows what is happening. He knows what every person has done, so it is foolish to deny past failures or to believe we can get away with wrong choices. Jesus claims that all hidden and secret things will one day be revealed because God is a witness to all our deeds (Luke 12:1–3). Part of the future is thus determined by the past, so we must be aware that there are consequences for the way we live. Exercising freedom of choice is not the highest ideal for us; the discipline to make the right choice is much more important.

This passage suggests that God deals with sinful people in two ways: in surprising and undeserving grace, and in deserved justice. (1) In grace, he sends his prophets and preachers to convict people of their sins and warn them of his ways (Amos 3:7–8). This is what Micah is doing in this sermon. In his grace, God is patient and long-suffering with the wicked so that they may have an opportunity to repent (Jer. 26:17–19 shows that Hezekiah repented because of Micah's preaching in Mic. 3:12). God did not destroy Israel immediately after Jeroboam I built the golden calves (1 Kings 11–12) but sent prophets to warn them until their final end two hundred years later. God did not immediately destroy Nineveh (Jonah 3–4) but was gracious and extended the life of that nation about one hundred and fifty years. There is no need for God to be gracious, no necessity for him to show compassion. Yet, if God immediately executed just judgment for every sin, who of us would still be alive?

(2) The second way God deals with people is in deserved justice. This is the main emphasis of Micah's message, and it is an integral part of God's plan that the church needs to hear. Both God's grace and justice are based on the premise that he rules over all nations and individuals (1:2), is a holy God who witnesses what they do (1:2), and has the unlimited power to execute his will over human beings and nature (1:3–5). If these truths are accepted, it is not difficult to believe that God will eventually bring deserving punishment on people when his undeserved patience and compassion are ignored. Divine justice should be expected for sinful rebellion against God's revealed will, and especially for putting any person or thing in God's place (1:6–7). This will surely lead to divine justice and destruction.

Theodicy. In a certain sense, this passage answers some of the questions that lead people to question the justice of God's action. When a disaster happens, people often approach this issue from the perspective of what we do not understand about God's justice *after* the event; that is, we try to figure out the past (the problem of theodicy).[19] In this sermon Micah raises the question of theodicy (God's just rule of the earth) from a different perspective: the prophetic declaration of divine justice *before* it happens. This suggests that one can come at this question from the perspective of what one already knows about how God rules the world so that one will better understand what the future may bring.

In this context, the purpose of the prophet's message is to warn people of God's just punishment so that they may understand what he will do. This knowledge will give them and us an opportunity to respond and avoid his judgment (see this principle in Jer. 18; Jonah 3). Micah's message encourages his readers to examine what they believe about God's justice.

If the church can provide people with a broad theological perspective on how the justice of God works *before* they face such disasters, it may be easier to accept some of the unanswered theological questions *after* the fact (though, of course, all the emotional issues will not be solved by this approach). Micah is telling his audience in Judah about the nature of God, and he helps his listeners understand the future administration of God's justice. He does not answer every possible question, nor does he does try to deal with all the various ways God acts in different situations. Rather, he speaks to the needs of his audience in their historical circumstances.

In other words, Micah's application of the justice of God does not raise issues of Satan's role in bringing disaster into people's lives (cf. Job 1–2), the mysterious wisdom of God's different ways of bringing glory to himself (cf. John 9:1–3), or the testings that come to people (cf. Gen. 22; Deut. 8; Judg. 3:1; Heb. 11:17). His picture does not include these additional points because he is not trying to give a complete, systematic description of God's justice and because these issues have nothing to do with God's plans for Israel and Judah at this point in their history. It is thus inappropriate to make this brief treatment of God's future just dealing with his people in Judah and Israel into a paradigm that explains all of his past and future dealings with the human race. Nevertheless, this passage can help us understand what may happen if we reject God. Nothing can stand when his judgment comes in its full power.

---

19. P. Yancey, *Where Is God When It Hurts?* (Grand Rapids: Zondervan, 1990), deals with this problem of making sense of things after a tragedy strikes. For a discussion of key Old Testament passages, see *Theodicy in the Old Testament*, ed. J. L. Crenshaw (Philadelphia: Fortress, 1983).

Micah 1:8–16

⁸Because of this I will weep and wail;
    I will go about barefoot and naked.
  I will howl like a jackal
    and moan like an owl.
⁹For her wound is incurable;
    it has come to Judah.
  It has reached the very gate of my people,
    even to Jerusalem itself.
¹⁰Tell it not in Gath,
    weep not at all.
  In Beth Ophrah
    roll in the dust.
¹¹Pass on in nakedness and shame,
    you who live in Shaphir.
  Those who live in Zaanan
    will not come out.
  Beth Ezel is in mourning;
    its protection is taken from you.
¹²Those who live in Maroth writhe in pain,
    waiting for relief,
  because disaster has come from the LORD,
    even to the gate of Jerusalem.
¹³You who live in Lachish,
    harness the team to the chariot.
  You were the beginning of sin
    to the Daughter of Zion,
  for the transgressions of Israel
    were found in you.
¹⁴Therefore you will give parting gifts
    to Moresheth Gath.
  The town of Aczib will prove deceptive
    to the kings of Israel.
¹⁵I will bring a conqueror against you
    who live in Mareshah.
  He who is the glory of Israel
    will come to Adullam.

¹⁶Shave your heads in mourning
 for the children in whom you delight;
make yourselves as bald as the vulture,
 for they will go from you into exile

MICAH'S LAMENT IS marked off by his initial determination to begin lamenting (1:8) and his final
encouragement for others to join him (1:16).
Although some see a strong connection between
"this" (*zo't*) at the beginning of verses 5 and 8 and thus put verses 8–9 in the
first paragraph, doing so improperly separates the announcement of a lament
(1:8–9) from the lament itself (1:10–16).¹ The section is organized into the
following structure:

 1:8–9 Announcement of a lament
  v. 8 The prophet's determination to lament
  v. 9 The reason for his lament

 1:10–12 Lament for six cities in Judah
  vv. 10–12a The cities lamented
  v. 12b The reason for the lament

 1:13–16 Lament for five cities in Judah
  vv. 13–15 The cities lamented
  v. 16 The reason why others should lament²

This structure shows that the prophet was not just interested in lamenting by himself to put on a good show. The rationale that ends each paragraph
highlights the reason why lamenting is necessary and why others should
join him. Death and destruction are coming to Judah in the near future, so
people should stop fooling themselves into thinking that nothing will ever
happen to them (2:7; 3:11). God will bring a great disaster right to the gates
of Jerusalem (1:12).

The date of this lament is before the attack on Jerusalem in 701 B.C., but
no one knows how long before that event. Those who place it at 701 B.C.
when Sennacherib is already attacking Jerusalem interpret the perfect verbs
in verses 9 ("it has come"), 12 ("disaster has come"), and 16 ("[have gone]

---

1. Hagstrom, *Coherence of the Book of Micah*, 46–47, discusses these options. Allen, *Joel, Obadiah, Jonah and Micah*, 266–69, finds two paragraphs in 1:2–9 (vv. 2–5 and vv. 6–9).
2. This follows the general analysis of B. Renaud, *La formation du livre de Michée: Tradition
et actualisation* (Paris: Gabalda et Cie, 1977), 37, but organizes the material in a different way.

into exile") in a past tense, but it is better to view these verbs as pointing to future events (called the prophetic perfect)[3] that God *will* accomplish. These cities are not now in exile or even being attacked, for the prophet is using puns on the name of each city to tell the people who still live in these places what will happen. We date this lament either around 720 or 714–711 B.C., when the Assyrians were conducting campaigns in the area around Judah.[4]

The predictions in this prophetic lament were at least partially fulfilled by Sennacherib's invasion and conquest of forty-six cities, including his attack on Jerusalem in 701 B.C. (Isa. 36–37).[5] Like Amos's lament in 5:1–17, Micah is warning people of an impending problem that will strike them if they do not humble themselves and lament.

The lament nature of this message is introduced in verse 8.[6] In other texts this mourning theme is connected to the death or funeral of a loved one (Gen. 23:2; 50:1–4; 2 Sam. 1:17–27) or a nation (Lam. 1–4). People also lamented the approaching threat or death of a person because of sickness, oppression, injustice (Ps. 6; 13; Jer. 11:18–23), or the impending demise of a nation (Isa. 15:1–9; Jer. 48:36–44; Ezek. 26:27–36).[7] When people mourned, they often shaved their hair, wore sackcloth, sat in ashes, wept, and sometimes employed professional mourners.[8]

Since these were the normal cultural behaviors for people giving laments, one can assume that Micah follows some of these practices. This suggests that Micah is weeping as he sings this dirge. Maybe his plaintive cries would cause some in his audience to listen with a sympathetic ear to his warnings. Perhaps this lament, which identifies the prophet with the future sorrows of the people and reveals the agony of his heart, would cause some to realize that God is truly about to judge them. The fulfillment of this lament gives credibility to his words as he preaches in the following years.

---

3. See GKC, par. 106n; Shaw, *Speeches of Micah*, 56–67, reviews various possible dates and ends up dating this passage early in the time of Jotham.

4. The fact that the people of Judah are still in Gath suggests the date is before 711 B.C., when the Assyrians took it. See Allen, *Joel, Obadiah, Jonah and Micah*, 242. Wolff, *Micah*, 49, prefers a date not later than 722 B.C.

5. *ANET*, 287–88.

6. T. Longman III, "Lament," *Cracking Old Testament Codes*, ed. D. B. Sandy and R. L. Giese, (Nashville: Broadman and Holman, 1995), 197–213, gives a good introduction to the lament. See also the article by C. Westermann, "The Role of the Lament in the Theology of the Old Testament," *Int* 28 (1974): 20–38.

7. C. Westermann, *Praise and Lament in the Psalms*, trans. K. R. Crim and R. N. Soulen (Atlanta: John Knox, 1981), 261, describes the different kinds of laments.

8. G. Stählin, "κοπετός," *TDNT*, 3:836–41.

Announcement of a Lament (1:8–9)

THE LAMENT BEGINS with Micah's decision to "weep and wail" and go "barefoot and naked."[9] The Hebrew cohortative verbs "I will . . ." express the prophet's firm resolve to act.[10] No matter how strange this sounds to Westerners, Micah is following the ancient Near Eastern cultural pattern that expressed profound grief and sorrow over the approaching death and destruction of a nation (cf. Isa. 15:1–4; Jer. 48:37–38). This symbolic action is also meant as a sign act of things to come in the future; that is, Micah is behaving as the people will behave when this terrible disaster finally reaches Judah (cf. Isaiah's behavior in Isa. 20:1–4).

Micah's bitter cries have the weird and eerie sounds of the howling jackal and the loud screech of the ostrich (not "owl," as in NIV). The louder and more overt the expressions of grief, the stronger the pain that is communicated to others. Micah's ravings are a sign of his deep anguish over what is about to happen. Such a demonstration of wailing is sure to draw a crowd, which will be sympathetic to the pain of the grieving person.

The reason for this commotion was the "incurable" or inescapable wound that has hit the northern nation of Israel, which "will" (not "has," as in NIV) be inflicted on the city of Jerusalem (1:9). It is unclear if this wound refers to a military disaster, to the coming of the Lord (see 1:3 and 12), or to both these two factors. Though no military army is mentioned, Micah's audience knows that the Assyrians are the major international power at this time and probably assume that God may use them. Although this is shocking news, if the people of Judah follow in the footsteps of the Israelites (1:5), it should not be surprising that they will suffer a similar destiny.

Lament on Six Cities in Judah (1:10–12)

THE LAMENT PROPER begins with a series of puns on the names of six towns in the Shephelah near Moresheth Gath, the hometown of Micah. These towns seem to be chosen because puns can be made with their names.[11] The puns are like saying: Watertown will be covered with water, Washington will be washed away, and Waterloo will meet its waterloo. The puns that play on the sound or meaning of the name of the towns are as follows:

---

9. "Because of this" in 1:8 is usually taken to refer to what is said before it, but does it make much sense that Micah wails the destruction of Israel's idols (1:6–7)? Micah 1:9 and 12 pick up the theme of the coming of God in judgment from 1:3, which may be the connecting reason that "this" refers to.

10. B. K. Waltke and M. O'Connor, *An Introduction to Biblical Hebrew Syntax* (Winona Lake, Ind.: Eisenbrauns, 1990), 573, 34.5.1a, describe the possible uses of the cohortative form.

11. The location of some of these towns is unknown, and most have not been excavated.

the city	meaning/sound	the pun
Gath	the sound *gat*	the sound *tag* (Heb. verb "tell")
Beth Ophrah	"house of dust"	roll[12] in the dust
Shaphir	"pleasant/beautiful"	nakedness and shame
Zaanan	(similar sound)[13]	not come/go out
Beth Ezel	"house of taking away"	protection taken away
Maroth	"bitter"	good

In each case a disaster will happen and the town will suffer an evil end related to the meaning of its name. The themes of weeping (1:10), nakedness and shame (1:11), mourning (1:11), and calamity from God (1:12) give the listeners some insight into the nature of the terrible events that will happen in Judah.

Where will this disaster come from? Why will someone destroy Judah and Jerusalem? The answer is clear. The God of Judah is sending it on them. Since this problem will reach the gates of Jerusalem, one is left with the impression that the central government will be unable to protect any of the cities in Judah and that the enemy will attempt to wipe the whole nation off the map—including Micah and his listeners.

This claim probably sounds preposterous to some in Micah's audience, and it raises all kinds of theological questions: Will the God of Judah purposely try to destroy his own people? Why will he become a traitor to those who serve him? Is he not the God who lives in Jerusalem and protects it? What good will be accomplished by having a pagan king destroy Jerusalem? Can any army actually defeat Jerusalem and breach its strong walls? Does Micah really know what he is talking about?

Lament on Five Cities in Judah (1:13–16)

THE SECOND STANZA of the lament continues the puns of the first stanza. This additional set of towns adds to the force of the lament by showing how extensive the devastation will be. Town after town will be affected, from the smaller villages to the major fortresses like Lachish.

the city	meaning/sound	the pun
Lachish	(similar sound)	to the horses/team
Moresheth Gath	"to be betrothed"	you will give parting gifts

(chart continues on following page)

12. The Hebrew written text (*ketib*) has "I will roll myself," but the spoken text (*qere*) and Mur 88 (one of the Qumran group) have the imperative "(you) roll yourself," which is more fitting in this context. The NIV follows the spoken text.

13. The comparison between *ṣ'nn* and *yṣ'h* is a little stretched, but there is some overlap in sounds between the two words.

... the city	meaning/sound	the pun
Aczib	"deception"	will prove deceptive
Mareshah	"conqueror/possessor"	a conqueror against you
Adullam	the place where David fled	glory of Israel will flee there

Even Micah's home town of Moresheth Gath will be included in this destruction from God. Micah has probably visited many of these villages. These are not just far-off places he has only heard about. The friends he grew up with and his parents and relatives who live in these towns will have to face this terrible day of disaster. This makes the coming attack personal for Micah. His family will have to suffer as well.

Interpreters are unclear about the meaning of the prophet's comments about two of the towns. (1) Micah gives special attention to Lachish, a key defensive fortress protecting Judah's southern flank (1 Kings 9:19; 10:26; 2 Chron. 11:9). Mays believes the sin of Lachish that has affected the rest of the nation is her trust in military strength (see also 5:10). B. Waltke's suggestion that Lachish has borrowed pagan worship from Israel and led the Daughter of Zion into the sin of idolatry is less likely.[14]

(2) What is the meaning of the "glory of Israel" in 1:15? Does this refer to the king himself hiding out in a cave like David (1 Sam. 22:1), the men of rank in Judah running to hide (Isa. 5:13), or the riches of Judah being hidden? Rather than identifying one specific person, it is probably better to suggest that the "glory of Israel" points to all that is glorious in the nation. It will all be debased and forced to run for cover in a cave. This will not be a pretty ending for the people or the nation.

The lament ends (1:16) with two imperative exhortations to Jerusalem (using a second feminine singular form). The people should join Micah in shaving their hair (as in Isa. 3:24; 15:2; Jer. 16:6; 47:5) and mourning for many dear people (including delightful children) who will be killed or exiled in the near future.[15] This provides a final rationale for the lament. Surely some people will be moved to respond by the enormity of the destruction surrounding this event. People should cry out to God because of the devastation it will cause to others but also because it will reach to the very gates of Jerusalem (1:12). The unnamed conqueror will come (Assyria is never

---

14. Mays, *Micah*, 58; Wolff, *Micah*, 62; but see Waltke, "Micah," *Obadiah, Joel, Micah*, 155. Archaeologists have found several pagan temples in the excavation of Lachish; see *The New Encyclopedia of Archaeological Excavations in the Holy Land*, 3:897–911. They found a Middle Bronze Canaanite Fosse temple that was in use from 1550–1250 B.C. and a Canaanite acropolis temple. From the united monarchy of Israel there was a cultic area near a solar shrine.

15. The prophetic perfect verb refers to a future event as if it is already complete.

mentioned by name), and it is clear that this enemy will not be stopped by Judah's army.

It is a little surprising that Micah does not focus on Judah's sins in this lament. This is perhaps because he simply wants people to sense the tragedy that lies ahead. If they can feel the pain and start to wail, they will almost automatically be moved to ask Micah (or God) why this is happening and will want to ask God to stop it. When they are ready to plead for God to act on their behalf, then Micah can give the answer to their questions and lead them to the next step. But if the audience is unconcerned about the future, there is no hope they will ever change their ways.

Bridging Contexts

LAMENTING. Since this lament focuses on what will happen to specific towns in Judah, these warnings contain little in the message itself that we can relate directly to our day. The area where some lasting significance can be developed is in what Micah is doing. When the prophet of God sees people headed for sure destruction, he is moved to outwardly express his sorrow and encourage others to respond appropriately to what God is planning. This raises an important question. What is the purpose for laments in the Bible? The answer to this question will enable us to ask another question in the next section: Should Christian people lament today, and if so, under what conditions?

Lamentation and wailing seem to be a normal practice in the Hebrew culture of the Old Testament, and it is mentioned from time to time in the New Testament. People lamented for several reasons, such as the death of a friend or ruler (David lamented the deaths of Saul and Jonathan in 2 Sam. 1:17–27) or troubles with an enemy (many examples in Psalms). But the better parallels to this passage in Micah (as well as Amos 5) are those examples where someone weeps because people have not responded to the ministry of a prophet and will be judged. The prophet Jeremiah lamented his own personal trials and failures (Jer. 11:18–23; 15:10–21; 20:7–18), but he also mourned and interceded with God when he heard that God was going to judge his covenant people and send them into exile (8:18–9:2; 14:17–15:2). Listen to his anguish and his call for mercy in 14:19, 21:

> Have you rejected Judah completely?
>   Do you despise Zion?
> Why have you afflicted us
>   so that we cannot be healed? . . .

> For the sake of your name do not despise us;
>   do not dishonor your glorious throne.
> Remember your covenant with us
>   and do not break it.[16]

Although Jesus wept when Lazarus died (John 11:33–35), much more significant was his weeping over Jerusalem when he wanted to gather these people together into his kingdom as a hen gathers her chicks (Matt. 23:37; Luke 19:41). Paul also seems to be in mourning and anguish over the stubborn resistance of the many Jews who refused to respond positively to the messianic claims about Jesus (Rom. 9:1–3).

In each of these cases a messenger of God declares God's message, an audience does not accept that revelation, and the messenger expresses deep sorrow over the coming judgment. The first two elements are common to many forms of prophetic speech, but the third is unique to the lament. In the process of persuasion, the lament is a powerful alternative to accusations and condemnations. It expresses an attitude of identification and sympathy rather than opposition and conflict. The speaker takes the side of the audience and expresses regret (sometimes even uncomfortableness or disagreement with God—see Jer. 14:17–15:2) for what is about to happen.

This process should lead an audience to react appreciatively because of the support offered by the messenger rather than defensively because of the speaker's severe condemnation. In other words, the lament builds a bridge of commonality with the ones who will suffer, yet it does not deny the truth that God will bring judgment. In many ways the lament may be a more effective persuasive tool than the judgment speech because the listeners finally realize the emotional depth of the speaker's concern for the people being judged.

The reason for a lament must arise from the inner agony of the messenger, not from a desire to manipulate the emotional response of the audience. The apostle Paul was willing to have himself "cursed and cut off from Christ for the sake of my brothers" (Rom. 9:3), and Moses was willing to have his name blotted from God's book for the sake of the children of Israel (Ex. 32:32).[17] Jesus expressed deep sorrow for the stubborn and unresponsive people of Jerusalem, and surprisingly for the hypocritical Pharisees in Matthew 23.

---

16. See A. R. Diamond, *The Confessions of Jeremiah in Context: Scenes of Prophetic Drama* (Sheffield: JSOT, 1986), and M. S. Smith, *The Laments of Jeremiah and Their Contexts: A Literary and Redactional Study of Jeremiah 11–20* (Atlanta: Scholars, 1990), for a discussion of the interpretation of these laments.

17. J. I. Durham, *Exodus*, 432–33, makes the point that Moses goes through the emotional responses of pleading for mercy, anger, reasoning, taking control of the situation, and seeking forgiveness for the people.

It is essential to notice, however, that the movement to a lament is not accompanied by a modification of the speaker's theological beliefs. Micah still predicts the destruction of many towns in Judah—even Jerusalem. Moses and Paul do not all of a sudden change their minds about the sinfulness of their audience and take a mushy position that God's love will somehow overlook all their evil. These kinds of laments are not a sign of weakness, pastoral compromise, denial of responsibility, or softening of a belief in God's justice. Intercessory laments are personal expressions of deep sorrow that God is ending his long-suffering patience and bringing death. Why should we then not lament as Micah did when God decides to bring death on an individual or a nation? Do we not care?

THE NEED TO LAMENT. When I think of a past situation evoking lamentation, my mind remembers my mother-in-law, Dorothy, who died in her early fifties of Amytrophic Lateral Sclerosis (Lou Gehrig's Disease), or Glen, a close friend and neighbor who died a few years ago of an incurable cancer called Multiple Myeloma. If a friend or relative has one of these diseases, there is usually little hope of an extended survival unless God provides a miraculous deliverance.

In such contexts there seems to be little choice but to lament. You must learn to accept the inevitable, center your energies on whatever medical treatment is available, enjoy the pleasures of each day, try to keep your spirits up, and hang on to your trust in God's sovereign plan. Although you could easily slip into denial and avoid any discussion of death, the disease and its emotional consequences cannot be managed by refusing to acknowledge it. Most visitors feel uncomfortable talking to people with incurable diseases because there is little hope and no explanation as to why this is happening. In private there is plenty of lamenting and mourning, but a public expression of sorrow is usually silenced by social pressure.

This is a tragedy, for a great and horrendous darkness will befall millions of people in this world in the near future. Many will die in military battles similar to the one that fell on Judah. A few people will lament the loss of life in senseless wars and intertribal fighting, but there seldom seems to be enough will among national leaders or in the church to head off the deaths of thousands of innocent people. Some of these victims will die without any knowledge of the true God of Scriptures, and others will purposely reject the saving grace of God.

Unfortunately, there is little talk in the church today about lamenting the lost of this world, who will suffer the punishment of eternal death, and far too little talk of ending war. Moses, Amos, Micah, Jeremiah, Jesus, and Paul found grieving a fitting way of communicating to the people in their audiences their deep sorrow for those who will die (many without a relationship with God). But this cultural pattern of communicating one's deep feelings of sorrow is largely lost in many cultures. Why is this? Is there a fear of showing emotional weakness and vulnerability? Has the loss of this means of expression been caused by a theological weakness in the church? Has it resulted in any theological loss? Would it be appropriate for people in the church to lament today?

It is instructive to see the way people deal with the threat of physical death. Lamenting may be rejected because it is seen as blaming God. Or perhaps it does not seem to be a mature way of faith but a surrender to the negative instinct of giving up all hope. Others with good intentions may object to any sorrow by asking:

> Haven't the New Testament and resurrection morning effectively eliminated the need for lament? Aren't the Old Testament cries of anguish superseded, rendered unnecessary? Might they even be a sign of unbelief now that God has raised Jesus from the dead? . . . If Jesus' followers really believed in the resurrection, if they really believed in the power of God to overcome evil and provide joy and comfort in his Spirit, the lament wouldn't be needed. Maybe laments are for those who can't really believe as they ought.[18]

This kind of reasoning may sound like good theology, but it seems to imply that the coming age of victory is here already and that this present evil age of suffering is past. In one sense death was defeated by Christ's death and resurrection, but the final elimination of death and sorrow must yet be fulfilled at some future time (Isa. 26:19; 1 Cor. 15:26). Death still has power over believers and unbelievers. Those who want to eliminate grief fail to bring any comfort by their pious remarks and only increase the weight of grief for those who need to lament. Criticisms of mourning should not be centered on the sufferer's unbelief because the lament is simply an honest confrontation of God with questions and struggles that are not understood, plus emotions that are overwhelmed with sorrow and confusion.

A. Resner suggests that part of the reason for this dilemma about grief is that the church has lost the legitimate use of the Old Testament lament tradition.[19] R. Davidson suggests that our truncated canon, our lopsided liturgy, and our incomplete preaching of the whole counsel of God has created a need

---

18. A. Resner, "Lament: Faith's Response to Loss," *Restoration Quarterly* 32 (1990): 129.
19. Ibid., 132.

for psychotherapy and self-help groups.[20] He quotes a therapist who says that "churches have not learned that the best way to pass from defensive rationalizations to secure faith is to let doubt, inconsistencies, confusion and rebellion come out in the open instead of using various forms of spiritual coercion to keep them hidden."[21]

Believers do not need to deny feelings of pain and loss, for God was willing to listen to the groaning and weeping of his people in the past. He repeatedly responded to the cry of his people, comforted them, and helped them. Those who do not cry out to God make him irrelevant to their lives and delay healing by not embracing the pain they experience. The Old Testament believers did not exclude God as part of the solution to their misery but openly expressed their exasperation and grief over the calamities of life. The prophet Amos, Job, and the psalmists allow us to face the deepest fears and sorrows simply because they voiced their grief. They did not face their sorrow alone but brought it to God, who could do something about it.

Underlying the sorrow of these saints was a faith that believes God is trustworthy and understanding; he is a resource who can change the lament orientation into assurance and praise.[22] The effort to eliminate human laments to God has the effect of making God impotent to change our sorrows and unable to bring comfort to our spirits. It also eliminates the questions of theodicy and about the purpose, meaning, and justice of human life with God.[23] It discourages honest and open interaction with God based on what people really feel.

Those who discourage lamenting take away a canonical form of expression that was an accepted and meaningful way for saints in the past to deal with their grief.[24] The church should not teach people to suppress their deepest feelings and pretend we are big enough to handle the trials of life on our own without God. E. Kubler-Ross's study of the five stages of grief suggests that accepting death is only possible if people stop their denial and isolation, deal with their anger and depression, and gain the loving support of others.[25] Although she does not employ biblical laments, Old Testament laments were the Hebrew way of handling this issue constructively.

---

20. R. Davidson, *The Courage to Doubt* (London: SCM, 1983), 16.

21. Ibid., 17.

22. W. M. Soll, "The Israelite Lament: Faith Seeking Understanding," *Quarterly Review* 8 (1988): 79–85.

23. W. Brueggemann, "The Costly Loss of Lament," *JSOT* 36 (1986): 60–63.

24. S. P. McCutchan, "Illuminating the Dark: Using Psalms of Lament," *The Christian Ministry* 24 (1993): 14.

25. E. Kubler-Ross, *On Death and Dying* (New York: Macmillan, 1969), 38–88. W. Brueggemann, "The Formfulness of Grief," *Int* 31 (1977): 267–74, makes positive and negative comparisons between laments and Ross's approach to grief.

Lamenting God's judgment. If the church can come to the place where it will allow laments, then Micah's lament in 1:8—16 begs us to ask a second, more difficult question. Should Christians, or the church community as a whole, lament God's legitimate punishment of people and nations (like God's coming judgment on Judah, which Micah lamented)? This raises all kinds of disturbing thoughts. Do not rebellious people deserve God's wrath? Should we feel sorrow for those who have freely chosen to reject God and his will? Can one or should one really try to change God's mind on these issues?

Such questions reveal some of our deepest attitudes toward the ungodly. Should we pray against them or for God's mercy on them? Do we love them enough to have a theodicy crisis when God judges them? Do we just tell them a few Bible verses, or do we cry out to God in intercession for their lives? Do we show them our deep emotional hurt (assuming we do feel it) that God has rejected them? Moses, Paul, and Jesus lamented over those whom God would destroy, and I have seen a mother lament her son's death, but the church seldom follows these examples by expressing its profound grieving love for lost souls. Have we just lost our ability to lament, or have we also lost our compassion on those who will die and experience God's wrath?

Micah 2:1-11

¹ Woe to those who plan iniquity,
   to those who plot evil on their beds!
At morning's light they carry it out
   because it is in their power to do it.
² They covet fields and seize them,
   and houses, and take them.
They defraud a man of his home,
   a fellowman of his inheritance.

³ Therefore, the LORD says:

   "I am planning disaster against this people,
      from which you cannot save yourselves.
   You will no longer walk proudly,
      for it will be a time of calamity.
   ⁴ In that day men will ridicule you;
      they will taunt you with this mournful song:
   'We are utterly ruined;
      my people's possession is divided up.
   He takes it from me!
      He assigns our fields to traitors.' "

⁵ Therefore you will have no one in the assembly
            of the LORD
      to divide the land by lot.

⁶ "Do not prophesy," their prophets say.
   "Do not prophesy about these things;
   disgrace will not overtake us."
⁷ Should it be said, O house of Jacob:
   "Is the Spirit of the LORD angry?
   Does he do such things?"

   "Do not my words do good
      to him whose ways are upright?
⁸ Lately my people have risen up
      like an enemy.
   You strip off the rich robe
      from those who pass by without a care,
      like men returning from battle.

⁹ You drive the women of my people
    from their pleasant homes.
You take away my blessing
    from their children forever.
¹⁰ Get up, go away!
    For this is not your resting place,
because it is defiled,
    it is ruined, beyond all remedy.
¹¹ If a liar and deceiver comes and says,
    'I will prophesy for you plenty of wine and beer,'
    he would be just the prophet for this people!"

THESE VERSES ARE all part of one sermon. The idea of taking people's homes and inheritance is found both in 2:1–5, which refers to the powerful who covet and steal property, and in 2:6–11, which focuses on how the powerful reject God's instructions and take the property of the weak. The two paragraphs are also linked by "these things" (2:6), which refers back to the judgments discussed in 2:3–5. The date of this sermon is unknown but is usually placed in the reign of Ahaz, when wickedness was rampant in Judah. The opposition to a righteous prophet's words noted in 2:6 fits this period.

The audience seems to be made up of powerful people who abuse the rights of others.[1] The reference to taking garments from "men returning from battle" (2:8) suggests that this is shortly after a war. This may refer to booty taken from the defeated or to the taking of things from those who are fleeing to escape the ravages of war. Some see this reference as indicating that powerful people in the military are in Micah's audience.[2] The accused are called a "family" (*mišpaḥah*) in 2:3 ("people" in NIV), which suggests an identifiable class of powerful people in Jerusalem. A. S. van der Woude believes Micah is speaking to a group of false prophets, based on the interaction against prophesying in 2:6–7.[3] Instead, we think this dispute is against the powerful leaders in Jerusalem who have rejected Micah's announcement of divine justice in 2:3–5 and have accepted the positive hopes of the false prophets (2:6–7).

---

1. Wolff, *Micah*, 74–75, thinks Micah is preaching in his home town of Moresheth Gath before the elders in the gate about the evil ways of the civil and military authorities, but this is just a hypothetical guess. It seems more likely to place Micah in Jerusalem.

2. Wolff, ibid., 83, suggests this.

3. A. S. van der Woude, "Micha ii.7und der Bund Yahweh mit Israel," *VT* 18 (1968): 388–91. Allen, *Joel, Obadiah, Jonah and Micah*, 294, seems to take this approach also.

The first paragraph (2:1–5) is a short woe oracle that follows the traditional pattern of other woes (see Isa. 30:1–5; Amos 6:1–7) by beginning with a cry of woe (2:1), followed by a series of accusations (2:1–2), and concluding with a statement of judgment that begins with "therefore" (2:3–5).[4] The paragraph is held together by the contrasting use of the repeated vocabulary. The "plan" of the wicked is the "evil" of "taking away" houses and "fields" (2:1–2), but the "plan" of the Lord will bring "disaster/evil/calamity" on them and cause them to "take up" a taunting song because their "fields" will be assigned to traitors (2:3–4).[5] These people will reap what they have sown.

Several woe oracles in the Old Testament are associated with a lament for the dead or for those who are about to die (1 Kings 13:30; Jer. 22:12; 34:5), so one should hear this message as sorrowful words, similar to the lament in the preceding section. In a similar manner, the prophet Amos mourned in a woe oracle over the northern nation's deceptive misunderstanding of the Day of the Lord (5:18–20) and their foolish complacency because of their riches and power (6:1–7).[6] The woe oracles in both Amos and Micah lament the blindness of their audience's understanding and the tragedy that will soon engulf them.

The second paragraph (2:6–11) is a disputation speech,[7] in which the audience argues with Micah about his earlier prophecy (2:1–5), his theological perception of the nature of God (2:7), and God's relationship to his covenant people (2:6, 8). Other prophets dispute with their audiences over similar ideas (Isa. 49:14–21; Ezek. 33:23–29; Amos 3:1–8; Mal. 1:6–9; 3:13–4:3). In most cases the audience has misunderstood how God relates to his people and has accepted pious phrases, half-truths, and unbalanced teachings that assure their own prosperity and security. Tragically, these deceptions cause them to fail to deal seriously with the human responsibility to love and follow God completely and to treat their neighbors justly.

The Powerful Covet and Steal Property (2:1–5)

THIS PARAGRAPH BEGINS by explaining why Micah is lamenting in this woe oracle (2:1–2). The "woe" introduces a funeral-like lament (see 1 Kings 13:30; Jer. 34:5), which actually precedes the death of anyone in this setting; thus, it functions as a warning of what will happen. To persuade his audience

---

4. C. Westermann, *Basic Forms of Prophetic Speech*, trans. H. C. White (Philadelphia: Westminister, 1967), and W. Janzen, *Mourning Cry and Woe Oracle* (BZAW; Berlin: W. de Gruyter, 1972), 40–80.

5. Hagstrom, *Coherence of the Book of Micah*, 48.

6. See G. V. Smith, *Amos*, 238–39, on the background of the woe oracle.

7. A. Graffy, *The Prophet Confronts His People: The Disputation Speech in the Prophets* (Rome: Pontifical Biblical Institute, 1984), and D. F. Murray, "The Rhetoric of Disputations: Reexamination of a Prophetic Genre," *JSOT* 38 (1987): 95–121, describe this form of speech.

successfully of God's evaluation of the deeds of Judah's powerful military and political leadership, Micah must present an accurate portrayal of the situation and communicate his evaluation in a way that causes his listeners to consider seriously what he has said. The emotional appeal of his mournful cry and the logic of his accusation will help convince his audience. They are on the way to destruction and the grave if they do not change their ways.

Micah regrets the fact that some powerful people spend their evenings planning evil so that in the morning they can carry out their strategies of injustice (2:1).[8] The timing of these evil deeds is not when one usually expects crimes to happen. Most thieves work at night when no one can see them; ironically, these powerful thieves brazenly operate in broad daylight by using legal and illegal means to take what they want from others. Since they are people of status, wealth, and political influence, many have successfully added new land and property to their holdings.[9]

The spiritual problem is that these greedy people covet (*ḥmd*) in their hearts what belongs to others, in direct rebellion against the tenth commandment (Ex. 20:17). Their inappropriate and lustful desires lead to actions that ignore the theological principle that God owns the land (Lev. 25:10, 23; Num. 36) and has given it as an eternal gift to each family forever.[10] The powerful people rob some, oppress others, and defraud whomever they wish. The results are the same: People lose their homes and fields and become destitute. As Mays suggests: "In Israel's social order a man's identity and status in the community rested on his household or family, dwelling place, and land.... Lose it, and he lost all the rights which were based on its possession; he had no 'place' in the community."[11]

This loss of land also involves the loss of a sacred trust that God has granted to each family. Micah probably knows people from Moresheth Gath who have suffered in this way and has heard the sad stories of some who were tricked or legally outmaneuvered in the courts (2:8–9). The nation is in a terrible state, with many destitute people who have lost everything.

The abrupt "therefore" of 2:3 marks the change to the announcement of punishment and demonstrates a connection between the crime and its consequences. The messenger formula, "the LORD says," and the direct first-

---

8. According to Prov. 4:14–16, God does not want us to stay up nights planning evil actions against others (cf. Ps. 36:4).

9. Isa. 5:8–10 has a similar group of people in mind.

10. No land could be lost to a family for more than forty-nine years, according to the laws in Lev. 25. See J. A. Fager, *Land Tenure and the Biblical Jubilee* (Sheffield: JSOT, 1993); J. E. Hartley, *Leviticus* (WBC; Dallas: Word, 1992), 425–50.

11. Mays, *Micah*, 64; for an extensive discussion of property rights see J. A. Dearman, *Property Rights in the Eighth-Century Prophets: The Conflict and Its Background* (Atlanta: Scholars, 1988).

person address by God ("I am planning") emphasize the authority and sureness of what will happen. God's plan (counter to the plans of the wicked) is to send a severe and inescapable calamity against these wicked, oppressive people. They will no longer walk around in pride with their heads held high because of their wealth and privilege. The fact that "you will not be able to remove your necks from it, or walk upright" (lit. trans. of 2:3b) suggests that they will be under the binding yoke of someone else and will have no power or freedom (see Isa. 9:4; 10:27; Jer. 28:14). Once the wealthy are subdued, it will not be hard for this enemy to take their property away from them.

Micah then sings a brief sarcastic lament (2:4b), which will be sung by an unidentified lamenter, such as (1) the conquerors of the wealthy, (2) one of the poor people left in the land, singing to ridicule these former leaders in Jerusalem, or (3) one of the powerful leaders lamenting over what he and his friends have suffered and lost.[12] The sorrow of this lament song focuses on the hopelessness of the powerful, their loss of property, ("we are utterly ruined"[13]), and the giving of what was theirs to traitors (2:4).[14] Today one might mockingly say: "Isn't it too bad! It is so unfortunate, what these rich people had to go through. What they coveted and stole is now being coveted and taken from them. They're going to end up with nothing. Doesn't it just break your heart to see them get what they deserve!"

Some of these words are no doubt similar to what Micah has heard the poor people saying as they lamented when the Hebrew land barons were taking their land (2:1–2). Micah's lament suggests that these powerful landowners will soon be singing a similar tune. The wealthy will ask: How can God allow this to happen? How can my land be taken by the rebellious traitors of the nation who conquer the land?

Verse 5 is Micah's concluding comment after the mocking lament. When this disaster comes upon these elite leaders, they will lose all their rights to own land in the future. They will be excluded from participating in the redistribution of the land after the restoration of the people to the land. This picture imagines a reenactment of Joshua's original division of the land by lot

---

12. R. Smith, *Micah–Malachi*, 25, believes that one of the rich landowners will sing this song, but this is unlikely. The NIV translation suggests someone else is taunting them. Waltke, "Micah," *The Minor Prophets*, 639, thinks those who defeat Judah will mock the rich landowners.

13. There is repeated alliteration of the *s* and *d* consonants in this saying to give it a little extra flair.

14. The NIV uses the verb "divided" in the phrase "my people's possession is divided up," which is based on reading the verb *mwr* (to change, exchange) as *mdd* (to measure, divide), following the Old Greek translation of this word, which seems like an unnecessary textual emendation. Waltke, "Micah," *The Minor Prophets*, 640, also keeps the present Hebrew text.

(Num. 26:55–56; Josh. 14:1–2; 19:51). The exclusion of these evil leaders from the assembly of the Lord implies that these covetous people will all die or be purposely excommunicated because of their treasonous deeds against the poor. Hidden behind this devastating word of judgment is also the hopeful implication that some day the faithful people of God will again inherit the land (see Mic. 2:12–13; 7:11–12); the promise to Abraham will be fulfilled in spite of the destruction God will bring on the nation in the near future.

The Powerful Reject God's Word (2:6–11)

MICAH'S PROPHETIC WORDS do not please his audience. Consequently, they dispute his theological perspective on God and his relationship to his people, and they even try to get him to stop prophesying (see also Isa. 30:10; Amos 7:10–17). This paragraph is held together by its reference to the topic of who should be prophesying what, both at its beginning (2:6–7) and end (2:11). The main issue here is the audience's unwillingness to accept the prophecies of God given through Micah but their openness to accept whatever useless drivel a drunken prophetic deceiver may have to say. Of course the reason why they do not approve of Micah's messages is his condemnation of them as the enemy whom God will judge. Therefore, Micah weighs in with additional evidence to support his claim that these military and political leaders are oppressing God's people (2:8–10) and deserve his judgment.

The reconstruction of the dispute is difficult because one is not always sure who is speaking in each verse. L. C. Allen and J. L. Mays, after making some emendation of the Hebrew text, have the wealthy leaders of the house of Jacob being quoted by Micah in all of 2:6–7, while H. W. Wolff (cf. NIV; NASB) properly maintains the first-person pronoun in 2:8a ("my people") and sees this as Micah's rebuttal of the faulty theology in 2:6–7a.[15] There is also a debate about who is speaking in 2:6b, but this is heavily dependent on whether one follows the Hebrew text or emends it slightly.

First, Micah's opponents want the godly prophet(s)[16] to stop prophesying immediately. The word for "prophesy" (*nṭp*) is not the usual one by which prophets declare a divine revelation. The word *nṭp* means "to drip, flow" (Judg. 5:4; Amos 9:13) and may here be a derogatory term for the overenthusiastic sputtering and blabbering of a prophet.[17] Micah thus quotes his

---

15. Allen, *Joel, Obadiah, Jonah and Micah*, 292–96; Mays, *Micah*, 67–69; Wolff, *Micah*, 81–82.

16. The first imperative is plural, so it appears that there were other prophets with Micah (Hillers, *Micah*, 36). There is no other mention of other prophetic support for Micah in other passages, though one might assume that Micah and Isaiah encouraged one another.

17. Wolff, *Micah*, 81, thinks it "refers to a passionate, zealous manner of speech in which spittle sprays forth," a disparaging term for prophecy. See also R. Hess, "נטף," *NIDOTTE*, 3:97.

opponents' pejorative reference to himself, but then calls them the same term (Heb. "they drip/sputter," for NIV "their prophets say").

Some believe the last line of verse 6 gives the reason for this opposition to Micah (if the false prophets are speaking). These prophets believe that the disastrous things Micah has predicted in 2:3–5 will never "overtake"[18] them (cf. Amos 9:10; Mic 3:11). After all, they are God's chosen people, and the covenant promises guarantee them protection from God. The other option is to follow the Hebrew text (giving Micah a rebuttal both in vv. 6b and 7b) and take this line as Micah's prediction of shame and disgrace on the nation (see the preceding footnote).

Although both approaches make good sense in the context, we prefer to adopt the original Hebrew reading.[19] Thus 2:6 can be interpreted:

A. [The charge of the false prophets] "Do not give sputtering prophecy," they sputter.
B. [The rebuttal of Micah] "They are not sputtering prophecies concerning these things;
    shame will not be removed."

The second argument against Micah (2:7a) is that God will not do the kind of things Micah is predicting because he is not an angry God. They remember the ancient authoritative traditions that emphasize God as patient, long-suffering, compassionate, and slow to anger (Ex. 34:6; Ps. 86:15; 145:8; Jonah 4:2), and they use these truths to defend their position. In this case the wealthy leaders are not in error about the character of God; they are just half right—and at least half wrong.

A change comes again in verse 7b because this too is Micah's rebuttal. His response initially affirms what they say. Yes, God and his words are good. But then he suggests a major adjustment to their theology by claiming that God's goodness and blessings are experienced only by the upright, not universally by every Hebrew. The other half of the story is that he "does not leave the guilty unpunished" (Ex. 34:7), "will not acquit the guilty" (23:7), and "if you forsake the LORD and serve foreign gods, he will turn and bring disaster on you and make an end of you, after he has been good to you" (Josh. 24:20).

---

18. The final line can be interpreted with the NIV ("disgrace will not overtake us") as a statement by the false prophets, but the Hebrew text seems to have Micah saying, "Shame will not be removed." Allen, *Joel, Obadiah, Jonah and Micah*, 292 n. 40, emends *ysg* to *yśg* to get "overtake." The NASB and Waltke, "Micah," *Obadiah, Jonah, Micah*, 159, keep the Hebrew text and see this as a reply by Micah.

19. E. A. Neiderhiser, "Micah 2:6–11: Considerations on the Nature of Discourse," *BTB* 11 (1981): 104–5, also sees 2:6b as Micah's rebuttal and does not emend the Hebrew.

The wealthy land barons who have bought into the theology of the false prophets downplay or deny the reality of God's anger by forgetting that God unleashed his burning anger on Pharaoh and the Egyptians at the Red Sea (Ex. 15:7). He also burned in anger against Israel when they refused to go into the land from Kadesh Barnea (Num. 14:11–12) and in anger threatened to bring the covenant curses on the nation that worships other gods (Deut. 29:25–28).

The optimistic approach, which deliberately overlooks one whole realm of God's action and reimagines the Creator into a humanly synthesized and sanitized version of a great loving Santa Claus, has little basis in history, in revelation, or in personal experience.[20] Such reconceptualizations by the false prophets pervert what is known into what some wished for. The wealthy leaders are foolish to believe this comfortable but false view of God. Such theology turns God into an immoral being who does not distinguish between right and wrong and has no standards of justice. Thus 2:7 could be interpreted:

A. [The question of the false prophets] Should it be said, O house of Jacob:
   "Is the Spirit of the LORD angry? Does he do such things?"
B. [Micah's rebuttal quotes God] "Do not my words do good to him whose ways are upright?"

If God has promised to give good to the upright (2:7b), the key question is: Are the people in Micah's audience upright people, whom God will bless? Micah answers this question in 2:8–10, boldly claiming that God's covenant people are acting like enemies of God (2:8). This conclusion is based on the assumption that justice will characterize the way covenant people should treat one another. Since Micah's audience has grossly mistreated others, they cannot be upright and cannot expect anything good from God. To support this line of argumentation, Micah gives several explicit examples of injustice where the powerful have become enemies of God.

Using direct address ("you"), the prophet accuses some in his audience of taking the clothes of innocent people who are peaceably walking down the road just a couple days previous. This text is cryptic,[21] but it appears that the

---

20. Although it is true that all people filter their view of God in light of their own experience and what they have been taught, every view must ultimately be evaluated as an adequate or inadequate portrayal of all the revelation in Scripture. P. Berger and T. Luckmann, *The Social Construction of Reality* (New York: Doubleday, 1966), 129–47, discuss this process of internalizing the worldview of the society in which a person lives. The danger is that people internalize the misunderstandings of one's culture instead of allowing God's Word to redefine reality as he sees it.

21. See the various attempts to get at an acceptable translation in the commentaries. Many emend the text, while others try to explain the present text by finding later

Hebrews strip or unclothe unsuspecting people as if they are gathering the booty after a war (NIV), or that they steal clothing from people who are turning/returning from a war, or that they take clothing from peaceful people— that is, from defenseless people who are not armed like soldiers to defend themselves.[22] It sounds as if they are treating their own fellow citizens as they would treat some hated foreign enemy. No wonder God sees these oppressors as the enemy of his people. This verse probably does not refer to wealthy people not returning a pledged cloak to poor people who are in debt (see Ex. 22:26–27; Amos 2:8).[23] The exact circumstances of the innocent person who is attacked and robbed are not fully explained, but it is clear that the powerful leaders are unjust in their treatment of others.

Even worse is their relationship with the widows of the land. After suffering the loss of their husbands (possibly in war, though the text is silent on this point), widows would have great difficulty maintaining their homes and land. If they are not already in debt, soon they will find themselves so overwhelmed with debt that they will have no hope of repayment. Before long they will be "driven out" of the one piece of security they have left—their precious and pleasant homes. Such unjust heartlessness by the wealthy is devoid of all sympathy.

This problem, which is repeatedly addressed by the prophets, still existed in New Testament times (Mark 12:40) and is not unknown today. Instead of freely opening their hands to help the poor with generous gifts to meet their needs—which is the standard God desires (Deut. 15:7–18)[24]—the powerful take everything they can get their hands on. They leave people with no possessions, no dignity, and no hope for future generations.

In this unjust process God says these powerful people "take away my blessing from their children forever" (2:9). Some think the "dignity" of these small fatherless children is taken away, but the word used here (*hdr*) probably describes the "glory, splendor" of something given by God, specifically, the riches of land that each family could pass on as an eternal inheritance to their children (Jer. 3:19).[25] Many will never know the blessing God gave

---

redactions. See Mays, *Micah*, 67, or the suggestions of H. G. M. Williamson, "Marginalia in Micah," *VT* 47 (1997): 360–64, for further discussion of these problems.

22. Commentors like J. L. Mays, *Micah*, 69, see those living without a care as "averse to war," but this is not as good a translation as "those returning from war."

23. Kaiser, *Micah–Malachi*, 44, accepts this view but Waltke, "Micah," *The Minor Prophets*, 646, properly rejects it.

24. E. Merrill, *Deuteronomy* (NAC; Nashville: Broadman and Holman, 1994), 243–49, discusses the implications of this text.

25. Mays, *Micah*, 67, prefers "dignity," but Allen, *Joel, Obadiah, Jonah and Micah*, 297, sees the land as the glorious heritage God gave his people.

their ancestors because their eternal land grant has been removed from their control and enjoyment.

These brief accusations are concluded with a statement of judgment on the wealthy Hebrew landowners, who are God's enemies (2:10). Micah abruptly commands his audience to get up and leave this land, for it is not their resting place. Earlier God promised the people rest and security in the land he would give them (Deut. 12:9–10; 2 Sam. 7:1, 11; 2 Chron. 14:6; Ps. 95:11),[26] but Micah is nullifying that hope for these oppressive leaders. They will have no rest, no inheritance, no part in the future messianic rest that God will bring his people. They have "defiled" the land (i.e., made it unclean for God[27]); thus, it is "ruined" beyond hope and will be abandoned. Because they have destroyed the people to whom God gave the land, they will not enjoy its blessings but will be driven from it, just as Micah claimed in 2:3–5.

Having supported his original accusations against the powerful military and political leaders with additional evidence, Micah returns to the problem of the false prophets, who lead these people astray and cause many to reject God's revelation through Micah (2:11 picks up from 2:6–7). Why do the wealthy believe these sputtering, so-called prophets? Do the people in his audience have no perception of what a prophet is supposed to say and do (see 3:8 for Micah's view of a true prophet)?

With humor, scorn, and irony in his voice, Micah imagines a man "of the wind" (*ruaḥ*; not "of the Spirit,"[28] like the true prophet in 3:8), who is a deceptive prophet. If this known deceiver should come and "prophesy" (or "sputter"—the same root as in 2:6) about such insignificant issues as wine and beer,[29] he will be immediately embraced and accepted by these people as a fitting prophet. What a pathetic person to believe! What theology will this deceiver understand? The picture is meant to ridicule both the character and the message of the false prophets in order to undermine the bad theology these wealthy people follow.

These leaders are not interested in what God has said through Micah, but they are interested in hearing a windy discussion concerning what is the

---

26. See the excellent discussion of this theological theme in W. Kaiser, "The Promise Theme and the Theology of Rest," *BibSac* 130 (1973): 135–50, or G. von Rad, "There Remains a Rest for the People of God: An Investigation of a Biblical Conception," *The Problem of the Hexateuch and Other Essays*, trans. E. W. T. Dickens (New York: Oliver and Boyd, 1966), 94–103.

27. This concept is associated with the worship of idols in Jer. 19:13; Ezek. 22:15; 36:25, so one can see how detestable this oppression is to God.

28. For some odd reason the idea "spirit/wind" is omitted in the NIV, though in 2:6 and 3:8 it is included.

29. There is a nice wordplay between šqr (false, lies) and škr (beer).

best wine produced in the land last year. How can God accept the theology of people who rely on a prophetic source like this? This audience must critically evaluate the word of God they have heard from Micah and decide if it carries authority and is consistent with the theological framework of earlier revelation about God and his covenant relationship with his people. They need to recognize that Micah is a man who is filled with the Spirit (3:8).

THIS LONG SECTION deals with principles of God's equitable justice for powerful and wealthy leaders who mistreat others and who covet what belongs to others and the human problem of misunderstanding the nature of God and his revelation. The first issue is addressed in other contexts (see 3:1–4), so attention will be given to the last two areas.

Coveting what belongs to others. One of the central theological themes in this section is the disastrous consequences of coveting things that belong to someone else. Covetousness gets to the root of human sinfulness because it exposes a person's inner thoughts and the problem of self-control. E. J. Bush believes that Adam and Eve got into trouble in the Garden of Eden (Gen. 3) because they

> looked around with that anxious itch of covetousness in their hearts and said, "This is not enough. We're not really in control. We want to be like God." ... Nothing could stop them from grasping for the power and knowledge that would destroy their joyful, innocent relationship with their Creator.[30]

V. P. Hamilton agrees because "indulgence here would give to the woman something she did not, in her judgment, presently possess, and that is wisdom.... Here is the essence of covetousness. It is the attitude that I need something I do not now have in order to make me happy."[31] The decision to follow the inner desires of the heart led to a disastrous separation from God and the curse of death on all people. Adam and Eve could not control their selfish desires, so they took something that did not belong to them.

Coveting was also behind Ahab's murder of Naboth (1 Kings 21:1–29). Ahab originally was willing to pay for the field or trade Naboth's field for a better one, but when the deal fell through, the king became depressed and

---

30. E. J. Bush, "Last Commandment, First Sin," *Christian Ministry* 26 (1995): 34.

31. V. P. Hamilton, *Book of Genesis: Chapters 1–17* (NICOT; Grand Rapids: Eerdmans, 1990), 190.

angry. Naboth's unwillingness to accommodate the king demonstrates how important it was in Israel to maintain the family's inheritance on their ancestral land (1 Kings 21:3; cf. Num. 27:1–11; 36:1–12), based on the belief that God gave this land forever to his family.[32] Because of Ahab's deep desire for this property and his sullen attitude, his unscrupulous wife, Jezebel, concocted a plot to have Naboth stoned. This kind of event is similar to what is happening in Micah's day, perhaps even killing people to get their property (see 3:9–10).

The issue of the heart's desire (which can lead to coveting) is at the center of Jesus' new commandments in the Sermon on the Mount (Matt. 5:21–47). He is not content to argue that people should meet the minimum standards of not killing, not stealing, or not committing adultery, for he knows that some can outwardly keep these laws but still have deep internal struggles with their evil desires. Thus "Jesus ... focuses on a person's inner desires, intentions, and motives"[33] and reminds his listeners about the problem of coveting another person's wife or desiring to kill another person. As Olsen claims:

> The most important commandment is the first: you shall have no other gods.... Worshipping other gods ... wanting other things for our security or sense of happiness—that is at the root of why we break all the commandments. We worship things, so we steal. We worship pleasure, so we commit adultery. We worship power, so we kill.[34]

This worship puts our highest regard on something we want, and this attitude of coveting leads to actions God despises. Later, Jesus claimed that evil thoughts, murder, adultery, sexual immorality, theft, false testimony, and slander "come from the heart" (Matt. 15:8–19). These sins are committed because covetous desires motivate people to act in evil ways to get something that someone else has. Consequently, "for Jesus the inner attitude is of supreme importance."[35]

Jesus also told the parable of the rich fool, who built more and more barns for his crops so that he would have plenty of things laid up for a life of ease and fun in the future (Luke 12:13–21). Because this man was not rich toward God (12:21), Jesus warned his followers not to be anxious about

---

32. G. H. Jones, *1 and 2 Kings*, 2 vols. (NCBC; Grand Rapids: Eerdmans, 1984), 2:353–54, shows that people at Mari and Ugarit had similar customs in relationship to the sale of land, but there was a totally different approach in Babylonia.

33. D. T. Olsen, "The Beginning Is the End: The Coveting Commandment and the Sermon on the Mount," *Princeton Seminary Bulletin* 2 (1990): 159.

34. Ibid., 160.

35. D. A. Hagner, *Matthew 1–13* (WBC; Dallas: Word, 1993), 116.

---

the cares of this life (12:22–26). They should seek first the kingdom of God (12:31), for where their treasures were, there their hearts would be (12:34). A. B. Malherbe quotes the church father Chrysostom (*Oration* 17), who reminded his readers about the anxiety that wealth brings, warned about how covetous people carry out their plans at night, and argued for a proper proportion of goods and the avoidance of the pursuit of insatiable covetousness.[36]

It is interesting how John derives the source of sin from coveting things valued in our world or culture. He admonishes his readers: "Do not love the world or anything in the world. If anyone loves the world, the love of the Father is not in him. For everything in the world—the cravings of sinful man, the lust of his eyes and the boasting of what he has and does—comes not from the Father but from the world" (1 John 2:15–16). Coveting is self-seeking, an impulse or lust for satisfaction; it is one of the chief problems we must combat on a daily basis.[37] It is not just a sin that afflicts the poor, and it is not conquered by having great riches. Coveting comes from desiring more or better things so that one can have greater pleasure. Paul encourages the Colossians to "put to death, therefore, whatever belongs to your earthly nature: sexual immorality, impurity, lust, evil desires and greed, which is idolatry" (Col. 3:5).

Misunderstanding the nature of God and his revelation. The woe oracle and disputation define the nature and activity of God in unique and unexpected ways. The wealthy and powerful leaders in Micah's audience do not think that God will plan a calamity to remove them from their land (2:3–5), is so impatient with them that he will destroy Judah, considers them as his enemies, or reveals his will through a prophet like Micah. The central principle described here is that any person or group can fall into the trap of putting God in a humanly constructed box that inadequately captures the dynamics and richness of the Godhead.

A human theological construct may limit God's actions to a set of accepted beneficial activities, circumscribe his character around an incomplete set of attributes, or prescribe the revelation of himself only through a preset method or person. This limitation causes people not only to misunderstand how God has acted in the past but prevents them from comprehending his possible actions in the future. Such blindness leaves people unapproachable by the truth because they have ruled out certain things as impossible.

---

36. A. J. Malherbe, "The Christianization of a *TOPOS* (Luke 12:13–34)," *NovT* 38 (1996): 123–35.

37. See F. Buchsell, "θυμός, ἐπιθυμία, ἐπιθυμέω," *TDNT*, 3:167–72. He contrasts Greek views of this desire (which is a lack of rationality) and the biblical perspective (which sees this as sin).

To illustrate this point, it might be helpful to write down on a sheet of paper the different ways God reveals himself and to whom. Then compare this to what we know from the Bible to see how it matches up with what is written there. One might think that God would reveal himself only to his chosen people—maybe to people like Abraham and Joseph. But to our surprise, when Abraham sinned by lying about his wife, God did not speak to sinful Abraham but to Abimelech, the king of Gerar (Gen. 20:1–10). Later when Joseph was in prison in Egypt, God surprisingly revealed the future to the butcher, the baker, and Pharaoh, so that God could then reveal the interpretation of these dreams to Joseph (chs. 40–41).

Much later God instructed another pharaoh to fight the Assyrians, but the righteous king Josiah did not accept this news from God through Pharaoh and was killed at Megiddo in 609 B.C. (2 Chron. 35:20–24). To many people's disgust, Jesus mixed with sinners, touched lepers, talked to a Samaritan woman, ate with a tax collector like Zacchaeus, and called the traitor Judas to be his disciple. In all these cases God is revealing himself in untraditional ways to undeserving people.

Since his disciples were expecting Jesus to reveal his messiahship by defeating the Romans and setting up God's kingdom through earthly power, some seemed to be confused by his death. Amazingly, God chose to appear in a theophany to Saul, the unworthy killer of Christians, and miraculously transformed him into the great missionary to the Gentiles (Acts 9). Clearly there is a danger in limiting how or through whom God can reveal himself; yet many today have a narrow view of the possible ways God can work to reveal himself. Micah's audience also feels that God could never be speaking through this prophet and that he would not be saying the things Micah is prophesying.

Often the reason for limiting God (and thus rejecting truth) is a person's preconceived beliefs about the nature of God, the way he will act, or his view of us. Micah's view of God's character and his view of his audience deviate from the perspective of his hearers; therefore, he is excluded from the social role of prophet and considered a sputtering lunatic. They think God could not have said these things, which they perceive as contradictory to his character traits. In a similar manner, Amos prophesied that the Day of the Lord would bring destruction on Israel (see comments on Amos 5:18–20) and the end of the reign of Jeroboam II (7:9). Amaziah the priest then called Amos a traitor and rejected what he said (7:10–17).

Malachi knew that God loved his people, but they did not think this was true (Mal. 1:1–5). He preached the justice of God, but some in his listeners questioned if God really was just (2:17–3:5). The people in Jeremiah's day thought they were protected by God's presence in the Jerusalem temple, but

Jeremiah claimed they were trusting in deceptive words and that God would depart from the temple and destroy it and the city of Jerusalem (Jer. 7:1–15). Jesus attacked the legalistic teachers of the law and the Pharisees (Matt. 23), and Paul condemned those who wanted Christians to keep their old Jewish ways (Gal. 1–3). In each case we have people with incomplete, false, or wrongly applied ideas about God and themselves.

These types of misunderstandings lead people to reject the truth when it is declared by a true messenger of God. Such religious blindness and prejudicial views prevent people from seeing all of what God has revealed because their socially constructed view of reality excludes or reinterprets ideas so that the status quo is not disturbed.[38]

Every person has opinions about God based on culture and experience: Is he patient or impatient? Does he do only good or bring destruction also? Will he punish his own people? Which prophet or messenger of God should we believe? The answers to these questions are complicated, for God deals with real people in different ways and does not follow the same pattern in every case. Sometimes God even surprises his followers by unusual ways (e.g., Job, Jonah, Habakkuk, and Peter). God's ways are then a corrective to our slanted way of looking at things. If we remain open to learning new truth from Scripture, it is possible to renew our minds based on authoritative truth rather than church tradition, past experience, or personal preferences.

HOW HAS COVETING **affected our culture?** Does the problem of coveting exist in the economic systems of the world today? In many ways, coveting is at the heart of many economies. If all advertising removed any hints that might lead to coveting, how would this affect sales? If no one coveted for a month, would the sales rate fall precipitously in most industries and stores?

The rate of coveting is now measured by consumer debt and consumer confidence numbers—important numbers that signal future economic growth. This plague of coveting is not just part of the economy; it has infiltrated many parts of our materialistic culture. Ads in books and on television play on the lusts and desires of people. Coveting what others have is a major underlying cause of problems in situation comedies, romance and mystery novels, and movies. Coveting leads to immoral sexual relationships and even to murder.

---

38. Berger and Luckmann, *The Social Construction of Reality*, 19–46.

J. Stapert sees coveting and greed as a key problem in major-league sports.[39] Years ago players could not even imagine the idea of a strike because of their love for the game. Later, when unions were established, players began to covet the huge profits of the owners, who were being bankrolled by big television contracts. Deciding who is greedier is not the issue—neither group can manage their covetous desires. Stapert claims that "we fans would see both the club owners' and the players' greed for what it is, if we weren't so blinded by our own envy."[40]

This cultural acceptance of having and getting more and more has led to a cultural acceptance of coveting what others have. Paul encouraged people to be content with what they have and warned that the desire to be rich brings senseless and hurtful desires that will lead to destruction (1 Tim. 6:6–10). Many are now declaring personal bankruptcy because they cannot pay credit-card bills on the goods they have coveted. Is there any difference between shoplifting goods you have not paid for and leaving a store legally but later illegally refusing to pay for the goods by declaring bankruptcy?

The whole advertising industry knows the weakness of its audience and so appeals to the human desire to have more. If advertisers can appeal to a person's covetous desire to have the best and latest clothing styles like other people (certain labels on shoes and jeans), sales will be good, and the store owner's greed will be satisfied. Why have shopping malls become so popular? They offer "stimulations that arouse and titillate our acquisition fantasies, just as lustful people seek out stimulation that arouse them sexually. . . . It is not vicious to want to acquire things . . . it becomes vicious when it becomes disordered, when the desire for food or sex becomes obsessive."[41] Who has not felt a sense of greed after reading Ed McMahon's congratulatory news that you will be the next ten-million-dollar winner of the latest sweepstakes (if your number is chosen)?[42] Who has not felt a sense of envy and covetousness when they see the new car or house that someone has built because they won some money?

Coveting what others have motivates a great deal of crime. Those teenagers who cannot afford high-price labels on the latest fashions now steal the shoes off those who can afford them. Factory owners covet the success and power of other companies in their field, so they steal research information from their competitors to reduce their costs of research and increase

---

39. J. Stapert, "It's About Greed," *Perspectives* 10 (1995): 4−5.

40. Ibid., 5.

41. R. C. Roberts, "Just a Little Bit More: Greed and the Malling of Our Souls," *CT* 40 (April 8, 1996): 30.

42. P. Brasfield, "Fame, Fortune, and Greed: Ed McMahon and the American Dream," *Other Side* 27 (Jan.-Feb., 1991): 40−42.

their income. Violence erupts because one man covets another man's girl-friend. Robberies take place because people want the possessions that are in the home of someone else.

Generosity is an attitude that will counteract our natural desires of coveting and greed. "The generous person is loosely attached to goods and wealth and more deeply and intensely attached to God and his kingdom.... The generous person acquires goods in a different spirit ... she does not cling to the ones she has."[43] Generous people take joy in helping others, so they think of the needs of others and not just their own. They recognize the generous way God has blessed them and want to respond in the same way to others. Community good is often more important than individual success, and security in the future is not a major obsession. They have learned the truth of Jesus' statement that "a man's life does not consist in the abundance of his possessions" (Luke 12:15).

C. K. Lysons suggests three principles to guard against these sins: (1) practicing justice in paying people an appropriate wage (not too little or too much) and in charging people a fair price for goods (not inflating profits); (2) showing liberality and sympathy toward those in need, rather than selfish protection of possessions; and (3) living in simplicity or even poverty.[44] In the end each person must soberly assess his or her own attachment to things, learn to manage desires, and consciously reject any impulse to take what rightly belongs to another. Micah's audience has failed to do this, and God will bring disastrous destruction on them because of this.

How have we misunderstood the nature of God? Here's something to try. Ask the people in your congregation whether they think God is someone who will bring disaster on people based on their sinfulness. Is he a just God who rewards and punishes people fairly? Is Paul's admonition true in Galatians 6:7–8: "A man reaps what he sows. The one who sows to please his sinful nature, from that nature will reap destruction; the one who sows to please the Spirit, from the Spirit will reap eternal life"? Will God respond justly and judge my own sinful attitudes and behavior? Are our audiences deceived with the impression that God will not punish them?

This sense of invulnerability and of having a special and secure place in the mind of God is a common trap for religious people because many tend to think he will always bless them. Some will say, "Since I keep the Golden Rule, go to church from time to time, and believe that God exists, God will bless me. After all, I have never killed anyone." The wise man Job had to struggle with the dilemma of not always receiving the blessing of God, and

---

43. Roberts, "Just a Little Bit More," 30.
44. C. K. Lysons, "The Seven Deadly Sins: Avarice," *ExpT* 97 (1986): 241–42.

Christians today are frequently just as shocked and confused as Job when tragedies happen to them.

Part of this problem is created by pastors who concentrate almost entirely on the good news of God's love and forgiveness. It is right to emphasize that God is compassionate and long-suffering; it is appropriate to tell the world about his matchless love. But when a congregation comes to the point of denying God's deeds of judgment or acts of anger (like Micah's audience in 2:7), something is wrong. What are the danger signs? Micah gives several suggestions that might apply today.

(1) If a person stops listening to one of God's messengers who is faithfully preaching from a biblical text (cf. 2:6), it may be a sign of deceptive beliefs. People may express this resistance by complaining about the preaching or, in more severe cases, by trying to fire the pastor and remove "the problem" from the church. A less confrontational approach is to switch churches so that the individual can listen to someone with a more acceptable message. The reputation of Christ and the church is damaged when the effectiveness and liberty of faithful preachers are undermined by complaints about good biblical preaching or more trivial issues. These problems deflect the energies of those who preach the whole counsel of God and put the messenger on the defensive, lest someone be offended and raise more problems.

A sense of boldness is needed if the Spirit is going to convict people of sin and stretch a congregation to new heights of commitment and service. When a spirit of resistance and division arises, it is important for people on both sides to evaluate their theology and motives. Like Micah, a pastor must reflect on what is being said and determine if it is consistent with God's Word, or whether anything was said out of impure motives. Likewise, those who complain must examine their hearts and get together with the leadership to work out their differences.

Church conflict based on doctrinal differences takes on a more serious tone than problems of personal style, differences on changing a single phrase in the constitution, what color paint to use in the church kitchen, or developing a new motto for the church. Micah's difficulty relates to basic theological beliefs. His audience thinks that God is not impatient or angry with his people (2:7), so that the punishment Micah predicts (2:3–5) cannot happen to them (2:6). This false sense of security is partially created because of a slanted reading of past revelation, unbalanced preaching by other prophets, and a failure to apply principles of divine justice to themselves.

Many in the church also do not have a healthy fear of God's just anger at sin, even though this concept is repeatedly illustrated throughout Scripture. Some have wisely given up the fire and brimstone preaching of the past but in its place have substituted an anemic message focused on the common felt needs of their parishioners. If the issue of God's hatred of sin is avoided and God's help in becoming "all you can be" is the primary emphasis, it is not surprising to find that people have trouble applying any negative thoughts or actions to him. It is only logical to conclude that he will never bring disaster on us, if we are his people who worship him.

Micah presents two solutions to this problem. (1) The messenger of God can clarify the theological witness of Scripture to restore a balanced presentation of God's character. God is only good to the upright (though, to be sure, the rain falls on the just and unjust), not to everyone (Mic. 2:7). He is a just God, who distinguishes between his righteous followers and his wicked enemies (Ex. 34:6–7; Mal. 3:13–4:4). God's action toward any individual or group is not based on their size, might, financial or social status, education, skin color, or country of origin (even if it is Hebrew). His blessings or curses are influenced by the sin or obedience of people (Deut. 27–28). It is true that God sometimes gives grace because others are so wicked or because he is fulfilling a promise made years ago (Deut. 9:4–6), but it is dangerous to presume on that grace. Whatever the theological dispute may be in the church, all parties need a thorough and balanced understanding of the teachings of all of Scripture on a topic in order to resolve the conflict.

(2) The other approach Micah employs clarifies how God views those who reject his Word (2:8–11). Although they may think of themselves as religious people whom God would never punish (2:6), God looks at those who oppose his teachings (2:6), oppress the weak in society to enrich themselves (2:8–9), and follow the teachings of deceptive people (2:11) as his enemies (2:8). Not all of these conditions are necessary to be the enemy of God; in fact, any one of them can bring opposition from God.

The point of application comes in evaluating ourselves, our churches, and our leadership. Do we oppose the teachings of God in any way by twisting the intent of some verses or by ignoring others? Do we oppress or take advantage of the weak by what we say or do? Are we open to following the leadership of people who do not tell the truth but deceive people with pleasant words that entertain? Are people like this friends or enemies of God?

Since it is so easy to be self-deceived in any self-evaluation, often an outsider (note that Micah is not part of the group he condemns) can throw more light on the evaluation process and raise questions that will allow the Holy Spirit to begin the process of conviction and repentance. Such a person does not have social friendship with one party in the conflict, which could prevent complete honesty and a neutral perspective.

My own view of the church was altered by being immersed in another culture for a year. Seeing the way other people did things opened up new possibilities, plus the time away allowed for a fresh look at old accepted habits.

When I returned from my sabbatical year, what surprised me was the strangeness of the way things were done back home. In this passage Micah is the outsider whom God uses to give a shocking picture that the insiders are unable to see. Perhaps more church experiences in overseas areas by leaders and laypeople will assist in this process of self-evaluation at home.

Micah 2:12–13

12 "I will surely gather all of you, O Jacob;
    I will surely bring together the remnant of Israel.
I will bring them together like sheep in a pen,
    like a flock in its pasture;
    the place will throng with people.
13 One who breaks open the way will go up before them;
    they will break through the gate and go out.
Their king will pass through before them,
    the LORD at their head."

Original
Meaning

THE LARGER SECTION of Micah 1:1–2:13 is completed with a salvation oracle that provides the
possibility of hope for a future gathering of a remnant after the judgment of the nation. In some
ways this brief positive note is unexpected after the long series of negative
messages. Consequently, scholars have doubted the authenticity and meaning of these verses. A. S. van der Woude interprets these words as the foolish hope of the false prophets whom Micah is quoting,[1] but why would these
people be talking about a return from exile if they never believed the nation
would see disaster in Jerusalem (2:6)? Mays's interpretation of "breaker" (prṣ;
NIV "one who breaks," 2:13) causes him to view this as a judgment oracle in
which God sovereignly leads the people out of Jerusalem into exile.[2]

Some scholars see these two verses as an exilic or postexilic addition dis-
placed from its original location in 4:1–8,[3] while others see it as Micah's statement about the gathering of refugees because of Sennacherib's invasion in
701 B.C.[4] L. C. Allen makes the connection with 701 B.C. because he notices
similarities between the wording here and Isaiah's oracle of hope to Hezekiah
when Sennacherib was attacking Jerusalem (2 Kings 19:31; Isa. 37:32). He also

---

1. A. S. van der Woude, "Micah in Dispute with the Pseudo-Prophets," *VT* 19 (1969):
244–69, thinks these words are the lies and deceptions mentioned in 2:11.
2. Mays, *Micah*, 4–5, 28, but this destroys the balanced pattern of negative and positive
parts in each section.
3. Shaw, *Speeches of Micah*, 75–76, reviews the postexilic evidence (it has vocabulary similar to Jer. 50:8 and Isa. 52:12), but these words are not limited to exilic usage. Also one must
ask why an editor would take a verse from an appropriate context (4:1–8) and add it here
where it does not fit as well.
4. R. Smith, *Micah–Malachi*, 28.

believes this verse contrasts victory at the gates of Jerusalem with the destruction at the gates in 1:9, 12.[5] If Micah is predicting the coming of an army against the cities in 1:10–15 (including Jerusalem in 1:9, 12), it should not be surprising for him to give a word of hope about what God will do for the remnant after the time of judgment (2:12–13).

These words cannot be dated exactly (i.e., during Sennacherib's attack), because the description is too vague to be an eyewitness account of what happens.[6] The rhetorical purpose of 2:12–13 is to encourage the righteous (following the hints of hope behind 2:5), who are being oppressed in Judah. They need to know that God has not forgotten them and that there will be a radical change in their situation in the future, when God acts as king among his people (2:13).

The Lord describes what he will do in 2:12 in first-person language. Then, using third-person verbs, Micah writes in 2:13 how God will do this. God promises in strong overtones (using an infinitive absolute plus a finite verb[7]) that "I will surely gather all of you," giving the listeners great assurance of the promise of God's care. It arouses determination to walk by faith, knowing that in the future God will transform their situation. This promise is first pronounced on all of "Jacob," and then specifically given to "the remnant of Israel." These are not contradictory, for all that will be left of Judah after God's judgment of the powerful leaders (2:3–5, 10) will be a remnant.

This "gathering" and "bringing together" of many people "like sheep in a pen" implies a threatening force around them, possibly the destructive forces that come from God (alluded to in 1:10–16). God's shepherding is an activity of care and guidance that was the ideal of Hebrew kings (2 Sam. 5:2; Ezek. 34:1–6) and God himself (Ps. 23; Isa. 40:10–11; Ezek. 34:11–19). God will properly shepherd his people and not abuse them like the powerful leaders in Micah's audience. There is no indication of who will scatter the flock, how the one who scatters will be defeated, where the people will be gathered to, or when this gathering will happen.

Since the exact historical setting is hidden in the future (some think it may relate to Sennacherib's attack on Jerusalem), the focus falls only on God's gra-

---

5. Allen, *Joel, Obadiah, Jonah and Micah*, 301. Waltke, "Micah," *The Minor Prophets*, 652, has a fairly complete survey of the different ways interpreters have struggled to make sense of these verses.

6. Shaw, *Speeches of Micah*, 91–96, surveys the options of dating this to 722, 715, 701, but his own suggestion that it be put way back in the time of Menahem (2 Kings 15 at 738 B.C.) seems unlikely.

7. Waltke and O'Connor, *An Introduction to Biblical Hebrew Syntax*, 581–88, give examples of places where the infinitive absolute intensifies the verbal root; thus God says "I will *surely* gather."

cious care for his people. God has not and will not forget his faithful people in the midst of their trials. The final line of verse 12 describes the noise and excitement among those who are gathered together, not "confusion" as Waltke suggests.[8]

Additional information is provided in 2:13 to explain more about this promise. There are three references to God ("one," "their king," "the LORD"), who will lead his people out of a gate. This probably does not refer to God's breaking his people out of Babylonian captivity but to his breaking out of the gates of a city in power and victory.[9] Elsewhere God does "break out" in his anger to defeat his enemies (Ex. 19:22, 24; 2 Sam. 6:8).[10] Willis connects this idea to Davidic tradition, which recalls how "the LORD has broken out [*prṣ*] against my enemies before me" (2 Sam. 5:20).[11] This imagery suggests that the people will be trapped in a city and God will deliver them. Verse 13 focuses on God as the sovereign King, who will bring about this great event, not on how this breaking out will actually be accomplished. God's people do not need all the details spelled out; they act in faith, trusting that God will do what he has promised.

THIS PASSAGE CANNOT be taken as a promise that God will always deliver his people from harm's way or that God will always give us victory over our enemies. Sometimes God allows his people to suffer because of the sins of others (the powerful are oppressing people in Micah's day), and at other times he miraculously intervenes in his sovereign power to care for and guide the remnant who will follow him. This promise does not eliminate the need for the death and destruction of Judah's powerful

---

8. Allen, *Joel, Obadiah, Jonah and Micah*, 300, translates this line "bleating in fear of men," but there is no word for "fear" in this text. The NIV adds to the verse "the place" and then translates the verb *hwm* as "will throng" rather than the more usual translation "be excited, agitated, noisy." Although this word can mean "confusion" as Waltke, "Micah," *The Minor Prophets*, 653, maintains, this idea does not provide hope and seems to ignore the strong leadership of God at this time.

9. This may refer to God's breaking out of the city of Jerusalem against the Assyrians in 701 B.C. Kimchi has this same general idea but applies it to Zedekiah's breaking out of Jerusalem in 597 (Jer. 52:1–7). See W. McKane, "Micah 2:12–13," *JNSL* 21 (1995): 84–85.

10. Kaiser, *Micah–Malachi*, 45, thinks "the breaker" is the Messiah himself, but this finds in these words more than Micah seems to say (where is "breaker" used for the Messiah in earlier passages?). This approach opts for an eschatological interpretation of this promise rather than a historical one for Micah's audience.

11. J. T. Willis, "The Structure of the Book of Micah," *SEÅ* 34 (1969): 26, and G. Brin, "Micah 2, 2–13: A Textual and Ideological Study," *ZAW* 101 (1989): 118–24.

leaders (and it also negatively impacts many innocent bystanders caught in this setting), for God also promises to destroy them (2:3–5, 10). This promise offers hope and a future to those who can see only more and more hopelessness ahead.

The character of God. Two principles are fundamental to all believers as they look to the future hope that God promises. People need to be sure about his character and what he will do for them. This passage says little directly about God's character, although his kingly role and his "breaking out" imply that he has great power. His shepherding of his flock implies that he is loving and caring for each one of his sheep. He knows about the scattering of his people, so he will act on the behalf of the remnant.

The explicit promises in 2:12 (based on God's character) provide the listener a great sense of security. The followers of God can be assured that he has a plan ("I will ...") for the future and is not at wits' end trying to deal with calamities that happen to pop up unexpectedly. He will gather people (he will "surely" do so). This is not something that is just in the process of being thought out. His action is for his people, and he will provide safety for many. He will give good leadership because he is their king and leader. He will face the foe, and his power will overcome the enemy as he breaks out before them.

All of these factors function to support the rhetorical aim of this promise. As a messenger of God, Micah wants people in his audience to choose to trust God for their future, for he will sovereignly act on their behalf. Hope based on God's character, and his promises can transform people to act in faith.

CERTAINTY IN GOD'S **promises.** The character of God has not changed, and his actions on behalf of his people will continue into the future. These facts bring assurance and hope to God's people everywhere and cause them to trust him as they struggle through trials. Although no one can predict what God will do in any specific situation (not even Micah does this), Scripture contains promises (Ezek. 36–39; Dan. 7–8) that assure people today that God knows what will happen and that he will ultimately have victory over all forces of evil.

In his Olivet Discourse (Matt. 24; Luke 21) Jesus reveals some of God's plans. After the abomination that causes desolation appears in the temple (Matt. 24:15), the Son of Man will come in the clouds with power and great glory to gather his elect up into heaven (24:29–31). Knowing the future does not come from reading astrology charts in the newspaper; it comes from reading the Scriptures and understanding the character and plans of the Creator of the universe.

It is clear that God's justice brings judgment on humankind, but his plans also include the eventual restoration of his people to himself. God is not powerless to deliver and restore his people. Believers must stand fast in their faith in God, wait for his timing to reveal the next step, and rest in the assurance that he will do what he has promised. We have hope because God is still in sovereign control of all that happens.

How does one prepare people in a congregation for these future events? One way is to follow Micah's example and preach both God's judgment of sin and his glorious hope for his people. As J. N. Oswalt contends:

> There is no hope apart from judgment, and there is no judgment apart from hope. . . . He will be just and that means judgment, but he will be merciful and that means hope, and hope comes through judgment. What else is the Cross of Christ than the eternal vindication of the justice of God and the eternal proclamation of the mercy of God.[12]

If one believes in this supreme act of justice and mercy, the future justice and mercy of God fit as part of his eternal plan. A steady diet of basic Christian doctrine sprinkled into every sermon should provide a solid foundation for believers to face the future with hope. Then we can look through the eyes of faith to see and follow the divine plan God has revealed. There is hope because an all-powerful God who loves us is in charge of the future. He will not forsake his own but will gather them to himself.

---

12. J. N. Oswalt, "Judgment and Hope: The Full-Orbed Gospel," *TrinJ* 17 (1996): 201, illustrates this specifically in the writings of Isaiah.

❦

THEN I SAID,

"Listen, you leaders of Jacob,
   you rulers of the house of Israel.
Should you not know justice,
²   you who hate good and love evil;
who tear the skin from my people
   and the flesh from their bones;
³ who eat my people's flesh,
   strip off their skin
   and break their bones in pieces;
who chop them up like meat for the pan,
   like flesh for the pot?"

⁴ Then they will cry out to the LORD,
   but he will not answer them.
At that time he will hide his face from them
   because of the evil they have done.

⁵ This is what the LORD says:

"As for the prophets
   who lead my people astray,
if one feeds them,
   they proclaim 'peace';
if he does not,
   they prepare to wage war against him.
⁶ Therefore night will come over you, without visions,
   and darkness, without divination.
The sun will set for the prophets,
   and the day will go dark for them.
⁷ The seers will be ashamed
   and the diviners disgraced.
They will all cover their faces
   because there is no answer from God."

⁸ But as for me, I am filled with power,
   with the Spirit of the LORD,
   and with justice and might,
to declare to Jacob his transgression,
   to Israel his sin.

⁹Hear this, you leaders of the house of Jacob,
    you rulers of the house of Israel,
who despise justice
    and distort all that is right;
¹⁰who build Zion with bloodshed,
    and Jerusalem with wickedness.
¹¹Her leaders judge for a bribe,
    her priests teach for a price,
    and her prophets tell fortunes for money.
Yet they lean upon the LORD and say,
    "Is not the LORD among us?
    No disaster will come upon us."
¹²Therefore because of you,
    Zion will be plowed like a field,
Jerusalem will become a heap of rubble,
    the temple hill a mound overgrown with thickets.

THIS MESSAGE BEGINS the sermons given by Micah in the time of Hezekiah (3:1–5:15; see Introduction to Micah). Like the first section (1:1–2:13), this one has a similar series of negative judgment speeches (3:1–12), but it ends with a much longer series of positive promises of hope (4:1–5:15). The reference to Micah's preaching to Hezekiah (and Hezekiah's positive response) in Jeremiah 26:17–19 helps to date Micah 3:1–12 to an early period, before Hezekiah decided to follow God completely. Although some deny Micah's authorship of chapters 4–5 and give it an exilic or postexilic date,[1] I believe that the reference to the people's present travails (4:9–5:1) describes events in the years preceding 701 B.C. The positive promises of hope in 4:1–8 could be an encouragement to Hezekiah shortly before or during Sennacherib's attack on Jerusalem.[2]

Although Micah probably speaks the oracles in this section at different times during 714–701 B.C., in their present literary arrangement chapters 3–5 are connected by repeated themes. Willis suggests these sections are unified

---

1. Wolff, *Micah*, 117, and Mays, *Micah*, 95, think 4:1–8 is postexilic from the Persian period because of its dependence on Isaiah and the reference to the temple standing.

2. J. T. Willis, "The Structure of Micah 3–5," *ZAW* 81 (1969): 199, believes the purpose of 4:1–8 is to encourage Israel to trust God in a time of great distress. Allen, *Joel, Obadiah, Jonah and Micah*, 246–48, dates 4:11–5:15 to the Assyrian crisis in 701 B.C. but dates 4:1–10 later because of late vocabulary and a reference to Babylon (see discussion of these points in the commentary).

by five linking ideas that contrast Jerusalem's present unjust leaders in 3:1–12 with God's future just leadership in Zion in 4:1–8.[3] If God is going to remove the unjust leaders in Jerusalem by bringing judgment on Judah (3:1–12), there is hope for the oppressed. If God will one day set up his kingdom and cause the Messiah to lead his people and the nations to a time of peace and justice (4:1–5:4), there is hope for all humankind. If God is going to remove the nation's enemies, there will be no need for their sources of false trust—horses, strong cities, idols (5:5–15).

Such evidence leads to the logical question: Should the nation not turn from its evil ways and walk in the ways of the Lord today (4:5)? Jeremiah 26:17–19 indicates that Hezekiah and many of the people respond to Micah's preaching here by humbling themselves and trusting God. Thus, God delivers Hezekiah and Jerusalem from Sennacherib (Isa. 37), but he does not remove the Babylonian threat (Mic. 4:10) because of a lack of trust in God (Isa. 39).

The three judgment oracles in the first sermon (Mic. 3:1–12) are unified by their common condemnation of the leaders of Judah, who are unjust in their treatment of people. There is also a progression from God's giving no answer when people cry for his help (3:4), to his giving no answer when the false prophets look for help (3:6–7), to the implied no answer from God when the temple is destroyed (3:12). This is in stark contrast to the leaders' naive trust in the theological cliché that "the LORD [is] among us" (3:11). Both the first and third oracles (3:1, 9) are addressed to the leaders and rulers who are supported by false prophets (3:5), as in 2:6–11.

All three judgment oracles have a similar structure of an accusation and punishment. Part of the unifying glue that ties these pieces together are the ten common words found in at least two of these messages.[4]

The exact setting in Jerusalem for these oracles is unknown, although there is no doubt that the audience is Judah's powerful and unjust religious, civic, and political leaders. Micah's rhetorical purpose is "to persuade his audience that disaster will be the outcome of their actions ... shattering the

---

3. The five points of contrast of Willis, "The Structure of Micah 3–5," 196, are: (1) ch. 3 refers to the imminent future of Jerusalem, while ch. 4 refers to the distant future; (2) in 3:12 Zion is to be destroyed, but in 4:1 it is exalted; (3) the "heads" are condemned in 3:9, 11, but in 4:1 the mountain of Zion is the "head" (chief) of the mountains; (4) the unjust judges of 3:11 will be replaced with God's just judgment between nations in 4:3; and (5) in 3:10 Jerusalem is a city of bloodshed, but in 4:2–3 Zion is a place where God teaches all people and they beat their swords into plowshares. Willis's chiastic structural analysis of chs. 4–5 is given in a chart on page 212. See Hagstrom, *Coherence of the Book of Micah*, 68–83, for a discussion of different ways of looking at the structure of chs. 4–5.

4. Hagstrom, *Coherence of the Book of Micah*, 40, lists these words: my people, answer, prophet, divination, head, ruler, hear, justice, Jacob, Israel.

false security of his audience."[5] By the use of questions (3:1), an appeal to his own experience (3:8), the quotation of their own misplaced theological beliefs (3:11), and his confrontational and emotional style, Micah tries to get his audience to consider seriously their future and transform their thinking.[6] Although there is no direct call for repentance, Hezekiah's response of fearing God and seeking his favor (Jer. 26:18−19) demonstrates the convincing power of Micah's message and the working of God's Spirit in the king's heart.

The Removal of Judah's Unjust Leaders (3:1–4)

MICAH BEGINS WITH a call to hear what God has to say (cf. also 1:2; 3:9; 6:1). This message is given to the "leaders of Jacob, you rulers of the house of Israel" (3:1), a reference to the political and civic leaders responsible to ensure that justice governs all human relationships.[7] These officials include judges, who adjudicate civil and criminal trials (one of which is the king), and the elders of tribal clans, who serve both as military leaders and local judges to settle minor disputes (Ex. 18:25; Josh. 10:24; Isa. 22:3).[8]

The rhetorical question, "Should you not know justice?" has an obvious answer: yes. These people are to be knowledgeable of civic government regulations and religious laws in the Torah so that they can give normative rulings based on good reasoning and authoritative tradition.[9] This is the people's and God's expectation (Deut. 16:18−20; 17:8−13; Isa. 1:16−17; 5:7). By asking this question Micah raises doubts about what these people in leadership really know and do. Is justice actually being served?

God's dissatisfaction with the justice being carried out in Judah is evident in 3:2−3. These leaders "hate good and love evil"—just the opposite of what should be. To support this argument Micah uses the metaphor of cannibalism to exaggerate the depravity of this injustice. It is as if the leaders savagely and unmercifully tear the skin off people[10] and rip the muscle from

---

5. Shaw, *Speeches of Micah*, 121−22.

6. G. V. Smith, "Persuasive Rhetoric in Divine Inspiration," *Didaskalia* 8 (1997): 60−74.

7. J. R. Bartlett, "The Use of the Word רֹאשׁ As Title in the Old Testament," *VT* 29 (1969): 1−10. This word is used as early as Ex. 18:25 to refer to the leaders of the tribes of Israel who helped Moses administer justice during the desert journey.

8. Mays, *Micah*, 78, and Shaw, *Speeches of Micah*, 110, strongly support this military background, but probably the same person functions as the leader in all areas of life (military, family, judicial).

9. K. W. Whitelam, *The Just King* (Sheffield: JSOT, 1979), deals with the different people who helped carry out justice in Israel. V. H. Matthews and D. C. Benjamin, *The Social World of Ancient Israel: 1250−587 B.C.E.* (Peabody, Mass.: Hendrickson, 1993), 121−31, deal with the role of the elder, while 159−74 describe the monarch.

10. The Heb. text is unclear in the next to the last phrase in 3:3. Based on the parallelism, the NIV and most commentators suggest that *prś* (to spread out) be read as *prs* (to divide,

the bone to eat them. This picture is drawn from the behavior of a wild animal that has no conscience but only a desire to quickly satisfy its hunger. Half-starved beasts tear their victims apart, breaking bones. Drawing on another analogy, Micah claims these people are like cooks preparing a meal. The leaders chop up people for stew and throw their flesh in the pot to boil (3:3).

These are grotesque and violent pictures of inhumanity and barbarous acts.[11] Micah's analogy apparently refers to the leaders' unjust stripping of people of everything they have and treating them like animals. The government and civic institutions, created to protect justice, use strong-arm pressure and outright violence to get what they want. Micah may have witnessed some of this brutal lawlessness and lashes out with this scathing description to bring out in the open the dirty secrets of the powerful leaders in Jerusalem.

There is no indication that the people who are being butchered by these unjust leaders have done anything wrong, nor does the text say that they are just the poor people of the land.[12] This injustice ignores God's view that these are "my people" (3:3), a covenantal term of endearment that describes the solidarity between God and his people. These ruthless leaders ignore the biblical view that every person is made in God's image (Gen. 1:26–28). These acts are not what God-fearing, trustworthy, and fair leaders should do (Ex. 18:20–21). They are not following God's statutes in the Torah or making just decisions after prayerfully taking the case to God for his direction (Ex. 18:15–16). Certainly this kind of language gets the listeners' attention, puts their behavior in a new light, and brings everyone's focus back to the basic issues of justice.

God's response to their unjust behavior is to refuse to answer their prayers when they cry out for help (3:4). No mention is made of the punishment they will get, possibly because that is already presumed in an earlier oracle in this book (2:3–5, 10). They will soon find themselves in trouble and alone, but they will be without assistance from God when they lament their situation (see Deut. 1:42–45; Ps. 13:1; 27:9; Prov. 21:13; Isa. 59:1–2; Amos 8:11–12). Usually God is pictured as near and ready to answer and save people in need (Ps. 50:15; Isa. 55:6; 58:9; 65:24), but his grace and mercy will not be available to these leaders. As God said many years earlier, if the people fall into sin, "I will

---

break) and that the relative *kᵃ²šr* (as, like that) is a copyist's error of metathesizing the middle two letters and should be *kš²r* (like flesh). Both of these minor changes help to make sense of the problematic clause in this context and are accepted by almost everyone.

11. Similar grotesque imagery is used of oppression in Ps. 14:4; 27:2; Prov. 30:14.

12. Allen, *Joel, Obadiah, Jonah and Micah*, 307, and Mays, *Micah*, 79, believe this refers to the abuse of the poor. The identity of the oppressed is not clarified here, but probably includes both poor and those with money.

become angry with them and forsake them; I will hide my face from them, and they will be destroyed" (Deut. 31:17). This is a terrifying state to be in.

The Removal of Judah's Prophetic Leaders (3:5–8)

THIS SECOND PARAGRAPH focuses on the unprincipled prophets who "lead my people astray." God's covenant people are wandering aimlessly, being misled by greedy spiritual leaders who are out to get rich.[13] These prophets are supposed to be trusted as the voice of God to his people. Micah does not say that they are the worst pagan scoundrels that ever existed, that they are trying to get the people to worship false gods (Deut. 13:1–4), or that they give false prophecies because they are deceived by a lying spirit sent from God (1 Kings 22:19–28). In fact, some of them are perhaps receiving messages from God (Mic. 3:7). They look like normal Hebrew prophets and talk the right "God talk," but this has only made these prophets more deceptive.

Their downfall is that they love money and treat those more favorably who happen to slip a little extra cash in their hands (3:5). These spiritual leaders are not focused on faithfully delivering God's message to his people but slant and misrepresent the full force of his words based on a person's ability to give a financial gift. Those who give food or money to these prophets receive words of peace, salvation, health, God's blessing, and success. But if a person cannot afford a gift or does not give as much as the prophets expect, then the one who comes for divine advice will receive a hostile prophecy of war, death, divine judgment, and hopelessness.[14]

Holy wars were usually viewed as holy "crusades against infidels"[15] who rejected God, but in this case such dire invectives are pronounced on godly people simply because they cannot pay enough to meet the prophet's financial demands. A person's righteousness or love for God is not the basis of these prophets' blessings or curses; rather, the key factor is one's willingness to grease the hand of the messenger.

God is not pleased with this prostitution of the prophetic office. The logical result of their perversion is tit-for-tat. If they cannot deliver God's message faithfully, God will not deliver his message to them. These prophets will soon be "without visions, ... without divination," in "dark[ness] ... ashamed ... disgraced ... because there is no answer from God (3:6–7)." God will reject them, and they will lose all their enlightenment. Their perceptions of the

---

13. The verb $t^c h$ can mean to wander about (Gen. 21:14), stagger (of drunks in Isa. 28:7), or mislead (3:12; 9:15).

14. The false prophets sometimes did give negative messages; they were not positive about everything. Especially when they were not paid, they could be negative.

15. Allen, *Joel, Obadiah, Jonah and Micah*, 312.

---

future will be blinded. In this useless state, they will suffer disgrace and failure. Those who try to merchandise their prophetic gift to make a tidy profit will have it taken away from them. This implies that people will no longer come to them or pay them for their services.

Although it is legitimate to argue about what gifts these prophets really have, whether their messages actually come from God, or whether divination is a legitimate way of receiving a divine message, Micah chooses to skip these arguments and focus on an ethical question that is beyond the point of argumentation. No matter what one may think is the right answer to the earlier questions, these people are disqualified to be prophets. They are not primarily committed to giving God's words but to manipulating revelation to please the wealthy and punish those who do not line their pockets with cash.

Micah's prophetic role, by contrast, is centered around different priorities (3:8). The emphatic contrast is emphasized by the presence of the strong adversative *ʾulam* ("on the other hand" or "but as for me") and the emphatic personal pronoun *ʾanoki* ("I, myself"). Micah highlights the source of his inspiration (being filled with the power from God and the Spirit), whereas when the other prophets are described, attention is primarily on the methods of inspiration (dreams, visions, and divination). Micah speaks with bold conviction based on divine justice in order to make the sins of Judah known, while the other prophets speak based on financial payments in order to get rich. Micah's filling by the Spirit is the opposite of the false prophets' abandonment by God.

Micah 3:8 is not a reference to Micah's call to be a prophet[16] but to his continuing way of functioning in his prophetic role. He does not speak his own words from his own imagination but is filled with powerful words from the Spirit of God. God's power is the source of his "physical and psychic strength to stand up against opposition and discouragement."[17] His life is filled with, not merely touched by, the fire and motivation of God's Spirit. Micah does not let his own agendas determine what he will say; he surrenders his will to let the Spirit guide and empower him for his task. This filling by the Spirit results in a strong sense of God's justice and the courage to declare his words to others. Fear does not immobilize Micah, and favoritism does not guide his thinking.

This filling leads to the conviction that people in Micah's audience must hear what God thinks about their sinful behavior. His role is "to confront,

---

16. R. Smith, *Micah–Malachi*, 34, calls it "a kind of call narrative," while Mays, *Micah*, 84, believes it has the basic elements of a call story.

17. Wolff, *Micah*, 105.

stand opposite to"[18] their rebellion (rather than NIV "transgression") against God's authority. Micah and God are on the same wave length, for God's purpose in coming to earth in great power in 1:5 is also to reveal the sins of his people. Micah knows what justice is (contra the leaders in 3:1), and he has the fortitude to stand up for it in front of the nation's political and religious leaders. This sermon undercuts the theological message and motivation of these prophets. If they cannot be trusted by the leaders of Judah, these leaders will need to reevaluate all the positive messages from these prophets.

The Removal of Judah's Political, Civic, and Spiritual Leaders (3:9–12)

THE FINAL PARAGRAPH returns to address the same audience in 3:1–4, the leaders and rulers who despise the idea of limiting their behavior options by the principle of justice.[19] This paragraph is made up of accusations against these oppressive leaders (3:9–11) and a final announcement of judgment on the city of Jerusalem, the place where these leaders live (3:12).

In this oracle Micah specifies the injustice of politicians who build Jerusalem without concern for the cost of human life (3:10). The archaeological discoveries of Hezekiah's Broad Wall in the Jewish Quarter of the walled city (ca. 24 feet wide) and Hezekiah's Tunnel (2 Chron. 32:3–5, 27–30) in the Kidron Valley, plus new storage areas, testify to the expansion of Jerusalem and the need to protect and provide for many people within the city. These enormous construction projects would require thousands of manhours of hard physical labor to cut and move tons of rock.[20] Since the large army of Sennacherib may soon threaten the city's existence, there is no time to waste. These leaders do not worry too much about who gets trampled in the process; they are intent on getting the job completed. Consequently many people die.

Micah also accuses other civic and religious leaders of injustices (3:11). The judges accept bribes rather than conduct their work without showing partiality (see also Isa. 5:23) in direct rejection of the admonitions of the law (Ex. 23:1–8; Lev. 19:13–15; Deut. 16:19). Once again the desire for money in the judges' pockets, not doing what is right, determines what they do. The

18. Ibid. Although *ngd* means "to declare" in many contexts, it is not always a neutral term of informing people but can move over to the idea of "to confront."

19. Isa. 3:1–3 lists the hero, warrior, judge, prophet, soothsayer, elder, captain of fifty, man of rank, counselor, skilled craftsman, and clever enchanter as some of the leaders in Jerusalem whom God will judge.

20. Jer. 22:13–14 complains of a similar problem in the reign of Jehoiakim a hundred years later (cf. also Hab. 2:12).

priests and prophets are just as bad because they have devised schemes that will enable them to sell their theological expertise for money. Yes, the spiritually minded priest charges people when they come to be taught at the temple.[21] The prophets, of course, have gotten in on the same scam by telling the future for a fee.

The corruption and duplicity are unbelievable, but the leaders cover this all over by public expressions of piety (3:11b). They profess to trust, rely, or lean on the Lord; they are not pagans who worship other gods or secularists who do not think they need God. Their reliance is based on God's presence in their midst in the temple. They think that if the all-powerful God of the universe is in their temple in Jerusalem, it will be impossible for any nation to destroy them. They are immune from disaster; God's presence makes them untouchable.

What hypocrisy! With one hand they reject God's justice, but with the other hand they welcome his protection. This belief in God's presence goes back to the people's experience of God's being in their midst in the fire by night and pillar by day in the desert journey (Ex. 13:21–22; 14:19–20). It symbolized God's presence with them (33:2–5) and God's presence above the ark in the tabernacle/temple (25:8–22; 40:34; 1 Kings 8:10–13). The great Psalms of Zion also proclaim its invulnerable status (Ps. 46; 48; 84; 87). But Micah's audience has turned a conditional promise of divine presence based on the people's covenant faithfulness and love of God into an absolute, guaranteed right unrelated to their faith or behavior. Why would God protect these unjust and selfish hypocrites?

Micah interrupts this series of accusations with a powerful "therefore" (3:12), signaling the beginning of an unequivocal announcement of the removal of Jerusalem from the ancient Near Eastern map. In pointed style, Micah identifies the cause of Jerusalem's problems. It is "because of you" leaders that Zion will be devastated. God holds you accountable for your actions; therefore, Micah's audience will lose everything—their power, money, beautiful homes, stately buildings, even the walls of Jerusalem. Parts of the city will be leveled into a field for plowing, and the temple site will be a grove of trees and underbrush. There is no ambiguity in this statement. It is a powerful claim, warning of the end of Jerusalem. This action will prove that God is not a protector of unjust people and that he is not imprisoned in the temple. God is free to leave if his people reject him (see Jer. 7 for a repeated emphasis on these points).

There is an important footnote in Jeremiah 26:17–19 that needs to be added to this passage. It explains something about how the audience reacts

---

21. Mays, *Micah*, 89, thinks that this refers to the priest making judicial decisions (see Deut. 17:10–13) in parallel with the problems of the judges, but this is not described as "teaching" in those contexts.

to Micah's sermon. An elder at the time of Jeremiah remembers how Hezekiah and the people of Judah heard this divine message. When the king and all Judah realized what would happen, they feared the Lord and entreated his favor so that this disaster would not fall on them. Because they turned to God, God graciously decided not to destroy Judah at this time.

This demonstrates the true persuasive power of Micah's message and how God's Spirit is able to use these words to pierce the hearts of unjust and deceptive people. This response by Hezekiah (see Isa. 36−37) changes the course of history for Judah. But it happens only because Micah is willing to declare the sins of Judah.

THESE THREE PARAGRAPHS emphasize that God will hold political, civic, and religious leaders accountable for their actions. Although the context, responsibilities, and specific problems may be different for political, judicial, and religious leaders today, such people have a large impact on preserving justice for people in the cultures where they live. Because leaders, by the nature of their role, have unusual power to control the lives of others and easy access to the financial resources of the organizations they work with, there is great temptation to slightly (or grossly, in some cases) misuse these advantages for their own selfish gain or for the benefit of a friend.

Social and political power can bring special considerations and put unusual pressure on decision makers to do what influential people want. The desire to be powerful and financially well off can cause people in any culture or at any age to treat others unjustly so that they can reach the next higher level of status or authority. Micah's warnings, and the reasons behind those warnings, set down key criteria for evaluating leadership in the church, in government, and in civic organizations. These principles also have some parallel application to family and business life, but these are not the focus of this contextual setting in chapter 3.

Political and judicial leaders. The paragraphs dealing with political and judicial leaders (3:1−4, 9−10) center around the issue of justice and the far-reaching consequence of loving evil and hating good. This relates to the internal values a leader uses to act with integrity and fairness, both in legal relationships as well as common social relationships with others. Justice is a central characteristic of God (Ps. 145:17; Jer. 12:1; Dan. 9:14), for he acts rightly according to the terms of his agreements, with due respect for the duties and rights of each person.[22]

---

22. See D. J. Reimer, "צדק," *NIDOTTE*, 3:744–69; G. Schrenk, "δικη, δίκαιος, δικαιοσύνη, δικαιόω," *TDNT*, 2:174–78, 188–90, 195, 204.

Although right judgment is frequently associated with decisions that are consistent with the law of God, justice is not just an impersonal observation of some legal mumbo-jumbo. Since the will and justice of God is expressed in the covenant instructions, any breaking of a law is actually a rebellion against the authority and person of God.[23] Thus, justice is not primarily an abstract conception but a relational term that describes the appropriate behavior between two parties. In the case of earthly judges, just judgments are those decisions that impartially and fairly settle the claims of one person against another, based on the consistency of these actions with the will of God and the law of the land (Deut. 1:9–18; 16:18–20).

The establishment of justice functions to preserve the unique identity of the community by establishing a divine order and human respect between individuals. Principles of just behavior plus illustrations of unjust actions can be found throughout the Old and New Testaments.[24] One can point to examples where leaders operate on the basis of just decisions as well as those where justice is not carried out (e.g., Abraham's behavior in Gen. 12 and 20). A lack of just behavior changes King David's future leadership potential (2 Sam. 11–12), but the just and gracious behavior of Nehemiah toward financial matters gives him great leverage in transforming the behavior of the unjust people in Judah (Neh. 5).

Since God and most people watch what leaders do and have great expectations of their selfless service, it is essential to stand firmly on the side of justice if one wants to continue in a leadership position. Those who abandon God's way and forget about justice will sooner or later be abandoned by God and their followers when their deeds are uncovered (Mic. 3:4). Ripping God's people apart rather than leading them will not be tolerated for long. Leaders cannot treat people like objects to be sacrificed for their own pleasure, for injustices cannot be hidden from God.

Spiritual leaders. The second paragraph (3:5–8) deals with principles of spiritual leadership by providing both a negative and a positive example. Messengers of God who fail to give godly leadership can cause people to go astray by giving preferential treatment to people who provide special financial benefits, mistreating people who are of no value to them, and twisting the words of God based on how they feel about the person to whom they are speaking (3:5). Having the privilege of sharing what God has said carries with it a heavy responsibility to speak *only* what God has said as well as

---

23. W. Eichrodt, *Theology of the Old Testament*, trans. J. A. Baker, 2 vols. (Philadelphia: Westminster, 1961), 1:240, supports this position from the studies of Cremer, Weber, and Pedersen.

24. J. R. Clinton, *Leaders, Leadership and the Bible* (Atlanta: Barnabas Resources, 1993), gives many examples.

all that God has said. Micah realizes that this task requires one to share the truth consistently even when it involves negative news for close friends or good news for enemies—something the prophets of Micah's day will not do.

The messenger does not create the message; the messenger carefully hears what God says to each audience and then faithfully delivers that news to those for whom it is intended. If spiritual leaders let personal friendship or financial gain become a criterion that determines the message they speak to an audience, they may lead people astray from the truth and fail to carry out their divine responsibility (3:5). Micah presents some criteria that may open the blind eyes of those who are quick to point the finger at other spiritual leaders who are failing.

The person who gives godly leadership is filled with power and passion, commodities that are not common in the status quo culture of many churches. Of course, loud yelling should not be confused with power or passion, because the kind of power Micah is referring to is power that comes from the Spirit of God (3:8). This "filling" by the Spirit is not precisely defined, but the messenger has an overwhelming sense of complete control that results in submission to the divine presence. This power is partially manifested by the leader's commitment to stand for justice in all relationships, rather than be influenced by other factors.

H. W. Wolff quotes a wise statement by Pascal (*Pensées*, 298) that "justice without power is powerless. Power without justice is tyrannical. . . . Justice and power must therefore be connected."[25] A dedication to speaking about justice requires courage and powerful convictions because sooner or later one is going to offend people and cause controversy by rejecting commonly accepted patterns of unjust behavior. God considers these commonly accepted patterns of behavior sin, and a spiritual leader must be able to identify sin without hesitation. This will be impossible if a leader is not walking close to God.

Those religious leaders who fool themselves by winking at the minor ways they lead people astray must take seriously the warning of Micah (3:6–7). It is a serious matter to teach and preach what God says, for accountability is high (James 3:1). Those who treat this responsibility lightly will find themselves abandoned by God, just like unjust political and judicial leaders (3:4). God will not give them his messages, trust them with his words of advice, or answer their prayers. They will be disgraced before their followers (rather than being bold and courageous; 3:8) and will be cut off from God (rather than being filled with his Spirit).

A false sense of security. The final paragraph (3:9–12) addresses some of the same issues of injustice dealt with in earlier paragraphs, but it adds one

---

25. Wolff, *Micah the Prophet*, 152.

more characteristic that makes these civil, political, and religious leaders especially dangerous. They have a false sense of security and assurance about their work and their future, based on a deceptive conception of the presence of God in their midst (3:11). They think that since God's Shekinah glory has been in the temple and he is the almighty God, Jerusalem will be protected and not suffer any calamities.

Amos addressed the same deceptive false sense of security that arose earlier in Israel (Amos 9:10). It was based on a false trust in the nation's size, their wealth, and their military conquests (6:1–14). They had a false trust in the grace of God that had delivered them from Egypt (9:7–10). Over one hundred years after Micah, Jeremiah will again face this same false trust in God's presence in the temple (Jer. 7:1–15). It is a common problem for people to presume God is for them and will graciously protect them from all danger, based on some true biblical information. But frequently this conclusion is based on a misapplied text, a series of half-truths, unbalanced suppositions, or incomplete information.

It is true that God lives in the temple and that he is almighty, but these facts do not mean that he will protect the people in Judah if they reject him and act unjustly. God's relationship with his people is based on a covenant that requires his people to love him with all their hearts (Deut. 6:5), to fear him, to walk in God's ways, to serve him (10:12), and to be a holy people (Lev. 19:2). If the people enter into this covenant relationship and maintain a close walk with God, his blessings and protection will be provided; but rebellion against God brings his curse (Deut. 27–28). The truth is, important political, judicial, or religious leaders today have no guarantee of God's protection if they are unjust or lead people astray.

Contemporary Significance

MICAH'S CONFRONTATION OF the evil characteristics of leaders in his audience presents the possibility for the church to apply his three criteria to political, judicial, and religious leaders today. Micah is not just concerned about the affairs within the temple itself—the political, judicial, and priestly decisions the religious leaders make. He is concerned about justice within and outside of the temple; therefore, this application will address issues of justice within the church as well as in society in general.

(1) First, however, one needs to ask (based on Mic. 3:1–4) whether it is appropriate to apply criteria of justice to policies and practices of our political leaders. Although some question the propriety of being concerned about the moral life of a leader, God demands all leaders to be just. If the Bible

emphasizes this point, should not people in the church take a stand on injustices? We should support politicians who call for independent counsels to investigate shady practices and congressional committees that censure the flagrant breaking of rules. Unfortunately, it seems the more liberal the church, the more interest there is in political and social justice.

(2) Closely related is another question: How does the church evaluate its spiritual leaders? Should the church and society not reject religious leaders who lead people astray (3:5)? Do we accept as leaders in the church only those who are filled with the power of the Spirit, who courageously stand for justice, and who declare to people their sins? Are these the criteria pulpit committees look for? Are these the prominent characteristics of our denominational leaders, or are they chosen because they have been faithful to the denomination, are theologically safe, and have a popular reputation? Should we not ask about a leader's spiritual and moral character?

(3) Do the leaders of the church promote deceptive theological teachings, or do they attempt to uncover and expose the false cultural interpretations of the faith that parade around as the real thing? A similar question can be asked of politicians. Does this person I am about to vote for buy into some of the deceptive philosophies of our day (political, criminal, educational), or does he or she critique the culture and try to move people to a more realistic view of reality?

What kind of leaders are needed? In 3:1–4, 9–10 God condemns leaders who have a lifestyle of violence, oppression, selfishness, and injustice toward others. These are not, of course, the success traits that are held up as ideals in modern leadership books. J. O. Sanders lists egotism and jealousy as two of the main perils of leaders, but injustice and oppression are not at the top of the list.[26] Yet all too often selfishness and jealousy eventually lead to injustices toward those who are weaker. God rejected violence as an acceptable behavior pattern as far back as Noah's flood (Gen. 6:11–13), and he judged the Egyptians for their oppressive injustice to the Hebrews (Ex. 3:7–9; 5:14–16).

The legal traditions in the covenant stipulations present a strong case for civic and judicial justice for others (especially in the courts in Deut. 16:18–20; 17:2–7), and they specifically forbid oppression (Lev. 25:35–43; Deut. 15:7–18; 24:15). If modern leaders behave oppressively or unjustly, it is a sign that they do not fear God (Lev. 25:43). Leaders who act in this way have either thoroughly rejected God's instructions about justice in the Scriptures or are so perverted by their selfishness and rationalization of improper

---

26. J. O. Sanders, *Spiritual Leadership* (Chicago: Moody, 1994), 154–55. Other perils he identifies are pride, popularity, self-perceived infallibility, indispensability, and depression.

behavior that they no longer fully comprehend the distinction between right and wrong (Mic. 3:1).

This gets to the heart of integrity, a fundamental characteristic repeatedly highlighted in modern books on leadership.[27] If leaders cannot be trusted to do the right and just thing, how can one respect their decisions and follow them? Too often a leader's selfish goals and desires are given higher value than justice (3:5, 11). Money corrupts, and the pressure for big donations can tempt leaders to do things in secret that are not above board. Although it may seem contradictory and surprising to some in leadership, many citizens and church members wonder if their leaders (political and religious) are not far more interested in their salary packages and benefits than in issues of justice. God sees when any leaders treat others unjustly and will hold each of them accountable for acts of injustice and selfish attitudes toward money.

The veteran leader Paul encouraged the new leader Timothy to "command those who are rich in this present world not to be arrogant nor to put their hope in wealth, which is so uncertain, but to put their hope in God, who richly provides us with everything for our enjoyment" (1 Tim. 6:17). Paul also warned that "people who want to get rich fall into temptation and a trap and into many foolish and harmful desires that plunge men into ruin and destruction" (6:9). The desire for wealth can became a stumbling block to a leader's trust in God and a source of temptation to sin against another person, and it may lead to a false perception of reality.

James also confirms that God will judge unjust leaders who have "hoarded wealth in the last days. Look! The wages you failed to pay the workmen who mowed your fields are crying out against you.... You have lived on earth in luxury and self-indulgence. You have fattened yourself in the day of slaughter. You have condemned and murdered innocent men, who were not opposing you" (James 5:3–6).[28] These passages should cause church leaders and politicians to ponder their attitudes toward money and lead them to question whether money has in any way led to injustices in their personal life or in their community.

The broader principles of Scripture condemn people (leaders or followers) who center much of their attention on gaining possessions, are unprincipled or unjust in the way they achieve status and power, or place their hope and satisfaction in money or power (see Mic. 3:5, 11). If leaders center their hearts on God, they will value justice, serve others, and enjoy what-

---

27. W. Bennis, *On Becoming a Leader* (Reading, Mass.: Addison-Wesley, 1989), 160, connects the traits of constancy, congruity, reliability, and integrity as keys to giving people confidence in a leader.

28. For a survey of biblical statements about these selfish desires, see G. A. Getz, *A Biblical Theology of Material Possessions* (Chicago: Moody, 1990).

ever God has given them. If people take what God has given to another or obtain goods stolen through unjust dealings, God will correct the injustice by removing the unjust gains and eliminating that person from a leadership position. This is a prophetic message that every moral culture and every biblical church must live by and proclaim in the world today. Bonhoeffer said that "our being Christian today will be limited to two things: prayer and doing justice among men."[29] Such statements should not be taken lightly, for the level of devotion to prayer and justice reveals a great deal about a person's relationship to God.

Spiritual leaders like Billy Graham are respected and used by God because they do not get entangled with financial controversies and have a deep sense of the presence of the Spirit, filling their lives (3:8). Dr. Graham speaks boldly about sin, includes themes about God's justice, and is not shy about calling people to forsake the selfish cares of this world. Although no human leader is perfect or should be set up as the ideal example to follow, God can powerfully use leaders who allow the principle of justice to critique all their financial dealings and all their relationships to others. But God will abandon those who lead people astray through unjust behavior.

Dealing with theological deceptions. Like Micah (3:11), preachers and teachers must identify and confront the modern deceptions in our culture and in the church. Will being baptized in a church automatically guarantee a place in heaven? Will faithful attendance at church services and putting money in the collection plate result in God's hundredfold blessing? Will taking Communion magically produce forgiveness regardless of a person's true attitude? Will confirmation or church membership necessarily bring God's favor for the rest of a person's life? Does keeping the Golden Rule guarantee that a person will be treated kindly by God? Are these wise maxims to live by or deceptive myths that will eventually lead to ruin? Unfortunately, some people attempt to comfort themselves by rationalizing deceptive ideas that contain a portion of the truth but miss the overall thrust of what is needed to please and glorify God.

Sociologists call this kind of self-deception a reification[30]—a process whereby people view a social phenomenon as the only right way of doing things and give it an ontological status that makes it unchangeable. Thus, a person may believe that a human social institution like the church must always operate like the divinely designed pattern used by the early disciples in Acts 4:32–35. If one reifies this pattern, then no one may change any part

---

29. D. Bonhoeffer, *Letters and Prayers from Prison* (London: Collins, 1959), 300.

30. Berger and Luckmann, *Social Construction of Reality*, 89–92; see comments in the Contemporary Significance section of Hosea 10:1–15.

of this formula or adapt it to different situations or cultures. But if the church pattern in the New Testament was a human social institution guided by God to meet the needs of Jewish people during the famine in Jerusalem while the church was in its infancy, then the concept should not be reified and is open to change. People today are then free to ask how to conceptualize and organize the church to meet the needs of people today in different cultures, such as China, Brazil, Kenya, and Sweden.

Many in the Amish community have reified certain man-made cultural patterns of behavior and dress. They have given certain outward signs of their identity an absolute status, but other Christians look at the principles of modesty, humility, and separation from the world and conclude these ideas can be implemented without maintaining such a reified lifestyle.

The most serious reified self-deceptions are theological.[31] This happens when leaders or laypeople give divine authority and status to humanly created perceptions that do not fully represent what God has said or what he desires. Church leaders need to know what kind of false religious or theological securities people in the church, and those outside the church, depend on today. What beliefs or practices assure people that everything is right between them and God? Why do people believe God will bless them and protect them?

Naturally, the answers to such questions will vary, depending on the religious traditions practiced and the spiritual maturity of the person. I have spoken to people who believe they will be treated kindly by God because they have kept the Golden Rule. Others feel that their baptism as a child or the fact that they have taken Communion recently will please God. Others depend on a ritual prayer (the Lord's Prayer) or the repetition of some pious formula (the Rosary). There seems to be a widespread feeling that, if I do certain things, God will repay me with his favor. This is based on a general belief in the justice of God and biblical passages that connect God's covenantal blessings to human obedience (Deut. 27–28).

Like the Hebrews in Micah's day, people today still can be confused or deceived about God's presence and protection. Usually there is a partial basis in Scripture for deceptive thinking, but there is an overdependence on the goodness of God and a failure to appreciate the enormous impact of human sinfulness. Even though we may partially misunderstand the nature of the new covenant relationship we have with God, God will not be fooled. Thus spir-

---

31. R. Perkins, *Looking Both Ways: Exploring the Interface Between Christianity and Sociology* (Grand Rapids: Baker, 1987), 156–66, believes reification leads to exclusivity, parochialism, confrontationalism, pride, absolutism, and self-contradiction by modern Christians in the church. For example, not long ago Christains claimed that the Bible supported racism and slavery.

itual leaders (like Micah) have a serious responsibility and play an important role in giving members of their churches a balanced presentation of the whole message God has revealed in order to remove any false expectations about his protection.

Three issues raise problems with overly optimistic expectations of divine protection. (1) Human experience demonstrates that good people sometimes suffer unexpected tragedies. This has happened in my own family and in the families of two of our friends. It is a deceptive security to depend on your Christian beliefs or your good behavior to automatically bring material blessings, good health, and protection from all disasters. This is much like the case of God's righteous servant Job, who suddenly had God's blessings removed and his health destroyed (Job 1–2). When these things happen, it is not unusual for people to question God (cf. Job 9) because we live with the false security that bad things will not happen to good people.[32] Such incidents do not mean that God does not exist or that he is unjust; rather, they point to the fact that there is not always a one-to-one relationship between our actions and God's response in this world. People may try to limit what God can and should do, but such positive formulations only make the reality of life more bitter when God does not follow our plans.

(2) The Bible does describe the prophets being persecuted (Jer. 15:10–21; 20:1–6; 28; 37–38), Paul's many painful experiences (2 Cor. 11:23–29; 12:10), and Peter's advice that his audience should not be surprised if they suffer persecution (1 Peter 4:12–19). Yet many in the Western world today have a false security that they will not suffer or be persecuted because of their faith. In contrast to this view is the fact that many Christians in other countries are in fact persecuted because they believe in Christ (particularly in Muslim countries closed to the gospel). Their lives are anything but peace and prosperity, yet they live lives pleasing to God.

(3) It is all too apparent that many false securities are not based on a fundamental belief that every good thing a person receives is an act of God's grace (people somehow think they have earned it). It is a perversion to conclude that we will always get what we think we deserve in this life. If that were true, there would be no basis for any security for anyone, for everyone falls far short of God's holiness and rightly deserves God's immediate judgment.

The essential point these examples have with Micah's message is that people create false expectations and develop an empty security based on inappropriate theological grounds. At this point in Micah's sermons (3:9–11),

---

32. P. Yancey, *Where Is God When It Hurts?* (Grand Rapids: Zondervan, 1990), and P. Giesbrecht, *Where Is God When a Child Suffers?* (Hannibal: Hannibal Books, 1988) struggle with these questions.

the prophet does not attempt to create a positive set of criteria for authentic security but simply gives his own testimony about the things that make him tick (3:8). His main purpose is to remove those deceptive factors that cause people to develop a false sense of security. Spiritual leaders today must also warn people about imaginary securities that have no basis in Scripture or that twist biblical teachings to create false impressions of an easy way to earn God's approval. We must confess that we live totally by God's grace. A selective reading or slanted interpretation of the Bible needs to be challenged so that the blindness that covers people's eyes can be removed.

Micah 4:1–8

IN THE LAST DAYS

the mountain of the LORD's temple will
be established
as chief among the mountains;
it will be raised above the hills,
and peoples will stream to it.

²Many nations will come and say,

"Come, let us go up to the mountain of the LORD,
to the house of the God of Jacob.
He will teach us his ways,
so that we may walk in his paths."
The law will go out from Zion,
the word of the LORD from Jerusalem.
³He will judge between many peoples
and will settle disputes for strong nations far and wide.
They will beat their swords into plowshares
and their spears into pruning hooks.
Nation will not take up sword against nation,
nor will they train for war anymore.
⁴Every man will sit under his own vine
and under his own fig tree,
and no one will make them afraid,
for the LORD Almighty has spoken.
⁵All the nations may walk
in the name of their gods;
we will walk in the name of the LORD
our God for ever and ever.

⁶"In that day," declares the LORD,

"I will gather the lame;
I will assemble the exiles
and those I have brought to grief.
⁷I will make the lame a remnant,
those driven away a strong nation.
The LORD will rule over them in Mount Zion
from that day and forever.

> [8] As for you, O watchtower of the flock,
> O stronghold of the Daughter of Zion,
> the former dominion will be restored to you;
> kingship will come to the Daughter of Jerusalem."

THIS SALVATION ORACLE has two paragraphs: 4:1–5 and 4:6–8. These promises of salvation stand in stark contrast to the situation in Jerusalem described in 3:1–12. The problem of the Lord's absence in 3:4 is contrasted with his presence in Zion in 4:2; the destruction of the temple hill in 3:12 is starkly different from the exaltation and abundance of that same hill in 4:1, 4; the wicked "leaders" (*roʾš*) in 3:9 are contrasted with the glorious "head" (*roʾš*) of the mountain in 4:1; the oppressive bloodshed in Zion in 3:10 is the opposite of the end of war and the destruction of swords in 4:3; the wicked judges in 3:1–2, 9 function very differently from God when he judges in 4:3; the poor are abused in 3:2–3, 9–10, but they are gathered and strengthened in 4:6–8; the fake confession of trust in God in 3:11 is contrasted with the true confession in 4:5; and the prophets and priests do not give God's words in 3:5–7, but God himself teaches the people in 4:3.[1] These changes in Jerusalem show how godly leadership can transform this world.

The origin and date of these promises about the establishment of God's kingdom in 4:1–8 are viewed from various angles in commentaries. Since the contrasts between 3:1–12 and 4:1–8 are so pronounced, some authors conclude that 4:1–8 are postexilic additions by a later redactor, intended to soften the harsh judgment in 3:1–12.[2] But 4:1–8 does not contradict 3:1–12, since 4:1–8 does not rescind the earlier message by saying Jerusalem will not fall.[3] The contrast is over the approaching demise of Jerusalem because of its failed leaders and the future glory of Jerusalem because of the leadership of God himself.

---

1. Waltke, "Micah," *The Minor Prophets*, 676, describes fourteen contrasts; J. T. Willis, "The Structure of Micah 3–5," *ZAW* 81 (1969): 196, mentions several; E. Nielson, *Oral Tradition* (Chicago: Allenson, 1954), 92–93, also emphasizes these connections between chs. 3 and 4.

2. Mays, *Micah*, 29, 95, and Wolff, *Micah*, 21–22, 114–18, take this position because (1) Jeremiah 26:17–19 remembers Micah as a prophet of doom, (2) his calling in 3:8 is to announce to Judah its sins, (3) 4:1–8 assumes the exile when the temple was rebuilt, and (4) the people are not at war. Hillers, *Micah*, 51–52, and E. H. Scheffler, "Micah 4:1–5: An Impasse in Exegesis?" *Old Testament Essays* (Pretoria, South Africa: Univ. of South Africa, 1985), 52–53, refute all of these points: The text does not say Micah *only* spoke words of judgment against Judah, and Jeremiah only refers to one sermon of Micah's. Allen, *Joel, Obadiah, Jonah and Micah*, 244, sees only 4:6–8 as a late exilic addition.

3. Hillers, *Micah*, 53, makes this point.

A. S. van der Woude believes 4:1−8 comes from the time of Micah, but he surprisingly views these words as the deceptive hopes of the false prophets (Micah does quote them in 2:6)[4] that Micah is trying to deny. This view is unacceptable, for every indication here and in Isaiah 2:1−4 (the same verses are found there) is that these are true prophecies from God.

Because of the identity between Micah and Isaiah, the question arises as to who first spoke these words and who copied them. E. Cannawurf and B. Waltke think these words were revealed to Micah and copied by Isaiah. L. Allen concludes that Micah and Isaiah were both drawing on earlier Zion ideological traditions found in certain psalms. H. Wildberger, by contrast, argues that Isaiah originally received this vision and Micah copied it.[5] There is no clear answer to this problem, though these words seem to be an authentic revelation to Micah.

The date of this message is the time of Hezekiah, when he and his followers needed words of hope during Sennacherib's siege in 701 B.C. Outside the walls of Jerusalem were hordes of enemy troops (4:9, 11; 5:1). What would become of Jerusalem? Would God ever fulfill his glorious promises about that great city of God, that beautiful city of Zion (Ps. 46; 48)? Would the son of David reign forever over the whole earth (2 Sam. 7; Ps. 2), or were those promises forfeited? How could the small nation of Judah ever bring peace and prosperity to the earth and end the military terrorization of the nations? How could the nations be brought to the place where they would accept Judah's God and serve him?

Micah's words answer these questions and serve as a secure foundation for hope in a dark and hopeless day. King Hezekiah and his faithful followers can put their trust in God. There is hope in the future because no evil people (Hebrew or Assyrian) can prevent God's ultimate plan to transform Zion and all the people on earth. This hope does not promise a quick and painless deliverance from Sennacherib (only Isaiah speaks to that point in Isa. 37); it first and foremost calls the listener to trust in God's transforming power. Micah knows that everyone can rest secure, for eventually God will transform this world and set up his kingdom.

God's Transformation of Zion and All Nations (4:1−5)

THIS PROPHECY PROVIDES Micah and his audience with a vision of what God will ultimately do in Zion. It begins by pointing forward to a future time "in

---

4. A. S. van der Woude, "Micah in Dispute with the Pseudo-Prophets," 244−60.

5. E. Cannawurf, "The Authenticity of Micah IV 1−4," *VT* 13 (1963): 26−33; Waltke, "Micah," *Obadiah, Jonah, Micah,* 170−75; Allen, *Joel, Obadiah, Jonah and Micah,* 243; H. Wildberger, *Isaiah 1−12* (CC; Minneapolis: Fortress, 1991), 83−96.

the last days"[6] when the people of the world will experience God's presence in a totally new way. This era will inaugurate a new relationship between God and humankind, Israel and the nations, and humanity and nature (see related promises in similar prophecies in Isa. 4:2–6; 11:1–9; Hos. 2:16–23; Amos 9:11–15). God will enter the human realm in time and space and give the people of Judah and the rest of the nations of the world a type of leadership that will be effective and transformational. God's original purpose for humankind will be fulfilled as God Almighty finishes his plan.

God's role is hinted at when Micah describes God's mountain in Jerusalem[7] where his temple is. When it is raised up as the "chief" and highest place, it symbolizes God's supremacy. It is as if God's heavenly dwelling place and his earthly temple are joined as one, an idea hinted at in certain hymns of worship (cf. Ps. 11:4; 46:4; 48:2). This exaltation of God's dwelling represents to the nations the greatness and importance of the Lord God. This future status will be different from the useless briers that will cover the temple area when it is destroyed (Mic. 3:12).

Micah 4:1b–2 picture throngs of endless people streaming[8] to Jerusalem from many nations (cf. Isa. 19:19–25; 56:6–7; 60:4–14; 66:18–21; Amos 9:12). This worldwide pilgrimage to Jerusalem will feature the mutual admonition (one of the functions of the cohortative form of the verb) by fellow pilgrims, "Come, let us go up to the mountain of the LORD" (cf. Ps. 42:4; 122:1–4). The purpose for coming to Jerusalem is not just to see the exalted mountain or the temple, but to hear the words of God,[9] to be taught his ways, and to understand the "law" (*torah*) from God himself. God's ways describe how he acts and reflect who he is. His words contain his spoken will, which reveals his glorious wisdom, and his instructions direct people to walk in godly ways.

No specific mention is made of the new covenant or covenant making in this context (see Jer. 31:31–34 for this). The goal of God's teaching is the practical direction of people's lives so they will end up walking in ways consistent with God's ways. His powerful presence and persuasive message will transform the thinking and behavior of millions in the last days.

---

6. R. Smith, *Micah–Malachi*, 36, sees this as referring to eschatological events.

7. Micah and all the other prophets think this new era will take place at the geographic location of Jerusalem (and that is how we should interpret the meaning of this verse), but as Allen, *Joel, Obadiah, Jonah and Micah*, 327, reminds us, Jesus seems to downplay any specific geographic location for later worship when talking to the woman at the well in John 4:21–24.

8. Mays, *Micah*, 96–97, and several other commentaries suggest a connection between this streaming of people to Jerusalem and the streams of living water that will flow from Jerusalem (Ps. 46:4; Ezek. 47; Joel 3:18), but I see no connection.

9. Hillers, *Micah*, 51, thinks this word of Yahweh is a prophetic word since it is used in that sense elsewhere, but there is no mention of prophets here, only direct instruction from God himself.

Not only will the lives of individuals be eternally changed, but the self-ish and brutal political purposes of nations will follow an altered course (Mic. 4:3). God will sit as royal judge among the nations of the world to settle their disputes and iron out their differences. He will remove the reasons for international conflict so that people will not need to go to war again. Weapons of war and death will be destroyed and transformed into instruments of agriculture, which will preserve life. This seems to be a voluntary decision by these nations because they will renounce all intentions to plan or carry out warfare against any other people.

As a consequence of this transformation, every individual will have plenty to eat, be free of anxiety, and have a peaceful sense of security (4:4). These conditions will fulfill the people's dreams. They offer paradisiacal hopes of joy and prosperity (Isa. 65:20–25; Hos. 2:18)[10] without fear of violence. Micah's fantastic vision of the future ends with a reassuring promise that these words come directly from the mouth of God, the LORD Almighty. There is no doubt about the author of this message, the authority of these words, or their fulfillment. What God says, he does.

Verse 5 is a response of faith and commitment by some of the godly people listening to Micah. Although they are surrounded by the powerful Assyrian army (in 701 B.C.), which worships Assyrian gods, Micah, Hezekiah, and the faithful in Jerusalem are determined to walk in ways pleasing to Yahweh, Israel's God. This contrasting source of faith is clearly displayed in Sennacherib's letter and his servant's speech in Isaiah 36–37. The Assyrians believe it is foolish to trust in the power of Israel's God (36:7, 15, 18–20), but God destroys the Assyrian army and causes King Sennacherib to go home because he has blasphemed God's name (36; 37:6, 23–24).

The Assyrians have come to Jerusalem trusting in themselves, their gods, and their military might, not because they want to learn God's ways. In contrast, the hopelessly outnumbered Hebrews in Jerusalem are ultimately victorious only because they trust in God. Part of the reason why they are able to trust God in this disastrous situation is found in the promises of Micah 4:1–4. Since God will have the ultimate victory over all nations, since he has the answers to resolve military conflicts, and since he alone can provide people with true security, trusting God is the most sensible act of faith that anyone can propose. This commitment to God is a life-and-death matter for God's people, and it is an unending commitment

---

10. I do not see these as symbolic of a modest lifestyle but of an ideal situation with plenty of food and security. W. Brueggemann, "'Vine and Fig Tree': A Case Study in Imagination and Criticism," *CBQ* 43 (1981): 188–204, correctly sees this as a different ideal from those coveting more land (2:1–4) or those who work only for the sake of getting more money (3:9–11).

("for ever and ever") rather than a momentary foxhole cry for help while they are in a tough spot.

God's Transformation of the Weak into the Strong (4:6−8)

GOD'S PROMISES ARE for "that day" (4:6), so no one can blindly assume that everything is going to be roses and joy from the present time until the end of time; those who trust God know better than this. Many cities in Judah have already been captured, and thousands of people in Judah are dead. Many have been taken captive by Sennacherib's Assyrian army. Micah 4:9−10a, 11, and 5:1 [4:14 in Heb.] refer to these battles when Judah is attacked. Of course, Micah also vividly remembers hearing the news about the ten northern tribes of Israel exiled in 722 B.C. (just twenty years earlier) by the Assyrians when Samaria was destroyed (2 Kings 17).

A natural question to ask is: What will happen to all those people who suffer and are taken captive to places far away? In 4:6−8, Micah assures his listeners that God has not forgotten any of them. They are not so far away that God cannot bring them back to Jerusalem. They are an important part of God's future plan for Jerusalem. Not only will people want to come from many nations to Jerusalem to learn God's ways (4:2), but God himself will gather and assemble his weak, afflicted exiles and bring them back to the land (the same idea is promised in 2:12−13).

This theme of God's gathering his people as a shepherd gathers his injured sheep is a reassurance that God has not forgotten these people, nor is he unaware of their miserable condition. The lame person in exile, who feels rejected and of no value to God or the community, will be transformed into the precious remnant of God's people;[11] the weak exiles banished from their land will be transformed (śym)[12] into a strong nation (4:7; cf. the similar term in 4:3)—though there is no hint that this strength will be used for military purposes.[13] This change will be a marvelous work of divine power and grace, for these people will be helpless and unable to heal or regather themselves.

The final theme in this section is a reassurance that in the future God will reign as king in Zion forever (4:7b−8). There will be no more defeats, no more exiles, and no hopeless years serving foreign kings. God's kingship will last forever. Ideas about the reign or kingship of God go back to the Song of

---

11. Wolff, *Micah*, 123−24, questions whether this is a reference to the limping or lameness of Jacob (as B. Renaud has suggested), for there is no mention of Jacob. He prefers to connect this text to Ezek. 34, where the gathering of Israel is described, but that text never mentions the lame.

12. Wolff, *Micah*, 123, suggests the translation of śym here in 4:7 and in 1:6 as "transform."

13. Mays, *Micah*, 101, says "The dispersion will not be transformed into a mighty nation in order to resume a political career that is the expression of their own power and will."

Moses in Exodus 15:18, reappear in the Gideon story when he refuses to be a king because God already rules over them (Judg. 8:23), and are argued about when Saul does become king (1 Sam. 8:7). The idea of God's kingship is a fundamental part of covenant theology, for he is the King of kings and Lord of lords (Ezra 7:12; Ezek. 26:7; Dan. 2:37; cf. Deut. 10:17), who rules his covenant people. This divine king sits enthroned above the cherubim on the ark (Isa. 6), and his kingship is repeatedly celebrated in temple hymns (Ps. 47; 96–99). When God is king in Jerusalem at the end of time, a new world reminiscent of the nation's past glory will come into existence (Mic. 4:8).[14]

Using direct address to "you" (4:8), Micah reminds his listeners of ancient images of Judah's former stronghold in Jerusalem (the tower and the Ophel hill). The people in Jerusalem are given new names that describe their future condition. This "Daughter of Zion," who will be weak when the nation is defeated (4:10), will arise like a fortified tower and a strong citadel. Although these terms usually relate to warfare, in the context of "no war" in 4:3 they are symbols of stability and unmovable strength rather than protection from outside attack by an enemy. These pictures remind one of the strong but bygone power of the Davidic and Solomonic empire.

God's promise that "the former dominion will be restored to you" further emphasizes this return to Judah's ideal state. These promises give hope for the future to a people who have little to look forward to. There is always hope when God's people know that their king will reign over them and fulfill all his promises.

Bridging Contexts

ON INTERPRETING **Old Testament prophecy.** The application of this passage to people today can take different approaches because interpreters choose to use different hermeneutical principles to determine how to apply these promises. Is the determinative context for interpreting this text (1) the meaning the original author Micah wants his Hebrew audience to understand, (2) the way the New Testament deals with this topic,[15]

---

14. See the fuller discussion of God's kingship in G. V. Smith, "The Concept of God/the Gods As King in the Ancient Near East and the Bible," *TrinJ* 3 (1982): 18–38.

15. Waltke, "Micah," *The Minor Prophets*, 678, strongly supports this approach because Old Testament prophecies are fulfilled in Christ; the prophets speak of the new age under the symbols of the old; Old Testament prophecies have heavenly realities behind their symbols; Christ's coming has done away with the old reality; and the prophets supercharge their old symbols with hyperbole. These points may help one do a systematic theology of prophetic issues, but they do not help one understand what God reveals to Micah or what Micah means as he addresses his audience.

or (3) whatever significance a reader (ancient or modern) might choose to give to it?[16]

If the first option is chosen (which seems necessary to me), one must then ask: To what extent is Micah speaking literally or figuratively?[17] Interrelated to this issue is the question of how God's promises in the Old Testament are connected to the church of the New Testament and today. Is there primarily continuity (everything that applied to Israel in the Old Testament can now be related to the church) or discontinuity (Israel and the church are separate) between the Testaments? Or is it not an either/or issue but some continuity and some discontinuity? Can or should one interpret an Old Testament passage through the eyes of a later New Testament expansion or application of these Old Testament verses, or keep the comments of later authors separate from the exegesis of the Old Testament verses?

This latter approach seems necessary (at least in the exegesis of the present text), for it has the important advantage of maintaining authorial integrity. It also recognizes that through progressive revelations by later authors, new information is added that was not revealed at the earlier stages. The contemporary significance one gives to applications of prophecies will be directly affected by what decision one makes on these hermeneutical questions.

It seems wise, if one is a firm believer in interpreting the original meaning of the biblical author, to bring together the literal and figurative meanings rather than making a sharp distinction between them. This approach maintains that Isaiah actually, for example, saw the Lord sitting on a throne, high and lifted up in the temple, and the seraphim touching Isaiah's unclean lips (Isa. 6). There is no need to deny the literal aspect of what he saw, but one only gets half the point if we do not see these physical acts have a symbolic or deeper inherent truth (Isaiah's lips are cleansed by God's touch). Would not a different message be conveyed if the Lord had appeared on a lowly donkey or if the seraphim had touched Isaiah's feet?[18]

---

16. E. D. Hirsch Jr., *Validity in Interpretation* (New Haven: Yale Univ. Press, 1967), stresses that the only valid principle is to base an interpretation on the meaning given by the original author. R. H. Stein, *Playing by the Rules: A Basic Guide to Interpreting the Bible* (Grand Rapids: Baker, 1994), gives a popular explanation of the Hirschian approach to the process of interpreting Scripture.

17. Some may divide these into the literal hermeneutic of dispensationalism and the figurative approach of covenant theology, but adherents to both of these systems take some verses literally and some figuratively. See the contrasting articles from both sides of this question in *Continuity and Discontinuity: Perspectives on the Relationship Between the Old and New Testaments,* ed. J. S. Feinberg (Westchester: Crossway, 1988), 263–307, where B. Waltke and W. Kaiser explain their contrasting approaches to prophecy.

18. See J. N. Oswalt, *Book of Isaiah: Chapters 1–39* (NICOT; Grand Rapids: Eerdmans, 1986), 177–85, who quotes Calvin's claim that it is impossible to separate the sign from the truth.

Of course, whenever a prophet speaks, the imagery is always limited by the cultural meaning that exists in that day. Thus, there is no need to take Micah's reference to beating swords into plowshares "overliterally" and thus exclude any reference to what will happen to rifles or machine guns in the future. Micah is saying that the metal used to make swords (or any other comparable weapons) will be put to peaceful purposes, like making tractors, plows, or combines. In ancient Israel and even today, pious symbolic claims to be a peace-loving nation are empty without the literal redistribution of a nation's use of its metal for peaceful purposes. The symbolic principle is inherent in the act, but it is a meaningless symbolic concept without real action.

This approach does not allow one to conclude that "the great and powerful nations began to discern [Zion's] true heavenly quality when the Lord raised Zion out of its ashes, and peoples of all nations came to their full senses about it when God raised his Son from the dead and set him at his right hand in heaven."[19] On a factual basis one may ask what nations recognized the "heavenly quality" of Zion when it was rebuilt after the Exile and whether the resurrection of Jesus is prominently used to promote the greatness of Zion in the New Testament churches in Acts or Paul's letters. Is this what Micah thinks God is conveying to him?

These attempts to focus exclusively on specific Old or New Testament fulfillments of Micah's words about the final exaltation of Zion can have the effect of distracting the modern reader from the main theological point Micah is trying to communicate to his audience (remember, they do not know how or when these things will be fulfilled). It is true that later revelation about the new Jerusalem in the Old Testament and the New (Isa. 65; Heb. 12:22−24; Rev. 21) may add to or clarify some of these, but these new facts are not a part of the meaning of Micah's message in 701 B.C. Although the fulfillment of this prophecy is of paramount importance for the future of the world, a more practical basis for application of this passage to the church is based on the key theological themes Micah uses to transform the thinking of his audience (not on the issue of when this will be fulfilled).

Four bridging principles. (1) In difficult times believers should follow God's leadership (4:5) because God has a future plan to establish his kingdom (4:1−8). The challenge to walk in God's ways and trust him for the

---

19. Waltke, "Micah," *Obadiah, Jonah, Micah,* 168. A somewhat similar approach is used by M. Luther—see *Luther's Works,* ed. H. C. Oswald (Saint Louis: Concordia, 1975), 18:238, who thinks "this mountain became very famous because of Christ." Later in 4:6–7 Luther sees God as restoring a small Jewish remnant after the Babylonian exile but then strangely twists the reference to these people becoming a strong nation into a reference to the church.

future is of paramount importance both in a crisis situation, where there is mass confusion and little hope, and in times when everything is going smoothly. Knowledge of God's sovereign control over the future gives comfort and confidence to those who do not know which way to turn. Since God's plans are sure and he has the power to complete them, he is a worthy leader to follow. This principle can be used to challenge people in the church to examine whom they are following. Do they consciously look for God's leadership in crisis situations? How does God's character and leadership motivate us to action?

(2) God's exaltation (which is the reason for Zion's exaltation) will bring many nations to him and cause them to want to learn his ways and follow in his paths (4:2). Two factors give hope in this principle: God will exalt himself in the eyes of all the nations of the world, and the nations will come to him and learn his ways. This evangelistic effort will be the most successful missions outreach ever seen.

The date and means by which God will exalt himself are unknown, but the effect is clear. Nations will willingly change their plans and gladly learn new behavior patterns. This principle encourages people never to give up on unbelieving people or nations but always to believe that transformation can happen through God's grace. This passage also suggests an effective strategy for evangelism: to declare God's exalted glory before the nations.

(3) God's wise judgment can bring about peaceful and secure coexistence among nations (4:3–4). Since God knows the motivations and hidden agendas of every nation (and individual), he has the ability to secure peace by justly arbitrating differences. This principle gives the believer confidence that no matter how difficult or impossible international relationships among nations become, God can bring about peace. By the extension of this principle one can also suggest that God can solve the conflicts between individuals, such as between parents and children and husbands and wives. Justice is one of the keys to developing these relationships today.

(4) God's leadership involves caring about his afflicted people and strengthening them when he comes to rule as king (4:6–8). He does not abandon the wounded or give up on his people after punishing them. His strategy is to gather them like a shepherd and to strengthen those in need. He is able to do this because he is the eternal king who will reign in power forever.

It is important to notice that each of these principles focuses primarily on what God will do, but each one also calls for a response of change from some group of people. Thus, having a correct theological conception of God's ways and his future plans is foundational if a person, a church, or a nation is going to respond by trusting God in the turbulent times of life.

Contemporary
Significance

WE MUST DISCOVER the meaning given by Micah if we hope to develop practical applications for the church. Micah 4:1–8 does not clarify when these events will take place in the future, so speculations that try to identify a fulfillment in the Millennium or at some other time are not based on what this passage says. Micah does not know the time, Jesus did not know the date when the kingdom will arrive, and certainly we do not have access to the answers to these fascinating questions. Thus, application should move away from setting dates and focus on the theological message.

Strictly speaking, most of these promises apply in their primary application to Hebrew believers, but Micah says that Gentile nations will also seek God and benefit from his coming in the last days (4:1b–3). Thus, Micah's promises of hope provide encouragement to people in the church because we are among the Gentiles. All humankind will respond when God comes as king. People will seek to transform their own behavior based on God's teachings. Since there are still many Jews and Gentiles who have not come to God today, since there is still plenty of war around the world, and since God is not reigning as king on the earth, I conclude that this prophecy was not fulfilled in the New Testament period. Therefore, its primary purpose is to provide hope for people who trust in God today, just as it provided hope for those who trusted God in Micah's day. What hope is provided from the four bridging principles listed above?

Walking in God's ways. Since God has a future plan to establish his kingdom, all believers should commit themselves to walk in God's ways and trust in his leadership, for he is the only basis for hope (4:5). Although this seems basic and taken for granted by many, if this principle were actually practiced by every believer, every church committee, and every leader, the church would be transformed with the removal of petty politics and anemic faith.

Three factors are involved in this application. (1) Foundational to all the rest is that each person must accept that God has a plan for his or her life and for this world. God sovereignly controls people and events. The timing of history's final chapter is programmed to accomplish the goal of setting up his divine rule over all the world.

Of course, God's plan includes the church today, before the final eschatological period. This plan was established when he decreed what would happen to accomplish his eternal purposes and bring glory to himself.[20] His plan should not be viewed as a patchwork sewn together on the spur of the

---

20. J. O. Buswell, *A Systematic Theology of the Christian Religion* (Grand Rapids: Zondervan, 1962), 163–70, describes some of the ways different theologians have tried to explain the decrees of God.

moment out of a confused and uncontrollable series of accidents of history. The decrees that make up that plan have their origin long before their fulfillment, and the parts of the plan purposely mesh together to demonstrate God's exalted glory. Although some have viewed God's decrees as secret and incomprehensible, the revelation of his will for the future in Scripture uncovers a small part of what is unknown and unveils a few threads of the marvelous mystery of God's plans.[21]

(2) Knowledge of God's sovereign control over the future leads to the second factor. When people have confidence in God's sovereign plan, they will acknowledge his control, submit to his will, and want to walk in his ways. Through the revelation of his power and plan, God will transform the hearts of people on the earth so that his desires are accomplished in and through them. Confidence also leads to a commitment not to walk like other people, but to follow the leader who has the winning plan. This confidence will naturally express itself in trust and faith to do what seems difficult.

(3) Confidence in God's plan leads to another factor, hope. Hope is of paramount importance, particularly in a crisis situation where there is mass confusion and no solution readily at hand. Hope is a future trust that the things planned will be accomplished because the person in charge is able to make good on the promises that were made.

Practically, this means that people do not have to fear that the world is totally out of control. Prosperity, natural disaster, disease, accidents, or persecution may cross a person's path, but nothing can undo or frustrate the final goal God has established. One may not understand why things happen the way they do or know how God is ever going to straighten out the mess the world is in, but we can look confidently at the future, knowing that eventually God will work all the parts together in such a way that his plan is accomplished.

We must have the final plan of God in mind as we carry out our little corner of service in the worldwide ministry of the church. If we do not know that God's program is an absolutely sure winner that will succeed in the end, we may be discouraged by the small size of our group or feel there is no hope of seeing God transform unbelievers. For example, because many Christians did not know the details of God's plan, they used to think there was no hope for Russia except divine destruction. But now God's plan has become clear, and through his grace many churches are being planted in that former Communist country. Knowing that plan for Russia would have helped people be optimistic about what God could do, even when things looked discouraging. Hope and confidence are a central part of every person's life;

---

21. G. W. Bromiley, "The Decrees of God," *Basic Christian Doctrine*, ed. C. F. Henry (New York: Holt, Rinehart and Winston, 1962), 42—48, shows that some relate the decrees only to issues of election, while others use the term in a broader sense.

thus, it is important for every believer to know about the great plans that God has for the world.

Strategies for evangelism. The mission program of God is to bring unbelieving Jews and Gentiles to see the glory of God so that they will transform their lives and follow him. God's exaltation of himself in the future will bring many nations to himself and cause them to desire to learn his ways and walk in his paths (4:2).

Earlier we noted the twofold emphasis on God's exaltation of himself and the coming of the nations in response. This suggests a strategy for evangelism in the church today. We must make sure every man, woman, and child is aware of the glory of our exalted God. The 1976 Urbana conference of Intervarsity Christian Fellowship focused on the theme of "Declaring His Glory Among the Nations." In that conference E. Clowney talked about how Israel declared God's glory to the nations after the Exodus (Ex. 15) and in their worship (Ps. 96:1–3), and then suggested that we too can evangelize the world today by exalting God's name and glorious deeds to those who do not know him.[22]

J. Piper's book on missions also emphasizes the goal of making God supreme in the church through worship, prayer, and suffering, as well as by declaring his supremacy among the unevangelized peoples.[23] This involves talking about who God is (holy and all-powerful), what he has done in the past (Creator and Redeemer), what he is doing today (in our experience and in countries around the world), and what he will do in the future (set up his glorious kingdom). If the focus remains on God rather than on denominational distinctives, cultural mores, or the personal or political agenda of the believer, many people will desire to know more about this gracious and loving God.

This principle encourages the church to never give up on unbelieving people next door or in distant nations that speak different languages and have strange cultural and religious beliefs. We know that transformation can happen through God's grace; what the nations need to see is a true vision of the glory of God and the encouragement to come and learn of his ways. The history of missions is full of illustrations of this principle. Many years ago there were no Christians among the Quichua Indians in South America, but today there are hundreds of thousands who gather to worship and praise God.[24] They have seen something of the glory of God and have submitted their lives to him.

---

22. E. Clowney, "Declare His Glory Among the Nations," *Declare His Glory*, ed. D. M. Howard (Downers Grove, Ill.: InterVarsity, 1977), 95–108.

23. J. Piper, *Let the Nations Be Glad: The Supremacy of God in Missions* (Grand Rapids: Baker, 1993).

24. My parents, who were Gospel Missionary Union missionaries in Colta, Equador, during their retirement years, have referred to towns where all the people were Christians.

Fairness, justice, and peace. A third application is that God's wise judgment can bring about peaceful and secure coexistence between people and nations (4:3−4). This principle suggests that believers should do the work of God by practicing fairness and justice so that peace will characterize both personal and international relationships. Coveting, stealing, strife, bitterness, revenge, fighting, and war are not behavior patterns that please God; but justice, forgiveness, grace, peace, and suffering for the sake of others are. Psalm 34:14 encourages people to "seek peace," Jesus refers to the peacemakers as a blessed group (Matt. 5:9), and Paul encourages the Romans to "make every effort to do what leads to peace and to mutual edification" (Rom. 14:19) and to "live at peace with everyone" (12:18).

The Scriptures make it clear that lasting peace is a gift of God (Num. 6:24−26; John 14:27) and cannot be fully attained without him. J. I. Durham claims that real peace "is a gift of God that can be received only in the presence of God";[25] thus, attempts to manufacture temporary truces by separating fighting parties usually do not solve the basic problem unless the parties have a confrontation with God and give up some of their own selfish desires. Since God knows the motivations and hidden agendas of every person and nation, he has the ability to secure peace by justly arbitrating differences, convicting people of sin, and giving them a forgiving spirit.

This principle also gives the believer confidence that no matter how difficult or impossible international relationships among nations become, God can and will one day bring about peace throughout the earth. Although this passage is about peace among nations, this principle can also be extended to the problem of developing peace among individuals: parents and children, husbands and wives, workers and bosses, pastors and parishioners.

Caring about the afflicted. A final application comes from God's example of leading by caring about the afflicted and his strengthening of them (4:6−8). Our Lord did not abandon the wounded and weak who could not help themselves, and neither should we. Nor did he give up on those who deserved to be punished or write them off as hopeless cases of no value, and neither should we. This attitude also characterized Jesus, who cared for the blind, the lame, the lepers, and the outcasts of society. His strategy was to heal and teach them in order to demonstrate that God's grace and love are not based on status or humanly created value systems. Jesus pictured himself as the good shepherd, who cares for his sheep and strengthens all who are in need (John 10).

---

25. J. I. Durham, "*šālôm* and the Presence of God," *Proclamation and Presence: Old Testament Essays in Honor of G. H. Davies*, ed. J. R. Porter and J. I. Durham (Richmond: Knox, 1970), 292.

Micah 4:9–5:9

⁴·⁹ Why do you now cry aloud—
    have you no king?
  Has your counselor perished,
    that pain seizes you like that of a woman in labor?
¹⁰ Writhe in agony, O Daughter of Zion,
    like a woman in labor,
  for now you must leave the city
    to camp in the open field.
  You will go to Babylon;
    there you will be rescued.
  There the LORD will redeem you
    out of the hand of your enemies.

¹¹ But now many nations
    are gathered against you.
  They say, "Let her be defiled,
    let our eyes gloat over Zion!"
¹² But they do not know
    the thoughts of the LORD;
  they do not understand his plan,
    he who gathers them like sheaves to the threshing floor.

¹³ "Rise and thresh, O Daughter of Zion,
    for I will give you horns of iron;
  I will give you hoofs of bronze
    and you will break to pieces many nations."

You will devote their ill-gotten gains to the LORD,
    their wealth to the Lord of all the earth.

⁵·¹ Marshall your troops, O city of troops,
    for a siege is laid against us.
  They will strike Israel's ruler
    on the cheek with a rod.

² "But you, Bethlehem Ephrathah,
    though you are small among the clans of Judah,
  out of you will come for me
    one who will be ruler over Israel,
  whose origins are from of old,
    from ancient times."

³ Therefore Israel will be abandoned
    until the time when she who is in labor gives birth
  and the rest of his brothers return
    to join the Israelites.

⁴ He will stand and shepherd his flock
    in the strength of the LORD,
    in the majesty of the name of the LORD his God.
  And they will live securely, for then his greatness
    will reach to the ends of the earth.
⁵   And he will be their peace.

When the Assyrian invades our land
    and marches through our fortresses,
  we will raise against him seven shepherds,
    even eight leaders of men.
⁶ They will rule the land of Assyria with the sword,
    the land of Nimrod with drawn sword.
He will deliver us from the Assyrian
    when he invades our land
    and marches into our borders.

⁷ The remnant of Jacob will be
    in the midst of many peoples
like dew from the LORD,
    like showers on the grass,
which do not wait for man
    or linger for mankind.
⁸ The remnant of Jacob will be among the nations,
    in the midst of many peoples,
like a lion among the beasts of the forest,
    like a young lion among flocks of sheep,
which mauls and mangles as it goes,
    and no one can rescue.
⁹ Your hand will be lifted up in triumph over your enemies,
    and all your foes will be destroyed.

Original Meaning

THIS LONG UNIT can be divided into two sections: 4:9–5:4 (4:9–5:3 in the Heb. text) and 5:5–9 (5:4–8 in the Heb. text). Commentaries differ on their understanding of the structure and relationship between the paragraphs, based on whether they accept the structural analysis of Hagstrom, Nielson, Renaud, Allen, or Willis.[1] Nielsen, Allen, and Renaud see a chiastic relationship between the paragraphs in 4:1–5:15, based on similar themes in corresponding A, B, and C paragraphs, while Willis finds seven parallel pericopes with each having a negative beginning and a positive conclusion. Hagstrom finds only three paragraphs (4:1–7; 4:8–5:3; 5:4–14). Although these scholars have almost the same verses in each paragraph, they relate them to each other in different ways. The chiastic structure seems to work for some paragraphs but not all, and Willis's approach is not consistent for every paragraph.

This passage begins with three parallel paragraphs (4:9–10; 4:11–13; 5:1–4), each introduced with ʿattah (lit., "now," 4:9, 11; 5:1). This structure is difficult to see in the NIV because the translators have omitted "now" in 5:1 (cf. NASB). Each paragraph includes the description of the approaching disaster the nation is facing in the near future, a promised deliverance by God, and the eventual establishment of the messianic kingdom.

These factors point to a major break after 5:4 because the next verses do not follow the pattern in 4:9–5:4, but begin a new literary pattern. Micah 5:5, 7, and 10 are each introduced by wehayah (lit., "and it shall be") and are all grouped together in one unit by Hagstrom. Nevertheless, 5:5 is closely connected to 5:4—in fact, so close that NIV, NASB, and D. Hillers end the preceding paragraph after 5:5a, while B. Waltke and L. Allen put 5:1–6 together as a paragraph.[2] These studies properly see valuable points of continuity but tend to ignore the Hebrew rhetorical marker (wehayah) that separates 5:5ff. from what goes before it.

I prefer to make 5:5–9 a second section closely related to what precedes it. The absence of the initial "now" and the absence of a clear contrast between "now" and the future sets these paragraphs apart as a separate section. The topics in 5:10–15 are then put in a third paragraph by themselves because of the consistent "I will cut off" phraseology at the beginning of each verse and its distinctive themes.

---

1. Hagstrom, *Coherence of the Book of Micah*, 72–87, surveys and analyzes the strengths and weaknesses of each and then gives his own views.

2. Hillers, *Micah*, 64; J. T. Willis, "The Structure of Micah 3–5," *ZAW* 81 (1969): 198–212; Waltke, "Micah," *Obadiah, Jonah, Micah*, 181; Allen, *Joel, Obadiah, Jonah and Micah*, 339–41.

The date and setting of 4:9–5:9 is hinted at by a reference to the approaching problem of leaving the city (4:10), "many nations are gathered against you" (4:11), "a siege is laid against us" (5:1), and the comments about "when the Assyrian invades our land" (5:5). Some do not believe Micah wrote these verses and give an exilic or postexilic date to this material.[3] I believe these words were spoken while the Assyrian army of Sennacherib surrounded Jerusalem in 701 B.C. If this is correct, Micah is persuasively exhorting Hezekiah and the people of Jerusalem to face the reality of Assyrian aggression honestly but not to lose sight of the long-term plans God has for his people. They must trust him, for he will redeem them and eventually bring the Messiah from Bethlehem to shepherd his people.

Zion Will Be Attacked and Later Delivered (4:9–5:4)

THE FIRST PARAGRAPH (4:9–10) begins with *ʿattah* (lit., "now") and three questions. Why are crying and distress in Zion, pain like a woman in labor? Micah responds to this lamenting with two rhetorical questions: "Have you no king? Has your counselor perished?" This could be a sarcastic remark about the inability of King Hezekiah to protect the people of Jerusalem from Sennacherib. It seems more likely, however, in light of the kingship terminology in 4:7–8, that this is an inquiry about why the people do not call on God, their King.[4] Is he not able to hear their painful agony?

Micah sees three steps in the near future that will cause the people to writhe in agony: They will leave the city of Jerusalem (a reference to its conquest), then camp in the open field for a period of time (a reference to their journey into exile), and finally end up in Babylon (4:10a). This brief oracle makes no mention of Assyrian exile and ends with a promise of God's plan to deliver his people from the grasp of their enemies at some time in the future. Ending this oracle with the good news of hope should have caused Micah's audience to look realistically at their present danger, to cry out to God

---

3. Wolff, *Micah*, 136, and Mays, *Micah*, 104, are influenced strongly by the reference to going into exile in Babylon, which happened about 120 years later; but Isaiah's prophecy to Hezekiah (Isa. 39) indicates that the prophets already knew before 701 B.C. that God was going to give Judah into the hand of Babylon. Shaw, *Speeches of Micah*, 157, places these events back to the reign of Pekah and the Syro-Ephraimite war in 734–732 B.C., but why would Micah give the evil King Ahaz such wonderful promises of hope?

4. Allen, *Joel, Obadiah, Jonah and Micah*, 333; Mays, *Micah*, 105; and Kaiser, *Micah–Malachi*, 61, point to the inadequacy of the earthly king, while Wolff, *Micah*, 139, and Waltke, "Micah," *Obadiah, Jonah, Micah*, 178, think the king is God. If 4:1–8 and 4:9–5:4 are intended to encourage the people of Jerusalem with some thread of hope during Sennacherib's attack, it seems that Micah would be focusing their attention on trusting God and building up the people's trust in the good King Hezekiah—not ridiculing him.

for help, and to put their present problems in the larger framework of God's ultimate plan for his people. God is not totally giving up on them; he is committed to them in spite of their present failures and setbacks. They can look forward to better days in the future.

The second paragraph (4:11–13), also beginning with "and now," has an announcement of many nations gathering against Jerusalem (4:11).[5] These enemies will proudly gloat over Zion and purposely plan to defile and desecrate the holy city and its temple. This gloating is evident in the messages announced by Sennacherib's messenger (Isa. 36). God himself condemns the Assyrians for their arrogant attitude that proudly proclaims their superiority over everyone else (10:5–15; 37:23–29). The defilement of Jerusalem's sacred temple precincts, which are open only to the holy priests, will seek to deny the power and sacredness of the God who lives there.[6]

To emphasize the foolishness of this haughty people, Micah contrasts the attacker's ideas with God's thoughts (4:11–13). They think they have a brilliant plan to gather at Jerusalem, but actually it is God who is gathering them. They want to destroy Jerusalem, but in the end God will thresh and destroy the nations who attack Jerusalem. They want to desecrate Zion and loot its temple, but Zion will end up consecrating the enemies' wealth to God.[7] Some time later this was all fulfilled when God miraculously destroyed 185,000 Assyrian troops.

In explaining the positive hope for the future, Micah pictures Zion as a mighty ox that is threshing sheaves of grain in a threshing floor (4:12b–13). In almost a summons to battle (Num. 10:35–36), God provides his people with the ability to accomplish this task. Judah will arise and thresh with "horns of iron" (implying such great strength that no one will be able to stop her from doing this) and "hoofs of bronze" (symbolizing the crushing power that will bear down on what was threshed). There is no doubt that God will defeat Zion's enemies; Zion will be invincible. Using imagery from the practice of holy war, God predicts that all the wealth of these nations will be like booty devoted to God (see Josh. 6:18–19; 7:11–12). Micah's rhetoric is meant to convince his audience that the gloating Assyrians will not have the last say. If the people put their trust in God, he will reverse the proud plans of those who wish to defile his holy place.

The third paragraph (5:1–4) follows the same pattern of describing an approaching siege that is "now" about to begin, but there are many interpretive problems that complicate an attempt to understand what Micah

---

5. The idea of many nations gathering against God's people is common to Zion tradition (see J. J. M. Roberts, "The Davidic Origin of the Zion Tradition," *JBL* 92 [1973]: 329–44).

6. Waltke, "Micah," *The Minor Prophets*, 696, reports that this was commonly done; also, enemy nations plundered a nation's gold that was consecrated to its gods/God.

7. Mays, *Micah*, 107, points out these contrasts.

is communicating. Some commentaries think the first verb in 5:1 (*gdd*) means to gash, cut oneself, and consequently conclude that Micah is describing the people in Judah who are lamenting their hopeless military plight so strongly that some are slashing themselves with knives as they grieve.[8]

B. Waltke and W. Kaiser (along with the NIV and NASB) prefer another meaning of *gdd*, to gather troops (e.g., Ps. 94:21; Jer. 5:7).[9] Since Micah is speaking to the militarized populace in Jerusalem (this "city of troops"), he is probably encouraging them to prepare to defend their city because of the approaching siege in 701 B.C. The prophecy indicates that the enemy will strike a Hebrew "judge" (NIV "ruler" is an appropriate translation since kings were judges) on the cheek with a rod, a sign of great humiliation (1 Kings 22:24; Ps. 3:7; Isa. 50:6). This may refer to the coming humiliation of Hezekiah,[10] who cannot prevent the Assyrians from defeating many cities in Judah. He has to pay a large amount of tribute (2 Kings 18:13–16) and listen to Sennacherib's messenger mock and undermine the people's trust in Hezekiah (Isa. 36:14–18).[11]

The positive message of hope in 5:2–4 looks forward to a day when a strong ruler will arise from Bethlehem Ephrathah, the city of Boaz, Jesse, and David (Ruth 4:11; 1 Sam. 16:1; 17:12). This mention of a new king from the line of David reminds the people about their tradition of the messianic promise of the eternal reign of David's Son (2 Sam. 7:4–17; Ps. 2; 89; 132). Several things are said about this messianic ruler. From a human standpoint, he will come from one of the smallest families in the tribe of Judah; but from the divine standpoint, he will go out "for me" ("for God" as in 1 Sam. 16:1, though not reflected in NIV)—that is, in order to do God's will and to be God's "ruler" over Israel. The reference to his origins "from ancient times" has been connected to the eternal preexistence of Christ the Messiah,[12] but the parallelism with the preceding line suggests Micah is probably pointing back to the ancient line of David.

---

8. Allen, *Joel, Obadiah, Jonah and Micah*, 341, translates "gashing yourself," and Wolff, *Micah*, 129, 131, translates the verb from this root "gash yourself." The RSV "Now you are walled about with a wall" is based on the emendation of the root *gdd* (troop) to *gdr* (wall), based on the Old Greek.

9. Waltke, "Micah," *Obadiah, Jonah, Micah*, 181; Kaiser, *Micah–Malachi*, 63.

10. Mays, *Micah*, 115, and Kaiser, *Micah–Malachi*, 63, think this refers to the humiliation of Zedekiah, who was tortured after the fall of Jerusalem about 120 years later, but it makes more sense to see it as a reference to Hezekiah (as Allen, *Joel, Obadiah, Jonah and Micah*, 341, suggests).

11. K. Barker, "Micah," *Micah, Nahum, Habakkuk, Zephaniah*, 95, also suggests it may refer to Zedekiah, who was blinded by Nebuchadnezzar's soldiers (2 Kings 25:7; Jer. 52:10–11) or even to Christ (Matt. 27:30), but Hezekiah seems more likely.

12. See Kaiser, *Micah–Malachi*, 64.

Verse 3 briefly interrupts the flow of thought with the clarification that this ruler will not come immediately and prevent the present disaster the nation is facing. First, there will be a period in which the nation will be abandoned and in exile (cf. 4:10). Sometime after that a woman will give birth to this child (see a similar tradition in Isa. 9:6–7), and then the exiled brothers[13] will return to their land.

After this brief clarification Micah begins to describe the reign of this new messianic ruler in 5:4. He will "stand" or establish himself as ruler in order to accomplish God's plan. Like David his ancient ancestor, he will shepherd God's people by leading, protecting, and providing for their needs (cf. 2 Sam. 5:2; 7:7). This will be possible because this ruler will get his strength from God and rule by the sovereign authority of God's name.

In 5:4b Micah reminds his audience that this ruler will bring true security to the nation (in contrast to their present distress because of Assyria), just as the original messianic prophecies said (see 2 Sam. 7:10). His kingdom will be a universal rule, including all the nations of the earth (see Ps. 2:8; 72:8). This great hope that the nation dreams of will surely come; therefore, Micah's audience should face their present crisis in light of the big picture. Their temporal setback is part of God's plan and will not prevent him from establishing his rule over the earth in the future. Micah's audience can be confident that God knows what he is doing.

The Conquest of Zion's Enemies (5:5–9)

THIS SECTION IS made up of two paragraphs (5:5–6 and 5:7–9), each beginning with *wehayah* (lit., "and it shall be"; see comments above on this issue). Most maintain that the *zeh* ("he"; lit., "this one") in 5:5a refers to the Messiah as described in 5:2–4. The universal and secure reign of the Messiah will result in a period of peace (cf. also 4:1–4). Isaiah also saw this coming king as the "Prince of Peace" (Isa. 9:6).

This announcement is followed with a somewhat surprising announcement of what "we" will do when the Assyrians invade "our" land. Some view these statements as positive affirmations about how Micah, the people of Judah, and the Messiah together will defeat all their enemies in the messianic era of the future (following in the spirit of 4:13).[14] Instead, these

---

13. This may be a hint that both Judah and the northern nation of Israel will return. I do not follow Waltke, "Micah," *The Minor Prophets*, 706, who claims that "the prophecy was fulfilled at Pentecost" but believe there is much more to this prophecy than what happens in Acts 2.

14. Wolff, *Micah*, 147, and Mays, *Micah*, 119, see the name Assyria as a code word for Judah's enemies and not a specific reference to Sennacherib's forces, which are invading the land at the time.

expressions seem to betray a significant contrast between what Micah has said about what God will do through the Messiah and what the audience is confidently saying about what "we" will do through "our" military strength. Allen suggests that 5:5b–6 is patterned after a nationalistic song of victory.[15] Micah is probably quoting what he has heard people say in order to correct their misunderstanding of what God intends to do in the future.

This proud song represents the audience's overconfident attitude about what they and their leaders (seven or eight kings symbolize powerful military resources through alliances) will accomplish rather than what the Messiah will do. This overconfident zeal is also revealed by the emphasis on their belief that "we" can conquer the Assyrians (this seems to contradict 4:9, 11; 5:1). They even think that their military rulers will go on the offensive and rule over all the territory of Assyria and Babylon ("the land of Nimrod"). Maybe they think that the promise of victory over their enemies in 4:13 will enable them to defeat Assyria.

But Micah does not say that the Messiah will come immediately, deliver them from the Assyrians now, and set up his universal kingdom over their enemies at the present time. First there will be a time of agony and exile (4:9–10; 5:1, 3a). Micah calls the people to trust in God and his coming king, but his audience seems to be more focused on what "we" will do with "our" military strength now.

D. Hillers (cf. also RSV) emends "he will deliver us" in 5:6b to "they will deliver us," meaning the seven or eight leaders will deliver us.[16] L. Allen keeps the singular verb in the Hebrew text and sees this as Micah's correction of this proud national claim of self-sufficiency. Micah objects, "No, *he* (this one who brings us peace in 5:5a) will deliver us, not the human leaders in 5:5."[17] A third approach takes this singular verb to mean the collective military forces of seven or eight leaders, just as "it" in the last line refers to the collective forces of Assyria. Either of these last interpretations makes good sense in this context, though I prefer the last one.

If this is an appropriate interpretation of 5:5–6, then verses 7–9 offer corrective ideas to the proud statements of the military leaders of Judah. These verses also begin with *wehayah* ("and it will be") but include no "we" statements. Instead, Micah pictures "the remnant of Jacob" among the nations in exile, a

---

15. Allen, *Joel, Obadiah, Jonah and Micah*, 347, compares it to Judg. 16:23–24 and Jer. 21:13.

16. Hillers, *Micah*, 68–69, does this because of the preceding plural verbs.

17. Allen, *Joel, Obadiah, Jonah and Micah*, 348, has a solution that makes good sense. We do not follow Waltke, "Micah," *The Minor Prophets*, 709, who sees this fulfilled in the messianic era, when God's people are attacked. The reference to Nimrod and Assyria suggests that Micah is not just using code words for Israel's enemies but referring to real people at that time.

point made earlier in 4:7, 10. The analogy between the remnant and "dew" or "showers" is not clear. Since Israel does not have any rain from June through September, any living plants depend heavily on the moisture from the dew each morning. Thus, dew or showers may be symbols of fertility (Gen. 27:28; Ps. 65:10), but the negative analogy of the remnant to lions in 5:8 seems to present two contradictory pictures. Based on the reference to dew in 2 Samuel 17:12, a few interpret the dew in a negative sense.[18] Others see the blessing of many dew drops as a comparison to the enormous size of the seed of Abraham or a sign that the Hebrew exiles will be dew (a blessing) on the Gentiles.[19]

It seems better, therefore, to focus on the interpretation Micah provides at the end of 5:7. The real purpose of this analogy is to show that dew and showers are mysterious gifts of God not controlled by humankind (all we can do is wait). Micah's rhetorical point is to persuade his listeners not to count on what "we" can do (5:5–6) in "our" strength, for humans can do little to determine the future; people cannot even control the dew. All they can do is trust the sovereign plan of God and wait for him to act. The divine initiative will accomplish all he has promised in its appropriate time.

The second analogy in 5:8 compares the remnant to a lion that mauls and destroys. Here Micah points to the truth in the people's claims about defeating their enemies in 5:5–6. But the final line of 5:8 focuses the listeners' attention on the divine control over these events, for "no one can rescue" these nations if God has determined their destiny. The dew analogy shows that Judah is not in control of its future, and the lion analogy shows that the nations are not in control of their future. Micah is trying to persuade his audience that God is the One who sovereignly determines the coming events, so they must realize their own dependence on him and look to him for hope. There is no room for human pride or triumphalism about what "we" will do.

This oracle ends with a statement of victory over Judah's foes (v. 9). Some interpret the verb used here as an irregular imperfect that predicts what will happen to "you," the remnant, as you defeat your enemies.[20] This does not seem to be the best approach, however, for the jussive form of the verb suggests that this is a prayer addressed to "you," that is, to God.[21] Supporting this view is the idea that when a human being lifts up his or her hand, it is usually a negative sign of pride, rebellion, or violence. Having illustrated the limited power and control that both the remnant and the nations have over the future, Micah now cries out to God for help by requesting that he assert his authority and destroy his enemies as he has promised. Micah is putting his

---

18. Hillers, *Micah*, 71, relies on the views of Wolfe and McKeating for this interpretation.

19. Barker, "Micah," *Micah, Nahum, Habakkuk, Zephaniah*, 103.

20. Waltke, "Micah," *Obadiah, Jonah, Micah*, 188, and Allen, *Joel, Obadiah, Jonah and Micah*, 355.

21. This is the view of Wolff, *Micah*, 157, and Mays, *Micah*, 123.

total confidence in God. Some of those who hear this prayer, Micah hopes, will follow his example and commit their lives to his care and protection.

THE SIGNIFICANCE ONE gives to these prophetic messages is dependent on the hermeneutical principles used to interpret and apply them. Some of these prophecies were fulfilled in the past and do not apply directly to people today. The Assyrian attack on Jerusalem took place in 701 B.C. (4:11; 5:1). Some years later Judah was taken into Babylonian exile for seventy years (4:10a; Jer. 29:10), and later a portion of these people returned to the land (Mic. 4:10b; Ezra 1–2). Some seven hundred years after Micah's prophecy Jesus was born as King of the Jews in Bethlehem (Mic. 5:2; Matt. 2:6), but his universal rule of the whole earth is still anxiously awaited (Mic. 5:4). The primary principle learned from these fulfilled prophecies is that God's prophecies are true; what he says happens.

One also realizes that some parts of prophecies are literally true down to the detail (e.g., the reference to Babylon and Bethlehem Ephrathah), while the predictions in other verses are more nebulous (e.g., "I will give you hoofs of bronze" in 4:13) or symbolic (e.g., the dew and lion in 5:7–8). General time frames of reference are provided, so that one can distinguish between "now" and what "will" happen in 4:9–5:4, but the main purpose of these prophecies is not to provide a precise timetable or dates for the listeners. A person's hope for the future is primarily based on what God will do, not when it will happen.

Theologians interpret the unfulfilled portions of these prophecies in either a more literal hermeneutic, which applies all prophecies about Israel to the people of Israel, or a less literal hermeneutic, based on Paul's statement that the Gentile believers have been grafted into the vine of Israel (Rom. 11:17). Followers of the first approach often identify the remnant of Israel as the Jewish revival in the Millennium, while the second view usually insists that these prophecies are fulfilled in the ministry of the church.[22]

T. McComiskey strikes a good balance when he says that "while the remnant is specifically Israel, there is a sense in which the church forms a part of the remnant."[23] If a person focuses only on what Micah communicates to his audience, there is little question that he is thinking about Israel's future,

---

22. See the contrasting approaches in *Continuity and Discontinuity: Perspectives on the Relationship Between the Old and New Testaments*, 263–307; esp. the two chapters on the "Kingdom Promises" by W. Kaiser and B. Waltke. R. Saucy and M. Woudstra also give two different approaches to the question of "Israel and the Church," 221–62.

23. T. McComiskey, "Micah," 7:430.

for he has no knowledge that the church will come into existence at some later date.[24] Many years later, however, New Testament revelations seem to allow a broader application to some information about the future, while keeping other prophecies specifically for Israel (Rom. 11:23–28).

Human overconfidence versus God's sovereign plan. If we focus only on the fulfillment issues in this passage, we may miss the underlying theological message that is the basis for these promises. One of these themes is that people can have a warped understanding about their own ability to control their environment and bring about God's plan (5:5–6). This usually is also accompanied by some confusion about God's role in determining the future.

In this section the Hebrew people in Jerusalem cry out and lament their situation because the Assyrians are threatening them (4:9), yet they inexplicably fail to go to God as the King who has the ability to change their situation. By contrast, the many strong nations attacking Jerusalem think that they are in control of their future and that by their own strength they will be able to desecrate Jerusalem (4:11); yet these nations fail to understand that God has higher purposes and plans to destroy them (4:12).

All the positive hopes presented by Micah encourage his Hebrew audience, but in their overconfidence they proudly claim what "we" will do when the Assyrians attack (5:5–6). They ignore the fact that God's plans "do not wait for man" (5:7). This basic theme is a central lesson of all prophecy. God is the sovereign power who plans the future, not human beings; nations do not determine the future political maps of this world, God does. Through a new messianic ruler who governs in God's strength, God will bring about his worldwide kingdom on earth (5:4).

God provides hope for the future. God gives people hope for the future because he knows the end from the beginning and the timing of each aspect. In a crisis where people feel overwhelmed by circumstances beyond their control (the Assyrian attack, in Micah's case), it is easy to despair and think that there is no possibility of finding a solution. Micah's message teaches that hope involves waiting, having faith that a promise will come true, developing confidence in the One who has made the promise, and possessing a degree of peaceful assurance that things will change.

Hope involves the removal of fear and a subjective attitude of strong expectation for what has not yet happened. Trust in God's promises produces hope.[25] W. Zimmerli has traced the message of Israel's hope through

---

24. I do not follow Waltke, "Micah," *The Minor Prophets*, 709, who sees the prophecy about the seven or eight leaders fulfilled "in the church: Christ raised up elders and gifted people to protect it against evil people."

25. E. Hoffmann, "Hope, Expectation," *NIDNTT*, 2:238–46.

---

each section of the Old Testament and finds hope as a fundamental thread flowing throughout its pages.[26] Proverbs provides hope of a good result for the people who discipline themselves and follow God's wise advice, while Job struggled to discover if one can put any hope in God's administration of justice. Although trials test our faith and may temporarily shake our confidence, in the end even Job found that God's wisdom and power provided a solid foundation for hope (Job 38–42).

Abraham went to an unknown place, based on his hope that God would fulfill his promises (Gen. 12:1–7; Heb. 11:8–10). The psalmists repeatedly waited on God to deliver them from the sword of their enemies (Ps. 13; 27:13–14; 33:20–22), and the prophets pointed to an ideal period in the future when God's rich blessing would be a reality in the lives of his people (Amos 9:11–15). Micah adds to this hope in chapters 4–5, not simply in order to give people more detailed information, but to challenge them to put their trust in God in the midst of their present trials. Micah's message encourages them to face the unpleasant facts of exile (4:10a), but he couples these ideas with words of hope because God will redeem them (4:10b).

Hope is not just related to what God has done for others in the past but is also connected to his ultimate plan to bring the messianic Ruler who will some day shepherd his people in the strength of God (5:2–4). This messianic promise guided the wise men who followed the star and then followed the prophecy of Micah to Bethlehem to find the baby Jesus (Matt. 2:1–6). We still look forward to the final fulfillment of that prophecy, when the "greatness [of the Messiah] will reach to the ends of the earth" (Mic. 5:4).

THE APPLICATION OF the central portion of this passage (5:2–4) in the church is heavily influenced by the fulfillment of this prophecy recorded in the New Testament (Matt. 2). For the person who has accepted Christ as Savior, the birth of Jesus wonderfully confirms what Micah says. This fulfillment gives great assurance that the other prophecies in the Bible will be fulfilled. God's promises are taken seriously because they are not empty talk. God accomplishes his purpose (Isa. 55:10–11).

In certain situations the fulfillment of a prophecy has apologetic and evangelistic value.[27] P. E. Little uses Micah 5:2 and various prophecies in

---

26. W. Zimmerli, *Man and His Hope in the Old Testament* (Naperville, Ill.: Allenson, 1968).

27. I have a tract in Hebrew and English that uses these verses in Micah to demonstrate to Jewish people that the Messiah whom Micah spoke of has already come in the person of Jesus Christ.

Isaiah to prove that the Bible is a reliable document and the Word of God.[28] The birth of Christ in Bethlehem helps a believer demonstrate to the doubter or unbeliever that this person, Jesus, is the One whom the prophets spoke of. Since Jesus was from the line of David according to the genealogy of Matthew 1 and functioned in his ministry as the good shepherd of his sheep (John 10), he fits the picture Micah presents. Since he is not presently reigning on earth as the Ruler of all nations, we look forward with anticipation to the time when that part of his mission will be fulfilled—that is, when he comes a second time. Micah originally gave this prophecy to provide hope for people thousands of years ago, and it continues to engender trust and confidence in God's promises for people today.

How should people respond to a crisis situation? The crying and agony in 4:10 are a typical and natural reaction to a crisis situation (such as the coming of the Assyrians). There is nothing inherently wrong with crying when difficult situations arise in our lives. Thus, Micah's exhortation focuses on what people often do not do in a crisis situation: The Israelites do not turn to their King and Counselor, God himself (4:9).

Why not? Micah does not explain the reason here, but a person's view of the nature and character of God may well explain the issue. Those with a high view of God, who recognize that God is the sovereign King of this world, will be more likely to bring their problems to him. If, however, you live around self-reliant and independent people who proudly struggle through problems with a stiff upper lip, then calling on God for help may not be an immediate response to troubled times. These people work hard, don't complain, and don't bother God with the little details of life. Looking at this idea from the positive side, one can exhort people not to follow the mistakes of the past but to seek God's help in times of crisis. A good biblical example is Nehemiah, who repeatedly calls out to God for help throughout his ministry (Neh. 1:4; 2:4; 4:4, 9; 5:19; 6:9, 14; 9:5–38; 13:14, 22, 29).

One factor that determines how people respond to a crisis is their belief about God's sovereign plans in relation to "our" plans for the future. The Assyrians think their plans can determine their future and that of Judah (4:11), while the proud Israelites in Judah think their own plans and strength will enable them to defeat their enemies (5:5–6). This tendency to depend on what "I/we" can do and the desire to control the future through "my/our" own wisdom leaves no room for God to demonstrate his power, accomplish his plans, or demonstrate his glory.

---

28. P. E. Little, *Know Why You Believe* (New York: Pyramid, 1973), 60–62, says that "fulfilled prophecy is one of the evidences of the supernatural origin of the word of its prophets (Jer. 28:9)."

In some ways life is a struggle of wills, a contest to see whose plans will win out. It almost seems like second nature for two-year-old children to say no to their parents when it is time to go to bed. They have their plans and want things their own way. It is not always easy to teach them that they do not have the ability to control everything around them.[29] Just about the time that parents finally think they have regained some order in the family, junior-high students going through puberty challenge every rule and principle the parents have established in their first dozen years of life. Parental plans about dating, curfews, and doing things as a family are often thrown out the window. Although at this stage parents must allow these children to develop their own identity and permit some independence,[30] this does not mean that anything goes.

Anyone involved in marriage counseling knows that the problem of wanting *my* plans to happen and wanting to control the future are common forces that drive couples apart.[31] At work, bosses and employees often have different perspectives on how companies should be run, and one person or group in the church may try to force their wishes on the rest of the congregation. In all these cases there is the problem of *my* control of the future and *my* ability to make things go according to *my* plans. We often want to solve our crisis situations ourselves.

Micah's message reminds us that God is in control of the future. Although we (as children, teens, or married adults) may independently demand to do things our way and follow the example of Judah's enemies in 4:11, God knows our thoughts and will eventually bring us into submission to his plans (4:12). Equally objectionable is any claim that we can determine the future by our own strength (like the military-minded inhabitants of Judah in 5:5–6). We are like the dew, sent by God according to his gracious plan, yet we must admit that our future is not controlled by human forces (5:7). All we can do is bring our future to God and pray for his will to be done on earth as it is in heaven (5:9; cf. Matt. 6:10).

Proverbs 27:1 encourages us not to boast about what will happen tomorrow because we do not determine what will happen. James 4:13–16 warns us not to predict what we will do because "you do not even know what will happen

---

29. B. Narramore, *An Ounce of Prevention* (Grand Rapids: Zondervan, 1973), 97–109, talks about the need for parents to discipline children. He opposes the approach of A. S. Neill, *Summerhill: A Radical Approach to Child Rearing* (New York: Hart, 1960), 114, who insists that "to impose anything by authority is wrong."

30. J. Kessler, *Ten Mistakes Parents Make with Teenagers* (Brentwood, Tenn.: Wolgemouth & Hyatt, 1988), 57–63, provides some helpful hints to parents about allowing teenagers to develop their own identity.

31. J. O. Balswick and J. K. Balswick, *The Family: A Christian Perspective on the Contemporary Home* (Grand Rapids: Baker, 1996), 231–44, deal with the issue of power and control within a marriage.

tomorrow.... As it is, you boast and brag. All such boasting is evil." This does not argue against planning for the future, but it does remind us that our plans are always subject to God's will. We may think we can accomplish great things (cf. Mic. 5:5–6), but it is actually God who is accomplishing them through us.

Balancing present realities with future hope. The hope apparent in Micah's oracles is not utopian, for imbedded in the very structure of these promises are realistic words about the present siege "now," which will bring humiliation to Judah's king (5:1). Even the bright messianic promises are qualified by "Israel will be abandoned until the time " (5:3), and redemption is only after a Babylonian exile (4:10). This reminds every preacher and teacher to declare the whole counsel of God. The day of the Lord's coming and the establishment of the Messiah's worldwide kingdom is not yet here, so today we live in the real, sinful world of wars and trouble. Nevertheless, hope is not destroyed by our present reality in this world, for this hope produces faith in God's promises, a commitment to walk in his ways, and patient endurance as we wait for the confirmation of the promises (Rom. 5:2–5).

Hope is practical because it is seen in the eyes and the smiles of those who believe, it influences attitudes toward what can be done, and it looks beyond the present problems toward the One who has the power to control the solutions. Without hope there is no reason to go on. Having the blessed hope that Micah describes gives people a reason to live joyfully and to serve willingly in submission to God's plans.

At the funeral of John F. Kennedy, Senator Edward Kennedy quoted a portion of one of his brother's speeches:

> Our future may lie beyond our vision, but it is not completely beyond our control ... the work of our own hands, matched to reason and principle, will determine our destiny. There is pride in that, even arrogance, but there is also experience and truth. In any event, it is the only way we can live.[32]

I would beg to differ, Mr. President. The future is not ours to control. It is sinful and proud (as you admit) to claim that we control what must be left in the hands of God. There is another way to live. We can trust in God's sovereign power rather than the work of our own hands. Hope is not secure if it is founded only on human plans, human reason, and human experience. Lasting hope is only found in God.

---

32. B. L. Shelley, *The Gospel and the American Dream* (Portland: Multnomah, 1989), 174, quotes from this speech and then notes how far this secular view of reality has drifted from the biblical perspective.

Micah 5:10–15

I N THAT DAY," declares the LORD,

"I will destroy your horses from among you
and demolish your chariots.
¹¹ I will destroy the cities of your land
and tear down all your strongholds.
¹² I will destroy your witchcraft
and you will no longer cast spells.
¹³ I will destroy your carved images
and your sacred stones from among you;
you will no longer bow down
to the work of your hands.
¹⁴ I will uproot from among you your Asherah poles
and demolish your cities.
¹⁵ I will take vengeance in anger and wrath
upon the nations that have not obeyed me."

Original Meaning

MICAH ENDS THE long section of 3:1–5:15 with a final oracle about purging all false sources of dependence—anything other than God himself. Allen calls it an announcement of punishment, while Mays give a more appropriate name: a message of salvation through purging.[1] Although some see a certain chiastic parallelism between 4:1–4 and 5:10–15, this is unlikely, for the only common element to both paragraphs is the destruction of instruments of war.[2] Each verse in 5:10–15 is constructed in an identical manner, except the final statement about the destruction of the nations that do not obey God (5:15); thus, the material is tightly unified in a single paragraph.

---

1. Allen, *Joel, Obadiah, Jonah and Micah*, 356; Mays, *Micah*, 124–25. Hagstrom, *Coherence of the Book of Micah*, 68, believes "this unit proclaims future hope for Israel in spite of YHWH's destruction of her own weapons." Wolff, *Micah*, 153, thinks this passage is related to an excommunication ceremony at the temple (Lev. 17:10; 20:3, 5–6), but this is primarily based on just one common word, "I will cut off." Excommunication is the cutting off of people, not cities, fortifications, horses, or idols, which are the objects mentioned in this passage.

2. Hagstrom, *Coherence of the Book of Micah*, 74, lays out the connections hypothesized by Renaud, while Allen, *Joel, Obadiah, Jonah and Micah*, 258–60, briefly lays out E. Nielsen's and his own chiastic structure but without much evidence or explanation.

Some scholars relate this oracle to the approaching Assyrian attack on Jerusalem.[3] Isaiah told Hezekiah about the foolishness of trusting in the horses and chariots of Egypt (Isa. 30:1–3; 31:1–3). Hezekiah himself then downplayed the importance of military forces to his people (2 Chron. 32:7–8) and worked hard to rid the nation of all forms of pagan worship (2 Kings 18:1–4). This sermon is probably a supportive message to legitimate Hezekiah's actions in the eyes of some doubters in Jerusalem (see Mic. 5:5–7). The prophet is apparently trying to persuade the leaders and citizens in Jerusalem to support the king's religious reforms.

The central theological message of this section is that God wants his people to stop worshiping and putting their hope in objects made by humans, which cannot save them (5:13b). Strong walled cities like Lachish and Jerusalem, strong armies from Egypt or Babylon, idols and Asherah poles, even witches who cast spells in the names of these gods—all these are of no value. They are human creations, which provide no lasting security. Hope is found only in God. He will purge all these feeble human attempts to provide hope. Only those who listen to God and obey him will escape his judgment (5:15).

False Political and Military Hopes Will Be Purged (5:10–11)

VERSE 10 BEGINS the same as 5:5, 7, 8 (5:4, 6, 7 in Heb. text) with *wehayah* (lit., "and it shall be"). This section adds the modifier "in that day," which links it with the identical phrase in 4:6 and the similar phrase ("in the last days") in 4:1. Thus, it seems to describe what God will do in an eschatological period. What Micah writes regarding what will happen in the last days has a repetitious regularity that builds force and emotion as you progress through them (a common technique used by African American pastors today). "I will destroy" is pounded into the psyche of the listener at the beginning of both of these verses to emphasize God's decisive action to end all trust in false, humanly created hopes. God sovereignly controls the future.

God will cut off both horses and chariots (5:10), the main means nations in that day used to destroy their enemies and assert sovereignty over land they owned or wanted to own (see also Isa. 2:7; 30:15–17; 31:1–3; Hos. 14:3). Micah is reacting against the nationalistic fervor of war that optimistically imagines that military might is the key to the success of a nation (see Mic. 5:5–6). The early covenant instructions warned kings not to

---

3. J. T. Willis, "The Authenticity and Meaning of Micah 5.9–14," *ZAW* 81 (1969): 353–68, lists thirty-one arguments scholars have given for a preexilic date at the time of Micah and thirty-nine reasons scholars have given for an exilic date. Mays, *Micah*, 124, sees it as exilic but connects the message to the 701 B.C. Assyrian crisis.

multiply horses (Deut. 17:16). The nation needs to put its confidence in the name of God rather than in horses and chariots (Ps. 20:7). Since God will judge between the nations and bring an end to war (Mic. 4:3–4), his promise to remove these instruments of war is not surprising. The purging of this source of human power and control comes when people put their total trust in God for security.

In a second, more drastic step, God will cut off and tear down the major walled cities in the land as well as the mighty fortresses (5:11). Whenever war came in Palestine, people from the countryside rushed into the heavily fortified cities for protection from an approaching enemy (Jer. 4:16; 5:6). These cities were built on strategic hills and had thick walls (the Broad Wall that Hezekiah built in Jerusalem was twenty-four feet thick), high towers, and three-chamber gates to make them almost impregnable. As a result, people tended to put their trust in human resources rather than in God. Later in Lamentations, the people mourned the fact that God "swallowed up all her palaces and destroyed her strongholds" (Lam. 2:5), leaving the people without any human basis for hope. Although such massive buildings and huge walls appear to provide hope to the nation, God's removal of them will leave the people with nothing to depend on but God.

False Religious Hopes Will Be Purged (5:12–14)

ISAIAH 2:6 AND 8:19 describe some of the witchcraft and sorcery that gradually infiltrated into Judah in the years preceding this message (during Uzziah's and Ahaz's reigns). Although Hezekiah attempted to remove the high places (2 Kings 18:1–4), not all the people who worshiped at these temples immediately changed their superstitious ways to follow God. Moses condemned such practices (Ex. 22:18; Lev. 19:26; Deut. 18:9–14), but they remained a part of the popular religious beliefs throughout the divided kingdom. The final purging of the land will remove this stumbling block and enable the people to listen to God.

Part of the false religious hope in Judah was tied to the people's dependence on idols of foreign gods. These included cultic stone pillars representing the Canaanite god Baal and the wood carvings of his female partner, Asherah (Mic. 5:13–14). These man-made representations of foreign gods seduced the Israelites into trusting in magical formulas, accepting false theological understandings of divine power and divine transcendence, and participating in the gross sexual practices of the Canaanites. The Israelites are to worship only Yahweh as their God (cf. Ex. 20:4; Deut. 7:5, 25; Isa. 44:9–20). Idols are useless objects that have no power; they cannot give people hope. By purging the nation of these idols, God will help the people focus on their true source of hope. As Ward maintains, it is impossible "to reduce the transcendent majesty of God to measurable certainty and manageable size."[4]

The reference to the removal of cities in the last line of 5:14 seems repetitive of 5:11 and out of place in this list of idols. L. Allen and T. Gaster translate the word "idol" rather than "cities," based on a Ugaritic cognate root meaning "idol."[5] Waltke follows Fisher, who believes there is a second meaning to this Hebrew root (i.e., temple quarters, inner room of a temple), based on its usage in 2 Kings 10:25.[6] The solution for this problem is unclear, but these two options help alleviate the problem without rejecting the present Hebrew text.

The Purging of Those Who Do Not Obey God (5:15)

THIS SECTION'S CLIMAX features a final statement about God's purging of people who do not listen or obey. Almost all commentaries regard 5:10–14 as the purging of God's people, while 5:15 is a condemnation of Israel's enemies, the foreign nations.[7] Although this is certainly part of the meaning of "nations" or Gentiles (*goyim*), disobedient Israel is lumped with these nations and given this same name on more than one occasion (Ezek. 2:3; 36:13–15; 37:22).[8] Thus, I maintain Micah is referring to the execution of God's anger and fury against the people in all nations (including Judah) who do not obey God by submitting to his will.

The word translated "vengeance" (*nqm*) does not mean spiteful, vindictive revenge. Waltke's study of this word finds it is used as "a legal term that signifies a ruler who secures his sovereignty and keeps his community whole by delivering wronged subjects and punishing their guilty slayers who do not respect his rule."[9] Thus Waltke translates the first part of 5:15, "and I will avenge my sovereignty." This refers to the just execution of divine control over the affairs of the world. In the process of exercising this full control, some who have ignored God's ways and not obeyed him will reap their just reward.

This final statement is therefore both a challenge to Judah (lest it be among these nations) as well as a great basis for hope (God's judgment of their enemies who reject him). Judah will not have to worry about its powerful enemies forever, for God's sovereign power will one day eliminate all opposition to his

---

4. J. M. Ward, *Hosea: A Theological Commentary* (New York: Harper and Row, 1966), 147.

5. Allen, *Joel, Obadiah, Jonah and Micah*, 360, depends on T. Gaster, "Notes on the Minor Prophets, *JTS* 38 (1937): 163–65.

6. Waltke, "Micah," *The Minor Prophets*, 721; L. R. Fisher, "The Temple Quarter," *JSS* 8 (1963): 32–41.

7. Wolff, *Micah*, 160; Mays, *Micah*, 127; Allen, *Joel, Obadiah, Jonah and Micah*, 360.

8. See A. Cody, "When Is the Chosen People Called a Gôy?" *VT* 14 (1964): 1–6.

9. Waltke, "Micah," *The Mnor Prophets*, 722.

rule. The Hebrews in Micah's audience need to be concerned primarily about their own faithfulness to what God has spoken to them. In the end nationalism really does not matter; what matters is a people's relationship to God.

THIS SECTION IS focused on what God will do to remove humanly created sources of false hope. The prophet gives no exhortations here to the audience of his day, nor does he demand that they act in any certain way. Nevertheless, if God is someday going to destroy certain things, implicit in Micah's statements is the idea that true followers of God should desire to implement his divine will into their lives today. In other words, knowing that God will bring an end to war in the last days (4:3) and bring in peace (5:5a), a believer should support this divine ideal today. Likewise, if God is going to purge the world of all false religious hopes in the last days (5:12–14), we should follow the Lord God today.

Since this prophecy functions as a support for Hezekiah's policy of removing idols from Judah, it should support similar attempts to remove false worship practices that humans have created to give themselves a false sense of security. As Allen suggests, "Micah issues a clarion call to Israel for true faith in their God, a faith that transcends nationalism and addiction to religion and to the metaphysical, a faith that is grounded in the revelation of God's character and will."[10] If the passage is dealt with in this way, several principles can be developed that will set the basis for modern application in the church.

No dependence on the military. God's people should not depend on military forces or defensive systems to assure them of military victory (5:10–11). The clear and consistent message of Scripture is that the outcomes of battles on earth belong to the Lord (1 Sam. 17:47).

This was true of the battle between the mighty horses and "six hundred of the best chariots" (Ex. 14:7) of the Egyptian pharaoh and the frightened Israelite camp, which had no military power. Although the Israelites feared immediate slaughter by Pharaoh's army, Moses encouraged them with the promise that "the LORD will fight for you" (14:14). God's purpose was to gain glory for himself through his destruction of Pharaoh and his chariots (14:18). This happened in two ways: when the Egyptians confessed that "the LORD is fighting for them against Egypt" (14:25), and when the Israelites sang their song of victory: "The LORD is my strength and my song; he has become my salvation. . . . The LORD is a warrior; the LORD is his name. Pharaoh's chariots and his army he has hurled into the sea" (15:2–4).

---

10. Allen, *Joel, Obadiah, Jonah and Micah,* 361, sees an application to Micah's audience and to us today because both groups need to know if they are depending on false hopes.

God's power also overthrew stronger military forces when the Israelites defeated the Amalekites (Ex. 17:8–15) and when he destroyed the mighty walled city of Jericho (Josh. 6). Although Gideon was weak in his own faith, God miraculously enabled a small force of three hundred Israelites to confuse the large Midianite encampment and defeat them (Judg. 7). Through God's power the young, militarily inexperienced David overcame the skilled giant soldier, Goliath, in order that everyone would know "that it is not by sword or spear that the LORD saves; for the battle is the LORD's" (1 Sam. 17:47).

Hosea complained that "Israel has forgotten his Maker and built palaces; Judah has fortified many towns" (Hos. 8:14), rather than trusting in God for military protection and security. The psalmist argues against any false trust in military power because God "makes wars cease to the ends of the earth; he breaks the bow and shatters the spear, he burns the shields with fire. 'Be still, and know that I am God; I will be exalted among the nations'" (Ps. 46:9–10). According to Revelation 19, God will win the final battles at the end of time. Thus, people should not depend on military strength, which is only a false hope, for their security.

No dependence on the humanly created religious activities. Another principle is that people should not depend on humanly created religious means of pleasing God (5:12–14). Many of these are only deceptive charades that provide no contact with God and bring no eternal hope. From the giving of the commandments about not making a graven image (Ex. 20:3–4) and the condemnation of the worship of the golden calf (Ex. 32), to the constant fight against the worship of Baal throughout the history of Israel (Judg. 2; 1 Kings 11:1–13; 18; 2 Kings 17; 21), God's people continuously desired to reimagine God in a form that was humanly controllable. People want to be able to have the security of knowing that a divine being will act in a predictable way if they pull the right strings and say the right liturgy.

Such reduction of the incomprehensible God, who is glorious beyond understanding, into a set object or series of defined behavior patterns is a deluded attempt to achieve religious security on human terms rather than on the basis of a dynamic relationship with a living God. This manipulation of the divine being in order to get human control of the future can exhibit itself in many forms. Idols and the soothsayers are one form of perversion, but more sophisticated people today are more apt to re-create an image of God in their minds by redefining him in terms acceptable to their philosophical beliefs and modern cultural assumptions. This is evident in arguments over God's gender by feminists, his racial features by minorities, his limited power by those who have an open view of God, and the rejection of eternal judgment by universalists.

Equally as serious are the widespread prejudices by church members against conceiving of God as anything but loving, or the strange view that God will automatically take us to heaven if we are fairly good people. Many are deluded by false hopes that have no basis in Scripture. Those who truly follow God should not wait until he purges the world of these human creations in the last days (idols or any other false understanding of God), but should attempt to remove as many of these as possible today, just as Hezekiah did in his day.

Listening to and obeying God. The final principle (in 5:15) is that God's treatment of people will be based on their willingness to listen to what he has said and their commitment to follow his will faithfully. God will execute his sovereign will over all humanity, and those who pay no attention to what he has said or are fooled into believing some false understandings about him will discover the error of their ways. As Jesus taught in the parable about the wise and the foolish builders, "everyone who hears these words of mine and puts them into practice is like a wise man who built his house on the rock. . . . But everyone who hears these words of mine and does not put them into practice is like a foolish man who built his house on sand" (Matt. 7:24–26). Someday the reign of God will come and the house built on false hopes will come crashing down.

THIS PASSAGE ADDRESSES three modern cultural trends that people in the church need to take a stand on: the tendency for nations and individuals to anchor their hopes for the future on the military strength of a nation; the belief that any religious expression will be honored by God and provide a legitimate hope for the future; and the contention that a loving God would not establish his rule by punishing people who look at things a little differently from the biblical way.

Although there is nothing wrong with having an army, religious beliefs, or a positive view of God's character, every conceptualization of reality (especially spiritual reality) is in danger of being incomplete, unbalanced, culturally biased, or half-true. Such ideas may have the form, vocabulary, or flavor of true faith in God but in actuality be deceptive and misleading. Of course, some tolerance of religious diversity is necessary for people from different backgrounds and belief systems to live together in peace, but toleration should not be seen as the approval of behavior and beliefs that are inconsistent with what God has said. Micah is clear: Either you listen to what God has said and follow it, or you will have to answer to God himself (5:15).

Since many people in the church still struggle with what they should believe on various issues, spiritual leaders have the responsibility to provide

guidance and correction with teachings that alleviate confusion and misunderstandings. Like Micah, leaders must move people to levels of greater spiritual maturity. We know we will not achieve perfection, but we press on,
looking forward to the day when God's goals will be perfectly accomplished
at the coming of his glorious kingdom.

Trust in military resources? The Old Testament does not restrict kings
from having military forces, nor does it argue that cities should never have
defensive walls. Military conquests were necessary for the nation of Israel to
inherit the land of the Canaanites, but God repeatedly reminded the covenant
people that he was the One who was actually going before them to defeat
their enemies (Deut. 7:1–6; 9:1–3). God assumes that kings will have an
army (Deut. 17:16; 1 Sam. 8:11–12) but gives regulations about their size
(Deut. 17:16), treatment of captives (20:10–14), the destruction of whole
cities, and the dedications of all the booty to God (Josh. 6:17–24; 1 Sam.
15:1–3). The problem comes with the consequences of having large military
forces.

God insists that his people should not put their hope in a large army
(Deut. 17:16), trust in military alliances to bring success (Isa. 30:1–3; 31:1–
3), or use a superior military force to inhumanely mistreat people (Amos 1).
When kings have large armies, they are tempted to think in their pride that
they are sovereign over the world (Isa. 10:5–15; 36:13–20; 37:22–29).

The prophets teach that God is the One who removes rulers from power
and raises up kings and nations (Dan. 2). Sometimes he uses armies to defeat
his enemies (Josh. 6; Hab. 1), but at other times the divine warrior himself
defeats his enemies without human military effort. The Egyptian army was
drowned in the Reed Sea (Ex. 14–15). God miraculously defeated the Assyrian army at Jerusalem when the angel of the Lord killed 185,000 troops (Isa.
37:36). Jesus never condemned the military might of Rome but reprimanded
Peter because people of the sword often perish by the sword (Matt. 26:53).
Some heroes of faith (e.g., Heb. 11:32) were military men.

Some believers today are pacifists, who oppose war and military service
and take a nonviolent approach to conflict. They maintain that Christians
should turn the other cheek and be more concerned about the spiritual battle for people's souls rather than earthly battles for power and land.[11] R. J.
Regan and other Christians have proposed a just-war theory, which suggests
that at certain times it is appropriate and the just obligation of peace-loving

11. W. Klassen, *Love of Enemies* (Philadelphia: Fortress, 1984), focuses mainly on the ideal
of peace, but he fails to adequately deal with Israel's military tradition. He sees God's commands to destroy the Canaanites as "aberrations which come from weakness and failed to
draw upon that faith in Yahweh which is the cornerstone of Hebrew faith" (39).

people to intervene by going to war to protect the mass slaughter of innocent people.[12] Such approaches deal with the ethical questions of going to war, but more focus needs to be given to the proper use of military forces, the limitations of their use, and the psychological and religious impact of military power on people's acceptance of the sovereignty of God.

Micah and Isaiah argue for trusting in God rather than in military forces (Isa. 31:1–3). The same key practical questions come back to people today: In what do we put our trust? Who do we think controls the military powers of this world? Are we willing to hold rulers and military leaders accountable for the misuse of power? What is a legitimate size for an army in God's eyes? How can we as individual Christians and as a body of believers be involved in the process of determining the appropriate use of military forces? Are we willing to trust God instead of our military and defensive strength?

For a practical application of some of these questions, one could use Regan's discussion of World War I (1914–1918), the Vietnam Wars (1946–1975), the Falkland War (1982), the civil wars in Nicaragua and El Salvador (1978–1992), the Gulf War (1991), the intervention in Somolia (1992), and the Bosnian War (1992–1995). An analysis of the behavior of armies on both sides of these conflicts helps one address thought-provoking questions at the end of each section to sharpen the reader's understanding of the complexity of the political and ethnic conflicts. When one sees the enormous loss of life through massive killing of innocent people by powerful armies, one cannot help but pray that the day will come quickly when there will be no need for instruments of war. In the meantime, Christians must be a part of the political process of helping each nation understand its limitations and responsibilities.

What religious expressions engender false hopes? Few would argue that idols and graven images do not present a false hope to the worshiper, and most would concede that the flimflam con artists in the religious world provide no real hope to those who are deluded by a lot of fast talk. Equally serious are the deceptive false hopes that are more realistic imitations of the truth, especially the hope offered by cults that make some use of the Bible.

In 5:12–14 Micah describes deceptive forms of worship that are rejected because the worshiper does not distinguish between proper and improper conceptions of God. Modern missionaries must contend with people who actually have images of gods in their homes or places of worship. This passage supports a missionary's exhortations to remove all idols since God will

---

12. R. J. Regan, *Just War: Principles and Cases* (Washington, D.C.: Catholic Univ. of America, 1996). A dialogue of four different views on this issue is found in *War: Four Christian Views*, ed. R. G. Clouse (Downers Grove, Ill.: InterVarsity, 1991).

judge people who worship false gods. Other more sophisticated intellectuals may not worship an idol in their homes, but they believe in the predictions of the horoscopes, trusting in the alignment of the stars and planets instead of the Creator of the stars.

A contemporary area where the church may need to apply lessons from this passage is seen in the new interest in Sophia, the goddess figure that some feminist groups have deified. Is this a true reflection of God or a clever deception that God would want to remove? *Sophia* is the Greek word for wisdom, used to describe the wisdom of God (Rom. 11:33; 1 Cor. 1:24; Eph. 3:10). The strong connection between God and wisdom is especially prominent in Proverbs 1–9, where wisdom says: "I was appointed from eternity, from the beginning, before the world began" (Prov. 8:23). Wisdom is personified as a female figure, yet closely identified with God himself.

Although some modern authors use Sophia as just another name for God,[13] others have crossed far beyond that threshold by introducing a foreign female goddess. Those attending the "Re-Imagining" conference in 1995 heard about a "Second Reformation" for the church. S. Cyre reported that "working from a basis in feminist theology, conference participants looked to pantheistic religions and the heritage of the Gnostic gospels to 'reimagine' a new god and a new road to salvation. The attendees blessed, thanked, and praised Sophia as a deity."[14] Mack B. Stokes viewed the conference as "theologically ignorant ... ontologically superstitious ... Christologically blasphemous ... ecclesiastically irresponsible."[15]

T. Finger takes a less confrontational approach to the subject but clearly recognizes wisdom in Proverbs 1–9 as "a personification of one of Yahweh's attributes."[16] He finds traces of the idea of wisdom in Proverbs 1–9 and Wisdom of Solomon 7:24–26, where *sophia* "pervades and penetrates all things. For she is a breath of the power of God, and a pure emanation of the glory of the Almighty ... a reflection of eternal light, a spotless mirror of the working of God" (NRSV). Finger also sees a connection between *sophia* and Jesus as the "Word" in the Gospel of John (both were with God at creation, and both manifest God's glory). The wisdom connection with Jesus is also evident in 1 Corinthians 1:24,

---

13. E. Schüssler Fiorenza, *In Memory of Her: A Feminist Theological Reconstruction of Christian Origins* (New York: Crossroad, 1983), 130–33, identifies feminine images of God with Sophia but later speaks positively of the integration of Egyptian Isis goddess language into Jewish monotheism. In spite of this, she warns of "ditheism" and says that "goddess-language is employed to speak about the *one* God of Israel."

14. S. Cyre, "Fallout Escalates over 'Goddess' Sophia Worship," *CT* 38 (April 1994): 74.

15. Ibid.

16. T. Finger, "In the Name of Sophia: Seeking a Biblical Understanding of Holy Wisdom," *CT* 38 (Nov. 1994): 44.

where Jesus is called the "wisdom of God" (see also Col. 1:15–17).[17] Finger does not object to the use of Sophia as a name for God to enrich our appreciation and understanding of God, but he does object to the current trends because "much current Sophia worship ... is so focused on an immanent divine presence, and seems to regard Jesus as so little different from us."[18]

L. Lafebure has traced the history of Sophia in the church and finds that Catholics have often identified Sophia with Mary, while Russian Orthodox thinkers have developed a mystical tradition around reflection on Sophia.[19] He has also found that second-century gnostics developed elaborate mythologies about Sophia while the early church tended to follow the lead of Philo of Alexandria, who made a connection between Sophia and the Logos.[20] Origen saw that Christ was called wisdom and suggested that Sophia was "begotten beyond the limits of any beginnings that we can speak of or understand,"[21] but Irenaeus identified Sophia with the Spirit, not Jesus.[22] This desire for a female goddess by some women will continue to challenge the limits of church tolerance and inclusiveness. Although there is nothing wrong with imagining God as a mother caring for a child, a failure to distinguish between metaphor and reality could lead the church into further strife and even into heresy.

Many people are not even aware of the Sophia movement, but everyone is involved with reimagining God based on biblical metaphors, church traditions, and meaningful cultural models. Thus, there is a danger that anyone could imagine God in a way that is so far from the truth that a false god is created in the minds of worshipers. Drawing the line between heresy and an unbalanced picture is not our concern here. The main need is for each person to evaluate one's own conception of God and for pastors and teachers to make sure that their representations of God are not out of focus or a lopsided picture of the fullness of the mystery and majesty of God.

Do we use the term *Father* too much and thus give a male gender to God? Do we emphasize God's love, grace, and mercy but ignore the fact that God hates and despises evil? In a world of democracy and individual rights, do we ever picture God as the all-powerful King of kings, who is to be absolutely obeyed? Have we caused people to be afraid of God by making him a stern Judge who is just sitting up in heaven, watching us so that he can catch us in some small mistake? Or has God become so much a friend and buddy

---

17. Ibid.
18. Ibid., 45.
19. L. D. Lafebure, "The Wisdom of God: Sophia and Christian Theology," *Christian Century* 111 (Oct. 1994): 951.
20. Ibid., 954.
21. Origen, *On First Principles* 1.2.1–2.
22. Irenaeus, *Against Heresies* 4.20.3.

that there is no majesty or fear? What emphasis is placed on the holiness of God? Do we emphasize the justice of God and therefore encourage justice in relationships between genders, races, employees and employers, and nations? How do we imagine God makes a difference?

People tend to develop their worldviews (including religious images) from their social relationships, so the church has an awesome responsibility to give the world an accurate picture of God that is biblically based rather than culturally based. God's decision to destroy Israel because they have misconceived who he is (5:15) demonstrates that the way one reimages God does matter to him. In that instance the nation adopted a popular cultural model (a Canaanite or Assyrian image) rather than our modern concept of God. The threat of allowing our culture to remold God into its own image is a mistake each generation must resist.

Consequences for disobedience (5:15). Micah's sermon ends with a clear indication that God will deal with all nations (and the individuals within them) based on obedience. Disobedience is the act of not listening to (šmᶜ, to listen, obey) or following what God says. God's response to rebellion will eventually come; he will not be long-suffering and patient forever. Someday he will exercise his divine justice by ruling in power over all nations. This warning is not just applicable to nations in the time of Micah but applies to all nations. If our nation consistently chooses to turn from God's revealed will, it will experience horrible consequences when his just rule is established. Obedience is not optional but is a natural response to hearing what God has said. Once a person or nation has heard the truth, responsibility is required.

This idea can be applied to innumerable practical issues in the church. Although divine justice will be established at the end of time when God sets up his final kingdom, no one should think that God will let people get away with unjust behavior today. If one does not listen to what he has said about sexual purity, one should expect to be confronted by him on this act of disobedience. If one lies and deceives people about the truth, one should not be surprised at God's attempts to establish justice by holding one accountable for past deceptions. If one cheats another person in a slick business deal, one should expect God's disapproval for this injustice.

If God has commanded believers to go into all the world and make disciples, will he be pleased with people who refuse to listen to his instructions? If God requires from people just relationships with others, a deep love for steadfast covenant loyalty, and a circumspect walk with God (6:8), will he deal kindly with those who do not accept his requirements? In the end, obedience is an issue of choosing to do our will or to submit to God's will. If people are unwilling to listen to and do God's will, they are not his disciples. If one is not a disciple, one is an enemy of God and subject to his punishment.

Micah 6:1–16

Listen to what the LORD says:

"Stand up, plead your case before the mountains;
    let the hills hear what you have to say.
² Hear, O mountains, the LORD's accusation;
    listen, you everlasting foundations of the earth.
For the LORD has a case against his people;
    he is lodging a charge against Israel.

³ "My people, what have I done to you?
    How have I burdened you? Answer me.
⁴ I brought you up out of Egypt
    and redeemed you from the land of slavery.
I sent Moses to lead you,
    also Aaron and Miriam.
⁵ My people, remember
    what Balak king of Moab counseled
    and what Balaam son of Beor answered.
Remember ⌐your journey⌐ from Shittim to Gilgal,
    that you may know the righteous acts of the LORD."

⁶ With what shall I come before the LORD
    and bow down before the exalted God?
Shall I come before him with burnt offerings,
    with calves a year old?
⁷ Will the Lord be pleased with thousands of rams,
    with ten thousand rivers of oil?
Shall I offer my firstborn for my transgression,
    the fruit of my body for the sin of my soul?
⁸ He has showed you, O man, what is good.
    And what does the LORD require of you?
To act justly and to love mercy
    and to walk humbly with your God.

⁹ Listen! The LORD is calling to the city—
    and to fear your name is wisdom—
    "Heed the rod and the One who appointed it.
¹⁰ Am I still to forget, O wicked house,
    your ill-gotten treasures
    and the short ephah, which is accursed?

¹¹Shall I acquit a man with dishonest scales,
 with a bag of false weights?
¹²Her rich men are violent;
 her people are liars
 and their tongues speak deceitfully.
¹³Therefore, I have begun to destroy you,
 to ruin you because of your sins.
¹⁴You will eat but not be satisfied;
 your stomach will still be empty.
 You will store up but save nothing,
 because what you save I will give to the sword.
¹⁵You will plant but not harvest;
 you will press olives but not use the oil on yourselves,
 you will crush grapes but not drink the wine.
¹⁶You have observed the statutes of Omri
 and all the practices of Ahab's house,
 and you have followed their traditions.
 Therefore I will give you over to ruin
 and your people to derision;
 you will bear the scorn of the nations."

Original Meaning

THIS CHAPTER IS a covenant lawsuit brought by God against his people (somewhat similar lawsuits are in Deut. 32; Ps. 50; Jer. 2; Hos. 4).[1] Some extend the lawsuit form only to 6:1–5 or 6:1–8, but the judgment speech in 6:9–16 can be integrated into the lawsuit form if it is seen as the verdict of the Lord's case against his people.[2] C. Shaw extends this section even further to include 6:1–7:7, but we will argue that

---

1. The content and structure of biblical lawsuits are discussed in G. E. Wright, "The Lawsuit of God: A Form-Critical Study of Deuteronomy 32," *Israel's Prophetic Heritage: Essays in Honor of James Muilenburg*, ed. B. W. Andersen and W. Harrelson (New York: Harper and Row, 1962), 26–67; J. Limburg, "The Root רִיב and the Prophetic Lawsuit Speeches," *JBL* 88 (1969): 291–30; G. W. Ramsey, "Speech-Forms in Hebrew Law and Prophetic Oracles," *JBL* 96 (1977): 45–58. L. Allen also suggests that Micah is using a cultic "entrance liturgy," an inquiry about whether a person is able to be admitted into the sanctuary for worship (Allen, *Joel, Obadiah, Jonah and Micah*, 363), but it is doubtful that the questions in 6:6–7 are the questions that would be asked by any priest.

2. R. Smith, *Micah–Malachi*, 50, and Mays, *Micah*, 136, find the lawsuit in 6:1–5 and a Torah liturgy in 6:6–8, but Mays believes the two form a rhetorical unit.

7:1–7 is an integral part of the lament form present in chapter 7, but not in chapter 6.[3]

The imperative exhortation to "listen" (*šimʿu*) in 6:1 and 6:9 signals the main breaks between the two halves of this prophetic sermon. The dialogical interaction between the Lord and his people includes both the Lord's accusation (6:1–5) and the people's response of misunderstanding about sacrifices (6:6–7), plus God's response (6:8–16). The lawsuit includes the traditional elements of: (1) a call to attention (6:1); (2) a calling of witnesses (6:2a); (3) the announcement of a case (6:2b); (4) a defense of God's action (6:3–5); (5) a defense by the accused (6:6–7); (6) the basis of God's judgment (6:8); (7) additional accusations (6:9–12); and (8) God's verdict of judgment (6:13–16).[4]

These elements can be grouped into two paragraphs: 6:1–8 and 6:9–16. This literary form communicates the seriousness of the breakdown in God's relationship with his people. Some in Micah's day apparently think that everything is fine, that God should be happy with them. They are not listening to what the prophet has said over the years. In order to emphasize the seriousness of the situation, God is now willing to prove his case against them in an imaginary court of law. This lawsuit is a final wake-up call. The people should not assume that God's covenant relationship with them will continue if there is no commitment to worship and serve him. In fact, severe judgment is just around the corner because of their sinfulness.

The setting and tone of this sermon is very different from the spirit of 4:1–5:15. There are no positive promises, and this message does not refer to the immediate danger of the Assyrian crisis (701 B.C.) in terms similar to 4:10–11; 5:1, 5. Although Willis suggests a date around 701 B.C., Mays attempts to find an exilic or postexilic date, and Lecow proposes a fourth-century date for this speech. Though no date is given, the wicked conditions described in both chapters 6 and 7 could fit the final days of Hezekiah, when Manasseh was taking over from his father and turning the nation away from God.[5] The other possibility is to push these final chapters back

---

3. Shaw, *Speeches of Micah*, 165–84, based on a similar historical setting of social disorder, but this only suggests that chapters 6–7 come from the same time period, not that they are a literary unit.

4. In light of the judgment in 6:9–16 it is odd that J. M. P. Smith, "Micah," *Micah, Zephaniah, Nahum, Habakkuk, Obadiah, and Joel* (ICC; Edinburgh: T. & T. Clark, 1911), 122, thinks that a redactor changed an original judgment speech in 6:6–8 into the present Torah liturgy. J. T. Willis, "The Structure of the Book of Micah," *SEÅ* 34 (1969): 35, properly finds the sentence to the lawsuit in 9:13–16.

5. See the survey of opinions in Allen, *Joel, Obadiah, Jonah, and Micah*, 249–50, and Wolff, *Micah*, 170.

to the time of Ahaz (735–715 B.C.), to an unknown time after 722 (preferred by Allen).[6]

If Micah has a chronological order and if we are to make sense of the great disappointment of Micah in 7:1–2, then one can connect these sermons in chapters 6–7 to the early years of Manasseh when the people return to the pagan practices of earlier years (6:16). The rich take advantage of the weak (6:9–12) and follow the Baalism of Ahab (6:16; cf. 2 Kings 21). Micah sees these disappointing changes taking place at the end of his ministry (Mic. 7:1–2) as Manasseh begins his rule and quickly confronts it with this challenge. He warns the people about God's judgment if they do not come back to him and maintain their covenant relationship.

God Brings a Covenant Lawsuit Against Judah (6:1–8)

As Micah begins to deliver this sermon based on the characteristics of a lawsuit in a nation's courts, his audience undoubtedly quickly realizes the significance of the analogy he is using. But it is probably a surprising concept to many. Why does God bring charges against his own covenant people? What is the basis for his accusations against them? Have they done something so wrong that God is turning against them? Will God actually take his own chosen people to court because they are not faithful in keeping some minor part of the covenant relationship? Will he destroy Judah as he destroyed the northern nation of Israel a few years back (in 722 B.C., see 2 Kings 17)? This paragraph is held together by the repeated use of *mh* ("what") in 6:3[2x], 5[2x], 6, 8[2x], which inquires about "what" has gone wrong with this relationship.

The initiation of God's lawsuit (6:1–2). After an initial call to attention in 1:1a, God exhorts his prophet[7] to arise as a plaintiff in the court (Deut. 19:15) and plead this case before the mountains. The role of the mountains is unclear, but heaven and earth were witnesses when God made his covenant with Israel (Deut. 32:1; Ps. 50:1) and when his people sinned on the mountains of Judah.[8] The mountains (personified) know about the people's

---

6. Allen, *Joel, Obadiah, Jonah and Micah*, 250. I do not follow Lindblom or F. C. Burkitt, "Micah 6 and 7: A Northern Prophecy," *JBL* 45 (1926): 159–61, who identify the city in 6:9 and 7:10–11 as Samaria just before its destruction in 722 B.C.

7. Waltke, "Micah," *The Minor Prophets*, 727, appropriately differs from the NIV section heading (which imagines God addressing Israel), because he sees God asking Micah to arise and present this case in 6:1. Wolff, *Micah*, 167, takes the unlikely view that the hills are symbols of the nations, who are addressed in 6:1.

8. D. R. Daniels, "Is There a 'Prophetic Lawsuit' Genre?" *ZAW* 99 (1987): 339–60, suggests that the mountains are not called as judges or as witnesses to an earlier covenant, but

immorality and false worship of other gods; there is no way the people can deny what has happened.

Verse 2 reveals the purpose of God's lawsuit. With deep sadness yet stern resolve, God indicates that his covenant lawsuit is against his own people. He has serious accusations of covenant unfaithfulness to bring against them. All is not well in this relationship; thus, an adversarial confrontation is invited to resolve the conflict and restore mutual understanding and commitment between the partners. The Hithpa'el reflexive form of the verb "lodging a charge" (*ykḥ*) suggests that this will be a dialogical dispute in which they will argue with each other.

A defense of God's action (6:3–5). Instead of immediately accusing the people of Judah with a whole series of failures, as one might expect in a lawsuit, God begins his speech by rhetorically asking two questions about what he has done wrong. This may be understood as a response to the people's attitude toward God or simply as a wise rhetorical strategy that would be more successful than a direct frontal attack. The way the questions are asked projects God's tender love and deep care for "my people" rather than a hostile desire to end their relationship.

With strong pathos in his words,[9] God appears to be searching his own heart to determine if there was some evidence of unfaithfulness on his part or some unreasonable burden he has put on his covenant partner. Why is there such neglect by Israel, such boredom with the things of God? These questions will remove the listeners' defensive posture and open them up to considering God's failures—that is, their supposed objections to what God has done for them. Of course, if they cannot find any failure on God's part, then they will have to look at the possibility that they have failed in some way. The questions end with a request for some response from the people of Israel to explain what God has done wrong.

Since no response is presented to accuse God of any failings, he defends his past behavior by reciting his great acts of grace on behalf of his people. Four examples are given: the Exodus from Egypt, the giving of great leaders to the people, the deliverance of the nation from the requested curse of Balak, and the crossing of the Jordan and entering the land (6:4–5). In brief references to past traditions in the Torah, Micah calls the people to remember God's righteous deeds on their behalf. Through this process they will be

---

as entities affected by the behavior of the Israelites. I think both of these last two functions are appropriate, for the hills are invited to "listen" to what God and the people have to say— presumably, for the purpose of verifying its truthfulness.

9. Allen, *Joel, Obadiah, Jonah and Micah*, 365, emphasizes the Lord's tender pleading in these questions.

led to evaluate his faithfulness and ask whether the present covenant problems are God's fault.

God's saving deeds or "righteous acts" are celebrated in hymnic material (see Ps. 77:6–20; 105–106), in prophetic disputations (see Amos 3:1–2; 9:7–10), in confessions in covenant-renewal ceremonies (Josh. 24; 1 Sam. 12), and in prayers (Neh. 9). God's people were in Egypt and helplessly oppressed in slavery (Ex. 5–6) when God delivered/redeemed[10] them by miraculously bringing them out of bondage (Ex. 14–15). This fundamental righteous act of God's grace established Israel as his chosen people and functioned as a rationale for the establishment of the covenant relationship (19:4; 20:2). This use of ancient tradition is a powerful persuader that God has not been unfaithful to his people; no wrong can be found in his actions.

His great saving deeds involved the capable leadership of Moses, Aaron, and Miriam (Mic. 6:4b; see Josh. 24:17; 1 Sam. 12:6–8; Ps. 77:20; 105:26). Although these leaders were not perfect (Ex. 32; Num. 12; 20), they did lead the people through these perilous years.

God also calls the people to remember how he reversed the evil plans that Balak concocted and how he caused Balaam to pronounce blessings on Israel (Num. 22–24). Balak requested Balaam to curse the people (22:6, 16; 23:8, 13, 27; 24:10), but Balaam spoke only good news. Through his mouth God promised multiplication of the people, their strengthening, the coming of a future ruler, and the defeat of Israel's enemies.

The final glorious deed mentioned by God through Micah was crossing over the Jordan from Shittim on the east side to Gilgal on the west side (Josh. 2:1; 3:1).

This gracious list of deeds for Israel shows God's care for his people and the fulfillment of his promise to bring them into the Promised Land. The rhetorical force of these illustrations in Micah argues for the position that the people of Judah have no basis for complaining against God.[11] He has not failed to keep his side of the covenant relationship. An obvious implication of this evidence is that the fault does not lie with God.

A defense of Israel's action (6:6–7). Sensing the force of this conclusion, Micah imagines what some in his audience might say, or perhaps he is actually quoting the response of some Israelites. This is not a Torah liturgy made

---

10. The Hebrew root *pdh* can mean "to redeem" by paying a redemption price (Ex. 13:13; 34:20), but also the more general idea "to deliver" when no redemption price is paid.

11. Waltke, "Micah," *The Minor Prophets*, 730, calls 6:5 a "call to renew covenant," but it is not clear that "remembering" always or necessarily leads to accepting something or committing one's self to God. This is what God wanted to happen when the people remembered the Passover and celebrated it with a Passover meal, but there is no indication here that Micah is asking the people to remember things in this participatory way.

up of questions a priest would ask a person when coming to the temple.[12] Note how the entrance questions recorded in Psalms 15 and 24 deal with moral qualifications, not the size of one's offering. Note too that the present passage has nothing to indicate inquires about entrance into the temple.

These questions in verses 6–7, in other words, are rhetorical statements in which the people try to defend themselves by explaining how faithful they have been to God. Their questions match the earlier questions of God in 6:3 (*mh*, "what"), and they seem to protest their innocence by asking God similar questions. What have they done that God should find fault? They do not know what more they can do to please him. They bow low and humble themselves when they come into the glorious and powerful presence of God; is that not enough? Does God just want more burnt offerings? Would he be pleased with a greater quantity of sacrifices—as many as a thousand rams? How about ten thousand containers of oil or even a person's firstborn? Are not the Israelites obedient, full of reverence, and generous in giving to God?

But something seems out of line with these questions. They focus on excessive giving, as if God is primarily interested in the size or cost of the gifts. The nonsensical extremes (a thousand, ten thousand, a precious child) become absurd and reveal a fundamental problem in understanding what God requires of his people. What purpose did animal sacrifices have in restoring a person's relationship with God? Were they just a means of bribing God by giving him an enormous quantity of gifts? No, they were much different. They were an outward sign of the inner attitude of a person's broken and contrite heart.

What God requires (6:8). The answer to the audience's question is based on past traditions revealed earlier to the people ("he has showed you," or "he has told you"). Thus, Micah is not attempting to reveal some new standard of conduct or give an expanded or secret list of requirements previously unknown. God has already communicated what he requires. He wants from "man"—that is, from the creatures he created on the earth—three basic things.[13] By explaining these three principles Micah hopes to correct the misunderstanding of his audience in 6:6–7 and to explain the basis for God's verdict of this lawsuit in 6:13–16.

Earlier God required that his people love him with all their heart (Deut. 6:5); obey rather than sacrifice (1 Sam. 15:22; Hos. 6:6); fear, serve, obey, and

---

12. Hillers, *Micah*, 78, and Mays, *Micah*, 137, think that verses 6–7 come from "entrance liturgies" or priestly instruction regarding qualifications for coming into the temple area, but the differences between Psalms 15 and 24 and these verses suggest that this is not the background here. Wolff, *Micah*, 168, realizes that these verses do not have the expected content of an entrance liturgy.

13. Allen, *Joel, Obadiah, Jonah and Micah*, 371, sees this as contrasting the divine glory and stressing the subordination of humans to God.

not rebel (Deut. 10:12; 1 Sam. 12:14); and return to God, maintain loyalty and justice, and trust in him (Hos. 12:6). These past examples and Micah's present admonition do not really answer the question concerning *what sacrifices* one is to bring to the temple. As Mays comments, "The question is focused on 'with what' [in 6:6–7], on external objects at the disposal of the questioner. The answer [in 6:8] is focused on the questioner himself, on the quality of his life."[14] God is more interested in the person than any gift one might bring. One's character and behavior are what matter to God.

(1) Micah's list of core requirements first focuses on "acting justly" toward others. Since the people are covenant partners with God, they must demonstrate mutual respect for one another within the community. "Justice" describes right social relationships between people based on God's view of what is appropriate. These behavior patterns were described in covenant documents (Ex. 20–23), covering both legal and normal social relationships in and outside the courts. Such instructions included protection for foreigners, the poor, slaves, orphans, and widows, who could easily be wronged or taken advantage of by others (Isa. 1:17).

This characteristic of justice prohibits violent acts of physical abuse or any kind of behavior that attempts to take something that rightfully belongs to another. When people in Micah's audience forcibly confiscate other people's land or possessions (Mic. 2:1–2, 8–9), treat people inhumanely (3:1–2), and selfishly cheat others so that their financial position will be enhanced (3:9–11), these are unjust social relationships. Since the entire nation is a united covenant partner with God, it is important that people within that group not mistreat others who are essential members of this partnership with God.

(2) The second principle is to love "mercy" (*ḥsd*, i.e., "steadfast covenant loyalty"). The semantic range and usage of this term makes its interpretation somewhat unclear. Is this word used as a near synonym of "justice," pointing to the need for people to relate to other people in a merciful manner with loving affection rather than with injustice?[15] Waltke sees covenant loyalty being done when "anyone who is in a weaker position due to some misfortune or other should be delivered not reluctantly, but with a spirit of generosity, grace and loyalty. Acts of justice and succor motivated by a spirit of mercy guarantee the solidarity of the righteous covenant."[16]

If the word is not taken just as a parallel to justice, an even broader scope may be in view. *Ḥsd* describes the nature of a relationship characterized by

---

14. Mays, *Micah*, 137. This is similar to Wolff's comment that "it's you, not something, God wants" (*Micah*, 180).

15. Wolff (*Micah*, 181) focuses only on the merciful and heartfelt love between humans.

16. Waltke, "Micah," *Obadiah, Jonah, Micah*, 195.

loyalty to covenant obligations as well as acts of mercy that are not obligatory. In God's own steadfast covenant loyalty, he constantly is attentive and faithful to his covenant relationship. Like God, his people are also to relate to him in a spirit of steadfast covenant loyalty. When God's people exhibit a deep love for this kind of relationship with him, its power impacts one's commitment to deeply love those aspects of covenant life that relate to interpersonal human relationships as well.

Thus, the heart of *ḥsd* as steadfast covenant loyalty is not just being merciful to people in need. That response is only one outworking of a deep commitment to covenant life within God's community. On a day when one is not required to be merciful to any unfortunate person, one is still involved with maintaining a faithful covenant relationship with God and other people within the covenant. In other words, loving to maintain steadfast covenant loyalty will impact a person's attitude to worshiping God on the Sabbath, leaving the land fallow every seven years, releasing slaves according to Mosaic instructions, caring for the poor, and giving a tithe each year. If there is no commitment to remain faithful to this divine covenant relationship, then covenant life will cease to exist. Understood in this way, *ḥsd* is a broad term that encompasses much more than merely acting mercifully toward others.

(3) The final requirement is related to a person's humble walk with God. The Hebrew root *ṣnᶜ* describes a life walk that is not proud (Prov. 11:2) but is attentive, careful, and prudent to follow God's will. Thomas translates this phrase "to walk circumspectly,"[17] while Hillers prefers "wisely."[18] This suggests that Micah is warning against carelessly or presumptuously doing things your own way, instead of being attentive to do God's will. Such a walk with God is humble in that it puts a person's will in a secondary position and gives prudent attention to doing his will. In some sense this requirement is the broadest of the three, for if one does this, one will certainly treat others justly and faithfully maintain all the covenant responsibilities.

Micah's delineation of God's requirements is noteworthy insofar as it includes no negative statements about what is forbidden to the Israelites. It presents a positive case of what God thinks is best for humankind. It is the key to a full life within the covenant. It draws attention to the main things that matter and consequently ignores the petty attitudes of trying to please God by bribery through more or bigger sacrifices. God's radical requirements are more comprehensive and more penetrating than the casual deed of just bringing an animal to sacrifice at the temple. His covenant relationship lays a claim on

---

17. D. W. Thomas, "The Root *ṣnᶜ* in Hebrew and the Meaning of *qdmyt* in Malachi 3:14," *JJS* 1 (1949): 182–88, concludes that "humble" is a secondary meaning.

18. Hillers, *Micah*, 75–76, notes that the Targum translation is "discreet."

every human relationship, calls every act into loyal submission to the covenant agreement, and desires that every attitude of selfishness be prudently submitted to God's will. This high calling requires discipline and full commitment on the part of anyone who wants to be part of God's holy nation.

Accusations and Verdict (6:9−16)

ACCUSATIONS OF COVENANT disloyalty (6:9−12). Having set the standards for proper covenant behavior in 6:8, God now raises specific examples demonstrating that the people in Jerusalem have failed to live up to their covenant agreement. There has been no justice for others, no deep desire or commitment to maintain their loyalty to covenant principles, and no attempt to walk circumspectly with God. The specific address to "the city" in 6:9 does not imply that this is a new message to a new audience, for Micah is speaking to the people of Jerusalem throughout this lawsuit. It is also unnecessary to relocate 6:12 right after verse 9.[19]

The address to the city (6:9), presumably Jerusalem, focuses attention on the government, business, and religious leaders. Jerusalem is a major center for trade, the place where many wealthy people live; thus, it is one of the key places where the dishonest commerce is going on in the days of Manasseh (6:10−12). The NIV translates the last line of verse 9 as "Heed the rod and the One who appointed it" in the text, but the footnote indicates this reading is problematic. Since the word *mṭh* can mean either "rod" or "tribe" (NASB, RSV), many commentaries translate this word as "tribe." We prefer "Give heed, O tribe," since it provides a better parallel with "Listen! The LORD is calling to the city" in the first part of the verse.[20]

Interjected between these two addresses is a brief comment or a bit of advice. It is about sound judgment and practical good sense. Micah advises that if the people are wise, they will fear God's name, implying that they should take the following words that God speaks seriously.

---

19. Wolff, *Micah*, 188, sees a great deal of discontinuity with 6:1−8, while Mays, *Micah*, 143−44, and Hillers, *Micah*, 80, move verse 12 right after verse 9 because they believe the feminine pronouns in verse 12 refer to the city in verse 9. Hagstrom, *Coherence of the Book of Micah*, 95, sees unifying factors between vv. 1−8 with 9−16, based on repeated vocabulary ("listen" and "voice" in vv. 1 and 9; "in order that/therefore" ends vv. 5b and 16b). Allen, *Joel, Obadiah, Jonah and Micah*, 377, believes the covenant curses in 6:13−16 also help connect 6:1−16. Finally, I agree with Willis that the covenant lawsuit in 6:1−8 is incomplete without accusations or a verdict. Thus, the accusations in vv. 9−12 and the verdict in vv. 13−16 are needed to complete the lawsuit.

20. Waltke, "Micah," *The Minor Prophets*, 736, 738, and Hillers, *Micah*, 80, combine the end of 6:9 with the first word of verse 10, change the word divisions, and come up with "the assembly of the city," but this is unnecessary and assumes major corruptions in this text.

The accusations Micah wants his audience to pay attention to in 6:10 are plagued with textual problems. The NIV "Am I still to forget" is accepted in several commentaries, but it is just an educated guess.[21] Since the "wicked house" and "ill-gotten [wicked] treasures" seem overly repetitive in this verse, Allen, Wolff, and Waltke have taken *byt* ("house") as *bt* ("bath, a liquid measure"), thus giving the translation "a wicked measure," which provides a good parallel to "the short ephah, which is accursed" in the last line.[22]

In spite of the difficulties in the transmission and translation of this verse, clearly God is accusing the merchants in the market of cheating people through the use of dishonest weights and measures (see Amos 8:4–5). If a person can sell you a bushel of corn for three dollars but uses a bushel basket that actually contains only nine-tenths of a bushel of grain, the seller will add to his cash in his wicked treasury. The same thing can be accomplished by having "deceptive weights" or a scale that is not true (6:11). If one pays three shekels of silver for a product, the merchant can quickly increase his profit by setting on one side of a scale a three-and-a-quarter-pound weight, which the buyer must balance with his silver. God cannot just look the other way and declare people innocent of any wrongdoing. Micah's case is persuasive because no one would ever expect God to approve these evil acts.

An additional accusation of injustice is that the rich people in Jerusalem are disloyal to covenant principles because they are full of lawlessness, violence, and oppression (6:12a). Being "full of violence" (lit. trans. of 6:12a) implies that almost all actions are affected by this negative behavior pattern. The way they express this aggressive behavior is related to their improper use of their tongues (6:12b). They lie and use deceit to get their way. This may refer to their aggressive browbeating of people who question their cheating, untruthful statements about the products they sell, insults that deny people their rights, and maybe even deceit in court cases.

Verdict of punishment (6:13–16). Because of Israel's infidelity, the present covenant relationship is unbearable to God. Thus, the only possible verdict for this lawsuit is: guilty as charged. By giving this terrible conclusion, Micah is hoping to convince his audience of the seriousness of their sins. God's people must realize that this kind of behavior is unacceptable and will no longer be tolerated. God does not enjoy punishing his own covenant people any more than a parent enjoys punishing a child, but "because of

---

21. This requires one to change the Hebrew *hʾš* (possibly "the fire" or "the man"). If it is a verbal expression, it could be *hyš* ("is there") or *hʾš* ("can I forget," from the root *nšʾ*, "to forget"). The most literal translation might be, "Are there yet, in the houses of wickedness, treasures of wickedness?" but this does not fit well with the next line.

22. Allen, *Joel, Obadiah, Jonah and Micah*, 375; Wolff, *Micah*, 185–86; Waltke, "Micah," *The Minor Prophets*, 736, 738.

your sins" God himself will "make you sick, smiting you," or "will sorely smite you" (not the NIV "I have begun to destroy you").[23]

In contrast to God's decisive "I will" action in 6:13 are the "you will" consequences on Israel in 6:14–15. This divine frustration of the natural order is what is called a "futility curse." These curses, which bring to naught the usual expectations of people, are common in ancient Near Eastern treaties as well as in the Bible (Lev. 26:26; Deut. 28:30–31, 38–40; Hos. 4:10; Amos 5:11).[24] The usual blessing of God on nature will be reversed into a curse so that eating will not satisfy, planting will not be followed by harvesting, treading on grapes will not result in wine, and storing up things will not produce a savings. Nothing will happen as it is supposed to; everything a person tries will be frustrated by God's curse. The second half of 6:14 does not follow this pattern as closely as the rest of 6:14–15, but part of the problem may be some misunderstanding of the vocabulary.[25]

The verdict ends with a brief conclusion that has a final accusation and punishment statement. To show the seriousness of the problem in Judah, Micah compares Judah to the northern kingdom under the reigns of Omri and Ahab, two wicked kings of Israel. Micah does not spell out what specific sins he is referring to, but his audience knows about these kings. First Kings 16:25–28 refers to Omri as a king in Samaria who did evil in God's eyes and was more wicked than all the kings before him—including encouraging the nation to worship idols. Ahab did even worse by building a Baal temple and altar in Samaria (16:29–33). Ahab and Jezebel cruelly killed the prophets of God (18:4) and lied to have Naboth stoned so they could take his land (ch. 21). Later, 2 Kings 21:3 states that Manasseh followed the worship patterns of Ahab, as Micah claims here. These actions are in direct contradiction of the Torah traditions that condemned the worship of other gods (Ex. 20:2–4).

Since the people in Jerusalem at the time of Manasseh are following the same practices as Omri and Ahab, the same thing that happened to the northern kingdom will happen to the southern kingdom. God will abandon the inhabitants of the city of Jerusalem and allow them to be ruined and

---

23. The verb comes from *ḥlh* ("to be sick") rather than *ḥll* ("to begin"), although Wolff, *Micah*, 187, and Waltke, "Micah," *Obadiah, Jonah, Micah*, 143, prefer "to begin."

24. D. R. Hillers, *Treaty-Curses and the Old Testament Prophets* (Rome: Pontifical Biblical Institute, 1964), 28–29.

25. In 6:14b there is confusion over *yšḥ* ("hunger, emptiness"), which NIV translates "empty," while NASB has "vileness"; Kaiser, "Micah," *Micah–Malachi*, 75, prefers "dysentery." H. G. M. Williamson, "Marginalia in Micah," *VT* 47 (1997): 367–68, suggests a new translation of 6:14c—"though you plant a protective hedge, you will not make (it) secure"— based on an Aramaic translation of *swg* ("to hedge, fence"), also used in Song of Songs 7:3.

annihilated by their enemies, and the nations will scornfully mock them. This is God's verdict if there is no immediate turning from their evil ways.

REMEMBER GOD'S GRACE. A key principle in the first part of this chapter is not to forget the grace of God (6:3–5). As early as the giving of the law at Sinai, God called on the nation of Israel to remember "what I did to Egypt, and how I carried you on eagles' wings and brought you to myself" (Ex. 19:4). If they did so, the Israelites would be willing to commit themselves to keeping the covenant stipulations as a good covenant partner. B. Childs concludes that memory indicates an active relationship to some object or person that exceeds a simple thought process.[26] It is a persistent and reflective examination of the implied meaning of an act so that its value is not lost to the people involved.

Thus, a major function of worship ceremonies is to help people remember God's gracious deeds in the past. In the covenant-renewal ceremony in Joshua 24, the initial covenant deeds of God are traced back to calling Abraham out of Ur, guiding the lives of Isaac and Jacob, bringing the people up from Egypt, defeating the king of Sihon, frustrating Balaam's curses, crossing the Jordan, defeating the Canaanites, and finally receiving the land. It was important for the people, having just been given the land, to remember what God had graciously done for them so that they would respond appropriately to him.

Elsewhere remembering God's gracious deeds in the past is associated with reciting them in worship to give praise to God (1 Chron. 16:12; Ps. 105). Not forgetting what God has done is an integral part of the motivation used to encourage covenant obedience in Deuteronomy (Deut. 5:15; 7:18; 8:2; 9:7; 15:15; 24:9). If one forgets about the past, there is no debt of gratitude, no sense of obligation, and no feeling of closeness because the intimate bond between the receiving and giving partners is broken. If the past is not remembered, a new generation of people might conclude that God has not done anything special for them. People who forget God's grace may be tempted to blame God for his lack of concern for them when difficult times come. But the past is reality; it can neither be erased nor denied. Only a proud and foolish person would try to deny the significance of the past deeds of God on his or her life.

What God really wants. The second principle is not to get confused about what God really wants and requires. Although he enjoys true worship

---

26. B. Childs, *Memory and Tradition in Israel* (London: SCM, 1962), 17–30.

that glorifies his name, he is not impressed with mere ritual observance or attempts to buy his favor with a huge quantity of gifts. Micah 6:6–7 deals with the improper attitude of the worshiper. The people in Micah's day do not understand what more they can do to please God because they do not understand the essential things God wants. They repeatedly come to sacrifice at the temple. What more could God possibly want? Does a person have to give a million dollars before he is satisfied? What does it take to keep him happy?

Psalms 15 and 24:3–6 describe the behaviors and attitudes God desires to see in those who worship him. In one of David's prayers he remembers that the sacrifice that pleases God most is a broken and contrite heart (51:17). God knows every person's heart and each deed of unrighteousness; therefore, it is impossible to fool him with a show of spirituality. A second-rate, outwardly pious deed does not function as a legitimate replacement for a first-class commitment to love God with all your heart and serve him. God is not impressed with the size or number of our gifts but by the quality of our relationship with him. If you do not love God, nothing else counts.

Honesty and integrity. God will judge those who do not conduct their business dealings with others honestly and without deception or lies (6:9–12). The Bible is full of admonitions about the importance of honest and ethical behavior in business (Deut. 25:13). Although many live outside the agricultural setting of selling grain, the trusting relationship between the sellers and buyers is regularly experienced at the farmers' market as well as in other places of business or trade. One cannot be spiritual and close to God while robbing or cheating others out of their money. There is a consistency between a person's acts and heart. Those who consistently lie with their tongues and cheat others with their hands (Mic. 6:11–12) are called wicked and violent people. They are not doing justice or walking humbly with God.

Moral requirements. God's moral requirements of his people are declared openly (6:8). They are to act justly toward others in all their dealings, remain steadfastly loyal to God and the principles of covenantal life together with his community, and reject any careless or presumptuous attitude of doing things their own way. Such a walk with God is humble in that it puts a person's will in a secondary position and gives prudent attention to doing his will. This kind of wise and circumspect life looks first at one's responsibilities to God and others rather than focusing on selfish, personal concerns. These three broad requirements connect real-life behavior with God to higher spiritual ideals that should cause everyone to put God first.

Blessings. Finally, Micah's message teaches that if people are not living in a proper relationship to God, they will never be satisfied (6:13–15). Deuteronomy 6:5 focuses on God's requirement that his people love the Lord with all their heart, while 10:12 requires them "to fear the LORD your

God, to walk in all his ways, to love him, to serve the LORD your God with all your heart." God does not need sacrifices (Ps. 50:7–13); he desires a broken spirit rather than many sacrifices (51:16–17). Isaiah 1:10–17 reveals God's weariness with meaningless ritual if the hearts of worshipers are not walking in God's ways. Those who do these things will see God's blessings, but those who do not will never be satisfied with life.

THIS LONG LAWSUIT in Micah 6 is based on the covenant relationship God has with the people of Israel. It includes certain expectations of both partners. God agrees to be their God, to dwell among them, and to bless them by giving them the land of Canaan (Ex. 6:4–8). But in order for this relationship to thrive, they agree to be a holy people, to obey God's voice, and to love, fear, and serve him (Ex. 19:5–6; Deut. 10:12). These basic factors still describe the nature of the relationship people have with God under the new covenant (Jer. 31:31–34; Luke 22:20; 1 Peter 2:9). We too must be holy people who love, fear, and serve God (Mark 12:28–31).

In some ways the condemnation of the churches in Revelation 2–3 is similar to the court case against Judah in Micah 6. When the church of Jesus Christ is not faithful to its covenant responsibilities, it must answer for its behavior. Someday, when individuals meet God face to face, they will have to answer for their behavior. There will be something of a court setting. The books will be opened, and a verdict will be proclaimed. God will either invite people to enter the joy of his presence, or he will command them to leave his presence and enter eternal darkness (Matt. 12:36–37; Rom. 14:10; 2 Cor. 5:10). Insights from Micah's description of God's judgment court should help us to prepare for our day in court by changing the way we live.

Remember the grace of God. One way church members today can ensure a proper relationship to God and avoid his condemnation is never to forget what he has done for them. This is why Paul encourages the church at Corinth to celebrate the Lord's Supper, basing it on the memory of what Jesus did at his last Passover and on the cross: "Do this in remembrance of me" (1 Cor. 11:24). He knew if believers forget that Jesus died for them, severe consequences will follow. Of course, just remembering is not enough; one must do what God has said (James 1:25). Although repeated remembering can become boring repetition, values and beliefs are cemented in the minds of believers by repeatedly emphasizing them.

The author of Hebrews reminds his audience not to forget the word of admonition in the Old Testament books "that addresses you" (Heb. 12:5–12), for by this means God's people endure in faithfulness through the discipline of remembering the past. Peter also maintains that those who lose sight of the importance of moral discipline, self-control, the need for perseverance, and Christian love and godliness do so because they do not "remember" the greatness of their purification from their past sins (2 Peter 1:5–9).

Jesus called his audience to "remember Lot's wife" (Luke 17:32) and not make the same mistake she did. He also prepared his followers for his death so that they would remember what he said (John 16:4) and not forsake him when the dark hour of his death came. Paul asked the church at Ephesus to "remember that formerly you who are Gentiles . . . were separate from Christ . . . without hope and without God in the world" (Eph. 2:11–12). The angel of God called to the church of Sardis was to "remember . . . what you have received and heard; obey it, and repent" (Rev. 3:3)—lest judgment come on them like a thief in the night.

The educational function of the church is heavily related to edifying people about the past history of God's dealings with his people. Through Bible study, people are reminded again and again that God has done many things for them. If we do not teach our children about the great deeds of God in the past, describe the teachings of Jesus, and drill into their minds the admonitions of Paul, how will they ever learn how to act in a Christian manner? A solid Christian education program is necessary if the church expects its members to maintain the faith.

In the secular realm, every ethnic and national group knows they must remind their young people about the past history of their group in order to create an identity and connection with the ideals and struggles of the group. When any group, and especially the church, forgets the suffering of the past and its many mistakes, it is doomed to a loss of significance for the next generation and is in danger of extinction. If we as believers do not remember what God has done for us and has said to us, how can we ever expect to maintain the church as a powerful force in society? As Micah knows, a group that does not remember what God has done for it will soon not please God with its actions.

Misunderstandings about what God wants from us. Today people may think they have done what God expects if they have been baptized or joined the church, just as Micah's audience thought they had done everything God wanted when they sacrificed a number of animals (6:6–7). Some think that they have pleased God because they celebrate Communion once every month or contributed at least a good part of their tithe every week. Others assume God will be pleased with them for saying the Rosary or the Lord's Prayer several times a day. A few think that following the Golden Rule or doing as well as the guy next door is all that is required. An Amish might tell you that all you have to do is to dress a certain way to please God, while an older saint may claim that you have to sing songs in a certain way to find approval in God's eyes.

These different options tend to be based not only on personal opinions but also on the belief that God is only impressed with repeated performance of duties or with what I find culturally comfortable. In most cases, a good thing (e.g., repeatedly saying a prayer) becomes a poor substitute for the most important requirement from God: truly communicating with him.

Some churches have so identified themselves with political, feminist, ethnic, or social causes that they have altered their reason for being. Fulfilling the ideals of the "cause" or ideology can easily become identified as what God really wants. This can even subtly grow into the misunderstanding that we can only please God if we sing out of a certain hymnbook or read a certain translation of the Bible. Cultural ethnocentrism can blind people who worship by lifting their hands into thinking that this outward expression of emotional conviction will get one more points with God than the deeply reflective chant of an Eastern Orthodox believer. Is a Spanish model of worship better than a Chinese approach? Will a Methodist model please God, while a Pentecostal pattern displeases him? Is the good old way we worshiped when we were kids the only thing God accepts?

In contrast to this trend to stick with what we have known from our culture and are comfortable with from the past is the experience of J. H. Townsend, pastor of the urban First Baptist Church in Los Angeles. His congregation has "church school classes for Korean, Spanish, Anglo and Filipino members.... But we worship as one body in Christ, every Sunday, surmounting the language barrier with simultaneous translation, heard over headsets.... Our abiding interest is in fashioning ourselves into one people."[27]

All these controversial issues about worship point back to the need for the church to again face the question: Have we misunderstood what will please God, or are we really just concerned about what pleases us? Micah clearly indicates that outward display of religious piety is not the key. This is especially true when it comes to the misconception that we can somehow please God more or earn his favor automatically by increasing the number of things we do for him. Many acts of grand display to show our colors cannot take the place of one truly sincere act of true devotion that glorifies God. The simple prayer of a righteous person can accomplish much more than the long, loud, and emotional displays of the TV pastor praying for the benefit of his watching television contributors. Eventually God will ask us all: Whom are you trying to please?

---

27. R. Chandler, *Racing Toward 2001* (Grand Rapids: Zondervan, 1992), 33.

What does God require? One could ask how every passage of Scripture applies to believers today and come up with an enormous list of things God requires. Micah also could have listed the 613 commandments in the Pentateuch or drawn several hundred more principles just from the book of Proverbs. Today we would have to add the teachings of Jesus and the admonitions of Paul, Peter, and John to this impressive list. Fortunately, all these applications from diverse contexts of the Bible point back to a few basic factors that determine a person's relationship to God. When the church gets its eyes off these central absolutes and starts focusing on the contextual applications of these principles in different settings, conflicts will arise and people will start to focus more on *how* they do things to please God, rather than *what* they do.

The exposition above has already defined what it means to act with a heart attuned to justice toward others, to maintain steadfast loyalty to the covenant principles that define our relationship to God, and to be circumspect by disciplining our attitudes so that we are always submitting our will to God's (6:8). These broad requirements are designed so that they can be applied in many different circumstances in the church and in a person's secular associations with others. The three points that Micah emphasizes are directed toward a person's inner spirituality as well as the actions these inner motivations produce.

Although there are numerous groups that promote spirituality as the umbrella for their concern for "earth-keeping" or the psychological healing of modern dysfunctionalisms, these causes will not produce people who please God unless they evidence the characteristics Micah mentions in 6:8. Ecology is not bad, and twelve-step plans to help people rid themselves of binding addictions are not bad; but if people involved with such programs do not act with justice, maintain a steadfast covenant loyalty with God, and walk wisely and in dependence on God, they will not please him.

One may find it a little too easy to condemn the values of some of the modern secular "movements" that have captured the imagination of so many (a substitute for their religion, in some cases). But it is more difficult to do a self-examination and ask how the various programs in your church are producing the spiritual values Micah mentions. When was the last time Micah 6:8 was mentioned in a sermon you heard? How many churches even attempt to build or evaluate their programs based on these criteria? Has any church attempted to test such issues through a questionnaire, addressed the areas that are weakest, and then retested to see if any progress has been made? Have churches consciously set these as goals they want to achieve?

Do congregations evaluate pastoral candidates on these three issues? How can a seminary curriculum get across that the nature of one's walk with God is more important than getting a B grade in a church history class? Should seminaries graduate students who have not achieved some level of mastery in these key ministry requirements? God looks at the heart rather than the outward facade; should we not pay attention to the things God holds to be most important?

Our acts betray our true beliefs. The proof is in the pudding. Yes, if it looks good but tastes terrible, it is never going to pass muster. God knows both our hearts and our actions; thus, it is not hard for him to point out shortcomings. Two of the telltale areas are: How do we deal with money, and do we always tell the truth?

In this commercialized age, there is a temptation to separate private piety from the secular practice of making a living. But if justice is required by God, this impacts how honestly we deal with others in business and how fairly we treat customers. Is it dishonest to fool customers by keeping the same size cereal box while reducing the weight of the product inside? Is it appropriate for a company or restaurant to brag about the hefty weight of its hamburgers and then have a small-print disclaimer admitting that this weight is connected to the product before it is cooked, thus allowing the company to include inexpensive and disappearing water and fat as part of its "quarter pounders"?

Misrepresentation of products can come in all forms, but all of it is motivated by the desire to show a product in a way that will deceptively encourage customers to buy it. Although some business people might respond that everyone else is making slightly deceptive claims, most books on business ethics maintain that "customs, conventions, and the accepted courtesies of a society are not the foundation of ethics."[28] Deeper convictions of right and wrong undergird ethical principles, and respect for the personal dignity of each person gives root to the honest and just treatment of others.[29]

Since buyers usually do not have enough information about the expenses of producing a product, the actual fair-market value plus a reasonable markup is unknown. This inequality of information can lead to unethical price-fixing by collusion among sellers. Charging whatever the market will bear is not an appropriate ethical pricing policy. Some merchants attempt to implement schemes that give the customer inflated costs for services or deflated rewards for producing goods.[30] Illustrations of ethical problems in doing business are

---

28. T. Garrett and R. Klonoski, *Business Ethics* (Englewood Cliffs, N.J.: Prentice-Hall, 1986), 1, claim that the law describes only the minimal regulations necessary for public order.
    29. Ibid., 3
    30. Ibid., 100–108 (on the issue of price-fixing and the alternatives of government controls on prices).

found in many business textbooks,[31] and these can function as case studies for ethical analysis and the development of appropriate moral responses to business situations.

Although some may think of "business ethics" as an oxymoron, as unthinkable as "military intelligence," this perception should be understood as a sign of the desperate need for principled and trustworthy business practices. Because many scandals are uncovered every year (often much worse than Micah's example of having two different sets of weights), an examination of business ethics needs to be addressed by churches to enable Christians to avoid the pitfalls of "business as usual." Theories of ethical egotism, ethical relativism, utilitarianism, religious ethics, and ethics determined by conscience should be examined for strengths and weaknesses.[32]

Although people often get uncomfortable when preachers start talking about money, an interactive seminar on business ethics could open the door to a more comfortable discussion about God's concerns with all financial matters. In the end it all comes down to whether people want to please God and do what he requires. If this is one's priority, honesty and justice will follow naturally.

---

31. M. Velasquez, *Business Ethics* (Englewood Cliffs, N.J.: Prentice-Hall, 1988), discusses the Union Carbide problem (3), Johns-Mansville's problems over asbestos (47), Ford and Chrysler (118 and 168), plus General Electric (205).

32. R. Green, *The Ethical Manager* (New York: Macmillan, 1994), 56–65, surveys these approaches to ethics.

Micah 7:1–20

¹What misery is mine!
I am like one who gathers summer fruit
    at the gleaning of the vineyard;
there is no cluster of grapes to eat,
    none of the early figs that I crave.
²The godly have been swept from the land;
    not one upright man remains.
All men lie in wait to shed blood;
    each hunts his brother with a net.
³Both hands are skilled in doing evil;
    the ruler demands gifts,
the judge accepts bribes,
    the powerful dictate what they desire—
    they all conspire together.
⁴The best of them is like a brier,
    the most upright worse than a thorn hedge.
The day of your watchmen has come,
    the day God visits you.
    Now is the time of their confusion.
⁵Do not trust a neighbor;
    put no confidence in a friend.
Even with her who lies in your embrace
    be careful of your words.
⁶For a son dishonors his father,
    a daughter rises up against her mother,
a daughter-in-law against her mother-in-law—
    a man's enemies are the members of his own household.

⁷But as for me, I watch in hope for the LORD,
    I wait for God my Savior;
    my God will hear me.

⁸Do not gloat over me, my enemy!
    Though I have fallen, I will rise.
Though I sit in darkness,
    the LORD will be my light.
⁹Because I have sinned against him,
    I will bear the LORD's wrath,

until he pleads my case
and establishes my right.
He will bring me out into the light;
I will see his righteousness.
¹⁰ Then my enemy will see it
and will be covered with shame,
she who said to me,
"Where is the LORD your God?"
My eyes will see her downfall;
even now she will be trampled underfoot
like mire in the streets.

¹¹ The day for building your walls will come,
the day for extending your boundaries.
¹² In that day people will come to you
from Assyria and the cities of Egypt,
even from Egypt to the Euphrates
and from sea to sea
and from mountain to mountain.
¹³ The earth will become desolate because of its inhabitants,
as the result of their deeds.

¹⁴ Shepherd your people with your staff,
the flock of your inheritance,
which lives by itself in a forest,
in fertile pasturelands.
Let them feed in Bashan and Gilead
as in days long ago.

¹⁵ "As in the days when you came out of Egypt,
I will show them my wonders."

¹⁶ Nations will see and be ashamed,
deprived of all their power.
They will lay their hands on their mouths
and their ears will become deaf.
¹⁷ They will lick dust like a snake,
like creatures that crawl on the ground.
They will come trembling out of their dens;
they will turn in fear to the LORD our God
and will be afraid of you.
¹⁸ Who is a God like you,
who pardons sin and forgives the transgression
of the remnant of his inheritance?

> You do not stay angry forever
>> but delight to show mercy.
> ¹⁹You will again have compassion on us;
>> you will tread our sins underfoot
>> and hurl all our iniquities into the depths of the sea.
> ²⁰You will be true to Jacob,
>> and show mercy to Abraham,
> as you pledged on oath to our fathers
>> in days long ago.

BECAUSE COMMENTATORS DISAGREE on many issues related to the interpretation of this complex conclusion to the book of Micah, it is important for us to be aware of the options and the strengths and weaknesses of each approach. (1) The first problem arises because the one lamenting in 7:1 is not overtly identified. Three major hypotheses have developed. (a) Some see the lament as a response to the announcement of judgment on the city of Jerusalem in 6:9–16. Thus, the first-person verbs represent the collective sentiments of the city of Jerusalem (7:1, 7–9), while the pronominal suffix on "your God" in 7:10d (feminine singular) agrees with the word "city."[1]

(b) Others see an individual righteous person (likely the prophet Micah) lamenting the anarchy of Judah in 7:1–6 and find the community lament of the city with answers of hope in 7:7–20.[2] This reconstruction is better than the first view for it does not have the difficulty of explaining why the wicked and unrepentant people in the city of Jerusalem during the time of Manasseh are lamenting their own wickedness.

(c) A third approach suggests that the whole chapter was the personal lament of Micah, plus his intercession for the depraved people in Judah (cf. 1:8–16).[3] This view is preferable, for it seems unlikely that the people of Israel would confess their own sins and look to God for help (7:8–11).[4] It is more natural to imagine that a righteous person like the prophet Micah

---

1. Mays, *Micah*, 31, 151, 153; Hagstrom, *Coherence of the Book of Micah*, 96–99.

2. Hillers, *Micah*, 90; Allen, *Joel, Obadiah, Jonah and Micah*, 393; Barker, "Micah," *Micah, Nahum, Habakkuk, Zephaniah*, 127; Waltke, "Micah," *The Minor Prophets*, 745, 754, all take a communal approach only for 7:8–20, believing 7:1–7 is by the prophet himself (or some righteous individual).

3. See Hillers, *Micah*, 89, and J. T. Willis, "The Structure of the Book of Micah," 35.

4. The feminine singular suffix in 7:11 may refer to Jerusalem as "your walls," but one cannot overlook that "to you" in 7:12 is masculine.

would lament about the evil in Judah. He would be the one disappointed about wickedness (7:1), mourn the loss of the righteous in Judah (7:2), confess the nation's sins (7:8–9; cf. Ezra 9; Jer. 14:1–9; Dan. 9:1–19), and intercede for God's grace and powerful deliverance (Mic. 7:14).

(2) A second problem relates to the date of this message. Willis believes the prophet is speaking as the nation's representative but concludes that the hope section in 7:7–20 was given much earlier (around 725 or 721 B.C.), when Assyria conquered the northern nation of Israel.[5] This oracle was adapted and added in the exilic period as the conclusion to Micah's teachings long after his death. Others question any connection with the northern kingdom and conclude that this passage assumes the fall of Jerusalem; thus, it must have an exilic or postexilic date.[6] Yet all the prophets predict the fall and restoration of Judah long before it happened, so I see no fundamental reason why Micah himself could not have received these words from God.

Chapters 6 and 7 fit well into the time of Manasseh, at the end of Micah's ministry. He feels so discouraged because many people who have originally followed Hezekiah's reforms turn against them (7:1–2). Thus, it seems as if there is not one righteous person left in the land (this certainly does not fit Hezekiah's reign after his reform). Although Micah has experienced the joyous and great revivals under Hezekiah (2 Kings 18–20; 2 Chron. 29–32), during Manasseh's initial years he witnesses the depressing reversal of Hezekiah's reforms, a broad decline in morality, and an acceptance of pagan worship (2 Kings 21).

(3) The rhetorical purpose of this sermon at the beginning of Manasseh's reign is to demonstrate the prophet's deep sorrow and anguish over the terrible social and religious problems in Judah and to intercede with God for forgiveness. He also wants to give hope to the righteous who still listen to his old-fashioned message. The only thing they can do is to cry out in confession, look to God in their misery, pray for his help, and rejoice in the hope that he will fulfill his promises by restoring Judah sometime after its judgment. The few righteous people left need to focus on God, his love, his forgiveness, and his power rather than their hopeless situation or the mocking of their enemies (7:10). God is faithful to his promises to Abraham and constant in his love, and he will fulfill his oath to their forefathers (7:20).

---

5. J. T. Willis, "A Reapplied Prophetic Hope Oracle," *Studies in Prophecy* (VTSup 26; Leiden: Brill, 1974), 69 and footnote 1 for a list of others who follow this interpretation. It is based on the many references to places in Israel (not Judah), the use of Israelite traditions, and because 6:1–7:6 (especially 6:16) may also be from Israel. Thus the city or community in view is Samaria, not Jerusalem.

6. Wolff, *Micah*, 218–19; Mays, *Micah*, 158–61; and Allen, *Joel, Obadiah, Jonah and Micah*, 252, 393, put it in the early postexilic period, think the enemy is Edom, and conclude that Jerusalem's walls (7:11) are about to be rebuilt by Nehemiah.

The structure of this sermon is complex, but there are similarities between certain lament psalms and this passage.[7] This chapter is composed of a lament over the terrible state of the nation (7:1–6), a confession of trust and confidence in God for forgiveness and help (7:7–10), an oracle of salvation (7:11–13), a petition asking God to deliver them (7:14), another oracle of salvation promising victory over enemies (7:15–17), and a final response of praise to God (7:18–20). The two oracles of salvation (7:11–13, 15–17) are a direct response to the requests before them, and the final hymn of praise responds to God's promise of hope in the salvation oracle.

Micah Laments Judah's Decadent Social Situation (7:1–6)

THIS SORROWFUL PRAYER begins with a cry of disappointment and hopelessness. Using the common metaphor of a harvester going out to gather his crops, Micah expresses his frustration and disappointment with the fruits of his ministry. Like a farmer who works hard to plant and cultivate his field, Micah has labored faithfully throughout the years and seen a good measure of success during the reform of Hezekiah. But now as he enters the last few years of his ministry, he finds that the fruit of his labor has disappeared.

According to his analogy, both harvesters and gleaners walk to the field with their saliva glands working overtime, for in their imagination they can already taste the wonderful experience of biting into that first fresh grape. They expect to find gorgeous large fruit on the vines, but in this case they find nothing. Micah does not say why the fruit is missing, and it is unnecessary to speculate on the cause. The main point is the exasperation and disappointment people feel when they yearn for something special and get nothing.

In this vein, Micah has yearned to see more and more righteous people filling the villages of Judah, but after the fervor of Hezekiah's reform wore off, Manasseh now allows the morality of the nation to decline. At the end of Micah's life, when he hoped to look back with satisfaction on what the Lord has accomplished through him, he sadly finds that there is official opposition from the political and religious leaders and a decline in public morality. Like Elijah, who thought he was the only righteous person left (1 Kings 19:10), Micah feels as if there are no righteous people left in Judah (Mic. 7:2). If he were to search for one person motivated by honesty and steadfast covenant loyalty, he doubts he will find any; they have all disappeared from the face of the earth. As with Elijah, this is probably an exaggeration.[8]

---

7. Wolff, *Micah*, 215; Allen, *Joel, Obadiah, Jonah and Micah*, 393. J. T. Willis, "A Reapplied Prophetic Hope Oracle," 65–66, makes the connection to certain psalms, but unwisely emends the Hebrew text in verse 15, thus making all of vv. 14–17 a prayer for help.

8. God had to remind Elijah that he was not the only one left, for there were still seven thousand who had not bowed to worship Baal (1 Kings 19:18).

Instead, "all men" (possibly another exaggeration) hunt down others with ambushes in order to kill them. The second half of verse 2 emphasizes the pervasiveness of these violent acts, the true intentions of the perpetrators, and the deceptive means of achieving these results. Instead of treating other Israelites as God's chosen people, they are hunting them down like wild animals.

Micah continues to weep over this decadent social situation (7:3). He clarifies that the "all" he is talking about (v. 2) are the leaders, officials, judges, and powerful people in society (cf. 3:9–11). These "great" men (NIV "powerful") are probably high government officials directly under the king,[9] the judges who control the court proceedings, and the civilian and military officials. They use their powerful positions in the social structure of Israelite society to get what they want. They are skillful in doing this evil because they are in charge of the process and "conspire together" (lit., "weave it") to benefit each other.

The verbs in verse 3 indicate why these leaders are successful. They sometimes have the gall to demand special bribes or financial rewards to grease the wheels of government. Their longings (quite in contrast to Micah's in 7:1) motivate them to get what they want by whatever means necessary, no matter what laws are twisted or what people are sacrificed. Although the covenant law forbids judges from taking bribes (Ex. 23:8; Deut. 10:17; 16:19) and requires the people to care for their fellow members rather than take advantage of them (Deut. 15:7–11), these officials work for the purpose of enriching themselves, not serving others.

Micah compares the best and most upright of these oppressors to "briers" and "thorns" (7:4), an ambiguous metaphor that is not explained. Perhaps they hurt people instead of help them, or they are thorny barriers to justice instead of God's instruments of reconciliation. In any case, this is a strong negative characterization of people who are hard to get along with.

Having wept over the problems in Judah, Micah gives a brief prophetic prayer of confidence or an announcement of punishment in 7:4b.[10] He reminds his audience that the day that God's watchmen (the prophets in Ezek. 3:17) predicted will soon come on the nation; the evil they are enduring will soon come to an end.[11] The time factor of "now" emphasizes that the disintegration of the present evil status quo will take place in the near future. Micah does not say how this will happen or what nation will wreak havoc on Judah to bring this about.

---

9. Wolff, *Micah*, 206.

10. Allen, *Joel, Obadiah, Jonah and Micah*, 387, sees it as a prayer of confidence, while Mays, *Micah*, 152, concludes that this is a punishment statement.

11. The verb *bʾb* (to come) can be seen as a feminine participle "is coming" (Allen, *Joel, Obadiah, Jonah and Micah*, 383 n. 5), but it probably is a prophetic perfect, a usage that sees a future action as already completed. English cannot convey both of these ideas at once.

After this confident statement of divine retribution, Micah returns to lament how the present social upheaval has destroyed the normal peaceful and trusting relationship within the family and neighborhood (7:5–6). He exhorts his audience to be cautious about whom they trust since deceit and disloyalty are destroying the solidarity within the most intimate relationships. People need to watch what they do and say at all times because a neighbor, a close friend, or even a spouse might turn against them.

This social reality indicates that the deceit and manipulation in the upper levels of government (7:2–4a) are filtering down to poison the most basic bonds of trust in the family. The dearest friend or relative might repeat something shared in confidence and get one in trouble, or a secret shared only in the bedroom might rise up to haunt one at a later date. When one member of the family tries to take advantage of another, there is a total breakdown in respect and order. Since Israelite culture emphasized the importance of the bonds of family loyalty, it is surprising to see it fall so far from this ideal. The moral depravity of such defiant rebellion against parental authority (7:6) is almost incomprehensible. This is a rejection of the fifth commandment about honoring parents and the opposite of all the admonitions in Proverbs. Children should not defy or attack a family member or an in-law; a relative should not be your worst enemy.

Confession of Trust in God (7:7–10)

THESE VERSES DEMONSTRATE an abrupt change of attitude and focus. Once the prophet moves his attention to God instead of the troubles all around him, a new sense of hope wells up inside. I interpret the "I" who is speaking in verse 7 as the prophet Micah. Beginning with verse 8 he is apparently confessing the sins of Jerusalem, not his own (cf. Ezra 9 and Dan. 9), and expressing hope for the nation.

Verse 7, then, becomes a key focal point for repositioning the prophet's mental perspective on God's sovereign control of life. Micah's concentration on God rather than his problems enables him to see a ray of hope for the future. The "watchman"/prophet (7:4) will "watch" (7:7) for Yahweh his God, for there is no other possible source of life. He will wait, trusting that his saving God will act. God will hear his prayers and understand his situation, for he pays attention to his people when they cry to him for help. These statements describe the deep personal relationship Micah has with God, reveal his dependence on God, and demonstrate that his confidence is not just wishful thinking. Therefore, he can face the future with assurance, for God is there with him.

Knowing that God is a holy God and Judah is sinful, Micah immediately expresses confidence that God will deliver them from their fallen state (7:8), forgive them of their sins (7:9), and shame those who have mocked God (7:10). This refers to a time of hope after a period of national decline and mockery by the wicked. Those who date this section in the postexilic period believe this refers to the national defeat of Judah by the Babylonians in 586 B.C. and the mockery of the Edomites (Obad. 10–14). B. Waltke rejects this dating and believes this is a prophecy that Sennacherib will defeat Jerusalem in 701 B.C. during the time of Micah (he did not know that the nation would repent and avoid that defeat).[12] If, however, this lament is given in the time of Manasseh, as I have suggested, we can date it some years after Sennacherib's attack. If so, the prophet is pointing ahead to the Babylonian conquest (as he did in 4:9–10).

Micah accepts the inevitability of the nation's judgment as a result of its sins (cf. 4:9–13), but in faith he believes that the nation will rise once again in the future (7:8). Darkness may come on them for a while, but light from the Lord will follow as surely as day follows night. Since God has a plan for the nation when he establishes his reign over the whole earth (4:1–4), no temporal defeat can annul his eternal purposes. This message of confidence provides hope in a time of hopelessness because the one praying knows that God will establish his eternal kingdom for his people in the eschatological future.

Yet the prophet does not expect this great transformation to take place without a change of heart on the part of the people of Judah. Since there is no evidence that Judah did repent, Micah confesses the nation's sins for them (like Moses in Ex. 32:30–34), recognizing that their punishment is fully deserved (Mic. 7:9). He also knows that God is not only the Judge who punishes them but also the One who decides when justice is served and when it is time for reconciliation and restoration. Then God will fight for Judah and right the injustices she suffers during her persecution by her enemies, and Judah's enemies will observe God's glorious deeds for her (7:9).

Some may mock the faith of the righteous in Judah when she suffers defeat and ask: "Where is your God? Why does he not have enough power to deliver you? If he exists and cares about you, why does he not deliver you from your enemies?" These unbelievers will laugh at the trust of the faithful and despise the power of the living God of Judah, but those who question the sovereign power of the Almighty will not stand for long. When the majesty and power

---

12. Wolff, *Micah*, 218; Allen, *Joel, Obadiah, Jonah and Micah*, 394; Mays, *Micah*, 159. Waltke, "Micah," *The Minor Prophets*, 754, also thinks this prophecy looks beyond the Assyrian crisis to anticipate the ultimate fall of Jerusalem to Babylon. I do not accept Waltke's dating of this chapter because the kind of wickedness in chs. 6–7 appears to fit better the evil present during the time of Manasseh, not Hezekiah.

of God are at stake, God intervenes to vindicate his reputation. These enemies are not identified, but their defeat will be total and shameful.[13] When these proud people are trampled into the dust of the earth, when their faces are shoved into the mud on the streets by their conquerors, they will totally submit in abject humility to a power much greater than their own.

Oracle of Salvation for Judah (7:11–13)

To STRENGTHEN THIS picture of restoration after conquest, either Micah reminds his listeners of earlier restoration traditions about the rebuilding of Judah (traditions like Isa. 11:11–16; 27:12–13; 60:11; Amos 9:11) and the desolation of the earth (Isa. 24:1–5), or he receives a new revelation about the restoration of Judah in response to his confession of trust in God. These promises confirm that the expectations of the prophet (Mic. 7:8–10) are not just pie in the sky or ungrounded imaginations of a false prophet. The audience should be persuaded to believe Micah's message of hope because it fits what God has already promised to do.

The coming "day" is left undefined (Micah does not say "in the last days" [4:1] or "in that day"[14] [4:6; 5:10]), so one can connect it to a restoration soon after Judah's defeat. Or perhaps it has the qualities that are similar to other references to that great eschatological day at the end of time.[15] On that unspecified day three things will happen: Judah will be rebuilt, people from all nations will come to Judah, and the rest of the earth will become desolate.

The rebuilding of fences marking Judah's boundaries (7:11; not "city walls," as in NIV[16]) implies that Judah will one day restore the domination of its territory. In fact, it will be so strong that it will even extend its boundaries

---

13. Hab. 2:6–20 also describes God's defeat of the wicked Babylonians after their defeat of Judah.

14. The beginning of verse 12 can be translated "that day" (there is no "in," as in the NIV) or more likely "it is a day." The DSS Mur 88 text does read the more usual "in that day," but it is probably not the more original text.

15. Allen, *Joel, Obadiah, Jonah and Micah*, 397, and Mays, *Micah*, 161, believe the rebuilding of the walls refers to the time of Nehemiah (445–433 B.C.), while Hillers, *Micah*, 91, connects these promises to Mic. 2:12 and 4:1–2 and calls them an "eschatological vision." Waltke, "Micah," *The Minor Prophets*, 756, however, claims that the "prophecy finds its fulfillment in the church, composed of all nations."

16. The Heb. *gdr* is a stone wall without mortar and usually refers to stone fences on a farm (1 Sam. 24:4; Isa. 5:5) rather than city walls. Ezra 9:9 uses this term to describe a "wall in Judah and Jerusalem." This could refer to Nehemiah's wall, but F. C. Fensham, *The Books of Ezra and Nehemiah* (NICOT; Grand Rapids: Eerdmans, 1982), 130–31, is right to suggest that this does not refer to a city wall but a boundary marker, for there never was a wall around all of Judah. We disagree with Allen, *Joel, Obadiah, Jonah and Micah*, 396, who thinks that "it is apparently the literal walls of Jerusalem that are meant here."

beyond the borders that presently exist (cf. a similar promise in Isa. 26:15). Micah is reminded that God will return the nation to its Promised Land and give it military strength to control all its land, not just the smaller portion now ruled by Manasseh. Through these acts God will bring glory to his name (cf. Isa. 26:15).

Part of the reason why the borders will need to be expanded is that many people from other nations will come to Judah (7:12; see 4:1–2). Some interpret this to mean Jewish exiles will return home from Egypt and Assyria[17] (as in Isa. 11:11–16; 27:12–13; Zech. 10:8–12), but it seems unlikely that those Jewish exiles actually come from "sea to sea," a rather universal description of their place of origin.[18] Other passages give similar universal images of people from all nations coming to Jerusalem to worship God (Ps. 2:8–12; 72:8–11; Isa. 60:11–12; Mic. 4:1–4; Zech. 9:10). These promises end with a prediction of God's judgment of all the nations of the earth who do not submit to his rule (Mic. 7:13). The fruits of their evil deeds will cause God to destroy those rebellious inhabitants (cf. Isa. 24:1–6; 26:21).

These traditions about God's great plans for Judah's restoration and exaltation in the sight of the Gentiles serve to legitimate Micah's message of hope for his audience. As the prophet and his audience remember what God will do to their enemies, they are not so fearful about their present suffering under Manasseh and the Assyrians or their future oppression by the Babylonians (4:9–10). God has not forgotten them; he is not impotent, and his purposes have not changed. Those who mock will be defeated and trampled into the dust when God annihilates the evil inhabitants of the earth.

Intercession for God to Act (7:14)

BEING REMINDED OF God's glorious plan for his people, Micah breaks forth into a prayer of intercession for the nation. He pleads for God's fulfillment of this great promise *now*. He does not enjoy the present state of the nation's social disintegration under Manasseh, nor does he look forward to the coming conflict and exile of the people under the Babylonians (cf. 4:9–10). This

---

17. It is odd that the Babylonian exile is not mentioned if this passage was actually written in postexilic times, as so many claim. Although an argument from silence, it probably points to the fact that the Babylonian exile had not been experienced when this prophecy was given.

18. Waltke, "Micah," *The Minor Prophets*, 757, and Mays, *Micah*, 162, believe those who come will be Jewish exiles, but Allen, *Joel, Obadiah, Jonah and Micah*, 397–98, sees a broader reference to the ideal geographic horizons of the messianic kingdom. Allen sees the problem with the usual exilic interpretation, but if his solution is the intention of Micah, why does he talk about it as "coming to you from," language that applies to the movement of people from one place to another. Since Allen sees 7:13 as referring to what Christians might call the Last Judgment, it is odd that 7:12 is not related to that same era of history.

petition, like David's much earlier prayer (2 Sam. 7:25), requests that God, as divine Shepherd-King of his people, take charge of his own flock by graciously ruling over them with his scepter.

These images take one back to two similar references to God using shepherd terminology. In 2:12–13 God reveals to Micah that he is the King at the head of the nation; he will gather his people together like sheep in a fold. Later in 5:4 Micah talks about the Messiah, who will rule Israel and shepherd his people through the Lord's strength. These figures of speech engender concepts of God's care by giving provisions and his divine rule by his royal scepter. He will restore his intimate covenant connection with the people he has chosen as his possession. Although the people presently live in loneliness and deprivation in a scrub land (not "forest," as in NIV)[19] that has little fertility in these difficult years of Manasseh, there is a yearning for the lushness of the pastures of Bashan and Gilead (Num. 32:1–4; Deut. 32:14; Ezek. 39:18), which they enjoyed years earlier when they first were given the land (Num. 32:1–4).[20]

Oracle of Salvation (7:15–17)

SOME INTERPRETERS SEE these verses as a continuation of Micah's prayer for God's help in 7:14, but this interpretation requires one to change the first-person verb "I will show" into a jussive, "let us see." If verses 15–17 are understood as God's answer to Micah's prayer in 7:14, the passage makes sense without changing the text.[21] These three verses are a series of promises by God, reconfirming that he will accomplish his plans and do what he has promised.

The yearning for the ancient situation in Micah's intercessory prayer (7:14) may be the impetus for God's response that recalls his marvelous deeds in the ancient past at the time of the Exodus from Egypt. God promises to answer Micah's intercessory petition by performing great and awesomely powerful acts on behalf of his people. The "wonders" he will show them are not described, so it is useless to speculate if this refers to another series of plagues like the ones that fell on Egypt (Ex. 7–11), another miraculous deliverance like the dividing of the Reed Sea (Ex. 14–15), or something new and unique. All God promises is that he will accomplish an amazing deed of power to help his people. This will be necessary because the nation is

---

19. Mays, *Micah*, 164, appropriately sees this as a reference to an area overgrown with thickets and scrub tree, a negative place when compared to a fertile pastureland.

20. Later Jer. 50:19 and Zech. 10:10 also lift up these areas as ideal pasturelands, which the nation will inherit again when God establishes his kingdom.

21. Mays, *Micah*, 163–65; Allen, *Joel, Obadiah, Jonah and Micah*, 392; Wolff, *Micah*, 212, all change the text and see this as the continuation of Micah's prayer; but Waltke, "Micah," *The Minor Prophets*, 759, keeps the Hebrew text and sees this as an oracle of salvation.

incapable of freeing itself from the mire of its own sinfulness or the military strength of other nations.

The future will be different. When God miraculously intervenes on behalf of his people, the nations that oppress them will see his power and be ashamed of their own puny strength (7:16). This response is similar to the trembling and dismay of the nations because of God's great deeds against Egypt (Ex. 15:14–16) and the melting of the hearts of the people of Jericho (Josh. 2:9–11). Isaiah prophesies that when these nations see the power of God, they will be ashamed of their gods (Isa. 45:16–17, 24) and will tremble in fear when his presence shakes the heavens and the earth (64:1–3). The nations will be powerless, devoid of ability to stand against God; thus, they will fearfully bow in submission before the God of the universe (Mic. 7:16–17).

Because of the awe-inspiring presence of God, the nations will not say a word. They will be speechless and no longer mock the God of Israel (cf. 7:16 with 7:10). Their humiliation is described in terms of "licking the dust" as they come before God. Isaiah likewise knows of a day when all flesh will see and know that God is the Lord of all the earth (Isa. 49:23–26). Then all people will bow their knees to him, swear allegiance to him, and declare that real strength belongs only to the Lord (45:22–24). Micah and Isaiah both prophesy God's ultimate victory, no matter how strong the enemy may be, no matter how distressed or weak the righteous may be.

Because God had already miraculously destroyed 185,000 Assyrian troops attacking Jerusalem (Isa. 37:36), Micah and his audience have good reason to believe what God says about the future. If he redeemed his people from Egypt and Assyria, certainly he can powerfully act on their behalf again.

This reminder of God's mighty deeds (past and future) legitimates a new way of looking at the social disintegration of society in Manasseh's reign (Mic. 7:1–6) and demands a transformation of the audience's focus. What determines the future is what God has done and will do, not what the evil people in society are now doing. They may rebel against God and effectively destroy his kingdom for a time, but they will soon lick the dust in fear of God's glory. Though difficulties will come, those who wait on God will rejoice because the Lord is their light and salvation (7:7–9). His promises do not fail, and his awesome power is unlimited.

Hymn of Praise to God (7:18–20)

MICAH'S TIME OF prayer ends (like many laments in the Psalms; see Ps. 13:5–6; 18:46–50; 21:13; 22:22–31) with words of praise to God.[22] The process of lamenting naturally brings a person from bitter complaints at the beginning,

---

22. C. Westermann, *Praise and Lament in the Psalms*, 267.

through petitions for help, to statements of trust and confidence, so that at the end one can refocus on the character and power of God in words of praise. This structural design helps transform the helpless person into a new creature because of a new vision of God. Instead of looking at the world through the human eyes of crisis and disappointment, the righteous are able to realign their concept of reality by perceiving the true character and glory of the sovereign King who controls the nations, their lives, and the future. As Micah ends his prayer on this high note, his audience can hardly help but be impressed with the change that overtakes the prophet.

This hymn is made up of two parts: a celebration of God and what he has done (7:18), and praise for what God will do (7:19–20). (1) The words of celebration begin with a rhetorical question: "Who is a God like you?" This comparative question draws attention to the uniqueness of Israel's God.[23] The obvious answer is: There is no other god who compares to Israel's God. The proof of this claim is related to God's unique way of dealing with sin; that is, he forgives his people. This passage juxtaposes several words for "sin" with several words for God's reaction to sin. Sin may be iniquity, rebellion, or a fractured relationship, but it does not forever destroy all hope for having a peaceful relationship with God. Confession of sin and repentance make it possible for sins to be removed, for God's anger at sin to be appeased, and for God's steadfast covenant commitment to blossom again.

For the remnant who love God, past experience teaches them that only Israel's God offers a solution to humanity's fundamental problem with sin. The Israelites experienced this when they built the golden calf at Mount Sinai, where God did not destroy the nation (Ex. 32:9–14). Instead, after confessing the nation's sins, Moses requested that God forgive them (32:32). After this episode God proclaimed that he is a compassionate and gracious God, slow to anger and abounding in love; he is willing to forgive all kinds of sins (34:6–7).

(2) Micah then turns to the future (7:19–20) and proclaims that God will again act in compassion toward his people. He will totally remove the sin problem that threatens to destroy their relationship to God. "He" (not "you," as in NIV) will not be angry forever, nor will he just wink at these sins by pretending they do not exist. He will deal with these sins by removing them and casting them in the depth of the sea (7:19—just as he handled his other enemies in Egypt) or by removing them as far as the east is from the west (Ps. 103:12; Isa. 43:25; 44:22). God will trample down his enemy (sin), defeat its power, and remove all, not just some, sins.

---

23. For a full discussion of the development of this theme, see C. J. Labuschagne, *The Incomparability of Yahweh in the Old Testament* (Leiden: Brill, 1966).

The final stanza (7:20) moves beyond the problem of sin to focus on the results of forgiveness. How will forgiveness affect the relationship between God and his chosen people? God will be a trustworthy source of help and will be faithful to his people. He does not change his loyalty from one group to another, based on their looks or behavior; he is a God characterized by faithfulness. When he makes an oath to establish an eternal covenant relationship with a people, he does not back out halfway along the road.

When God swore an oath to Abraham (Gen. 22:16; 26:3; Ex. 13:5, 11) and his descendants many years earlier, he did not speak lightly without considering the cost and commitment of his promises. His eternal plan to use the seed of Abraham to bless all the nations of the earth and to make of them a great nation (Gen. 12:3) is the only plan he has. He did not hold some cards in his back pocket in case things did not work out well but committed himself to bringing about his kingdom through this one people. For Micah and his audience, that plan may have seemed like a lost cause in the days of Manasseh, but through God's love and forgiveness he will miraculously accomplish his will on earth. Micah's bold hymn of faith in God's victory over sin gives real hope for the future.

IF A PASSAGE gives a clear prophecy of a future event, that event should be noted and the principle behind God's actions identified so that a more general application can be drawn by people who do not live at the time of its fulfillment. Several dangers exist with this kind of text. One may fail to identify the specific event that is being prophesied, one may identify the event but fail to draw any theological principle from it, or one may overexegete a passage by illegitimately inserting New Testament information into the verse and consequently making the prophecy say things that are not revealed to the Old Testament author.

We can identify two general guidelines here. (1) We must not try to turn broad statements about what God will do in the future into prophecies about specific fulfillments that the Old Testament author does not know about. When there is specificity (e.g., the ruler will be born in Bethlehem [5:2]), then a specific fulfillment is understood by the prophet. (2) We should try to compare each prophecy with similar prophecies (particularly earlier ones) to see how they fit together to give a clearer understanding of the events being described.

The danger of ignoring these principles of interpretation is seen in those studies that interpret Micah 7:11, for example, simply as a prophecy of

Nehemiah's coming rebuilding of Jerusalem's wall.[24] Although Nehemiah did do this, the above exegesis suggests that Micah does not have city walls in mind, but something much bigger—the boundaries of the nation. Thus, the prophecy fits better with other similar eschatological fulfillment passages.

Another questionable example brings New Testament evidence into this passage to enlighten it. Is it appropriate to suggest that the "crucial vocabulary of Micah 7:18 is used in connection with the Suffering Servant of Yahweh in Isaiah 53"[25] and therefore conclude that it is appropriate to see this as a prophecy of Christ? Certainly we know today that Christ is the ultimate One who has brought the forgiveness of sins, but this passage never says anything about the Suffering Servant or what God will do to make forgiveness possible for the sins of the whole world. Not every passage that uses these words is automatically about the Suffering Servant. The interpretive focus that looks to specific fulfillments not clearly explicated in the text twists the intention of the author and moves the reader's attention from what is being communicated to a specific historical example that may or may not clarify the meaning.

Lamenting oppression in society. Micah sets an example for his audience and the reader today by lamenting the corruption, lawlessness, and scarcity of righteous people in his day (7:1–6). Several factors characterize his response to these events. (1) Micah does not try to hide his disappointment. He recognizes his own humanness and admits that the circumstances of life have an impact on his disposition. Since God knows his state of mind already, he faces the reality of his own sense of frustration and deep sorrow.

Micah's example provides a principle for all people involved in ministry. Whether the situation is good or bad, it is important to be aware of and acknowledge how your setting affects your attitude toward God and the people in that social context. It does no good to just "keep a stiff upper lip" and try to ignore what is going on in your heart. Refusing to reflect on the actual facts of life will only result in living in an imaginary world. This subversion of reality also reduces the possibility that a person will grow through the experience.

(2) Another aspect of this lament that is an inevitable part of virtually all ministry experience is a periodic sense of loneliness and inability to trust others (7:2, 5–6). When people feel there are no others around them that truly understand their tensions, their burdens, their temptations, and their holy zeal, a certain sense of being all alone against the rest of the world arises. If people in ministry do not have some trusted friend to bear their

---

24. Allen, *Joel, Obadiah, Jonah and Micah*, 397.
25. Waltke, "Micah," *The Minor Prophets*, 762.

burdens, it is not unusual for them to feel as if the odds are so stacked against them that there is no hope for change. If you cannot trust a spiritual leader, if your mother or father have turned against you, if the elders or deacons seem to be enemies rather than fellow laborers in ministry, life will be very lonely. How can people share their deepest doubts and fears with others they cannot fully trust?

Nevertheless, how can a person ever expect life's circumstances to change if the risk of sharing your deep thoughts of life are never exposed? People tend to make one of two choices. Some continue to live in the unhealthy inner world of loneliness and distrust; they try to fit in with the status quo in order to survive. Others cry out to God for help, boldly admit the frustrations of life, and reach out to others to transform the present situation. Both alternatives have a high cost connected to them, and both can have dire consequences.

(3) The third point that stands out in this lament is that one can only progress out of the struggles in life by identifying the good as good and the bad as bad. Although every person must face reality and enter the real world, one can choose to take a pluralistic view of different moral activities and call them all acceptable alternatives, or one can view some acts as evil and others as good. The moral alternative is aligned with the second approach, but those who fall into this category must also choose how they will respond to the evil activities of others.

Should an internally motivated moral person let others "do their own thing," or should one try to impact the morality of others? Micah is determined not only to differentiate between the righteous and the wicked, he also speaks out against violence and oppression (7:2–4). This choice makes him unpopular with certain segments of society, but his stand against violence and official corruptions in high places is a result of his moral stand. All believers today end up by default taking a position on crime, sexuality, and all other types of oppression by what they say and do, or by what they do not say and do not do.

Looking to God for hope. Micah's lament exhibits a dramatic reversal of tone in 7:7. The depression of hopelessness turns not only to the possibility of hope, but the confidence that victory over sin is sure. This reversal of perspective is directly connected to the focus of the prophet. When the evils of this world are center stage, life can seem dreary and uninviting; but when God becomes the focus of attention, the "things of this earth grow strangely dim, in the light of his glory and grace." What factors lead the prophet to change his perspective? What does he see, hear, or remember about God that causes him to view his situation so radically differently?

(1) The prophet remembers that his personal relationship with God provides him with special privileges, the certainty of a divine advocate, and

assurances based on the character of God. Because I as a believer have a relationship with God, I have the privilege of talking to God, of knowing that he hears me, and of having God as my light and "my Savior." Without this personal connection, there is no hope of God's sovereign intervention into my life's problems.

But if this relationship exists, then there is a basis for the confidence that God can and will do things as an advocate for a covenant partner. I can be certain that the wait for salvation will end with rejoicing over my enemy, with light and not darkness (7:7–8), for God is pleading my cause (7:9–10). The value of God's actions produce confidence since he is motivated by principles of righteousness and justice (7:9), not the power or status of the one seeking help.

(2) The prophet remembers what God promised earlier prophets. When one knows God's earlier promises, this becomes a resource for answering national and personal questions that cry out for solution. If God already said that after a time of punishment his people will come back to their land and their enemies will actually end up joining his people in worshiping God (4:1–8), that makes a big difference in a crisis situation (7:11–12). If fellow prophets are proclaiming a similar message (Isa 45; 49; 60), the future is not some totally unknown mystery.

Yes, there will still be questions about when this will happen, how God will accomplish this transformation of the world, and how much suffering is required. These unknowns must be approached with an attitude of faith and trust. But the fundamental basis for hope is securely founded on what God has already decided, on the oaths he has already sworn to fulfill (7:20). This source of strength has always been a source of hope for believers.

(3) The prophet and every believer draw strength from knowing that God has a solution to the primary problem of all humanity, the problem of sin. Yes, sin angers God and brings judgment, but his anger will not last forever (7:18). A much more important divine response to sin is his offer of forgiveness and atonement for sin (7:18–19). Micah does not explain how this miracle happens; he only sings about God's compassion and his removal of sin. Because God bears the iniquity of our sins (7:18a), it is appropriate for him to have compassion on those he is angry with. If God is able to solve the basic problem of sin, there is hope for the transformation of my life, my situation, and my world.

Intercession for God's people so that God's will is done. Micah's prayers for his people fit in with a long line of godly people who have pleaded with God:

(1) Abraham interceded for Sodom and Gomorrah (Gen. 18).
(2) Moses prayed for God's mercy on the Israelites after the golden calf incident (Ex. 32).

(3) Amos asked God not to destroy Israel with locusts or fire (Amos 7:1–6).

(4) Jeremiah confessed Judah's sins and pleaded with God not to reject his people (Jer. 14: 19–22).

(5) Daniel sought God's fulfillment of his promise to return his people in seventy years (Dan. 9:1–20).

(6) Ezra confessed the sins of the exilic community that was defiling the holy seed of Israel by marrying pagan unbelievers (Ezra 9:5–15).

(7) Jesus interceded for the future unity of his disciples (John 17).

(8) Paul repeatedly mentions his prayers for the saints at the various churches he established (Phil. 1:3–4, 9–11; Col. 1:3, 9–12).

(9) Paul encourages Timothy to make prayers, intercessions, and thanksgivings for everyone—even kings—so that all will come to a knowledge of the truth and be saved (1 Tim. 2:1–2).

(10) This role is so important to the success of God's work that both the Spirit and Jesus are continually interceding for people in this world (Rom. 8:26; Heb. 7:25).

The prayers of believers may request many different things, but they should always be consistent with the known will of God revealed in Scripture. The faithful prayer warrior wants God's kingdom to come (Matt. 6:10), not his or her own wants and desires (26:42). Micah intercedes for God to plead Israel's case for them, to bring them out into the light (7:9), and to shepherd his sheep as in the days of old (7:14). Possibly no deed of Christian service is more effective in changing this world than the prayers of the saints. It is not an act of rebellion to reject the way things are or even to approach God boldly with requests that oppose what he may do in the future. God hears the prayers of the righteous and acts because they care enough to ask him for mercy and grace.

Contemporary Significance

MICAH'S FINAL SERMON raises a variety of themes that are developed in the New Testament: God's great love for the world (John 3:16), his forgiveness of our sins (1 John 1:9), and his promise to bring victory over our enemies (Matt. 16:18). The danger in developing these themes is the temptation to reinterpret concepts in Micah in forced ways,[26]

---

26. Waltke, ibid., 760, says: "The exodus Christ affords the church—bringing them out of a world of sin and judgment and setting them on their heaven-bound journey through the wilderness—is a far greater wonder. The wondrous Passover, the baptism into the Red Sea whereby they put Egypt behind them and set out for the Promised Land, the heavenly manna, and the water from the rock—all typify Christ and his salvation (1 Cor 10:1–4; 2 Cor 5:17)."

rather than allowing the historical development of these ideas to unfold naturally as progressive revelation unveils more and more insight into God's ways. Thus, it seems better to focus on all of God's powerful wonders throughout history, which are a continuation of his Exodus miracles (7:15), rather than tying his wonders just to Christological events in the New Testament. The promises in 7:15–17 focus on God, the revelation of his power, and the defeat of the nations. These are wonderful promises of hope, and they do not need to be twisted into "better" Christological promises.

Do we lament oppression in our world? When Micah saw the powerful in his society turn against the weak, he cried out to God for help. When he saw all the efforts of Hezekiah's reform and his own ministry fall apart, he wept. When the prophet realized that the glue of trust that held the family together was disintegrating the very fiber of social order, he lamented. The question that must be raised is: How does the church respond to this kind of social decay?

Three applications can be suggested. (1) It is necessary for individual believers and churches to look carefully outside their four walls and see what is happening in the world and evaluate how they want to impact the lives of people in their neighborhood. This will happen only when the church gives up its "fortress mentality" and is "unleashed"[27] to influence the sinful world around it. In Frank Tillapaugh's paradigm, the first step in reaching out is to see the invisible target groups within our community.[28] Just as Jesus went to the forbidden city of Samaria and did the unlawful thing (John 4:9, 27) by speaking to a Samaritan woman to find out her needs, the church must open its eyes to the sinful mess in the secular culture all around it. If this does not force us to our knees, then there is no hope for the future.

(2) A clear vision of rebellion against God in our neighborhoods should produce a second step of inner reflection if the love of God still dwells in us. We should be concerned about what can be done about this mess. What can we do to change this situation? Such questions usually result in feelings that it is impossible to change things, feelings of inadequacy because the task is too big, or frustration and loneliness because few share a similar vision for the church today. But one individual or one church should not let the plague of loneliness immobilize its behavior or quench its prayers. If we are stymied by loneliness, we should ask God to reveal the seven thousand who have a similar conviction (1 Kings 19:18).

(3) Like Micah, Jesus cried in disappointment and frustration over the rebelliousness of the people of Jerusalem (Luke 19:41). Should we respond

---

27. F. R. Tillapaugh, *The Church Unleashed* (Ventura, Calif.: Regal, 1978), contrasts these two approaches to church life and ministry.

28. Ibid., 48.

differently if we have the mind of Christ in us? If one is not disturbed by sinful behavior, one will probably not weep. It is common to hear people complaining about oppression, drugs, and the breakdown of the family, but complaining to others is different from lamenting before God. Like Micah and Jesus we have two choices: (a) to continue to live in the unhealthy inner world of loneliness and distrust and fit in with the status quo in order to survive,[29] or (b) cry out to God for help, boldly admitting the real frustrations of life and reaching out to others to call for a transformation of the present situation.

Is there any hope for us or this world? It seems apparent that many people who call themselves Christians do not believe the church has any hope of transforming sinners, for they attempt to do nothing to change lives. How can this hopeless plague be removed so that people can face the future with hope? For Micah, the depression of hopelessness turned not only to the possibility of hope but to the confidence that victory over sin is sure. Like Micah, we can gain some semblance of hope by focusing not on the terrible plight of our world but on God, his past promises, and his ability to deal with the source of hopelessness—sin itself.

(1) Because we, like Micah, have a covenant relationship with God, we know the Lord is a God who listens when we pray. Prayers do not just go up to the ceiling and bounce back as if God does not exist. Since people in the church have experienced the sovereign power of God in their lives, they are convinced that he is alive, that he can bring light out of a dark situation and deliverance from bondage. Because he is "my Savior," who pleads my case and forgives my sins, it makes sense to believe that he can do the same for others. Since God is sovereign, holy, just, faithful, and merciful, we can view the future with confidence and hope. The powerful oppressor, the rebellious sinner, and the distrusting family member do not control the future; God does. Assurance of victory is possible because God is on my side. Hope is born out of an intimate relationship with him and a solid understanding of his character.

(2) A second reason why a person can have hope about the future is because God will rescue the righteous and punish the wicked (7:11–13, 15–17). Although it is difficult to suggest how this specific promise applies to my church and its fight against the forces of evil at this time and place in history, the Old and New Testaments do give promises about what God will do in the future. These promises provide hope, even though God may ask some

---

29. P. Tournier, *Escape from Loneliness* (London: SCM, 1962), discusses the general feelings of loneliness present in society by looking at some of its causes. His final chapter on "The Spirit of Fellowship" (159–89) is esp. important.

to endure persecution or frustration for many years. What is clear are the final results of God's battle with evil.

Micah certifies three results. (a) God will restore and expand the boundaries of Judah (7:11)—a promise that does not apply to any concrete situation in any specific church. (b) People from many nations will come to God (7:12)—a promise that gives hope that many wicked people in this world will choose to repent of their sins and serve God. (c) Those who refuse to come to God will be defeated (7:13, 16–17)—a promise that gives assurance of victory over the forces of evil. These promises communicate the fact that God has a clear plan, he is sovereignly in charge of that plan, and it will be victorious. When he promises and swears by an oath, we can have confidence that it will happen. These promises encourage believers to step out in faith, stand up for what they believe, and act with confidence because they are on the winning team.

Why can a believer be so sure that God can pull all this off? Why can the members of the church sing God's praise even before he has fulfilled his promises? Micah knew beyond doubt that God will be victorious over sin; in justice he will judge sin and in grace he will forgive sin (7:18–19). This was ultimately accomplished when Christ died for the sins of the world. Although Micah does not know all the details of how God eventually worked it out, we do. This should give us even greater confidence and greater determination to address the evils in the world. When all sin is removed, what can prevent the coming of God's kingdom? "Victory in Christ" is not just a slogan; it will be a reality when all sin is removed from this world.

What can a believer do to bring about God's kingdom? There are many answers to this question throughout Scripture, but the practical answers derived from this chapter are to pray for the righteous who remain faithful, to intercede with God for his grace and forgiveness (7:9), and to plead earnestly for God to come in power and shepherd his people in order to fulfill his promises (7:14). Prayer does not excuse anyone from action, but prayer empowers all the activities of the church with divine power.

Without God's intervention to convict a person's heart, there will be no success in evangelism. Without God's transforming power, people do not have the courage to turn from the darkness of their past to a new way of life. If the church wants God's will to be done on earth as it is in heaven, prayer is needed. Without prayer nothing should be ventured for God, and without prayer nothing can be accomplished. Because the church knows the broad outline of God's plan for the future, we can boldly approach God with requests that his will be done. God hears the prayers of the righteous and acts because they care enough to seek his grace.

Scripture Index

Subject Index

Bring ancient truth to modern life with the
NIV Application Commentary *series*

Covering both the Old and New Testaments, the **NIV Application Commentary** series is a staple reference for pastors seeking to bring the Bible's timeless message into a modern context. It explains not only what the Bible means but also how that meaning impacts the lives of believers today.

Exodus
The truth of Christ's resurrection and its resulting impact on our lives mean that to Christians, the application of Exodus is less about how to act than it is about what God has done and what it means to be his children.

Peter Enns
ISBN: 0-310-20607-3

Esther
Karen H. Jobes shows what a biblical narrative that never mentions God tells Christians about him today.

Karen H. Jobes
ISBN: 0-310-20672-3

Ezekiel
Discover how, properly understood, this mysterious book with its obscure images offers profound comfort to us today.

Ian M. Duguid
ISBN: 0-310-20147-X

Available at your local Christian bookstore

ZONDERVAN™

GRAND RAPIDS, MICHIGAN 49530 USA
WWW.ZONDERVAN.COM

Daniel

Tremper Longman III reveals how the practical stories and spellbinding apocalyptic imagery of Daniel contain principles that are as relevant now as they were in the days of the Babylonian Captivity.

Tremper Longman III
ISBN: 0-310-20608-1

Mark

Learn how the challenging Gospel of Mark can leave recipients with the same powerful questions and answers it did when it was written.

David E. Garland
ISBN: 0-310-49350-1

Luke

Focus on the most important application of all: "the person of Jesus and the nature of God's work through him to deliver humanity."

Darrell L. Bock
ISBN: 0-310-49330-7

John

Learn both halves of the interpretive task. Gary M. Burge shows readers how to bring the ancient message of John into a modern context. He also explains not only what the book of John meant to its original readers but also how it can speak powerfully today.

Gary M. Burge
ISBN: 0-310-49750-7

Available at your local Christian bookstore

GRAND RAPIDS, MICHIGAN 49530 USA

WWW.ZONDERVAN.COM

Acts

Study the first portraits of the church in action around the world with someone whose ministry mirrors many of the events in Acts. Biblical scholar and worldwide evangelist Ajith Fernando applies the story of the church's early development to the global mission of believers today.

Ajith Fernando
ISBN: 0-310-49410-9

Romans

Paul's letter to the Romans remains one of the most important expressions of Christian truth ever written. Douglas Moo comments on the text and then explores issues in Paul's culture and in ours that help us understand the ultimate meaning of each paragraph.

Douglas J. Moo
ISBN: 0-310-49400-1

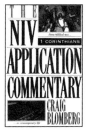

1 Corinthians

Is your church struggling with the problem of divisiveness and fragmentation? See the solution Paul gave the Corinthian Christians over 2,000 years ago. It still works today!

Craig Blomberg
ISBN: 0-310-48490-1

2 Corinthians

Often recognized as the most difficult of Paul's letters to understand, 2 Corinthians can have the same powerful impact today that it did when it was first written.

Scott J. Hafemann
ISBN: 0-310-49420-6

Available at your local Christian bookstore

GRAND RAPIDS, MICHIGAN 49530 USA

WWW.ZONDERVAN.COM

Galatians
A pastor's message is true not because of his preaching or people-management skills, but because of Christ. Learn how to apply Paul's example of visionary church leadership to your own congregation.

Scot McKnight
ISBN: 0-310-48470-1

Ephesians
Explore what the author calls "a surprisingly comprehensive statement about God and his work, about Christ and the gospel, about life with God's Spirit, and about the right way to live."

Klyne Snodgrass
ISBN: 0-310-49340-4

Philippians
The best lesson Philippians provides is how to encourage people who actually are doing quite well. Learn why not all the New Testament letters are reactions to theological crises.

Frank Thielman
ISBN: 0-310-49340-4

Colossians/Philemon
The temptation to trust in the wrong things has always been strong. Use this commentary to learn the importance of trusting only in Jesus, God's Son, in whom all the fullness of God lives. No message is more important for our postmodern culture.

David E. Garland
ISBN: 0-310-48480-4

Available at your local Christian bookstore

ZONDERVAN™

GRAND RAPIDS, MICHIGAN 49530 USA

WWW.ZONDERVAN.COM

1 Peter
The issue of the church's relationship to the state hits the news media in some form nearly every day. Learn how Peter answered the question for Christians surviving under Roman rule and how it applies similarly to believers living amid the secular institutions of the modern world.

Scot McKnight
ISBN: 0-310-49290-4

2 Peter, Jude
Introduce your modern audience to letters they may not be familiar with and show why they'll want to get to know them.

Douglas J. Moo
ISBN: 0-310-20104-7

Letters of John
Like the community in John's time, which faced disputes over erroneous "secret knowledge," today's church needs discernment in affirming new ideas supported by Scripture and weeding out harmful notions. This volume will help you show today's Christians how to use John's example.

Gary M. Burge
ISBN: 0-310-486420-3

Revelation
Craig Keener offers a "new" approach to the book of Revelation by focusing on the "old." He stresses the need for believers to prepare for the possibility of suffering for the sake of Jesus.

Craig Keener
ISBN: 0-310-23192-2

Available at your local Christian bookstore

ZONDERVAN™

GRAND RAPIDS, MICHIGAN 49530 USA

WWW.ZONDERVAN.COM

Praise for the NIV Application Commentary Series

"This series promises to become an indispensable tool for every pastor and teacher who seeks to make the Bible's timeless message speak to this generation."
—Billy Graham

"It is encouraging to find a commentary that is not only biblically trustworthy but also contemporary in its application. **The NIV Application Commentary** series will prove to be a helpful tool in the pastor's sermon preparation. I use it and recommend it."
—Charles F. Stanley, Pastor, First Baptist Church of Atlanta

"**The NIV Application Commentary** is an outstanding resource for pastors and anyone else who is serious about developing 'doers of the Word.'"
—Rick Warren, Pastor, Saddleback Valley Community
Church, Author, *The Purpose-Driven Church*

"**The NIV Application Commentary** series shares the same goal that has been the passion of my own ministry—communicating God's Word to a contemporary audience so that they feel the full impact of its message."
—Bill Hybels, Willow Creek Community Church

"**The NIV Application Commentary** series helps pastors and other Bible teachers with one of the most neglected elements in good preaching—accurate, useful application. Most commentaries tell you a few things that are helpful and much that you do not need to know. By dealing with the original meaning and contemporary significance of each passage, **The NIV Application Commentary** series promises to be helpful all the way around."
—Dr. James Montgomery Boice, Tenth Presbyterian Church

"If you want to avoid hanging applicational elephants from interpretive threads, then **The NIV Application Commentary** is for you! This series excels at both original meaning and contemporary signficance. I support it one hundred percent."
—Howard G. Hendricks, Dallas Theological Seminary

"**The NIV Application Commentary** series doesn't fool around: It gets right down to business, bringing this ancient and powerful Word of God into the present so that it can be heard and delivered with all the freshness of a new day, with all the immediacy of a friend's embrace."
—Eugene H. Peterson, Regent College

"This series dares to go where few scholars have gone before—into the real world of biblical application faced by pastors and teachers every day. This is everything a good commentary series should be."
—Leith Anderson, Pastor, Wooddale Church

"This is THE pulpit commentary for the 21ˢᵗ century."
—George K. Brushaber, President, Bethel College & Seminary

"Here, at last, is a commentary that makes the proper circuit from the biblical world to main street. **The NIV Application Commentary** is a magnificent gift to the church."
—R. Kent Hughes, Pastor, College Church, Wheaton, IL

Look for the NIV Application Commentary *at your local Christian bookstore*

ZONDERVAN™

GRAND RAPIDS, MICHIGAN 49530 USA

WWW.ZONDERVAN.COM

"Academically well informed ... this series helps the contemporary reader hear God's Word and consider its implications; scholarship in the service of the Church."
—Arthur Rowe, Spurgeon's College

"The NIV Application Commentary series promises to be of very great service to all who preach and teach the Word of God."
—J. I. Packer, Regent College

"The NIV Application Commentary series will be a great help for readers who want to understand what the Bible means, how it applies, and what they should do in response."
—Stuart Briscoe, Pastor, Elmbrook Church

"The NIV Application Commentary meets the urgent need for an exhaustive and authoritative commentary based on the New International Version. This series will soon be found in libraries and studies throughout the evangelical community."
—Dr. James Kennedy, Ph.D., Senior Minister,
Coral Ridge Presbyterian Church

"... for readers who want a reliable synthesis with a strong emphasis on application.... [Provides a] freshness that can benefit students, teachers, and (especially) church leaders ... makes good devotional reading, precisely because it emphasizes the contemporary application.... This approach refreshes and challenges the reader, and would make helpful material for sermon-preparation or Bible study.... At a time when many pastors are deeply in need of inspiration and encouragement, these volumes ... would be a good investment for congregations, even if it means adding a line to the annual budget."
—*Christianity Today*

"This commentary needs to be given full marks for what it is attempting to do. This is to provide a commentary for the English reader that takes exegesis seriously and still has space left for considerations of what the text is saying in today's world.... One will understand everything that one reads. May its tribe increase!"
—*Journal of the Evangelical Theological Society*

"... a useful, nontechnical commentary.... In the application section are illustrations, which, to pastors seeking a fresh approach, are worth the price of the book.... Other useful features include same-page footnotes; Greek words transliterated in the text of the commentary; and an attractive, user-friendly layout. Pastors and Bible teachers who want to emphasize contemporary application will find this commentary a useful tool."
—*Bookstore Journal*

"... one of the most helpful commentary sets from recent years."
—Alabama Southern Baptist Convention

"Some commentaries build walls that isolate you back in the ancient world. The **NIV Application Commentary** builds bridges that make the Bible come alive with meaning for contemporary life—and the series does so concisely, clearly and accurately. No wasted words or academic detours—just solid help and practical truth!"
—Warren Wiersbe

Look for the NIV Application Commentary at your local Christian bookstore

GRAND RAPIDS, MICHIGAN 49530 USA
WWW.ZONDERVAN.COM

We want to hear from you. Please send your comments about this book to us in care of the address below. Thank you.

GRAND RAPIDS, MICHIGAN 49530 USA

WWW.ZONDERVAN.COM